I0815115

The Art of WEAVING

The Art of WEAVING

MASTER THE TECHNIQUES, UNDERSTAND THE WEAVE STRUCTURES, CREATE YOUR OWN DESIGNS

BETTY BRIAND

FOREWORDS BY ERICA DE RUITER AND ANTOINETTE ROZE

STACKPOLE
BOOKS

Essex, Connecticut
Blue Ridge Summit, Pennsylvania

STACKPOLE BOOKS
An imprint of The Globe Pequot Publishing Group, Inc.
64 South Main Street
Essex, CT 06426
www.globepequot.com

Distributed by NATIONAL BOOK NETWORK
800-462-6420

Original French title: *L'Art du Tissage*

Graphic creation and layout: Anne Krawczyk

British Library Cataloguing in Publication Information available

Library of Congress Cataloging-in-Publication Data

Names: Briand, Betty, author.
Title: The art of weaving : master the techniques, understand the weave structures, create your own designs / Betty Briand ; forewords by Erica de Ruiter and Antoinette Roze.
Other titles: Art du Tissage. English
Description: Essex, Connecticut : Stackpole Books, [2023] | "Original French title: L'Art du Tissage, 2021 Éditions Eyrolles, Paris, France"—Title page verso. | Includes bibliographical references and index. | Summary: "This comprehensive guide to floor loom weaving begins with the basic but then goes so much farther, explaining the different types of weaves and how to read and weave from charts, and exploring a variety of weaves in depth. The author covers each topic in detail, with illustrations and photos and charts to guide you. *The Art of Weaving* is extensive in its scope, and a reference book for all skill levels"—Provided by publisher.
Identifiers: LCCN 2023008386 (print) | LCCN 2023008387 (ebook) | ISBN 9780811771849 (cloth) | ISBN 9780811771856 (epub)
Subjects: LCSH: Hand weaving. | Hand weaving—Patterns.
Classification: LCC TT848 .B72513 2023 (print) | LCC TT848 (ebook) | DDC 746.1/4041—dc23/eng/20230303
LC record available at https://lccn.loc.gov/2023008386
LC ebook record available at https://lccn.loc.gov/2023008387

Printed in India

First Edition

Forewords

The author, Betty Briand, has brought together her extensive knowledge and experience. Here she delivers good advice and tips to make quality weavings and to avoid or correct mistakes.

There are three parts to this book that cover all aspects of weaving: equipment, weaving structures, and artistry. It is enhanced by many very clear drawings and color photos illustrating the weaving structures presented.

Erica de Ruiter
Internationally recognized Dutch weaving teacher[1]

Weaving is one of the oldest crafts in human history. Fabric, very sensory and protective, has met and continues to meet many of our needs. Aren't textiles a part of our lives 24 hours a day? But what do we really know about them?

Many techniques have been developed throughout the world depending on available raw materials, living conditions, and financial resources, with the desire to make something useful and good, but also beautiful. Whether with plant or animal materials, while living a nomadic or sedentary life, and in all economic conditions, wool was spun, hemp was worked, weaving was done in houses. The practice of weaving leads to some very fun intellectual reasoning with an infinite field of possibilities, both technical and visual, the two being connected, and is accessible to all.

There is no pecking order among the different types of fabrics. From a plain color to a striking, large design, from silk to other textile fibers, from a fabric made in Peru, India, or elsewhere, it is always a question of finding the best balance between the use of the fabric, the materials, the techniques, the available tools and equipment, and the investment that can be put into it, both in time as well as money. The game then consists in finding a number of tricks to achieve the goal, add a decorative or qualitative element, and get around any obstacles imposed by the way the loom works.

Accessible to all, weaving becomes difficult and requires experience and patience when your first priority is perfect results. Next comes the search for type of decor and then we see how it is the simplest fabrics that are the most demanding.

"Hasten slowly, and without losing heart, go back to your work twenty times more," says Boileau. Weaving teaches patience and it is, above all, a complete art.

---

1 Author's note: Erica de Ruiter was my mentor, the one who taught me everything.

In this book, Betty Briand invites you to get to the heart of a fabric, meaning the world of fibers, in order to understand how it is made, how to go about making it, to place each thread where it should go, to work the fibers in a binary movement of “raising” and “lowering,” to interweave warp and weft, discovering little by little the whole realm of possibilities.

When you start to pull on the first thread, with Betty’s guidance from the beginning, your hand and your fingers lost in this fun-filled maze, you won’t see the other end.

Antoinette Roze
Textile expert and president of the association *Tours Cité de la Soie*

Acknowledgments

To Erica de Ruiter, my weaving teacher, whose lessons I followed for many years. She revealed to me that weaving was a language. And so, reading and writing this language became the first steps of this craft. An unconditional thank you!

To Antje Scharmer, from the German weaving school of Kukate, and to Yves le Duff, who also participated in my training by exposing me to new ways of weaving.

To all the weavers who attended my classes, who asked questions, to those who trusted me, to those who dared to try new things, to those who pushed me to my limits. To the weavers I met during events or workshops and with whom the discussions were often technical. Without you, I really wouldn't know as much! A nod to the rare male weavers, to whom I address the same thanks.

To the great weavers whose publications I was able to read to improve my knowledge. Living in the age of the web opens the doors to an infinite library.

To Patrick and our sons for all the help, support, tinkering, and now this beautiful workshop-school in Chinon. The thread of your story, in spite of you, has very often been linked to weaving; I am grateful for your patience and your affection. Our four sons and my thousands of threads, my entire life . . . .

To the founding members of ARTissage, I am profoundly grateful. Without their commitment at the beginning, I probably would not have dared. I owe this amazing adventure to them!

To the hosts who lent me their houses for the writing residencies. These pages were birthed in the air of the sea, the mountains, Normandy, Occitania, and Paris.

To Bach, Beethoven, Handel, Einaudi, and Camille, who helped me to isolate myself to concentrate throughout the writing of this manual.

To the wonderful friends who comforted me during the long work sessions. To the computer specialists and technicians who often came to my rescue. Building relationships really makes sense.

A special shout-out from the bottom of my heart to all the collaborators who have woven, illustrated, photographed, proofread, and corrected with such great care. It was a real team effort. You have been so conscientious and thorough, and made many improvements. This book is really yours as much as mine.

Of course to Eyrolles Editions as well, who, by publishing this book, give purpose to all this work, along with special thanks to Aude Decelle and to Sophie Hincelin, whose personal and professional support was a rare gift!

Finally, this manual is illustrated. Alix, Angèle, thank you for the joy of discovering your drawings as they arrived. I am awed by the fabulous quality of your work, your ability to transform my explanations into images, and your steadfastness in starting over, refining, improving until your drawings were just right. With the photographs, Jacques, you offered me your talent, your energy, your eye, and your sensitivity. I'm already feeling nostalgic!

Contents

Preface

Per laborem ad artem—By working, I become an artist

Fronton de la manufacture des Gobelins à Paris, 1667

Why is weaving so captivating and enjoyable? Everyone has their own reasons, and there are many. Creating a piece of fabric with only intertwining threads dazzles me. I feel it with every piece of weaving and I often observe it in those who discover this field. It is tremendously moving for me to be able to participate in this craft passed down from our ancestors, that millions of humans have invented and perfected depending on the region or the use. Using your own fabrics in your daily life, wearing a garment whose fabric has just come off the loom transforms what is familiar to us.

For a long time I have been weaving, training, researching, reading, making samples. I am fascinated by the field of possibilities that leads me to unceasingly explore this universe. The day I was introduced to coding, I discovered that textiles could be written like a text, which opened the doors to an infinite world.

Today, we have the immense opportunity to share our knowledge on the Internet. There is an unlimited exchange of expertise and discoveries among the vast community of weavers around the globe. Innovations and questions related to textiles circulate freely on the web, and many books are published revealing this wealth of knowledge.

As a teacher, I witness the special joy that each person finds in weaving, from choosing beautiful materials, to creating a useful fabric, searching for a good color combination, or simply making original creations. Some explore technique to craft a sophisticated weave while others follow their intuition. Eyes and hands work together. We are enriched through the creative process. Weaving leads to meditation, calling for serenity and patience. The passage of the shuttle through the shed brings a rhythm to our thoughts.

In 2010, supported by precious friends, I created the ARTissage workshop-school in Chinon to share my knowledge. Teaching weaving answers several of my wishes: to allow everyone the joy of designing their own fabric, always moved by the smile and the impatience of every ARTissage weaver when their fabric drops from the loom; to accompany the different steps with adequate explanations of the technique so that it is not an obstacle to creation; to pass on the language of weaving in order to decipher the countless publications and learn to how to write one's own project.

During my training courses, the student weavers often tell me about their fear of putting the warp on the loom and their hesitation about their choice of the right yarn or the appropriate density. They confide in me their desire for resources in French that would help them to better understand the weave patterns, encourage them to try more elaborate structures, and invite them to become inventive and autonomous. They urged me to fill this gap.

Every book has goals and aspirations, but also certain boundaries, and this one is no exception. You won't find many patterns to replicate, but rather the keys to understanding, explanations, and samples to accompany the process of making your own weaving. It will not replace either training or personal experience, but I hope it will give you the confidence to overcome any hesitations you may have and calmly dive into the weaving process.

This book is the one I would have liked to find when I started out. The first steps, the basic knowledge, are found in part one. It's a bit like kindergarten where we explore the tools and materials. Then we move on to the primary grades to learn to read and write. We enter middle school and high school (in part two) to study the fundamental structures with a fine-tooth comb: plain weave, twill, and satin. This is followed by a brief presentation of some common structures. Supplementary concepts are addressed in the last part for those who wish to go further.

In my workshops and courses, students of different levels interact and learn from each other. In the same way, in this book, I wish to address beginning, experienced, and highly qualified weavers. The experience gained in my ARTissage workshop-school has helped me to do so. It is up to each of you to find your way through these pages, going back and forth from one chapter to another as needed; it is a support tool to browse through.

In offering you this illustrated manual, I hope to spread the word in a way that is worthy of the richness and generosity of the teachings I have received, to continue to pass on the threads of this craft.

Betty Briand, Chinon, July 5, 2021

MORA

PART ONE

SETTING THE SCENE TO WEAVE

Staging means building a concrete foundation for the play, like for a howitzer. And let's go for the shot!

Jean Giraudoux, *L'Impromptu de Paris*, 1937

Before weaving, before starting to handle shuttles, threads, and treadles, we will familiarize ourselves with the elements that go into weaving, which we must understand to then organize them. Know the material, know what it's called. Choose the yarns, appreciate their uniqueness. Decide on a structure, distinguish its advantages depending on our project. Learn to read, write, draw a draft, and have a common language, to be able to illustrate on paper what our weaving will be. Then finally, wind and beam the warp and "dress" the loom.

This part is undoubtedly the most abstract, a little difficult sometimes. So, everyone at their own level, and depending on their desire to improve and know more details, will turn to the following pages depending on what they need to know. It is a reference text to be looked through as needed, without having to read everything from the beginning. I have chosen to group together topics that beginners may not understand the first time they read it or that more advanced weavers may find simplistic. I hope that the index, appendices, and illustrations will make the work easier for some and the reading more enjoyable for others.

I hope that this "setting the scene" will enlighten you and that the props you need will be ready on stage . . .

1

The Main Characters: The Loom, the Tools, the Materials

Weaving is interlacing two sets of threads at right angles, those of the weft through those of the warp. The warp threads are the threads stretched on the loom, held in vertical perforated supports, the heddles, attached to the shafts. Some of these threads are raised, other are lowered, creating an opening that we call the shed. Through this opening, a shuttle is slid that carries the weft thread. When this opening is closed, the weft threads are interwoven with the warp threads, then beaten with the reed. The fabric is created. Each layer of warp threads is called a **thread layer**. The beginner often confuses warp and weft; remember that the *weft* goes *left* and right.

Primitive societies worked with few materials. Warp threads were stretched between stakes or trees, fingers crossed the fibers, and a fabric took shape. Little by little, the loom made the work easier and faster.

Which Loom Is Right for You?

While the French word *métier* has, since the 12th century, applied to the exercise of any profession, it is only in the textile field that it was used to designate an implement: the loom.

Claude Fauque, *Les Mots du textile*, 2013

Surprisingly, the question of the choice of loom is often asked of me before any other. No loom is perfect except the one that suits us. It may take years to find the right one, and most likely will require several intermediate purchases and sales. It is by weaving that, little by little, we discover the one that is made for us.

Two main types of looms are available to us:

- floor looms or treadle looms;
- table looms or looms with levers.

Several criteria help inform the choice:

- what size loom will fit in the space available at home;
- what will it be used for, to produce and be efficient or to try out different things, to be as free as possible in creating fabrics; will it be for professional or amateur purposes;
- what is the budget.

Treadle looms are sturdy, and sometimes bulky. Different types are the **jack loom** or **rising-shed loom** (the shafts are raised when pressure is applied to the treadles), the **sinking-shed loom** (the shafts drop), the **countermarch loom** (some shafts rise while all the others drop, allowing a balanced tension on all threads), the **counterbalance loom** (the same idea as the countermarch but based on a system of pulleys that balance each other). They provide a weaving width from 20 to 80 inches, sometimes more. The very wide ones are equipped with a fly shuttle, without which you cannot throw the shuttle manually from one selvedge to the other. This system increases the width of the loom by about three feet and makes it more cumbersome. On the warp beam of these looms, it is very easy to wind very long warps as their circumference is larger. The beater is either suspended or attached to the bottom of the loom. One or more shafts are connected to each treadle.

Table looms take up little space and sometimes can be folded, even with weaving in progress, to store between uses or for transport. Each shaft is connected exclusively to a single lever. From 12 to 36 inches wide, they are equipped with 2 to 40 shafts, which is ideal for making samples. For most amateur weavers, these looms may be sufficient at first to try your hand at it. In any case, they should not be neglected just because they are small, as they are real looms.

There are other types of looms on the market, some very simple like the **rigid heddle loom**, which, without manipulations or an additional reed, can only be used to make plain weave, or conversely, the **Jacquard loom**, which individualizes each warp thread. **Dobby looms** are an intermediate between the two. **Damask looms** are almost two looms combined, one for plain weave, the other for patterns. **Tapestry looms**, with low or high heddle, have only two shafts. I'm listing these types of looms from memory, but none of them will be expanded on in this book; they are either very simple or very complex, and I am not a specialist at all.

Figure 1 Table loom with levers

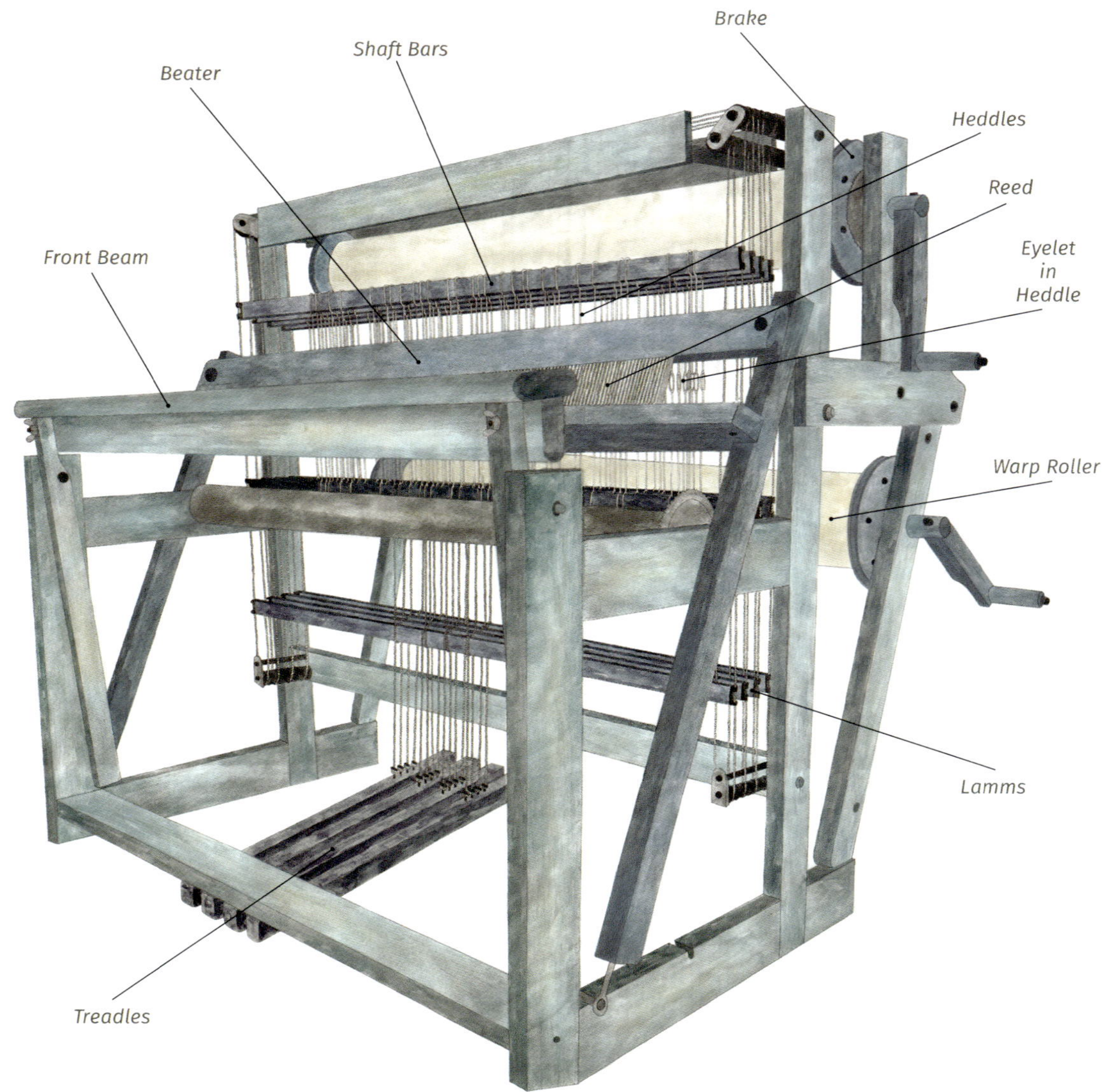

Figure 2 ***Floor loom***

It is very easy to find a used loom. Before you buy one, make sure it really works well. A handmade loom can be very nice, well thought out, but difficult, sometimes even impossible, to adjust. You don't want the moving parts to be out of alignment or to catch on each other. A factory-made loom is often more reliable and faster to adjust. It is also more expensive.

It is probably best to purchase a loom after trying your hand at weaving, with a weaver or a friend, or by taking a course. There is such a large amount and variety of equipment on the market that you must put together your own selection criteria. I also think that one should not hesitate to start small and then change equipment as you progress in your weaving knowledge and your needs. Some weavers create wonders with only two shafts, while others can only express themselves with 8, 16, or 40 shafts. It is by weaving, by experimenting, that you will discover which "family" you are comfortable with. If you are like me, you will probably fall into the common trap of having to find a larger space to accommodate the new, essential, but bulkier loom, as well as the threads and other materials that go with it. It is easy to want all the nice stuff very quickly!

Anatomy of a Loom

In the tradition of Islam, the loom symbolizes the structure and movement of the universe, and the two beams are called heaven and earth. By this very separation, the work of weaving is a work of creation, of giving birth.

Patrick Paul, *Interactive Newsletter of the International Center for Research and Transdisciplinary Studies*, No. 20, March 2008

We must become familiar with what the different parts of a loom are called and their functions. Sometimes, depending on the region or translation, the names can change. A glossary is included as an appendix (see p. 266).

The **loom frame** is often made of wood with four legs, metal elements, pulleys, cords, etc. Depending on the type of loom, the layout varies. However, its function remains the same: to be a support for all the parts of the loom, to be very solid and rigid to resist the tension of the warp and to absorb the beating of the reed.

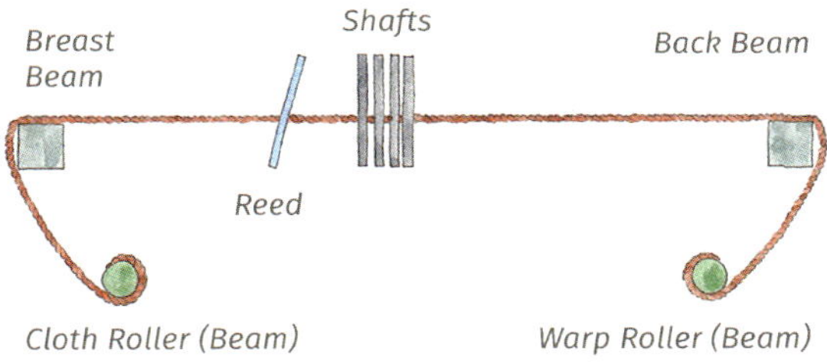

Figure 3 *Diagram of a loom*

Two **rollers**: these rollers (also called beams) allow the warp threads to be wound at the back and the fabric at the front. The back roller is unwound as the warp is needed, and the fabric is wound around the front roller.

Two **beams**: these are wooden bars, one at the front and the other at the back, each directly above the rollers, that keep the warp threads taut and parallel to each other.

The **shafts**: from 2 to 8 in general, they are made of wood and/or metal. The lighter and thinner ones are preferred. They carry the metal, cotton, or nylon heddles. These vertical rods have an eye in the center through which the warp is threaded. This eye, about ⅜ inch in diameter, guides the thread and carries it up or down to allow the passage of the weft. Older metal heddles are sometimes rusty. Depending on your preference, you may choose to replace them with new metal or nylon heddles. Many retailers offer Texsolv heddles, which are lighter, quieter, and more durable; they are ideal. Nevertheless, the little jingling of metal heddles is still quite pleasant, and some people also prefer them for their rigid eyelet that they can see better.

Figure 4 *Metal heddles*

The **reed** is set into the beater. Depending on the loom, the beater either hangs from the top of the shaft and swings out, or it is attached to the bottom and pivots, or it slides horizontally with a ball bearing system. It is used for beating the weft after each pass, maintains the width of the fabric, and determines its **density**. It is an expensive part of the equipment that must be taken care of. To pass the threads between the dents of the reed, always use a flattened **threading hook**, which is very flexible, so as not to risk twisting some of the dents; a damaged dent will always remain damaged and the fabric will be marked at that point. A single reed is often delivered with the loom, with a density of 10 dents/inch (40 dents/10 cm), which makes many weaving options possible. We will see later how to use the reed and how to choose the weaving density. One day you may want to supplement your collection of reeds. I always buy stainless steel reeds, which are more expensive, but do not rust. Depending on whether you prefer coarse or fine threads, you will choose the reed of the density you imagine using most frequently. But above all, wait to start weaving, then add to your equipment according to your needs, which will perhaps change over time.

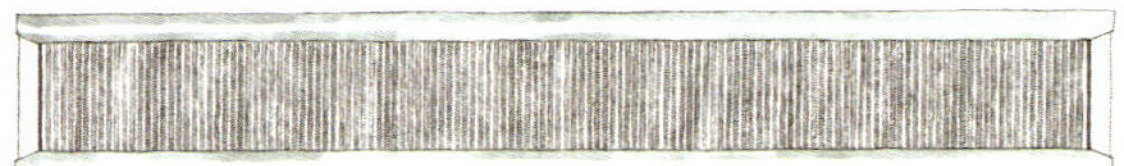

Figure 5 ***Reed***

Warp rollers, beams, shafts, and reeds are all parallel to each other. The warp threads, wound onto the warp beam, will go over the back beam, be threaded through the eyes of the heddles in a preset order, pass through the dents of the reed, and then, transformed into fabric with each insertion of the weft, go over the breast beam and be wound onto the cloth roller.

Some parts of the loom are mobile: the **shafts**, operated by **treadles** or **levers**; the **brakes**, which block the **rollers**, released by **handles**; the **lower lamms and upper lamms**, wood bars located between the shafts and the **treadles**, which pivot on an axis; the **jacks**, located under the shafts to connect the shafts to the treadles, which also pivot on an axis. The upper part of the loom is sometimes called the castle.

> . . . [A dancer] appears, slender and dainty, like a marionette in a puppet theater.
>
> André Levinson, *Les Visages de la danse*, 1933[1]

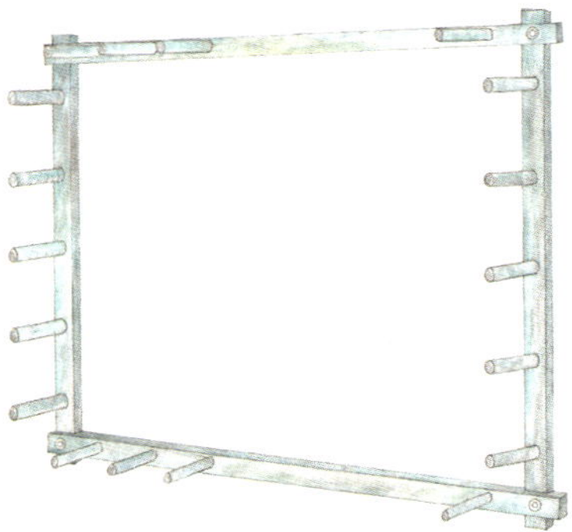

Figure 6 ***Warping board***

Figure 7 ***Warping mill***

Tools

A few tools are needed to prepare the warp.

A **warper** is used to prepare all the warp threads so they are the same length and have the same tension. Often this will be a warping board, which is a wood frame with pegs. For longer warps, a rotating warping mill is faster and more relaxing for the body. When starting out, a more economical simple wood bar with pegs can work, but it is recommended to get a sturdier and more practical device for winding the warp as soon as you can. This is the first tool that will be used to obtain good tension!

An **umbrella swift** is used to unwind skeins. It will very quickly become essential as the threads often come in skeins or hanks.

Figure 8 ***Yarn swift***

1. This quote shows the connection between a loom and a puppet theater, as the word "marionette" is the same as the French word for "jack," and the French word "castelet" means both "puppet theater" and "castle" (the castle on a loom, that is).

Lease sticks or **cross sticks** are used to preserve the cross made when warping; they separate the even and odd threads of the warp. **Warp sticks** are wound at the same time as the warp onto the warp beam to keep the threads in place. They both come with the loom. If they don't, it's easy to make your own. Lease sticks are usually flat and made of wood. But those used by silk workers are round and made of glass and they are beautiful!

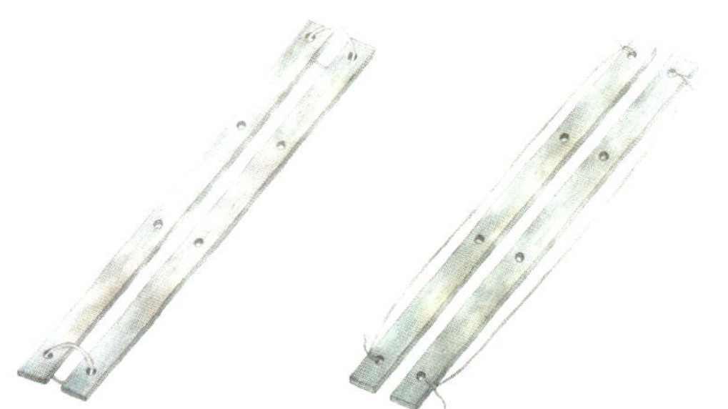

Figure 9 ***Lease sticks***

Warp sticks can easily be replaced by sheets of paper.

Figure 10 ***Warp sticks***

The **raddle** is placed on the loom to center the warp when it is wound and to spread it according to the selected density. It guides the threads on the warp beam so that they are wound at the desired density.

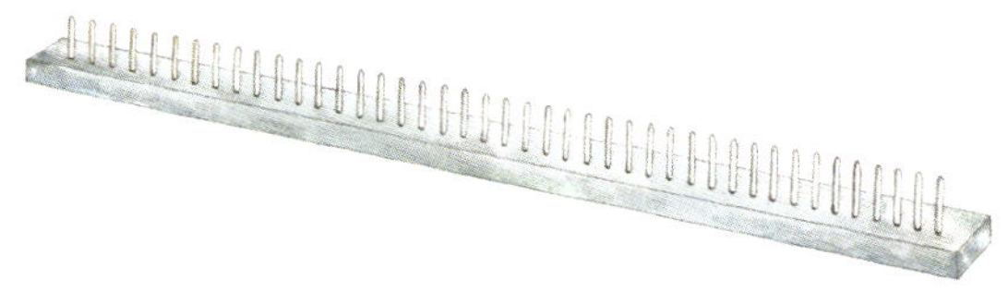

Figure 11 ***Raddle***

Weights are also needed for winding. Small bottles of water held by the threads will do the trick. Preparation of the warp on the loom will be described in chapter 4 (see p. 80).

A **threading hook** is needed to bring the warp ends through the eye of each heddle and between the dents of the reed. Sometimes, in order not to risk damaging the reed, a very flexible hook is chosen. For very deep looms, generally those with 4 shafts, a long metal hook is more practical.

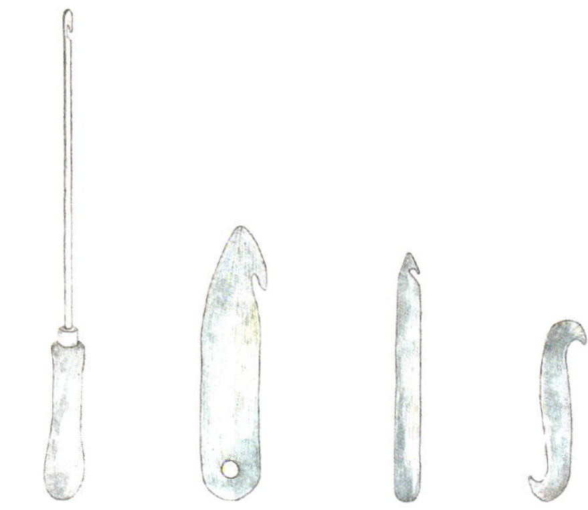

Figure 12 ***Threading hooks***

Shuttles are used to pass the weft through the **shed**, the opening of the warp threads into two layers. On flat shuttles, the weft thread is wound from one end to the other. Boat shuttles have bobbins on which the weft thread is wound using a bobbin winder.

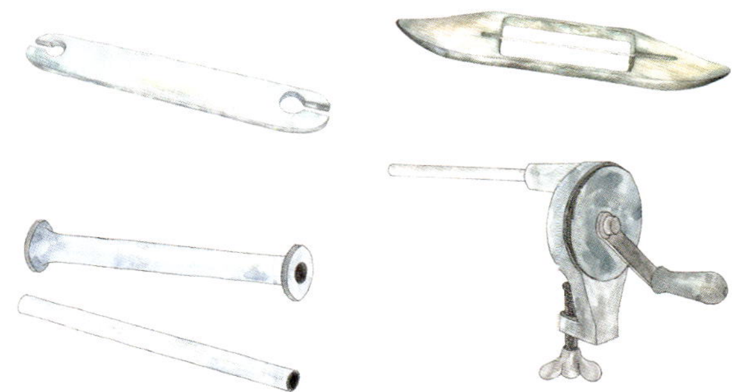

Figure 13 ***Flat shuttle, boat shuttle, bobbins, and bobbin winder***

Ski shuttles with single or double runners are used for making rugs.

Figure 14 ***Single or double ski shuttles***

Make sure you always have pins, scissors, a tape measure, and some sturdy cord in a small container nearby; you will use them constantly.

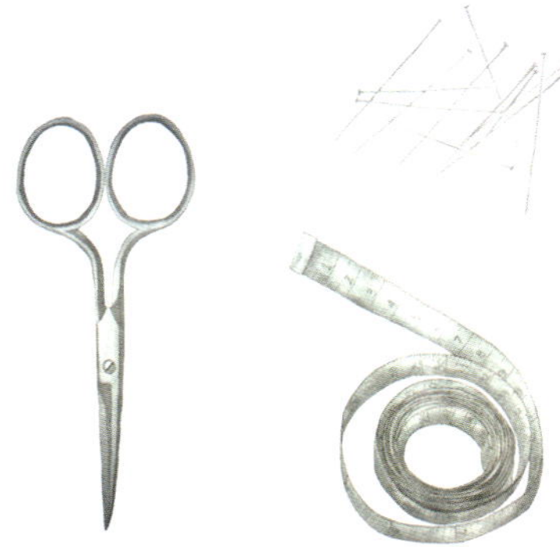

Figure 15 ***Small tool kit to have on hand***

Some weavers like to use a **temple** to ensure their weave width is even. This accessory stretches the fabric so that it does not shrink in width. It is attached to the selvedges between the reed and the cloth beam and is adjusted to the reed width.

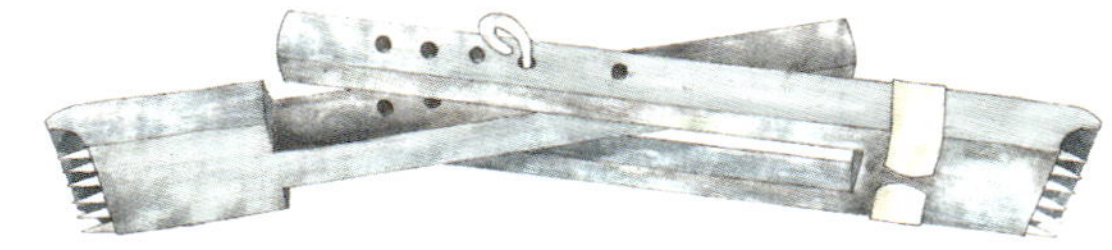

Figure 16 ***Temple***

A yarn **ball winder** quickly transforms a skein into a nice ball of yarn that can be easily stored on the shelves and used afterward without having to set up the yarn swift.

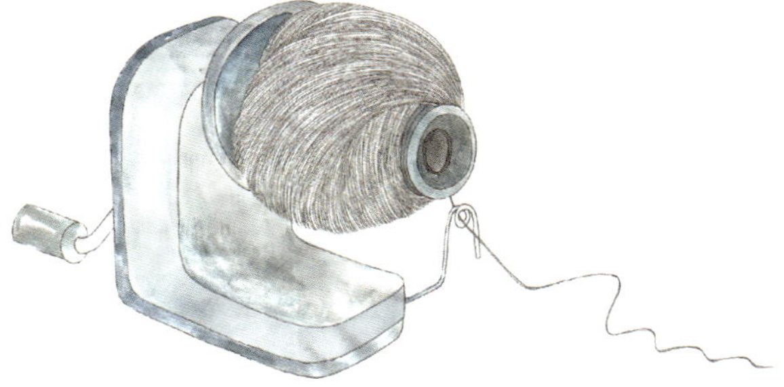

Figure 17 ***Ball winder***

The list of additional equipment could go on and on, but your needs, which will become clearer as you go, will determine how you expand your arsenal of tools. Weaving equipment is expensive, so you will have to make real choices and not simply fall for a beautiful accessory.

Yarns

The choice of yarn is essential for a successful weaving project. Each kind has its advantages and disadvantages and will not be suitable for all projects. That said, most yarns can be used by weavers: supple, dry, thick, thin, shiny, matte, fuzzy, etc. Although it is necessary to have some theoretical knowledge, nothing can replace experience.

Thread or yarn is a set of strands twisted together, in two to twelve strands, in one direction ("S") or in the other ("Z"), with more or less twist per inch (from two twists for wool to 75 for a very tight silk). A **two-ply yarn** is usually two S-twisted strands plied together with a Z-twist, or the reverse. A **singles** yarn is soft and airy but not as strong.

There are technical books devoted to yarns; the field is vast and fascinating and I present here only a brief overview. Reference works are listed in the bibliography in the appendix (see p. 275). In the next chapter, the properties of the fibers will be studied from the point of view of their use by the weaver.

There are two main categories of fibers: **natural fibers** of animal, vegetable, or mineral origin; and **man-made fibers**, which are either artificial or synthetic. A list in the appendix summarizes all the fibers that will be discussed here (see p. 273).

Figure 18 ***S twist and Z twist***

Natural Fibers

Animal fibers or protein fibers

Wool comes from the fleece of sheep, shorn once a year. The quality varies according to the breed of the animal, the region and its climate, as well as its diet. Long or short, the fibers are sorted, degreased, carded, combed, and spun. There are several categories of wool: merino wool (long, thin fibers), lambswool (lamb's first shearing), Shetland (dense and hardy wool), astrakhan (fur of the newborn or fetal lamb, either stillborn or killed between 2 and 4 days). Wool is sorted according to its qualities, then washed, which removes the lanolin. It becomes brittle and will be treated with a mineral, vegetable, or animal oil to allow carding, a sort of untangling of the fibers. It is then smooth and soft and can be formed into a roving to then be spun and stored on bobbins or in skeins.

Hair is a protein fiber. It bears the name of the animal from which it comes:

- the **cashmere goat**, native to the region of the same name, produces a very fine undercoat to protect itself from the cold. The yarn is soft and silky;
- the **angora goat**, native to the Ankara region, produces a lustrous white fiber called mohair;
- the **angora rabbit** provides the angora fiber, a particularly long hair;
- llama is a generic term for four different animals from South America: the **llama**, whose down is used; the **alpaca**, which has a very fine and silky fiber; the **vicuña**; and the **guanaco**. These last two are wild and their fleece is often prohibitively expensive;
- the **camel** provides a coarse, hard outer hair and very soft undercoat, which has antistatic properties;
- other fibers come from **mouflon**, **yak**, **dog**, **horse**, and **cow** (tail hair and hard hair). **Feathers** are also used.

Silk comes from the work of the caterpillar of the Bombyx mori moth. It is said that silk thread was discovered around 2700 B.C. by the Chinese princess Xi Ling Shi, the young wife of the emperor Huang-Di, who was having her tea under a mulberry tree. While recovering a silkworm cocoon that had fallen into her cup, she unwound the long silk filament, the hot water having dissolved the sticky substance, sericin, that coated it. After this discovery, the empress convinced her husband to develop the breeding of the silkworm. Its precious thread became a highly prized medium of exchange. For 30 centuries, Chinese know-how was improved and the manufacturing process—the trade secret—was fiercely preserved. Looters, monks, perhaps princesses—many legends tell how silk finally left the country. Production began in France at the end of the Middle Ages, after having crossed the Mediterranean Basin.

Silkworms are raised in silkworm farms. This type of cultivation is called sericulture. When the silkworms reach a size of 3 to 4 inches (8 to 10 cm), they make their cocoon with a single filament, the silk bave being about thirty thousandths of a millimeter in diameter and about two thousand meters in length for a cocoon, sometimes even reaching four thousand meters in length.

The silk filament is unwound, or reeled, directly from the cocoon, which must be intact, before the chrysalis pierces it. Cocoons are therefore treated with hot air to suffocate the chrysalis. The sericin, a type of natural gum that covers the thread, is then removed from it by plunging it in a bath of hot water, causing the sericin to soften. This process is called scouring or degumming. The **raw silk** obtained directly from a cocoon is so fine that the filaments of at least 7 cocoons must be unwound together; they are stuck to each other by the sericin. This is the silk throwing process. Depending on the desired thread thickness (see p. 34), 4, 5, 6, or 7 thrown threads are wound together with a very slight twist.

Schappe is made from waste silk (pierced cocoons, thread ends, etc.) which undergoes various processes (maceration, carding, drawing, spinning, etc.) to make these long fibers usable. They are combed and spun the same way as cotton fibers. **Silk noil** comes from the coarser and shorter waste.

- Each type of silk, depending on the direction of the twist or the number of twisted threads, has a specific name: **silk crepe**, made of several threads of raw silk twisted at 50 to 77 twists per inch; **organza silk**, made of two or three threads twisted in opposite directions; **soie ovale**, composed of two to sixteen threads with low twist; **grenadine silk**, a double organza with a hard twist; **cordonnette silk**, composed of three threads of raw silk or schappe assembled in the opposite direction with medium twist. **Tussah**, **shantung**, **eri**, and **muga** come from caterpillars living in semifreedom, on oak trees for the tussah, on the castor-oil plant for eri silk, and on the sal tree (endemic to eastern India) for muga silk. The thread is less regular and less fine than raw silk thread.
- We also find **spider silk**, coming from a Malagasy spider, caught without stress. It is a question of getting the silk directly from the spinneret on the abdomen and pulling on it. The thread is very strong with a naturally golden color.
- The **large mother-of-pearl shell** (*pinna nobilis*), from the Mediterranean, was sought after in ancient times. Its filaments, called byssus, were transformed to form a rare and beautiful thread. The Golden Fleece would have been woven with this sea silk.

Plant or Cellulosic Fibers

Fibers from stems

Flax is a plant with a long stem, pulled up and not cut to keep its full length. It is then retted, i.e., soaked in warm water in order to eliminate the pectose, a resinous vegetable gum that binds the cellulosic fibers. The pectose disintegrates through the combined action of maceration and bacterial decomposition. As retting is a source of pollution, it is now done directly in the open air and only through the alternation of sun and rain. The flax is then dried before being crushed to separate the long fibers, called long line, from the shorter fibers, known as tow. This operation is called scutching. The flax is then brushed by running it through hackle combs to produce roving, which is moistened and then spun. Though it has very little elasticity, this yarn is known for its great capacity for absorption. Flax is considered to be the oldest plant fiber known to have been used by humans.

Hemp is a fiber obtained after retting and scutching of the stalk of the plant that bears the same name, which grows in temperate regions.

Jute is a reed that, after retting, results in fibers that are longer than linen but less resistant to humidity.

Ramie, extracted from the stem of a nettle native to China, results in fine, long, and shiny fibers.

Fibers from seeds and fruits

Cotton comes from a plant or shrub, sometimes even a 15 to 20 foot (5 to 6 m) tree in certain tropical zones. The seeds of the cotton plant are surrounded by downy fibers that form a cotton boll. These fibers are short, ½ to 2 inches (1 to 5 cm), hollow, and sometimes called called silks. Once the flowers fade, the walls of the absorbent cotton fibers retract, forming small air pockets that give this fiber, once spun, a feeling of softness and warmth. The cotton is then ginned and spun. It is undoubtedly one of the most mechanically and chemically processed fibers, often bleached, dyed, printed, etc. Mercerization is an additional treatment with caustic soda that makes the yarn stronger and causes it to swell, thus facilitating the penetration of pigments. This process is very polluting.

Kapok is the fruit of the kapok or silk-cotton tree. A silky down, very light and waterproof, surrounds the seeds when mature.

Coconut fiber, called **coir**, from the outer husk of the coconut, can also be used.

Fibers from leaves

These are mainly fibers from **pineapple**, **raffia** (palm tree), **sisal** (agave leaf), and **abacca** (a kind of banana tree).

Fibers from Minerals

Asbestos rock is crushed to obtain a soft, cottony fiber. Regulations today forbid its use for health reasons. Metal threads such as gold, silver, and copper are obtained either by wire-drawing (transformation by stretching then pulling through dies, instruments pierced with holes through which the material flows in order to stretch it into threads), or by winding very thin strips around a core made of cotton, rayon, or silk cord. Lurex is one of the commercial names of this type of thread.

Man-Made Fibers

These fibers are often described as chemical in nature, as they are all created and manufactured industrially. Those made from cellulose or natural proteins, which undergo chemical treatments, are called **artificial fibers**; this is the viscose and rayon family. Those called **synthetic fibers** are petroleum-based. Chemists have invented many of them in an effort to compete with the fineness of silk and its price. This resulted in the creation of polyamides, polyesters, and acrylics. It is often difficult to tell these fibers apart, though a burn test helps identify them. In the appendix you will find a classification of yarns or threads together with the results of their burn test.

Artificial Fibers

Various chemical treatments are used to dissolve cellulose and produce new threads. This field is very complex and is beyond the scope of this book. I present these fibers under their commercial names, which will probably speak more to the amateur users that we are. Although they are often advertised as an alternative to synthetic fibers, they require dissolving and then transforming the cellulose into thread, operations that consume so much water and products that are toxic for the environment (caustic soda, carbon disulfide, sodium hydroxide, sulfuric acid, etc.) that they leave us perplexed about the natural or even organic designation of these products, despite their plant origin.

The **viscose process** transforms wood pulp into:

- **fibranne**, viscose with short and spun fibers;
- **rayonne**, having a continuous viscose rayon filament.

The cellulose comes from hardwood fibers such as beech or birch, from softwoods such as spruce, from bamboo, from soybeans, etc. The purpose of the chemical processing is to transform the fibers into very fine structures able to pass through dies. Often called artificial silks, these fibers have the qualities of flexibility while being inexpensive.

Bemberg, used for linings, comes from this same process using a mixture of plant fibers. **Bamboo** yarn is also easily available. **Alginate** is an extract of brown algae that produces a very pretty yarn. Fermented and distilled sugars from **corn starch** are separated and refined into polymers (Ingeo, Sorona). **Lycra** is an elastane derived from corn dextrose, more environmentally friendly, and has been an alternative to petroleum-based elastane since 2014.

The **Lyocell process**, LYOphilization of CELLulose, uses organic and low-polluting solvents to directly dissolve cellulose. Eucalyptus, bamboo, and hardwood pulp is ground and extruded and then mixed with the solvent in high-temperature water. This is how Modal and Tencel are produced. The solvent is recovered and reused several times. Bamboo is only peeled and not cut, which avoids deforestation. For the moment, this is the only slightly ecological alternative for artificial fibers. This process is in full development and the qualities of the fibers obtained are interesting: stronger, stable, easy to spin and dye, biodegradable, etc. But the solvent used is expensive, which compromises the future of this process.

Fibers based on animal proteins are also being manufactured. **Lanital** is made from milk casein, and chitin is produced from the shells of crustaceans.

Mineral-based fibers include **glass fiber**, made from silica; **carbon fiber**; and basalt fiber.

Synthetic Fibers

Industrial processes produce synthetic polymer fibers by synthesizing chemical compounds from petroleum and coal. **Polyamides** (Nylon), derived from petroleum, are often mixed with other fibers. **Polyesters** (Dacron, Tergal, etc.) are obtained by another polymerization process. **Acrylics** come from coal, lime, and nitrogen from the air (Courtelle, Dolan, Dralon, etc.). There are also **chlorofibers** (Rhovyl) **elastane** (Dow XLA, PBT, etc.), and **fluorofibers**.

The spinning processes make it possible to create a wide variety of fiber presentations such as flat blades, strands that are round or hollow, thick or very thin, shiny or matte, swelling, frizzy etc. With its constant research, the textile industry is always proposing new products.

2

Fabrics: Behind the Scenes

The most important thing in a play is the structure.

Alain Françon, director, 1971

Whatever the weaving project may be, the preparation phase is crucial. It involves calculations and decisions that can sometimes be intimidating. It is a matter of keeping it simple and efficient by answering a few questions.

- Which project, for what use?
- Which yarns to choose? What material, yarn count, color?
- Which structure or weave pattern?
- What size?

It is surprising to note that the motivations of weavers are very different. The need for a certain fabric, the desire to use a yarn that has been set aside or an unusual color, the plan to try out a new structure, the emotion of the colors of a landscape, a gift to make, and so on, the sources of inspiration are abundant. It is then a matter of making the right choices so that the result corresponds to our vision.

It is the relationship between the thread, the structure, and the density that determines the success of the planned weaving project. Will it be a rug, a garment, a frequently used household linen, a throw blanket, a shawl, curtains, a tapestry to hang on a wall? Each of these weavings will require a particular yarn, an appropriate structure, and a suitable density. Even if at first a person weaves just to weave, to play around without a plan, there will undoubtedly come a time when the use of the piece being made will matter.

What Is the Intended Use?

The soul, laundry freshly dried by the sun, lovingly folded.

Christian Bobin, *L'Homme-joie*, 2012

Household linens (placemats, table runners, napkins, hand towels, etc.) are often one of the first projects chosen. They are excellent for learning about weaving by testing colors, structures, and patterns, and are also useful finished pieces that we can enjoy every day. These woven items must be washable at high temperature, a placemat must be firm and not too thick to avoid having a glass set on the edge fall over, the napkin must be absorbent, etc. Plant-based yarns, such as linen and cotton, are well suited to these uses.

Scarves, wraps, and throws are probably the most commonly made items, as they are quick to weave, they provide the opportunity to try out a wide variety of yarns and structures, and are always fun gifts to give or wear. The fabric can be warm or light, thick or soft, treasured or ordinary, classic or adventurous. The most daring may use a structure with long thread crossings, called **floats**; a fragile, fuzzy, or very fine thread; or strong colors. The risks are low! Wool, cotton, linen, silk, mohair, cashmere, mixed fibers, bouclé, high-pile yarn, and so on—so many yarns that sometimes require a little more attention, but a simple project is the perfect time to try one or more of them.

Regular or half **curtains** require other criteria. They are exposed to light, they will hang, they must be a specific dimension and integrate with the colors of the room. Wool will degrade very quickly in the sun, wefts that are not tight enough will slide down, and bright colors will fade in the light. The dimensions must be calculated accurately and verified by a sample so that when installed the curtain is neither too long or short nor too wide or narrow. Depending on whether it is hung from a rod or the window, the hem length will not be the same. So I maintain that making a sample is really necessary, and if possible at a later stage in the actual width to check that the final dimensions after removal from the loom and washing match the preliminary calculations and that the fabric behaves well and that the colors go well with the other colors in the room.

Openwork or lace fabrics, such as for short curtains, are less heavy and therefore do not have the same issues. However, the final measurements are crucial. Once installed, these curtains must fit the size of the glass and the shape of the window. Very thin linen and cotton are perfectly suited to this type of item. Seaweed yarn, although still not well known, is also suitable for this purpose. It is fine and easy to weave, and its flexibility is attractive.

Rugs have very different functions and, here again, we must ask ourselves the right questions: will it be in a high-traffic area, will it get wet, such as in a bathroom or kitchen, will it be mainly useful or decorative, bring warmth, brighten up a room? In this book, we will only present the techniques that are similar to weaving, we will not talk about ryas, kilims, or knotted stitches. There is already a lot to say about weaving structures suitable for rugs, such as weft- and warp-faced reps, rag rug weaving, and corduroy. The choice of yarn and structure will bring stiffness or flexibility.

Garments are probably what is most attractive, but also what intimidates for a long time. Very often, we will start with a pattern that will not require too many cuts, such as sewing rectangles together for flowing garments that sometimes have an ethnic look. Some Japanese patterns propose sewing rectangles together in a very inventive and simple way to create an original garment. Nevertheless, nothing prevents you from considering your own weaving as a real commercial fabric and daring to cut and sew it, provided of course that you respect certain rules of cutting that are less necessary with an industrial fabric. It is so gratifying to wear a piece of clothing made from fabric you have woven and cut according to a pattern! A sample is then essential, at a smaller width at first, then tested in its final width. It should be washed and ironed so that you can judge its flexibility and how well it is suited to your project.

To remove some legitimate concerns from the outset, here are some tips inspired by the experience of ARTissage course participants.

- Draw your cutting plan beforehand, even before warping, to avoid running out of fabric. With our artisanal weavings, the question of the straight grain does not arise; it is either the warp thread or the weft thread. For industrial fabrics, the straight grain indicated in the cutting plan is the warp thread. Indeed, in order to save work time, the density of the weft is often less than that of the warp. The fabric is therefore stronger if it is cut following this thread parallel to the selvedges. In artisanal weaving, we try to have the same density in warp and weft. We can therefore lay the pieces in either direction, without worrying about the warp and the straight grain.
- When your weaving is taken off the loom, as with any fabric, it is essential to wash and dry it, stretching it well.
- Secure the fabric where you will be cutting by sewing zigzag stitches down either side of the cutting line, then ⅜ inch (1 cm) on each side, sew a straight stitch along the whole length, and cut between the two zigzags. This way, the threads will not unravel and the straight stitch offers additional security.
- This can be done directly on a serger, which does this zigzag and straight stitch at the same time and cuts flush with the seam.

Figure 1 ***Seams to secure the cut***

- Nevertheless, handmade fabric, less compacted than industrial fabric, deserves some precautions. To limit the excess thickness of the hem of a skirt or the button band of a jacket, it is advantageous to use the selvedge of the woven fabric; this way, only a single fold of fabric is needed.

With all this care, I encourage you to go for it! It's a real pleasure to wear a garment for which you have created the fabric.

Which Yarn Should I Choose?

Our days fabrics of silk
On a background of wool
Our destinies fabrics of joy
On a background of sorrow.

Charles Péguy, *Complete Poetic Works*, "Ballade de la grâce," 1941

After the general introduction to the main yarns we can use (see the previous chapter, p. 26), we are going to approach the question of the choice of yarn through the eye of the weaver. All can be woven, or almost all, but not all are suitable for all projects. It is undoubtedly the appropriateness of the choice as much as the quality of the yarn that will make the result satisfying. Which yarn? What size? What color? Having some reference points will help us a bit in making our selections.

Characteristics of Yarns

Sheep's wool is soft and retains heat, qualities preserved by weaving. Its fibers can be long or short, depending on the breed of sheep. It is a soft and stretchy yarn that a beginner can use easily because it lessens any unevenness.

The outside of the fiber is made up of flat scales that overlap and give it its elasticity. Under strong friction along with sudden changes in temperature and soap, these scales open and close by clinging to each other and the wool felts. But it is fine when washed gently in lukewarm water by hand with a suitable shampoo.

Worsted wool, with its long parallel fibers, reflects light better than carded wool, whose fibers are more tangled. Wool twisted into several strands will be stronger and is preferred for warp. The number of twists per inch changes the flexibility of the yarn. A wool singles, not twisted, can be used in weft to add loft and brightness. It will be more difficult to use in warps.

Yarn can be burned to test for fiber origin. When burned, wool gives off a smell of burnt horn.

Wool is suitable for all structures. For plain weave, the beat should not be too forceful to leave room for the increased loft after washing. Floats highlight the qualities of the yarn.

Twill, overshot, lace, and deflected doubleweave are some of the many variations of structures very suited to using wool to its best advantage.

This fiber is ideal for blankets, throws, coats, etc.

Other animal-origin yarns are sometimes more intimidating because they may be fine or fragile.

When handled very carefully, **mohair** is easy to use, even in warp. Use a reed with few dents per inch and place two threads together in each dent, remove the lease sticks to limit places of friction, and opt for winding from the back to avoid passing the threads twice through the comb. If the yarns really start latching on to each other through the heddles or the comb, you can apply starch as they come out of the warp beam. This way, the rogue hairs will stick to the yarn and slide easily. When brushing mohair to lift the pile, it is recommended to brush while the fabric is still under tension on the loom, as the work progresses.

Alpaca is a very soft and warm fiber. The absence of lanolin, a fat naturally present in animal hair, gives it hypoallergenic qualities. Today, makers have found spinning methods or blends that produce beautiful yarn qualities.

Cashmere, a soft, fine, and silky yarn, is wonderful to weave in warp and weft.

Silk requires a lot of patience as the number of threads in the warp and weft can become very high. The price and fineness of the fibers often put off the novice. Yet it is a strong yarn that requires little more attention than wool. It is so fine–some silk goes up to almost 298,000 yards per pound–that in the end the weight used is low, which mitigates the cost of the weave. Of course, the cost of a silk project remains high, but not exorbitant.

This yarn burns slowly, with the characteristic animal fiber smell of burnt horn.

Smooth, shiny, and soft, it looks great when woven with floats. Satin is the weaving structure where floats best show off the yarns, and is why silk satins are so renowned. Openwork structures, such as Bronson lace or huck lace, become delicate with silk. The effect is vibrant with structures where floats are wisely placed like a Summer-and-Winter crackle, or overshot weave. It even brings out the best in a simple twill.

Silk fabric is soft, lightweight, insulating, and somewhat wrinkle-resistant. It absorbs water very easily, and therefore dyes can be very intense. Silk is also very strong. The parachutes of the American soldiers during the landing of 1944 were made of silk.

Figure 2 ***Blanket in Holst Garn Tides, 70% pure new wool and 30% silk. Block twill on 8 shafts.***

Figure 3 ***Silk scarf. Leno, two-ply silk, 15,378 yd/lb (31,000 m/kg)***

Cotton is a strong, highly twisted yarn. Inexpensive, it exists in a wide variety of colors and yarn counts (see next section, p. 34). It is easy to work with and brings out the best in all structures, and it has the added advantage of being very sturdy. It can withstand any type of washing. Therefore, it is ideal for household linens or fabrics that will be subject to friction. Cotton fabrics have a greater capacity to absorb water if the yarn is not too twisted and if the structure does not have threads cross as often, such as loop pile or floats in waffle weave. They also wrinkle easily. One disadvantage is that shrinkage in the wash can become significant. Finding the appropriate density is therefore essential, and several washes are necessary to obtain a fabric that will no longer change in size.

Linen is a fiber suitable for household linens. It is very resistant to wear and washing and absorbs moisture very well. Of course, it is easier to use in weft for a beginner, because in warp, it wears very quickly due to friction from the reed or the eyes of the heddles, and sometimes breaks. It still has the reputation of being reserved for experienced weavers. It is better to practice with a twisted yarn and a short warp before daring to weave precious curtains with a single strand thread, both in weft and in warp. When used in warp, the work can be made easier by sizing the threads with starch to better withstand the friction.

With linen, more than with other fibers, it is essential to have the right reed density to avoid shrinkage, and to have perfect winding with an equal tension on all the threads. The use of a temple also helps to maintain the same width.

Linen fiber is heavy, and the fabric hangs beautifully. This stiffness gives it a certain elegance that it retains wash after wash.

To overcome the drawbacks of linen, it can be used in a mix with cotton. Some suppliers offer a cotton-linen with such a wide range of colors that it has become the most widely used yarn in the ARTissage courses. Placemats, hand towels, table runners, and curtains are made in many weave patterns: plain, twill, huck, waffle weave, Summer and Winter, overshot, etc. The softness of the cotton combines well with the freshness and the absorption qualities of linen.

Figure 4 ***Crackle weave. 8 shafts. Venne 100% Organic Cottolin Nel 22/2. Filoeuvre.***

Viscose has a shiny appearance like silk; wrinkles like cotton; and is soft, comfortable, and highly resistant to wear and to light. It gives fabric a pleasant and soft touch as well as a comfortable style. The fabric absorbs moisture well. Only its ecological impact hinders its use.

We cannot neglect the synthetic yarns. **Polyamides, polyesters, and acrylics** are light and often strong. They can be found in a very wide range of colors and materials, are very easy to obtain, and are inexpensive. When mixed with natural fibers, the range of yarns available expands significantly. The great advantage of synthetic fibers is that they are used to create a wide variety of fancy yarns that are very fun to use: furry, curly, shiny, with sequins or glitter, chenille—a whole range of yarns not to be looked down on that provide a different aesthetic.

Their ability to absorb water is low. Their manufacture has a negative environmental impact and they are not biodegradable. Moreover, polyamide produces static electricity, and polyesters and acrylics will pill.

We often find yarns that combine synthetic fibers with natural fibers, which is a good way to lessen the downsides of synthetics. As you can tell, I'm not a fan, but I don't reject them outright. I even enjoy using them sometimes.

One of the joys of weaving is working with beautiful and high-quality yarns. It makes me happy every time I do, because industrial fabrics rarely bring such satisfaction. Likewise, using natural materials, locally produced, gives me great joy. These materials are now more readily available at affordable prices. With them, you are almost guaranteed to weave an item that is pleasing to the eye and to the touch. Whatever the weave pattern, natural yarn shares its intrinsic qualities with the fabric it makes.

Yarn Count

Yarn count refers to the thickness of a yarn. It is the ratio between its weight and its length. Also included is the number of strands that make up the yarn. For example, 8/2 cotton has a length to weight ratio of 8, and is made up of two strands of yarn plied together. It is fundamental to be able to identify yarns this way, because this is how they are presented and described, and it is important to correctly name the yarns we want to use and know how to talk with those who sell them. Following are some detailed explanations. There will be no homework at the end of this.

Yarn count describes:

- either the yarn's **length at fixed weight**, easily understood as **yards per pound or meters per kilogram**;
- or its **weight at fixed length** (which would be **ounces per yard**, a measurement used for fine yarns).

Weight at Fixed Length; Typical Yarn Count System

In the typical yarn count system, the first number indicates the "size" of the singles in the yarn (the second number indicates the number of plies). It is measured by the length of a single ply (of arbitrary thickness) contained in a hank weighing one English pound, which has been set at 840 yards for a size 1 cotton. So the standard 1/1 cotton yarn is made of a single strand of 840 yd/lb.

Each number increase would then be an increase of 840 yards, i.e., a cotton with a number "2" first refers to a yarn twice as long: 1,680 yd/lb (840 yd × 2), "3" refers to a cotton yarn that is 2,520 yd/lb (840 yd × 3). The higher the number, the finer the yarn.

Yarns made of different fibers have a different standard "1" size, but "1" will always be the thickest size. Here are the standard yards per pound for different fibers:

- Cotton, silk: 840 yd/lb
- Woolen spun wool: 256 yd/lb
- Worsted spun wool: 560 yd/lb
- Linen, jute, hemp, ramie: 300 yd/lb

Most weaving yarns have multiple plies, and this is indicated by the second number. So, for example, a 3/2 cotton yarn would be constructed from two singles of 2,520 yd/lb yarn twisted together.

When evaluating your yarn needs, also keep in mind that yarn count always refers to undyed yarn. The dyeing operations involve some transformations that can change the weight of the yarn. Cotton and linen are sometimes bleached, the fibers are dyed, the skeins contract during drying, or the pigments of the dyeing material make the yarn heavier. We do not know exactly the length indicated by the yarn count; our skein will inevitably be a little longer or shorter than shown on the label. This applies especially to hand-spun and hand-dyed yarns, and less to synthetic yarns, which are calibrated . . . industrially!

Tex

Although it is not widely used outside the industry, the international unit for yarn count is Tex, short for Textile. It is used for very fine yarns. **Tex** measures weight to length, not length to weight like previous units. A kilometer of yarn weighing one gram is 1 Tex. This unit is used mainly in industry because weavers rarely work with such fine yarns.

1 Tex = 1 g/km, 2 Tex = 2 g/km, and so on.

Depending on the fineness of the yarns, subunits are introduced for convenience:

- militex (mtex): 1 mtex = 1 mg/km
- decitex (dtex): 1 dtex = 1 dg/km
- kilotex (ktex): 1 ktex = 1 kg/km

Denier

Like the Tex, the denier measures the weight of a fixed length of a very fine yarn. **This length is 9,000 m.** This unit was developed in Piedmont during the 18th century.

1 denier (D or den) = 1 g/9,000 m, 3 den = 3 g/9,000 m

Finding the Yarn Count of an Unknown Yarn

Sometimes you have a "mystery yarn" in your stock, given by a friend or found here or there. To get an idea of the count of this yarn, you may use a yarn balance to find the approximate number of yards per pound.

Let's try an example.

1. Follow the instructions for your balance to set it up. Lay a length of yarn in the notch of the balance and allow it to hang freely.
2. Use scissors to trim the yarn a little at a time until the balancing arm is level.
3. Remove that piece of yarn and measure it.
4. Multiply that measurement by 100, and this will be the number of yards per pound (e.g., 8.4 inches × 100 = 840 yd/lb).

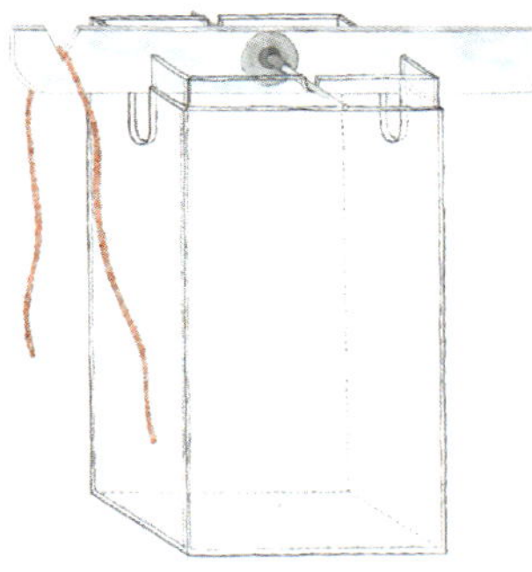

Figure 5 ***Yarn balance***

The Influence of Colors: The Lighting Designer at Work

Let's look at colors like an expert, but let's also know how to experience them with spontaneity and a certain innocence.

Michel Pastoureau, *The Little Book of Colors*, 2005

The feeling of having successfully made a woven item often comes from our reaction to its colors. The field of knowledge of color is vast; many scientists and artists have researched and written on the subject. We will not include here the history of color or the series of scientific discoveries related to it. Specialized works are readily available; some are mentioned in the bibliography in the appendices (see p. 275). The book by Deb Menz, in particular, is a valuable source, because she uses textiles exclusively to illustrate all her examples.

Colors inhabit the realm of emotion and the unconscious. Thus, the rational and scientific approach, even known and used by artists, is not always a good guide for an artistic choice. We like certain colors, either because they are linked to our stories and our own leanings, or because fashion influences us. The country in which we live and its culture also lock us into certain habits and rules. Marketing professionals know this and use it in their marketing strategy.

Even if we can say that nothing is beautiful or ugly, and that there is only what we like, some basic principles are unanimously adopted. It is necessary to know some fundamentals.

The Color Spectrum

Objects do not have their own color, rather they absorb or reflect light rays. The color is born in the eye and the human brain, which have the ability to decode the wavelengths emitted by light. These wavelengths are measured in nanometers (1 nm = 10–9 meters) and allow us to classify colors in the order they appear in the rainbow: red (780–658 nm), orange (658–600 nm), yellow (600–567 nm), green (567–524 nm), blue (502–431 nm), and purple (431–390 nm).

In 1695, Newton was the first to present the colors on a spectrum. They are classified into groups. The three **primary colors**, red or magenta, yellow, and blue or cyan, are pure colors; they form an equilateral triangle on the **color wheel**. They are impossible to reproduce by combining other colors. Between the primary colors we find the three **secondary colors**, mixtures of the two primary colors on each side of it in the circle: orange, green, and purple. A new mixture of a primary color and a neighboring secondary color produces the six **tertiary colors.** They are also inserted in the color wheel. Black and white are not part of the circle; these two colors are said to be neutral. They are used to reduce the intensity of pure colors.

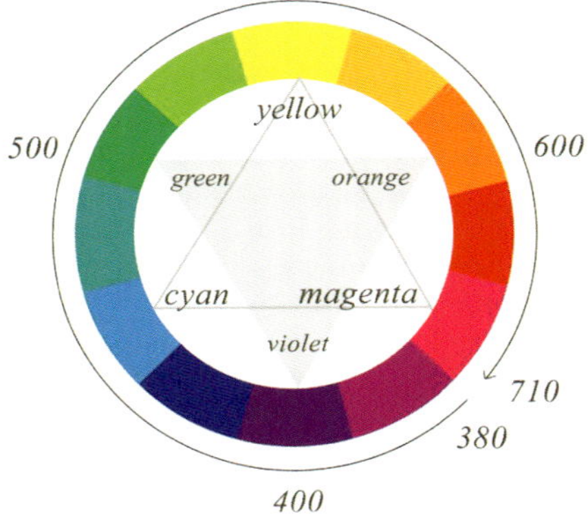

Figure 6 *Color wheel and color wavelengths*

Hue, Value, and Saturation: A Spotlight on the Properties of Color

Color is the only thing that is intrinsically impossible to describe, it is pure thought.

Daniel Buren Interview, *France Culture*, May 2020

Colors have three distinct and fundamental characteristics that determine their appearance: hue, value, and saturation.

When we call a color by its name, we are in fact talking about its **hue** or **tone**. We could say that the six basic colors, the primary and secondary colors, represent the "family name," while the infinite other hues are qualified by a "first name" such as vermeil red, poppy red, blood red, etc.

The brightness of a color is given by its **value**. Black-and-white photographs show only the values of colors. The gray scale is usually broken down into thirteen levels, going from black to white with regular increments. We can make it simpler by dividing the gray scale into three parts: dark grays, medium grays, and light grays. Black, white, and all intermediate grays are values of a colorimetric point of view. Of each of the colors, we can say if it is dark, medium, or light.

Saturation expresses the purity of a color. A bright color is said to be saturated if it is pure, and it is desaturated if it is mixed with black, white, or any other color of the palette (figure 7). Saturation is determined in percentage of primary and secondary colors. The more saturated a color is, the brighter it is. We also talk about intensity.

Figure 7 ***Color saturation***

By isolating the colors orange and blue located opposite each other on the color wheel (figure 8), we see that they seem to be more lightened than the colors in the center. We go from a pure color to its companion by adding a bit of the latter, little by little. We can establish a simple graduated scale: the prismatic color, the muted colors, the chromatic gray, the achromatic gray, the chromatic gray of the other color, the second muted color, and to finish the other pure color. That is why grays are pinkish or bluish.

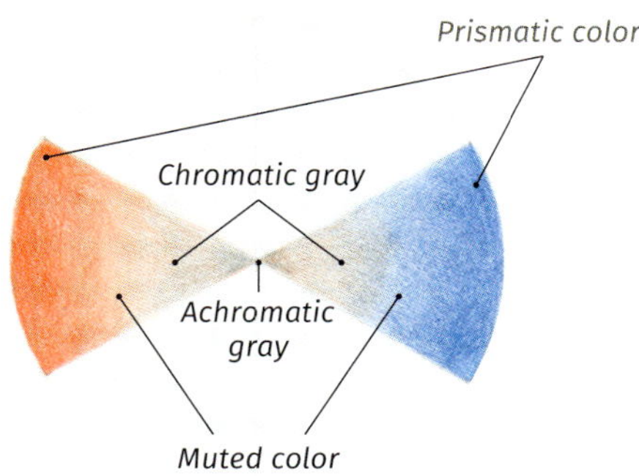

Figure 8 ***Prismatic colors and gray***

Knowing these few properties will sometimes help us to organize the choice and the associations of the colors in our weaving, knowing how to place them on the color wheel, knowing that some are light or dark, knowing why some are brighter. Let's say that this first preparatory work gives us some keys of understanding and the knowledge of a common language.

Other More Subjective Properties

We can list many other keys to classification, including these which are perhaps more familiar to us: the color will be **matte** or **shiny** (a matte color reflects less light), **bright** (yellow is the brightest color of the palette), **strong** (reds are the most powerful), **warm or cold** (red and its neighboring colors suggest warmth while at the opposite, blue evokes coldness). The color wheel is thus divided in two by a line going from red-violet to green-yellow. We will also use this chromatic circle to associate colors knowing that they are **complementary**. The color that is opposite of a color on the wheel is said to be complementary. The complementary color of each primary color is the mixture of the two other primary colors.

Effects of Contrast and Harmony

> In terms of visual perception, a color is almost never seen exactly as it is—as it is physically. This makes color the most relative element of art.
>
> Josef Albers, *Interaction of Colors*, 1810

Colors interact with each other so strongly that it is more judicious to choose a color depending on those colors that will surround it rather than just on its own. It is obviously easier with paints that are mixed than with yarns put side by side. Nevertheless, when choosing our yarn, it is necessary to cross them, to braid them, to twist them together to approach the effect that will be obtained by weaving.

Contrasts are optical phenomena that influence the perception we have of some colors in relation to others. The contrast of **complementary** colors is probably the most known. Two complementary colors (on opposite sides of the color wheel) are strengthened and appear brighter when they are placed next to each other. Playing with **light-dark** contrast makes it possible to lighten a color by putting it next to a dark color or to intensify it by placing it closer to light colors. Finally, the contrast of **quantity** seems rather obvious: the larger the surface area of a single color is, the stronger that color becomes.

Easier to use, softer to look at, the **monochromatic harmonies** are built by playing with different values or by using neighboring colors on the color wheel. This can consist of staying on the red color for example, and accompanying it with light and/or dark red, or choosing a pink or an orange.

Chevreul's Law of Simultaneous Contrast of Colors

> The frequent occasions that I have to look at the wide variety of colors and gradients required by the work at the royal tapestry factories put me in the position to make observations which will not be useless, I hope, to those who deal with matching diversely colored objects, in order to bring out the best possible match that is most pleasing to the eye.
>
> Michel-Eugène Chevreul, *Memorandum on the influence that two colors can have on each other when we see them simultaneously,* 1828

Figure 9 ***Chevreul's color wheel***

Figure 10 ***A "simultaneous dress" by Sonia Delaunay***

We cannot go on without talking about the work of **Michel-Eugène Chevreul**. Chemist and then **director of dyes of the *Manufacture Royale des Gobelins*** starting in 1813, he conducted extensive research based on an experimental method directly related to his work on tapestry dyes. He became known for his law of simultaneous contrast of colors. He affirms that the most tricky problems about colors are neither chemical nor physical, but physiological, that it is not the pigments that are in question, but the seeing of colors in relation to each other when they are side by side.

As soon as he became director of dyes, he received complaints about the quality of certain colors coming out of his workshop, which he attributed in part to poor contrast between them, stating that when two colors are close together in proximity, or when they are looked at one after the other, each one influences the perception that the eye has of the nuance and the tone of the other. "[. . .] where the eye sees two contiguous colors at the same time, they appear as dissimilar as possible. It is," he says, "a modification which occurs in us."

Thus, a color gives new **intensity** to a neighboring color (the lightest appears lighter and the darkest darker, an effect of contrast) and a new **nuance** (the complementary colors lighten each other and the noncomplementary colors mute each other).

Thus, when he arrived at Gobelins, he began by analyzing the colors, cataloging them, and naming them in a very scientific way. Through this work, it became possible to reproduce each color identically for the Gobelins tapestries. From then on, the research on color that he conducted in his laboratory took precedence over his work as a chemist. With knowledge from his previous experiments, including on fat and saponification, he studied colors from a physicochemical point of view to which he added aesthetic considerations.

So, he proposed a classification based on a color wheel with 72 segments. Each one is gradually modified in its intensity according to 20 tones, and then toned down with proportions of white or black. He listed 14,420 tones!

Chevreul's research was intense and methodical. He continued working on it until the end of his long life. A pioneer with Goethe, at a time when science was in its infancy, he inspired many painters and provoked controversy. Inspired by Chevreul's theory, in 1912 Robert and Sonia Delaunay founded Simultaneism, which consists in seeing in color contrasts the only possible variant of a painting, with these contrasts alone illustrating movement, space, and time, in the same way as music. Sonia Delaunay applied simultaneity to textiles and created her first dresses.

The painter Georges Seurat was inspired by the law of simultaneous contrast of colors. He used colors in small juxtaposed touches instead of mixing them on his palette, and pointillism was born. The mixture of the colors is made by our eye when we look at a painting from afar.

From the Gobelins Factory to Our Weaving Workshop—A Change of Scene!

Weaving is a crossing of threads where the warp and weft threads often appear equally, which is not the case in tapestry, where all the warp threads are completely covered. The hues of the yarns thus show on the surface depending on the interlacing of the selected weave pattern, the yarn count, and type of yarn. The size of a spot of color, its brightness, and its visibility will depend on the length of floats, on the contrast of the warp and weft colors, and on the yarn's thickness, twist, and type.

Type of fiber: A short fiber absorbs more light and appears duller, darker. A long fiber reflects the light more strongly and is more lustrous. Short fibers, even if they are made parallel by carding, will never have the appearance of a long combed fiber. Cotton and carded wool fibers are short. Silk, ramie, linen, worsted wool, and mercerized cotton fibers are long.

Yarn count: With two yarns of the same color, the thicker one appears darker. With two yarns of the same size and the same color, the one composed of several fine threads appears lighter than the one made up of fewer and larger threads, because it has more reflective surface. The fine threads tend to mix optically, and give more subtle hues, while the eye tends to isolate the thicker threads and see their true color. Finally, the thicker the yarn, the more structured the fabric will be, and the darker it will appear.

Weave structure: A tight weave allows little light to pass through and the color appears darker. For the same reason, a weave with a lot of intertwining does not allow the eye to analyze each thread individually. The floats are too short. Plain weave or tabby, which is a systematic crossing of all the threads, does not make it easy to analyze precisely; our brain merges the colors together. Conversely, floats highlight the yarn and the brain can more easily analyze the wavelength of the color carried by the float. To anticipate the effect of these colors being together, we think about the contrast of their values. The more contrast between the values, the more they will retain their effect despite being mixed together by the weaving and intersections. A plain weave in low-contrast colors shows the texture while colors that strongly contrast highlight the pattern.

The size of floats: The larger the float, the more light it reflects and the brighter it appears. To accentuate this effect, we can use combed yarns, and floats that are repeated or juxtaposed. The monk's belt weave structure, woven with linen or mercerized cotton, is a perfect illustration. I often take advantage of floats and accentuate them by choosing a brighter, more luminous yarn or a more prized one. I put it right at center stage.

The fabric patterns or the block: The larger the surface of the pattern is, the stronger its color appears. If we make two fabrics with the same yarns and colors, the one with the larger patterns will appear darker than the one where the patterns are smaller. If we want to obtain the same optical effect when the patterns are of different sizes, the smaller pattern should be made with a more luminous yarn. Similarly, colors that are not very strong are enhanced by using structures with blocks that visually define the color zone creating a frame effect.

The distance and angle of view of the weave: A color appears brighter when seen close up. From a distance, colors are not identifiable, and the whole piece looks duller. It's the effect of pixilation. A plaid fabric seems very colorful close up, but more like a single faded color seen from far away. For a placemat, which is sure to be seen up close, each color keeps its value regardless of the size of the patterns. For a curtain, which is likely to be seen from farther away, the colors and patterns appear

*Figure 11 **Linen floats with an overshot structure on a cotton plain weave***

*Figure 12 **Monk's belt. The plain weave is Venne 16/2 cotton and the floats are mercerized 34/2 cotton.***

more merged together. Garments, which are seen both up close and far away, nicely show a color effect seen from afar (bands, stripes, etc.) and very detailed patterns that can only be seen up close.

Finishes: Essential to the manufacture of a fabric, they give it its final character. They can sometimes alter the fabric, such as felting or fulling, and change the appearance of colors. A felted fabric, which is tighter, will appear duller. A mohair weave can be brushed and the very airy pile will lighten the fabric, but this carding will mute the strength of the colors. Linen, stiff and matte when it comes off the loom, regains its shine after washing.

Two Simple Tools Not to Be Neglected

Making a sample takes time, so being able to anticipate the effect of color on our weaving will save us time. To do this, I use two tools: **a small strip of cardboard and a camera**.

After cutting a piece of cardboard 2 inches (5 cm) wide and 4 to 6 inches (10 to 15 cm) long, I wrap the yarns chosen around it, following the color scheme I want to use. Then I look at it and evaluate. If necessary, I make several. This representation is obviously not true to the actual finished look since the yarns are not crossed and the colors appear pure. It is a first step in looking at a sample.

In cases where I use many colors, I sometimes make a small braid or a cord to mix the yarns and colors a little.

Of course, I may have chosen the colors based on the theoretical data stated above, using the color wheel, looking for or rejecting contrasts. Most of the time, looking at the strip of cardboard and changing the colors or their proportions to suit my taste is enough. Of course it may take a little time and experience to trust yourself. But it will come.

A **camera** in black-and-white mode allows us to assess **value of the colors**. By photographing the spools of selected threads or the cardboard strip in black and white, one can see that the value of the colors is independent of their hue. By analyzing the black-and-white photo, one might shift the order or quantity of the intended colors in order to achieve a pleasing harmony and balance. It is often very curious to realize that a color that does not appear to stand out often dominates the others in value on a black-and-white photograph.

The result will be even more eloquent if the threads are twisted together or braided. The black-and-white photo

Figure 13 ***Cardboard strip with the selected threads wound onto it***

Figure 14 ***Cardboard strip photographed in black and white to consider the color values***

will reflect the weaving. Either the contrast remains visible, in which case the effect of each color is preserved—each one is clearly visible—or the grays have barely any shades of difference, in which case it is certain that the mixed colors will dull each other, and none will really stand out.

Colors Surround Us

Steering clear from the theories or rules stated, I dare to offer a piece of advice. Nature, cities, store windows, posters, magazines, architecture, works of art, and fashion—a whole palette of colors and choices surround us. We must allow ourselves to look, to be inspired, to question ourselves, to judge, to criticize, to free ourselves from others' eyes and dare to include a bold color. The question of color, if it is looked at only in a theoretical way, can become too intimidating. Let's allow our intuition to guide us. There is no risk involved, just admiration or critique. A game to try!

I like sampling—it lets us try, test, check if the thread we're hesitant about will be just right. And sometimes, this exercise allows us to dare to choose a color that's out of the ordinary, even one that we don't like as much, and why not also one that seems in poor taste? In fact, it's because weaving is an interlacing of yarns that the interactions, so strong, prevent our brain from analyzing the original color. We will be able to see, like Chevreul, that the whole woven piece transforms the color and that, changed in that way, we will perhaps love it against all odds. So please, don't deprive yourself of this pleasure.

However, the sample, made to a smaller size will not be able to reflect the final effect as the size of the weaving will change the effect considerably. Many surprises still await us; it is also part of the charm of weaving

Which Weave Structure Should I Choose?

We call it dressing the loom, [. . .] attaching the cord to the treadles, pairing them, tying up the upper and lower lamms, distributing all their movements, establishing their connections, raising or lowering the heddles, dividing and opening the warp . . .

Encyclopédie Méthodique, "Manufactures et Arts," Volume Two, 1784

If the yarns and colors have been selected, the next step is to determine the method of interlacing. We are about to enter an infinite world, the world of **weave structures**. Dressing a loom consists of preparing the loom for weaving: threading the heddles, tying up the treadles to the shafts, attaching the lamms to the jacks, making all the adjustments necessary so that the weave structure selected can be created using the threads chosen.

The Basics

A **fabric** is the result of the interweaving of warp and weft threads. The **warp threads** are parallel to each other and arranged along the length of the fabric. The weft threads are perpendicular to the warp threads; they cross the warp threads and go back and forth from one edge to the other.

The weft thread is often called a **pick** when it crosses the fabric in the shed from one selvedge to the other. If the warp thread passes over or under several weft threads in a row, we get a **float**. If the warp passes over 2 weft threads we call it a 2-thread warp float. It is the same principle for weft floats. The edges of a piece of fabric are called **selvedges**.

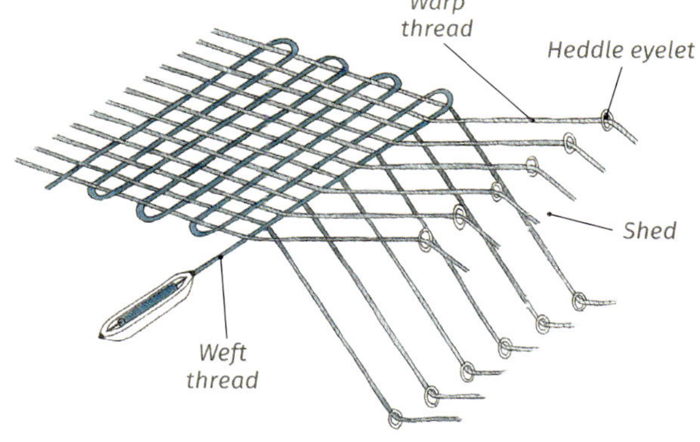

Figure 15 ***Interlacing of the yarns***

The **structure of a fabric** is the method of interweaving the threads used to make it. The warp threads are stretched on the loom, each held and guided exclusively by the eye of a heddle. When some of the shafts are lifted, the corresponding threads are lifted as well. The space between this layer of lifted threads and the threads below them is called the **shed**. Through this shed we slide the shuttle that carries the weft. Then we lower these shafts and raise other ones, another pick is sent through, and so on.

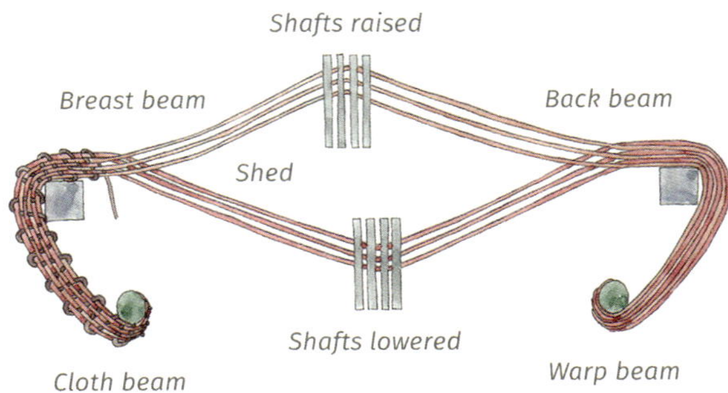

Figure 16 ***The shed***

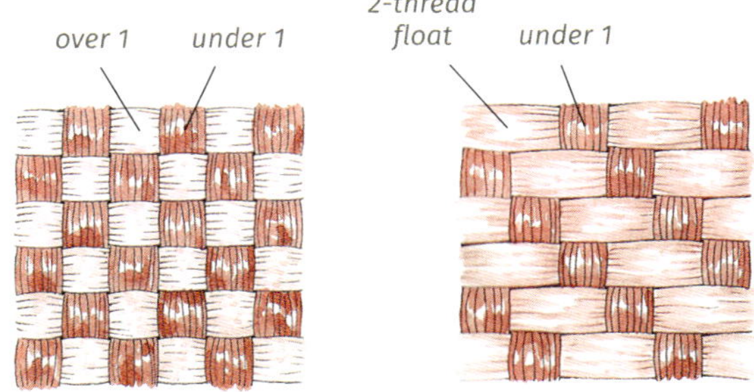

Figure 17 ***Different interlacings***

The Three Components of a Structure

Each fabric, depending on the structure chosen (threading, tying up, and treadling) has three characteristics:

- intersections, **interlacings**;
- **yarns** crossing the fabric, snaking between the other yarns, alternating passes above and passes underneath;
- **floats**, yarns that cross less often and go over several yarns at once.

Anyone who does a little weaving knows all this.

Nevertheless, let me insist on this idea: whether it is a warp or a weft thread, the story is the same. When the yarn goes from the top to the bottom, it slips between two other yarns, forcing them apart to make room for it. And it happens again each time they cross. **The interlacing creates the fabric.** Without it, we would have only parallel threads that would have to be joined together in another way. Crossing over and under forces the yarn to stay in place and creates the fabric. The more intersections there are, the more durable the fabric. Thinking about the preparation for a weaving project forces us to think about the amount of space needed for the weft to pass through, to interweave with the warp.

The weft is visible all the way through as it passes **over** the warp threads, when the latter are not lifted. Then it moves to the bottom, which in turn makes the warp yarn visible. It is the **yarn** that we are looking at, not the intersecting. It is the yarn that gives the fabric its identity, its color, its softness, its appearance. **The yarn is the artist.** It is at center stage. If it goes across with no stopping, it only shows a very small part of itself. When it floats, it is more generous because it crosses over several yarns in a row. The appearance of the fabric thus changes completely depending on the frequency of those intersections and whether the weft yarn bypasses one or more warp threads. The weft yarn, especially if it is fine, is hardly visible if it passes over a **single** warp yarn. On the other hand, this same yarn becomes more visible if it floats over two, three, or four warp yarns. Intersections "break" the visual line of the yarn, altering its charm. Their only role is to ensure sturdiness. It is the number of floats, the length of each float and where they are placed, and their arrangement in the weaving that will give it its identity and a name to the structure of the fabric. From a plain weave, basket weave, gabardine, and twill to a satin or damask, it is only the number of intersections and the length of the floats that differ.

One last thing to remember: **yarn is a good companion**. As soon as it can, as soon as it is free, it will move closer to its neighbors, the other yarns. This is how several floats that are next to each other will touch and stick together until a new intersecting yarn will separate them. This effect is particularly sought after in some structures, notably those of the openwork family (e.g., huck lace, Bronson lace).

Figure 18 ***Huck lace or Swedish lace. The noninterlaced threads draw closer to each other, creating open spaces.***

We will play with these two parameters according to the desired use of the fabric: maximum intersections to make it durable and the presence of floats to make it pretty.

The Three Basic Structures

In weaving, we use only three structures: plain weave, twill, and satin. Most of the time, the other structures are combinations or derivatives of these three.

Plain weave is the fundamental weaving structure, the one we begin with when we start to weave. It is the simplest to make. The majority of fabrics made in the world are made in plain weave. It is a very sturdy solid fabric because it has the maximum intersections. Each weft passes over and then under adjacent warp ends. No yarn can move, systematically surrounded by intersections all around it. The construction of plain weave is simple and uniform. Its basic unit is two warp and two weft; each weft thread alternates passing below, then above each warp end, with a shift of one thread for each pick. To prepare for a weft row, all even warp ends are lifted. For the return of the shuttle, these same even-numbered yarns are lowered and the odd warp ends are raised. Two shafts are enough to weave the fabric.

Twill contains floats, portions of warp or weft yarn that cross over or under two or more neighboring threads. The floats are not at the same place from one pick to the next. Each row is **offset** by one from the row above, so the floats create a diagonal pattern. At least three shafts are needed for twill, but most are made with four shafts, which allow for the weaving of the three basic twills. In 2/2 twill the weft thread passes **under 2**, then **over 2 warp ends**; for 1/3 twill the weft thread passes **under 1** then **over 3 warp ends**; and for 3/1 twill the weft thread passes **under 3** then **over 1 warp end**. The two sides of 2/2 twill are identical; the back of 1/3 twill is same as the front of 3/1 and vice versa.

Like twill, **satin** is composed of floats. The difference is that **the intersections never touch each other!** So the floats become much freer, and move closer to each other, laying over interlacing points until they are hidden. This gives the impression that the yarns are simply laid next to each other without the interruption of any intersections. The yarns appear to be continuous, without any break, and so reflect the light more and become brighter. At least five shafts are needed. The offset of two or three shafts in threading or tying up gives the name to the type of satin. A satin offset by 2 or 3 is called a 2 or 3 satin. Satin cannot be woven on six shafts. It is actually twill weaves that are offset by 1 and 5, and those with 2, 3, and 4 never activate some of the six shafts. With seven or more shafts, we multiply the alternatives: offsets of 2, 3, 4, 5, 6, 7, and more are possible. All this will be explained in much more detail in the section about basic structures (see page 123).

These three basic structures can be used to produce derivative structures that will combine them, repeat them, move them, or group them in different ways. These new structures are grouped by families, according to their similarities.

Some other fabrics do not come directly from these three basic structures, although they are made on a loom, and take certain liberties by introducing knots, twists, and hand sorting of yarns, such as velvets, brocades, knotted stitches, leno, etc.

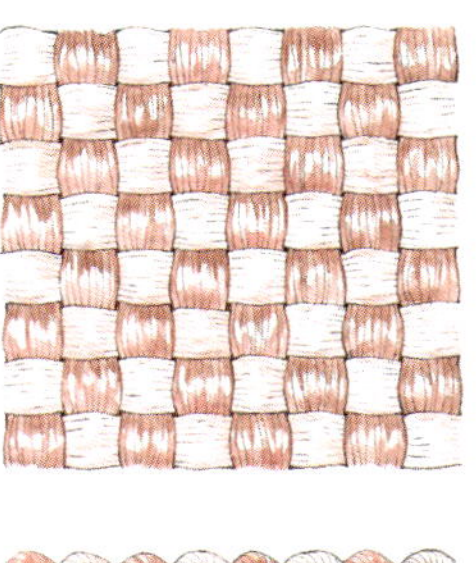

Figure 19 ***Plain weave***

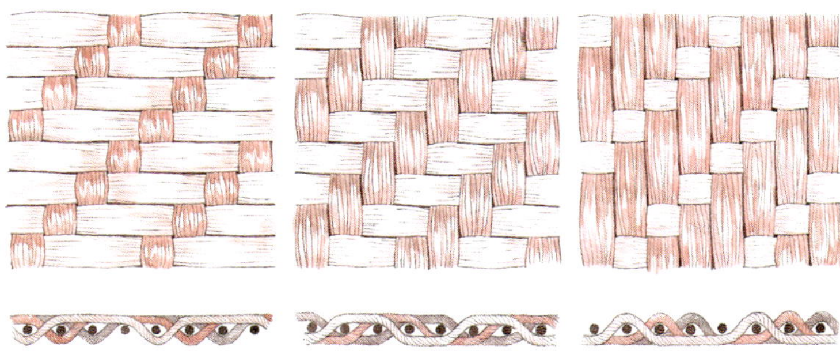

Figure 20 ***1/3, 2/2, and 3/1 twills***

Figure 21 ***Warp- and weft-faced satin***

What Should the Density Be? Do I Need to Make a Sample?

Initially, we don't know where we're going, it's very creative. We make samples. Then at some point two or three samples stand out, and those are the ones we want to push, to develop, to go farther with. At that moment, it's magic. What fun!

Interview with Caroline de Salins, winner of the 2016 Métiers d'Art Young Creative Craftworker's Award

The **thread count** of a fabric provides information on the densities and is defined by four values:

- the number of warp and weft yarns in a square inch of fabric;
- the respective yarn counts of these threads.

This concept is mostly used in industry. In artisanal weaving there is little talk of thread count, which is a pity. The yarn count and the **density of the warp and weft, or the warp count and weft count,** are presented separately.

The density of the warp is defined by sleying the reed. Density of the weft depends on beating with the reed after each weft pick. We call the warp yarn an end, and the weft a pick. Thus we speak of ends per inch (**epi**), i.e., the number of warp threads per inch, and picks per inch (**ppi**), the number of weft threads per inch.

The most frequent question from weavers is without a doubt about density: **"What density should I choose with this yarn?:** And always, the most accurate answer is: **"It depends!"** It's pretty annoying, I know, but that's the way it is. Because that choice depends on several options.

The first is the **function** of the fabric. Obviously, you don't want the same density for an upholstery fabric as for a wrap. For the first, a high density will be necessary, while lightness is desired for the latter.

The yarn used will also affect the density of the weave. The thickness of the yarn obviously plays a part in what we choose. A mohair yarn requires a much lower density than another yarn of the same count, otherwise its softness will not be highlighted. The flexibility and fluidity of the yarn also come into play. Some wool yarns swell a lot after washing; it is then necessary to anticipate this in the density calculation in order to leave room for the yarn to expand.

Another very important criterion to consider is the weave structure chosen. Depending on the structure, the weft thread will go through more or less often. The space to be left between the warp threads so that it interlaces fluidly is different. So the warp ends will then be more or less close together. It is the **interlacing** that requires space. Depending on whether the weft thread crosses often, as in plain weave, or less often, as in twill, the space to be left for the weft will be more or less large. In plain weave, the weft crosses around each warp thread, so there should be enough space left around each warp thread to let the weft pass. In twill, the intersections are fewer; the weft thread floats over two and then under two warp threads. Therefore, we need to leave less space. The number of warp threads will be higher in twill, and the density higher as well. We can see that by using an identical yarn in warp and weft, the density changes depending on the structure. This is why plain weave and twill cannot be woven one after the other with the same weft yarn without the selvedges curling. Remember, yarn is a good companion. It doesn't like empty space, and it draws close to its neighbor. Have you planned a density for the fabric? Then you decide to weave in twill? The density will be too low, and the warp threads will do everything they can to get closer together, taking advantage of any free space. **You will therefore have a lot of shrinkage**, and a fabric that is a lot less wide in the area where you wove a twill, unless you chose a thicker weft, or you beat more firmly on the weft.

Let's look at the **example** below. The first line shows the threads lined up next to each other, as we do on a ruler to estimate the density. Let's imagine 40 threads over 1 inch (2.5 cm) on our ruler. The second line shows that in **plain weave:** every other thread was removed to leave room for interlacing of the weft. Of the 40 threads placed side by side on the ruler over 1 inch, we keep 20 for the warp, and the 20 spaces freed up are replaced by the weft. We get a density of 20 threads per inch (8 per cm), which is the density of the plain weave.

For **2/2 twill**, shown in the third line, we use the same logic. With our 40 threads, the weft only intersects 6 times, so the density of the warp is 25 threads per inch (10 per cm). For **warp satin**, shown in the fourth line, or **weft satin**, just below that, 5 warp ends are separated by two weft threads.

For each of these structures, adding together the density of the warp and the number of weft intersections, we get an initial number of 40 threads: 20 + 20 in plain weave, 25 + 15 in 2/2 twill. The count for a 5 satin is over 35 threads: 25 + 10.

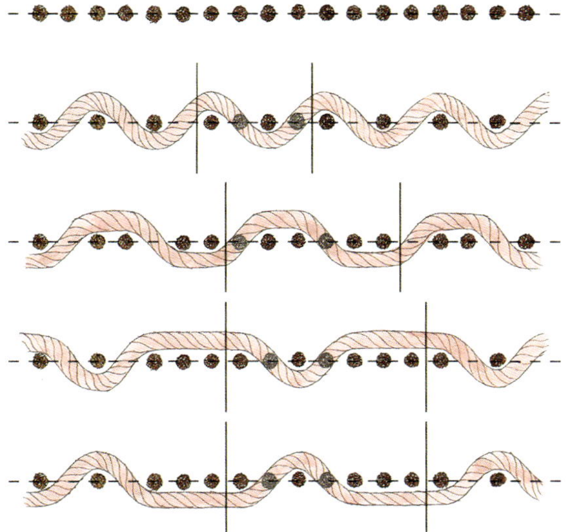

Figure 22 ***Cross-section view showing the space needed for the weft to pass through different structures: plain weave, 2/2 twill, weft satin, and warp satin***

The last criterion is purely subjective. Some people like dense, tightly compacted fabrics, while others prefer more pliable fabrics. This is really just a matter of **taste**.

Choosing the density consists of determining the number of warp ends over 1 inch (or 1 cm) or over 4 inches (10 cm) when the yarn is thick, and **the space needed for the weft** between the warp, so that each thread has its place, all of its place, nothing but its place, without being too squished and without excessive extra room.

Calculating Density

First, the warp density will be estimated and then tested with a sample. Some weavers will trust their intuition, their usual practices, or even reference tables (see p. 47). Others will prefer a more rational approach and will do the necessary calculations. A little overwhelming at first, this method is nevertheless very useful and becomes simple with a little practice.

Ashenhurst's Formula

The **warp density** is chosen first. Three pieces of information are essential to guide our choice:

- the number of warp threads that can be wrapped around a ruler over one inch = **R**;
- the number of warp threads in a **weave unit** (the smallest width of the threading sketch that must be repeated to get the complete draft) = **Wa**;
- the number of times the weft crosses the warp in this weave = **We**.

1. To calculate R, we wrap the yarn around a ruler over 1 inch (2.5 cm) or 4 inches (10 cm), depending on the size of the yarn, and then count the number of wraps. This requires a little practice, because you have to cover the ruler well, keeping all the wraps together, without pulling too much on the yarn. The yarn must be placed on the ruler with the same elasticity that it will have in the fabric, freed from the tension of the loom. For easier handling, you can also put a strip of glue on a piece of cardboard and wrap the thread around it, as we did when choosing colors.

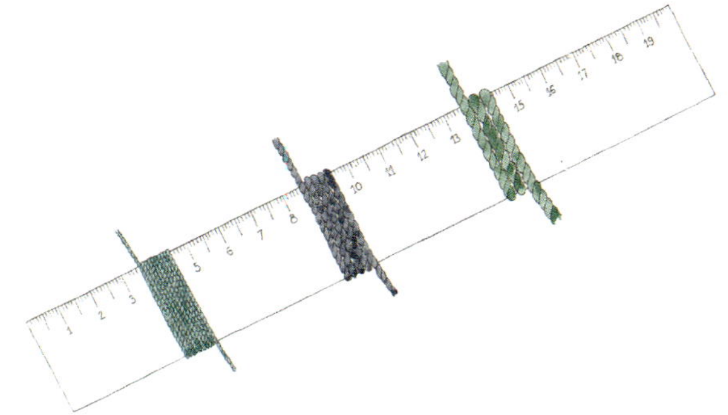

Figure 23 ***Wrapping the thread around the ruler to estimate density***

2. **The weave repeat is then drawn and the number of intersections counted.** Let's take a plain weave, for example, and choose the same yarn in warp and weft. The weft thread crosses each warp end, going over one and under the next. In the weave repeat, i.e., the smallest section that repeats, we find 2 warp ends and the number of intersections to leave room for the weft is also 2. We get Wa = 2 and We = 2.

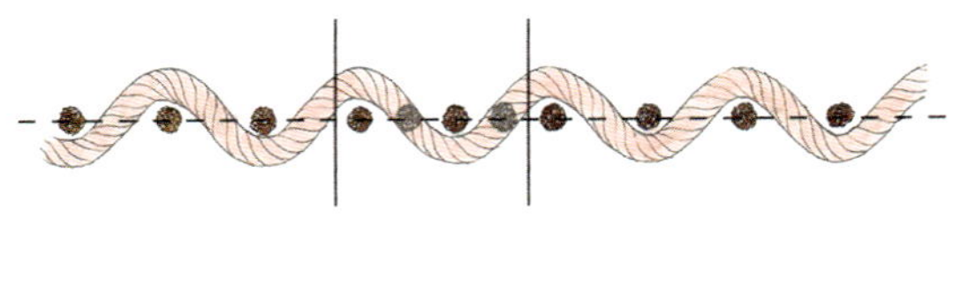

Figure 24 *Weave repeat for plain weave*

The **magic formula** used to find the density is the one from Thomas Ashenhurst, who worked in the textile industry in Bristol around 1880.

$$\textbf{D}\text{ensity} = \frac{\text{No. of wraps of yarn around the }\textbf{R}\text{uler} \times \text{No. of }\textbf{Wa}\text{rp ends in a weave unit}}{\text{No. of }\textbf{Wa}\text{rp ends} + \text{No. of }\textbf{We}\text{ft threads in the same weave unit}}$$

$$D = \frac{R \times Wa}{Wa + We}$$

For this example in plain weave, let's imagine that we wrap the yarn around the ruler 40 times per inch, with an 8/2 cotton for example. The density to choose will be:

R = the number of wraps per inch around the ruler = 40

Wa = the number of visible warp threads in the weave repeat = 2

We = the number of times the weft crosses the fabric = 2

$$D = \frac{40 \times 2}{2 + 2} = 20$$

We test the density with a sample by putting 20 threads per inch in the reed and beating to 20 threads per inch in weft to check our calculated assumption.

Let's continue with the same yarn in **2/2 twill**:

R = number of wraps per inch around the ruler = 40

Wa = the number of visible warp threads in the weave repeat = 4

We = the number of times the weft crosses the fabric = 2

$$D = \frac{40 \times 4}{2 + 4} = 26.7$$

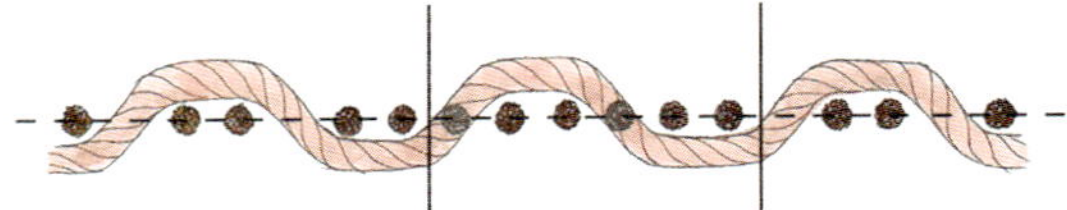

Figure 25 *Weave unit for twill*

With a sample we test a density of 26, then of 27 threads per inch. However, there is nothing to prevent us from sleying the reed at 26.5 threads per inch; I will explain how in the section "The Reed: The Tool to Obtain Your Desired Density" (see p. 51). I know, it may make you smile, but why approximate density too early?

It's up to you to do the calculation with the same yarn but this time in satin. I'll just give you the solution:

$$D = \frac{40 \times 5}{2 + 5} = 28.6$$

The correct density is around 28 or 29 threads per inch in the reed.

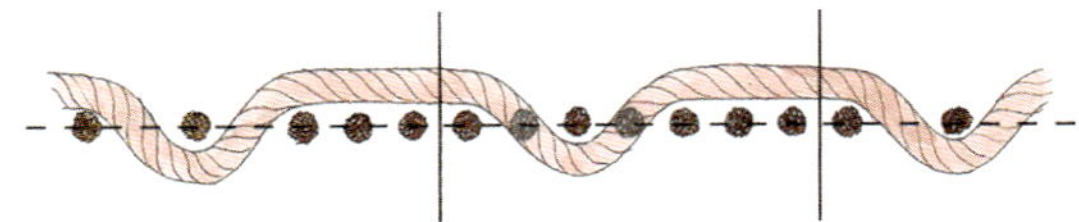

Figure 26 *Weave unit for satin*

This formula only works when the warp and weft have the same yarn count. Otherwise, of course, the space reserved for each place where the weft intersects must be changed.

When **using warp and weft that have different yarn counts**, it is wise to make wraps on the ruler or cardboard with both threads, reproducing the weave repeat exactly.

Example: for plain weave, one warp thread and one weft thread are wound alternately on the ruler. For a 2/2 twill, we wind 2 warp threads and 1 weft thread. Then, we count the number of warp threads wound on 1 inch This will be the warp density to choose from when sleying the reed.

Depending on the yarn count, we wind on several inches and take the average to obtain the result for 1 inch.

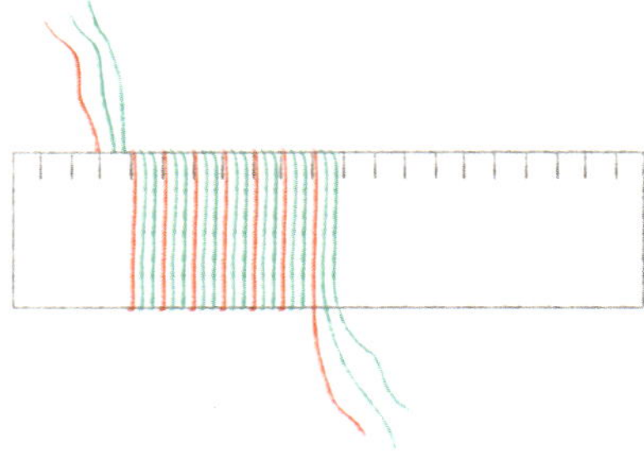

Figure 27 *Estimate of density with different warp and weft yarns*

Simplified Calculations: Percentages

We can make this work easier by using **simple percentages** that in most cases will do the trick for calculating warp density with a 4-shaft loom:

- Plain weave: 50% of the number of yarns wrapped around the ruler;
- Twill: 60% to 75%;
- Satin: 80% to 90%;
- Huck: 40% to 50%.

These percentages are derived directly from Ashenhurst's formula described above, but they do not help to understand its meaning. It is important to remember that they can only be used if the warp and weft have the same yarn count. Otherwise, it is much more precise to use the formula, winding the different yarns onto the rule in proportion to their use in the weaving.

Using a Table to Save Time

The following table allows you to estimate the density in the reed, but it should not be taken at face value. Density depends so much on the intended use of the fabric and on our own tastes in terms of flexibility of the fabric. It is a guide, nothing more, to always be checked by a sample!

Table 2 Yarn count and approximate density in plain weave and twill

Yarn Count	Density per inch in Plain Weave	Density in Twill
	Cotton	
20/2	25–30	32.5–35
10/2	25	27.5
8/2	15–22.5	22.5–30
8/4	12.5–15	20
5/2	15	17.5
4/2	12.5	16.25
3/2	10–12.5	15
	Linen	
20/2	20–22.5	25–27.5
12/1	22.5–25	27.5–30
4/1	12.5–15	15–17.5
	Wool	
20/2	20–22.5	27.5–30
12/3	15–17.5	20
12/2	17.5–20	22.5–25
7/2	12.5–15	15–17.5

Making Samples: The Dress Rehearsal

The only tool that will allow us to check our choice of density is the **sample**. This step can seem unnecessary, long, and costly. However, without it, we cannot know how the yarn will react, what constraints will be imposed by the weave structure, what kind of beat we will have, or how we will like our choice of colors. But above all, what density we will choose! It is so much more prudent to confirm our choice by making a sample rather than finding out, after a lot of work, that the result is disappointing. The weaving will have been in vain and expensive, and you will have wasted time.

What width should we make it? Beware of a sample that is too narrow because it is difficult to see the true effect of the color or weave. It is also tricky to beat in the same way; since it is easier to beat a narrow piece of weaving, we can press it too much. Six to eight inches (15 to 20 cm) of width are necessary, for sure not less!

What length? Once the weaving, tying on, and treadling are determined, all that remains is to check the **density**. In this case, I wind a fairly short warp, which will allow me to cut and re-sley the reed once or twice. 4 or 5 feet (1.2 to 1.5 m) can be enough.

But the sample pushes me to **try new things and be creative**. From experience, I often find that I lack the length of warp to "try everything," which is why I have a weakness for long samples. The first few picks always lead me to new ideas. So I cut, I rethread, hoping to find better effects. All these changes consume yarn length. I prepare a warp so it's possible to have at least one meter of weaving, so I never warp less than 5 feet (1.5 m). Much more often, for a sample I will warp 13 feet (4 m). This gives me the freedom to explore without restraint.

The sample has two jobs, the first concerning **aesthetics**. This consists of checking if our choices of yarns, colors, and structure match the idea we have in mind and if the fabric is suitable for our project. The other job is more **technical**, weaving to check the estimated density. Once out of the loom, washed, dried, and possibly ironed, we look at the sample to see if we like it, if we're happy with the colors and order of the yarns and if we are satisfied with the flexibility. This subjective impression of the fabric to the touch is called "the hand": rough, flowing, supple, hard, etc.

A Valuable Method for Testing the Same Density in Warp and Weft

Details make perfection, and perfection is not a detail.

Léonard de Vinci, *Notebooks*, circa 1500

Most weaves are **balanced weaves**. This means that they have the same density in warp and in weft when the yarns used are both the same weight. In order for the sample to truly test the assumed warp density, it must be **woven with the same yarn counts in warp and weft**.

The method consists of weaving the sample by beating the weft picks in such a way as to get precisely the same density for the weft as the one in the reed for the warp. To obtain this result, there is no other way than to put a tape measure on the weaving. Check frequently, for the first few inches woven, that the weft count is the same as the warp count. If the density chosen in warp is 10 threads per inch (2.5 cm), check that you have woven 1 inch after throwing 10 picks! The trick is to make the beating uniform to obtain this balance. Very quickly, you will measure your movements by eye and the strength of your hand. You can quickly do without the tape measure.

After having woven at least 4 to 6 inches (10 to 15 cm), cut this sample weave, wash it, and decide if the result is satisfactory. If it is not, you can always re-sley, re-weave following again the even weave, re-cut, re-wash, and re-decide. And maybe even re-re-do it???

More simply, you can use a piece of cardstock with a 45-degree angle cut off, to lay frequently over the weaving to check that the diagonal of the fabric follows that of the card stock. This method is perhaps less obvious with plain weave, but is convincing with twill rib or compound structures.

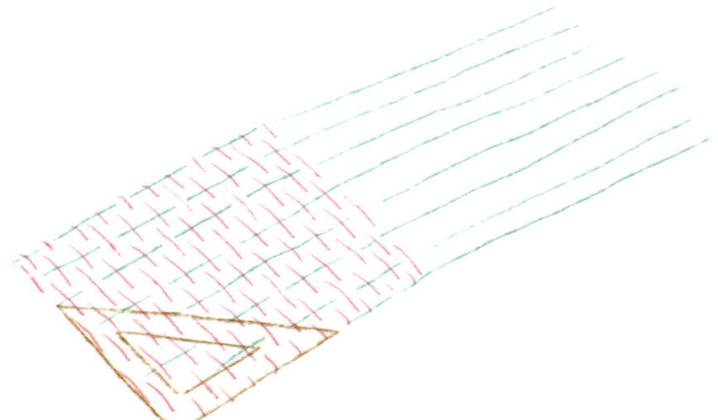

Figure 28 ***A 45-degree diagonal to check the balance of the weave***

Inevitable Shrinkage

There are many terms that describe the inevitable contraction of your woven fabric: **shrinkage, draw-in, take-up,** and others. However, they are all simply contraction and there are two kinds. One is related to the making of the fabric and the other to washing or other post-weaving finishing processes.

Shrinkage related to weaving

This is explained by undulations of the yarn when interlacing. The distance across the fabric is not a straight line, but rather, the weft travels over and under the warp. This up and down movement requires some length of thread. **Take-up or shortening** is a **contraction in length**. **Draw-in** is a **contraction in width**. For our nonindustrial uses, without distinguishing warp or weft, I will speak of the **shrinkage of fabric taken off the loom**. For most balanced weaves, where the number of threads per inch is the same in warp and weft, the percentages of take-up and draw-in are equivalent.

Nevertheless, it is important to really understand what is happening and to remember that this shrinkage depends on several factors:

- the type of yarn: its diameter, its elasticity;
- the structure used: the amount of interlacing;
- the density of the warp and weft: the closer the threads are to each other, the greater the up and down movement will be, and thread will hardly lie flat;
- the tension of the warp ends: the more tension on the warp, the more the weft will have to go up and down;
- the force on the beat: the more firm the beat, the more the weft will go over and under the warp.

In a **balanced structure**, which is the case for most weaves, if the warp and weft threads are identical, the shrinkage is the same in length and width, provided the warp is not excessively taut. Very low shrinkage indicates a good choice of density.

Conversely, in the case of a **warp rep** or a **rag rug** (see "Basic Structures" on p. 141), the warp threads are going to move up and down considerably over the very thick weft, so a much greater length of warp is required. The percentage of shrinkage can come close to 50 percent.

With a **weft-faced rep** like *boundweave* or *krokbragd*, the warp ends are very taut to allow the weft to go around them. In this case, there is almost no shrinkage. However, it is necessary to plan for a longer weft so that the yarn can wind through easily.

The **waffle weave** is undoubtedly the structure that contracts the most. We cannot calculate theoretical shrinkage for it and choose an appropriate density beforehand as neighboring floats, unequal in length, can slide over one another and overlap. This structure sometimes gives us a hard time. It is only when it comes off the loom and after washing that it takes on its full volume. What it loses by shrinking it gains in volume, thus offering to the weaver an astonishing three-dimensional structure.

Shrinkage related to wet finishing

Yarn reacts to various types of wet finishing of the woven fabric, such as washing and ironing, dyeing, or felting. This shrinkage acts on all yarns, whether they are woven or not. Fringe will shrink in the same way.

Whether you are the type to improvise or instead to reason everything out in advance, there is nothing more frustrating than to have to stop your weaving because of a lack of material or to discover after washing that the fabric intended for the curtains is so short that you will not be able to put it on the windows as planned. Knowing the difference between these two types of shrinkage will avoid this kind of inconvenience. This is also what a **sample** is for!

A Very Simple Application

If I have convinced you, you are now ready to make a sample. We're going to do it together. Let's start with a warp 6 inches (15 cm) wide and 5 feet (1.5 m) long. First estimate the density using Ashenhurst's formula or the table, either will do.

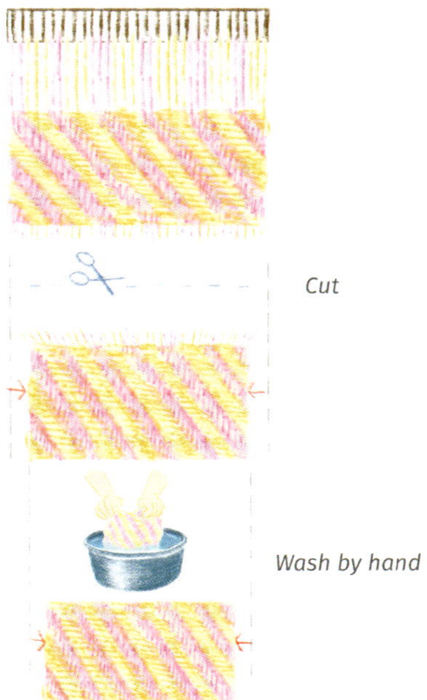

Figure 29 ***Calculating weft shrinkage***

Weave about 6 inches (15 cm), watching very carefully that your weft count is exactly the same as your warp count. Then cut this sample piece. You will note precisely the reed width and the width of the weave once it comes off the loom.

Wash, dry, iron, and again measure the width of the finished fabric. Using these three widths, you can find the percentage of weft shrinkage (Figure 29).

Warp shrinkage is more difficult to calculate. For balanced weaves, we will apply the same percentages in warp and weft. For other weaves, the only way is to unweave a warp yarn from the sample, and measure the difference between the length of the yarn removed and the length of the fabric.

Percentage calculations can be a bit daunting.

However, I can only imagine your joy in seeing how the following new formulas can help you. First the one for take-up, or how much the yarn rebounds after being removed from the tension of the loom, then the shrinkage due to post-weaving wet finishing.

$$\text{Percentage of shrinkage when removed from the loom} = \frac{\text{Width of fabric on reed} - \text{Width of fabric off the loom}}{\text{Width of fabric off the loom}} \times 100$$

This percentage should be as low as possible, and in any case, less than 10. I always look for a percentage close to zero, but never more than 3 or 4 percent. I have made it a challenge for my students, and those who do not exceed 2 percent are applauded!

We must always remember that a piece of yarn takes up its whole place, but nothing but its place. A high percentage of shrinkage means that as soon as the warp threads are released from the reed, they will move closer to each other, leaving only enough room for the weft thread that runs through. The fabric is then less wide than what we had planned with the reed. This is how the warp threads do not remain parallel on the edges. As a result, the reed rubs the selvedge threads a lot and they eventually get worn down and break. If the edges break a lot, it is a sign that the density of the warp is not high enough, that the weft threads are not able to fill the space left free. So you must re-sley the reed and increase the density so the warp ends are closer and decrease the width in the reed.

It is possible to cheat and weave without significant shrinkage, filling in the gaps by beating harder. But we will no longer get a balanced weave. This is not serious in itself, but the fabric will not be as pretty, twill will not have a 45-degree slant, the pattern blocks will not be the same width and height in a compound weave, and colored stripes will not be identical in width and height in the case of a plaid pattern.

$$\text{Percentage of shrinkage from post-weaving wet finishing} = \frac{\text{Width of fabric off the loom} - \text{Width of fabric after wet finishing}}{\text{Width of fabric after wet finishing}} \times 100$$

This shrinkage depends only on what you do to the fabric: washing, ironing, dyeing, etc. It has nothing to do with any defect in weaving or prior calculations.

These two percentages are then used to calculate the amount of yarn needed for the project. A specification sheet shown in the next chapter will guide you through this next step. But most importantly, for these percentages to be relevant, **the beat must be done in such a way that the weft count is the same as the warp count**.

A sample is most valuable when it is finished. This means that it must be taken off the loom, released from tension, then washed, dried, and ironed. It is only with this finished fabric that you can make any decisions. If, in the end, the fabric is not to your liking—too loose, too soft, too tight, too anything—then you must sley the reed again, and test a new density by weaving, cutting, washing, and measuring. This may seem tedious, but then what a pleasure it is to weave with confidence!

However, let's not get carried away by these calculations. These are tools that can either suit us or deter us. In the latter case, let your intuition speak for itself and make sure that you like your sample! This is **THE fundamental criterion**. The table on p. 47 shows the density for some common yarns by their yarn count. It can be useful and sufficient at first. Then with experience, little by little, the use of these formulas will become easier. Please, no worrying beforehand!

A Trick for the Unwilling

I smile when talking about samples because I see so often that course participants resist this exercise. With perseverance, I can sense that things are changing. And to lighten up my insistence, I suggest two ways of doing it.

The **"real" way** is to set up a warp as I have just explained. Enough length so as to not run out, not too wide so as not to consume too much yarn, and with a density chosen according to Ashenhurst's formula, or more empirically according to your mood. This warp should allow you to weave several samples in a row with densities that can be changed. We weave, measure, cut, wash, and evaluate. If necessary, we re-weave until the density is just right. The length of the warp allows for several trials. The many successive tie-ups require a length of warp that will not be woven, but which should nevertheless be taken into account when calculating quantity. Nothing is more frustrating than arriving at the end of the warp without having found the ideal density for your project.

The most difficult part of this exercise is to **use consistent force when beating the weft**. Over a large width of weaving, it is difficult to reproduce the same force as that practiced on the small sample width.

If, by chance, the density is found quickly, then some warp remains. This is the opportunity for new research on colors, tying up, treadling, etc.

This method is ideally suited for wider weaving projects. So, before warping, threading, sleying the reed, and many tie-ups, we test our project over a small width, therefore with less yarn.

A second way of doing things is often sufficient for a narrower weave. It is then a matter of winding and beaming the warp of your final project with a length greater than that of your project, and devoting the beginning of the warp to weaving the sample.

Figure 30 ***A sample directly before weaving***

This method is tempting because it has the advantage of not having to beam two warps. But it has many disadvantages. As with the "real" method, weave 4 to 8 inches (10 to 20 cm), then cut, wash, and examine. If the density has to be revised, then **the whole warp** has to be re-sleyed! Easy when the weave is not very wide, but longer anyway than for a sample warp that is 6 to 8 inches (15 to 20 cm) wide. Moreover, let's imagine that the density is too low, the fabric is too supple, so the threads must be narrowed in the reed. The width of the weaving will then be decreased, sometimes by a lot.

Conversely, if the density is to be reduced, then the weave will expand and, being limited by the width of your loom, you may be forced to remove warp ends. This can be annoying if the weave has a pattern that will be cut off.

To be extra thorough, I combine these two methods. When the width of a weave must meet very precise dimensions, such as for a garment or curtain, I make the usual sample on a small width. Then, while winding the warp for my project, I add 20 inches (50 cm) of length, and that part will be used to verify my assumptions in real width.

As you can see, for me, making samples is essential. And if "wasting" a bit of material is stopping you, imagine all the things you can make with these little pieces of fabric: a case, a purse, buttons, etc. It's up to you to create your own sample library.

Above all, remember that you can't judge the result until the sample is finished—cut, washed, and ironed! Don't decide too hastily: a simple glance at the sample still on the loom is useless.

The Reed: The Tool to Get the Density You Want

Suppliers offer reeds with many different densities. Most of the time, we receive a 10-dent or 12-dent reed. As time goes by, we add to our collection, but very often, we don't have the right reed, and we are stuck. It is actually very easy to get around the problem: you just have to change the **sleying sequence**. Here are some examples on a 10-dent reed.

By putting one thread per dent, 1-1-1-1-1, we have a density of 10 warp ends per inch (per 2.5 cm). If we skip one dent after every three ends, 1-1-1-0, we get a density of 7.5 ends per inch (epi). By doubling the number of ends, 2-2-2-2, we obtain a density of 20 epi. Doubling warp ends in every other dent, 1-2-1-2, gives 15 epi. By doubling warps ends in every fourth dent, 1-1-1-2, we get a density of 11.5 epi. You see, everything is possible. The only absolute rule to respect is to always repeat this sequence in the same order! Otherwise, it would be a sleying error that will be visible throughout your weaving and forever.

With thicker yarns, it is much wiser to calculate the density over several inches, or even over the entire width. It is just as clear and not more complicated. What to think, after having wound the warp around the ruler and having applied Ashenhurst's formula, of a density of 5.64 epi, for example? It seems a bit ridiculous. But if you calibrate to 4 inches, that translates into a density of 22 to 23 ends per 4 inches. Now let's imagine a 5-dent reed. Over 4 inches we have 22 ends for 20 dents, or 11 ends for 10 dents. The reasoning is very simple: we place 1 end per dent in the first 9 dents then 2 threads in the 10th dent (1-1-1-1-1-1-1-1-1-2)! If you'd like to play—don't look ahead—maybe you can do the same exercise with a 6-dent reed? The answer is 1-1-1-1-1-1-1-1-1-1-1-0. As you can see, sometimes we have to round off. But not too much, not too soon.

For the math whizzes, it is a matter of finding the greatest common denominator. Let's look at the following example. I want to weave 280 threads on a width of 32 inches (80 cm) with a 10-dent reed. With this reed and this width, I will use 320 dents (32 inches × 10 dents per inch) in which I want to distribute 280 threads. 320 and 280 are divisible by 40; this is their largest common denominator. We get 8 dents (320/40) for 7 threads (280/40). We then sley by distributing 7 threads for every 8 dents, always skipping the same dent in each repeat. Did you follow me?

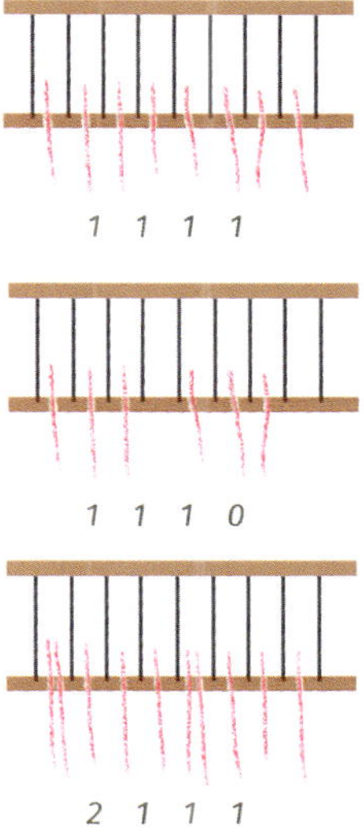

Figure 31 ***From top to bottom: regular sleying, 1 thread/dent; irregular sleying, 1 thread/dent 3 times then 1 empty dent; 2 threads/dent 1 time then 1 thread/dent 3 times***

The following table can save you some time and calculations. It indicates the sleying sequence for 12-dent, 10-dent, and 8-dent reeds according to the desired warp density. In this way, you can sley the density you want without worrying, for any one of these three reeds.

Table 3 ***Sley sequence by warp density and reed density***

Number of ends per inch (2.5 cm) by reed density			Sleying Sequence
12-dent reed	10-dent reed	8-dent reed	
4	3	2.5	0-0-1
6	5	4	0-1
8	7	5	0-1-1
9	7.5	6	0-1-1-1
12	10	8	1
15	12.5	10	1-1-1-2
16	13	11	1-1-2
18	15	12	1-2
20	17	13	1-2-2
21	17.6	14	1-2-2-2
24	**20**	16	2
27	22.5	18	2-2-2-3
28	23	19	2-2-3
30	25	**20**	2-3
32	27	21	2-3-3
33	27.5	22	2-3-3-3
36	30	24	3
39	32.5	26	3-3-3-4
40	33	27	3-3-4
42	35	28	3-4
48	40	32	4
200	160	120	4

Let's take an example. If I want to sley with a density of 20 epi, I can choose:

- a 12-dent reed with a sequence of 1 end in one dent and 2 ends in the next 2 dents;
- a 10-dent reed with a sequence of 2 ends per dent;
- an 8-dent reed with a sequence of 2 ends in one dent then 3 in the next.

I repeat: the only absolute rule to respect is to always repeat this sequence in the same order!

The project, the yarn, and the structure all interact, and it is only when we have found the right balance between these three parameters, through precise sample making, that the preparations for weaving can really begin. The foundations are laid! Changing one of these three parameters necessarily requires us to revisit the initial project. Rather than thinking of this as a chore, remember that it is often a nice way to look a bit further for a better idea. Of course, if you replace mercerized cotton with mohair, you probably won't still be weaving a placemat. More subtly, by changing only a yarn color, you might feel that another structure would enhance this yarn more. The search for a new balance is once again necessary. However, you also have to know when to stop and make a decision, even if this time of research is magical and a big part of the fun of weaving. I know some whose greatest pleasure is to weave only samples!

What Size Should It Be?

Things that have the right proportions delight the senses.

St. Thomas Aquinas, philosopher and theologian, 13th century

The last questions to ask yourself before starting to handle the yarn concern the dimensions of the item itself. This will allow us to calculate how much warp to wind to obtain the desired width. Then what length the warp should be so that the fabric has the expected dimensions. Then we will know quantities of yarn, without coming up short or having far too much material.

There are standard dimensions for various items, which we can refer to when in doubt. But since we are now creating for ourselves and can make all the decisions, we should not deprive ourselves of this opportunity and choose freely what we think will be best.

These few examples may serve as a place to start:

- napkin: 12 × 12 in. or 16 × 16 in. (30 × 30 cm or 40 × 40 cm);
- placemat: 12 × 18 in. or 14× 20 in. (30 × 45 cm or 35 × 50 cm);
- tea towel: 16 × 20 in. or 10 × 10 in. (40 × 50 cm or 25 × 25 cm);
- potholder: 7 × 7 in. (17 × 17 cm);

- scarf: 10 to 14 in. (25 to 35 cm) wide, 4 to 6 ft. (120 to 180 cm) long;
- shawl, wrap: 2 × 6½ ft. (60 × 200 cm);
- baby blanket: 40 × 40 in to 48 × 48 in. (100 × 100 cm to 120 × 120 cm);
- bath mat: 16 × 28 in. (40 × 70 cm).

Sometimes, in search of inspiration to draw balanced shapes or colored areas in proportion, we can simply use a famous "divine" mathematical proportion: the golden ratio. Approximately equal to 1.62, it is the harmonious ratio between the large and the small side of a rectangle. Applied to a rug, a napkin, or a placemat, it can sometimes guide us in choosing dimensions to be sure that the rectangle will be well-proportioned. We can also rely on the Fibonacci sequence: 1, 1, 2, 3, 5, 8, 13.

In all cases, there is neither an ideal dimension nor an absolute rule. By dint of doing, you will train your eyes and become very attentive to the objects around you. You'll see—you won't look at them in the same way again.

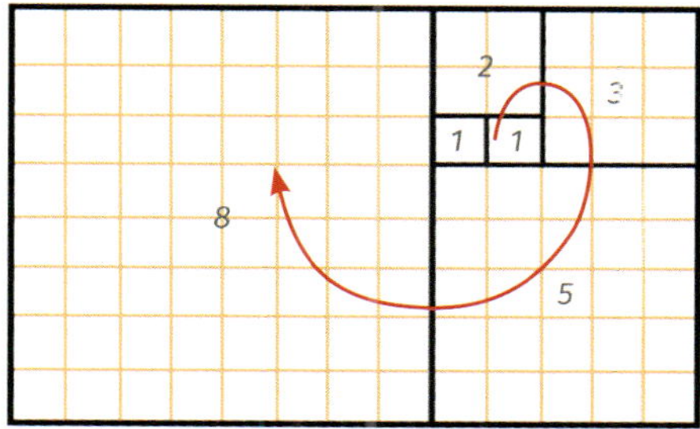

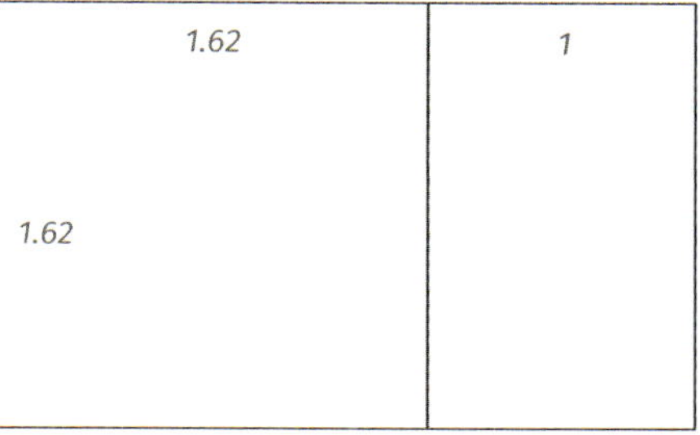

Figure 32 ***The golden ratio and the Fibonacci sequence may help with decision making.***

3

The Reading and Writing of Weaving: Stage Left then Stage Right

Just as the etymology of the word "text" (textus, woven fabric) draws a parallel between textiles and writing, weaving among the Dogon is associated with language. It is claimed that a single hero, Nommo, taught the techniques of both, and the first word is said to be intermingled with the first strip of cotton created.

Dogon, Exhibition File at the Quai Branly Museum, 2011

The day I met Erica de Ruiter (even though I already knew how to weave, wind, and prepare my warp, calculate my yarn quantities) I understood that the essence of my joy in weaving would forever more come from my understanding of it—recognizing the logic of a weaving process, understanding the essential role of tying up the treadles, studying treadling to find the ideal rhythm for the back and the feet, all of that. A few years later, during a training course in Kukate, Germany, I realized that the way to write and draw future weaving projects on a sheet of graph paper well before weaving would give me the joy of deciphering. I got into a class where I learned to read and write!

Noticing also that each structure can be recognized by its threading order, and that we can thus group certain types of weaving into the same family, freed me. Suddenly, things got organized in my mind, which is necessary for me to assimilate them. Weaving books written in English became understandable and I felt like I was becoming a part of a great community through reading books by Madelyn van der Hoogt, Tom Knisely, Mary E. Black, Sharon Alderman, and many others.

What I propose to present here on these next few pages is an understanding of how a structure works, what role each part of the loom plays, and how all of this can be foreseen on a sheet of paper. We will discover the reading and writing of threading, treadling, tying on, and weaving.

Then we will try to match them to each part of the loom: shafts, treadles, lamms. The weaving diagram, called a draft, will become a representation of the loom: the connections, ties, and cords connect the parts of the loom in the same way that our eyes connect the parts of the picture. If you are a beginner and want to take full advantage of the following explanations, I invite you to take a sheet of paper and colored pencils to draw as you go along.

I know that some people prefer to learn by trying things out in a more experiential way. If you are one of those people, just bypass this chapter. One day maybe you'll come back to it and won't want to put it down!

How to Read and Understand Threading, Treadling, and Tie-Up Drafts

Like reading, writing is a journey.

Alexandre Najjar, *Kadicha*, 2011

The basic weaving draft consists of four parts: threading, treadling, tie-up, and the drawdown, the graphic representation of the weaving, a sketch on paper. Sometimes they are called grids.

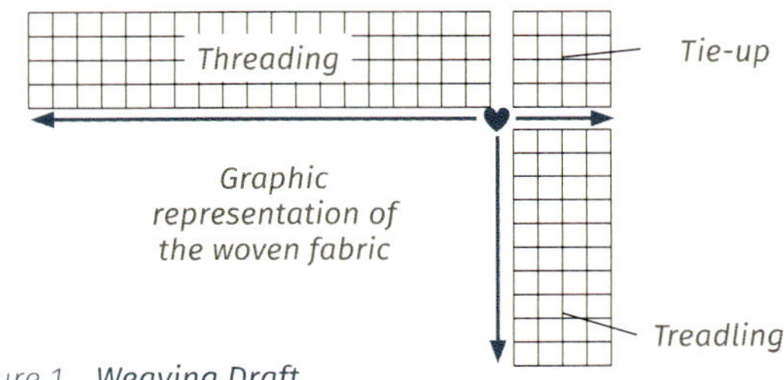

Figure 1 **Weaving Draft**

The small heart in the center shows that everything depends on what is around it. To continue in this vein, we will read the diagrams starting from the heart. So the threading draft is read from right to left, the tie-up draft from left to right, and the treadling draft from top to bottom. Not everyone shows it exactly this way. Nevertheless, the idea remains the same. Each line of the threading rectangle corresponds to a shaft. Each column of the treadling draft corresponds to a treadle. The tie-up draft connects the shafts and the treadles.

Threading

Threading is shown in horizontal lines. Each line corresponds to a shaft. The number indicates in which shaft the yarn is threaded. Line 1 is on the bottom, and line 4 is on the top. Shaft 1 is the one closest to us on the loom, shaft 4 the furthest.

Even if this is not the natural reading direction, I suggest you read from right to left, so that you always have the same starting point for reading: the heart of the pattern. In the example above, we will read the threading order as: 1-2-3-4-1-2-3-4, the first thread is threaded in a heddle on shaft 1, the second is in a heddle on shaft 2, etc.

This right-to-left writing direction is perfectly suitable for people who thread from right to left, a method that suits right-handed people. However, the reading direction is of little importance since it changes the weaving so little; for example, the slope of the twill will simply be reversed. You will therefore adapt your writing direction to the way you thread. The idea is to make it as simple as possible so that you can thread the heddles as automatically as possible. If you are more comfortable threading from left to right, then choose to write it as shown below, which starts from the left.

Depending on the region or country, we will find some differences in presentation that can be confusing, like using crosses, squares, or dashes. In Scandinavia, the threading draft is at the bottom of the diagram, under the graphic representation of the weaving, and the order of the shafts is reversed. The first shaft is at the top, closest to the drawdown (the weaving graph). You get used to these differences quite quickly, since the logic remains the same: the horizontal lines represent the shafts.

Treadling

Treadling is shown in the columns on the right. It shows the treadle number for each of the picks. I read this diagram from top to bottom, but again, there are many variations. The Scandinavians write it from bottom to top, which is quite logical, since the drawdown, the representation of the fabric, is drawn in the same direction as the weaving.

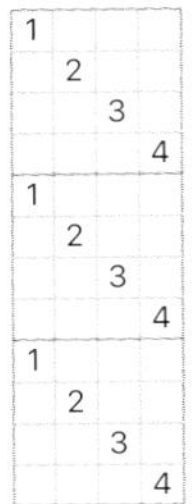

Habits die hard. I learned to read from top to bottom, and I continue to do so. Again, the heart of the pattern is a great reference for me. Everything starts from it, so my reading of the picks starts from the top.

The writings and symbols are as varied as for the threading. Some drafts use circles or crosses, others use numbers that indicate the number of times the pick passes through the same shed, and still others where the number designates the number of the treadle. Depending on the author of the draft, there is always a little decoding to do.

Each column corresponds to a treadle. In this example, treadle 1 is pressed to allow the first pick to pass through, treadle 2 for the second pass, and so on. Here, the number indicates the number of the treadle.

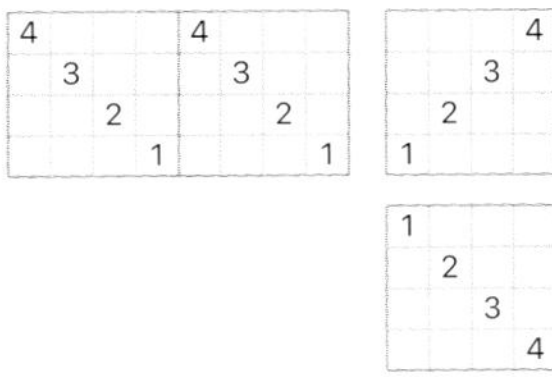

Changing the reading direction, going instead from bottom to top, will simply change the direction of the diagonal in the fabric. Most of the time, it doesn't matter if the direction of the twill in the weave is one way or the other. In any case, if you are confused reversing the direction, it is always very easy to draw your draft in a different direction to match the resulting fabric exactly.

Tying Up the Treadles

This part of the draft is often not well known. This is unfortunate because it makes the work of reading so much easier and the weaving more effortless that it is a shame to miss out.

The tie-up draft indicates which shafts must be operated by each of the treadles to allow the shed to open. Each structure has its own coding. Sometimes only one shaft needs to be lifted, sometimes two, sometimes three with a four-shaft loom. The principle of tying up is to tie several shafts together to a single treadle, and not a single shaft to a single treadle, as is so common.

This table is the crossroads, the connection point between the threading draft and the treadles (shown in the treadling draft). It is placed where they intersect, at the top right for English speakers and the bottom right for Scandinavians.

It has as many lines as the threading table, representing the shafts, and as many columns as the treadling table, representing the number of treadles needed. It indicates which shafts will be lifted for each weft pick. It is the instructions, the "how to," the roadmap of the weaving process.

Let's take the example of 2/2 twill, for which there are 4 different tie-ups: 1-2, 2-3, 3-4, 4-1.

The indication for the first pick is drawn in the first line of the treadling table. To read it, go back to the tie-up table, which indicates which shafts must be lifted. For the first pick, shafts 1 and 2 must be lifted together.

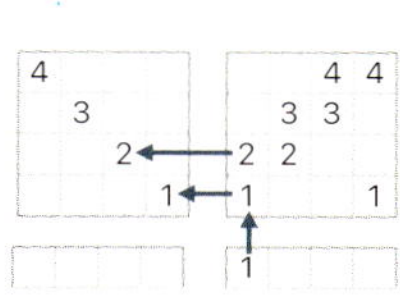

For the second pick, shafts **2** and 3 must be lifted, then shafts **3** and 4, and finally shafts **4** and 1 for the next two picks.

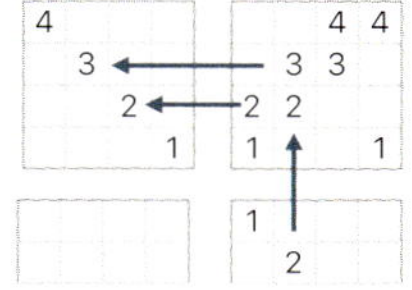

Again, there are various notations such as crosses, numbers, squares, or dots. Certain conventions apply depending on the loom. If it is a jack loom (rising shed loom), an "o" is commonly used as a sign, while with a countermarch or counterbalance loom, an "x" is used. In our example, the presentation is for a rising shed loom. For the passage of the first pick, we will lift shafts 1 and 2. If we had a counterbalance loom, we would replace these two numbers with 3 and 4 to indicate that we should lower these two shafts. Anyway, if by mistake you were to read backward, it would not have any serious consequences, except that you would have to contort yourself to see your real fabric because it would be on the reverse side. However, in many cases, the front and back sides are identical.

If you want to transpose the instructions from a counterbalance loom to a rising shed loom, simply replace the "x's" with a blank square and put an 'o" in the initially empty squares. In this way, the warp ends that were supposed to stay in their place will rise, while those that went down will remain horizontal.

In the next part, we will see more concretely how all this works on the loom. Even if you are a novice, or even reluctant to use this notation, I hope that the explanations and illustrations on page 95 will encourage you to at least try. This layout has proved so fundamental to me and has made my work so much more harmonious that I would be happy to persuade you of its merits.

The Drawdown

This last part, called the **drawdown**, is the depiction of the future fabric on paper. To understand, let's study the first row of the fabric drawn in our example.

For the first pick, the tie-up plan indicates that shafts 1 and 2 are to be lifted. So, on the entire first line, under the numbers 1 and 2 of the threading draft, a vertical mauve line is drawn to signify that these mauve warp ends will be raised for the first pick and will be visible. The yarn threaded in shafts 3 and 4 will not be lifted. The weft yarn can be passed through and will be seen horizontally; here it is shown in white.

In the second row, the mauve line will be drawn vertically under the numbers 2 and 3. Threads 4 and 1, not being lifted, will be covered by the weft in white. It can be seen that all the warp ends threaded in shaft 2 will remain raised for two consecutive picks. We will thus have a 2-thread float. Each purple line will represent a warp float of 2 and each white line, a weft float of 2.

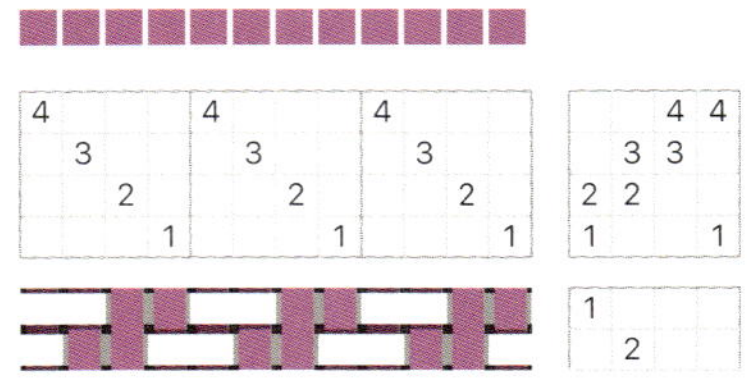

Most weaving patterns or software show squares rather than lines. It seems to me that a line represents a thread more than a square does. A warp thread is a vertical line and a weft thread is a horizontal line. Thus, it is easier to make the connection between what the diagram shows and what we see on the loom: warp threads that are raised, and threads that are not raised and are covered by the weft.

Connections Between the Draft and the Loom, or How to Dress Your Loom

> Like many, I was happy with the notion of warp and weft, and thought I knew about how fabrics are woven; in a word, I was not at all aware of what a fabric structure really is.
>
> André Lhote, *Peinture d'abord*, 1942

The point of these graphic representations is to be able to design the fabric on paper, or on screen, since now a project can be drawn using several different softwares, some of which are free. The following illustrations try to show the connection between the weaving draft and the set-up of the loom.

We can now imagine that the **threading draft** is the part of the loom that supports the four shafts, and that the numbers are the heddles. Knowing how to read and then write the threading chart yourself prepares you in advance for the task of threading the heddles, which will be done later; memory records, a bit like a nursery rhyme, and this will make the threading much easier. It is often a question of identifying a sort of sequence that is repeated and then retaining it like a little tune. To help, you can say that this draft answers the question: Where do I put the heddles? It shows a location.

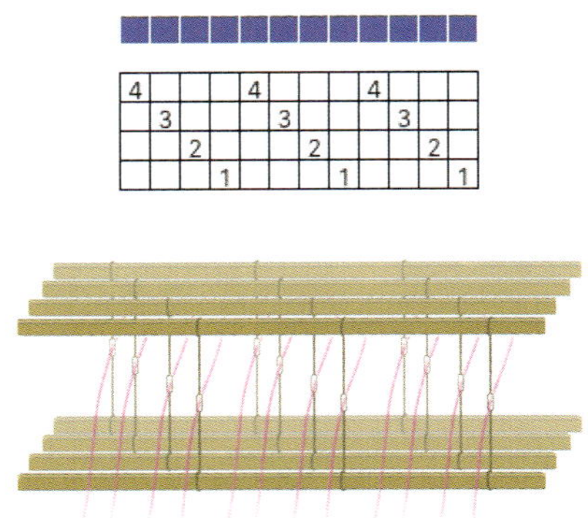

Figure 2 Connection between the threading draft and the shafts on the loom

The **treadling draft** requires little explanation. You follow the order given, pressing the correct treadle. The first column on the left indicates treadle 1, the second column, treadle 2, etc. Each notation in this table corresponds to the passage of a pick in the open shed according to the roadmap. Later on, we will see that we can change this order so as to design a treadling easier for the feet. Much like the hands on a musical instrument, we will need to find the position that will give us a smooth movement. This chart gives us information about a progression in the work: **Which** treadle should I press when I weave?

Let's move on to the **tie-up draft**; this is the fundamental part of the draft. It gives us the program and answers the question: **How** will the shafts rise when I follow the treadling order?

Here we see that the first treadle is connected to shafts 1 and 2. It is operated by the left foot. Then the second treadle, connected to shafts 2 and 3, is operated by the

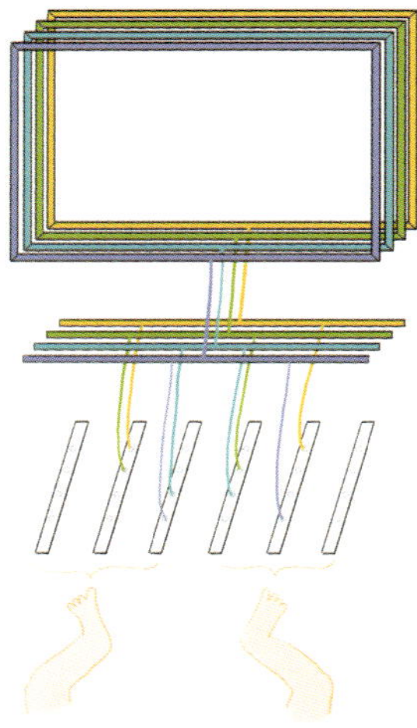

Figure 3 Connection between the treadling draft and the treadles on the loom

right foot. The third treadle, connected to shafts 3 and 4, is operated by the left foot. The last treadle, tied to shafts 4 and 1, is operated by the right foot.

Those who are novices, or haven't had any great interest in tying up, might be hesitant. Sometimes you may even be resistant. Especially since with each new weave, it is very likely that you will have to change the tie-up. If you have never done this, more often than not, treadle 1 is tied to shaft 1, treadle 2 to shaft 2 and so on. A treadle is attached to one shaft. This is called a single or individual tie-up. I know that some people recognize themselves in these words, don't they?

How about I try to persuade you? Okay, here goes! When it comes to lifting shafts 1 and 2, you use both your feet. Then, to lift shafts 2 and 3, you move both your feet together and so on. Should you do an overshot and have to insert a tabby each time, things get more complicated for your feet, which will cross over each other: tabby 1-3, pattern 1-2, tabby 2-4, pattern 2-3, tabby 1-3, pattern 3-4, tabby 2-4, pattern 4-1, and so on. How do you not get your feet caught in the treadles?

I can see four drawbacks to this method:

- With a 3/1 twill, you have to press three treadles with only one foot.
- With 4 shafts, it is still easy to manage this process, sometimes by pressing one foot on two treadles. With 8 shafts, this simply becomes impossible.
- You have to systematically lift both feet together to move them. This uncomfortable position is tiring and stresses our joints. I have so many projects in my head that I prefer to spare my back and my knees. So I make sure that I have the best ergonomics possible.
- When lifting both feet at once, we don't exactly know where to put them down again. We lose our bearings and we're often forced to look at the treadles. This slows down the rhythm, the ease and the fluidity of the movement, as well as the pleasure.

The great satisfaction of tying up is to be able to attach one single treadle to all the shafts that are above it in the same column of the tie-up draft, in a methodical way, so that you have to use alternately the left foot and then the right foot, and in this way, weave with the impression of walking. In Quebec, treadling is called walking, and the treadle is called a step. This expresses the idea of a regular and comfortable foot movement.

Dressing a loom means to prepare it by attaching, threading, and tying up everything as needed, matching each part of the weaving draft to the part of the loom that relates to it. Tying is no longer just conceptual but real. Preparing a loom properly, according to "best practices," completely frees the weaver afterward. Each foot slides from one treadle to the other, alternately, without ever having to look at the feet, being able to move fluidly. The mind thus freed of this constraint will be able to focus on the rhythm of the hands and the shuttle. The weaving will become more regular.

The real work consists in organizing the tie-up of the treadles in such a way as to always alternate right and left feet, while also setting it up for a more limited movement of the feet. We'll look at a concrete example later in this chapter.

Honestly, I have fond memories of times when I was able to witness the marvel of a weaver discovering the pleasure and the freedom of treadling with a real tie-up. I do not completely lose hope for those who still resist a little.

On the other hand, table looms with levers are often used in classes. These looms have the advantage that they take up little space and can be easily transported from school to home, like the student musician who returns home from band or orchestra with his instrument. But these small looms are not the exact reproduction of their big brothers; it is not possible to attach several shafts to a single lever. This has the advantage of giving the designers complete freedom and to be able to lift the shafts as they wish without being constrained by a tie-up. But I often miss the fact that you can't connect several shafts to one lever; it's a bit of a weak point. Whereas with my treadle looms, I make my work easier by pressing on a single treadle, here for a single pick, I have to operate one, two, or three or more levers to get the same result.

For table looms, to be able to interpret the tie-up draft, you have to imagine that there is a tie-up and always associate in your mind 1, or 2, or 3 shafts together according to the tie-up chart. So we do a virtual tie-up, more complicated to understand and remember. Nevertheless, I often notice that weaving is easier when we have linked, even mentally, each column to a "tie-up."

We can use a kind of code to remember only one number instead of several by replacing a group of levers with this number, as if the shafts were attached to each other.

Let's take for example the coding of a 2/2 twill:

- 1 is the code to activate levers **1**-2;
- 2 is the code for levers **2**-3;
- 3 for **3**-4;
- 4 for **4**-1.

So, the treadling sequence to memorize is clearly simplified.

Then for a 3/1 twill, the mental work is made even easier since each number replaces three others:

- 1 is the code to activate levers **1**-2-3;
- 2 for **2**-3-4;
- 3 for **3**-4-1;
- 4 for **4**-1-2.

Go ahead and try it; it will make me happy!

A Plot Twist: New Notations

Just when we thought we had everything figured out, it happens we discover a new way of writing. And suddenly, all reference points disappear. Fear and disillusionment set in.

No need to worry! The differences among draft notations are small and we quickly find new reference points. The shafts with the heddles are still represented in horizontal lines and the order of the picks, the treadling, is still in vertical columns. Only the symbols change. Nothing too difficult though, provided you focus a bit and translate into the usual language.

Sometimes the colors are mentioned directly in the lines. You may find "R" for red or "G" for green in the threading or treadling draft. You may also see thick yarns represented by a large circle and thin yarns by a dot, in warp or weft.

Also, more condensed writing can be confusing. Instead of writing the same group of threads several times, brackets or merged columns are used to show that this section is repeated.

In the following example, we will follow the draft from right to left:

- We thread 1, 2, 3, and 4, then repeat this sequence 5 times; 20 threads have been threaded.
- Next we thread 2, 1, 4, and 3, a sequence that is also repeated 5 times. Thus, a total of 40 warp ends have been threaded.
- This sequence of 40 threads is repeated 3 times. We have threaded a total of 120 warp ends.
- We finish by threading 1, 2, 3, and 4, repeated 5 times. This diagram indicates that 140 threads will need to be warped.

The reasoning used for the order of the weft picks is exactly the same.

Table 1 ***Condensed*** *notation of threading and treadling*

				3×							
5×				5×				5×			
4					4			4			
	3			3					3		
		2					2			2	
			1			1					1

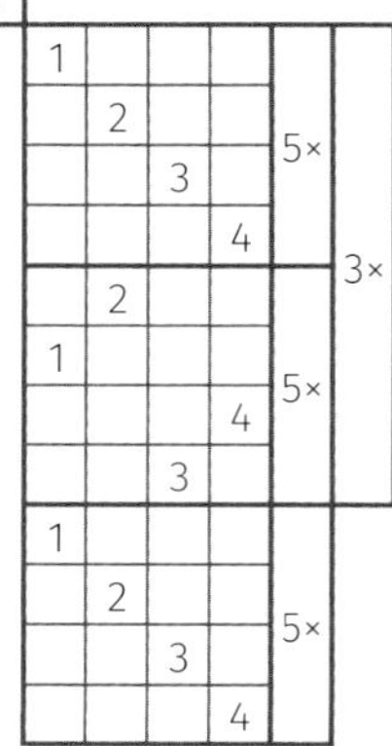

1				5×	3×
	2				
		3			
			4		
	2			5×	
1					
			4		
		3			
1				5×	
	2				
		3			
			4		

It is rather surprising, but this way of writing makes the weaving steps much easier. For threading the heddles, we remember 1, 2, 3, 4, then 2, 1, 4, and 3; that's it. Agree with me that it is simple. Moreover, the same numbers in the same order are used for throwing the picks! Don't have reservations about your memory—anyone can do it. What is surprising in this whole thing is that you gain a lot of fluidity in your work. Believe me, it will show in your weaving!

Being able to easily incorporate the rhythm of this sequence allows you to detach from the draft and free your hands for the threading, and your feet for treadling so that they work with harmony and consistency. Of course, at the beginning, you don't believe it! But I assure you, just try it!

It also happens that some authors of weaving books put a number in the treadling draft that indicates not the number of the treadle, but the number of times the pick passes through the same shed. Marguerite Davidson and Anne Dixon use this notation. It certainly uses fewer lines and is more condensed. Nevertheless, I prefer to write and repeat the number of the treadle rather than the number of repetitions of each pick; in this way the eye sees on the paper what will appear on the fabric. The weaving replicates the drawdown in such a way that some expect to see it appear as soon as they start weaving.

For the same reason of legibility, if we want to make the drawdown of a structure composed of a ground cloth of plain weave on which a pattern of floats will be placed, as with Overshot or Summer and Winter, the plain weave picks will not be shown in the treadling graph. The text accompanying the weaving project will note that it is necessary to use a binding pick, commonly called "tabby." Thus, markings for a plain weave will not interfere with the pattern, which will then be very obvious on the drawing.

The term "use tabby" means that we place a plain weave pick between each pass of pattern picks, those that will make the floats. Most of the time, the tabby pick is woven with the same yarn used for the warp. We will talk about this at length in the chapter on compound structures (see p. 180).

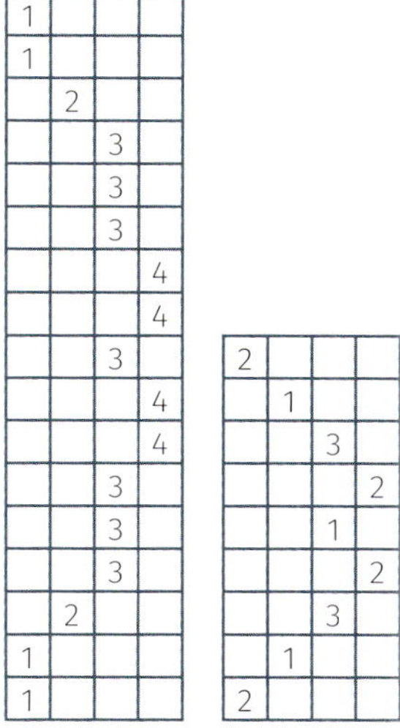

1			
1			
	2		
		3	
		3	
		3	
			4
			4
		3	
			4
			4
		3	
		3	
		3	
	2		
1			
1			

2			
	1		
		3	
			2
		1	
			2
		3	
	1		
2			

Table 2 ***On the left: Coding where the numbers indicate the treadle numbers. On the right: The same treadling where the numbers indicate the number of repetitions.***

Tying Up Treadles: A 14-Letter Alphabet

Remember when we talked about the three basic structures: plain weave, twill, and satin (p. 123)? We are going to show that these structures come out of tie-ups.

I'll repeat here the definitions of a pick and a float, just to be precise:

- The passage of the weft thread through the shed is often called a pick, even though this is tapestry terminology.
- If the weft passes over several warp threads in a row, it is a **float**, and we specify with the number of ends crossed in a row, such as 2- or 3-thread float. The warp is also called a float if it crosses several picks in a row.

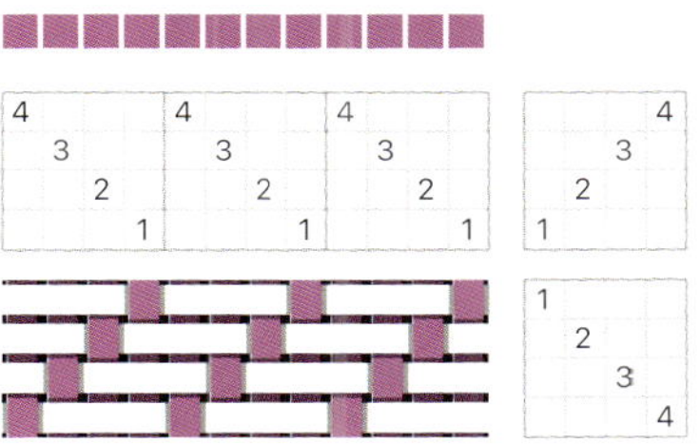

Figure 4 ***Tie-up for 1/3 twill***

Figure 5 ***Tie-up for 2/2 twill***

With 4 shafts, we have 14 different possibilities.

- It may be that **a single shaft is raised** at a time: shaft 1, or 2, or 3, or 4. From this we get a **1/3 twill**. A single warp end is raised, the three others remain down. The weft thread goes over these 3 warp ends while the one warp end crosses the weft.
- If two consecutive shafts are lifted at a time, **1**-2, **2**-3, **3**-4, **4**-1, we get a **2/2 twill**. Two warp threads are lifted per pick; the weft goes on top of the two warp ends not lifted. So we have a 2-thread weft float and two warp ends cross over the weft.

- If **two nonconsecutive shafts are raised** at the same time, 1-3 and 2-4, we get a plain weave.

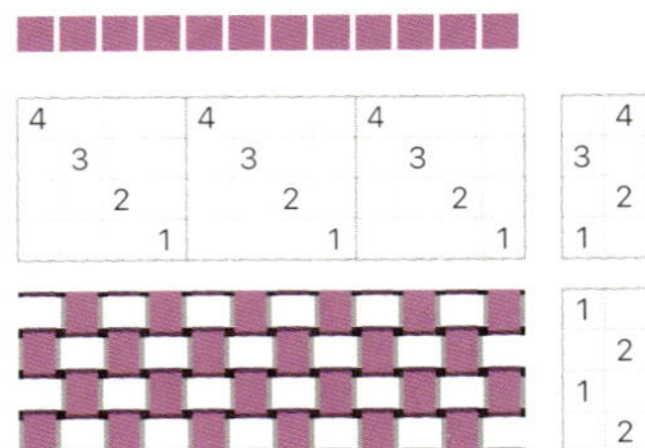

Figure 6 *Plain weave tie-up*

- If **three consecutive shafts are raised** at the same time, **1**-2-3, **2**-3-4, **3**-4-1, **4**-1-2, we get a 3/1 twill. Three warp threads are lifted per pick; the weft goes on top of a single warp thread not lifted. Each warp thread will remain lifted for three picks to make a float of 3.

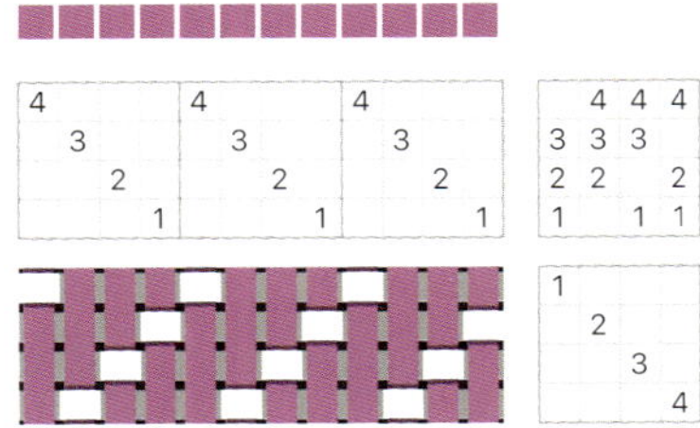

Figure 7 *3/1 twill tie-up*

The following lines will allow us to play with these 14 tie-ups and see that there is an infinite number of combinations offering us an infinite number of weaves.

Example 1. Let's take a straight threading, 1-2-3-4, 1-2-3-4. The first eight picks are woven with a 1/3 twill tie-up, the next eight with a 2/2 twill tie-up, and the following eight with a 3/1 twill. The treadling is consistent, wisely using only one type of twill at a time.

The exercise ends with a few picks of 1/3 twill then 2/4.

In this example, we will say that the first column of the tie-up draft corresponds to the first treadle, the second column corresponds to the second treadle, and so on up to the fourteenth treadle.

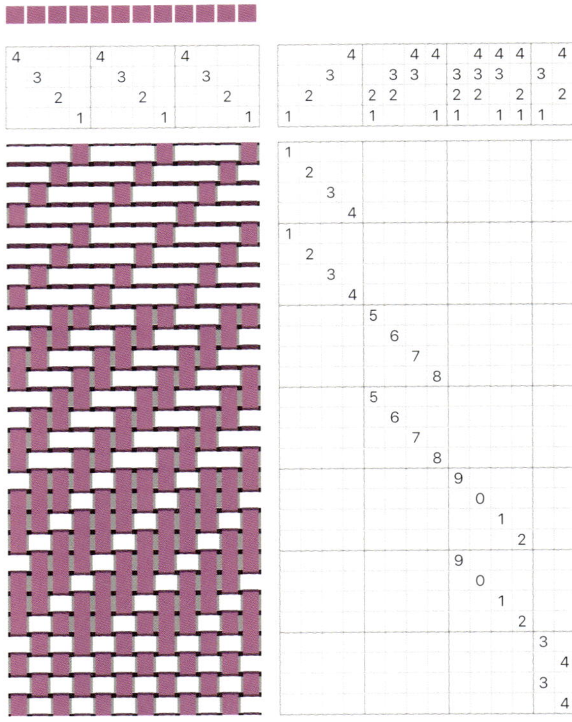

Figure 8 *The 14 tie-up combinations with 4 shafts*

Example 2. Things get fun and inventive when you select a few combinations from among these 14 tie-ups in a new structure, without forcing yourself to stay in one type of twill. In this example, the first and fourth picks are 1/3 twill, the second and fifth are in 2/2, and the third and sixth are in 3/1 twill.

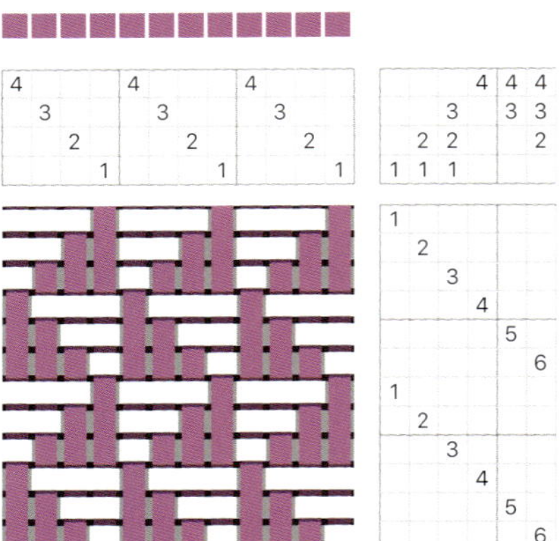

Figure 9 *Six tie-ups to make triangles*

Example 3. On a day you are less inspired, you could absolutely decide at random what tie-up and what treadles to use. Here, I selected 5 different tie-ups completely at random in this order: treadle 1, 7, 5, 12, 1, 11. I deliberately omitted plain weave. I wove for about 3 inches (8 cm) to be able to see what I thought of it.

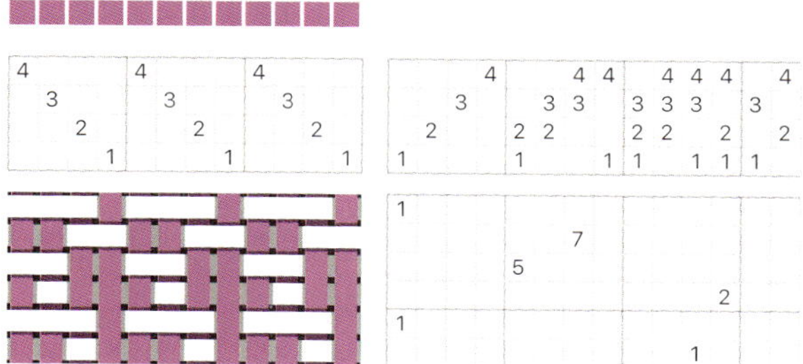

Figure 10 ***Random choice of tie-ups***

Of course, reading of the previous table is much easier if we show the only tie-ups used. We have a draft that is simpler to read and remember. We will use the treadles in this order: 1-2-3-4-1-5.

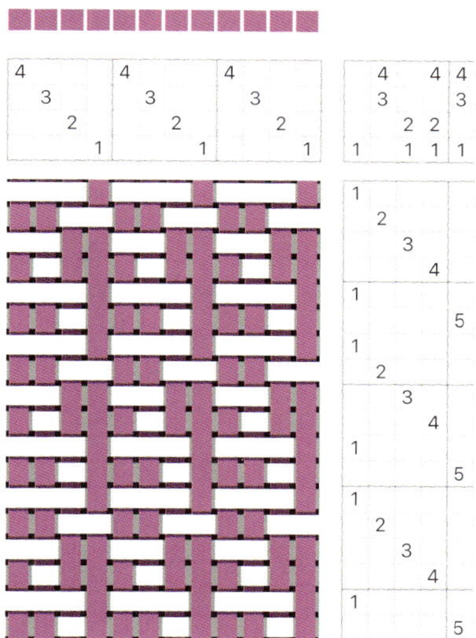

Figure 11 ***Reorganization of the choice of random tie-ups with 5 treadles***

To finish with this same example, it is no doubt simpler to choose to tie up 6 treadles instead of 5 and to double the "1" tie-up. This can make the reading even easier and the treadling certainly smoother. (Figure 12)

When it comes to inventing your own personal tie-ups, sometimes good things happen by chance. Nevertheless, it is a good idea to follow a few principles:

- **Each sequence should be fairly short**, no more than 8 to 10 picks. If the sequence is too long it will lose its legibility and identity and will be lost in the piece.
- **Each sequence will be repeated over about 3 inches (8 cm) of weaving**, otherwise the effect will not be seen. Above all, never decide to choose or to abandon this tie-up too soon! You can't see anything at the beginning, but as you keep adding picks, a pattern will appear.
- In each sequence, each weave unit, we must absolutely ensure that **at least once, each warp and each weft thread crosses the others**. There must be enough interlacing to ensure that the fabric is solid. In other words, the floats should not be too long. On the tie-up draft, check that in each row and each column, there is at least one notation and at least one empty square!

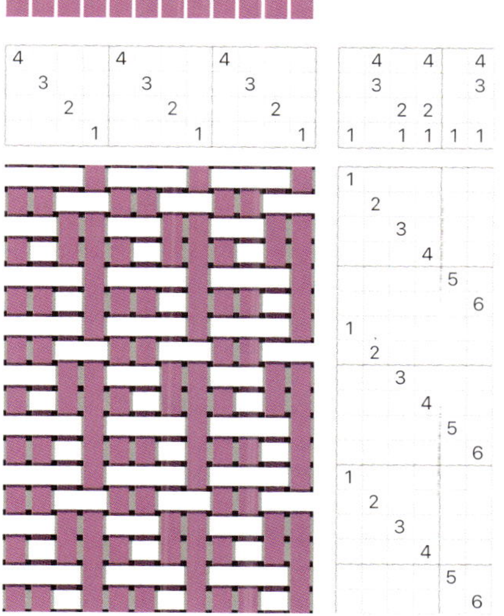

Figure 12 ***Transformation of this tie-up with 6 treadles***

Completely inventing your own weave can be scary at first. But that's just at the beginning, before you have discovered that there are so many weaves already invented, that everyone should test "their" pattern. I find that it is when you are just beginning to learn that it is so exciting to design one yourself. It is not uncommon that a course participant, excited to have "discovered" a new structure, wants to test it by weaving "her" project. The resulting scarf or pillow will bear witness to this impulse. It is really an immense pleasure and a bit of a source of pride!

Later on, we will be infected by another game, that of seeing some weaving on a piece of clothing or on the Internet and not being able to stop analyzing it to know how it was made. We will then want to verify our analysis by weaving it. It is incredible how this method allows us to expand our knowledge base. The more we look the more we decipher; the more we experiment the more we accumulate knowledge conducive to creation. This opens up to us a world of weavings to be made that a whole life will not be enough to explore.

I would like to conclude this chapter by borrowing a word that Erica de Ruiter often used in her workshops with a mischievous little smile: "serendipity." It conveys the idea that chance has a lot to do with discoveries.

I invite you to cultivate the art of paying attention to everything around you and then draw your inspiration from it.

SERENDIPITY

Word created by Horace Walpole on January 28, 1754, in a letter to a friend where he mentions the Persian tale *The Three Princes of Serendip*, published in Italy in 1557.

". . . while their highnesses were travelling, they made all sorts of discoveries, by accident and wisdom, of things they were not looking for at all."

Writing and "Weaving" on Paper: Creating the Script

Remember, we are in an elementary class. We just learned to read drafts. Suddenly, a vast world opens up to us, with no doubt a frenzy of wanting to try lots and lots of new structures.

Now, I suggest you write and draw your own drafts. No longer just inventing at random, but planning, choosing. Perhaps you will feel you are growing wings. Yes, you will be able to invent your own patterns; only a few rules need to be followed.

Of course, it is very easy and tempting to do this step on weaving software. It goes very fast, one click of the mouse and the diagram of the weaving appears. I would dare to challenge you a bit and encourage you to test out colored pencils on a piece of graph paper. Again, doing this exercise by hand allows us to really prepare in our head for the work we'll be doing, so much that we may be surprised to have almost everything memorized before we even start weaving.

Act One: Drawing the Drawdown of a Draft

I think it is by practicing that you will assimilate this part, so I suggest a little practice. For this, we will use the grid of an already defined draft. The warp is in mauve, the weft in white. Go ahead and make your draft at the same time to practice. Get out your paper and pencils!

Let's start with the first row. For the first pick, we're going to lift threads 1 and 2. With the mauve pencil, we make a vertical line in each column that corresponds to the threads in shafts 1 and 2. Then we make a horizontal line in white wherever the threads are not lifted, where the weft will be visible.

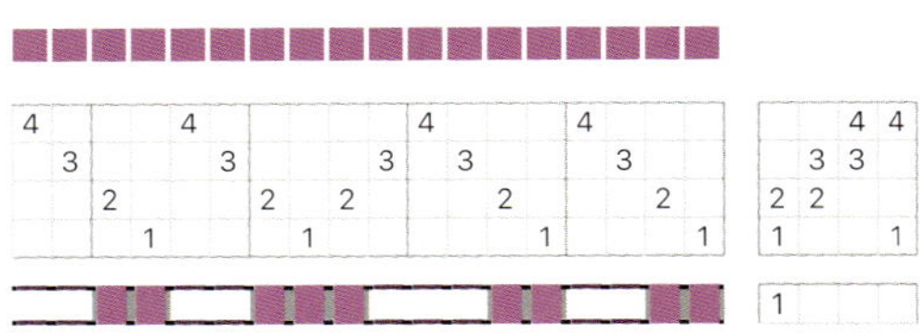

Then we continue with the second pick. In the same way, we draw a mauve line under numbers 2 and 3, on the second row, then we fill the gaps with horizontal white lines.

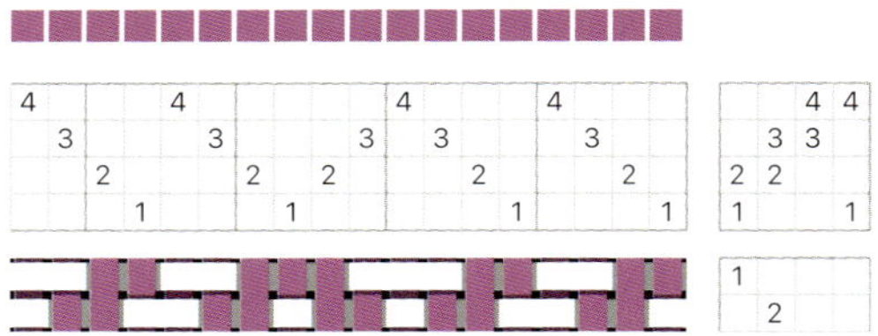

And so on for a few lines . . .

At the beginning, it is easy to make mistakes, to get lost in the rows and columns. But little by little, it becomes easy, even fun.

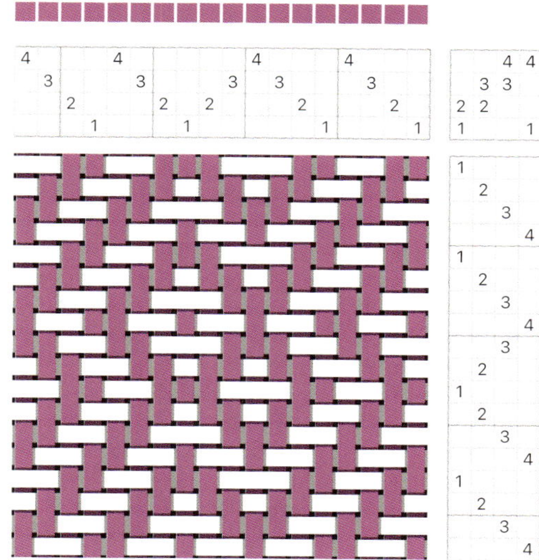

Some students almost never weave without drawing beforehand, in order to understand how things will play out with the thread.

This work, more painstaking at the beginning, allows you to immerse yourself completely in the structure. In addition, the time spent with your pencils will be mostly made up afterward when weaving. Having seen and understood what each thread was doing, you can then weave more easily. You can see a mistake right away and can correct it more easily, because the link is made between our memory of the drawing and what our hands are doing and our eyes are seeing. It's a little bit like in first grade, when you manage to not speak haltingly when you read, and without following your finger! A major victory!

You don't necessarily need to draw a large width of the pattern, or its entire length. But I would advise you to continue until you have really understood and succeeded in doing it without hesitation.

Act Two: Inventing Your Own Fabric and Writing It Out

Of all acts, the most complete is that of constructing.

Paul Valéry, *Eupalinos, or the Architect*, 1923

Let's practice something new. On your 4-shaft rows, let's draw a straight threading, with or without reverse, it doesn't matter (see a 4-shaft straight draw on p. 87, Figure 35). Then, again keeping things simple, we draw

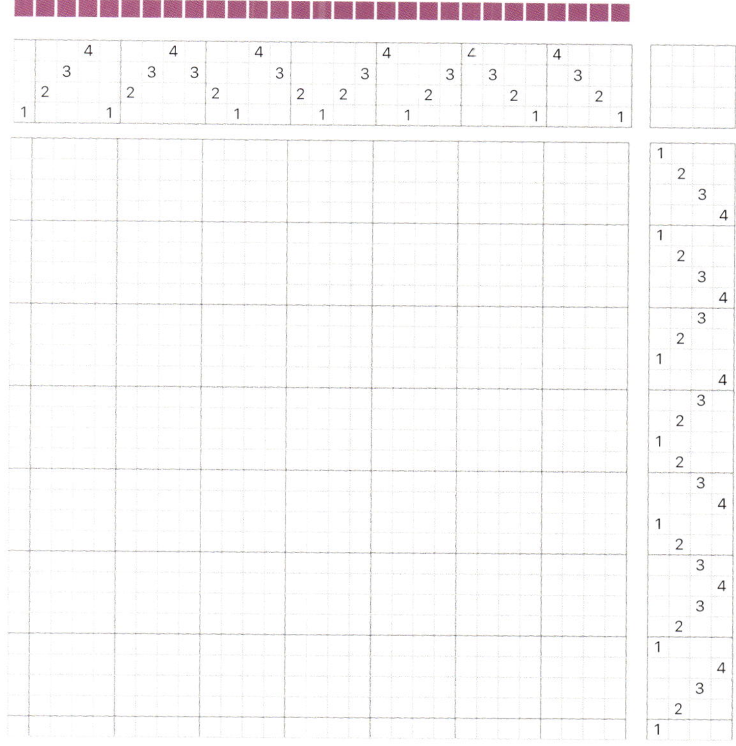

Figure 13 ***Inventing your own fabric***

the treadling like the threading. Sometimes the instruction "tromp as writ" comes up, meaning simply that the sequence of threading is repeated in the treadling. And continuing to keep things simple, we are using only 4 tie-up columns, no more for right now.

This is where the new game begins. In the tie-up grid, draw 4 of the possible 14 combinations. Do this on the paper and then, even better, check it right after on the weaving. It is quite magical.

Feel free to put in anything . . . as long as there is always, in each row and each column, at least one full marked square and at least one empty square! This is so there is always at least one, two, or three threads of warp that are raised. Never zero, never four. Weaving is interlacing!

Following are four inventions (p. 67), more or less pretty, but that are worth being tried and checked out on a weaving for at least about 3 inches (7 cm). You never know . . .

I have always had a lot of fun looking for new tie-ups. And I encourage you to try this method. Put on a fairly long warp, no less than 2 or 3 yards. Then test new tie-ups. The "tromp as writ" technique, i.e., reproducing the same diagram in the columns for treadling as the sequence used for threading, will ensure a balanced result, pleasing to the eye.

When you become an expert, you are free to add or remove tie-ups and to no longer "tromp as writ." Instead of four tie-ups, you can add more, and solidify with more tabby. Design new variations. For example, introducing a thread that is a different size or color is not always very eloquent on paper, but as you weave, you can try them out. Also try introducing a new yarn by associating it systematically with a single treadle. For example, each time you use treadle 4, play with a different color yarn or a larger yarn or a shiny yarn. You will relish the profusion of feasible and sometimes very successful attempts!

Weaving Software

There is a lot of weaving software available, some free to download, others very expensive. Some options are presented in the third part of this book.

Of course, watching the weaving being displayed instantly on the screen by simply tapping on the keyboard is both impressive and exciting.

It is true that with the computer tool you can immediately check out your ideas, because the fabric is "made" in real time before our eyes. I often use this method to check if a particular choice of threading, treadling, or tie-up works well and if the floats are not too long, or to count the heddles.

I am not a fervent user of the screen, which never replaces, for my taste, a piece of graph paper and my colored pencils. The speed of the computer leaves me little time to think, to imagine, to rectify. I am often disappointed because I cannot reproduce on fabric what the screen shows. With a pencil, I can enlarge the line or lighten it according to the thread used and thus better represent the effect of a mercerized cotton with a thin line or a mohair with a watercolor pencil over which I gently pass my wet brush. I make far fewer mistakes on the paper, because I have time to think. I would gladly advise the beginner not to be seduced by the speed of the software, but rather to be inspired by the slowness of one's hands. This is really how the fabric is made in our head: calmly.

Figure 14 *Four tie-up inventions with the threading and treadling remaining unchanged*

4

Staging Without Stage Fright: Dressing the Loom

What we must learn to do, we learn by doing.

Aristotle, Greek philosopher (384–322 B.C.)

Now that we have all the elements to choose from, it's time to get our hands dirty, so let's go! We will decide on a project, a thread, and a structure, and follow the steps one by one. For this exercise, we will use the loom, tools, materials—alternating with the weaving project record sheets that we will introduce here—and drawing paper. We will go from the record sheet to the loom, from theoretical preparation to actual implementation on the loom; we will go back and forth between theory and practice.

Afterward, I recommend that you start by drawing your project. Choose the threads, the structure, and then fill in the record sheet completely before starting to prepare the threads and the loom. In other words, do all the theoretical preparation before you start the actual setup.

The project record sheet I propose is quite complete; it will keep you from forgetting anything. This sheet is a help for some, for others it is too complete—too complex. It is up to everyone to make their own version according to their own personal way of thinking.

Normally, dressing the loom is the second step, done after all the calculations have been completed and all the options have been selected.

In the appendices, the record sheet is presented in its entirety, whereas here, for this practical exercise, it is broken down step by step in order to go along with the setup:

- **winding the warp**: placing the warp threads on a warping board or mill to prepare them all to be the same length and tension;
- **"raddling"**: spacing out the warp between the teeth of a raddle to then beam the warp according to the determined width and density;
- **beaming the warp**: winding the whole warp with the same tension on the warp beam or roller.
- **threading**: passing each warp thread through the eyes of the heddles in the order defined by the structure chosen beforehand;
- **sleying the reed**: bringing the threads through the teeth of the reed to ensure the desired density;
- **tying on**: knotting the warp threads to the cloth beam (roller);
- **weaving**: finally!

The actions to come, the steps to follow, can be intimidating and seem complex, long, and meticulous. We might feel a bit afraid or timid, and put off by the number of different steps. What I am sure of is that, explained methodically, each phase of preparation is easy to understand and to apply. With a quick reference to use when starting out, you will be able to follow page by page, through the illustrations, and easily complete each part, without mistakes and without forgetting anything with experience. I think above all that it is important not to panic, because each step and each tool has a purpose, not to cause a struggle, but on the contrary to simplify each operation. In any case, explaining things simply while sharing the tips and tricks I have discovered over time will be my common thread to make the preparation for the project stress-free and give you confidence!

As far as the first step is concerned, I will only present the indirect warping method using a warping board. Apart from the illustration below, I will not go into direct warping on the sectional beam.

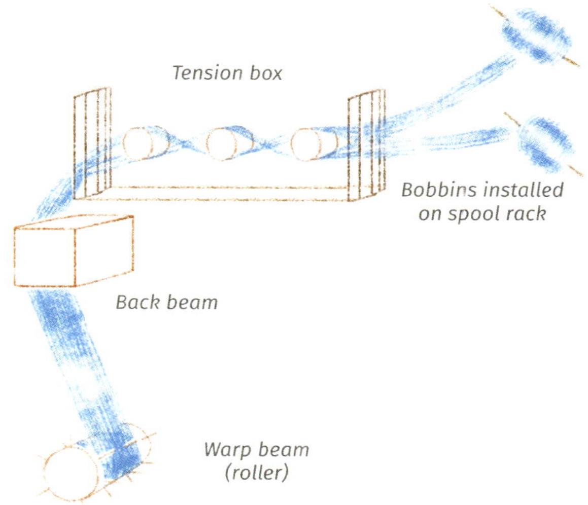

Figure 1 ***Direct or sectional warping***

I find that most amateur weavers wind **short warps** that do not require sectional warping. As soon as you want to wind with **many thread changes**, it is essential to know how to wind a warp with a warping board or mill. In any case, **not all warp beams are equipped to be sectional beams**, and you cannot use those for sectional warping. It is for these three reasons that I prefer indirect warping with a warping board or mill. A weaver who has learned to dress a loom with a sectional warp beam will find herself at a loss with a traditional warp beam. I agree that sectional warping with a tension box is very comfortable and ensures a perfect warping. This method is highly recommended for long warps, on a large warp beam equipped with sections.

This book is not a substitute for a practical course with an experienced weaver who would teach you how to perform the steps on the loom accurately and efficiently. Nothing replaces practice. The aim of this book is to bring you theoretical knowledge and to guide you step by step once the initial instruction is done, like being in the prompter's box, giving some tips to guide an uncertain actor.

The theater is the prompter. First of all, only he knows the whole play.

Jean Anouilh, French playwright (1910–1987)

Deborah Chandler's *Learning to Weave* explains in a very pedagogical way how to dress the loom and begin weaving. Other excellent resources include *Weaving for Beginners* by Peggy Osterkamp and *Next Steps in Weaving* by Pattie Graver.

The Script: Project Record Sheets

My play is done, I just have to write it!

Racine, French poet and playwright (1639–1699)

The record sheet has several functions: to **go hand in hand** with us so we do not forget anything throughout all the steps and to be our "**history logbook**" when one day we use the same thread or do the same project again, a bit like the magnificent books kept in the factories of the past. We will refer to it throughout the weaving. It must be clear, concise, and complete. And above all, it must be suitable for everyone's use. This chapter shows you the one I use at the moment, but it is constantly evolving. However, before starting, you must be able to answer the following questions.

- Which project, for what use?
- Which yarns: material, yarn count, color?
- Which structure or weave pattern?
- What size?

These are the first decisions to be made. If we know which project to make, then there is the question of which yarn to choose, often with a lot of wavering. Another scenario is that we have some yarn we want to use, we can roughly imagine the use of the fabric, but deciding on a structure takes time.

I really like these moments of looking around, researching, wavering back and forth. It is often the occasion to find a forgotten yarn or a weaving project put aside. The ideas flow, and I am often very excited, very eager to find **THE** right script.

And now, ask for the program! For a better understanding of the steps that follow, I have chosen to illustrate this chapter with a concrete example: a set of **placemats** in six colors from **slubbed linen/cotton** yarn from Les Linières de Saint Martin, woven in **varied twill**.

Figure 2 *One thread of each color is wrapped around cardstock*

- This yarn is 60% linen and 40% cotton. It is slightly twisted, and sometimes the fibers appear to be barely spun. It is therefore a slightly irregular yarn, which gives a rustic look to the weave. It is perfect for household linens. The range of colors is very nice. It is sometimes a little fragile in warp, but with careful preparation, it is not a problem.

Here is the threading draft. This will be our reference for what follows. Let's go ahead with the tests; our samples will become the rehearsals to get to the "performance." It's up to you if you will make it on the loom at the same time, but why not?

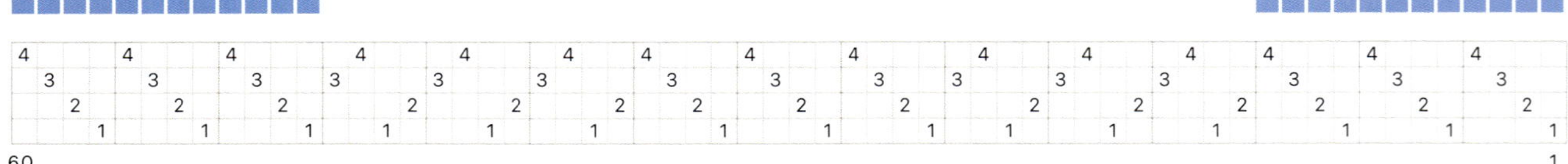

Figure 3 *The threading draft*

I propose this 12-thread sequence of broken twill:

- 12 threads in a regular straight threading in ascending order: 1-2-3-4, 1-2-3-4, 1-2-3-4;

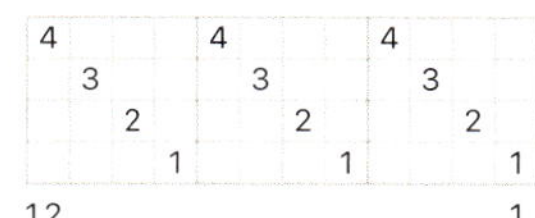

Figure 4 ***Threading of block A***

- then 12 threads in a regular straight threading, but in descending order: 2-1, 4-3-2-1, 4-3-2-1, 4-3;

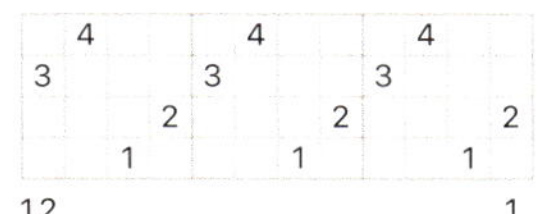

Figure 5 ***Threading of block B***

- At each change of direction, the continuity is broken by omitting a shaft. Thus, two even or two odd threads will be next to each other.

You have settled on a project, the yarns are chosen, the draft is drawn. There is still one important decision to make: **the density**. To do this, we will wrap the yarn around a ruler and practice with Ashenhurst's magic formula (see section on density on p. 45):

$$\text{Density} = \frac{\text{No. of yarn wraps around the ruler} \times \text{No. of warp threads in a weave ratio}}{\text{No. of warp threads} + \text{No. of weft threads in a weave ratio}}$$

By winding the linen/cotton slub from Linières de Saint Martin around the ruler, while making sure that the yarn touches its neighboring thread each time around, we note that 30 times around are needed to cover 1 inch (2.5 cm) on the ruler. To be more precise, you can even wrap over a couple of inches and determine an average. If using another yarn with a different yarn count, only the number of threads around the ruler changes in Ashenhurst's formula.

The twill weave unit shows 4 warp and 2 weft threads.

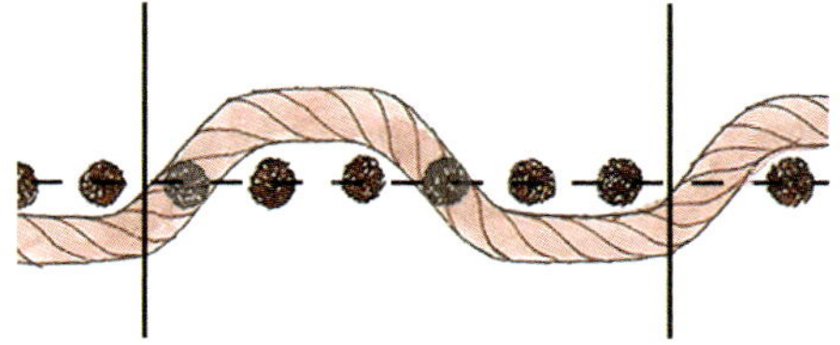

The density to test is therefore D = 30 × 4 / 4 + 2 = 8

$$D = \frac{30 \times 4}{4 + 2} = 20$$

Twill is a balanced structure, so the weft density will also be 20 threads per inch (8 per cm). I'm choosing a 10-dent reed, putting 2 threads/dent. The dents on a 20-dent reed are closer together and may wear down the linen thread much faster, so I prefer a low-density reed.

Part 1 of the record sheet allows us to summarize the first pieces of information.

Table 1 ***Project record sheet—Part 1***

Weaving Project	**Placemats**		
My source of inspiration	A series of twill with variations in tie-ups		
Final fabric measurements	8 placemats 16 × 24 in.		
Warp used	linen/ cotton slub	Thread count	2,727 yd/lb (5,600 m/kg)
Weft used	linen/ cotton slub	Thread count	2,727 yd/lb (5,600 m/kg)
Structure	Twill		
Warp density / in. (cm)	**20 threads/in. (8 threads/cm)**		
Reed: dents/in.	4	No. of threads/ dent	2
Weft density	**20 threads/in. (8 threads/cm)**		

Winding the Warp: Preparing the Yarn

Warping, from the Latin *ordiri*: to lay out threads to weave, to lay the warp, to begin. It [our soul] forms the link between our sensations, and weaves the fabric of our existence by a continuous thread of ideas.

Buffon, *Discourse on the Nature of Animals*, 1753. *The original quote is in French; the word "warping" translates to "ourdir" in French, hence the link to the Latin "ordiri."*

Winding the warp is the beginning of weaving. It is the preparation of warp threads so that **all have the same length and tension**. A warping board or mill is used.

So we need to calculate the following:

- How many warp ends does our project require?
- How long will they be?

Back to the project record sheet.

Warp Width

I introduced the different types of shrinkage in the chapter on samples (see p. 48). Whether in warp or in weft, as it goes back and forth and intertwines, the initial thread is longer than the fabric it is making. This excess depends on the structure selected, the density chosen, the yarn used, the tension we apply to our warp, and the firmness of the beat used.

In addition, the fabric contracts when it is removed from the tension of the loom. When we apply wet finishing processes to the fabric by washing and ironing, dyeing, felting, etc., there may also be shrinkage of the weave or swelling of the weave or swelling of the yarn. It is difficult not to have a small reduction.

We will only know the shrinkage percentages after a sample has been made. This is one of the roles of the sample: to allow us to evaluate this shrinkage in order to be sure to have enough yarn but also to verify that the dimensions obtained in the end are as needed.

Table 2 ***Calculation of warp width***

<table>
<tr><td rowspan="5">Warp width</td><td colspan="2">Desired width of finished fabric</td><td>16 in. (40 cm)</td></tr>
<tr><td>+ added amount due to finishing processes</td><td>7%</td><td>+1.1 in. (2.8 cm)</td></tr>
<tr><td colspan="2">= width of raw fabric off the loom</td><td>= 17 in. (43 cm)</td></tr>
<tr><td>+ added amount due to draw-in</td><td>5%</td><td>+ .85 in. (2.1 cm)</td></tr>
<tr><td colspan="2">= width of warp in the reed</td><td>= 18 in. (45 cm)</td></tr>
</table>

For our exercise, we will apply a percentage of 5 percent for "off the loom" take-up and 7 percent for "wet finishing" shrinkage, which is the percentage I usually adopt with this often used yarn and structure.

So to get 16 inches (40 cm) in width, we will have to prepare and weave 17¾ inches (45 cm) in width.

Warp Length

To make it easier to understand, we can separate the warp into three different parts.

The warp that will be woven, to which we will add the different shrinkages. In this example we are planning for 8 placemats at 24 inches (60 cm) each.

The warp that will not be woven, but is part of the project and will also be affected by washing: **the fringe**, **the hem**, the sections at the beginning and end of each placemat, sometimes the nonwoven parts inside lacework. In this example, we choose to have 1¼ inches (3 cm) of fringe around each placemat, which makes 2½ inches (6 cm) of fringe between each weave.

The warp that is used to tie it onto the loom:

- at the back of the shafts: this length varies depending on the loom and according to the method of tying. For this example, we will add 16 inches (40 cm);
- at the front on the beam or cloth roller: we will add 8 or 16 inches (20 or 40 cm) depending on the method used to tie it on.

This last part of the warp is considered lost, even if it can be used for other projects. To reduce these losses, whenever possible, it is best to weave several projects on the same warp, in order to share the unavoidable unused length.

I recommend a little caution with rounding, which should only be done at the end of the calculations. So we will wind a 21.4 foot (6.52 m) warp.

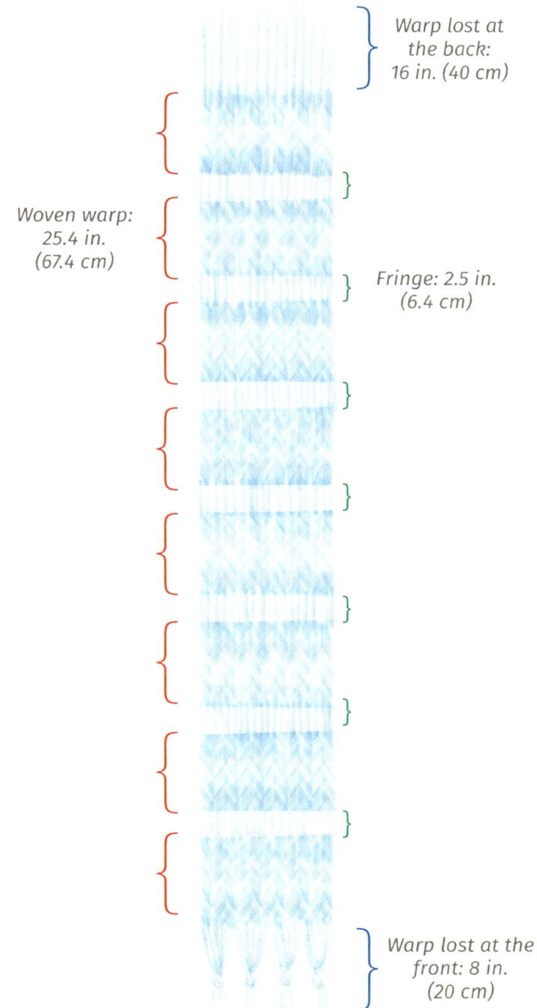

Figure 6 *Weaving setup and losses over the whole warp*

Table 3 *Calculation of warp length*

Warp length	**Desired length of finished fabric**		**24 in. (60 cm)**
	+ added amount due to finishing processes	7%	+ 1.68 in. (4.2 cm)
	= length of fabric off the loom		= 25.68 in. (64.2 cm)
	+ added amount due to shrinkage	5%	+ 1.28 in. (3.2 cm)
	= length of woven warp per item		**= 26.96 in. (67.4 cm)**
	+ fringe		+ 2.5 in. (6 cm)
	= warp length needed per item		= 29.5 in. (74 cm)
	× number of items	8	= 8 placemats @ 29.5 in. = 236 in. (8 × 74 cm = 592 cm)
	+ losses due to tying on at the front and back of the loom		+ 8 + 16 = 24 in. (+ 20 + 40 = 60 cm)
	= length of warp needed		**= 21.67 ft./7.2 yd. (6.52 m)**

Projected Amount of Yarn Needed for Warp and Weft

In weaving, we can know very precisely the amount of yarn needed. It is really easy to do, reassuring, and economical. There is little risk of discovering during the weaving process that you are short of yarn, or of buying too much yarn for fear of running out. I hope this sheet will be able to fulfill its purpose: to guide those who are not mathematically inclined!

On the opposite end, it happens that those who love math have fun finding the ideal dimensions of their weaving in order to empty their reserve of precious yarns, to the nearest meter. I smile when I think of the people who will recognize themselves in these words!

First the Warp

The next part of the record sheet is used to help calculate the amount of yarn needed for the warp.

Table 4 *Amount of yarn needed for the warp*

Number of warp ends	Width of fabric in the reed in inches (cm) × density	= 18 in. (45 cm) × 20 ends/in. (8 /cm) **= 360 warp ends**
Quantity in yards (m)	Number of warp ends × warp length	= 360 ends × 7.2 yd. = 2,592 yd. (× 6.52 m = 2,347 m)

So for this warp, we will need approximately 2,600 yds. (2,350 m).

Then the Weft

Calculating the quantity of yarn needed for the weft follows the same logic.

Table 5 *Amount of yarn needed for the weft*

Number of weft threads	Length of woven warp in inches (cm) × density × number of items	27 in. × 20 threads/in. × 8 placemats = **4,320 picks** (67.5 cm × 8 threads/cm × 8 placemats = **4,320 picks**)
Quantity in yards (m)	Number of picks × width in reed	= 4,320 picks × 0.5 yd. (18 in.) = 2,160 yd. (4,320 picks × 45 cm = 1,950 m)

So for the entire weft, we will need 2,160 yd. (1,950 m).

Once all this information has been calculated, we know all the elements concerning the **quantity of yarn**:

- 360 warp ends each 21.6 ft. (6.52 m) long, for a total of 2,600 yd. (2,350 m);
- 4,320 picks at a width of 18 in. (45 cm), for 2,160 yd. (1,950 m).

The amount of warp yarn is always a little more than the amount of weft yarn, since some parts of the warp are not woven (used at the front and back of the loom and the fringe). It is a poor reference to check our calculations, but it is sometimes useful.

Warp Color Order Charts

So, we know we need 360 lengths of yarn at 7.2 yards (6.5 m) each. But which yarn? In what order? In what color?

Warp color order charts provide an overall look at the number of threads in each color in the order of threading in a very visible and colorful way, if possible. They also help to check if the thread count is right and if the patterns chosen are feasible. Sometimes we will have to readjust the width of the weave to fit the selected patterns, so that they are complete.

The threading sequence presented in the section "The Script: Project Record Sheets" (see p. 70) showed 12 steel blue threads, 36 sky blue threads, and then 12 steel blue threads again. This arrangement will be repeated with new colors or in a new order.

The following warp color order chart shows the sequence for winding the warp with the number of passes of the yarns of each color for these placemats.

Table 6 Warp color order chart

Steel blue	12		12								36								60
Sky blue		36								12		12							60
Pink				12		12								36					60
Fuchsia					36								12		12				60
Lime							12		12								36		60
Lichen green								36								12		12	60

Placed near the warping board, this chart is easy to read and prevents mistakes. In this example, we first wind 12 steel blue threads, then 36 sky blue, then 12 steel blue again, then 12 pink, 36 fuchsia, and 12 pink, then lime and lichen, and the warping continues according to the instructions of the chart read from left to right, until the 360 warp threads have been wound. Let's never deprive ourselves of this kind of double entry table, which is a precious tool to check our counts and the total number of warp threads.

The Warping Board, an Essential Tool for Length, Tension, and the Cross

Absolutely necessary order, as without it, it would be impossible to recognize where you are, and all would be in danger of being lost.

Diderot, *L'Encyclopédie*, 1st Ed. 1751

Winding the warp is the process of organizing all the warp ends needed to cover the width of the desired weave with the same length and tension. It does not matter if you dress your loom from the back to the front or from the or from the front to the back. To each his own method!

A warping board, or a warping mill, is necessary because we are in a small space. If we lived in Peru or the Middle East, we would plant two stakes spaced 7 yards (6.5 m) apart. If we lived with the Dogon people in West Africa, we would use our house. We would plant two stakes in the earthen wall, and we would walk around the house.

If you don't have a warping board or mill, you can firmly attach some rods or pegs to a table, as long as the length and the cross are there.

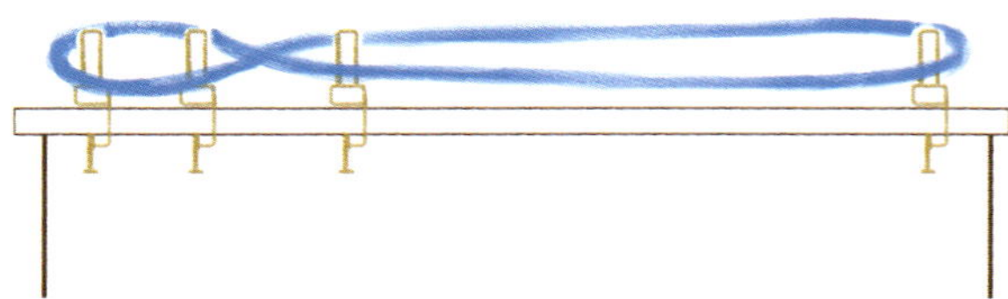

Figure 7 A makeshift warping board

However, a warping board is part of the list of basic materials. It is made using pegs. It takes up little space, is inexpensive, and is ideal for shorter warps. In any case, the idea is to set it up ergonomically, at a height that matches your height, preferably vertically, and never against the light, so as to be able to wind the warp with a smooth movement.

With a mill, while more cumbersome and more expensive, you can wind a much longer warp. It is simple and comfortable to use. One hand turns the mill while the other goes up and down to guide the yarn. In addition, by placing it at the right height, you can sit down, and that's pretty nice!

To understand how we are going to use this tool, let's imagine the warping board as an illustration of our loom, where each part of the warping board matches a part of the loom:

- The peg on the warping board at the beginning of the warp will be replaced, on the loom, by the front tie-on rod, which is connected to the loom's cloth roller;
- The pegs used to make the cross will be replaced by the lease sticks;
- The peg at the end of the warp will be replaced by the back tie-on rod, attached to the warp beam.

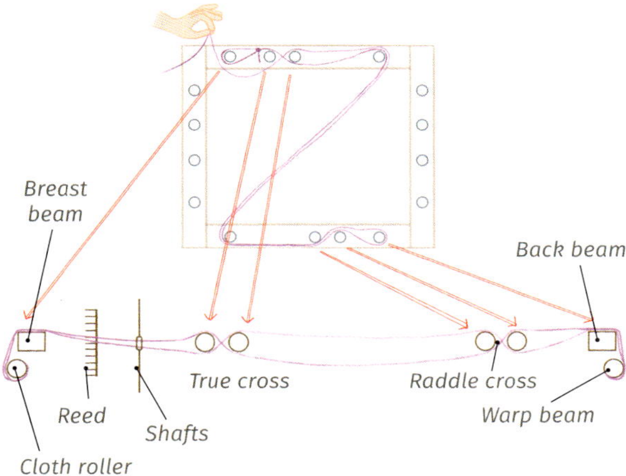

Figure 8 **Parallels between the warping board and the loom**

Let's complete this correlation between the warping board and loom and "spread out" the warping board to match up to our loom. Let me insist a little on this analogy. We are going to think as if we could warp our loom from one beam to the other. If the warping board was spread out, we would wind the warp from one peg to the other. We would then undoubtedly better understand this operation of winding the warp.

Having a more compact warping board, inevitable with our limited indoor space, seems to make the concept and the actual process of the warping unclear. During the whole weaving process, all warp threads must maintain equal tension. Warping is the first step! This is not a case of vigorously stretching out the yarn, but smoothly pulling it taut with the same tension throughout. We naturally associate the word "tension" with "hyper"; let's enjoy some "hypo" tension instead!

For this reason, we prefer to warp all our threads on the same day. Depending on our mood, we are indeed more or less tense.

Here's how to proceed. Stand relaxed in front of the warping board, hands swinging from right to left, body limber, as if you were ready to dance. No need to pinch the yarn, but with your hand, lightly move it from peg to peg. With a flowing movement, the left hand goes around the left pegs, the right hand around the right pegs. The body gets less tired if it is straight in front of a vertical warping board. The work will be easier if there is adequate light. Do not place the board in front of the window as backlighting is bothersome and tires the eyes.

In order for the threads to have the same tension, they must unwind easily and in the same way. We never warp two yarns packaged differently, for example one in a skein and the other in a cone! If that happens, transfer the yarns onto bobbins, so that they will unwind freely and identically. The balls will be placed in pots to prevent them from rolling around and getting tangled. Cones will be placed close by. Often, it is easiest to wind warp yarn on bobbins that will be placed on a creel, a frame with rods on which the spools are hung, so there is no risk of tangling or getting slowed down.

To wind the desired length of warp, I start by making a guide string of the same length by taking a solid yarn in a very different color than the yarn to be warped. With this guide string, on the warping board, I look for a path for the thread using a movement that will be the most natural for my hands. This thread will be my guide. There is no one way better than another, as long as you have the length and one or two crosses. I am most comfortable with a warping board or mill where four pegs are lined up. It is in the center of this line that I make the cross.

I start by tying a loose loop and then slip it around the first peg, the equivalent of the front tie-on rod on the loom. I finish in the same way.

Figure 9 **Starting to wind the warp**

So that the threads stay in the same order they are wound and don't get mixed up when we take them off the warping board, we will cross them each time we go between the second and third pegs. This is the indispensable **thread-by-thread cross**, the invaluable, almost sacred, method that no weaver can do without! For a flowing movement, carry the yarn as if writing a figure eight with your hand, in the direction that suits you. This movement will soon become quite spontaneous.

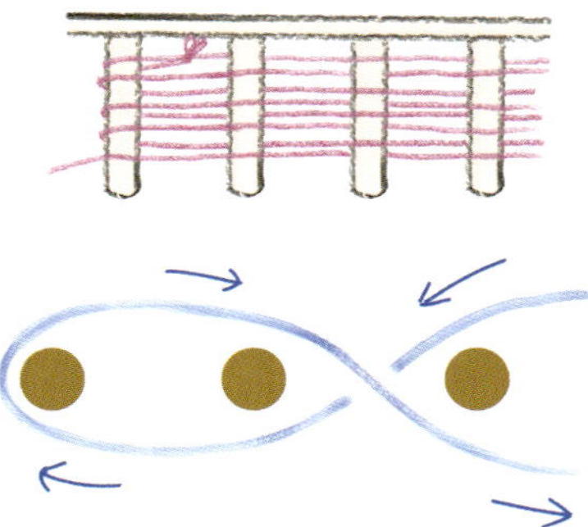

Figure 10 ***The thread-by-thread cross***

To keep count of the number of threads, you can take a contrasting color thread and simply slide it around every 10 threads. Don't make a knot as that will be in the way later on; a simple crisscross will suffice. Another efficient and practical method is to make what I call a **raddle cross**. I place it at the end of the warp, between the last four pegs, where I cross the yarn in sections, with the number of threads per section determined by the desired density.

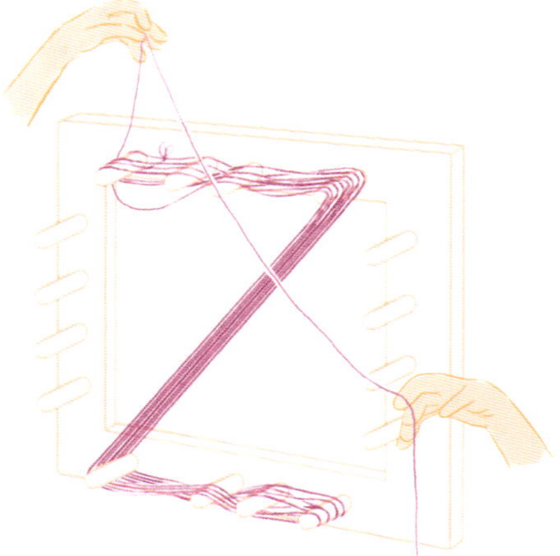

Figure 11 ***The two crosses made when winding the warp***

In our scenario, the density chosen is 20 ends per inch (8 per cm). So between the third and fourth pegs of the warping board nearest the end of the warp, I cross the opposite way every 20 threads. This trick makes it very easy to keep count of your threads; each group of threads corresponds to a 1-inch (2.5 cm) width of warp. This cross will make it much easier to distribute the warp between the teeth of the raddle during the next step of warping the loom.

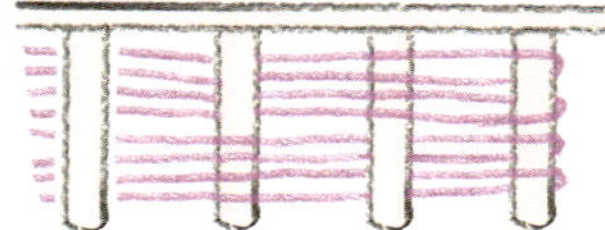

Figure 12 ***Groups of warp in the raddle cross***

This crossing of threads in sections is done automatically when several threads are wound on together, with or without pegs to wind around. There as well, to easily count the number of crosses, interlacing a colored thread will keep us from having to count and recount so often. Pass it around every 4 sections, for example. In our example, the multiple colors of the warp will be enough to identify the number of threads without having to add an additional marker. Putting on too many counting threads or making knots is often the mistake of the beginner who is afraid of not doing it right and who, as a result, gets more muddled. Sometimes less is more. The right marker will suffice!

Never tie a knot in the warp; if necessary, at the end of a ball, or when changing colors, **the knot will be at the beginning or end of the warp**, in an area that will not be woven.

Once all our warp is wound, before removing it from the warping board, **the yarn must be secured**, as some areas are very valuable. Remember the drawing on the previous page comparing the warping board to the loom. We want to move this warp, while protecting the four crucial locations: the first peg, which will be replaced by the front tie-on rod stick, the two pegs of the thread-by-thread cross, which will be replaced by the lease sticks, the two other pegs of the raddle cross, which will be replaced by the cross sticks at the beginning of installing the warp on the loom, and finally the peg at the end of the warp, which will be replaced by the back tie-on rod. We are therefore going to tie these critical places with sturdy pieces of yarn or string in a contrasting color to carry the warp to the loom. These are called transport ties.

If it helps you, I suggest using colored threads to help differentiate the beginning and end of the warp:

- **Green** thread, tied at the true cross near the beginning of the warp, which will be placed at the front of the loom;

- **Red** thread, tied at the raddle cross, which will be placed at the rear of the loom.

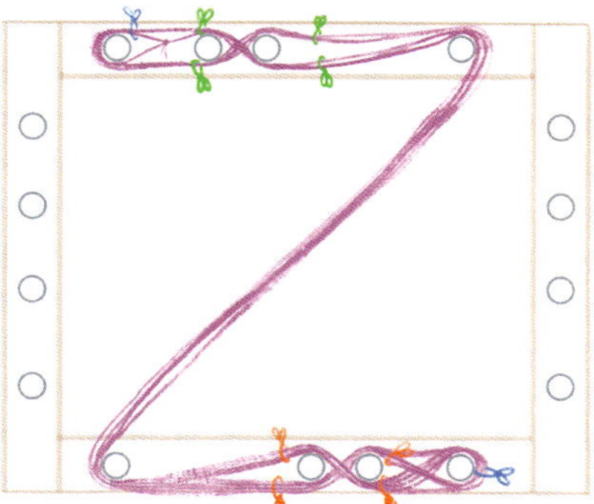

Figure 13 ***Ties used to keep the cross intact***

Moving the warp to the loom is sometimes a cause for concern, as it is true that a few mistakes are enough to make a mess of our warp and tangle with our nerves! So, if tying up the true cross with four green ties and the raddle cross with four red ties can take away a little stress, why not do it! And to help differentiate, I suggest using a yarn that is neither red nor green to tie the warp at the beginning peg and the turning (end) peg.

The start or end loops of the warp will be loose enough for the tie thread to pass through to tie up the warp so it can be carried to the loom.

Check that there are five ties at the beginning of the warp as well as at the end, the four protecting the cross and the one at the very end. Make knots that can be removed without the help of scissors, or a tie that is firmly attached but wide enough to allow a scissors blade to pass through without risk of cutting the warp. However, these ties must be firm so that they do not come undone by themselves. If the warp is very long, add some choke ties every yard or so to keep the threads together.

Once you have secured the crosses and the loops at the beginning and end, you can remove the warp from the warping board using the following method. First take the part of the warp that will be at the front of the loom, the one near the true, thread-by-thread cross. Then, gradually, remove the warp from the warping board by making a loose chain with your hands acting as a crochet hook. Stop when there are about 20 inches (50 cm) of length left.

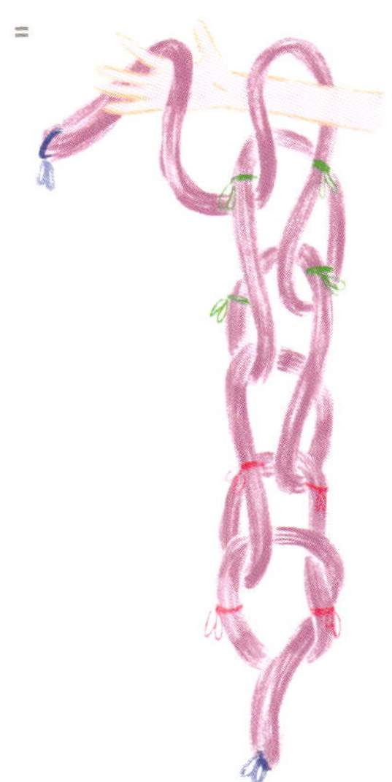

Figure 14 ***Chaining the warp for easier handling***

If you want to dress your loom from the front to the back, you will take the end of the warp first, so that the true cross is close at hand. In this case, there is no need to make a raddle cross.

Some people have difficulty making this chain. There is an easier option: simply wind the warp around a dowel or tube of some kind. The idea is only to free the chain from the warping machine and to place it in such a way that it doesn't move, especially unintentionally—by a cat or perhaps a child?

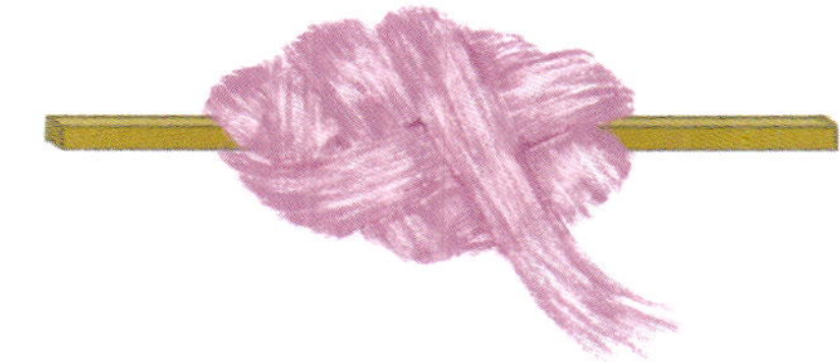

Figure 15 ***An alternative to the chain***

Our warp is thus safe and secure and can be transported, if necessary, by slipping it into a bag and attaching the last loop to the handle of the bag. When the time comes, the chain can be spread out on the loom.

Preparing the Equipment

Before beaming the warp, there are two or three small things to prepare or install on the loom. The main idea is to have everything at hand and to think ahead as much as possible in order to stay focused, relaxed, and calm.

Counting Heddles on the Loom According to the Threading

It is much more practical to count the heddles available on each shaft before starting to thread to make sure there are enough of them, and to add more if there are not. They are also counted in order to distribute the unused heddles equally on each side of the shaft, or to remove those not needed if the whole width of the loom is being used.

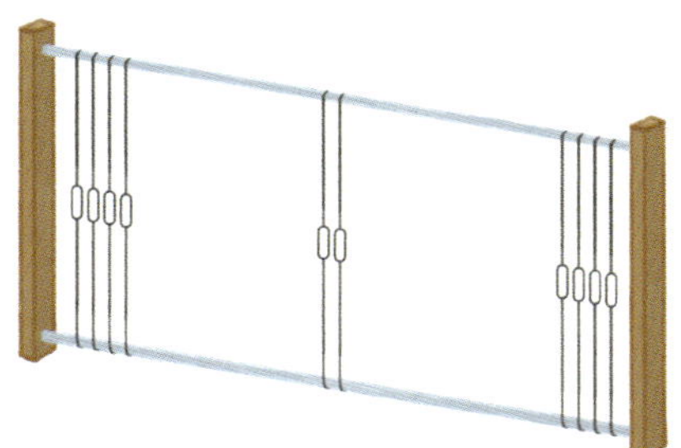

Figure 16 ***Counting the heddles on each shaft***

On some looms, it is easy to remove or add missing heddles, even if the warp is already partly threaded. On others, it is almost impossible. You might as well plan and count before you start threading. Here again, a table will allow you to check calmly and methodically.

The number of heddles needed depends on the number of warp ends to be threaded, which depends on the width of your weaving project and the density, but not only that! The number of heddles per shaft can vary depending on the weave pattern, sometimes considerably.

We look first at the weaving project for the best way to count the heddles. Sometimes they are counted by pattern, sometimes by block, or in some other way that helps to connect them, like the colors in our placemats example. The idea is to simplify the reading of the diagram as much as possible in order to facilitate the counting. Above all, step back, regroup, and do not count the warp threads in the threading draft one by one! Counting by groups is both easier and more accurate.

Let's get back to our threading chart.

I will explain later what a block is, and how it simplifies the reading and writing of a weaving pattern (see p. 235). Without going into too much detail for the moment, let's think of a block as a defined area with its own identity, and arbitrarily agree that in this example:

- the threading draft is read from right to left;
- the group whose order of threading is **1-2-3-4** is called **block A**;
- the group whose threading order is **2-1-4-3** is called **block B**;
- each block consists of 12 threads;
- blocks A and B alternate systematically.

Drawn in this way, the threading is much easier to remember. This is called a profile draft, a sort of outline of the future threading.

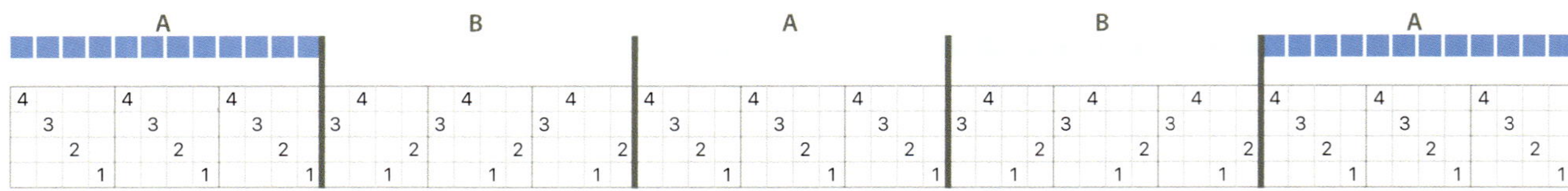

Figure 17 ***Threading draft of the example divided into blocks***

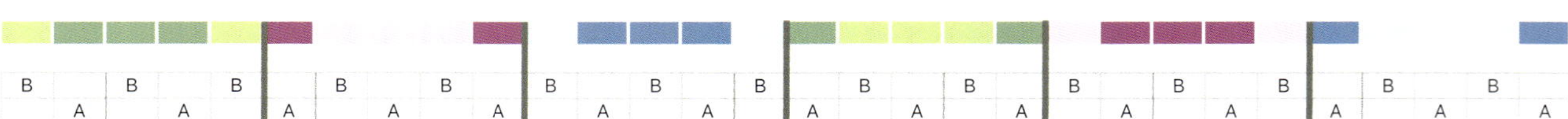

Figure 18 ***Profile draft of the entire threading***

Let's also get back to our warp color order chart.

Table 7 ***Warp color order chart***

Steel blue	12		12								36								60
Sky blue		36								12		12							60
Pink				12		12								36					60
Fuchsia					36								12		12				60
Lime							12		12								36		60
ichen green								36								12		12	60

In summary, the warp is made up of six groups, each consisting of two colors, a steel blue/sky blue group, a pink/fuchsia group, a lime/lichen green group (these three groups twice). In the outside columns of 12 threads, there is a single block, either A or B. In the middle column of 36 threads, 3 blocks will follow each other: A-B-A or B-A-B, depending on the block in the outer column. Blocks A and B, each made up of 12 threads, alternate systematically.

Now let's construct a heddle counting table.

Actually, for this weaving project, this table is hardly necessary, since each of the two blocks uses the same number of heddles, with the yarns distributed evenly over the 4 shafts. Let's call it an exercise. In other examples, it helps us to clearly visualize the blocks and to check that the number of warp ends wound does match the total number of heddles.

I like to look ahead and I have a weakness for tables that help with double checking. I can say that by constructing this project beforehand, it is surprisingly easy to set up afterward. Everything is clear and well laid out on our sheets, but also, interestingly enough, in our memory, a method to help avoid some mistakes.

So we come to the conclusion that we need 90 heddles per shaft. Now we must check that each shaft has the desired number.

I like this way of proceeding. This table is similar to a guardrail, and it is up to everyone to use the tool that suits them. The only rule is to do it in a very visual way, which leaves no doubt, and at the same time gives the opportunity to check that there are no counting errors. Here, the calculation gives us the expected result: 360 heddles for 360 threads!

Table 8 ***Heddle counting table—counting heddles per shaft***

Shafts	Heddles by group					Total	Each group is repeated 6 x, with the other colors	+ remainder	= total heddles per shaft
	Blue	Sky Blue			Blue				
	Block A	Block B	Block A	Block B	Block A				
4	3	3	3	3	3	15	15 × 6 = 90	0	90
3	3	3	3	3	3	15	15 × 6 = 90	0	90
2	3	3	3	3	3	15	15 × 6 = 90	0	90
1	3	3	3	3	3	15	15 × 6 = 90	0	90
Total	12	12	12	12	12	60			360 heddles

Backstage, Each Accessory in Its Place

Many weavers can't imagine being able to warp a loom without someone's help. However, the "someone" is not necessarily available, not necessarily competent, or necessarily patient. I like to work alone, without being dependent on a friend or family member. But sometimes, if someone could hold a thread or the warp or even bring me a tool, it would help me a lot. Still, I prefer to work alone. And to do this, it is important to organize and prepare beforehand. Everything in its place, as the prop master would say.

1—Installation of Helping Hands

The "helping hands" are two double threads placed on each side of the loom, stretched firmly between the two beams to be able to place the tools or the warp on a stable, horizontal, accessible support. These threads will also support the sticks without the risk of them falling before they are attached and wound.

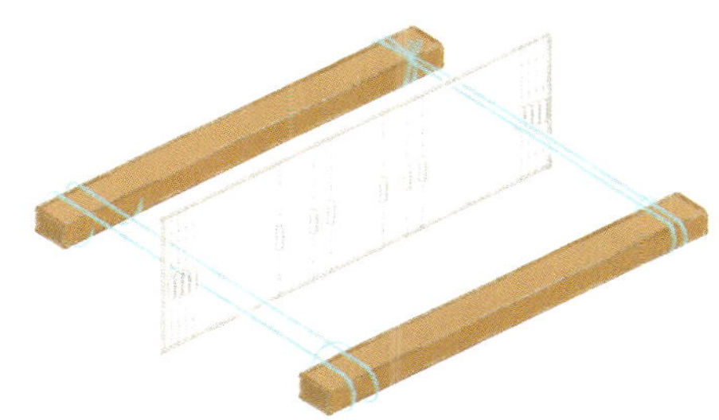

Figure 19 ***The helping hands installed between the front and back beams***

Over time, in my workshop, this tool has evolved. Now I use a waxed nylon thread, which stays on the loom's back beam. It remains attached when starting to dress the loom until the warp is connected to the front rod. It is unbreakable! I also prefer to double this thread to slide the lease sticks between these two guides.

Take a strong nylon thread, not too thick, twice as long as the space between the two beams. Take the middle of it and wrap it around the back beam, on one side of the side of the loom, taking the two strands across the shafts outside the heddles you need, tying it tightly and securely around the breast beam. Do the same on the other side.

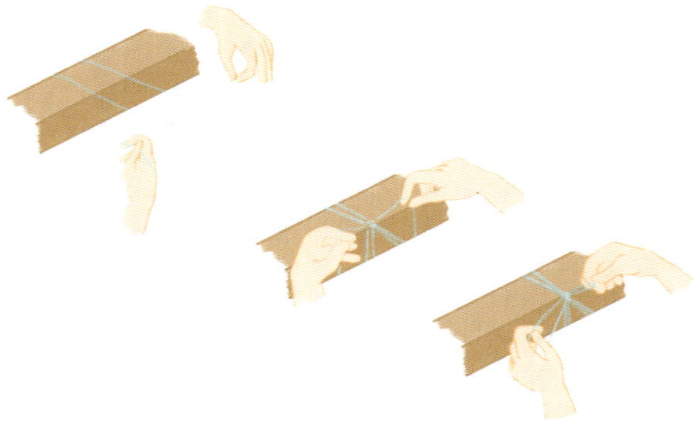

Figure 20 ***Adding on the helping hands***

These extra hands will be very useful, as you can lay the lease sticks and tie-on rods on them.

2—Materials to Keep Close at Hand

The raddle, rubber bands to hold it on the beam, the weights, the lease sticks and the rods or paper for winding, scissors, pieces of string, ties for the lease sticks, and a brush or a comb for untangling.

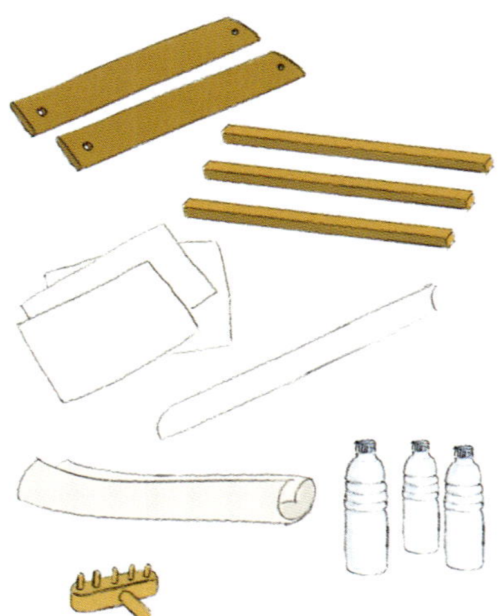

Figure 21 ***Preparing the materials***

The main idea is to remain calm and confident and to not make unnecessary movements. If everything is there, ready to use, the steps for dressing the loom flow from one to the next, without stress, and above all without the risk of dropping the warp during a crucial step. All of these materials can be placed on a little rolling cart so you can be comfortable and have them close at hand.

3—Placement of the Warp

Some weavers prefer to warp from the front, others from the back. I wind on from the back, because I learned this way and I'm content with that. This is the method I present here, but the other one is just as good.

However, I do highly recommend winding from the back for fragile yarns. Mohair would lose some hair and be at risk of catching or sticking too much with the double pass between the reed dents. Linen wears out so much from friction that it must be protected as well. For the other yarns, choose the method that seems most natural to you.

We will now move to the back of the loom. No kidding, sometimes with table looms that are turned in all directions, you can lose track.

I slide the two lease sticks into the raddle cross, the one where the threads are in groups of 20. The cross can be recognized by the red ties (**R**ed, **R**ear, **R**addle . . .). I secure my lease sticks by placing them between the two threads of the helping hands, then I tie them together. It is now impossible for them to fall out!

Figure 22 ***The lease sticks are secured***

I then slip a stick into the back loop of the warp. I don't directly use the back rod which, connected to the warp beam by numerous ties, does not make it possible for the warp to be completely spread out. I use an extra stick that I slide into the rear loop of the warp. Then I tie these two sticks together at their ends. This way, the warp can be spread out across its entire width without anything in its way.

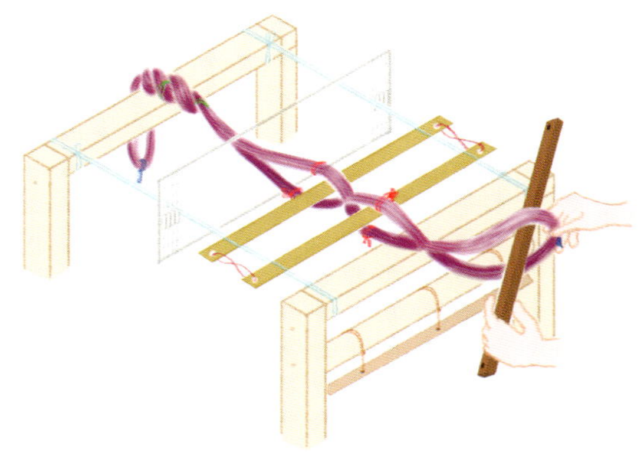

Figure 23 ***Warping the loom from the back***

I wind up warp a bit until the two tied sticks are close to the warp beam and it is no longer possible for them to fall. I temporarily weight the whole thing down in the front. Threads under tension are always easier to work with and the whole thing looks in order.

Figure 24 ***The warp is weighted at the front of the loom***

The lark's head knot is simple to tie and works well for attaching the ballast. A small bottle of water is the ideal weight.

Figure 25 ***The lark's head knot used to attach weight to the warp***

When all these sticks are secured, I remove the 5 ties, the 4 red ones in the cross and the 1 from the end loop. Once freed, the warp threads are very visibly seen to be in groups. In the next step, they will be placed between the teeth of the raddle.

Now we can sit. Here is a new "absolute" rule in weaving: **find a position that is comfortable and relaxing**. As soon as you can sit down, go ahead. And above all, never stay in an uncomfortable position. Always try to be set up in a way that suits you!

Setting Up the Raddle and "Raddling" the Warp

The raddle is a tool whose teeth are often spaced one half-inch apart. It is placed on the loom during the warping and is used to spread out the warp according to the desired density and width in order to ensure an even warping. The groups of warp ends are placed in each space between the teeth, the sections very visible now that they are separated by the lease sticks.

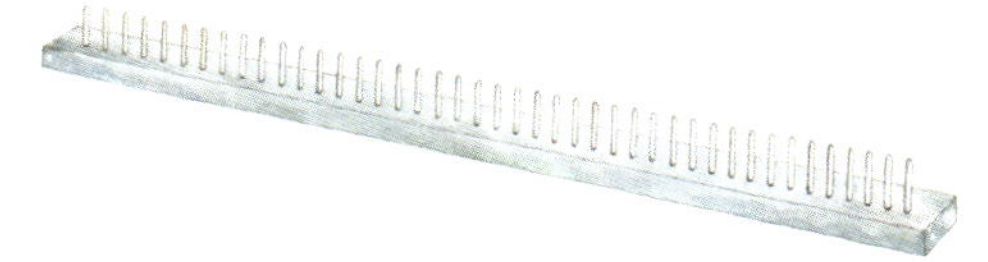

Figure 26 ***The raddle***

Purchased or homemade, with nails or pegs, the raddle is the tool used to spread out the warp according to the calculated density.

Two elements are fundamental.

In weaving, **the middle of the loom is THE reference point to always have in your line of sight!** The warp must be centered the entire time you are dressing the loom. The raddle is the first tool used for this purpose. For looms that don't come with a raddle, it can be attached to the loom with rubber bands. I prefer to attach it now to the back beam, so I have it directly in front of me. When beaming the warp, it is very easy for me to watch that threads do not get caught on each other or in the teeth of the raddle. Guesswork is out of the question! The middle of the raddle must be placed in the middle of the back beam so that the warp is wrapped around this valuable point of reference. So go ahead and draw a small permanent mark on the back beam and on the raddle. Then there will be perfect centering of the warp on this raddle!

The raddle helps with even winding. In our example, we must spread the warp over 18 inches and put 10 threads in a half-inch space (over 45 cm with 8 threads per cm). **The raddle is a guide, but only a guide.** If while warping you made a mistake in counting the number of threads per group, it's really not a big deal. The whole thing remains uniform. If you happen to get a raddle in approximate measurements, or you get one in centimeters rather than inches, don't panic!

There are 5 cm per 2 inches, so distribute what you would normally place in four one half-inch raddle spaces over 5 cm. Divide the threads as evenly as possible on both sides of the middle! And balance out the whole warp so that the width in the raddle is about the same width of the item to be woven, give or take half an inch or so. Only the centering of your warp should not be approximate.

The lease sticks show the separation of each group of warp ends. We take them one by one, putting them into each tooth of the raddle. In doing so, they are moved little by little onto the back rodstick so that they are straight below the raddle. This way, all of the warp ends are carefully arranged.

Tidy work properly done and clearly presented helps keep us from making setup mistakes and guarantees a balanced tension. The warp threads separated out this way are then secured on the raddle using thread or a rubber band, so that none of the warp moves out of these spaces during beaming. If the raddle is made with round pegs rather than tines or nails, a small rod or bar can be slid into the pegs, or sometimes a cover can be placed on top. Everything must be kept in order.

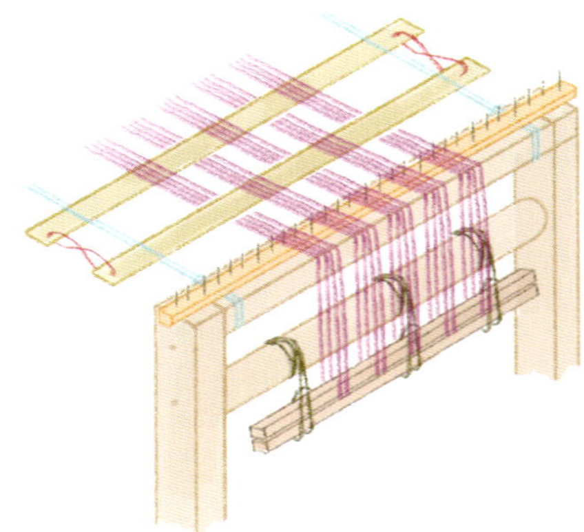

Figure 27 ***The warp is distributed between the teeth of the raddle.***

The two back rods, the one attached to the warp beam and the one that was added, are then securely tied together across the entire width before being wrapped around the warp beam. The raddle cross sticks can then be removed. They will be reused for the true cross a little later.

Beaming the Warp: Quiet on Set . . . We're Rolling!

While consistent tension on the warping board is important, it is essential to pay attention to keeping consistent tension when beaming the warp. The quality of beaming the warp will unquestionably ensure an even fabric. **All warp ends must be wound with the same tension**, across the entire width and length, but this does not mean a strong tension. This even tension should be maintained during all of the preparation and the weaving that follows. For this, two tools will suffice, as well as a little space around you and some peace and quiet.

Warp Sticks

These sticks will be slid between the layers of yarns during the entire winding process. Thanks to them, the circumference of the warp beam will always be equal over the entire width and the warp ends will stay in their place, without slipping to the side or overlapping. The sticks can be replaced by paper or heavy cardboard at the beginning, to protect the layer from the bumps of tying knots. Large recycled cardboard tubes cut lengthwise will be perfect. The ideal thing is to have a roll of paper the width of the warp beam, like wallpaper, kraft paper, a heavier type paper. Make sure that the sticks or the paper used are always wider than the warp to be wound by about an inch (2 cm) on each side. Otherwise, there is a great risk that the threads will slip over the edges, permanently compromising their even tension.

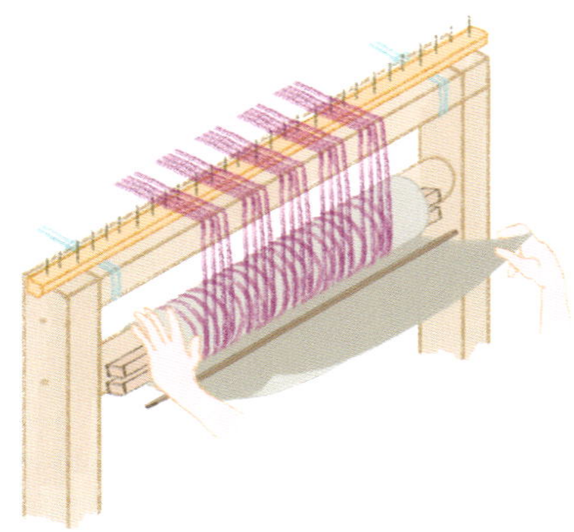

Figure 28 ***Winding the warp with paper or warp sticks***

Wound uniformly between the layers of warp, this paper will hold the warp ends in place. From time to time, for a long warp, some more firm warp sticks will be slid in to reinforce the edges. If you are using a table loom, these warp sticks should not be too thick, as the space between the roller and the beam is fairly limited.

Weights

It is so normal to warp a loom with a friend's help that it's hard to imagine being able to do it alone. It has almost become part of the legend: alone, it is impossible to beam the warp. But "helping hands" can replace the help of a friend. In this step, we use weights to be that help, and they will make it possible to wind on the warp all by yourself. Almost better than an extra pair of arms to evenly pull the warp taut, the weights will be attached to the warp at the front of the loom. One thing is certain, we are at least assured of an equal load distributed evenly and an identical tension applied to each section.

To ensure that all warp ends have the same tension, they are weighted in identical groups. From the front, we divide the warp into bundles of approximately 10 to 15 sections each. All the bundles must have the same number of warp ends! What good would equal weights be if they didn't weigh down an equal group of threads?

Figure 29 ***The sections are weighted at the front.***

In our example, we divide the warp into 4 groups of 90 warp ends, each occupying about 4 inches (10 cm) of width in the raddle. We firmly pull each section taut, like Ben-Hur with his leather straps to guide his chariot, or in any case, just as vigorously. We may want to do a bit of brushing to untangle yarn, if needed, and again, not with mohair, or wool, or linen, or single-ply yarns. Then we add a weight using a lark's knot at each section. The four weights do not need to be very heavy, as long as they are identical. Again, small water bottles will work just fine here. The length of the tie to the bottle allows it to be close to the ground and then to rise as the warp is wound up. Generally, the knot is at the height of the cloth roller, and the bottle is almost on the ground.

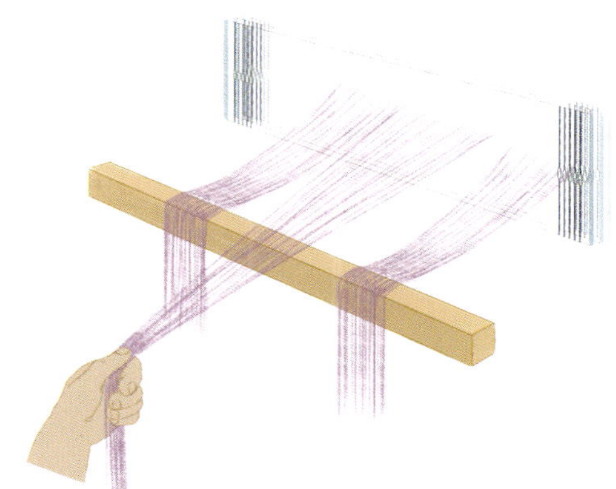

Figure 30 ***The sections of warp ends are pulled taut Ben-Hur style.***

Sitting at the back of the loom, with the warp sticks or the paper roll at hand, all that remains is to wind. When the bottles get near the raddle, we go back to the front and untie them, play Ben-Hur again, reposition the bottles, and then beam the warp some more. And so on until the whole warp is rolled up and the thread-by-thread cross, with the green ties, reaches the raddle at the back of the loom.

A Few Comments

Due to lack of habit or confidence, one may be confused when faced with a problem. I think it's important to remember that the raddle, and therefore the spreading out of the warp in the raddle, is just a guide in beaming the warp and not a step in itself. So, **no need to panic, we can all relax**.

Sometimes the **threads can catch on each other** between the weights and the raddle when winding on the warp. This is an area to watch out for because it is often where the warp threads break during winding, or at least weaken. Becoming stuck together because of fuzz in the yarn, they get jammed up at the raddle. If you feel a little more tension while winding, check that all the threads can slide freely between the teeth of the raddle. When installing the raddle on the back beam and sitting close by, I can easily see the threads on the raddle and on the warp beam at a glance, watching that the warp is winding smoothly. This is also why I recommend removing the raddle lease sticks. At the cross between the two sticks, the threads are very close to each other, so it is a risky area. There are already enough of these as it is; no need to add another. The warp ends like to move close to each other and can get caught on each other, until they break if you don't pay enough attention.

The direction in which the warp beam is wound varies depending on the loom. To be sure not to make a mistake in the direction, the warp beam **locking device must be left in place**. No mistake is then possible. It's common sense, but reverse winding is more common than you might think, so it's better to just bring this up.

End of the Act

After some winding, you will gradually arrive at the true cross, recognizable by its little green ties. This is the moment to use again the lease sticks that were used for the raddle cross and now slip them into the real cross. **The thread-by-thread cross is valuable** and warrants all our attention. **It is indispensable** in the next step, where it becomes the guide for presenting each warp end in the right order for threading.

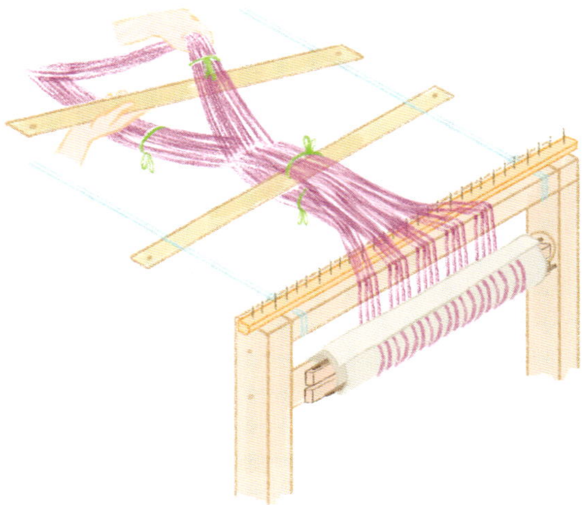

Figure 31 ***The lease sticks are inserted in the true cross.***

Insert the lease sticks in the cross, following that idea from the beginning that they "replace" the pegs of the warping board around which the warp was wound. As we just finished doing for the raddle cross, slide them between the sections of thread using the little green ties, which can be firmly pulled. Then slide them through the "helping hands" and tie them together on the other side. **When everything seems secure**, after checking things again, remove the ties from the cross so that finally the warp can be spread out over its entire width.

Caught up in the enthusiasm of beaming, it sometimes happens that the ties around the cross are removed too soon. As long as the raddle is in place, we can remain calm. If, inadvertently, the true cross becomes useless, the warp ends will be taken in the order they are in the raddle spaces. I'll talk about this a little later, so don't worry prematurely. Nonetheless, the cross is a valuable ally for weavers as it facilitates our work.

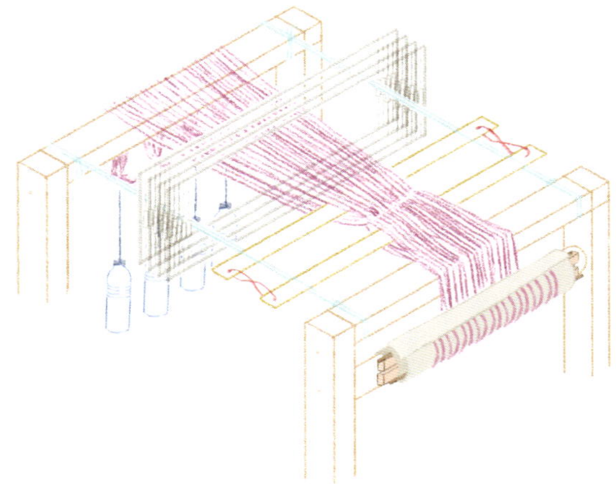

Figure 32 ***Beaming of the warp is finished.***

The essential part of the preparation is finished. You will not necessarily be very skilled at first, but practice will bring confidence. I promise you that one day, winding and beaming the warp will not be a problem. Don't hesitate to improve these steps in your own way, by installing little tricks and aids. Janine, a weaver friend, made a "lantern" inspired by something she saw in an encyclopedia. She winds warp sections on several spools with grooves on the side. These spools are installed on a wooden frame placed at the front of the loom, the "lantern." They are unwound little by little as the warp is being wound onto the warp beam. They are stopped by a thread wound in the groove and weighted down.

Of course, if you prefer to get help from the hands of friends, that's fine too! The right method is the one that suits you!

Heavens, the Cross Has Disappeared!!!

Present fears are less than horrible imaginings.

William Shakespeare, *Macbeth*, 1605

Yes, it happens sometimes! And a cold sweat runs down your spine! If by mistake, you lost the cross by removing the ties before having slipped in the lease sticks, **this is not too dramatic as long as the raddle is still in place**. While a less precise guide, it still shows you the threads in order and grouped in sections. Most of the time, this will be enough. The real cross contains the complete order of the threads, which is desirable because it makes the work of threading easier. The raddle cross offers a relative order, which is sufficient most of the time.

Take the threads arbitrarily from a single section, which is a very relative arbitrariness. Once again, the cross is an indispensable guide, but you must remain relaxed. You want to take them in the order in which they were wound onto the warping board and not mix them up. A few mistakes are not dramatic as long as the raddle is there! In any case, it is really useless to put wrongly crossed warp ends back in their place between the cross sticks. The cross remains a guide and not a goal in itself.

If your cross is well done, which is most often the case, and which is what we're always aiming for, then you can calmly and safely remove the raddle. You can now move the seat to the front of the loom as the preparation work at the back is finished. We're leaving the backstage area!

Tightening Loose Warp Ends

Despite everything we have done, there are times when the tension is disappointing. The series of mistakes made by beginners or those who are stressed out or daydreaming will have caused uneven tension. Fortunately, once the heddles have been threaded and the reed sleyed, it is possible to fix the tension, without even needing the little water bottle weights!

When the whole warp is ready—heddles threaded and reed sleyed—I unroll it completely at the front of the loom, making small chains as I go along. I then slip four lease sticks or smooth rods over and under each layer of yarn, in the manner of a tension control box, at the front of the loom, in front of the reed. I slide the four sticks through several sheds as if they were weft in a plain weave. It is as if we had four lease sticks. The friction of the warp on these four sticks allows for even regular winding without needing the bottles as weights. Now to simply play Ben-Hur again evenly along the front to loosen and untangle the threads.

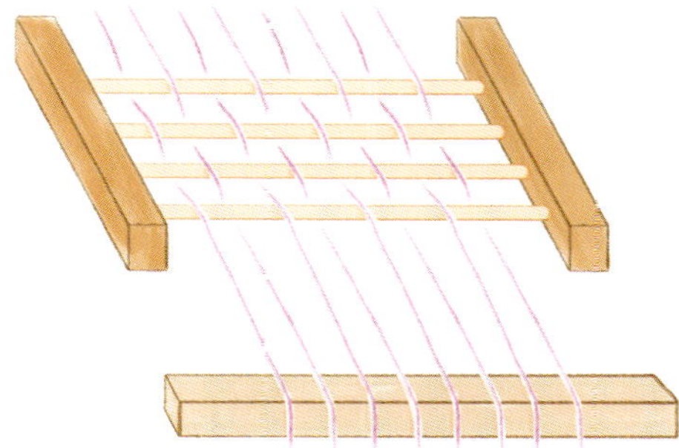

Figure 33 ***A method inspired by warping from the front to tighten a warp with poor tension***

This method is widely used by people who warp from front to back. They use a system of rods or sticks that can be attached to the loom's warp beam.

Threading

Threading consists in putting the warp ends through the eyes of the heddles, each one in its place, following two instructions: take the threads in the order they come from the lease sticks and thread them following the order shown on the threading draft.

It is at this point that we will begin to "dress" the loom, that is to say to connect the warp ends to the loom by transferring to the loom what is shown on the project record sheet (see "The Drawdown," p. 57).

The heddles are threaded according to the order shown in the draft that is required by the weave structure. Sometimes it has a family name: twill, Summer and Winter, huck lace, overshot, etc. The four rows of threading correspond to the four shafts or harnesses on the loom. The bottom row usually represents the first shaft, the one that is closest to the weaver, the top row represents the fourth shaft, the one furthest to the back. The way it is "coded" sometimes changes depending on the country. Scandinavians draw it exactly in reverse order! The drawing below shows the connection between what is written and what is on the loom, between the lines of the draft and the heddles of the shafts.

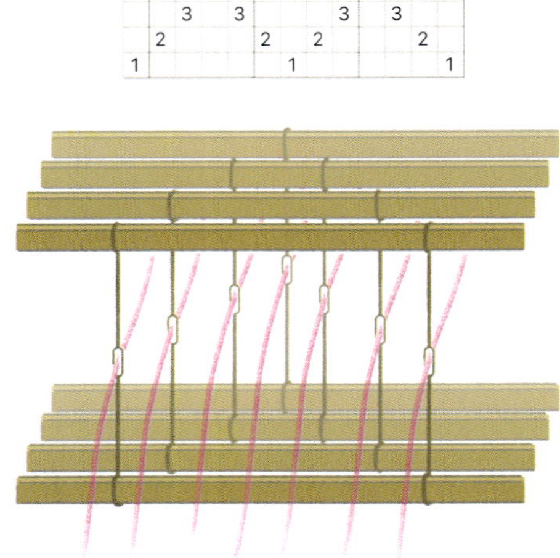

Figure 34 ***Connection between the shafts and the threading draft***

A Comfortable Position Is a Treasure Worth Seeking

When threading, above all make yourself comfortable. Here are my recommendations.

- Be sure that you are seated properly. This step can be time consuming and again, a **good position and good posture are necessary**. The breast beam sometimes pulls out of the loom. You can then slide a stool further into the loom to improve comfort. Otherwise, you can lean or rest on the breast beam. In any case, remove the reed and its beater if possible.
- Keep in mind that your body must find a comfortable position to then **arrange your work space** so that everything is ergonomic for your hands and eyes. The lease sticks should be at the right height, not too far from the heddles, so that you don't have to bend down or stretch too far to grab the warp.
- Choose to **raise the shafts** or to lower them, depending on which is more comfortable. I now slide two sticks under the shafts and place them on the back beam. In this way, the shafts are aligned at an angle, those at the back a bit higher than the front ones. This way it is easier to not mix up the shafts, which is all the more valuable when you have a large number of them. In any case, stabilize the shafts so that they don't move at all. Most treadle looms have systems to stabilize them using a rod or a piece of wood. If nothing is provided, you can find a way to do this with strings or clamps.
- Draw a clear and concise threading draft. The general idea is to understand the "music" of threading so that you don't have to keep your eyes riveted on a complex diagram on which you have to find your way by checking things off with a pencil or pointing with a needle. Having assimilated the logic or the rhythm of the diagram, you almost don't need it anymore; it is already almost memorized.

You don't believe it? Well, we are going to study how to take a step back, zoom out, and see the big picture.

A Bit of Method to Become More Efficient

Often, the pleasure derived from reading largely depends on the bodily comfort of the reader.

Alberto Manguel, *A History of Reading*, 2000

Whatever symbols are used in the threading chart—crosses, numbers, lines—and whatever direction it is written in, the idea is to follow the threading draft step by step.

Being right-handed, I prefer to thread from right to left; I hold my warp ends to be threaded with my left hand, and the threading hook in the other. There is absolutely no need to start in the middle, since the heddles will have been counted and can slide easily in the shaft. Sometimes the tie-up strings for the treadles pass through the middle of the shafts, sometimes metal links attach the heddle bar to the shafts; in any case, try to remove anything that hinders the heddles from sliding freely. Everyone will find their own way of doing it; it doesn't matter, as long as you are comfortable and relaxed.

To avoid mistakes, I usually divide the work as much as possible into steps, bunches, or blocks, in order to have ways to frequently check my progress, breaking it down either by color or by threading group.

Let's go back to our example and repeat the explanation given when counting heddles.

- the steel blue threads are grouped in block A;
- the light blue threads are grouped in block B, block A and block B again.

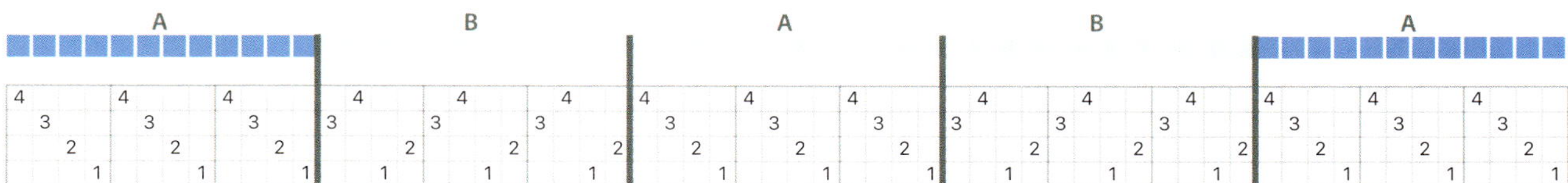

Figure 35 ***The threading draft from our exercise***

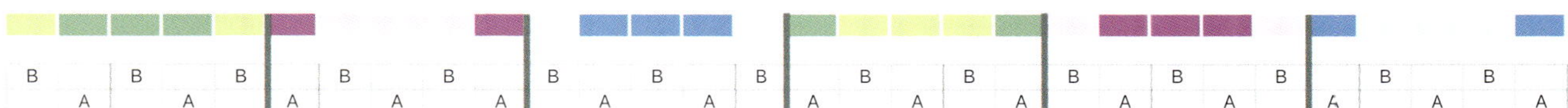

Figure 36 ***The threading profile draft from our exercise***

And now let's try to only follow the *profile draft* when threading.

Coded in this way, it becomes easier to memorize and do the threading. It is very likely that I would systematically prepare 3 heddles on each of the 4 shafts to thread the 12 threads in each block. I prefer to give myself the means to check by block and to correct as I go along so that I don't have to redo the whole threading process on the whole width in case of error. This way, I can move forward with complete peace of mind.

Then, for this first group of steel blue and sky blue threads I check that I have 15 threads on each shaft.

Sometimes, threading is not as visual as this one, not as easy to remember. The only advice I give here is to look for a logic, a common thread, to dissect the pattern, to make it readable and memorable and thus, to almost not need to follow the paper. Don't get overconfident, but don't be afraid either! My memory is really not always very sure, and in my early days, I had my threading draft right in sight and I followed it step by step. Today, I'm looking for a rhythm to group the threads in sequences, so that I can retain a series—not necessarily of 4 threads by the way. The idea is to take a step back to free yourself from the paper. I can assure you that it is a real way to avoid mistakes. You just have to trust yourself, but I think that's the hardest part!

Our previous example is obvious. In more complex structures, you have to rack your brains a bit and look for a rhythm to remember. The threading in Figure 37 is an example to explain this method. I thread from right to left, so I read the draft from right to left. This is probably how I would group the threads to have a simplified reading 1234321, then 434, 323, 21212, 34343, 232, 121, 4321234, 121, 232, 34343, 21212, 323, 434.

As always, to each his own. The important thing is to force yourself a little at the beginning to look for a logic, a simple way of working. Circle to visualize . . . . Try to sing 1234321, then 434, then 323, 21212, ... Try to remember, ... Try to thread by memory by using this refrain, ... This is an exercise that I gently make my course participants try out. They often resist at the beginning, then quickly agree that it is magical.

Then, for this example, I would prepare the heddles for the whole pattern: 11 heddles on shafts 1 and 4, 18 on shafts 2 and 4, 18 on shafts 2 and 3. This way, when I have finished threading each pattern, depending on whether or not there are any prepared heddles remaining, I will be able to conclude quite quickly whether I made a mistake or not. This process helps to check methodically, securely, and in sequence.

To make it even easier to place the heddles, I arrange each small group in the right order just before threading. Their placement is very graphic and looks like the diagram—a visual aid not to be overlooked either.

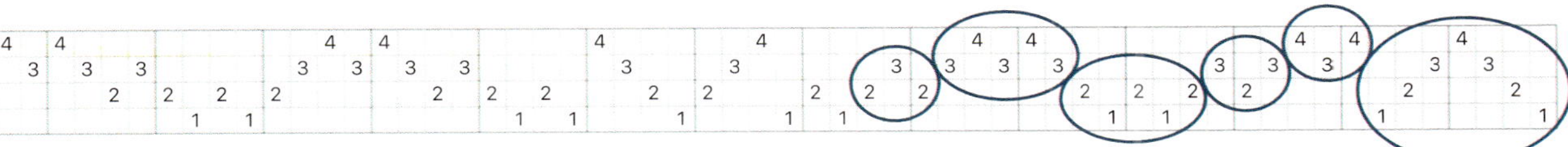

Figure 37 ***Complex threading dissected***

Now for a Little Dexterity

Once you have settled down in front of the loom, once the simplified and symbolized threading draft can be seen at a glance, once the cross is clearly visible and the warp ends are within reach, and once your body is in a good position, full speed ahead!

Follow the order of the cross. It is really the weaver's valuable ally. Let me emphasize it again! I will also point out that you should not worry too much if there are some mistakes in the cross. There is no risk of mixing the threads if they are in the right order. If sometimes two threads are side by side without crossing, and so you therefore made a mistake on the cross when winding the warp, it is of little importance. The principle of the cross is to organize and sort the warp threads. Whether it is thread-by-thread or two threads by two threads, or there is some confusion between some neighboring threads, it does not compromise the general order. I know that many people are troubled by these small mistakes. I advise a certain indifference—everything is relative. **The cross is a major tool, of course, but it is only a tool!** It is a matter of taking the threads in the order in which they were wound, or almost.

However, when inserting the lease sticks, if you realize that there are a lot of mistakes, you will decide to thread following only the order of the sections placed in the raddle. You will make sure to keep the stray threads close to their original place in the raddle. As always, let's think! What you need to do is take the warp ends in order to prevent them from getting tangled, which would increase the risk of them getting caught on each other and then breaking. **The ideal is the cross; the least bad is the raddle cross!**

If your winding on the warping board is so poorly done that no order is visible, there is still a chance to preserve both your warp and your calm! Thread in the order that seems best to you, and sley the reed as if nothing had happened. Then completely unroll out your warp toward the front, very carefully, making a chain. When everything is unwound, once the back rods are visible, put the warp ends in a bit of order on the back rod if necessary, then wind again with the 4-lease sticks method again as shown in the section "Beaming the Warp: Quiet on Set, We're Rolling!" (see p. 116).

Follow the threading draft. Contrary to the order of the threads in the cross, **no approximation is tolerated** in the threading order. So at the risk of repeating myself let me emphasize this again. From right to left, from left to right, or from the middle to the outsides, it doesn't matter, as long as you find a comfortable way to read and transcribe the draft in your heddles. I prepare the necessary heddles needed on my left, in order; I thread and then I slide these threaded warp ends to the right. Thus, I freely take the warp ends that come next off the lease sticks and I'm not bothered by those that are already threaded. I bring the lease or cross sticks as close as possible to the heddles, sliding them between the helping hands. The shafts in the back are slightly raised. I can easily look at the sticks without having to bend over.

Take the warp ends by block and spread them out between the fingers of the left hand. I pull them taut, the thumb and forefinger holding the heddle so that it stays in place when I insert the hook through the eye. In this way, each thread that comes next is taut and separated from its neighbor. It is very practical. The only regret is that there are only four spaces between my fingers!

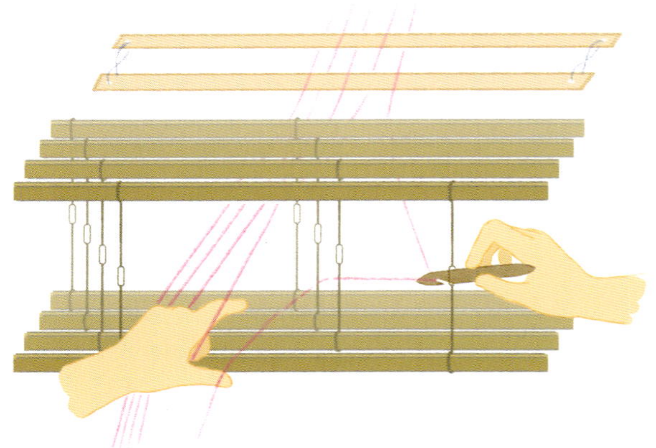

Figure 38 Threading method

Ensure that the ends don't come out of the heddles by tying a slipknot at the end of a group of threads. The knot should not be too tight or too close to the end of the warp. Otherwise, undoing these loops when you're sleying the reed will become tedious.

I can't say it enough: making yourself comfortable is an absolute rule. You may have to fiddle around, tie up, elevate, invent, or DIY something to find the best position.

Mistakes May Happen

In spite of all this attention to detail, checking and rechecking, it may happen that after finishing the threading we discover that we are missing or have some extra threads or heddles left over compared to our counts noted on the record sheet. This happens even to the most experienced among us. It may be a threading error. Most of these mistakes can be fixed quickly and easily, and it is very rare to have to start all over again! The biggest disappointment is not to find a few threading mistakes at this stage, but to discover them once the warp is fully woven. It is therefore not completely useless to systematically check for the most common errors. However, the final check will be done visually by examining the weaving after the first few picks are thrown.

As before, it is much better to take a step back and do the checks by groups.

- In the simplest case, **you have reversed the order of the heddles between two shafts and two warp ends are crossed**; it's really not that difficult to unthread these two ends and put them back in the right place by switching the two heddles.
- Less simple, you have threaded two warp ends on the same shaft, when they needed two different shafts. So a heddle is missing on one shaft. Here again, nothing serious. You can easily add a heddle. To make a new heddle from a cotton thread template or slide in a Texsolv heddle without unthreading everything, see explanations on page 113.
- A little more complicated: **you forgot a warp end**. If the heddle is there, so much the better; if not, adding another one is not a real obstacle. Make a small spool with the warp thread and let it hang off the back of the loom. This warp end will be treated as if it had been wound normally with the others, except that it will be hanging behind. When the time comes to weave, it will be weighted with a small weight, such as an old pill bottle with a few little pebbles or Legos wrapped around the thread. Nothing too heavy is needed.

You've checked once, twice, and you're afraid you've left a few mistakes in the warp? It happens. Maybe we'll find them when we sley the reed? Or perhaps when weaving the first practice weft picks? Let's be intrepid and move on to the next scene!

Sleying the Reed: Each Thread in Its Place

During this step, **each warp end must be threaded through the dents of the reed according to the desired density**. Still the same refrain: follow the notes made on the project record sheet.

Table 9 ***Project record sheet for our exercise***

Density of the warp	20 threads/in. (8 threads/cm)		
Reed: dents per in. dents per cm	10 4	No. threads/dent	2
Density of the weft	20 threads/in. (8 threads/cm)		

The weave for which we are following the steps is simple: 20 threads per inch (8 per cm) with a 10-dent reed (4 dents per cm), which means we sley 2 warp ends per dent.

In more complex cases, I advise you to refer to the section "The Reed: the Tool to Get the Density You Want" where we discussed the question of density (see p. 51).

In my classes, I often say that when it comes to density, we are the only ones in charge! It is our project; we're the ones who decide, and the materials won't limit us. If a density of 20 ends per inch seems not firm enough for you, don't hesitate to go to 22 ends per inch by sleying 3 ends together (instead of 2) every fifth dent. I will explain this in more detail later on.

While you can fix threading mistakes without having to redo everything, this is not the case for sleying the reed. You have to go back to where the mistake was made, fix it, and pick up the sleying sequence from there to the side closest to the mistake. A sleying error will always be seen in the fabric. You can't overlook it! Even if there's a lot of work to be done over, it is absolutely necessary.

Method, Attention, Precision!

Choose your reed, taking the one that will give you a simple sleying sequence.

Check the number of dents per inch. It is not uncommon to think the reed on your loom is the size you need, but it is a different size than you thought. Unfortunately, we notice this only after sleying the reed, by realizing that the width of the reed does not correspond to the initial project—that we have worked with the wrong reed.

When setting up the raddle, we carefully centered the warp on the warp beam, and **centering the reed is crucial** as well. A permanent mark at the middle of the reed beater and another one on the reed will encourage you to acquire this reflex. Centered, the threads stretched between the warp beam and the cloth beam will be parallel to the loom and the reed will be able to slide without wearing on the selvedges. Be careful: it is not a question of centering only the reed, it is about **centering the weaving!**

The reed is a rather fragile and expensive tool; **it must be handled very carefully**. A damaged reed cannot be repaired. I prefer to use a soft threading hook with which I won't risk bending any dents. For the same reason, I catch hold of the thread well in front of the reed.

Pay special attention to your setup again to facilitate this critical/key step: a comfortable seat, of course; a **light** neither too strong nor too direct, which could reflect off the metal of the reed and tire your eyes; as few distractions as possible (phone on silent mode and radio off?).

In Germany, I discovered sleying with the reed laid flat. This way, you can see the organization of the threading quite well, and mistakes are easier to spot. I tried this change a bit, and resisted a bit, and then I adapted and adopted it. And now, **I angle the reed at 45 degrees**. This way, I feel completely comfortable. My left hand is well in front of the warp ends and catches them easily with the hook, no contortions involved. My eyes can rest above the reed to get a good look. Finding ways to keep the reed at 45 degrees requires a little ingenuity depending on the loom. Small pieces of yarn or rubber bands often do the trick. Sometimes a reed can fall. My advice is to regularly tie the sleyed ends loosely in groups, as we did when threading the heddles. A vertical, horizontal, or tilted reed—the only rule is to be comfortable.

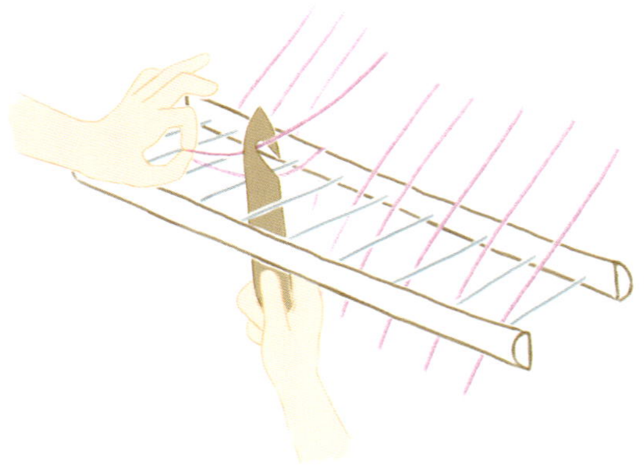

Figure 39 **Sleying the reed**

The question of the direction of work is posed in the same way as for threading: from right to left, from left to right, from the center to the edges? For beginners, it's better to start in the middle to ensure that the warp is perfectly centered on the loom. Because I am right-handed, I hold the hook in my right hand, and my left hand catches the ends I pull through. As for threading, I hold a group of warp ends between my fingers, grouping them in advance to keep the density. We have a density of 20 ends per inch with a 10-dent reed, so I prepare two ends together between each finger. The hook can almost no longer go wrong. It's up to you to test a method, a rhythm with which you feel comfortable.

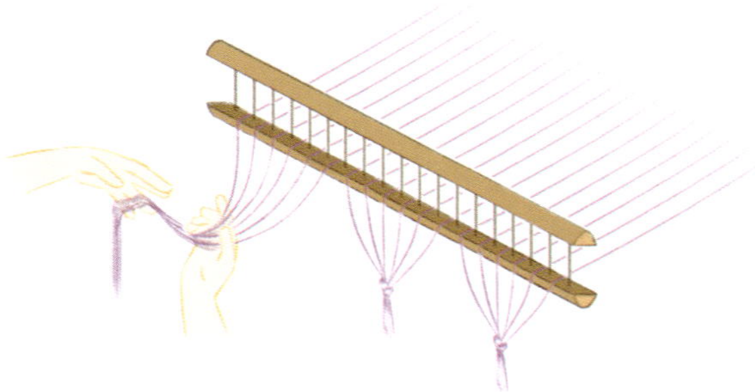

Figure 40 **Securing the threads with slipknots**

When everything is finished, all that remains is to place the reed in the beater and lock it into place.

Going Over Your Reed with a Fine-Tooth Comb

Checking back over the reed is a must, since an error is unacceptable!

First check whether **the planned width** per the record sheet matches the width in the reed. And I mean matches exactly. If this is not the case, even though there is no error in the reed, there is a problem somewhere. Either the calculation on the record sheet is wrong, or the reed doesn't have the density we imagined.

The second point not to be overlooked is **the centering of the warp**. And here again, no approximation is tolerated. If your weaving is off-center, your reed will rub on all the warp ends. Those in the selvedge, which have much more strain on them, will soon fray and break.

To finish, **check each dent**. Holding your groups of threads in your hand, pull them downward and shake them a little, pulling them taut. And look through them calmly to see if they are grouped correctly. Don't spend too much time on it and, especially, look from a distance; you will see much better.

Tying the Warp to the Cloth Beam

For me, this drawing (Figure 41) is the best summary of dressing the loom. The warp threads must first be wound onto the warp beam, threaded in the shafts, sleyed through the reed, then connected to the cloth beam, having gone around the back and breast beams so as to stay taut and horizontal. We are now here at the last step of dressing the loom: attaching the warp to the front of the loom.

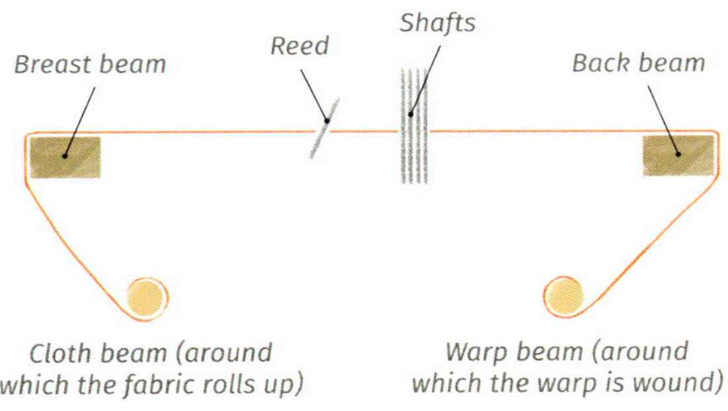

Figure 41 **Diagram of a loom**

As long as the warp is not permanently attached to the front, I keep those helping hands stretched out on both sides of the loom. They are used to place the front tie-on or apron rod horizontally, in front of me. Before attaching, I am careful to check that nothing is in the way of the free flow of the threads, and I remove the raddle, if it has remained on the beam. I also remove the lease sticks.

Be sure to check the tension. All the warp threads must be able to be tied to the cloth beam at the front of the loom with the same tension. The tying is the culmination of all the care previously taken to obtain this balanced tension. As always, make sure you are comfortably situated and tie on the entire warp in the same sitting.

There are several ways to connect the ends to the front apron rod. And again, only the method that works for you is the right one for you.

In all cases, I start by bundling the ends together in small groups, about 1 inch wide at the reed and only one half-inch at the selvedges. Then I place my apron rod on the helping hands, making sure to bring it around the cloth beam.

Tying with knots is quite common. It consists of dividing each bundle of threads in two, going around the front apron rod, and making a knot.

You usually start at the two ends, alternating, and work your way to the middle. Initially, only one knot is made per bundle. When the entire width is tied on, test the tension of each section of threads with your hand and rebalance by tightening a little more if necessary. When all the threads seem to have the same tension, you can secure them by tying a second knot on each group, which turns it into a final square knot.

Figure 42 **Tying to the front apron rod with a square knot**

A different way of **attaching the warp** to the apron rod is by **lashing it on**. Each group of warp ends is pulled taut, shaken for the usual untangling, and then a firm overhand knot is tied and pulled down until it tightens near the end of the threads. When all the warp is knotted, we take a long lashing cord, secure it to the apron rod, then take it back and forth between the center of each warp group and the front apron rod, tying a final knot at the end. Then we go back and pull on the lashing cord like harp strings to distribute any differences in tension. For this method to be effective, the lashing cord must be long enough to leave a space of about 6 inches (15 cm) between the knots and the rod.

I see two advantages to this method. You lose much less warp yarn than with the previous method, which is very valuable with expensive yarns, and it is not necessary to make and unmake knots one by one. Here they are all connected. A slightly loose group of ends can be tightened by relaxing a neighboring group that is more taut.

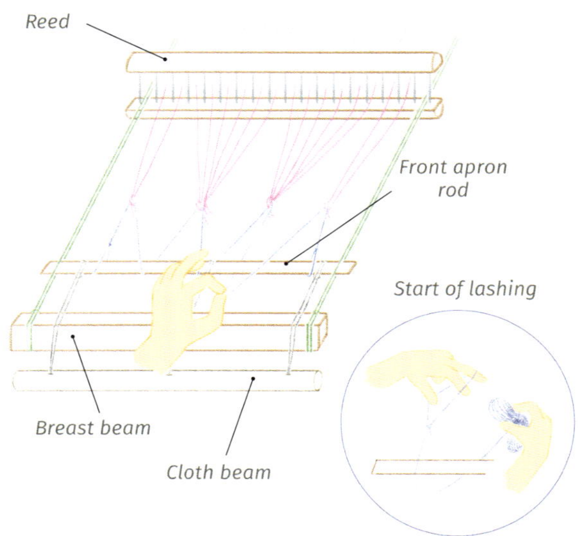

Figure 43 ***Lashing the warp onto the apron rod***

A combination of the two methods can also be created by using a little cord, called a leader, which is tied to the apron rod, and then pulled more or less to reach the desired tension. In this way, we tie on each group of threads individually and also do not lose any warp length.

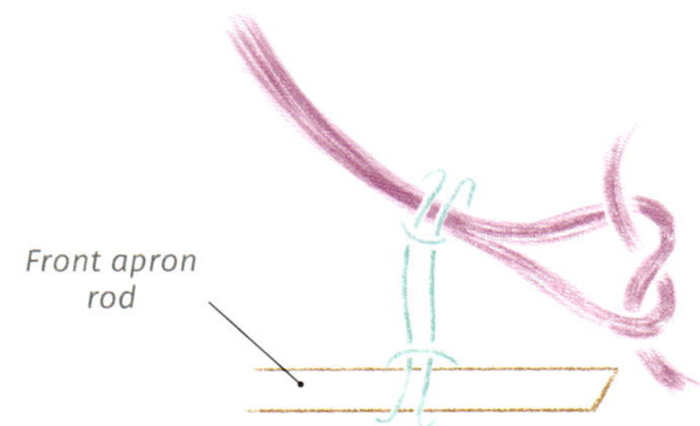

Figure 44 ***Tying with leaders***

In all cases, the goal is for **all the threads to have the same tension**. It is not a matter of stretching them a lot, but rather to obtain an even tension among all the groups of threads. This step is often not very reassuring because it is very subjective. We test, lightly bouncing a hand on the warp, we retension. It is also necessary to know when to stop and decide that the tension is satisfactory and that you can now start weaving.

At this point, the helping hands can be removed, as the warp is attached on both sides of the loom; it can stand on its own. The loom is now dressed and ready!

Tying Up the Treadles: The Stagehand at Work

In the section "Tying Up the Treadles" on p. 56, I explained the purposes of tying up. I'll take the risk of repeating how much we are depriving ourselves of a great tool if we do not take time to learn right from the outset how to properly tie up treadles and really understand best practice. Unfortunately, this cannot be done on all looms, such as:

- table looms with individual levers that cannot be connected;
- some treadle looms when they do not have lamms;
- four-shaft looms equipped with only four treadles.

The possibility of attaching several shafts to a single treadle has the advantage of allowing us to make a consistent motion while weaving. The feet slide from one treadle to the next and press one treadle at a time. I am convinced that when you bring fluidity to each step, the fabric benefits. Moving one foot at a time in a well-thought-out order frees up your attention and surely also releases tension.

Upper and/or lower lamms, or **sticks**, depending on the type of loom or manufacturer, are used to connect the treadles to the shafts. These wooden slats are positioned directly below each shaft, and are attached to the frame of the loom on one side.

So we have four shafts and four upper and/or lower lamms:

- each lamm is connected to its shaft with a string, metal, or leather tie;
- each treadle is connected to one or more lamms, depending on the desired weave pattern.

In Which the Weaver Becomes a Shipmaster

Equipping a four-shaft loom is perhaps less demanding than rigging a three-mast ship. However, you do have to think a little to tie things up correctly.

Shafts are raised or lowered, activated in the middle or at their ends. They are installed on the loom from front to back, while the treadles go from right to left. An intermediate is necessary so that all the treadles are connected to the center or the ends of the shafts: this is the role of the lamms. This is the first adjustment to make: **connect each shaft to its lamm**, making sure that the lamms are horizontal. This attachment is final.

Then, you have to **attach each treadle to the lamms**. It is not easy to explain this mechanism in a few words. Nevertheless, I'll try to use a concrete example: **attaching a 2/2 twill**, the one in our weaving example. We will see the order of the treadles later. For now, let's agree that shaft 1 and lamm 1 are the closest to the front of the loom, and that shaft 4 and its lamm are the furthest back:

- to treadle 1, we will attach lamms 1 and 2;
- to treadle 2, lamms 2 and 3;
- to treadle 3, lamms 3 and 4;
- to treadle 4, lamms 4 and 1.

With the example we have been following since the beginning of this chapter, treadle 1 is shown in the left-hand column of the treadling draft. This treadle 1 lifts shafts 1 and 2. Whenever the number 1 appears in the treadling draft, it means that you must press treadle 1, and thus shafts 1 and 2 are lifted together.

This **treadling draft** is read from top to bottom and indicates the number of the treadle. So, for the first pick, I press treadle 1, then treadle 2 for the second pick, treadle 3, then 4 and I repeat three times.

The **tie-up draft** reads from left to right:

- treadle 1: shafts 1 and 2;
- treadle 2: shafts 2 and 3;
- treadle 3: shafts 3 and 4;
- treadle 4: shafts 4 and 1.

Finding the order of the treadles must follow a logic that tries to allow both feet to work alternately as much as possible (left foot, right foot, left foot, right foot, etc.), to find a natural walking rhythm. In our rather basic example, I make the arbitrary choice to operate the odd treadles with my left foot and the even treadles with my right foot. First pick, left foot, second pick, right foot, and so on. It's only a choice—to each his own.

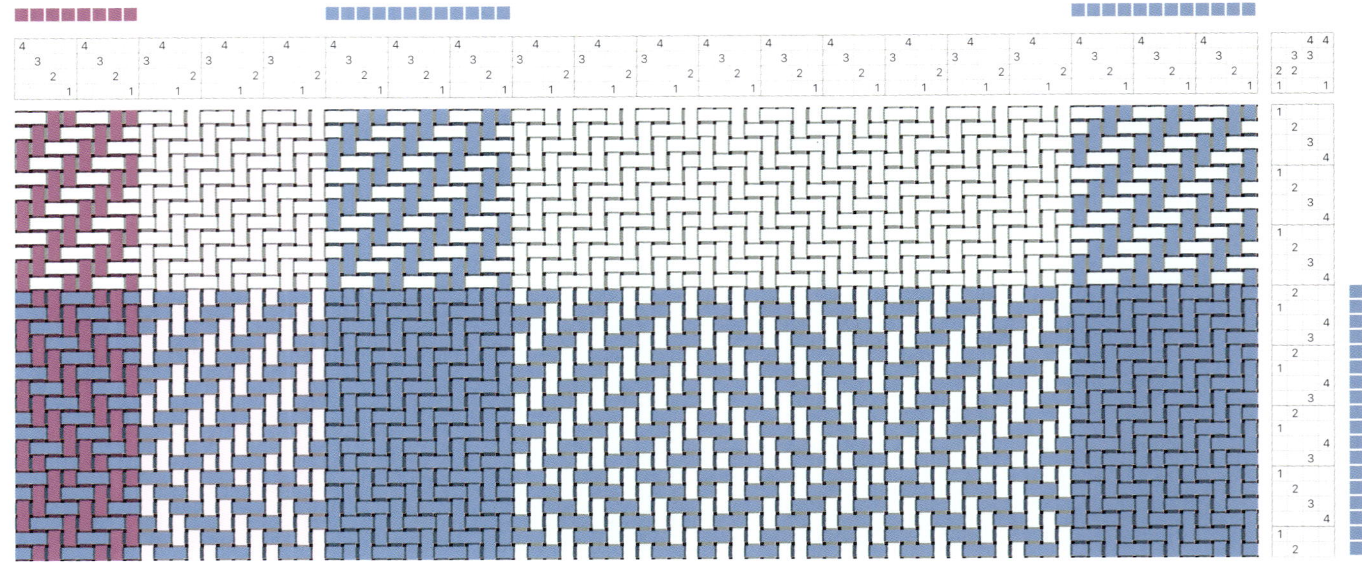

Figure 45 ***Tie-up for 2/2 twill and treadling for the weaving example***

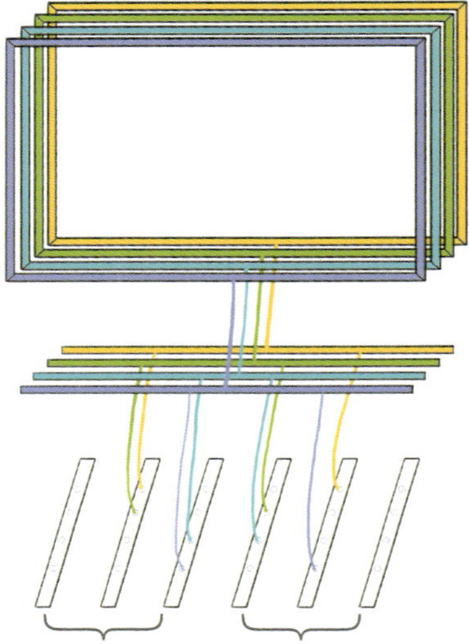

Figure 46 ***Tying up treadles in the right order***

The main idea of tying up is to choose which treadle will be number 1, then number 2, etc., and especially in which order they are placed:

- treadle 1: left foot;
- treadle 2: right foot;
- treadle 3: left foot;
- treadle 4: right foot.

In this way, the rhythm of my feet will be steady and relaxed. The two feet will never be lifted at the same time: one rises when the other is down. The left foot and the right foot move about alternately and slide constantly from one treadle to the next. There is little risk of making a mistake, and you don't even have to look at your feet. What rest, what fluid movement!

Figure 47 ***Set of hand towels with different tie-ups***

Now it's up to each person to decide how to assign the treadles. Depending on the complexity of the structure, one can choose to:

- put the most frequently used treadles in the middle, to reduce foot movements as much as possible;
- tie the middle treadles to the shafts that support the most heddles and will be heavier;
- find other options for easy treadling.

In the best of cases, the loom will be well thought out and the tie-up will be practical and simple. The ties will be of metal, nylon, or leather, with a predetermined length, and will be easy to install. But this is not always the case, and it can be discouraging.

Today, it is common to find looms that come with Texsolv cords. These have one-half-inch slots all along the length, which are attached to small pegs; these pegs lock in the treadle tie-ups. They are easy to remove and replace and simplify the tie-up process.

The system presented here is the traditional way. Simple to set up, it can be used in many cases. It is preferable to use linen or hemp cord, which will slip less than one made of nylon. We cut a piece of cord about 12 inches (30 cm) long, knot the two ends together, and then attach it to the treadle. Slip another piece of cord of the same length through an eyelet on the lamm and then through the loop of the lark's head knot on the treadle tie. Then, adjust the length of the tie by making a knot with the top tie. This knot should not be too tight because it must be able to relax without difficulty to adjust the treadles, which will often need to be adjusted. You can learn to get into this habit fairly quickly.

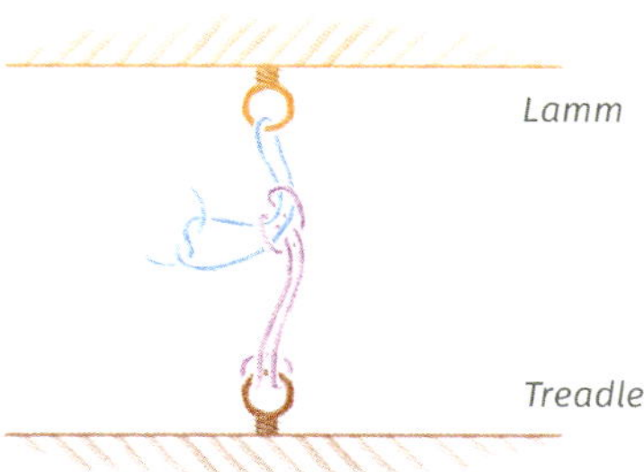

Figure 48 ***An easy tie-up to connect the treadles to the lamms***

If you need to equip your loom, invest wisely. The best materials will make your work easier. Going under the loom is already a bit daunting, and changing the tie-up for each different weaving project can be discouraging. I remember a weaver in Germany who spent half of her course time adjusting tie-ups on her loom. She was determined to succeed, to learn and do it again at home on her own identical loom. I know that if I were her, I would have immediately replaced the string ties with Texsolv.

To make these adjustments, everything must be horizontal: the shafts, upper and lower lamms, and the jacks. A small check with a level should not be overlooked. This step is done without the shafts being secured in place.

I won't mention again the advantage of attaching a single treadle to several shafts. Try it, and see if it works for you. As for me, I'll never go back, and I use every means possible to try to convert my course participants. I can be very persistent!

Drum Roll Please! The Countermarch Loom

My favorite loom is the countermarch. Its principle is simple: each time we press on a treadle, the shafts that we have chosen to be raised go up and all the others sink simultaneously. All the shafts are activated at the same time. The main benefit of this mechanism lies in the fact that all the warp ends are under the same tension. In many cases, it often takes less strength to operate the treadles, provided that the loom is well built.

On a rising shed loom, where only the shafts that are raised move, the warp ends have greater tension on them, while those that remain horizontal are looser. The warp ends are repeatedly subjected to increased tension. In addition, the ends that stay horizontal and therefore less taut have a harder time handling the boat shuttle, which risks dropping between the threads.

With a countermarch loom, **the tension on the warp ends is the same on the top and bottom of the shed and the shed is balanced** and large.

The adjustment of such a loom can be a bit intimidating. But then, when you understand the principle, there are no concerns. In the third part of this book, we show how to tie up the loom with details and illustrations (see p. 255).

Let's try it with our weaving example, shall we? Let's look at the structure of the loom, which is a little different. From top to bottom, we have:

- the upper lamms;
- the lower lamms;
- the treadles.

Four shafts, four lower lamms, four upper lamms, and four, six, or eight treadles!

With a countermarch loom, **a lower lamm and an upper lamm are paired with their shaft**. A shaft is attached to its lower lamm, located below it, like on a jack loom. And in addition, it is **also attached to its upper lamm**, located below or even above or next to it! The systems differ a little depending on the loom as do the names of each part, but no matter. Just remember: the **Lower Lamms Lift the shafts and the upper lamms sink them**.

All the shafts are attached to each treadle, either to lift via the lower lamm, or to sink, via the upper lamm.

Let's go back to our previous example of a twill with 4 shafts. Treadle 1 will be attached to lower lamms 1 and 2 that will allow shafts 1 and 2 to rise, and to upper lamms 3 and 4 that will allow shafts 3 and 4 to sink simultaneously:

- treadle 1: shafts 1 and 2 rise, attached to their lower lamm, shafts 3 and 4 sink, attached to their upper lamm;
- treadle 2: shafts 2 and 3 rise (lower lamm), shafts 4 and 1 sink (upper lamm);
- treadle 3: shafts 3 and 4 rise, shafts 1 and 2 sink;
- treadle 4: shafts 4 and 1 rise, shafts 2 and 3 sink.

The drawing on page 256 should help you better understand.

At the beginning, we might slip up and lose our footing (!) with all these upper and lower lamms and treadles, especially since we are under the loom, on all fours, often in an uncomfortable position. But with a countermarch loom, it would be a shame not to take advantage of the tie-up because the work becomes so fluid and the shed so clean that it is certainly rewarding to spend a little time to better understand the system.

Having a Good Treadle Stroke

We'll leave the world of the stage for a moment for that of the bicycle, as the definition of a "good pedal stroke" seems to me to fit perfectly: "it is said of a cyclist whose style is fluid, whose peddling is even and rhythmic." In fact, I hope you will find a tie-up logic that allows you to have an even and rhythmic treadling stroke!

Some tips:

- look at the columns of the treadling draft;
- imagine that you almost methodically alternate the right foot and the left foot;
- reserve the middle treadles for the picks used most often;
- rack your brains a bit, but it's actually quite fun;
- and try things out.

For weavers who would like to practice to make sure they understand these explanations, I present here the tie-up for another weave, a huck lace—a Swedish lace structure that is shown here in units of 5 threads: a threading that alternates two blocks of 5 threads, and a treadling with a sequence of 2 blocks of 5 picks:

- an **uneven tabby** (shafts 1 + 3), a **pattern** (shafts 2 + . . .), an **uneven tabby**, a **pattern** (shafts 2 + . . .), an **uneven tabby**;
- an **even tabby** (shafts 2 + 4), a **pattern** (shafts 1 + . . .), an **even tabby**, a **pattern** (shafts 1 + . . .), an **even tabby**.

The uneven tabby will be operated by the left foot and its related pattern with the right foot. The even tabby will be done with the right foot and its related pattern with the left foot. The feet do not move much; they slide happily from one treadle to another, always next to each other. The left foot stays on one of the three left treadles, and the right foot remains at its side.

What requires the most thought is to choose the right place for each treadle, in order to have a smooth movement. Then, the feet slide over the treadles, and you don't even have to look at them!

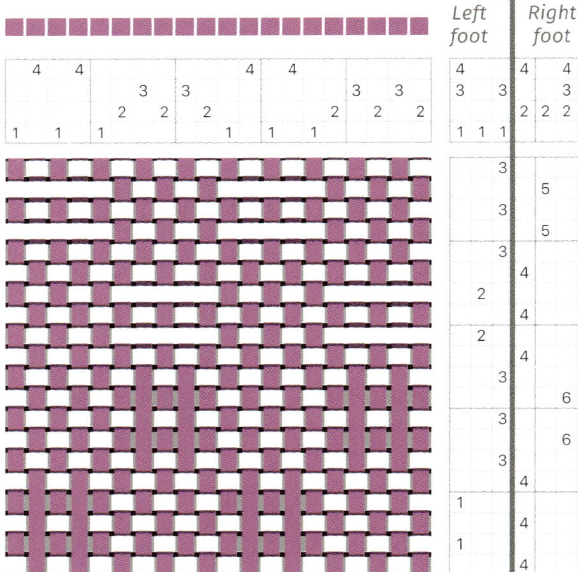

Figure 49 ***Suggestion for a huck lace tie-up***

A Short, Well-Thought-Out Summary

During a conference on blocks, Mary Alice Donceel, member of a group of American weavers, presented the weaving draft in a way that seemed very interesting to me and I was totally inspired by it.

- The **threading draft** answers the question of location: "**Where** does each thread go? In which shaft? In which heddle?"
- The **treadling draft** answers the question of time: "**When** will each pick be woven?" If I choose to read from top to bottom, the first pick is at the top of this grid. On the left is treadle 1, then 2, 3, then 4 on the right.
- The **tie-up draft** answers the question, "**How** will each shaft work?" This is the instruction manual! In our example, with the first treadle, we lift shafts 1 and 2, with the second one shafts 2 and 3, etc. This draft makes the connection between the two previous drafts.
- The last and largest table shows us the graphic representation, **the drawdown**, and answers the question: "**Which** weave structure is used?" It is a first view of the future fabric.

Figure 50 *Summary of the weaving draft*

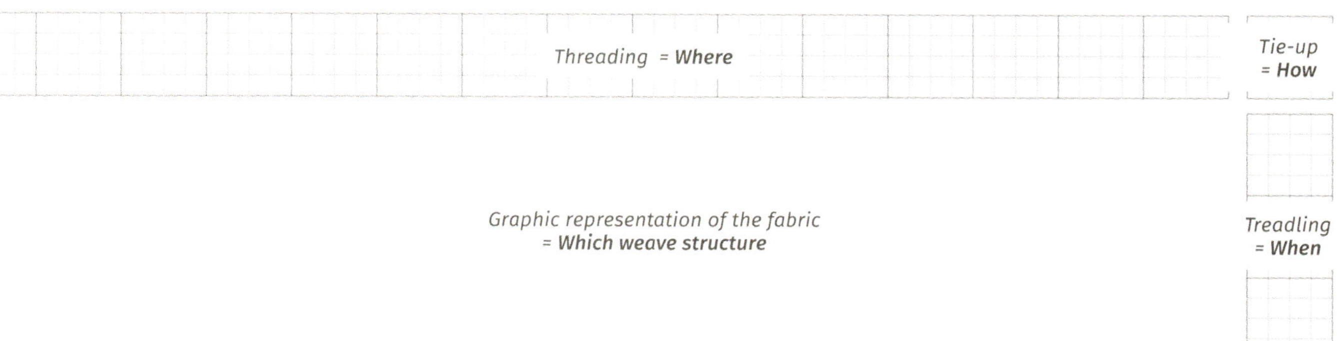

A Final Fine-Tuning: Adjusting the Shafts, the Reed, and Other Mechanisms

A clever man ought to so regulate his interests such that each will fall in due order.

François de La Rochefoucaud, *Moral Reflections*, 1664

This section aims to accompany you in a rather thankless task: adjusting the loom. Each loom has its own settings; I hope that you have the instructions and that they help you to understand what to do. One day, try to resist the frenzy of weaving and look at your loom from all angles to give it a little love.

The mechanical parts, like shafts and lamms, should all be horizontal on most looms. A single tool is needed: the level.

Adjusting the **height of the shafts** and the reed again depends on the loom, but it follows a very simple logic. We start with the height of the shafts, so that the warp ends are horizontal from one beam to the other. While they must be perfectly horizontal for counterbalance looms, some weavers prefer to lower the shafts a little for rising shed looms and, conversely, to raise them a little for sinking shed looms. Thus, the tension on the warp in movement is significantly reduced. These adjustments are made when the shafts are ready for weaving, not blocked in any way.

For **reed height**, the adjustments depend on the type of loom and are made at rest.

- With a rising shed loom, the warp ends should be at the bottom of the reed. So, when raised, the threads will free a space above the reed threshold. The shuttle will be able to slide easily.
- With a sinking shed loom, it is the opposite. The warp ends should be at the top of the reed and, when lowered, just reach the threshold to allow the shuttle to slide over the top;
- With a countermarch loom, the warp ends must pass through the middle of the reed. Thus, the threads that rise will go to the top of the reed, and the others to the bottom.

The difficulty lies in the relationship between all these parts. How do we dress our loom correctly? Well-designed looms have ties that are the exact length to connect treadles, lamms, shafts, etc. When this is not the case, we will have to fumble around to find the length of the ties that will allow the shafts to be lifted without having to press too hard on the treadle and still provide a large shed.

I must admit that I am not often a fan of looms made by independent woodworkers. Although beautifully made, their designs may not be user friendly. What I expect from a loom is to be able to weave effortlessly with a minimum of fatigue, to have shuttles that slide without catching, to have a reed that tilts smoothly, to have enough treadles to attach the shafts intelligently, to have the pressure on the treadles be transmitted with maximum leverage on the shafts via the jacks so that with only a little pressure on the treadles, the shafts will rise a lot. So, if I see a loom with less than six treadles, I won't take it. Ditto if the movement of the jacks is inefficient. Everything has to be flexible, light, and easily adjustable. I have too often been perplexed and annoyed by looms that were so pretty that I really wanted to use them, but the final adjustment of the shafts completely messed up the jacks, or I had other difficulties that led to a waste of time and onset of frustration. I'm sorry, but if a loom is difficult to use, it is not a good design. That's why I always prefer a well-tested brand name loom!

The **height of the bench** is also important. Some like to tower over their work; others prefer to have their arms higher. There are really no rules; it is up to each person.

The definitive criterion for the smooth overall operation of the loom is your own well-being—the comfort of your back, eyes, hands, and feet. You will have to sometimes be an inventor and DIY-er with the means at hand, always seeking to feel good. Weaving is a long-term activity; you might as well make it as pleasant as possible. Once the adjustments are properly done, there is typically little reason to modify them. So, I hope this encourages you to look once and for all at how your loom could work better.

To Conclude: Some Encouragement

This chapter is long and technical. It may seem boring or tedious. I agree that all these preparations may dissuade some potential weavers. I think that everything can be learned little by little. If you are patient and diligent, I recommend that you follow this advice step by step, take notes, and trust yourself. You can be sure that one day you will be able to happily follow all these steps without even thinking about it. If you are spontaneous and intuitive, then do it your way, and come back to this guide only when you encounter difficulties; there will probably be solutions to overcome them.

Some may find here an explanation that they have been missing until now. I did not invent these tips; at most I adjusted them to my own style. I have tested them, used them, and taught them. This is something I am really tenacious, even a pain, about! Weaving with method and without being nervous has given me such a sense of well-being!

Remember that **when you are well prepared, there are few bad surprises**, such as bad tension or a thread that breaks or defective selvedges or not enough thread to finish the project, or so on. And it is rather satisfying and pleasant to see that all this preparedness is paying off.

I sincerely hope that you will be able to pick up pointers you need as your experience progresses and that these explanations will be enlightening. My constant intent is to present the tools or methods that are useful to me, and that I have been teaching for many years, **so that technique is not an obstacle to creation**. It goes without saying that this way of doing things is neither universal nor exhaustive. So, may these tips and tricks allow you to find your own so that weaving will be a real pleasure and that you will be happy with the weavings you make.

Nothing will replace your own experience, as **it is by weaving that one becomes a weaver**.

Madelyn van den Hoogt, who was once asked if it was necessary to be patient to love weaving, replied, "Some people become patient by weaving, others weave because they are patient."

5

And Now, to the Stage: Let the Weaving Begin!

That is why woven material is called *soy*, which means "It is the spoken word." *Soy* also means 7, the rank of the Spirit who spoke while weaving.

Marcel Griaule, *Conversations with Ogotemmêli* (originally published as *Dieu d'Eau*), 1965

The staging is finished, the sets are ready, the props are in their place, the lines are down pat. The artist enters the stage. Now it is all up to him!

This analogy with a show is quite accurate. Beforehand, everything must be well prepared, not too much improvisation. But now, it is the actor's personality that will express itself. She has a job to do!

While preparation of the warp requires attention and precision, the weaving itself leaves more room for freedom, imagination, and creativity. There are still a few tips for successful weaving, but I won't be exhaustive. Everyone has their own way of doing things, and it's great fun to watch other weavers weave. You always learn! Again, what I present here is a little tour of what I am familiar with. But it's not a list of rules to follow!

The Entrance: Before the First Picks

The web of this world is woven of necessity and chance . . . human reason stands between the two.

Johann Wolfgang von Goethe, *Wilhelm Meister's Apprenticeship*, 1796

The weft, which is going to be slipped into the shed opened by the raised shafts, is carried by shuttles—a flat shuttle in the beginning, and perhaps a boat shuttle later on. The latter will be essential as soon as the weaving projects are larger, and is ideal for a loom whose beater has a shuttle race. There are small boat shuttles that are very practical even for narrow weaves.

The quality of a weaving depends partly on how the shuttle is handled. Very often, if the selvedges are disappointing, it is because the yarn has difficulty unwinding from the shuttle or that the shuttle catches on the warp threads. A bit of sandpaper or varnish on the edges of the shuttle can sometimes be enough.

Filling the Shuttle

To prepare a **flat shuttle**, I wrap the end of the yarn around the end of the shuttle several times so that it stays in place, without a knot. Then, I go from one end to the other, making figure eights, crossing the yarn on one side of the shuttle only. As with the cross, this prevents the threads from getting tangled. They will be able to unwind smoothly. This greatly decreases the risk of pulling on the selvedges. This way also, one side of the shuttle is thinner than the other and will slip more easily into the less open part of the shed. Of course, you can use both sides of the shuttle to wrap more thread on in a figure eight. But let's not overdo it! If the shuttle is too thick, it will rub against the warp threads, and this is how you end up wearing down the warp until some threads break. This can also cause the warp to snag and mess up the tension.

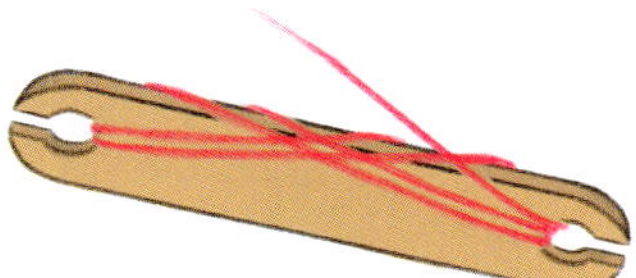

Figure 1 **Filling a flat shuttle**

For **boat shuttles**, the weft is wound onto a bobbin and requires the purchase of a bobbin winder. Do not try to wind by hand; it will definitely be done incorrectly. And remember that poorly made shuttles cause uneven selvedges. Drills, sewing machines, or electric mixers are sometimes hijacked by ingenious DIYers. I prefer the bobbin winder, of which I have several versions—one that works in low gear for beginners, another one that is faster for experts, one with a thicker tip to fill bobbins from a bobbin rack, and an electric one as well to go faster.

To wind the bobbin so that the yarn unwinds freely during weaving, there are a few little instructions you need to follow, which differ depending on the shuttle you use. There are two families of shuttles: **center-delivery boat shuttles**, which unwind in the middle from a bobbin spinning inside the shuttle, and **end-delivery shuttles**, where the yarn unwinds at the end of the tip of the cone-shaped pirn.

In all cases:

- Avoid looping at all costs. The yarn must be taut, otherwise there is a risk of tangling! And undoubtedly some jangled nerves.
- Hold the yarn as close to the bobbin as possible to keep good control of the area where it will be wound.

Of course, the two styles of shuttles are not loaded the same way. Following are some tips for **center-delivery boat shuttles**.

- Start winding the thread at both ends of the bobbin, near the edge if it has one. If it doesn't have one, make "little hills" like guardrails on each side, not too close to the edge, in case the thread slips a little. Then go back and forth a bit.
- When both hills are finished, little by little, move from one end to the other, filling in the middle, and shape like a "valley." You will get an even, concave shape. From that point on, fill in the center until you get a convex curve, "the mountain." Be careful to not overfill the bobbin; if it bulges too much, it might not fit in the shuttle anymore. And above all, it will rub against or get caught on the warp. Therefore, it is better to keep it light. No high peaks!

You can find cardboard or plastic bobbins on the market. You can also make them out of paper. Simply cut an oval out of a half sheet of 8½ × 11 inch paper, roll it up as tightly as possible around the shaft of the bobbin winder. Before the paper is all rolled up, slip the end of the yarn to be wound into it. Then wind as with a commercial bobbin. Drinking straws, preferably made of cardboard, are also very economical. This way I can build up a nice collection of bobbins prepared in advance.

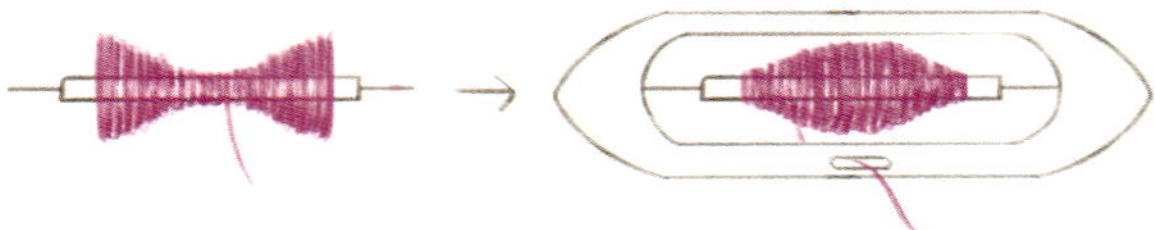

Figure 2 ***Winding boat shuttle bobbins***

For a shuttle where the yarns comes off the tip, an **end-delivery shuttle**, the yarn is first wound onto the thickest end of the pirn (a type of cone-shaped bobbin), moving it back and forth over a short section, and then gradually tapering it more and more toward the tip of this cone. The idea is to not go too fast toward the front. Unlike other shuttles, here the pirn does not turn, but rather the yarn slides out while unwinding. So it must be prevented from rubbing too often against the yarn wound on in the beginning, because it would certainly catch and drag it along, causing loops and tangles. Basically, when this happens, the only choice is to redo the pirn.

These shuttles are used for large width weaving with a loom equipped with a fly shuttle. They are often heavy and are not suitable for small looms.

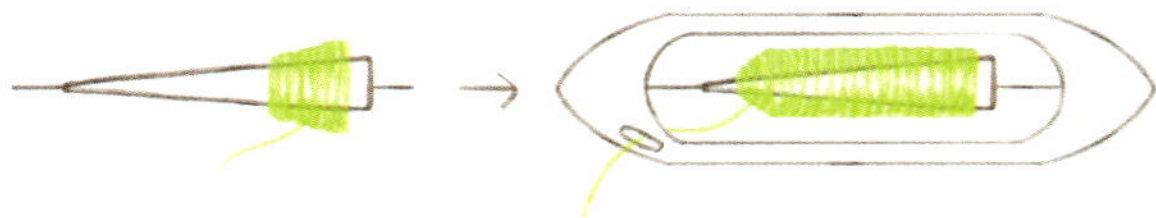

Figure 3 ***Winding a pirn for end-delivery shuttles***

The First Six Picks

The sections of yarn attached to the front tie-on rod are bundled together; the warp ends are not yet parallel. In order for them to become parallel quickly, we are going to throw half a dozen picks in plain weave that we will beat very lightly so as to **leave ¼ inch (1 cm) between each**.

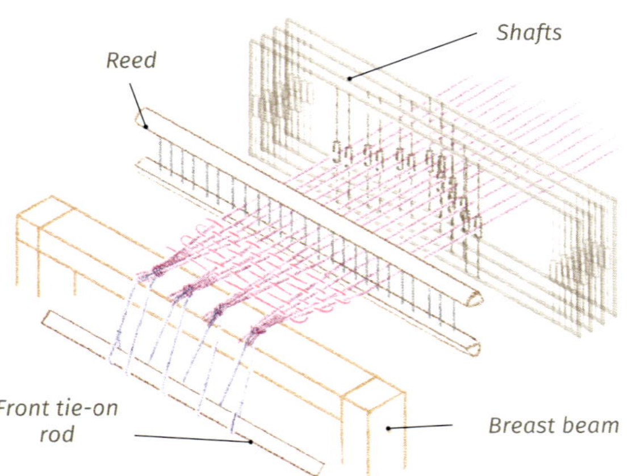

Figure 4 ***Weaving the first picks***

When these 6 picks are woven, we will beat them together with the reed and bring them back as close as possible to the knots from the start. Generally, this will be enough to make the large spaces connected to the knots disappear, to make the whole warp parallel and ready to be woven. Sometimes, if the warp thread is slippery, a few extra picks may need to be woven. The thicker the weft yarn used, the fewer wefts rows will be needed.

Any yarn (except for slippery yarns like viscose) will do for these preliminary weft picks. In any case, this method has the great advantage of putting all the yarn in place with only around a ½ inch (1 to 2 cm) of warp consumed.

As with the lashing brought up in the previous section to replace the knots, I appreciate these tricks that save me from wasting precious warp length. These first picks are not part of the project and are only used for the first adjustments. They will be removed from the final weaving, so it is a good time to use any unwanted yarn or leftover warp.

Plain weave is used for these picks so that it will be easy to unweave. Then when I start my real weaving, I can pull on this thread and it will come out very easily. I really like that even the start of my weaving looks pretty, too. Of course, other methods work just as well: a very thick thread, strips of a very large thread, gauze, or cardboard strips. This practice simply has the advantage of setting things straight in not much more than an inch.

Sometimes, before starting to weave, I like to check a few things to detect any mistakes in the threading or sleying. I do a bit of plain weave, then a few picks of twill with yarn contrasting to the warp in size or color. At the end of the chapter, see the most frequent mistakes and how to correct them.

The Paris Stitch and Hemming

Whether I need a perfect border for a weaving project or a sample, I'm always happiest when the whole thing is pleasing to the eye. I almost always start and finish my weavings with the Paris stitch. This embroidery stitch is best done when the fabric is still under tension on the loom. Made with the weft thread, it is not very visible and, in any case, it is more elegant than a machine zigzag stitch. Faster to do than knots, it also saves time. When I weave several pieces of fabric in a row, I separate them with this Paris stitch. Thus, as soon as they are off the loom, the woven fabric is ready to use.

On the other hand, if I need to do a real hem, I avoid doing this embroidery stitch, which gives volume to the fabric, making the hem too thick. In this case, I even do the first few rows of plain weave with a finer weft thread than the one chosen for the project, such as sewing thread, in order to obtain a simple, inconspicuous finish.

Here is how I do my Paris stitch finishing. With my shuttle, I weave a first pick in tabby, making sure to leave a length of nonwoven thread about three or four times the width of the weave on the right. Then I beat very lightly for the first 6 picks. (The space between the picks makes it easier for the needle to pass through to embroider the Paris stitch.) I then weave two more picks in tabby. Trading my shuttle for my needle, I do my Paris stitch over three or four warp ends at a time and over the three weft rows woven; the weft thread left in reserve becomes my length of thread. Start from whichever side you prefer, the right or the left. I usually sew starting from the right and I therefore start the first pick from the right.

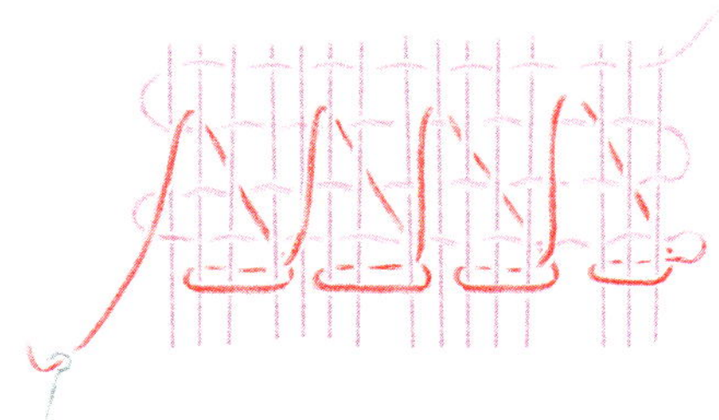

Figure 5 ***Secure the beginning of your weaving with the Paris stitch***

To finish, I slip the bit of thread remaining on the needle into the shed for a couple of inches. And because I am a perfectionist, the shed chosen to hide this little strand will be the opposite of the next shed, the first one of the weaving; otherwise there will be an extra thickness for an inch or so. The weaving of this project can now begin.

At the end of this chapter, I will briefly introduce other finishes. The Paris stitch is basic, but it's a sure bet!

Time to Perform: Weaving at Last!

I am the bonds that I weave.

Albert Jacquard, Early Childhood Colloquium in Lausanne, 2008

All of our actions and the movements of the loom will likely not result in the famous "bistanclaque-pan" that resounded on Croix-Rousse Hill in the city of Lyon. This onomatopoeia described the rhythmic noise of each of the silk weavers' actions. The **"bis"** corresponded to the noise made by the threads sliding against each other at the opening of the shed; the **"tan"** was the sound of the fly shuttle's hammer; the **"clack"** was the shuttle arriving on the other side and the warp closing; and the final **"pan"** referred to the reed beating against the fabric.

We will probably not have the same cadence as the famous silk weavers of Lyon, but each weaver will certainly find the rhythm that suits him or her and will settle in with regular, steady movements.

The Song of the Silk Weavers

We will weave the shroud of the old world,
For we already hear the rumbling of revolt.
We are the Silk Weavers;
We won't go naked anymore.

Aristide Bruant, *Le Chant des Canuts*, 1894

Soon a kind of automatic reflex will set in, and our hands will repeat these movements without really even being aware of it.

- **Raise the layer of warp for the shed** by pressing on the treadle or by operating the lever. We will see in the chapter on structures which shafts to lift depending on the weave pattern chosen.

- **Pass the shuttle** through the shed thus created. Some advice, of course: the shuttle, if it is flat, must be long enough so that your hand does not have to go into the warp, in order not to rub against the selvedge threads. Held firmly in your hand, it will then slide along the reed, resting on the warp threads below, a bit like a speedboat on the water. This is where the shed is the widest and the reed becomes a guide. The yarn in the shuttle must absolutely unwind freely, or even have the shuttle unwound in advance, with always this same care to not damage the selvedge threads by pulling on them. If you use a boat shuttle, you only have to be careful not to push it too hard, lest it fall; with this shuttle, the thread unwinds by itself.
- **Leave some length in the thread**. Once the shuttle is on the other side, pinch the weft thread with your fingers on the selvedge where it entered. It is made to run either diagonally or in a curve across the layer of threads. Remember that the weft thread goes over and under around the warp threads, so it should be given more length than the width of the weave. If it is too tight, the width of the fabric will decrease, the selvedge will be too stressed, and it will risk fraying. It is then inevitable that your reed, by rubbing more against these threads, will rip the selvedge.
- However, if the weft is not taut enough, it will not be able to not be placed correctly, even after beating. There is a risk of the selvedge curling. We must always be careful to maintain the same width of fabric as the reed width and reduce shrinkage as much as possible. This is difficult for beginners, as it takes some time to understand and practice the right movements. Even among experienced weavers, it can very frequently be seen that one selvedge is prettier than the other, proof that this is somewhat tricky indeed.

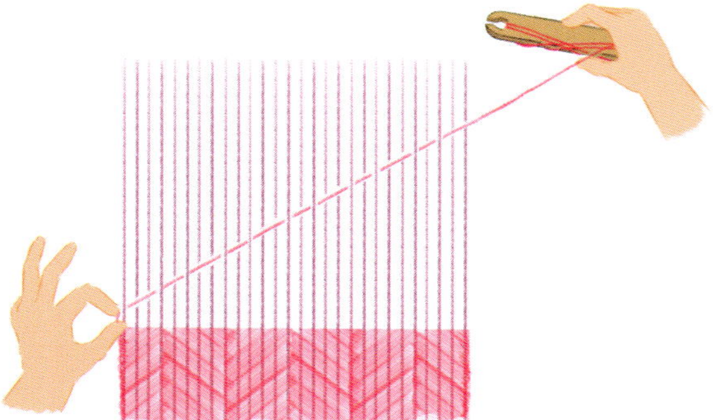

Figure 6 ***Positioning the weft***

- Beat the weft into place by taking hold of the beater bar and swinging it toward you and the fabric. The beat can be more or less firm, depending on the desired weave. One real rule is that the reed must remain parallel to the fabric, so beat with one hand in the middle or a hand on each side, it doesn't matter. It should be a single, smooth movement!
- Change the shed, i.e., the treadles or the levers, and reverse the warp threads. As for the movement of the reed, when it pivots from the bottom of the loom, you can choose to leave it against the weaving, change the shed, and then push the reed back. This is an important advantage for threads that get a little hung up on each other. This backward movement can untangle or loosen them.

Beating Pressure

Beating requires a lot of attention. Most weaves are balanced weaves. Plain weave, twill, and satin are mostly balanced, which means that the thread count in the weft is the same as the thread count in the warp and the density is the same in warp and weft. If necessary, go back to the chapter where we looked at density: "Making Samples: The Dress Rehearsal," p. 47.

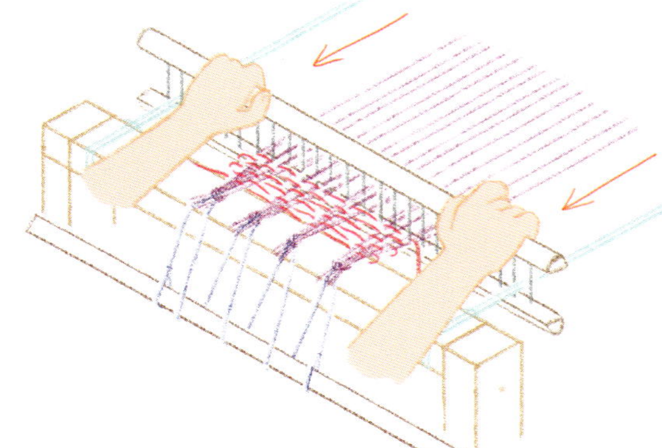

Figure 7 ***Beating the picks***

For weaves composed of plain weave and patterns such as Summer and Winter, overshot, crackle, etc., there must be the same number of tabby picks per inch as warp ends per inch; the picks in the pattern are not counted when checking density. I strongly stress the need to be very disciplined at the start of weaving so that you will obtain these same densities, until your hands and eyes are able to more automatically achieve the beat you want.

There are two tools for this: a **tape measure** or a **45/90 degree triangle ruler**. The tape measure checks whether you have the expected number of picks per inch and the triangle ruler checks if your diagonal is at 45 degrees. It's up to you to choose the one that works best for you. Let's just say that the tape measure will go with you the whole length of the weave, and the triangle ruler can help you with the initial measurement for consistency and for a check from time to time.

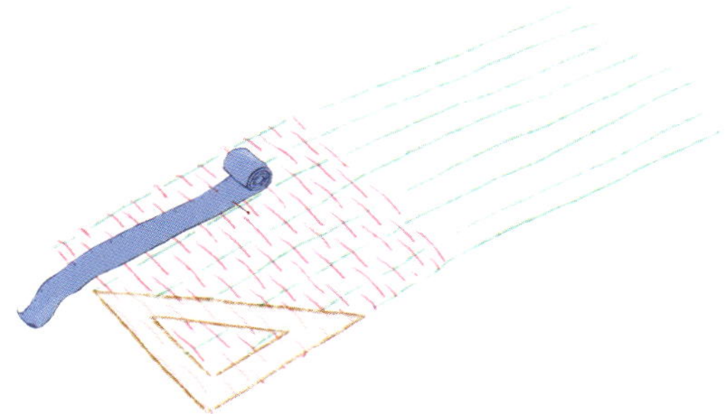

Figure 8 ***Using a triangle ruler or tape measure to check placement of weft***

I see a few smiles in the workshops when I insist on this balance between warp and weft. But eventually, everyone usually goes in that direction, because that way our weaving will be pretty, our plaids will be symmetrical, our blocks will be proportionate, our overshot roses or stars will be harmonious, and our twill diagonals will be at 45 degrees.

This method also has the advantage of confirming the choice of warp density. How so? If you have chosen a density of 20 epi in warp, then you beat so as to obtain 20 ppi (picks per inch). Of course! Presumably you have already woven a sample, and you have already decided on this density. The tape measure will be attached to the weave, and when you have woven 10 picks, you will verify that you have woven one half-inch. Don't worry, the eye will very quickly memorize this density, and you will use the tape measure to check only from time to time. You should also check again with the tape measure after taking a long break.

The method with the triangle is probably more visual and easier to use. It is often sufficient to find the right firmness for beating.

Open shed, closed shed, or opposite shed? When the **shed is open**, the pick will pack down much more easily. Necessary for weaves that you want to be quite dense, this practice is interesting since it leaves room for the weft yarn to spread out well. Always remember that the weft will go over and under around the warp threads and will require a greater length than the width of the weave. If this is not taken into account, the weave will draw in on both sides. Since this is often the cause of significant shrinkage for beginning weavers, choose to beat with an open shed at first. This will also solve the problem of wear on the selvedge.

Beating with **an opposite shed or closed shed**, on the other hand, makes it possible to manage weft placement with yarns that deserve flexibility. The density of mohair does not depend only on the yarn count. With mohair, adequate space must be left for the hairs to spread out. This low density must be the same in the weft. Beating with a closed shed will make this easier. Another yarn with the same yarn count would mean a larger thread count.

Some weavers like to beat with an **open shed and then closed shed**, without a firm beat. Others like to change treadling while the reed is still in the beating position. Returning the reed has the advantage of untangling the wool threads. It is up to every weaver to find their own motions so they become instinctive and the weaving is even, and so the fabric matches the desired outcome. No technique is better than the one that suits you.

There is only one rule: always hold the reed so that it is perpendicular to the warp threads, either with one hand in the middle or with one hand on each side. This seems very obvious, but in practice, when you are concentrated on weaving, you can make a wrong move without noticing.

Perfect Selvedges

The quality of a weave depends as much on an even beat as on the care given to the selvedges. Well-made selvedges are those that you can't see, because they look like the weave. No curls, no extra thickness, no higher tension.

As with commercial fabrics, you can **increase the density in the reed** for the last half-inch on each side. This does not mean doubling the density, but increasing it by a few threads; for a density of 20 epi, I regularly put 15 threads in the last half-inch of the reed at each edge. This more solid part of the fabric will help the selvedge threads stay parallel to the other threads.

The **floating selvedge** is a tool that quickly becomes indispensable. It is a thread, one on each side of the weave, that is wound on the warp beam, as part of the warp. It is not threaded in a heddle, but only through the reed. Therefore, these two selvedge threads never rise or fall. They always remain horizontal, from the back beam to the breast beam. Looking at the loom in profile, the floating selvedge should be in the center of the shed. If this is not the case, it can be moved using a small thread attached to the loom.

With each pick, the weft should always wrap around the floating selvedge on each side. When entering the shed, take the shuttle **over** this selvedge thread, and when exiting the shed, slip the shuttle **under** the other selvedge thread. While this is not necessary for plain weave, it is essential with twill or satin, or any other structure with floats. It is also necessary with color effect weaves like shadow weave. These two selvedge threads are an integral part of the weave. They are therefore the same threads as the warp threads: same color, same count, same tension.

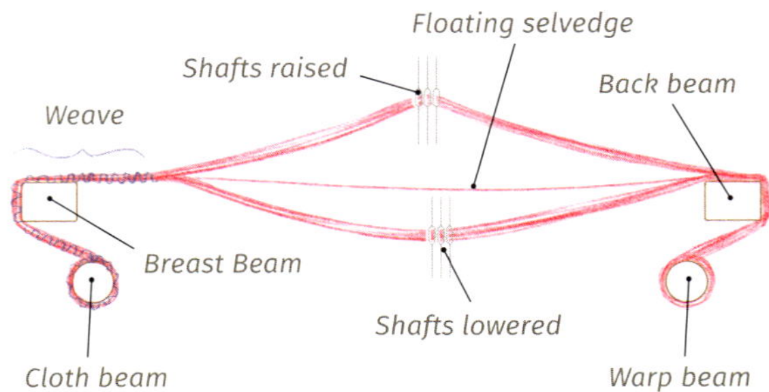

Figure 9 *The floating selvedge*

Sometimes it is tempting to put two selvedge threads on each side or to stretch them a little more than the other warp threads. This is sometimes a shame for the fabric to come. These thicker or tighter selvedges will be different and jarring. If the selvedges are tighter, there is a risk that the fabric will form a kind of pocket when it comes off the loom.

The floating selvedge is counted in the preparation of the warp and included in the winding, beaming, and sleying with all its companions. Sometimes it can be forgotten when winding the warp. In this case, it will be added by weighting a small spool of yarn on the back of the loom. This can be very useful if the selvedge thread breaks often, as it gives you a reserve of thread. You can use a small spool on which you can wind the thread, or you can put the little skein in an old film canister, weight the canister, and close the lid to trap the thread. You can also find small Kumihimo bobbins or little bobbins for fair isle or intarsia knitting.

Minimal Shrinkage

In the chapter on sampling, we talked extensively about the different types of shrinkage. The first, called draw-in, occurs during weaving and is measured in percentage. It is the difference between the width in the reed and the actual width of the weave when it comes off the loom. Two parameters affect this width.

Placement of the weft thread: It must unwind very smoothly from the shuttle. When this is not the case, for example because the thread on a flat shuttle or boat shuttle does not release properly, this too-short thread will pull on the edges.

Density in the reed: If the density chosen is too low, if the warp threads are too far apart, then the weft threads will not be able to fill all the free space. Threads are good companions and like to get as close to each other as they can. In doing so, they decrease the desired width. As we have seen, this shrinkage is the result of a poor choice of density, which depends on the quality of the warp yarn, the quality of the weft yarn, and the structure used. A sample allows us to confirm, or not, our estimates. If the weave is much narrower than the chosen reed width, it will be necessary to look at the density again. It goes without saying that this calculation only makes sense if, with the beating, you have scrupulously used the same count in weft as in warp! Otherwise, nothing can be concluded from it.

The **calculation formula**, discussed in depth in "Fabrics: Behind the Scenes" in the section "Inevitable Shrinkage" (see p. 48), is as follows:

$$\text{Percentage of Draw-in} = \frac{\text{Width of fabric on reed} - \text{Width of fabric off the loom}}{\text{Width of fabric off the loom}} \times 100$$

In the vast majority of weaves, this shrinkage expressed as a percentage should not exceed 5 percent.

In the case of a much higher percentage, the density is recalculated by counting the exact number of threads in the warp as well as the number in weft in the sample made. Then we will take the average of these two numbers, which will probably become the appropriate density. Be aware that this count in warp and weft is done once the fabric is taken off the loom or not under tension.

Let's add a few nuances. For instance, some yarns, because of their elastic quality, will pull on the weave and shrinkage will be inevitable, or even desired as in pleated weaves, such as the collapse weave. In the same way, some weaving structures take on volume once they are released from the tension of the loom. This three-dimensional expansion is at the expense of width. This is very characteristic of waffle fabrics and honeycomb. In these cases, shrinkage can be up to 40 to 50 percent.

To contain this draw-in, a temple (or stretcher) can be used. This is a wooden or metal tool with sharp little steel spikes that comes in different widths. It is placed near the reed, and it is adjusted so that it is equal to the width in the reed. Then it is placed on the weaving, on the last picks woven. The little spikes are set into the selvedge threads as close as possible to one edge, then the same is done on the other side while exerting pressure. The opening is blocked with a sliding metal ring. If there is too much pressure, the width of the temple is reduced a little. This tool stretches the weave and keeps it the same as the width in the reed. This way, the threads always stay parallel to each other so the reed can slide through the warp without causing wear due to friction. The reed moves more easily and the work becomes smoother.

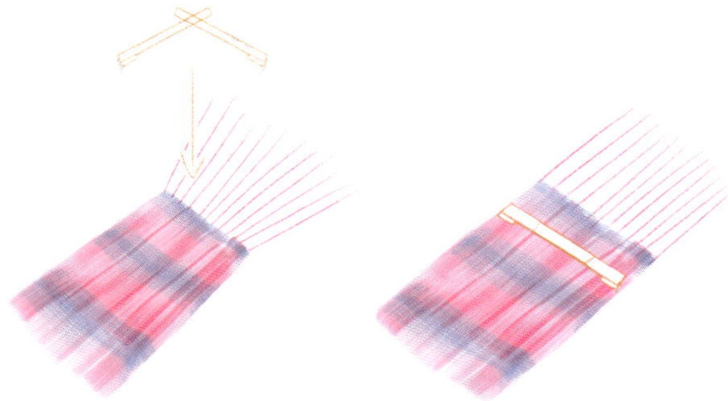

Figure 10 ***Positioning a temple***

Sometimes disparaged by experienced weavers, as it is true that when the density is appropriate and the shuttle is handled ideally, we could do without it, this tool is, however, used in many countries and has been for a long time, as testified by a stained glass window at the Chartres cathedral dating from the 14th century. It is almost indispensable for carpet weaving. Peter Collingwood, a remarkable English weaver who died at the end of the last century, adds that in addition to ensuring width without fear of too much shrinkage, it protects the selvedge threads from wear and tear, and makes it easier to go around the selvedge. The weft can be pulled more firmly, without having to leave any slack in the pick, and, in fact, neat selvedges are obtained.

To be effective, the temple must be moved often. This delays weaving and is an argument made by weavers who shun this tool. For me, it is an ally that I find helpful, and that I am not afraid to use when I have to be very careful with the selvedges. But as I don't always have the right temple at hand, I will resort to plan B when necessary. Instead of using a tool that pushes the fabric across its entire width, I install a device that stretches it outward: a simple pin on each side, knitting machine grippers, suspender clips with, to put them under tension, a wide rubber band that goes around the loom under the fabric or strings kept taut by a weight on each side. Admittedly less practical, these replacements are still better than nothing.

There are now temples inspired by industrial equipment, which advance automatically as the fabric is wound and which, when attached to a loom, can be adapted to any weaving width. These are worth considering if you do a lot of weaving.

Advancing the Weaving Every 1 to 2 Inches

There comes a time when, after so much weaving, the opening of the shed is no longer enough to send the shuttle through. It seems that, swept away by the fun, you forgot to wind up your weaving. Nevertheless, I advise you to wind your work well before you are forced to do so, and above all, often enough to obtain very consistent weaving.

As you weave, the weft and warp threads intertwine and undulate. Thus, as the weaving progresses, the warp threads become more and more taut. Over two or three centimeters, this is imperceptible to the eye, but beyond that, the difference can begin to show. It is therefore necessary to give the warp some ease.

It is also possible that, despite all the care taken to ensure even warp tension throughout the preparation work, the tension is not uniform across the entire width of the weave. Winding every 1 to 2 inches will erase these imperfections. Otherwise, by winding too infrequently, the new weft may not be pressed parallel to the previous one, and may form a small offset angle. We will then see some kind of striation appearing on the side with less tension.

It is also important that the reed hits the fabric at a right angle, so that each tooth hits the entire thickness of the weft. This does not apply to looms with a sliding reed, of course. For other systems, it is necessary to find the beating zone, between the breast beam and the reed, where the latter will hit the fabric while vertical. Depending on whether the beater is attached at the bottom of the loom or swings from the top, its span will be different, it will bounce more or less, and will pack the weft unevenly. Find the place where it beats consistently and always perpendicular to the fabric. This requires advancing the cloth about every inch.

In reality, the best frequency for winding the weaving depends on your comfort, your loom, and your position. You will be adding many, many rows of weft, so choose the weaving area that is most comfortable for you. The main thing is to advance the warp often enough to maintain your level of comfort the whole time you are working:

passing the shuttle, swinging the beater, and holding this position for a long time. Advancing the warp often will give you both a nice weave, without risk of unevenness, and some valuable relaxation. You will be able to weave longer.

Some looms have a warp beam brake disengagement system at the front of the loom. When this is not the case, it may seem cumbersome to get off the seat to disengage the pawl and then return to your seat. You may be able to DIY a system that makes it easier for you. Otherwise, look on the bright side: a little exercise will do you good.

Debriefing on Set in 5 Minutes!

As you continue adding the weft, the work advances. And as you advance the warp, the first wefts picks are no longer visible; they have already gone around the breast beam as the fabric winds onto the cloth roller. To follow the progress of the fabric, to check that the length is accurate for the project, to always know where you are, you can use helpers. Whether it's a ribbon, a long strip of paper, or a tape measure, the idea is to always know what is already woven and what is left to weave!

Attach the end of this helper to the beginning of the weave. If it is paper, first make marks on it for length or for color, thread, and treadling changes. As you work, pin this ribbon to the weaving and they will wind onto the beam together. This guide becomes indispensable when you want patterns to be positioned exactly or when you need very precise measurements, such as for absolutely identical curtains, a garment where the color changes will be at the same exact place on the back and front to allow for a perfect match, or a set of placemats that are all alike.

At the end of the work, this assistant will be preciously stored; it will perhaps be used for another project.

Winding onto the Cloth Beam

Quite quickly, the weaving arrives at the cloth roller. The apron rod is already rolled up, the lacing knots have also crossed the beam, and the fabric is ready. As with winding the warp onto the warp roller, we want to protect the woven cloth from the extra thickness of the knots that would deform the fabric. To do this, a slightly thick cardstock or warp sticks are slipped in as soon as the fabric arrives at the cloth beam. And then, for a long weaving, it is useful to insert stronger sticks between the different turns as the woven cloth is rolled up. Without these sticks, the fabric would be crushed at the edges, which would alter the tension of the selvedge threads.

Always Pay Attention to Warp Tension

One last point is the **warp tension**! When we first started weaving, we were often reassured by a strong tension. What is the ideal tension? This is an important question, but there is no standard answer.

A high tension has several disadvantages. It reduces the undulation of the warp threads and the weave appears unbalanced between warp and weft. Taut threads also wear out faster, with the risk of breaking. Remember also that on a rising-shed or sinking-shed loom, the warp threads under stress become more taut, so it is a bit risky to impose this extra tension on threads that are already extremely taut. You can only afford a little more tension with a counterbalance loom since all the threads move identically as they rise and fall.

However, the movement of the shuttle will be hindered by **insufficient warp tension**; it will not be able to slide easily between the upper and lower threads. Boat shuttles will fall off and flat shuttles will probably catch on warp threads. This is especially the case with table looms, which do not have a shuttle race to guide the boat shuttle as on other looms. Too little tension doesn't help with beating either, and keeping the selvedges in place becomes more complicated.

One more thing. When weaving warp-faced **reps**, you want to get the warp threads to move around the sometimes thick wefts; only a low tension will allow this, as well as very frequent winding to bring back slack to the warp threads. On the other hand, for weaves where the warp is completely covered, we will try to give it more tension so that the picks can slide in easily and be pressed down firmly, because this time, they are the ones that undulate. This is the case of weft-faced reps, boundweave, taqueté, etc.

Other cases: weaving wool with a low-tension warp will result in **a very supple fabric**. And since there will be space between each intersection, it is very likely that washing will accentuate this suppleness by making the threads swell. However, **some fibers need to be more taut**; otherwise they cling to each other behind the heddles, and it's difficult to open the shed. This is the case with mohair.

As you can see, there are no real rules. Your attention will be focused only on keeping a consistent tension, so that it is the same throughout the weaving. Your experience and, again and always, your well-being will guide you.

However, a small comment to finish. While it is true that each weaver will stretch his warp as he chooses and is comfortable with, sometimes our inner tensions are reflected in our weaving. And while weaving can help us to find our calm on stormy days, it is almost certain that the first weft picks will be more compacted and the work more taut when we are harboring inner turmoil. I think it will be necessary again to rely on the helper for a few picks. Use the tape measure or the triangle and check the beating of the first rows precisely, remembering that you will tend to overstretch and overcompact on those days.

The Conclusion: Finishing Your Weaving

The epilogue has its say and the curtain falls.

Théophile Gautier, *Mademoiselle de Maupin*, 1835

It is amusing to note that finishing a weaving does not mean the same thing for each weaver, and that once again, weaving is a bit of a mirror of who we are.

The most meticulous weavers will have been careful to follow a measuring tape or strip of some sort that will have served as a guide. The desired length is now reached; it is time to finish! Others will weave until the whole warp is finished, at the risk of making a scarf that is a little too long, and regret it; it is unthinkable for them to waste warp!

There is nothing to say except that the risks of mistakes are more significant at the end, once the back tie-on rod has gone around the beam: nothing holds or brakes the threads anymore, tension issues are at their peak and, very often, the warp threads do not rise consistently.

As far as I am concerned, the weaving is really finished when it is taken off the loom, the finishing touches are done, and the fabric is washed and possibly ironed. It is only then that the weaving has become fabric.

However, it is still a very special feeling when the last picks have been placed, possibly secured by the Paris stitch, and finally the weaving is cut and unrolled. In weaving, we never see the piece as a whole before it comes off the loom. While certainly less spectacular than a tapestry's "*tombée du métier*"—literally, the fall from the loom—when the piece is truly unveiled since the weaver works from the back side, this doesn't prevent the rest of us, also weavers, after some apprehension, from experiencing quite a moment when first seeing our whole piece. It sometimes takes a little time before fully enjoying it.

Different Ways to Finish Your Weaving: The Final Bow

The next step is to **secure the threads** in the weaving to prevent them from unraveling. These last steps serve to either protect before sewing, to highlight the charm of the weaving, or even to **embellish** it with accessories such as beads or braids or cutting fringe, making knots, etc.

The Paris Stitch

As at the beginning of the weaving, we can finish with the Paris stitch, but in reverse. So we will pass the needle horizontally over the warp threads not woven, then take it down diagonally into the weaving. For this embroidery stitch, I use the weft thread, leaving plenty of length.

It depends on your own dexterity, but, as at the start of the weaving, I am much more adept starting from the right. And I prefer to do it when the weaving is still on the loom, under tension. It's definitely one of the sturdiest finishes.

Figure 11 ***The Paris stitch to finish the weaving***

Zigzag Stitch

Using a traditional sewing machine or serger is the fastest way to secure your weaving. Be sure to adjust the stitch width so that several weft threads are sewn together.

I only use the machine when my weaving will be cut for sewing. Otherwise, I think it's a shame to finish a handmade work made of beautiful materials using a sewing machine.

Figure 12 **Sewing prior to cutting your weaving**

To make the stitching easier and more secure, I sometimes weave the last picks with a finer thread and, above all, I beat more firmly; a weave that is too supple and too slack would not be securely finished off by machine stitching. I sew two lines of zigzag stitch around the future cutting line and two lines of straight stitch on the fabric at ⅜ inch (1 cm) from this zigzag toward the inside of the fabric.

Chain Stitch

This is done directly on the loom. A little more slippery than the Paris stitch, because it does not sew the picks, I use it with thick weaves where the weft is very present. Like the Paris stitch, it can be sewn using the weft thread that has been cut leaving a long tail. You can use a hook to help you.

Knots

From a simple knot that serves to stop threads from unraveling, to very clever, attractive knots, there are a multitude of possibilities. Just browse through a book specifically on knot making to discover quite a wide variety. It is an art in itself that deserves to be used. On a shawl, a placemat, or a rug, these finishes will always be striking. On the other hand, they require a real know-how and a lot of consistency.

Use a pin to slide the knot in the right place, as close as possible to the weaving. It is important to not forget that knots consume a great deal of thread, which must be planned for beforehand.

Fringe

Of course, with knots, you can obtain fringe, but you can also do the opposite and make fringe without knots, which will be more decorative. To do this, divide a group of warp threads into two equal parts, twist them in the same direction as the twist of the yarn itself. When the twist is strong enough, bring the two strands together and twist them together in the opposite direction. Secure the twist by tying a knot at the end of the twisted strands. There is a small device with alligator clips that makes twisting easier.

Figure 13 **Fringe on a silk shawl**

Embellishments

Adding beads, tassels, or pompoms will add a touch of creativity to your weaving. You can of course consider all kinds of materials: leather, ceramic pieces, buttons, or more simply threads, either the same as those used in the weaving or others that will bring a shiny or bright touch. Be careful: some of them should not go through the wash.

There are several books on this subject: *Compendium of Finishing Techniques* by Naomi K. McEneely (Interweave, 2003), *Joinings, Edges and Trims* by Jean Wilson (Van Nostrand Reinhold Company, 1983). Peter Collingwood's comprehensive book *The Techniques of Rug Weaving* (Watson-Guptill, 1950) is an important resource for multiple finishes for rugs.

A Last Curtain Call, and We Keep on Weaving

Curtain call:

1 – Applause from the audience encouraging the performer to come back and take another bow.

2 – Exploit or exercise presented after the end of an act.

Dominique Denis, *Encyclopedia of the Circus from A to Z*, 2013

So yes, even after you are done, you can keep on weaving.

If there is still a lot of warp left, secure these threads with bow knots or sticky paper along the reed, cut and unwind the fabric from the cloth beam, then tie the warp back onto the front apron rod, as at the very beginning of the weaving. A few picks to even out the warp, possibly the Paris stitch, and the weaving begins again . . .

To avoid losing tension or too much warp length, another very easy method can be used. After having finished the weaving you wish to unroll, leave a couple of inches of warp free, then weave about two inches of plain weave with a yarn that is not slippery ❶, then insert one stick like weft in a plain weave shed, then a second stick in the second shed ❷. Add a few more rows of plain weave with the yarn ❸. At this point you can cut the warp between the finished weave and these few new picks ❹.

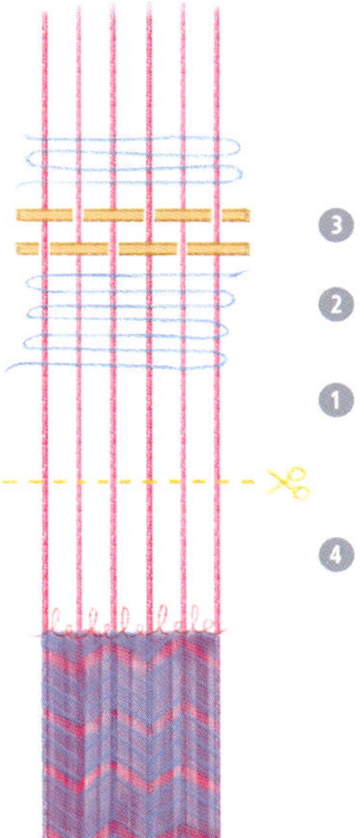

Figure 14 Cutting a piece of weaving and continuing to weave on the warp

Then, tie the apron rod very tightly to these two sticks inserted as weft. It's quick and very solid! The two sticks can be wood or metal, as long as they are thin, sturdy, and can be wound easily around the cloth beam.

The front apron rod tied to the weft sticks

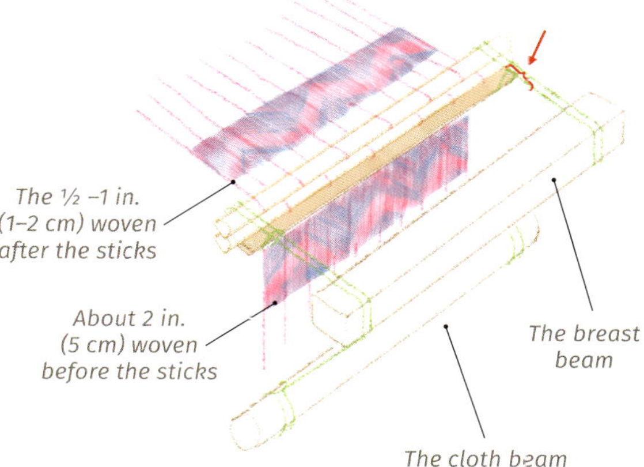

Figure 15 Attaching the two "woven weft sticks" to the front apron rod

Another advantage to this technique is that there are no knots on the front rod. This means that you can roll up the fabric without having to protect it with cardstock.

If there is no warp left to weave and you still want to make another weaving keeping the same threading and the same sleying of the reed, you can wind a new warp. Place it at the front of the loom, insert the lease sticks in the cross of the new warp, attach each thread to the thread of the previous warp in order, using the weaver's knot or the pull knot. Wind this new warp onto the warp beam with the usual care for tension and even winding. Pay particular attention when these knots go through the teeth of the reed and through the eyes of the heddles. The weaver's knot is fairly flat, so it is easy to pass through.

Figure 16 The weaver's knot

With a little experience, it is easy to catch the two threads in your hand, position them so that by twisting the two strands between the fingers, the knot is made quickly. This technique of knotting the warp threads together was constantly used by the silk manufacturers to avoid rethreading the many, many silk threads. It was even a profession in its own right, carried out by the twister. She would come outside the workshop hours, at night, with a little bucket filled with a secret glue made from milk and gum arabic. She would tie the new warp, stored on the warp beam, to the last lengths of the previous one, with impressive speed. Twisters were independent workers, and their fame was measured by the number of workshop keys entrusted to them.

In the Limelight: Mistakes to Correct, Tips and Tricks

As soon as the weaving process starts, the first picks are closely examined for defects. Some are very common; others are more or less easy to spot. Corrections are always possible, although sometimes very time-consuming. We are surprisingly "inventive" from this point of view, and I will not list all the possible mistakes. In the vast majority of cases, take a deep breath, smile, don't panic, and look inventively for ways to fix it. Even if the solution is not done according to the rules of the art, the important thing is to get around the problem by transforming, fiddling, or hacking to get everything back into working order or at least mitigate imperfections. I would like to use Erica de Ruiter's expression, when she would gently tell distressed course participants, "Let it go!—in the sense, of course, of putting one's perfectionism in brackets, of detaching oneself and tinkering without shame, maybe using a thread to support, a bottle to hang, a wooden stick to attach, a clamp . . .

In any case, if an error was detected too late and is visible in the weaving, if it cannot be repaired, then imagine playing with it, "highlighting" it, so that it appears to be a desired bit of creativity or whimsy and not a glitch. And very often the greatest inventions come from a mistake. Serendipity is a word I have heard frequently in English-speaking weaving classes. This exact word is not used often in French; we prefer "happy accident." Let us be inspired by these unexpected discoveries, because they have sometimes become pearls that catch on and are imitated.

I have one small comment, however. It is very easy to miss the mistake when one looks too directly at the details. This is true for preparing the work and it is equally true for fixing it. For example, you may choose to count your heddles one by one and check the threading several times in a row without finding a single error. Rather than zooming in, take a step back. Examine by groups or blocks, check the total width of the weave, compare with the record sheet and the draft for the number of heddles per shaft.

And a word of advice. Go slowly when analyzing the mistake. Don't panic, don't make a hasty decision, and above all, don't change anything too late in the evening or at night. The light is not as good and ideas are not as clear. Yes, believe me! What a pity, the next morning, to discover that there was a much simpler way to go about it!

The next part is to move beyond the mistake. Yes, it's hard to imagine that anyone could have made this kind of mistake. In everyday language, we often hear that there are no stupid questions. The same is true for mistakes; they may be caused by absentmindedness, lack of self-confidence, being overly laid-back, whatever. After some detective work to find the errors, you will have to roll up your sleeves and fix them. With a smile and tenacity!

Before Starting to Weave

The Warp Did Not Go Around the Breast and Back Beams

It sometimes happens that when taking the warp from the back to put it through the heddles, we forget to go around the back beam, and the threads go directly from the warp beam to the heddles. Of course, we may not discover this until after the heddles are threaded and the reed sleyed. So, plan B! We slip a stick under all the threads and attach it as close as possible to the back beam, so as to get back the horizontal position of the warp between the two beams.

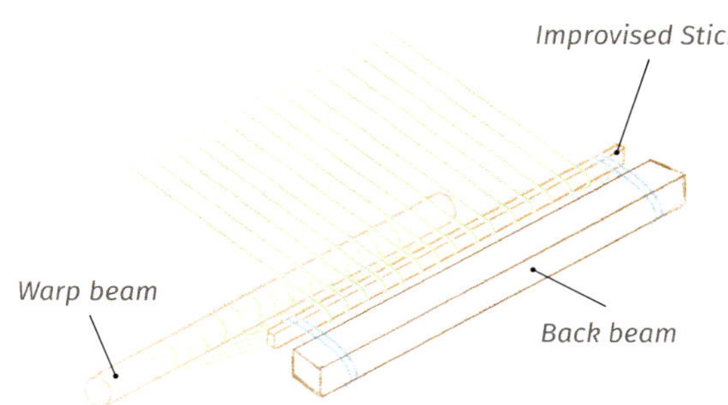

Figure 17 ***The warp did not go around the back beam.***

Less funny, but very surprising, is that this also happens with the breast beam. In this case, there is nothing else to do but unknot the threads or lacing and start again by going around the breast beam. You can do it. It won't take too long.

A Warp Thread Stays in the Middle of the Shed

This is the first check to be made before starting to weave, to be noted first on the list of potential mistakes to review. Each shaft is lifted individually and, looking through the shed, we check that no thread stays horizontal, neither rising nor falling, except for the floating selvedges whose purpose it is to do that.

If you find such a warp thread, either a warp end is bypassing a heddle next to it or two warp ends have crossed between the shafts and the reed, and the sleying order is reversed.

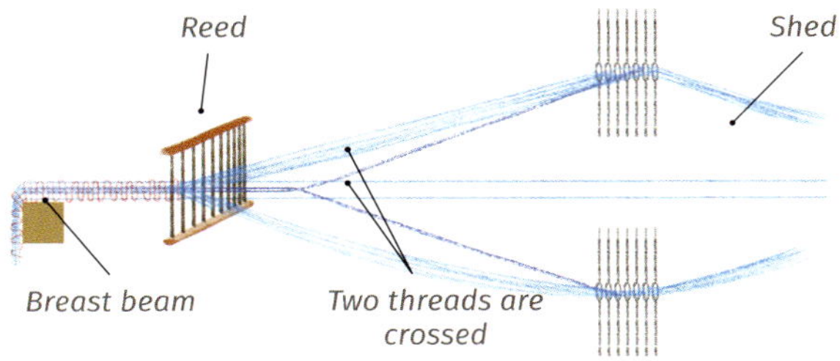

Figure 18 ***Two threads cross between the heddles and the reed.***

Figure 19 ***Two threads cross at the heddles.***

In both of these cases, two threads have crossed each other. Cut the two or three offending threads as close to the front apron rod as possible, and rearrange them in the correct order. A small piece of thread, tied to the two strands that have been put back in their place and tied "roughly" to the apron rod will do the trick. It's not necessary to do anything else. There is no need to undo the knot or the entire lacing.

After the First Picks

A Thread Is Never Woven

A warp thread floats above or below the weave and does not interlace with the weft. It is very likely that it does not pass through the eye of the heddle, which happens quite easily with Texsolv heddles. This error can be detected in the first few picks. Cut the misplaced thread as close as possible to the knot tying it onto the apron rod, slip it through the eye, pass it back through the reed, and attach it to the front, with a small extension. Tie on "roughly" again!

Two Adjacent Threads Follow the Same Path

Here's the second priority check to make: examine the first few picks by weaving plain weave with a contrasting color thread, and look for two adjacent warp ends that might interlace in the same way, giving the illusion of a thicker thread. This is a threading error. In the best case, two heddles have been reversed: you have threaded in 1-2-4-3 instead of 1-2-3-4. Cut the two threads, put them back in their place "roughly"—no heddle is missing, everything is fine.

Of course, a little more seriously, you may have threaded in 1-2-4-4 instead of 1-2-3-4. In this case, a heddle is missing on shaft 3. We will improvise with a Plan B again. Remove the third end threaded on shaft 4 that should be on shaft 3. The orphaned heddle will remain in place and will not interfere at all. There is no need to try to remove it.

Instead, you should **make a new heddle**, with a strong cotton thread, for example. Please note that it is essential to position the eye at the same height and to give it the same diameter as the neighboring ones. Use a heddle as a model. On a board or piece of styrofoam, attach this heddle with four pins at the ends and at the eye to form a template. Remove this template and make the heddle. Secure the eye preferably with a square knot that won't slip, and tie the ends around the two template pins. I find it just as easy to place a safety pin or a paper clip at both ends of this backup heddle, which I attach directly to the bars of the shafts; this makes the installation much easier.

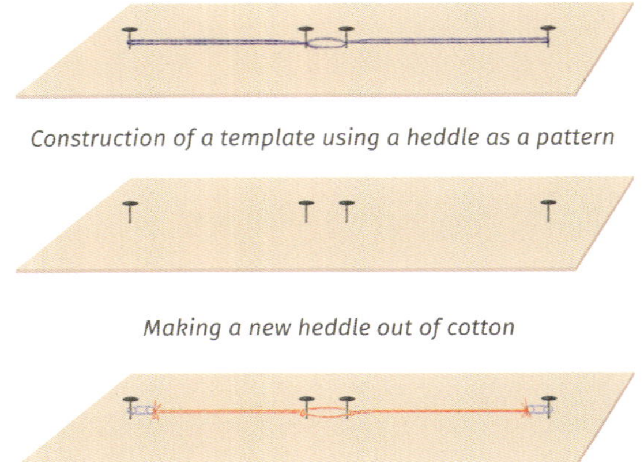

Construction of a template using a heddle as a pattern

Making a new heddle out of cotton

Figure 20 ***Making a missing heddle with a template.***

Rather than making a new heddle, I now choose to use a heddle from the loom that I attach to the shaft, whether it's made of metal or cotton; this way I can be really sure that the eye will have the same shape and height as all its neighbors. Otherwise, all it takes is a tiny shift in the height of the warp thread and the flat shuttle will definitely catch repeatedly on this thread that is not in line.

If you have a loom with Texsolv heddles, rejoice, because there is a simple method to make a quick, effective repair. Tie two heddles together at their ends, either with a square knot or with a small tie. Then wrap these two heddles around the bars of the shaft and join them with a short thread. Then make sure to thread the warp end through both eyes at the same time. This is the method I prefer; it's quick and easy, as long as you have a few back-up heddles.

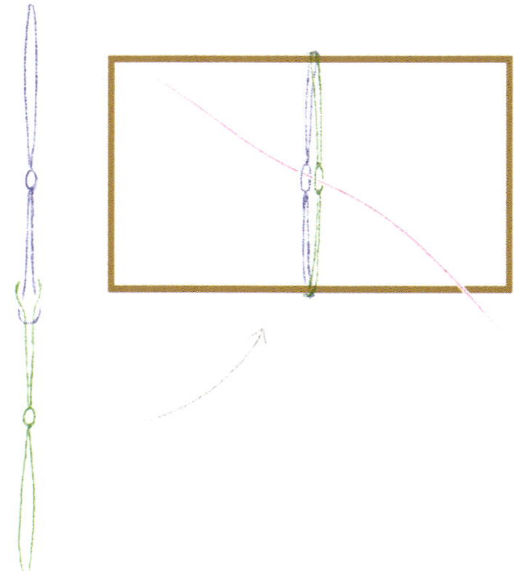

Figure 21 ***Installing a double Texsolv heddle.***

A Mistake in the Pattern Is Repeated Across the Whole Width

When the first checks with the plain weave are finished, we try with another treadling. Weaving ½ to 1 inch (1 to 2 cm) of 2/2 twill is perfect, and makes it easier to inspect the whole width of the work. If a **pattern error appears across the entire width of the weaving**, it is most likely just a problem with the treadle tie-up or a shaft that is not lifting properly. It's probably nothing serious.

Most of the time, though, a **few mistakes are scattered here and there**, randomly, and there is no escaping a check of the entire threading.

The first thing to resist is discouragement! Often, there is more fear than harm. The second is to be disappointed. We had been so attentive, we had taken so much care—all this time wasted to have to start again. The third is the temptation to check the whole threading from beginning to end, heddle after heddle, dominated by panic.

There are some things I am very insistent on and this is one of them: **zooming out, looking at things by taking a step back**. I am all the more insistent because experience shows that it is very fruitful to do so. I am also persistent because some people resist due to a lack of confidence. It really is more effective to correct by group, provided you find the right groups.

Let's take the example of a twill threading, like a rosepath. The block that repeats is the following: 1-2-3-4-1-4-3-2. So we'll check from group of 8 threads to group of 8 threads. To do this, I lift shaft 1, and I see if in this block of 8 threads, I correctly have 2 threads on each shaft. Then I continue this check on each of the shafts. This allows me to spot most mistakes.

However, you may at some point have to redo the whole threading process if there is a large number of errors. Above all, resist making this decision too quickly, or in any case, never in the evening. If rethreading is nevertheless necessary, make sure to reinsert the cross sticks if you had removed them. Resume slowly, taking all the threads out of the heddles rather than taking them out as you go, and opt to handle them in blocks.

A Pattern Is Not Finished

You may simply have forgotten a heddle and a thread. You'll need to make the heddle using the method you prefer, and add a new warp thread. If you have kept the guide string for your warp, you know exactly the length you need. Make a spool and place it in the back, weighting it down. I wind onto fair isle fish bobbins or Kumihimo bobbins, and weight with S painter's hooks. Avoid choosing a weight that is too heavy, as the higher tension on the yarn will damage it. At the most, try to get the same tension as that on the threads already warped. On the weaving, I wrap this yarn in a figure-eight around a thin-headed pin I inserted there.

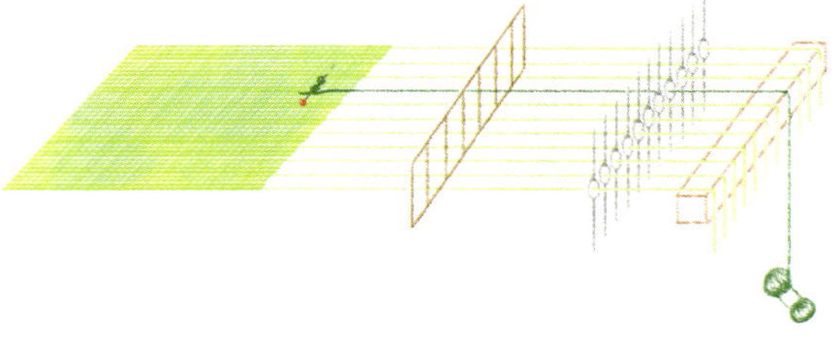

Figure 22 ***Adding a missing warp thread.***

An Area of the Reed Is Mis-Sleyed

This is a mistake that I curse, because there is no way to do anything else but to adjust the sleying of the reed. You will probably have put two threads instead of one in a reed dent, or left an empty dent that should have been filled. Nothing can be done except to take all the threads out of the reed from the mistake to the edge, and start again. Without question, a mistake in reed density will always show up! There is no way to escape it—we must re-sley. Sigh!

While Weaving, What to Do When . . .

The Shuttle Is Empty

Whether it's because the shuttle is empty or because you want to pick up another yarn, there comes a time when you have to change threads.

Very easily, you can leave the threads hanging over the edge of the fabric, and this is no problem for a fabric that will be cut and sewn. No need to waste time with finishing touches that won't show. For other fabrics, leave the thread loose until you tuck it into the fabric when it comes off the loom, slipping it between the selvedge threads. Some prefer to do this after washing.

For perfectly invisible changes **with the same thread**, and this is obviously what I prefer, use a ply-split join. Split the end of the thread from the shuttle over about 1½ inches (3 to 4 cm). Do the same with the beginning of the yarn on the new shuttle. As you weave, you'll overlap the two half-threads so that they replicate the thickness of the original thread. Pull the two remaining half-threads out of the weave and cut them after washing. Unraveled, these threads are very fragile, especially the cotton ones; they must be handled very gently. With linen thread, it is not necessary to split. Scraping the thread to remove a little thickness will suffice.

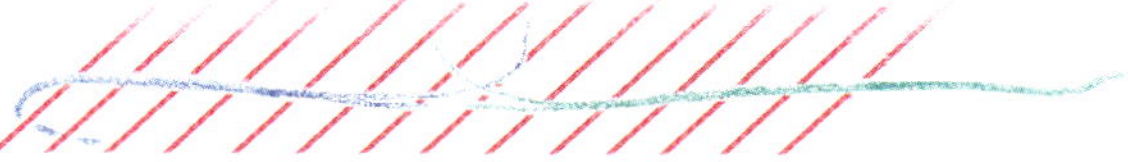

Figure 23 ***Joining yarn when the shuttle is empty.***

If you need to **change the thread**, and it's not just a matter of joining, you will do almost the same thing. Cut the current thread, leaving an extra 2 inches (5 cm). Split about the last 4 inches (10 cm), and weave one half-thread in the same shed, wrapping it around the floating selvedge and going back over the same thread. Then do the same with the new yarn, splitting the first 4 inches (10 cm), wrapping it around the selvedge and going back over the same 2 inches (5 cm) at the edge. To make these two overlapping strands look like one thread, they absolutely must pass through the same shed after going around the selvedge thread. Again, after washing, cut the half-thread not woven in.

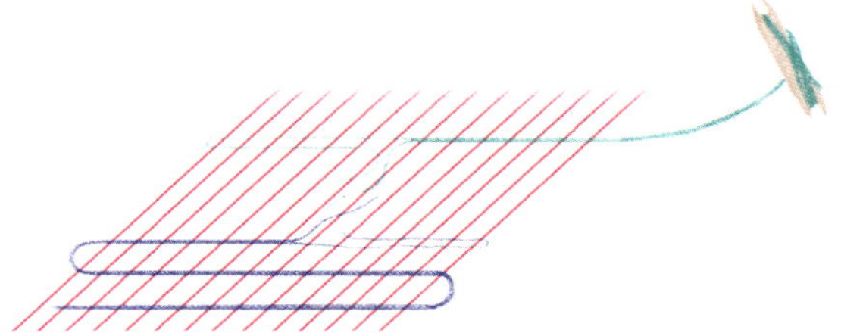

Figure 24 ***Changing the weft yarn***

Sometimes you may be a little reluctant to do this and prefer to simply double the threads over an inch or so at the beginning or end, or where joining. Of course, this is faster and more suitable for samples. But in any case, this extra thickness will always show, no matter how thick the yarn is. Even a very thin yarn, when doubled, is twice as thick. There are some weaves that deserve careful finishing, and this inevitably requires a little more attention and work. Unfortunately, imperfections always show.

I admit that I'm a little bristled by the expression "homemade" when it justifies slapdash work. I prefer to associate the homemade with polished, carefully crafted work, where all the smallest details matter, and to leave the approximate to commercial fabrics. It is undoubtedly also a way to increase the value of these items made with our hands, which require so much attention. That's why I don't mind a little extra handling. Some say I am meticulous, others say I am fussy. In fact, I am inspired by our grandmothers who chose to devote time, care, and love to embroidering napkins, the latest garment, a headdress. I subscribe to this simple, high standard that makes our daily life valuable.

A Warp End Breaks

There are several reasons this might happen, and the solutions are necessarily all a little different. The important thing is to **never make a knot** that would remain visible in the weaving. Change the thread by adding a connecting thread about a yard long, or by replacing it completely with a repair thread that matches the length of what is left to weave. Depending on the location of the break, slip it through the empty heddle if necessary and then through the reed. Then insert a T-pin at the exact location of the old thread, without making a mistake in the reed order, and wrap the replacement thread around it in a figure-eight knot to secure it to the weaving. When the weaving is off the loom, weave in the ends of the threads hanging out, as nicely as possible, in the direction of the warp, and why not also in the direction of the weft if it is the same thread, splitting it.

Now let's look at why this happened and how to fix it.

A single thread may possibly break because it is fragile or there was some bad movement or a one-time incident. If this is the case, add on a yard or so of yarn identical to the one that broke, a sort of **temporary repair end**, tying it to the broken yarn at the back of the loom. Slip the other end through the heddle, through the reed, and then, to secure this addition to the front of the loom, insert a pin into the fabric, wrapping the end of the thread around it in little figure eights. Then off the back hang a light weight on this repair end to put it under tension. As you weave, this knot will eventually reach the heddles. Remove the weight at the back, gently pull the rest of the repair end forward, the knot goes through the heddle, the reed, and reaches the weaving. Then cut the rest of this repair end off and wind the original thread thus recovered in a figure eight knot around a new T-pin inserted in the fabric. The trick is done, there is no knot left in the fabric, which is an absolute rule! Once the weaving is off of the loom, remove the two pins and tuck these little pieces of thread seamlessly into the fabric.

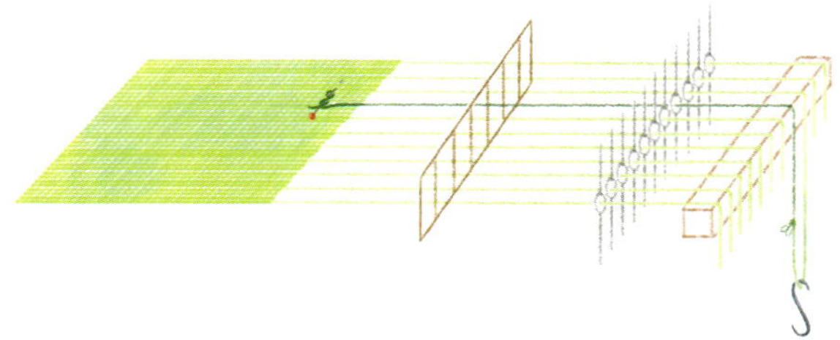

Figure 25 ***Repairing a broken warp end.***

The solution is different if it is **the selvedge threads that break**, which is likely due to a wrong choice of warp density. The fabric draws in and its width is no longer the same as that imposed by the reed. As a result, each time the reed moves, the teeth rub on these selvedge threads that are no longer parallel to each other, and wear on them. The moment comes when these frayed threads break. If you are only at the beginning of your weaving, cut the warp and re-weave with a higher density. If this initial density is the one you want, or if your work is already very advanced, then use a temple that will force the fabric to keep the width and density you want, or use any of the DIY systems presented in the section on the temple (see p. 106).

Some threads are more sensitive to wear. Linen is one of them; so are some mohairs and untwisted single-ply yarns. These yarns can be strengthened by spraying with starch or hair spray. I don't like these polluting products very much; I prefer to use powdered starch to be diluted, although it is less easy to use, I must admit.

How to Fix Loose Warp Ends and Uneven Tension

Tension is without a doubt the most tricky thing to maintain. Indeed, it depends on so many parts of the setup that it has to have been consistent throughout all the preparation: winding the warp, beaming the warp with sticks or paper, and tying on. All of that must have been done calmly and consistently.

The word "tension" makes us think (wrongly) that the warp has to be pulled very taut. However, it is not a question of pulling hard on the threads, but only of doing it consistently.

Differences in tension will always be visible, making the fabric curl, wave, or have little pockets. But above all, when there is uneven tension in the warp ends, this causes mishaps. The shuttle keeps snagging on these threads, passes over them when it should have passed under threads that didn't really move. This weakens the threads, and on the fabric, we see unwanted floats.

If the weaving has not really started, try to adjust the tension of these threads, maintaining the tension on the front of the weaving with a pin. If it's too late, place a weight at the back to tighten up the stubborn thread a bit. The common risk is to put too much weight, and to increase the distension of this thread. Often, a very light weight is sufficient.

If the problem is only with a small group of threads, you can also slip an extra thickness such as a slat into the warp against the warp beam to stretch the distended threads. But this will certainly not solve everything, and it's impossible to correct any major tension issues this way. Either the threads are stretched too much or not enough. This method is not reliable enough to be overused.

If it is the selvedge threads in particular that have become too loose, because the beaming was not done correctly, you can compensate by slipping in a slat on each side to increase the circumference of the warp beam on the side only. But always, always with finesse so as not to exacerbate the problem.

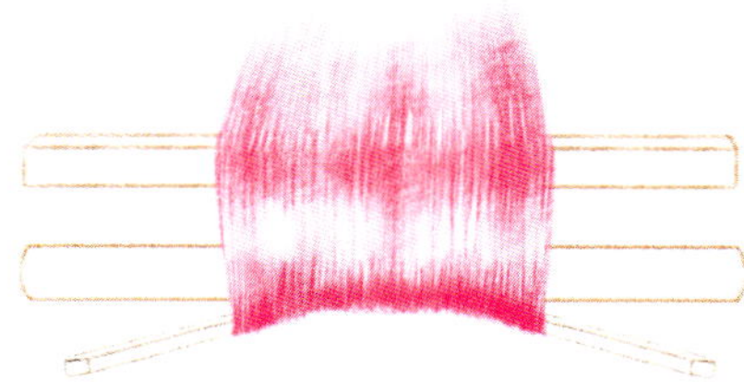

Figure 26 ***Fixing selvedge tension***

If the number of weights increases unreasonably because too many threads are loose, you can unwind the warp from the beam 12 to 18 inches, and rewind it, slipping bubble wrap over it. Keep doing this at regular intervals until the weaving is complete. This method has the great advantage of not stretching the threads unnecessarily, as they take the right path between the bubbles by themselves. And it may even be possible to solve the problem and realize that finally, none of the threads are loose. Good for you!

If this difficulty increases, and if it is possible to cut the weaving in progress, for example because you are weaving a series of hand towels, cushions, placemats, etc., you will benefit from taking the completed weavings off the loom and correcting the tension of the remaining warp. Unwind the rest of the warp from the front, slide four slats (lease sticks for example) on the back, opening the sheds of a plain weave, even and odd threads one after the other. Then wind on the warp beam with all the necessary precautions. Go back and reread the section on "Tightening Loose Warp Ends" included under Beaming the Warp (see p. 85).

Threads Are Fraying

The reed wears on the threads and some are more fragile than others. When choosing a reed, it is sometimes better to choose a lower density reed and to use two threads per dent. For example, for a density of 15 epi, it is better to use an 8-dent reed (2 threads in 7 dents, 1 thread in 1 dent). In this way, the threads are a little pampered. You can also strengthen them with starch.

The Shed Doesn't Open Completely

Everything is going well, then suddenly the shed opens less. Most likely, if not removed, the lease sticks were pulled forward when the warp was unwound to advance the weaving. They are therefore too close to the shafts and prevent them from lifting properly; they can simply be moved back and attached to the back beam. Often, they can just be removed with worry—but that's another issue!

There is dissension on this topic: do we keep or not keep the lease sticks in? As for me, trained by weavers who worshipped their presence throughout the weaving process, I found it very difficult to free myself from this practice. However, what is the purpose of the lease sticks? They show us the warp threads in the order they were wound so they can be threaded without getting mixed up. They have therefore played their role perfectly. Theoretically, you can remove them. I strongly recommend removing them when using fragile threads or ones that snag. But of course I recognize that, left in place, they help find a broken warp thread. Silk weavers leave their lease sticks in throughout their work. However, they are made of glass, highly polished, with no risk of snagging or jamming.

Here is my policy, and the one I teach: I remove the lease sticks. And if I see that I need them again, I put them back! I lift the even threads, slide in a stick, lift the odd threads and slide in a second one.

The Shed Is Not Clean

When there is a large distance between the first and the last shaft, which is the case with some artisans' looms, or for looms with 8 or more shafts, I find that we have to give up on having all the shafts aligned horizontally. The important thing is to adjust the height of the shafts so that all the warp threads are at the same angle. To make this adjustment, I raise and lower the first and last shafts and look through the shed to find the height of each that will allow the threads to all be at the same level where the shuttle will pass. You'll probably have to lower the first few shafts a bit and raise the last few. This, of course, is in cases where the back and breast beams are at the same height. Otherwise, keep in mind that the goal is for the shuttle to glide through a clean shed.

By Way of Conclusion

Sometimes I regret not listing all the mistakes that course participants or I myself have made. It's amazing to discover new ones all the time; it's a bottomless pit. Most often you just have to laugh about it. It's a good bet that with experience, blunders will be less frequent, adjustments will be more precise, and movements will be more skillful.

When it is your turn to innovate and invent an error not described in these paragraphs, you will have to in turn invent a correction. In any case, I invite you to take the time to analyze what seems to be the problem, and to use your practical sense to fix it. Don't panic! Wait for the next day. Let it go overnight if the repair is very involved.

There are many proverbs that speak of the haste to act. Take time to think before you imagine the worst and get discouraged: "Take time for all things: great haste makes great waste."

A tiny third of **confidence**, a slightly larger third of **reflection**, a good third of **imagination** . . . and a large third of **patience**. And there you have it!

"And that makes four thirds," Marius replies to his father, César, who is explaining to him the famous recipe for a picon-lemon-curaçao drink in Marcel Pagnol's play.

"Exactly. I hope that this time, you've understood," replied César.

"But in a glass, there are only three thirds," Marius replies, surprised.

"But, you fool, it all depends on the size of the thirds."

PART TWO

THE MELODY OF WEAVING: STRUCTURES

Fabric appeared very early, as soon as man knew about counting and enumeration, before writing, during the Neolithic period.

Patrice Hugues, *Le langage du tissu*, 1982

There are innumerable ways to interlace threads. Consider that with only the twenty-six letters of the alphabet, we can write a countless number of words that we classify as nouns, verbs, adjectives, etc. In weaving, the threading, treadling, and tying on would be the letters, while the patterns and the textile would be the words and the text.

It is the manner in which the threads cross each other that distinguishes a weave, what we call a fabric's structure or weave pattern. This is how it is recognized, named, and classified.

There are so many new weaving patterns and designs, and globalization has given us access to so many sources of inspiration (photos, books, magazines, blogs, etc.), that my desire in this book is not to add new ones. Rather, I would like to share the basics of weaving, its grammar, dissect with you the principles of some of the most used structures, so that you can really understand them, make them your own, and then adapt them as you wish. Knowing and deciphering sets us free. Then it's time to be inspired and fearless.

This analytical method, very commonly taught in Scandinavia, has fascinated me and taught me so much that I now teach it. Some people are afraid to invent, especially at the beginning, and prefer to copy a pattern, even though the yarn they have doesn't match the pattern. The result can be disappointing. On the contrary, drawn in by the freedom gained once they have become familiar with the rules of construction, they take to the game, and dare! When the timidness at the beginning is replaced by the joy of a weaver who unrolls his work invented from scratch, I feel that I was right to emphasize this. So yes, it is essential to understand the basics of construction in order to start creating!

It turns out that it's always easier to find things when they're neat and tidy; I've tried to apply this rule to weave structures. Of course, how they are arranged depends on each author. I obviously didn't invent anything—at most I organized differently.

I barely touched on structures in Chapter 2, "Fabrics: Behind the Scenes" (see p. 41). I will now describe the **three basic structures** in depth, and then I will present some other common structures, with record sheets and very simple examples.

First, a few words of clarification.

We are always confronted with the same **difficulty of vocabulary** in which the same structure may be described by different words. Adopting one name rather than another will perhaps hinder understanding—I am well aware of that. But what to do? I have therefore often chosen to use the vocabulary that I have been taught, that is familiar to me, that I am used to passing on to others. I hope that the glossary will serve as a guide for people who use other terms.

For the same reasons, I have chosen to **group certain structures together** to emphasize their details. As for the choice of names, my bias is inspired by what I have learned. Here again, it is not a question of being original, but of being as coherent as possible to facilitate research and understanding.

As a precaution, one last comment. Some structures could be **grouped in several families**. I had to decide, and sometimes follow one logic rather than another. In this case, I opted for what seemed to me the clearest, but how to know? I hope that the table of contents will guide you.

> Like all writing, weaving has its grammar, which is the art of combining, of composing sounds, the vibrations specific to each material, to each color, to each line, to each pattern.
>
> Jacques Anquetil, *Mémoires d'un tisserand*, 1997

This is why I have pushed this game of similarities by using a musical vocabulary for this second part. I invite you to join this new orchestra, and to read, write, and then play together some pieces of music. To your instruments!

Minuet 1

Cello Suite No. 1

J.S. BACH

6

The Basic Structures: Perfect Harmony

Total ignorance is preferable to knowledge that has lost its fundamental principle.

Gaston Bachelard, *The Formation of the Scientific Mind*, 1938

Fundamental means "serving as a basis supporting existence or determining essential structure or function," according to the dictionary. Even if this word is a bit imposing, this is how I like to present the three basic structures: **plain weave, twill, and satin**. They take center stage because all other structures are derived from them, with a few exceptions.

Weaving is an interlacing of threads. This means that one thread crosses other threads to be sometimes visible, sometimes hidden. **The intersections ensure solidity; the threads bring beauty.** The closer the binding points are, the stronger the fabric, but the less visible the thread is, the less it is highlighted. Conversely, the less frequent the binding points, the more the threads float on the fabric, the more visible they are, the more they show their characters, color, and material, the softer the fabric, but the less solid it is. Designing a weave consists in favoring either solidity of the fabric or highlighting of the thread! It is the essence of weaving to find the ideal compromise between these two criteria.

These three fundamental structures have their own specific features. They differ in **the number, order, and location of the binding points per basic unit as well as in the number and length of the floats**. I will now briefly introduce these three structures and then we'll look at them in detail.

Plain weave offers the most interlacings. Each thread, whether in warp or in weft, passes over and under a single other thread, systematically! The thread enters the scene to immediately dive backstage. Plain weave is solid, but we barely have time to see the thread. The intersections touch each other in all four directions.

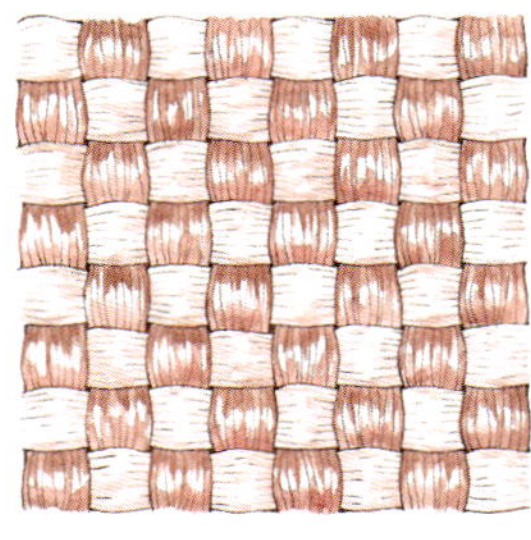

Figure 1 ***Plain weave interlacing***

Twill exposes a little more thread, but still provides good solidity. With a four-shaft loom, the thread can pass over 2 or 3 other threads, called 2- or 3-thread floats. Each interlacing adjoins only two other intersections in the diagonals, not four as in plain weave.

Figure 2 ***Twill interlacing***

Satin is a structure often associated with pomp and circumstance. Because no binding point is visible, satin leads us to believe that the yarns are laid next to each other, exposing the full range of their qualities, such as color and texture. Yet the intersections do exist, but they are spatially arranged in such a way that the floats can come close to each other and completely cover them. Note that floats in satin are not necessarily longer than those in twill. It is simply that the interlacings are no longer in contact with each other, allowing the floats to hide them. As a result, satin is a less solid fabric, but very soft and beautiful. To allow for distribution of the interlacings, a loom with at least five shafts is required. In this case, the weave unit is 5 warp, 5 weft threads, the binding points are set over by 2, and the order is 1 weft under warp, 4 weft over warp.

Figure 3 ***Satin interlacing***

The weaving of these three basic structures is absolutely square: 2 threads in warp and weft for plain weave, a minimum of 3 but often 4 in our weaves for twill, and a minimum of 5 for satin.

The other structures are also defined by the same parameters as these three fundamental structures: it is by **the number, the order, and the place of the interlacings**, and by **the number and the length of the floats** that they are grouped in families to better recognize them.

I find it particularly exciting that it is simply the place and number of binding points and/or the length and number of floats that open up a universe of such a variety of structures, just as the twenty-six letters of the alphabet open up a universe of literature.

Dynamic Plain Weave

Plain weave is the beginning structure, the oldest weaving structure, the most widespread, and still the most used. Eighty percent of the world's fabrics are made of plain weave.

It is the strongest fabric because it has the most interlacings possible. Each thread passes over and under its own neighbor, in warp and weft.

It is also the weaving of the beginner because this structure is easy to understand and the necessary material is elementary. Two shafts are sufficient, alternately lifting all even-numbered threads and then all odd-numbered threads.

Figure 4 ***Plain weave in silk and wool***

It is amusing to see how plain weave causes two very opposite reactions among weavers. Because it is simple, it is often considered as lowly. It is sometimes abandoned in favor of more complex structures that offer more diversity. The more numerous shafts invite a variety of threading, tying, and treadling. It is not uncommon to hear weavers apologize when praised for fabrics they have created by arguing that it is simply plain weave, as if the plain weave had no real value.

Conversely, other weavers, enthused by this simplicity, seek, invent, and—no longer having to think about structure and floats and blocks—concentrate on the materials and the colors. The "plainness" of the plain weave inevitably drives us to create. Everything must contribute to dress up this basic structure. We then take liberties by choosing different warp and weft threads with different thread counts and/or colors. The variety of yarns sometimes forces us to free ourselves from the balance of this weave, and never mind about differences in density between the weft and the warp! A few colorful yarns will become stripes that, depending on their arrangement, will bring softness or structure to a simple fabric. Similarly, incorporating more hairy, fuzzy, or thicker yarns of the same color will transform a basic plain weave, provided you balance these additions without overdoing it. Plain weave, a simple beauty that requires little makeup?

Figure 5 ***Plain weave with two mohair yarns with different yarn counts***

Plain weave can be transformed through the warp and/or weft. Inserting a slightly contrasting thread at regular intervals adds elegance to the fabric. We can also play with varying the density. This is easy to implement in warp thanks to the reed; it is trickier to pull off in weft with the beating.

Paradoxically, the plain weave is undoubtedly the most difficult structure to achieve, and teachers would approve a weaving student's plain weave in the days of weaving education. The slightest mistake was obvious. No random choices were made related to reed density, or beating the weft, or warp tension, and problems with selvedges were immediately pointed out. Consistency above everything!

Think about it every time you come back to your loom after an interruption, and beware of mood swings that will immediately impact your regular movements and be seen! Also make sure you advance your work often;

every inch or so, unwind a little bit of warp from the warp beam and wind your fabric at the front. This way, the warp tension, which increases with each weft pass due to the interlacing, will remain the same throughout the project. The distance between the beater and your fabric will remain approximately the same throughout the project, as will the strength you exert and the angle of the reed to the fabric. Every flaw in beating will be visible when held against the light and we will discover some kind of striping that will barely fade at all during washing.

One advantage to keep in mind when necessary: plain weave is very economical in its use of yarn. Indeed, this fabric has the maximum number of interlacings, so it requires a low density in warp and weft. The day we want to weave with a yarn that is precious to us or that we only have a small amount of, it is useful to think of plain weave.

Since for many decades all over the world this was the only possible structure, it is fun to now see the great diversity of fabrics that the industrial world has produced.

Plain Weave Fabrics

Depending on the type of yarn, or on its twist, or on the density in warp and weft, plain weave takes on different names, a real poem! There's more to it than meets the eye, so basic and yet so many variations!

Plain weave takes on different names when made from different materials. A plain weave in very fine linen is called batiste, from the name of the inventor of the process, Jean-Baptiste, a French weaver in the 17th century. A heavier plain weave fabric is called broadcloth. If made of linen, it is called lawn.

When made of cotton, it is called cretonne, after Paul Creton, another French weaver. Very sturdy and often printed, it was mainly used for furniture. It is called shirting when the warp threads are thicker. Percale owes its name to parkala, which means very fine cloth in Persian. It owes its lustrous appearance to its very tight structure, no less than 65 threads/cm^2, and a finishing treatment. This fabric is particularly appreciated for bed linens. Today, percale is made with a cotton/polyester blend, or with Lyocell. Also made of cotton, calico is a coarse plain weave. However, originally, calico referred to all cotton fabrics, even muslin imported from India or from Kozhikode (formerly Calicut), an Indian city. It is used for upholstery or furnishings or for patterns by pattern makers.

In silk, plain weave fabric is called taffeta. And depending on the type of silk, the arrangement of colors in warp or weft, also the number of threads in the shuttle, sometimes only by alternating a weft with an S-twist yarn and another with a Z-twist yarn, the collection of names grows: ombre taffetas, cameleon taffetas, chiné, crushed, moiré, bayadere, damier, or glacé taffetas. We are instantly transported into a world of luxury including high-end clothing, furniture, and décor. We are lucky enough to still be able to see and touch these marvels that dwell in our castles and certain interiors.

In Tours, Antoinette Roze runs the family business Jean Roze, which has been manufacturing silk for furnishings since 1650. The production of silk fabrics in Tours dates back to 1470, when Louis XI decided to set up a silk fabric factory in Touraine to counter the import of Italian silks. The Tours Cité de la Soie association is actively working on setting up a silk museum in the Loire Valley city. With the same intention of presenting the world of fabrics, the Musée des Tissus et des Arts Décoratifs in Lyon exhibits an unparalleled collection: 2.5 million pieces covering 4,500 years of textile production and honoring the history and know-how of the Lyon silk workers. A visit is not to be missed.

Figure 6 ***Taffeta, Tours Cité de la Soie collection. 18th-century lampas fabric made in Tours—Photo TCS***

Today, taffetas can be made from synthetic fibers. The weaving is very fine; the weight is 60 to 150 g/m^2. From silk and/or synthetic fibers, it is used for clothing, high-end or ready-to-wear, linings, furnishings, and home decor.

Poplin is a fabric where the warp threads are finer and closer together, so that the density of the warp is twice that of the weft. Made of cotton or mixed with polyester or silk, this weave is ribbed widthwise. It is widely used for shirts and blouses.

Muslins, originally woven in cotton, are now made of natural or synthetic thread. The name comes from Mosul in Iraq, where they were originally made. Depending on whether they are made of wool, cotton, or silk, their lightness varies. In wool, they are used for shawls; in cotton, for lightweight dresses. Silk muslin, for dresses or scarves, is of an incomparable lightness. The dress in fashion during the Restoration was from muslin, synonymous with romanticism. **Crepe de Chine** is woven with a raw silk warp and a weft with tightly twisted yarn. Two picks of Z-twist yarn alternate with two picks of S-twist yarn, each 2,200 twists/yard (2,400/meter). Weft trying to free itself from this strong twist causes its typical crepe texture, heightened by washing. Be aware that sometimes crepe only refers to a highly twisted thread, which is used to manufacture the crepe fabric. This is the case for silk organza, made of two, three, or four threads of raw silk which is S-twisted, then retwisted in a Z-twist. **Organdy** is also a muslin with fine and highly twisted threads. **Organza** is made with threads from which the sericin coating has not been removed, making it a stiffer fabric.

As its name suggests, **cheesecloth**, originally made of horsehair, is used in cheesemaking. It was then woven in cotton, silk, and wool. Used for furniture and clothing, it also has industrial uses. Loosely woven, it is made with highly twisted threads so that the roughness of the twists catch and hold the threads.

In worsted wool for the best qualities or carded and/or mixed with cotton for average quality, **flannel** undergoes a felting and brushing process called napping, which makes it softer and warmer. It originates from Wales, where the word wool is *gwlân* or *gwlanen*. Flannelette, in plain weave or twill, is a denser flannel.

Madras is a very colorful fabric; it was woven with cotton and banana threads. Originally from Madras, a city in southern India, now Chennai, it probably arrived in the West Indies with the immigration of those who came to replace the slaves after abolition. Then woven with silk in warp and cotton in weft, it is now mainly made of cotton.

It would be delightful and nostalgic to keep adding to this list of plain weaves, but I will stop with **chintz**. This printed cotton fabric was classified as an *Indienne*. Its colorful prints distinguish it from calico, chint meaning multicolored in Hindi. Chintz is also glazed to give it a glossy appearance. Previously done with agate stone, the process now uses silicone. In 1686, to protect French weavers, an edict prohibited the import of these *indiennes*, printed cotton fabrics from India. Their import was restored under Louis XV, and the first Oberkampf Manufactory was established in Jouy-en-Josas in 1760. Called "Toile de Jouy," one immediately imagines red or blue scenery printed on a white background with romantic and pastoral scenes. The factory had up to 58,000 workers in 1809 and closed its doors permanently in 1843. All kinds of contemporary fabrics are still called "Toile de Jouy" as long as the usual patterns are recognized. It is, however, sad to note that this rich vocabulary is lost in our fabric stores.

Let's Review: Plain Weave Explained

Two shafts are needed to separate the threads into two layers: even threads and odd threads. In each pick, the shuttle passes the weft thread over one warp thread, then under the next, systematically. The weave unit, i.e., the number of warp and weft threads that will consistently be repeated, is 2 warp ends and 2 weft picks. The binding points are offset or shifted by 1 from one pick to the next. They rhythm is 1: weft under one warp, weft over one warp. The weft crosses the fabric alternating going either over or under each warp end. Each of these interlacings strengthens the fabric and helps it to be very durable. No two adjacent threads ever follow the same path.

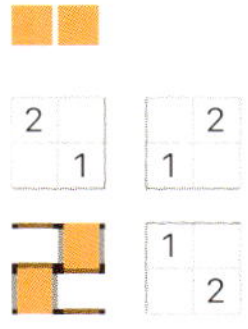

Figure 7 ***Weave unit of the fabric***

Nevertheless, even if 2 shafts are sufficient, it is preferable to weave with 4 or 8 shafts when possible, especially with fine threads or threads that cling together. This way, the number of threads is divided among all the shafts, the heddles not as close together so there is less wear and tear on the yarn due to friction. Honestly, with these particular threads, I recommend an "amalgamated" threading, not straight, on 4, 6, or 8 shafts, which distributes the threads much better by creating distance between them.

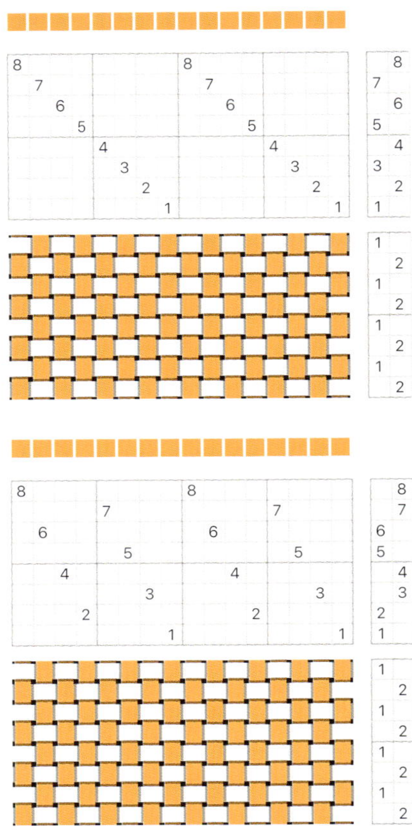

Figure 8 ***Straight and complex threadings***

With the same yarns in warp and weft, **the thread count is square, the weave is balanced. The warp and weft must have the same yarn count.**

Figure 9 ***Square thread count in plain weave vs. rectangular distortion***

The space between the threads must be perfectly square. To achieve this, the right warp density must be found in order to beat the right firmness to match this balanced density. If the warp density is too high, beating will not allow the weft to go where it should and we will see a kind of vertical rectangle. If the density is too low, the weft will slip a little too much in the fabric, and we will have a horizontal rectangle. To check the balance, it is really easier to count the number of warp and weft threads per square inch than to look at the little rectangle. I often use a thread-counting magnifying glass to check precisely, or I place a tape measure on the weave and check very, very often at the beginning of the weave, until my eye calibrates the weaving action. My experience has made me much more attentive to this balance of density in warp and weft. It's a simple way to weave comfortably. Knowing exactly how many wefts we need to weave per inch, there are no longer any questions to ask . . . as long as we have found the right density.

Plain weave wefts are sometimes combined with twill to make the weave sturdier. They are usually called **tabby picks**, and their role is to consolidate the weave by binding or interlacing the warp threads and thus limit the floats. Sometimes the tabby pick is used only for aesthetics, to highlight the weft or to lighten it. Depending on its use, it is made with a finer thread than the one used for the floats, or one in a different color. In some structures, plain weave is fully part of the weaving, which, depending on the sequence of the floats, will be called overshot, Summer and Winter, or crackle. The plain-weave ground cloth then forms a sort of framework, a grid on which the pattern floats will be placed. In these structures, I will not talk about tabby picks, since the fabric in question is a true plain weave. These picks woven in plain weave will be made with the same thread as the one used in warp, and the density to be found will be that of the plain weave, without thinking too much about the importance of the floats that will be placed on this plain weave.

Figure 10 ***Overshot floats in 266 Royal Linen 24/6 100% MERO pure fine linen placed on a linen plain weave***

Originally, tabby referred to a moiré silk fabric, the wavy effect created with ribbed rollers, mostly used in upholstery or bookbinding. The term "to tabby" was used to give the fabric a wavy volume effect. Al-Attabi is a district of Baghdad where this silk was manufactured. In English, *tabby* refers to both the coat of a tabby cat and this pick that goes between the pattern picks. In 1910, in his book *Hand-Loom Weaving*, Luther Hooper was probably the first to extend the term tabby beyond moiré taffeta.

Finally, tabby and taffeta are both plain weave, but the first refers to a plain weave when accompanied by pattern picks and the second is reserved for silk plain weave fabric.

How Is Plain Weave Made?

For any weaving project, the questions to ask are about choices concerning:

- **structure**;
- **yarn** (material, count, and color);
- **density**;
- **use** of the fabric.

The choice of **structure** is decided, as we are talking about plain weave.

The choice of **yarn** is the big door that opens up this structure because anything is possible. All yarns are suitable—all colors, all yarn counts. With no block or treadling requirements, use of a single color or many colors, and not necessarily yarn with the same qualities in warp and weft or the same yarn count, or the same colors, plain weave offers total freedom.

The choice of **density** depends on the choice of yarn. As much as the plain weave gives us complete freedom in the choice of yarn, the question of density requires us to be perfectly precise. During the learning process, to get comfortable with this technique, we will weave a plain weave with the same thread in warp and weft in order to work on balance, as plain weave is the balanced fabric par excellence and therefore a perfect teacher.

The choice of density is essential. Based on Thomas Ashenhurst's formula (see p. 45), the density of the warp is estimated by wrapping the yarn around a ruler. The threads should be positioned on the ruler depending on the use of the fabric, bringing them as close together as you would like them to be in the final project. Wrapped tightly for a seat cushion project, the threads should conversely be placed loosely to estimate the density of a shawl or wrap.

In the section on calculating density, we saw that in plain weave, interlacing is systematic. The yarn wrapped on our ruler represents half warp threads and half weft threads. We count the number of wraps per inch and divide by two. The number obtained determines the estimated density of the warp.

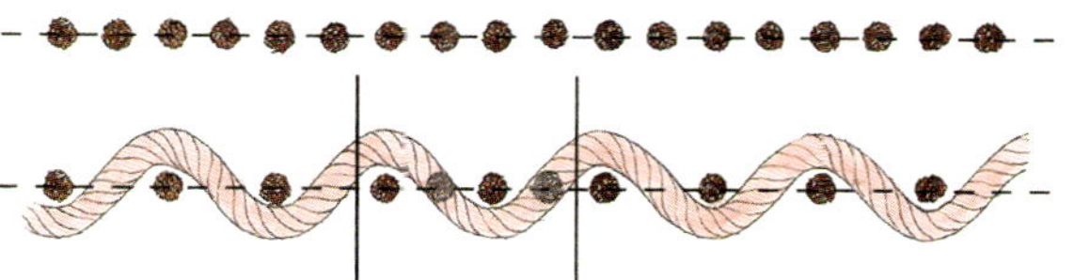

Figure 11 ***Plain weave interlacing and density***

A **sample** is essential to check that this choice of density is correct. To do this, weave the fabric, trying to obtain the same count in weft as in warp. The sample can be woven with a tape measure placed on the weave to verify this balance.

While weaving, we may get the impression that this weave is too loose, or on the contrary too tight. Don't forget that the threads are under tension! The effect will change a lot as soon as it comes off the loom, and just as much after washing. No premature judgment! As long as it is not washed, dried, or even ironed, a fabric is not finished. The yarn needs space to spread out; some become thicker, others lose their luster and open up a bit. It is only after all these steps that we can decide whether or not to change the density.

If you choose to re-sley, especially don't forget to use this new density in weft as well so that the weave is balanced again. And perhaps it will be necessary to make a new sample; you never know!

Welcome Creativity with Method

Because plain weave is a very wise structure, very even, where each thread systematically bypasses its neighbor, we often try to brighten it up in all sorts of ways. I would even dare to say that any idea is good, even one that initially just seems unreasonable; if it is interesting, it deserves to be tried Vary the colors, the yarn counts, the type of yarn in warp and/or weft, try a new density, etc.—the list is endless and will delight the innovative.

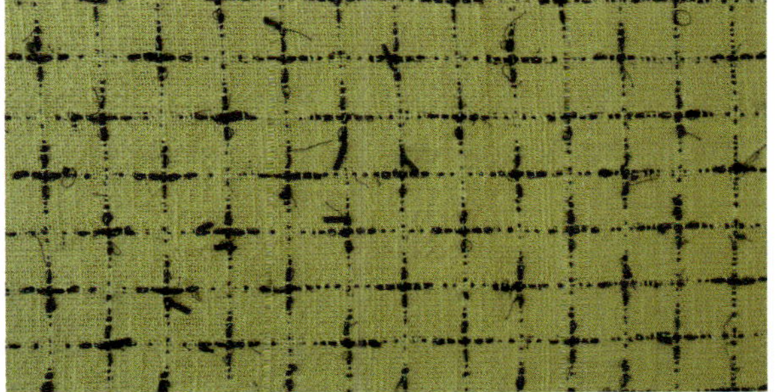

The question then is either to give free rein to one's creativity without second guessing, instinctively, or to think things out beforehand and draw out the whole project. It is important to take into account that as you weave, the weaving just made is rolled up on the cloth beam and is no longer visible, that we will never have an overall picture of the project before it's finished. We will resist the urge to unroll the fabric to see it all, as we would then take the risk of not rolling it back the same way and the point where we resumed weaving would very likely be visible. Go on an adventure, yes, but maybe not without a map. It is not useless to make a drawing of what you want. A simple sketch with a few colored pencils, to get an idea before starting, can do the trick. Or conversely, draw as you go and progress in the weaving to keep track.

For the more logical, a guide can be used for the order of changes, whatever they may be. There are a few iterations that are frequently used in art because they provide a restful and balanced pattern to the eye. Those who are intuitive or mathematically challenged should skip these few paragraphs. It will certainly scare them off! I know of others for whom these tips will save them a lot of time hemming and hawing.

Finding a basic "chord" and repeating or inverting it is a simple and effective way to invent a sequence. More easily, the diagrams below show the variations of colors, but we might imagine two different yarn counts or two different fibers. Alternating a thick yarn with a thin yarn following these iterations creates a nice effect.

The **Fibonacci** sequence can inspire you; it is a series of numbers in which each number is the sum of the two preceding it: 0, 1, 1, 2, 3, 5, 8, 13, 21, and so on. If you want to introduce a new yarn and make stripes following this order, we don't ask ourselves any questions and we make a stripe with 1 thread, then again 1, then 2, then 3, etc. We decide that the numbers refer to a ¼ inch or a centimeter rather than the number of threads. For example, 1 cm with the new color, 1 cm again, then 2 cm, then 3, and so on.

Figure 13 ***Stripes on a Japanese silk stole following the Fibonacci sequence***

There are other mathematical sequences that are sources of inspiration. The **Lucas** series is the Fibonacci sequence with 1 and 3 at the beginning (1, 3, 4, 7, 11, 18, etc.). The Pell numbers are the Fibonacci sequence with the sum of 2 times the preceding number and 1 times the one before that (0, 1, 2, 5, 12, 29, 70, etc.).

Weaving, because it is structured, has inspired people with a rational mind. Ada K. Diets, an American mathematics teacher, discovered weaving in 1946 and used her mathematical knowledge to create her own series. She developed (a+b)2 which becomes aa+ab+ab+bb. She placed thread "a" on shafts 1 and 2, and thread "b" on shafts 3 and 4. In another way, we can imagine that "a" is a group of two red threads and "b" is a group of two orange threads, with this order of colors, in warp and weft.

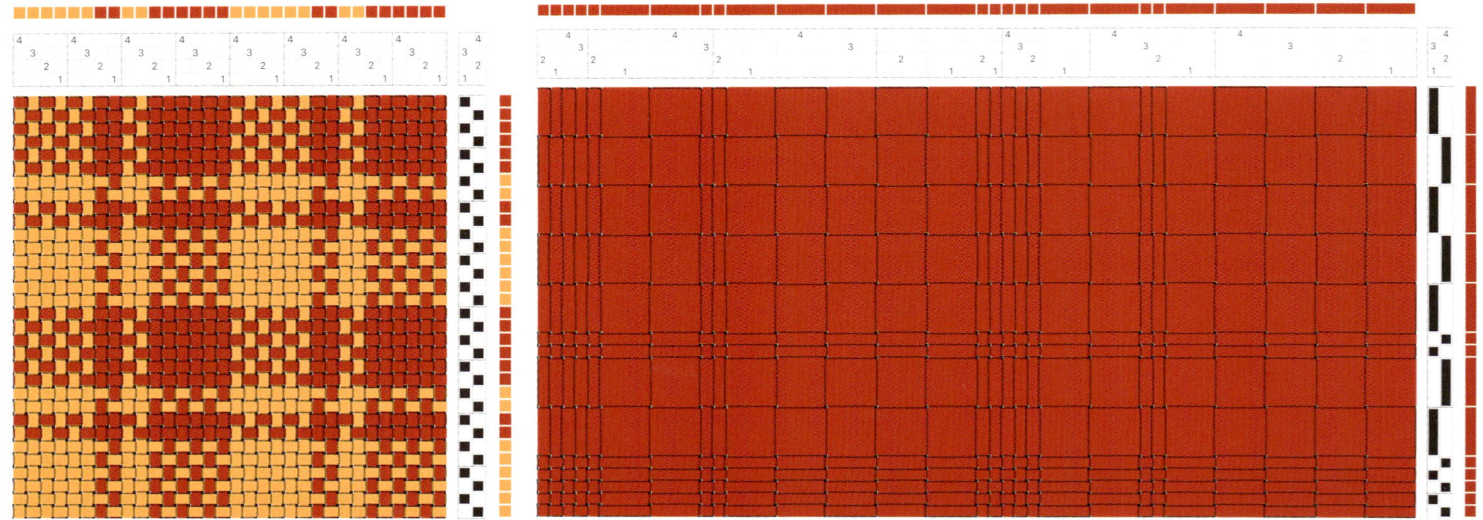

Figure 12 ***Basic rhythm in colors or thread counts, repeated straight or symmetrically***

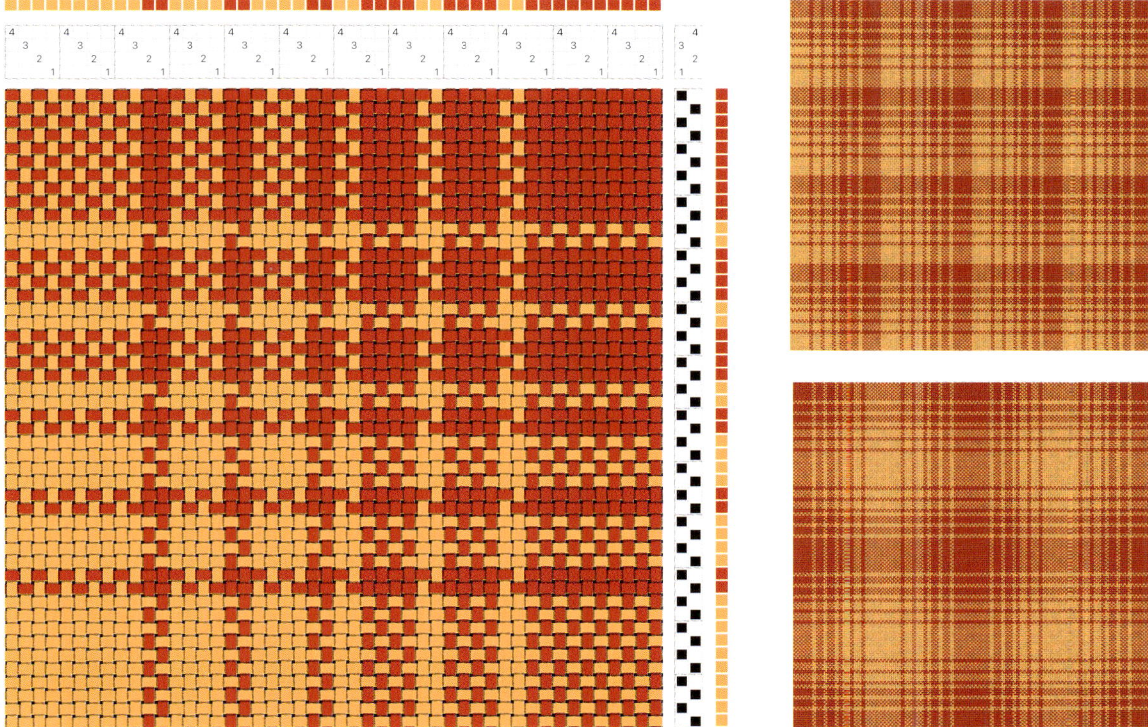

Figure 14 ***Inventiveness using the formula $(a+b)^3$ where the basic block is repeated or mirrored***

Of course, she tested other ideas. (a+b)3 produces a very different effect. Expanded, this formula gives aaa+aabaabaab+abbabbabb+bbb, keeping the same idea depending on whether "a" is placed on shafts 1 and 2 or a group of threads of the same color, and "b" on shafts 3 and 4 or the group of threads of the other color. Whatever the mathematics, we can use the suggestion without knowing its origin.

The basic block built on the development of the mathematical formula can be repeated straight or in mirror image.

For those who don't like numbers, let's play with letters. The idea is to use a code with letters, a little bit like games for children. We write a word and decide that the letter "A" corresponds to a ¼-inch stripe, "B" to ½ inch, "C" to 1 inch, "D" to 2 inches, "E" to 2½ inches, and then back to ¼ inch for the letter "F." The idea is to take a fairly short word and repeat it either sequentially or in mirror image. Let's take the letters of the word MUSIC from their place in the alphabet.

¼ in.	a	f	k	p	U
½ in.	b	g	l	q	v–w
1 in.	C	h	M	R	x
2 in.	d	I	n	S	y
2½ in.	e	j	o	t	z

Then let us give the stripes the widths indicated in this table in the order of the letters of the word MUSIC to determine the distribution of each color.

Figure 15 ***Each letter of the word MUSIC has a corresponding stripe color and width.***

It's up to you to invent your own code if it helps you to structure a new idea. This is only a guide to go along with some research. You can do with it what you want!

Playing with Colors

I suggest you go back and read the section in Chapter 2, "Fabrics: Behind the Scenes" (p. 36), having with you the wools and other yarns you wish to weave. Then test by winding the yarns you have selected around a small piece of cardboard to see how the colors resonate with each other. Try primary and/or secondary colors, arrange stripes with yarns of very similar hues, but lighter or darker, choose to combine a set of warm colors with a blue yarn, or include a color that you like less, interspersing it with other colors you instinctively like. The effect can be very pleasant. Of course, you can also change the look of a color you want to be dominant by framing it with other colors to test Chevreul's law of simultaneous contrast of colors; a color will stand out more or on the contrary will be softened depending on the colors that surround it. Or lines of dark colors give the impression they stand out when they are placed on a plain light background, while light lines will appear to be recede if they are surrounded by dark lines.

Figure 16 ***Vary the effect the colors have by playing with their placement.***

You can choose a single color for the warp and another single color for the weft, resulting in what will look, from a distance, like a solid color. This fabric is called Chambray. You may prefer to use wide or thin repeated stripes, or use some of the iterations previously presented for inspiration. Don't forget that you can take a black-and-white photo to check the harmony of the values. Remember also that the high number of interlacings in plain weave prevents the yarn from taking center stage. The more substantial it is, the more our eye will decipher its color. Too many fine yarns of different colors will be seen as a somewhat solid hue; our eye will not distinguish the nuances, and the effect will become drab.

Another very pleasant method is to dye the threads that we want to use. There are techniques for dyeing warp and/or weft that you can use to create beautiful fabrics, such as resist-dyeing or tie-dyeing, or using plants that leave an imprint from their tannins, and many other methods. It is fun to dye one's own yarns in order to add a personal touch. This area is beyond the scope of this book as there are so many processes to present, but don't hesitate to feel free to try it out sometime. Some instructors offer courses as an introduction to *ikat*, *shibori*, and *bogolan*, without having to go to the other side of the world, which is nonetheless very tempting. There are a lot of skills and expertise to be learned in Southeast Asia, Africa, and Central America. I admire these people, some of whom are considered as great masters in their country; they spend an immense amount of time in the preparation of yarns to then weave real masterpieces. Catherine Legrand, a great traveler and textile collector, reveals the skills and artisans from Japan to Peru, by way of Madagascar, Finland, or China, notably in her books *Indigo: The Color That Changed the World* and *Textiles: A World Tour*.

Less engaging, there is a process that I find particularly fun and simple to undertake. It involves painting the warp threads while they are stretched on the loom, as they are unwound, with fabric paint. These colors are applied either freehand or using stencils. Wooden wedges are inserted, protected by plastic, so that the threads are "laid" on this hard surface that will be used as support during painting. It is also possible to select certain warp threads by lifting some of the shafts and painting only those threads, protecting the others with a plastic sheet. Easy to implement, the result is very subtle. We choose a uniform weft, so that only the warp threads show a little color.

Figure 17 ***Painting with stencils on warp with straight threading on 4 shafts***

Weaving with colors is a continuous surprise, and it is difficult to anticipate the result. Indeed, not only does interlacing interfere with the yarn's ability to reflect light, but the quality of the yarn also counts: length of the fiber, twisting of the strands, permeability to dyes. A highly twisted yarn reflects light more easily, which is why mercerized cotton is very bright. Long fibers have more surface exposed to light. Thus, a wool with long combed fibers will have brighter colors. Silk has a very high water retention capacity. It therefore absorbs dye very deeply. Moreover, this fiber is very long and often strongly twisted. It is undoubtedly one of the most brilliant yarns.

To summarize, color on a plain weave can play tricks on us. But it is above all a beautiful way to make discoveries. There are bound to be some very pretty, unexpected, unusual ones. And there will certainly be some that you will be happy with.

Playing with Yarn Thickness

The character of this simple structure can be heightened by using yarns of different sizes. You can choose to incorporate a slightly thicker or thinner thread in the warp and/or weft. It can be the same color or a different color. Again, depending on the desired effect, you may want to go for softness or some shine.

If you double or triple a yarn from time to time, I recommend that, to keep this stripe uniform, you should thread these yarns in two or three different heddles on the same shaft, so they do not overlap, and so their placement always stays the same and the volume appears the same. If they are threaded together, they would twist as the weaving progresses, giving a more adventurous effect.

Choosing the right density with yarns that have different yarn counts requires a little thought at the outset. The idea remains the same, to **leave room for the weft yarn between the warp ends** so that it is neither too tight nor too loose. To estimate the density, we wrap all the threads used in warp and weft around the ruler according to their proportion in the weaving, and probably over a few inches, to then calculate the average.

To help understand, I propose you test this out. Let's say you are imagining using a fairly **fine warp yarn** and a **yarn two or three times as thick in weft**. You are going to surround the ruler with these two threads, alternating a thick thread and a thin thread over 2 inches. Count how many warp threads you have, then divide by 2 to get the average over 1 inch. The number obtained is the density of the warp and weft that you will use for your sample. Does this number seem low? Then you have forgotten that the weft threads will take up the space thus freed up!

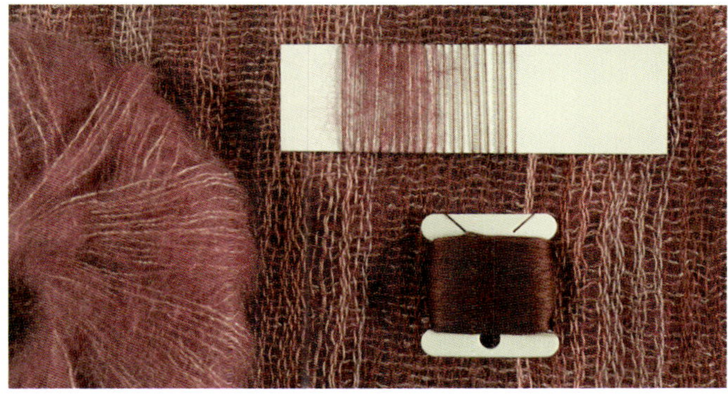

Figure 18 ***Warp 20/2 tencel and weft French mohair***

Playing with the Type of Yarn

Yarns react differently to weaving and then to washing. This is an effect you may want to take advantage of. When combining wool yarns with cotton yarns, little happens when they are woven, but when washed, they express their characters. If the wool felts, it will shrink, while its cotton neighbor will not be moved. This is an easy way to obtain fabrics that will make little waves if the threads concerned are only in warp or in weft. The fabric will bubble with alternating characteristics in both directions.

On the market, there are now yarns where strands of cotton are spun with a strand of Lycra. Integrating such yarns that are known to become elastic when washed opens up new horizons. These threads are relatively easy to use as long as you tie them together each time you cut them; otherwise the Lycra will twist around itself like a clown popping out of its box. The more daring will use real elastic threads. Using these on their own makes winding and beaming the warp a real challenge. I'll let you imagine using this thread as weft, alternating with the other yarn chosen for the warp. I assure you it is possible . . . but not easy!

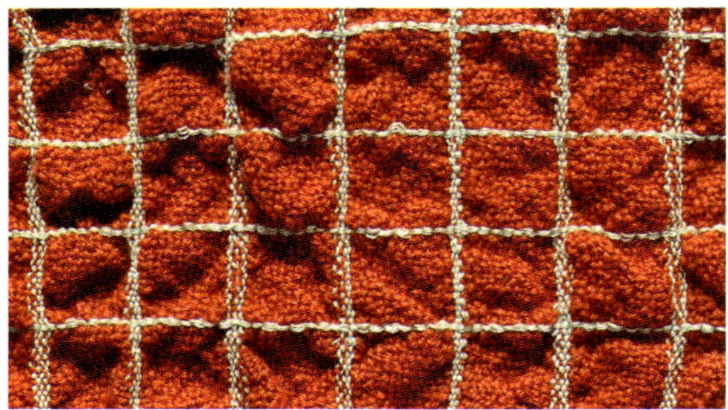

Figure 19 ***Plain weave, 4 shafts. Warp and weft Venne Colcolastic 34/2, Fonty Zephir wool***

Alternating two threads in warp and weft with opposite directions of twist, or an S-twist thread in warp and a Z-twist in weft, brings a small, subtle variation—on the one hand, because the threads will attract or repel each other; on the other hand, because the direction of reflection of the light will be different. Once again, a world opens up; just try it—anything is possible.

There are also novelty yarns that harmonize quite easily with the very even plain weave. Some yarns change color or size as they unwind. You just have to make sure that they pass easily through the teeth of the reed without too much wearing due to friction. If you are vacillating, it is always preferable to use a reed with a lower density and to put two threads in the same tooth; it's less risky.

Playing with Density

A very simple way to play with density is not to use the same density over the whole width of the weave. In some areas, the density is adapted to the yarn chosen; in others, the density is higher or, conversely, lower. To do this, we skip a few dents in the reed over a small portion of the width and/or we put several threads per dent in the adjacent area.

Figure 20 ***Plain weave with irregular structure. MERO 266 Royal Linen Nm 24/6 100% pure fine linen***

It is certainly a little more difficult to deal with this same unevenness in weft. "All" you have to do is press more or less firmly with the beater. If you want to reproduce the same spacing between several picks, you can slip small strips of cardstock to hold the wefts in place and remove them at the end of the weaving.

Chances are that these spacings will move over time with repeated use or washing. But a mark will certainly always remain. Of course, some yarns will stay in place better than others. It is illusory to want to succeed at this with viscose.

It is also possible to weave the entire width with the same density, but using different types of yarns or ones with different yarn counts; the fine yarns will let more light through while the others will appear darker. Reproducing this variety in the weft while respecting the density of the warp will still require some attention to sometimes beat normally and sometimes beat more gently.

However, this does not mean bringing too great a variety of elements, either in the type of yarn or its color or size. Too much going on may kill the desired effect. Your plan should be checked beforehand with a large enough sample to visualize the result. On the other hand, if the changes are very soft, or repeated very often, they liven up the fabric. For example, weaving the whole thing with two colors very close on the color wheel will bring a fineness to the fabric, with one color in warp and the other in weft. Or, if wool and cotton are woven one after the other for each pick, the waffle effect will be so soft that the fabric will appear barely wrinkled.

Stripes, Plaid, Log Cabin, and Other Color Effects

Weft stripes are easy to insert when inspiration strikes, while warp stripes need to be planned when winding the warp. When the two are combined, you get the famous plaid, regardless of the width of the columns or rows of colors, or their order.

When the colors and size of the stripes alternate in a consistent, identical pattern in warp and weft, you get a small checkered pattern, one of which is the very popular houndstooth, although this name is more correct when the weaving is a twill.

By systematically alternating two colors, and changing this order from time to time, we enter the category of color effect weaves. Shadow weave, color-and-weave effects, log cabin . . . , it really doesn't take much to transform this plain weave into a kaleidoscope.

Let's wind two contrasting warp yarns, take two shafts, and thread the heddles by systematically alternating even shaft and odd shaft. All that's left is to determine which colors and which order. For fun, I suggest you experiment with a few test runs on the same weaving to see how they look. Follow the example on the diagram below, in which I chose three color sequences. For the weft, you will choose at first to follow the same color sequence as in the warp. In this diagram, I show the treadling for the famous log cabin, where the sequence is only broken when repeating the red, in warp and weft.

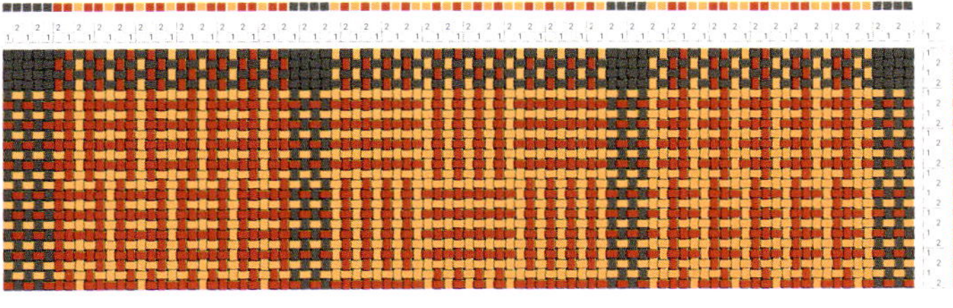

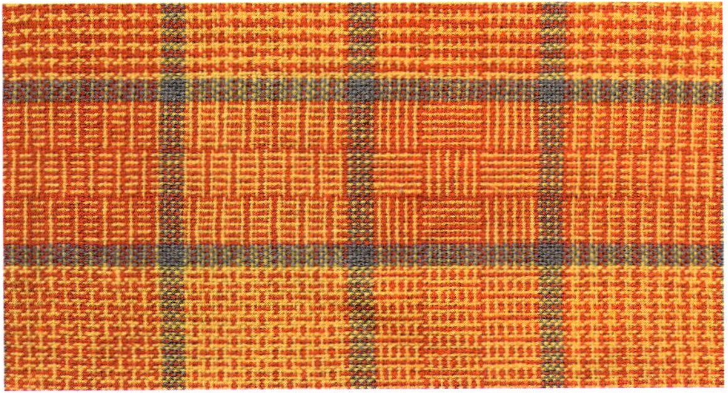

Figure 21 ***Color effects in plain weave, 4 shafts. Venne 22/2 Cottolin***

There is no obligation to follow these repetitive sequences. There is only one rule to follow: this is a plain weave. So, as much as your creativity can play with the colors, each thread must be threaded in a shaft the opposite of the preceding one: even shaft, odd shaft! 2 shafts, 4 shafts . . . .

If you like this technique, you can test it by alternating, not threads of contrasting colors, but threads of contrasting yarn count or fibers.

Figure 22 ***Color effect in Fonty Zephir wool, 3,720 yd/lb (7,500 m/kg)***

Log cabin or shadow weave can be made on a rigid heddle loom. We will see later that these alternating colors are just as noticeable with twills. Even in plain weave, their effects are simply magical!

Supplementary Yarn, Interchanging Warp, and Other Manipulations

Plain weave is such a simple structure, so basic, that it invites some embellishment. I am always very moved when looking at fabrics throughout history. Generations of men and women have sought to embellish this fabric in every way possible. For everyday people around the world, this was the way to combine the beautiful with the useful, setting aside daily tasks to spend ages making a special garment precious with ordinary materials. This is how clothes intended for a religious celebration were transformed into ornamentation. I also imagine our grandmothers embroidering linens thinking about a boyfriend, future children, a beautiful family, their future life.

It is for these same reasons, but with much more splendor, that religious or political leaders had sumptuous fabrics made that were nothing more than plain weave or taffeta—a taffeta with a jacquard or fancy woven design, such as damask, brocatelle, or velvet. To satisfy increasingly complex needs, we began to invent machines, but at the beginning, it was all done by hand and manipulating the threads with the fingers or some very simple tools like bars, originally from bone. Today, the shafts have been multiplied and the jacquard loom invented, which automatically makes the weavings.

Supplementary Warp or Weft

The idea of a supplementary warp or weft is simple: with your fingers, you add a thread as inspired, sliding it into the open shed over the whole width or only part of it. You can wind the yarn into a butterfly "bobbin," or use little bobbins for knitting color work or for kumihimo. For more elaborate patterns, we use small shuttles like those for silk weavers. I also use needles for mending fishing nets. It is easy to construct a geometric pattern by repeating the plain weave in certain areas with these supplementary threads. A bright or contrasting thread gives the beautiful effect of a brocade.

Figure 23 ***Wrap in French Mohair with supplementary threads inserted by hand***

With a multishaft loom, some supplementary warp is threaded in shafts that are not used for the plain weave. This will make the handwork go faster. But the shape is more geometric. In this example, the plain weave was divided into two blocks, and the supplementary warp is on shafts 5 and 6.

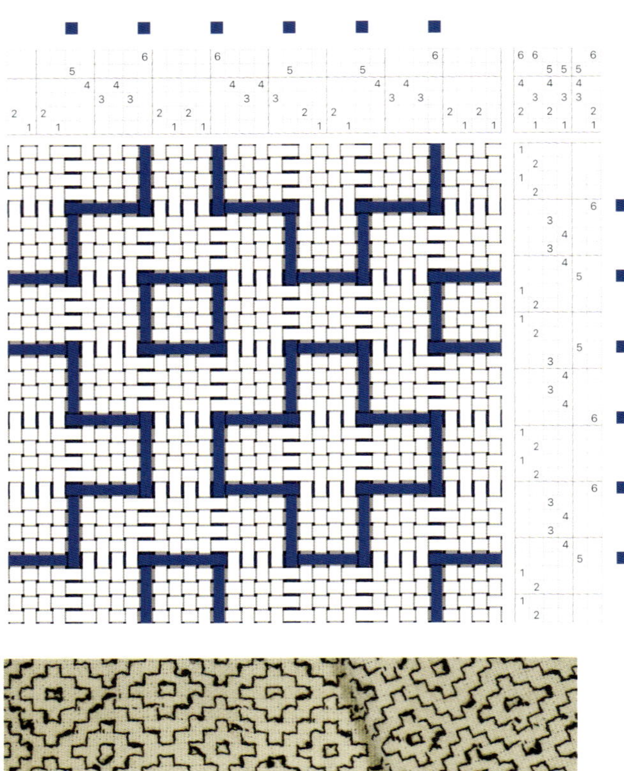

Figure 24 ***Plain weave with supplementary warp threaded***

Interchanging Warp

Without the assistance of shafts, many people have been able to weave patterns by adding warp ends underneath the weave, making them appear as needed by switching the real warp thread with the one underneath. This is a technique used by North African women to highlight colors from time to time in their rugs. The method of Peruvian women with their belt loom is not very different. In one strip, the two warp threads are switched around when needed according to the pattern. Suggestions made for rigid heddle looms or inkle looms can provide plenty of inspiration. Or you can even check out books devoted to braid and band weaving by Anne Dixon, *The Weaver's Inkle Pattern Directory* (2012, Interweave), and Barbro Wallin, *Moraband* (2012, Zorn Museum), which are true references.

Manipulating the Yarn

Again, there are many, many methods, and I would recommend browsing through the books on rigid heddle looms. Making knots, twists, adding threads or beads, embroidering to make openwork, adding a scalloped accent . . . the list is long. Some have their own name: Spanish lace, Italian festoon stitch, the Brooks bouquet, hand Leno, or the Swedish medallion, among others.

Clasped Weft, a Simple Way to Add Color

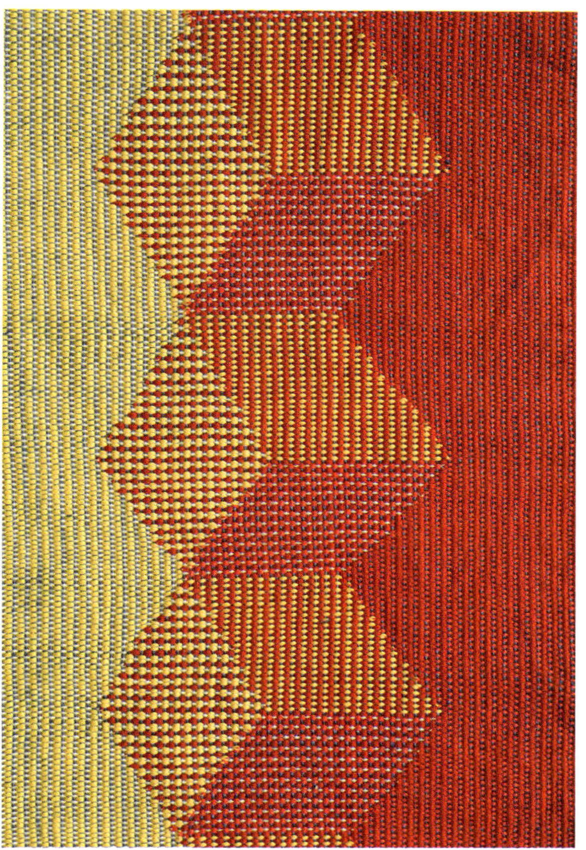

Figure 25 ***Clasped weft, 4 shafts. 266 Royal Linen 24/6, MERO 100% pure fine linen***

A clasped weft is one that does not go from selvedge to selvedge, but which loops around a second thread of another color coming from the opposite selvedge. To make it simple, place a spool or cone of yarn on the left side of the loom, pass your shuttle from right to left through the shed, then loop the shuttle around the yarn you placed on the left to grab it and draw it into the shed from the left to the right. Gently tug on one or both yarns to move the point where the two yarns are linked together to the place you want it in the fabric. Then we change the shed and start again. This system has the disadvantage of doubling the weft; it's something to think about when choosing the weft yarn. Either we accept that the new weft is twice as thick or we use other yarn twice as thin. This method can be used with all structures.

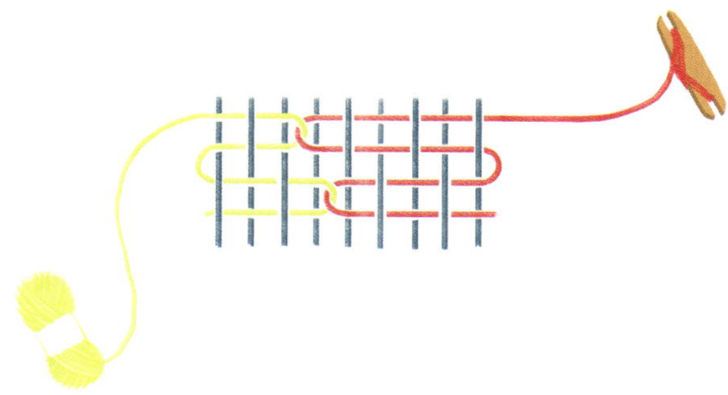

Figure 26 ***Interlacing of the two wefts***

By Way of Conclusion

Plain weave can be made with two shafts. But as soon as possible, try to set up the threading onto 4 or more shafts to avoid too much friction. The larger number of shafts also offers the possibility of dividing the threads into blocks, some on the first two shafts for example, and the others on the last two, to facilitate the interchanging of threads.

I will reserve a special spot later in the book on the technique developed by Theo Moorman, for the same reason, that having a good understanding of floats is essential to work more easily. This weaver wished to be able to weave in total freedom without the constraints of tapestry. She developed a very personal technique that allowed her to depict her inspirations in weaving. Like a kind of lampas, but not really.

Plain Weave Derivatives: Changing the Tempo

Jazz is swing, a way of interpreting the tempo even if it is binary; who can say where it starts and where it stops?

Didier Lockwood, jazz violinist

In this new section, we are going to leave behind pure plain weave, meaning the systemic alternating of odd and even threads, or the search for a balanced structure. We are going to introduce variations in density of warp and/or weft, or allow neighboring threads to be lifted together. In warp or in weft, changing the number of adjacent threads or changing the density is so easy and makes such a wide variety of fabrics possible that there is a very large number of terms for them. Let's try not to get lost among all the names of fabrics made by silk makers and the more or less precise translations of terms coming from all over the world

Cannelé or *cannetillé*, faille, ottoman, louisine, **basketweave**, etc. These names make me dream. **It is the number of adjacent threads in warp or weft crossing above or below the other that distinguish these structures.**

When we talk about **variations in density**, we speak of **reps** or **ribs**, **cords**, or ***repps***, etc., then there is **boundweave**, **weft rep weave**, or ***krokbragd***. To avoid misunderstandings or disagreements, I will speak of weft or warp reps.

Derivatives Due to Number of Threads

Figure 27 ***Louisine, basketweave, and cannelé, 4 shafts. Venne 22/2 Cottolin***

We saw earlier in this chapter that we could incorporate thicker threads into a basic plain weave to add a structural effect. Here, we'll take that action a step further by using identical threads but playing on a variation in threading, tie-up, or treadling.

Louisine

This structure resembles a plain weave in which the warp thread is thicker. This is done by threading two or three warp ends on the same shaft or by attaching the shafts to the treadles so that the adjacent threads rise together in the case of straight threading. Each weft is systematically different, contrasting. The result is a fabric with a slightly different grain than that of a plain weave.

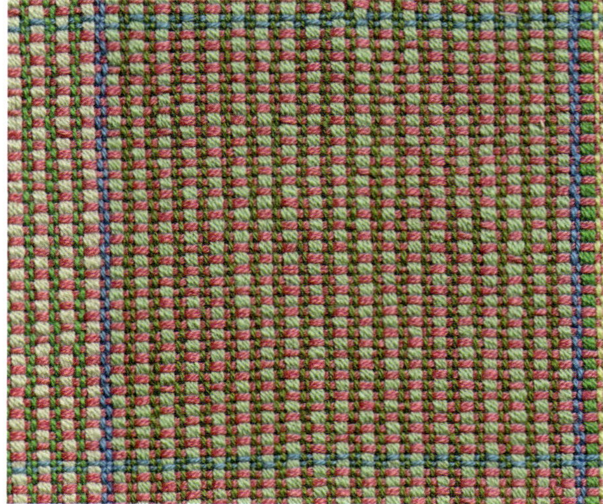

Figure 28 ***2/1 Louisine, 4 shafts. Venne 22/2 Cottolin***

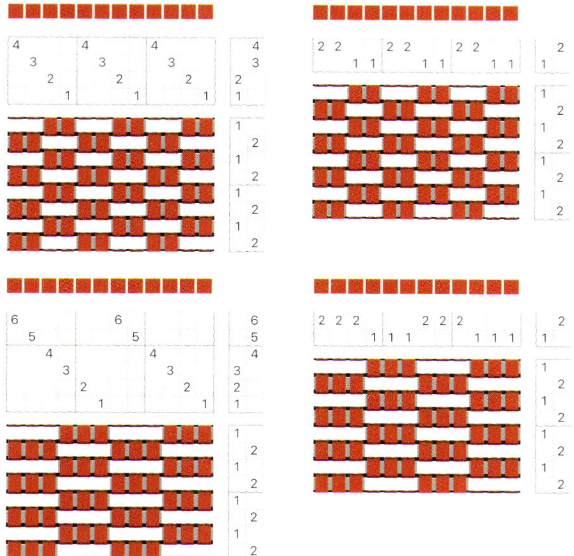

Figure 29 *2- and 3-end Louisine on 2, 4, or 6 shafts*

Cannelé

This is the same principle but in weft. This time, several wefts are inserted in each shed while each warp end is solitary. Horizontal ridges extend across the fabric covered by warp floats. Cannelé fabric is named according to the number of picks in each of the ribs or ridges. Gros de Tours is a 2/2 cannelé woven in silk.

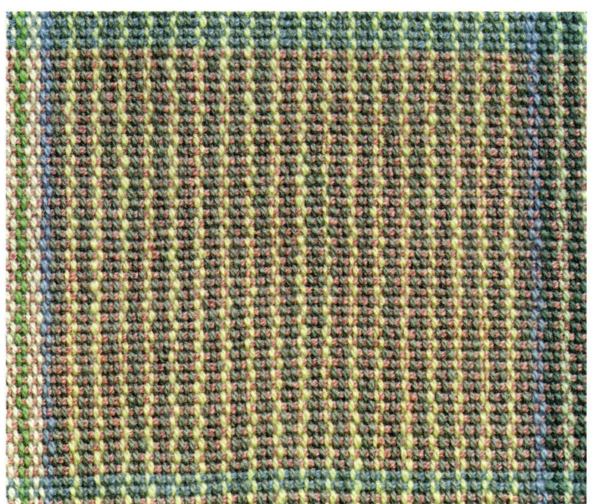

Figure 30 *2/2 Cannelé, 4 shafts. Venne 22/2 Cottolin*

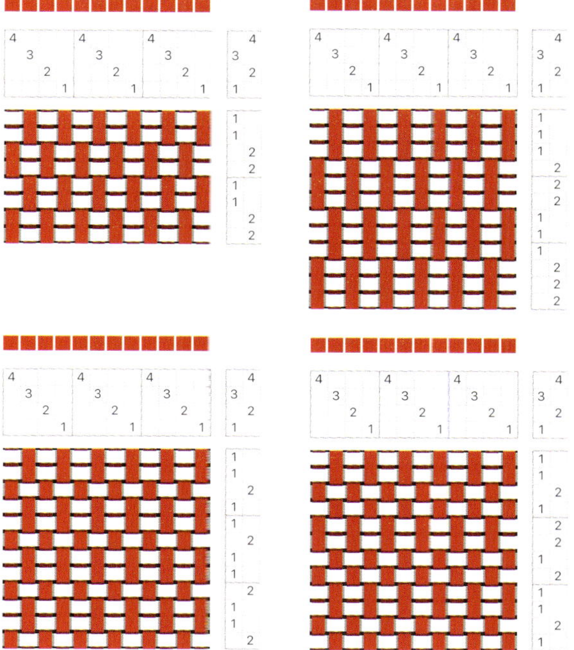

Figure 31 *2/2, 3/3, 2/1, and 2/1/1 Cannelés*

French faille is a derivative of these cannelés, woven with two warps, one making the rib and the other making the binding points. **Ottoman** resembles faille but with uneven ribs.

Basketweave

Basketweave is a combination of the two previous structures; it has the same balance as a plain weave, but expanded. Each warp end and each weft thread are doubled or tripled. In other countries, it is called *natté*, **panama**, or hopsack. A number is added to describe the number of threads grouped together.

Figure 32 *3/3 Basketweave, 4 shafts. Venne 22/2 Cottolin*

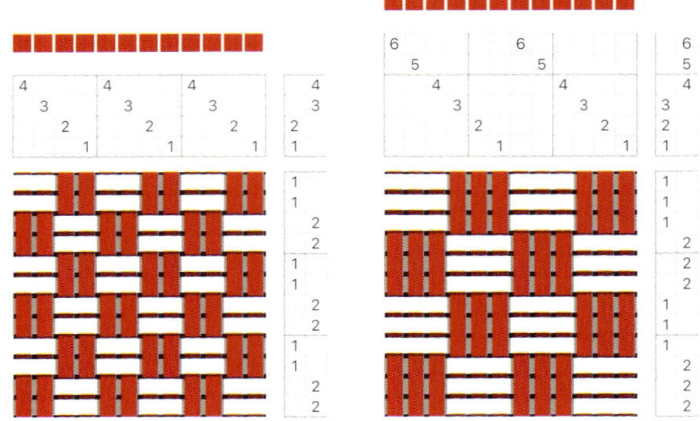

Figure 33 2/2 and 3/3 basketweaves

It is sometimes very interesting to thread in point twill because, this way, a binding point can be inserted, invisible under the floats but giving the fabric better stability. This method also greatly simplifies selvedge work, since with this binding point, having triple weft picks or even more is no longer a problem.

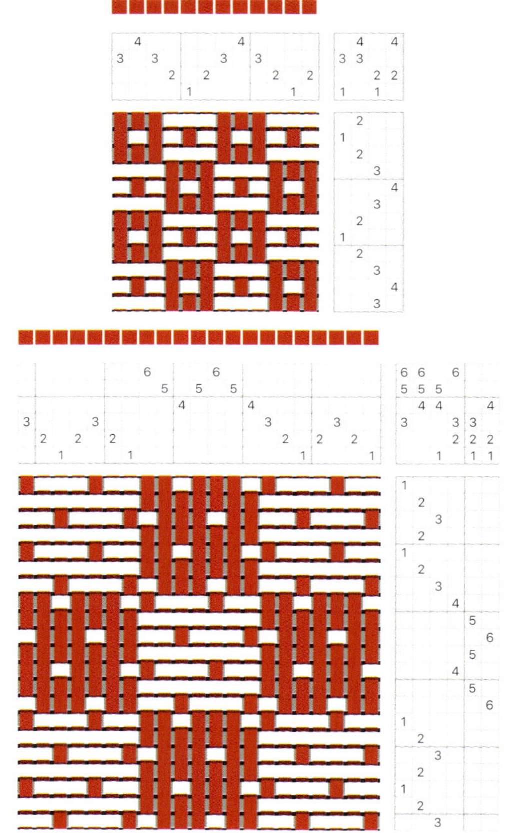

Figure 34 2/2 basketweave and 6/6 basketweave with interlacing

Many variations are conceivable as soon as you change the ratio between the number of threads crossing above or below. Some of them are listed and have a name.

Don't be satisfied with the ones presented here. It's up to you to invent; it's easy and without risk. Some weavers consider that this is not really basketweave. The important thing is to enjoy this weave in that it is very structured, visual, flexible, and has multiple uses depending on the yarn and density chosen.

Technical Aspects of Threading or Density: Staying in Harmony

Because we want each thread to keep its independence and not get so close to its neighboring float that it gets wrapped up in it, we recommend that **each warp end be threaded in a different heddle**, even if they are on the same shaft, so that each one stays in its place.

Sleying will contribute to this voluntary and necessary separation of the warp ends. Two shafts are sufficient, but it is preferable to weave in four or six shafts to avoid the heddles being too close together, especially if the density is very high with fine threads.

For **the weft**, the shuttle will be thrown several times in the same shed. The work is more tidy if a double boat shuttle is used to prevent the threads from overlapping. The idea and the attention remain the same as in warp: each thread in its place without getting entwined with the one next to it. No need to prepare your shuttle with several threads together in advance! Threading selvedges in single plain weave help to obtain a nice border, which is more complicated with multiple threads. Putting in **floating selvedges** is a must.

This family of structures is built based on a plain weave but with units of threads per group. Therefore, we look for a balanced density in warp and weft.

Beware, this fabric will be softer than its close cousin the plain weave because there is less interlacing than in the real plain weave. Therefore, its density is similar to that of twill; threads float over several adjacent threads. This can be verified with Ashenhurst's formula (p. 45).

Let's take an example with a 22/2 cottolin. Forty threads can be wound on 1 inch (2.5 cm) on a ruler. Let's do the calculation for a 2/2 basketweave and for a plain weave. The weave unit of the plain weave is 2 warp and 2 weft yarns. The full weave unit for basketweave is 4 warp and 4 weft yarns, the same as for a twill.

The formula for **plain weave** is:

$$D = \frac{40 \times 2}{2 + 2} = 20$$

the density to choose is 20 threads per inch (2.5 cm).

The formula for **basketweave is**:

$$D = \frac{40 \times 4}{4 + 2} = 26.67$$

so we will choose a density of 26.5 threads per inch (2.5 cm).

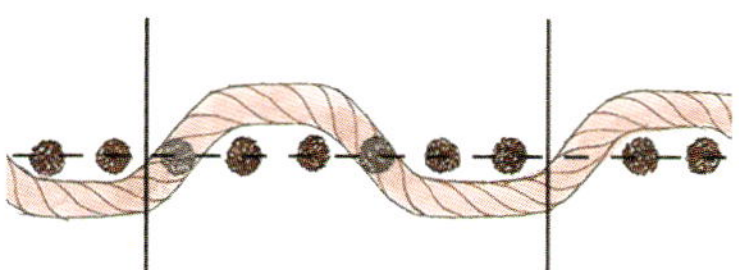

Figure 35 *Weave unit for basketweave*

To put it simply, most of the time, the density of twill will be suitable for the basketweave.

This is important to know when you want to alternate strips of twill and plain weave in warp. In this case, we will change the density according to the weaving chosen: we will alternate parts in plain weave with 20 threads per inch with parts in basketweave at 26.5 threads per inch. Otherwise, the proximity of two different structures would lead to a kind of crumpling of the weave and a waving of the selvedges.

As always, the choice of density is important. Here, you have to look for the combination of the softness of the floats and the solidity of the fabric . . . Sampling is essential!

When working on a weave pattern effect, it is preferable to use the same yarn in warp and weft, which will give a simple, soft, even sumptuous fabric. The light is not reflected in the same way on basketweave floats as on plain weave; these regular interruptions bring real structure.

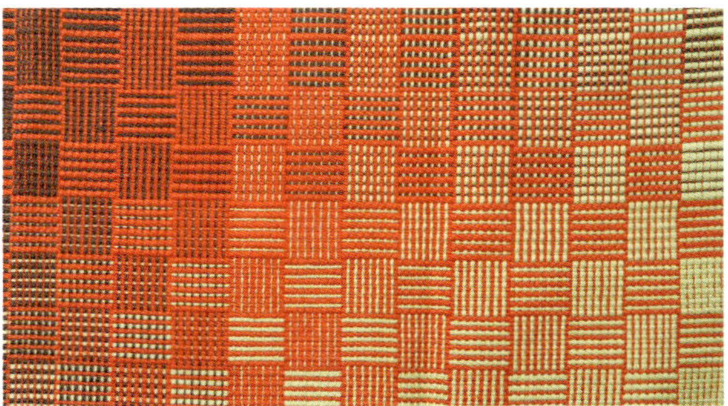

Derivatives Due to Density—The Rep Family

When changing the density of plain weave, everything changes. When the warp and weft counts are no longer identical, the fabric is no longer balanced. Pushing this difference to the extreme, the warp threads can be so close together that they will completely cover the weft. Conversely, by choosing a very low warp density, the threads are so far apart that they are hidden by the weft at each shuttle passage.

Well established in Scandinavia, weft rep rugs were often used to recycle old fabrics by preparing them in strips that became wefts. This is known as a *lirette*, or rag rug.

Some details about terminology are necessary once again.

The rep or rib (or *repp* or *reps*) designates the same weaving with a few variations. So, some more translation stories. With rep, the warp and weft threads do not intertwine so much, but go around each other. In warp reps, the warp completely covers the weft, which stays horizontal, supporting the warp ends. In contrast, in weft reps, the warp barely undulates and it is the weft that goes around the warp ends, covering them completely. We will see later that this is very important in calculating take-up or shrinkage which, unlike plain weave, is not identical in warp and weft.

The term "rib" is also used to describe a weave where the thread count is different in warp and weft. When the warp yarn is thicker, we see some kind of vertical ribs. Conversely, when weaving in a thicker weft, the ribs appear horizontal. Rib shows an interlacing with a more visible yarn. But in many books, rib and rep mean the same thing.

Depending on the region and/or the technique, the name for reps or ribs changes. For simplicity's sake, I will call them warp-faced reps when only the warp is visible, and weft-faced reps when only the weft is visible. In books you will sometimes find rag rug or cannelé or boundweave or *krokbragd*.

Warp-Faced Reps

Warp-faced reps is a plain weave in which the density is so high that the warp yarns completely cover the weft yarns. It is therefore the arrangement and color scheme of the warp threads that will make the pattern. The weft serves as a binding.

Figure 36 *Warp reps, 4 shafts. Venne 22/2 Cottolin*

Conventionally, a thick weft is alternated with a thin weft. The thick weft highlights the warp threads and reveals their color.

This weave has ridges, like speed bumps next to each other. Depending on the thickness of the weft, the bumps will be more or less plump. This structure is often used for rugs or placemats.

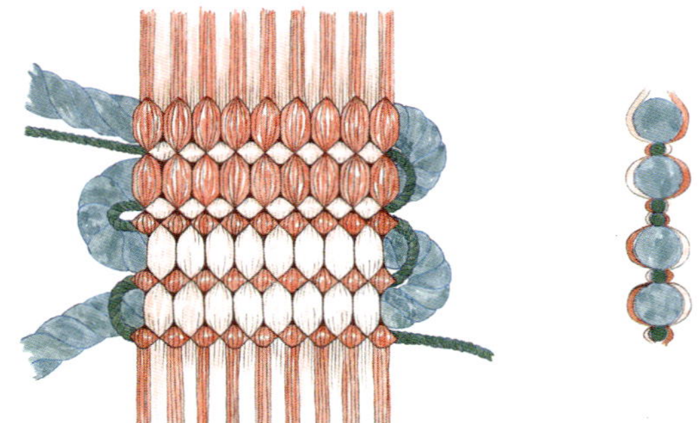

Figure 37 ***Warp reps***

We don't want to see the weft yarn, so the warp threads are very close together to hide them. They have a real tendency to catch on each other behind the heddles or between the heddles and the reed. This sometimes makes it difficult to open the shed. To alleviate this problem, we use "amalgamated" threading, trying to spread out adjacent threads as far as possible in separate shafts.

Warp reps are easier to achieve on a deep, solid loom, where the space between the shafts and the weaving area is larger, allowing the threads to separate and lift more easily. On these looms, the warp can also be tightened more firmly, which will help. On the other hand, it will often be necessary to free the warp from the warp beam, because going around the thick weft consumes a lot of warp. A balance must be found between tension to separate the warp ends and flexibility to let the thread undulate!

The job of separating the threads will also be easier if you attach a single shaft to a single treadle, and if you lift one shaft after the other so that each shaft rises to its maximum level, not held back by adjacent threads. This is probably the only time I advise tying a single shaft to a single treadle, as I am usually such a fanatic about tie-ups. Countermarch or counterbalance looms are ideally suited for this.

The work is easier with a flat shuttle than with a boat shuttle. Some yarns that cling too much to each other should be avoided, as well as yarns that wear out quickly from friction, like linen. However, wool that clings together is a very nice effect for a carpet because it swells when taken off the loom and completely covers the weft. Spraying the warp with a starched water will limit snagging.

Do not release the tension when you take a break; otherwise the spot where you resume weaving will inevitably show.

"There is no use or excuse for a sleazy mat," in the words of Mary E. Black, a legendary weaver in the U.S. **So, let's talk about density.**

To estimate density, we wrap the yarn around the usual ruler, then double the number of threads counted over 1 inch (2.5 cm). It is a bit as if the ruler became the weft, as it is entirely covered by the warp yarn above and below. As a result, the number of warp ends quickly becomes very high. For this reason, we might be reluctant to use a fine warp thread, it takes so much. However, the result is worth the trouble.

Figure 38 ***Two-color rep weave, 4 shafts. Venne 20/2 mercerized cotton***

It is also very prudent to count the number of heddles on each shaft before planning this type of weave. This structure uses a large amount of yarn because of its high density.

Both the choice of colors in the warp and the alternation of thick and thin weft produce the pattern. It is important to understand that the thick weft will reveal the warp ends, giving volume to those under which it passes, while the sole role of the thin weft is to provide interlacing in the plain weave. Each pick of thick weft lifts half of the warp threads, while each pick of thin weft lifts the other half. So we have a real plain weave, although it doesn't look like one.

It is not necessary for one weft to be very thick and another very thin. Not so long ago, we could find thin rep in our fabric stores for curtains where the two wefts had the same yarn count. The high density of the warp prevented any deformation of the fabric even though its full weight was suspended.

Blocks and profile drafts are explained in detail in the last part of this book (p. 234). Nevertheless, it is difficult to avoid them when teaching reps. To make it simple, let's say that a block is a group of threads that work together, that are woven in the same way. Writing a profile draft with blocks makes it possible to summarize, to condense the writing, to make it more readable by zooming out, by stepping back.

An example of warp-faced rep on 4 shafts with 4 blocks

Let's try to learn the rep technique with an easy example: 4 shafts, 4 blocks, 4 colors.

Figure 39 Warp-faced rep weave, 4 shafts. Fonty Cotton Club 3, 1,091yd/lb (2,200 m/kg)

Little by little we are going to put together the record sheet that shows the project in its entirety. First, the steps are described in detail, then comes the summarized record sheet. The idea is to understand the drafts that we find in publications.

The warp chosen is Fonty's Cotton Club 3, a blue for the background and three yarns from the red family: red, orange, and coral. It doesn't matter what is used for weft, as long as there is a thin yarn and a thick yarn and they are about the same color as the warp in the selvedges, as this is the only place they will be seen. In our example, a cotton sewing thread will be the thin one and the thick one will be the same as the warp, doubled or tripled.

Figure 40 Part of the profile draft

Threading Heddles

- The threading is divided into a series of 4 blocks: A, B, C, and D.
- The threading blocks are groups of 6 threads in this example:
  - Block **A : 1**-3-1-3-1-3 ;
  - Block **B : 2**-4-2-4-2-4 ;
  - Block **C : 3**-1-3-1-3-1 ;
  - Block **D : 4**-2-4-2-4-2.
- The blue is threaded in shaft 1 for Block A. in shaft 2 for Block B, in 3 for C, and in 4 for D. It's automatic: when you read "Block A," it means that the threading starts with shaft 1 and that it is with the blue thread!
- As for the thread from the red family, it is systematically in shaft 3 for Block A, 4 for B, 1 for C, and 2 for D.

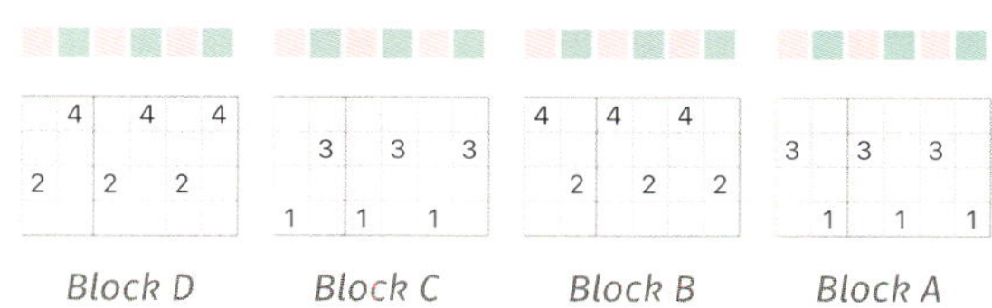

Figure 41 The 4 threading blocks

It's because I thread from right to left that I am finally writing the threading from right to left, just like the weaving software that I use.

In the following project record sheet, only a small part of the profile draft is expanded in threading. Get used to mentally converting the profile draft into a threading draft to thread the rest. I highly recommend you systematically adopt this conversion method.

Putting in a floating selvedge is essential.

Winding the Warp

Finally, the colors always go in pairs: one blue followed by one red. To save a little time when winding, we can absolutely take these two threads together, but with a few precautions:

- prepare the threads so that they unwind with the same tension, by transferring them to bobbins and possibly to a bobbin rack;
- be sure to prevent the threads from twisting together, possibly by keeping a finger between the two to separate them;
- make the cross between these two threads in the threading order, especially with thin or tightly twisted threads; otherwise there is a risk of them getting tangled at the back of the loom. In this example, you will systematically thread the blue first in each block.

Tie-Up

4 shafts, 4 blocks, and 4 **tie-ups** that are all different. In this example, the tie-up looks like the one for a 2/2 twill. However, it is in fact a plain weave in each of the blocks. Remember, however, it can be helpful to tie up a single shaft to each treadle.

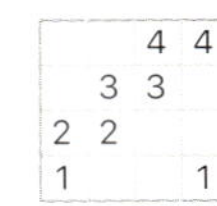

		4	4
	3	3	
2	2		
1			1

Figure 42 Tie-up for rep weave project

Treadling

As is often the case, the pattern is enhanced when the famous "tromp as writ" is used, the same one found in weaving software. And again, following the profile draft makes it much easier to decipher the treadling and helps your work flow smoothly.

A treadling block will include two picks, one with thick yarn followed by one with thin yarn. Only the pick with **the thick yarn is visible in the profile draft diagram**. The **thin yarn will systematically be on the shafts opposite** to those lifted with the thick yarn.

Block A will be repeated as many times as shown in the profile draft, then B, etc.

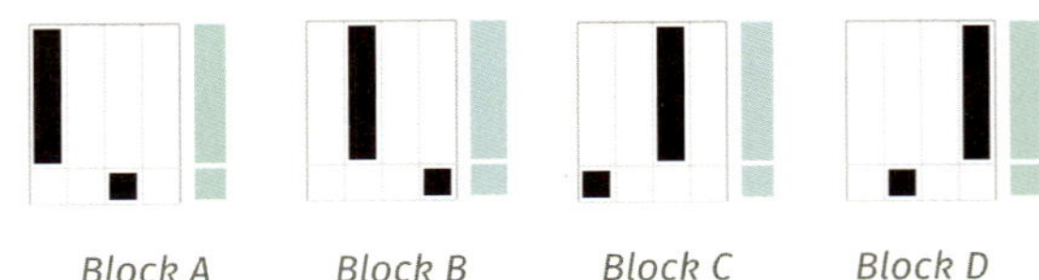

Figure 43 The 4 treadling blocks

Finishing

The traditional finishing is fringe. However, it is very advantageous to start and finish your piece by weaving several picks in plain weave (1-3, 2-4) with the thin yarn only and beating very firmly. This will strengthen the beginning and the end of the weaving. You can also finish each end with the Paris stitch, using this same yarn. This strip can be sewn like a hem, sometimes with a bias that will stabilize rebellious threads.

PROJECT RECORD SHEET—WARP-FACED REP WEAVE, 4 SHAFTS AND 4 BLOCKS

Warp: Fonty Cotton Club 3, colors 110 (blue), 117 (red), 118 (orange), and 119 (coral), 1,091 yd/lb (2,200 m/kg)

Weft: in blue, a cotton sewing thread and the warp cotton doubled

Sett: 35 epi (14 ends per cm)

Width in reed: 20.5 in. (52 cm)

Total number of ends: 720: 390 blue and 330 red

Project length: 39 in. (100 cm)

% of draw-in during weaving due to significant undulation: 20%

% of shrinkage when taken off loom: 20%

Fringe: 4 in. (10 cm)

Loss due to front tie-on and loss at back of loom: 24 in. (60 cm)

Total warp: 10 oz. (280 g) of red, 11.6 oz (330 g) of blue

Color												Total
(blue)	30	33	30	24	24	108	24	24	30	33	30	390
(coral)		33								33		66
(orange)			30		24		24		30			108
(red)				24		108		24				156

Figure 44 Warp color order chart

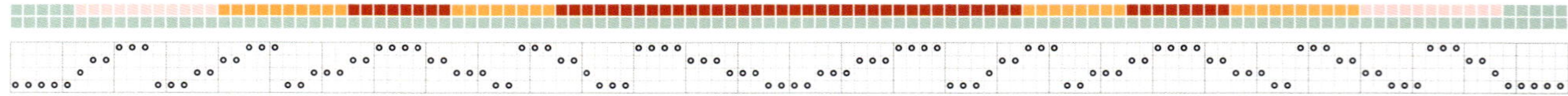

Figure 45 Profile draft of the entire threading

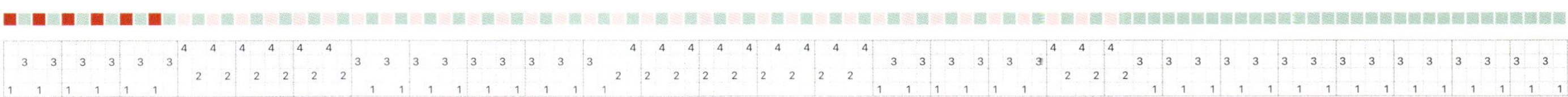

Figure 46 *Expanded threading of first 18 blocks from the right*

Figure 47 - **Profile draft: Threading and treadling**

Sometimes more is more: 6 shafts and 6 blocks

As is often the case, the greater the number of shafts, the greater the variety of patterns. With 4 shafts, the number of blocks is limited to 4. With 6 shafts, we can play with 6 blocks. With 8 shafts, we can combine 8 threading blocks.

Figure 48 *Plain weave and reps on 6 shafts—only the density changes*

We still use the same method, sketching out a profile draft, and for each block a coding that is the twin of the previous threading.

Figure 49 *Profile draft of a rep, 6 shafts and 6 blocks, and tie-up*

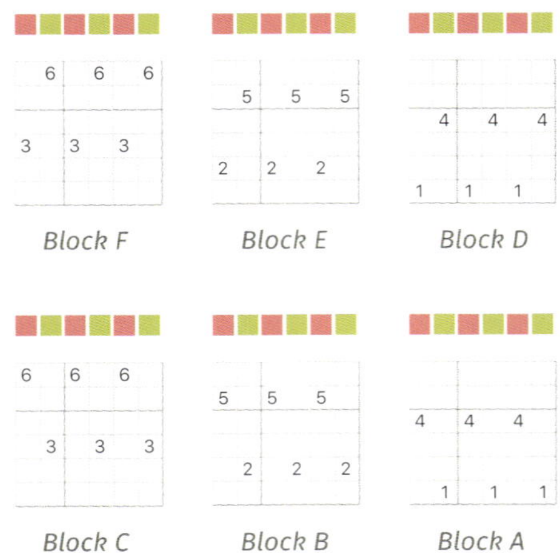

Figure 50 *The 6 threading blocks*

For the **treadling**, let's make it simple and keep the "tromp as writ"! The profile draft shows only the picks of thick weft; remember that it is always followed by a thin yarn that goes through the exact opposite shed. This is a plain weave on 6 shafts, yes, but it is a still a plain weave!

For the **tie-up**, we go between these 6 possible blocks. Like the previous rep on 4 shafts, we tie up in 3/3 twill or, more precisely, in plain weave for each of the 3 blocks. And I'll say this again: if the threads catch on each other, it is advisable to tie up each shaft separately so as to keep them apart more easily.

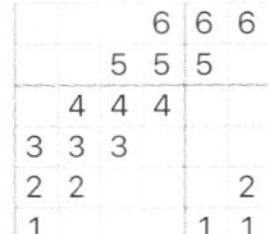

Figure 51 *Rep tie-up with 6 shafts*

This is a weaving to try out one day, following your own inspiration for threading. Remember only these few recommendations brought out in the previous example: alternate thick weft picks when half the ends are lifted, with a thin yarn for the opposite shed; put in a floating selvedge; and the significant take-up requires that you plan for a generous length of warp.

People using an inkle loom weave reps. Warp ends, not constrained to stay in place, move as close together as possible, completely hiding the weft. On your loom, whatever kind it may be, you can weave reps as on an inkle loom, but only over a limited width, by removing the reed and using a strong shuttle to beat after each pick, as Peruvian women do with their backstrap looms.

Weft-Faced Rep Weave

Weft-faced rep weave is the result of a strong cotton warp, very tightly wound, where the threads are spaced far enough apart so that each row of weft can be firmly beaten and **cover the warp completely**. The design will be made simply by the number of times each row is repeated and the order of the colors in the shuttles.

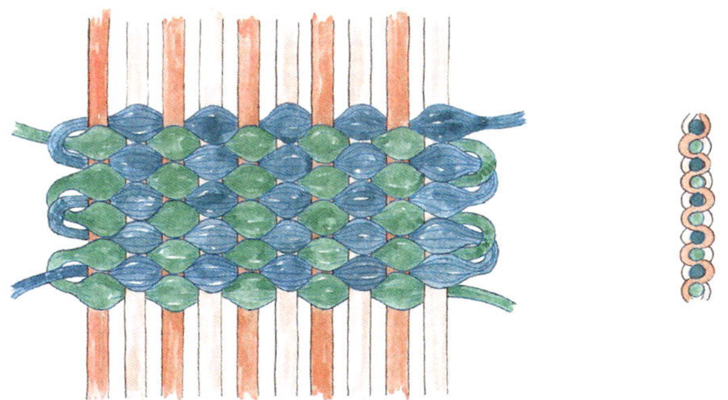

Figure 52 Weft-faced rep weave

The difficulty of this type of weave resides in the **balance between the warp density and the properties of the weft**. The warp is spaced out but at the same time it must be dense enough so that the fabric is not limp. The weft yarn should be twisted as little as possible so that it can open up completely, making it easier to cover the warp. This balance will undoubtedly require a few test runs.

Apart from this technical issue, creating this is very fun, playing with the colors and their placement. The threading in plain weave reduces the variety of designs, since we only use two different sheds. Nevertheless, it is already a lot of fun placing the colors at your leisure. Imagine how much the creativity is multiplied with 4 or 5 shafts in point twill or overshot threading, as we will discover later.

Let's look at an example. We'll wind a warp in strong cotton, called cable-plied cotton, and do straight draw threading, preparing three shuttles with Fonty BB merino wool, a wool that will flow well, has a good flexibility for this kind of weaving, and has a nice color palette. The warp density will be 5 ends per inch (2 per cm), meaning you must weave 50 rows of weft to make an inch of fabric.

Generally, weft-faced rep weave is shown for sinking shed looms, which is much simpler to think about. The shaft that is lowered pulls the covered warp ends down. With rising shed looms, there is a little mental exercise you can do. We raise shaft 1, and yet it is on shaft 2 that the weft is placed. We think 1, we see 2. Then, for the second pick, we lift shaft 2 and it is the threads from shaft 1 that are covered by the colored weft. You have to think backward, but it comes quickly.

Figure 53 Rug in weft-faced rep weave, 2 shafts, MERO cable cotton for warp, Fonty BB merinos for weft

Sketching the patterns

To draw the project, we first use a simple grid. Reading the usual draft is slightly different from what we know and requires a little explanation with this example woven on two shafts. Let's agree that we will systematically lift shaft 1 first and then shaft 2. Having done that, a whole row is covered.

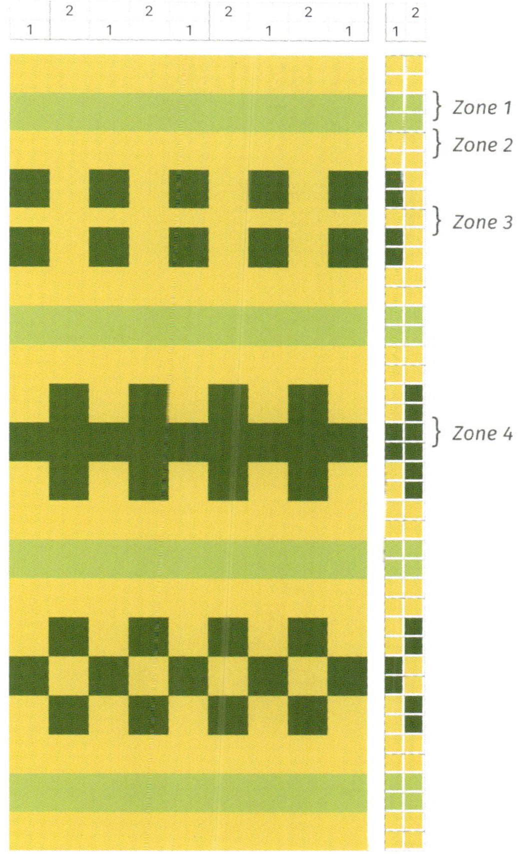

Figure 54 Weft-faced rep in plain weave

Depending on the thickness of the yarn, it will likely take several wefts to get the equivalent of a square of the grid. Because it's very visible to the eye, you will quickly realize how many weft rows are needed to clearly see the pattern. The columns, rows, or squares are all yours!

Nevertheless, here are some explanations to understanding the draft from bottom to top, in the direction of the weaving:

- zone 1: raise shaft 1, pass a yellow weft, then raise shaft 2 and pass a yellow weft again, sequence to be repeated as many times as necessary. In weft-faced rep, the word "pick" takes its true meaning: it is the back-and-forth trip of the shuttle that covers all of the warp threads, as in tapestry;
- zone 2: same thing, but in celadon green. To be repeated;
- zone 3: weft 1 in yellow, weft 2 in green, to be repeated until you get a green square;
- zone 4: weft 1 in green, weft 2 in yellow until you get a square, then two wefts in green, then the two colors alternate again.
- And so on.

A diamond grid rather than a square grid

Using a diamond grid is undoubtedly the method that best reproduces what we will see in the fabric. The diagonal lines take into account the compacting and the overlaying of the pick at an angle. Appropriate for elaborate designs, this "grid" will be necessary for those who need to see their pattern in advance. A full-page diamond grid is included in the appendices. Photocopy to your heart's content.

Figure 55 *A diamond grid for drawing the pattern*

Here, in Figure 56, are some patterns that describe the weaving pictured.

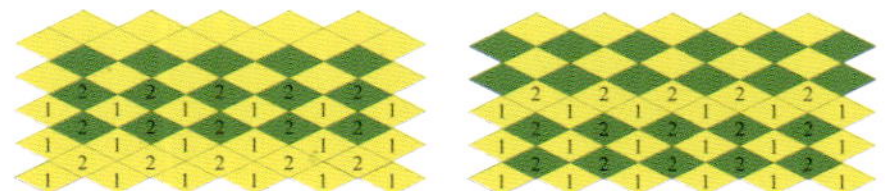

Figure 56 *Some examples of patterns on the grid*

With weft-faced rep weave, the only "inconvenience" is the slowness of it. In this example, you have to pass 5 wefts on each of the 2 shafts to get a square, which is a weft density of 50 threads per inch (20 per cm)!

We also gain by using 4 shafts instead of 2 as we can spread out the heddles on the shafts better. And finally, with so many shafts, why limit yourself to lifting even or odd shafts together? Sometime try lifting shafts 1 and 2 together, then the other two, as for a cannelé.

Rag Rugs

To finish this section on plain weave, I would like to talk a bit about lirette rugs, a type of rag rug that consists of using thin strips of fabric as weft. This type of weaving has always been a way to use up old clothing with a pretty result. Long rugs made this way are still in use in Northern European countries.

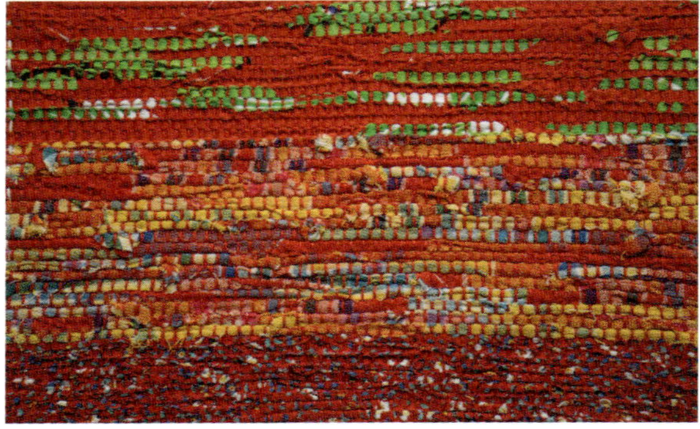

Figure 57 *Rag rug woven with fabric strips cut on the bias*

The thinner the strips, the lighter the weave. And if the strips are cut on the bias, the rug is much more subtle and polished. Here is a tip for cutting a long bias. Take a square of fabric ❶, cut it on the diagonal ❷, make two seams to join the sides of the square ❸, and you get a cylinder ❹. Now just cut it in a spiral starting along one side of the tube ❺.

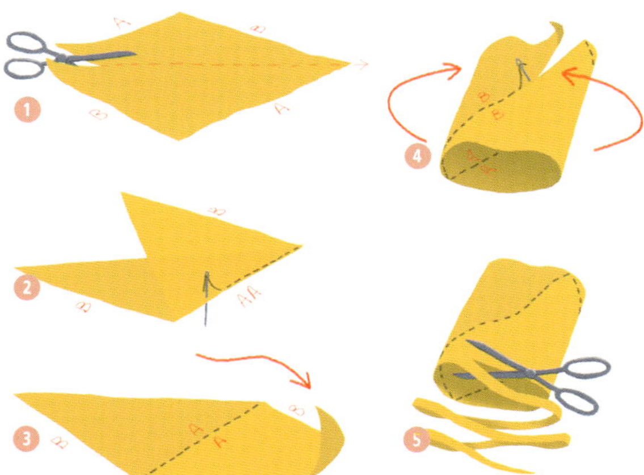

Figure 58 *A clever technique for cutting on the bias*

The color of the warp threads can be varied to liven up the rag rug. In this example, the weft is a strip of thin light green felt. When the warp thread is green, then our eye transforms the color of the felt. It's incredible how much it changes the effect on the fabric, even though the warp thread is very thin compared to the felt strip!

Some designers say that the limitations push us to be inventive. Plain weave is good proof of this, as you now know. There's more to it than meets the eye, hiding behind its modest appearance . . . .

Figure 59 ***Effects of a colored warp on a solid color light felt weft***

Twill

The number of variations to be gained in (twill) fabrics made by changing the sequence of the treadlings, by using different combinations of the tie-up of the harnesses, by adding color variations in the warp and weft, or both, cannot be figured even mathematically.

Marguerite Porter Davison, *A Handweaver's Pattern Book*, 1994

Figure 60 ***Concerto of twill dish towels, 8 shafts, Venne 22/2 Cottolin***

With plain weave, the interlacing was thread by thread, or group of threads by group of threads. With twill, the thread will now pass over several adjacent threads, to make floats appear. Each weft is offset by one warp end. The weave unit is square. The slope of the twill is theoretically 45 degrees.

Prelude: Some Definitions

The **float** is the passage of a warp or weft thread over or under at least two adjacent threads. This simple difference from the plain weave opens up a world of unlimited structures. And depending on the mood, I am either delighted with so many discoveries to make or I am saddened to never be able to explore them all.

Straight, point, or broken threadings highlight twill very naturally. They show a weave with diagonal lines called ribs or veins. Either the fabric is identical on the front and back, or it has two different sides: warp-faced, where the warp floats are more visible and more numerous, and weft-faced, where the weft floats are more on display. We speak of ribs in warp or ribs in weft. Each binding point is offset or set over by one warp end.

- **Twill** is the method of interlacing: the number of ends the weft goes under versus the number of ends the weft goes over. A 1/3 twill means that one weft goes under one end and then goes over three. For 2/2, the weft goes under two ends, then over two
- The diagonal line indicates the threading order: 1-2-3-4 for straight threading, 1-2-3-4-3-2-1 for reverse threading. We will talk about this at length coming up.

Figure 61 ***Vest made in 2/2 twill, straight twill threading, 4 shafts, Holstgarn Tides, 2,852 yd/lb (5,750 m/kg)***

When the same yarn is used in warp and weft, a **balanced weave** can be made where the density of warp yarns is the same as in the weft, just as in plain weave; the angle of the twill is 45 degrees.

What is the benefit of floats?

- The yarn, which passes freely over several consecutive threads without being trapped by an interlacing as in plain weave, is on display. It **shows its color, its material, its sheen**—contrary to in plain weave where, hardly seen, the thread disappears immediately.
- When a float is set over by one warp end, this shift from one weft pick to another gives movement and flexibility to the fabric.
- Since there are fewer intersections, the threads are freer and **the fabric is softer, more voluptuous**. It also becomes a bit more fragile depending on the length of the floats.

A minimum of three shafts are needed to weave twill. You can choose to show the floats in the weft direction, 1/2 twill, or in the warp, 2/1 twill. But in any case, the reverse side of 1/2 twill will be 2/1 twill. This 2/1 twill is traditionally called jeans twill. Depending on the direction the weft is set over, you get a vein or rib that leans toward the right or the left.

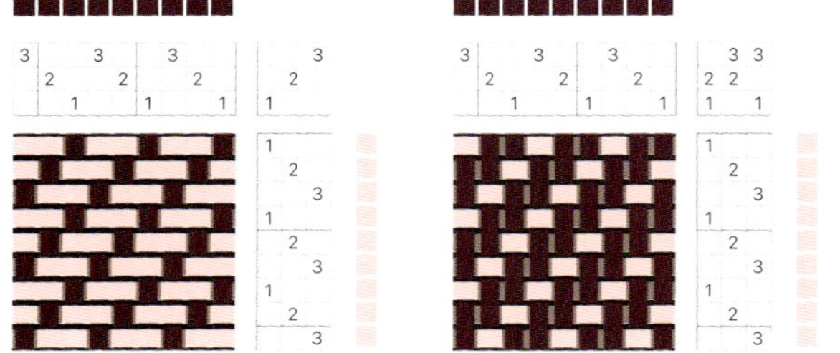

Figure 62 ***1/2 and 2/1 twills on 3 shafts***

Erica de Ruiter was very interested in three-shaft structures and has written extensively on the subject. For myself, I am more attracted to multiple shafts. The examples that follow will rarely use less than four shafts.

In twill, the twist of the yarn can amplify the diagonal or almost cancel it out. A few years ago, it was easy to find the same quality of yarn either S-twisted or Z-twisted, but it is more difficult today to find this variety for our crafting activities. Nevertheless, nothing prevents us from choosing one direction of diagonal rather than the other to emphasize this effect. The flexibility of the fabric is accentuated if the direction of the yarn's twist goes with the slope of the diagonal.

Tie-Up: The Conductor Sets the Rhythm

Twill is the way to intertwine! So let's focus on the little square at the top right of each draft: **the tie-up**.

We talk about a **simple twill** when the weft goes around a single warp end: under 1, over 3 or more, that is 1/3 or 1/4, 1/5, etc.

We have a **repeat twill** as soon as the group of binding threads contains at least 2 threads: 2/3, 2/4, 3/5—when the number of shafts increases.

Cross or **balanced** or **regular** or **straight twill** designates cases where weft and warp floats have the same prominence: 2/2, 3/3, 4/4, etc. These are the most used twills because the effect is pleasant; we see as much warp as weft. These weaves are identical on the front side and the reverse side. The 2/2 and 3/3 twills are sometimes called Batavia twill or *casimir*.

As soon as we leave the world of 4 shafts, we can make **compound twills**. We imagine a twill on 8 shafts as the combination of two twills of 4 shafts: 2/2 followed by a 1/3; or a twill followed by plain weaves: 1/3 followed by 1/1, 1/1; or any other variation. Blending weave structures together is valuable as it prevents long floats on straight twills. We will study some examples a little further on.

With 4 Shafts, 3 Twills Are Compatible

With a 4-shaft loom we can make 3 different twills:

- **simple 1/3 twill**: This involves raising shaft 1, then 2, 3, and 4. The weft covers the three other threads not lifted. This is a weft-faced twill;
- **regular 2/2 twill**: Shafts are systematically lifted in pairs. Shafts **1**-2, then **2**-3, 3-4, and finally **4**-1. All the floats are the same length in warp and in weft;

- **simple 3/1 twill**: This time, we lift 3 shafts; the weft covers the only thread not lifted. Shafts **1**-2-3, then **2**-3-4, **3**-4-1, and the last **4**-1-2. This is a warp effect twill.

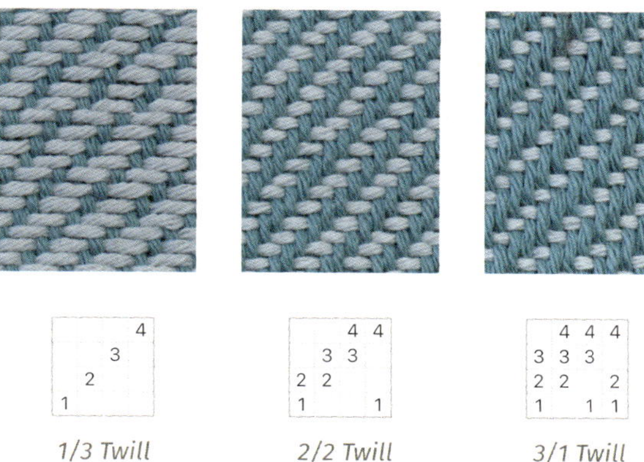

Figure 63 Three tie-ups on 4 shafts

With 8 Shafts, an Abundance of Chords

With an 8-shaft loom, the arrangements increase considerably. The following drafts show the possible combinations of **regular twills**.

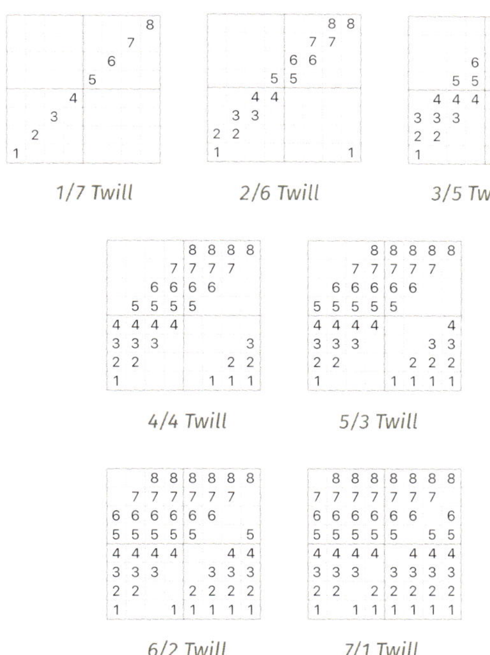

Figure 64 Tie-ups in regular twill on 8 shafts

Figure 65 Rows showing the 7 different tie-ups in regular twill on 8 shafts

Next comes the large family of **compound twills**. Neither to impress you nor to lose you, this abundance will be a very useful resource in some of your weaving to avoid floats that are too long. Mathematical precision helps us to classify and memorize them. Tuck all these possibilities away in a little corner somewhere, but don't forget them. And then, the understanding of what is happening here becomes very helpful when weaving more complex structures such as the echo weave, for example.

Following is a way to write out the treadling for a compound twill to help you remember the pattern to follow. For each treadle, start with a horizontal line above which you note which shafts are lifted and the order in which they are lifted, and under the line the shafts not lifted, which will be covered by the weft. This is the kind of transcription that will make your life so much easier when memorizing the treadling. Let's analyze this first draft in Figure 66.

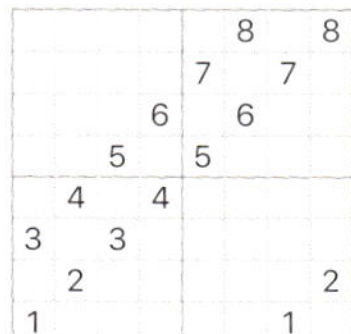

Figure 66 Example of compound twill tie-up on 8 shafts: 1/1/1/5

This tie-up draft shown as $\frac{1 \quad 1 \quad\quad}{\quad 1 \quad 5}$ means that one thread is lifted, the following stays down, the following is lifted, and the remaining 5 stay down. Now let's see how that is read during weaving by analyzing the columns of the tie-up draft from left to right:

- For the first column, the **shaft lifted** is **1**, the **shaft lowered** is 2, then the **shaft lifted** is 3, the **five shafts lowered** are 4-5-6-7-8;
- Let's look at the second column. **The shaft lifted** is **2**, the **shaft lowered** is 3, then the **shaft lifted** is 4, the **five shafts lowered** are 5-6-7-8-1;
- All the other columns show this same logic. This is the order that you have to follow for the tie-up of the

treadles or for manipulating the levers: one shaft lifted, one lowered, one lifted and five lowered.

Finally, we're going to read the first column with this **coding** by replacing the numbers of $\frac{1\quad 1}{1\quad 5}$ with the numbers of the corresponding shafts. On top, the shafts that will be lifted, on the bottom, the shafts that do not move. In the first column, we get $\frac{1\quad 3}{2\quad 45678}$ and $\frac{2\quad 4}{3\quad 56781}$ for the second column. While weaving, when the treadling table indicates 1, thanks to this mnemonic device, we know that shaft 1 is to be lifted and what comes next flows logically. I know, this memory exercise is terrifying. How many times have I heard fears, even objections. But I will never give up and will continue to be emphatic about it, because the astonished look a weaver who suddenly understands, applies, and fluidly weaves thrills me SO much. Eureka!

The following 8 tie-up codes will be read in a similar way. Code $\frac{1\quad 2}{1\quad 4}$ is read: one shaft is lifted, the following stays down, the next two are lifted and the four others remain down.

Sometimes we find other ways to write this: 1:1:2:4 or 1/1/2/4, but the principle remains the same.

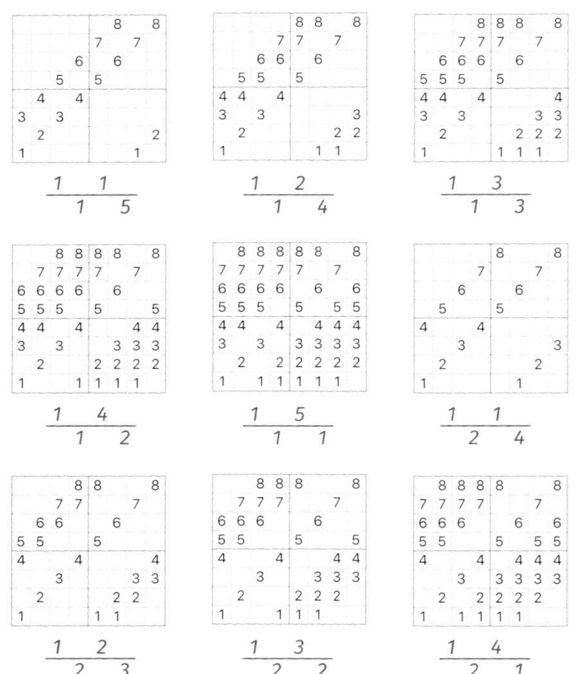

Figure 67 ***Compound twill tie-ups on 8 shafts***

Other tie-ups look like the tacking together of two 4-shaft twills: 1/3 twill followed by a 1/3 twill or by a 2/2 twill or by a 3/1 twill, as shown by the first three examples below (Figure 68). The last three twills shown are the merger of a plain weave on 4 shafts and a twill on the 4 other shafts. This ensures very good stability of the weaving, a bit as if a connection was made at the same time as the pattern.

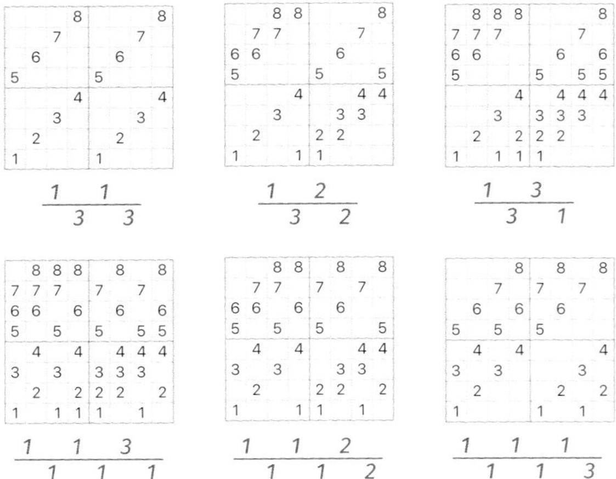

Figure 68 ***Twill tie-ups assembled on 8 shafts***

As in music, we start by creating chords: major, minor, perfect. This consists of combining the raising of shafts according to an established, repeated rhythm. Choosing one tie-up over another comes down to whether you want to show more warp than weft, or whether you want long floats. There is no hard-and-fast rule, only your choice depending on the usefulness of the fabric and the yarn you choose.

First Concert: A Suite of Twill Threadings on 4 Shafts

When we want to weave in twill, the most common threadings are straight, point, or broken twills. It is the order of the threads in the heddles that will set the tone! We will now talk about **threading**.

To begin with, I will only present **sequences on 4 shafts**. It is very easy to find threadings on 8 shafts in many publications. As always, the possibilities are multiplied and are exciting.

To better demonstrate, I will use the traditional **tromp as writ** approach, which shows each diagonal in its purest definition. I will adopt the regular 2/2 twill tie-up, as it gives as much prominence to the warp as to the weft. Perfect harmony! Just by using a different treadling or another tie-up, the inventions will be endless.

All the following drafts are executed with the same yarn in warp and in weft, Lang Baby Cotton. The diagonal is exactly 45 degrees.

One last comment. As we progress we become ambidextrous in writing and reading drafts. I show threadings from right to left, which matches my threading movement. Eventually, this direction will become natural for you as well.

Straight Twill

Straight threading is the easiest: 1-2-3-4, 1-2-3-4. It is likely to be what you use when just starting out. There are so many treadling and tie-up variations that you can easily keep entertained with this simple design; just change the direction of the treadling, alternate 2/2 twill with 1/3 twill, etc.

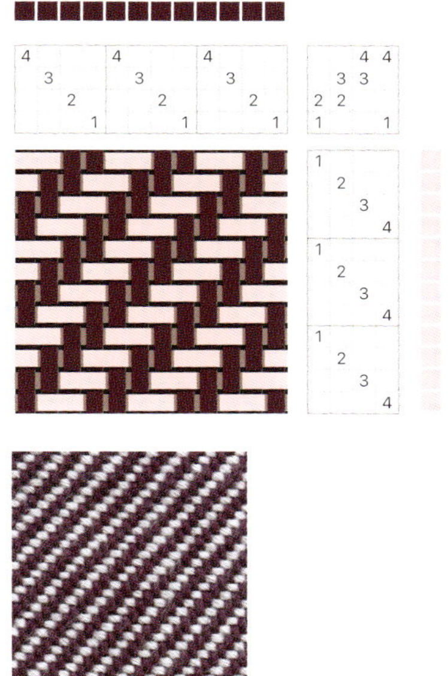

Figure 69 ***Threading and treadling in straight twill***

Point or Simple Reverse Twill

The threading is straight but with an out and back, 1-2-3-4-3-2-1. This little difference merits two comments:

- the block that is repeated is a group of 6 threads. It is composed of this sequence: 1-2-3-4-3-2, 1-2-3-4-3-2, etc. It is only at the end, in the last block, that a last thread will be added on shaft 1 to balance the pattern. The number of threads for this type of threading is therefore a multiple of 6, +1;
- be sure to count the heddles before starting. By block, there must be a heddle on shafts 1 and 4, and 2 heddles on shafts 2 and 3.

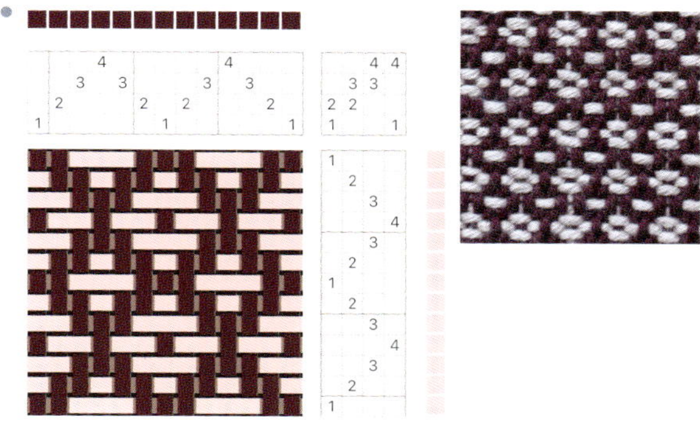

Figure 70 ***Threading and treadling in point or reverse twill***

This famous weave pattern is sometimes called bird's eye when it is done with a little reverse, or rosepath, or even goose eye, depending on the size of the point.

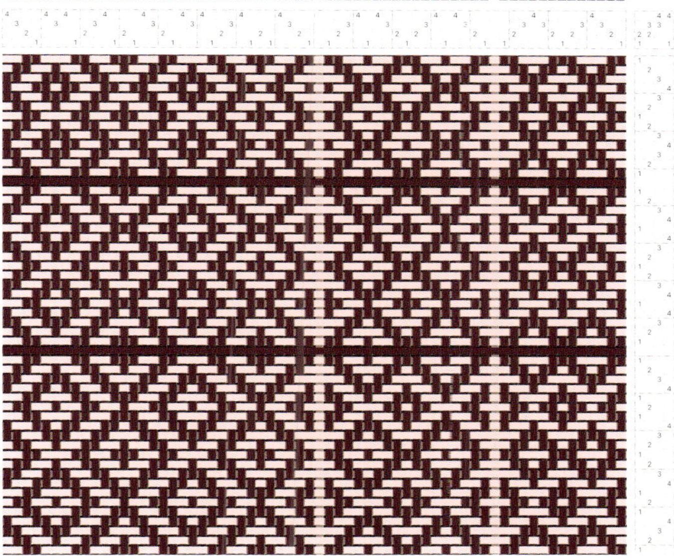

Figure 71 ***Left to right: Goose eye, rosepath, and bird's eye threadings***

M & W—An Extended Point Twill

As before, this is a point twill, but drawn in a way that resembles these two capital letters.

In the same way, it is completely possible to stretch them out or to make them go back and forth more, to thus thread the M & W in a "rosepath." Or why not in a "sunflower path"!

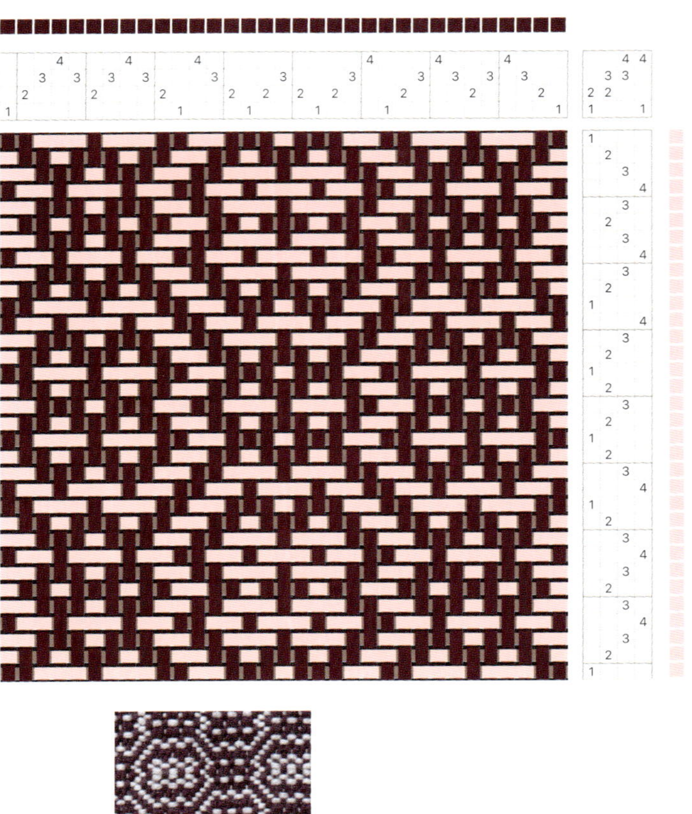

Figure 72 **M & W threading**

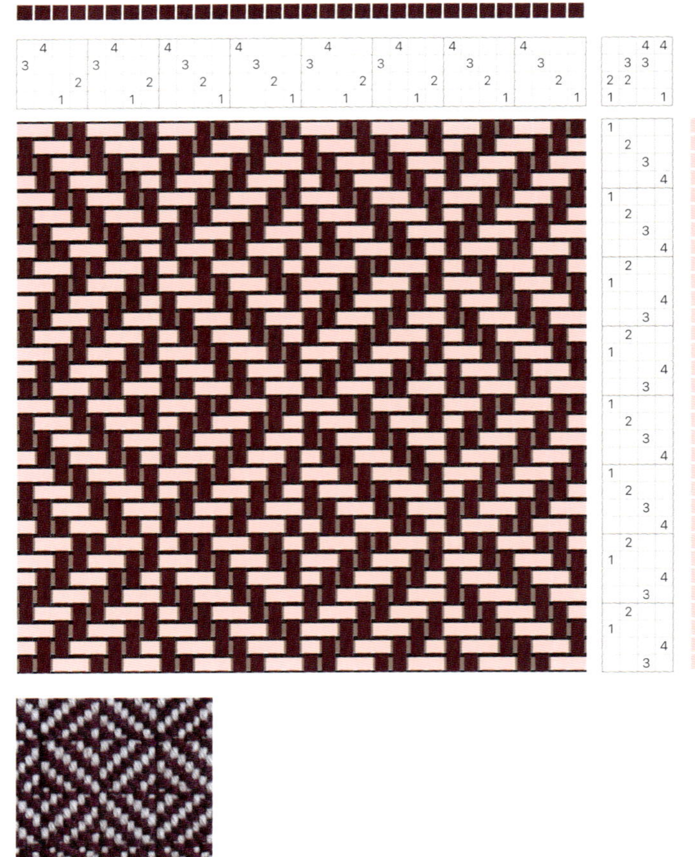

Figure 73 **Fishbone twill**

Herringbone Twill

This is probably my favorite one; it just gives this little breath, like in music, that allows you to savor the rest. It is a sequence in straight twill, with a break when the direction changes. As always, it can be extended *ad libitum*, in a regular or irregular pattern: 1-2-3-4-1-2-3-4 - 2-1-4-3-2-1-4-3, etc.

A small comment is needed, however. This is the first twill threading with which it is not possible to make a pure plain weave, since two even and two odd threads are juxtaposed at each change in direction of the herringbone. If the entire threading is done in a herringbone pattern, this repeated irregularity will be considered inventiveness. This will be less true if it is mixed with straight twill or with a plain weave where alternating and uniformity are observed. It will look like a mistake. So be careful about where you place it.

Broken Twill

This is a straight twill sequence, but shifted: **1**-2-3-4, **2**-3-4-1, **3**-4-1-2, **4**-1-2-3. Very pretty, but as with the fishbone, true plain weave is not possible because of yarns that are both even or odd being next to each other.

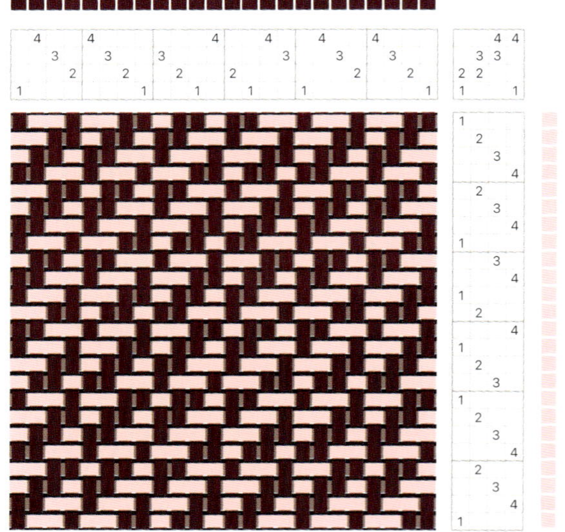

Figure 74 **Broken twill**

It's still the same story. You can break at two shafts: **1**-4, **2**-1, **3**-2, **4**-3, or at three shafts: **1**-2-3, **2**-3-4, **3**-4-1, **4**-1-2. You can also place the breaks with less regularity: 1-2, 4-1, 3-4, 2-3 twice, then repeat that in reverse, for example.

The Final Movement

Obviously, it is impossible to reproduce everything here, if there actually is an "everything" on this subject. Just know that you will not be risking anything if you invent your own threading. Combining what has been shown here or using other patterns are avenues to be explored. There are so many resources found in books or on the Internet, so why deprive yourself of this inspiration? It's like in music—we more often play the chords of other composers than those we have put together ourselves.

Intermission! A Few Clarifications to Stay in Harmony

There are, however, a few little dangers from which you have to learn to protect yourself: the selvedge, the density, and an excess of invention.

Floating Selvedge

This is essential! With twill threading, some warp ends do not move for several weft passes. If these ends are on the edge, the weft will not go around them.

Put in a floating selvedge by sleying the first and last threads on each side of the weaving in a single reed tooth, but **do not thread it** through a heddle. This way, it will neither rise or fall. Located in the middle of the shed, you systematically go around the floating selvedge with your shuttle by exiting the shed under it and entering over it (see p. 105).

Some people prefer to use two shuttles on either side and choose the one that will go around the floating selvedge. This is a clever method, but difficult to use when you have several colors and many shafts.

Density

We looked at this in part one of this book, but let's come back to it for a bit. Diagonals are successful if the slope is 45 degrees. By using the same yarn in warp and weft, the warp density should be the same as in the weft; this is a balanced weave. This is far from being only a question of principle, as it is the only way to equally show the warp AND the weft. A density that is too low will not hold the weft up adequately with each beat. The warp will be covered in part by the weft. On the other hand, too high a density will make the warp much more visible, unless you beat very firmly, which takes away the flexibility of the fabric.

Density can be estimated by wrapping the yarn around a ruler and multiplying by a percentage between 66 and 75 percent. More seriously, we can apply Ashenhurst's formula (p. 46) by finding the number of binding points in each threading block, meaning the space necessary for the weft to pass through.

Let's take a closer look.

With a **straight threading on 4 shafts**, whether with a 1/3, 2/2, or 3/1 twill, the number of binding or interlacing points is always the same in each block. For 4 warp ends, we must leave space for 2 weft yarns. Therefore, when wrapping the yarn around the ruler, we apply this same 2/3 proportion. If we have 30 wraps on the ruler, we will choose a warp density of 20 ends per inch (2.5 cm).

$$D = \frac{R \times Wa}{Wa + We} = \frac{30 \times 4}{4 + 2} = 20$$

Figure 75 Density of a straight twill

With a **simple reverse threading on 4 shafts**, it is easy to see that the weft interlaces less often and that it needs less space. In a block of 6 warp ends, the **weft interlaces twice**. The ratio is no longer 2/3 as previously, but **3/4**. This is the ratio that should be applied to the number of threads wound around the ruler. If there are 30 wraps on the ruler, the density will be 22.5 ends per inch (2.5 cm).

$$D = \frac{R \times Wa}{Wa + We} = \frac{30 \times 6}{6 + 4} = 18$$

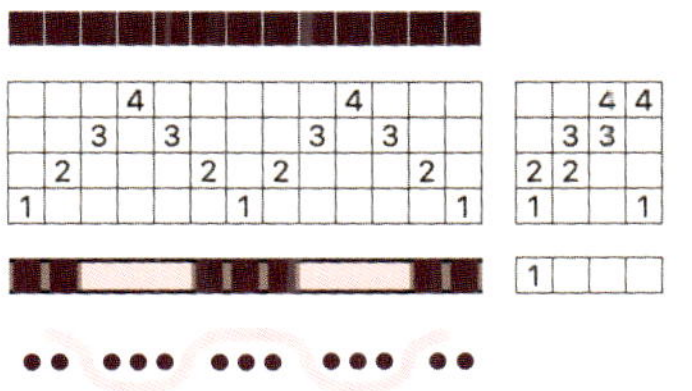

Figure 76 Density of the first weft of a simple reverse twill

On the other hand, with this reverse threading, we can see that in the second pass, the **weft interlaces** with the 6 warp ends in the block **4 times**. The density to choose will be 18 ends per inch (2.5 cm).

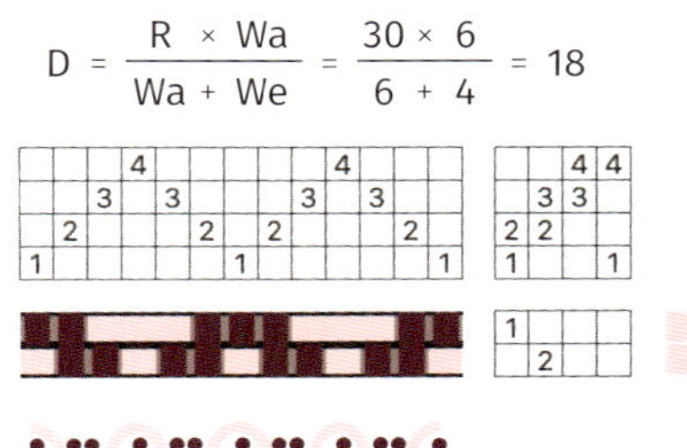

Figure 77 Density of the second weft of a simple reverse twill

With 4 shafts, averaging out the complete treadling block is almost superfluous. On the other hand, as soon as you go to 8 or more shafts, it is essential to understand and apply this principle, because the difference in the number of interlacements between two wefts can be as much as double and distort the density. It is important to simply remember that the higher the number of intersections, the lower the density, and vice versa.

In any case, the best method remains the sample. You estimate this density with Ashenhurst's formula, you test it in warp AND weft, you cut, you check that the shrinkage is less than 5 percent, you wash, you decide if you like it or if you want to re-sley.

Creation with Moderation

Creating in twill is almost limitless. And I hope that these paragraphs will give you the keys to dare to try. To remember a melody, it must include repeated patterns; the repeat bar lines used on musical scores play this role. It is a bit the same with threading and treadling. You chose a threading and/or treadling group, a block that is not too long that you will repeat several times so that it can be recognized. You will build a threading block of about ten different threads that you will repeat straight or in mirror image. Same thing with treadling. And little more than eight different tie-ups. This restraint is the best way to make your creation legible.

Color often plays a big role in twills. Alternate bands of color, in warp and weft, and you enter the world of plaids or tartans. Choose a straight or reverse twill, whichever you like, but something simple. If the sequence of the colors is the same in warp and weft with a straight twill and a 2/2 twill, we call these plaids tartans. If the bands of only two colors that are the same size are alternated, then it is called houndstooth.

Figure 78 Houndstooth, 8 shafts. Fonty 100% merino lace, 4,465 yd/lb (9,000 m/kg)

A Polyphony of Threading: Twill Gamp or Patchwork

All Anglo-Saxon weavers know what a gamp is, and although this term has entered the common language, nobody is sure of its precise origin. The word, British slang for a large umbrella, probably comes from the character Sarah Gamp, from a book by Charles Dickens. Like an umbrella, the gamp is a set of regular segments.

Regardless, weaving a gamp—one could say a patchwork—consists in separating a weaving into several sections all of identical size, but each with a different threading. This variety is carried over into treadling with the traditional tromp as writ. The weave is perfectly symmetrical in relation to the diagonal. The following example is a twill gamp.

Figure 79 Weaving a varied twill gamp, 2/2 twill, 4 shafts. Lang Baby Cotton, 1,785 yd/lb (3, 600 m/kg)

A gamp is interesting because it shows on one piece of fabric how each treadling influences each threading. The result is extraordinary and informative! It is also inspiring when trying to choose the pattern for a future project.

This pattern is a lot of fun to weave, because with each new treadling block, we discover what is going on in the next threading columns. It's like asking several musical instruments to play the same chord together.

To simplify the reading of this example, each of the 11 threadings is shown at least by a single block. In creating this, I repeated each block until I had about 60 threads per pattern. Our "umbrella" has 11 sections of about 60 threads, in purple for the warp and pink for the weft.

The warp sections are separated by a strip of basketweave in the color of the weft, in pink. This is the "refrain" of our rhyme with eleven verses whose threading is 2-2-4-4. At each selvedge, it is increased to 10 threads: 1-2-3-4-2-2-4-4-2-2.

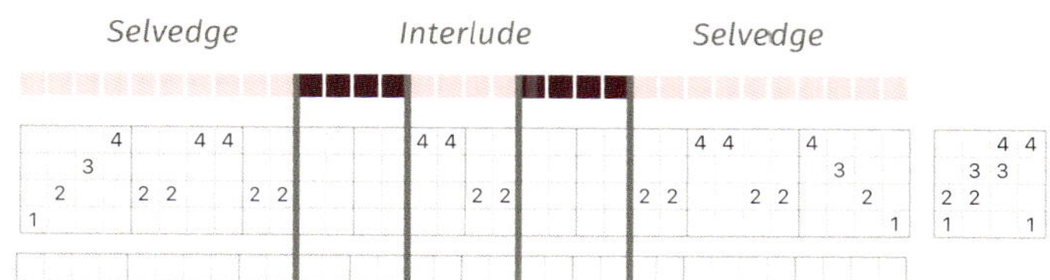

Figure 80 *Selvedges and interludes of the gamp made with the weft color*

Then the blocks come after that. The only thing to be careful about is to not start or end a block with an end threaded in shaft 2 or 4, reserved for the basketweave in the middle. If this is the case, you will thread the basketweave in 4-4-2-2 instead of 2-2-4-4.

PROJECT RECORD SHEET—2/2 TWILL GAMP

Warp: Lang Baby Cotton (197 yd per 1.8 oz), colors purple and pink

Weft: Lang Baby Cotton (197 yd per 1.8 oz), colors pink and purple

Sett: 16 epi (6.5 ends per cm)

Width in reed: 43 in. (110 cm)

Total number of ends: 720: 660 purple and 60 pink

Project length: 78 in. (200 cm)

% of shrinkage during weaving: 5 %

% of shrinkage when taken off loom: 6 %

Fringe: 2 in. (5 cm)

Loss due to front tie-on and at back of loom: 24 in. (60 cm)

Total warp: 22 oz. (620 g) of purple, 2 oz (60 g) of pink

Total weft: 1 oz. (20 g) of purple, 7 oz (200 g) of pink

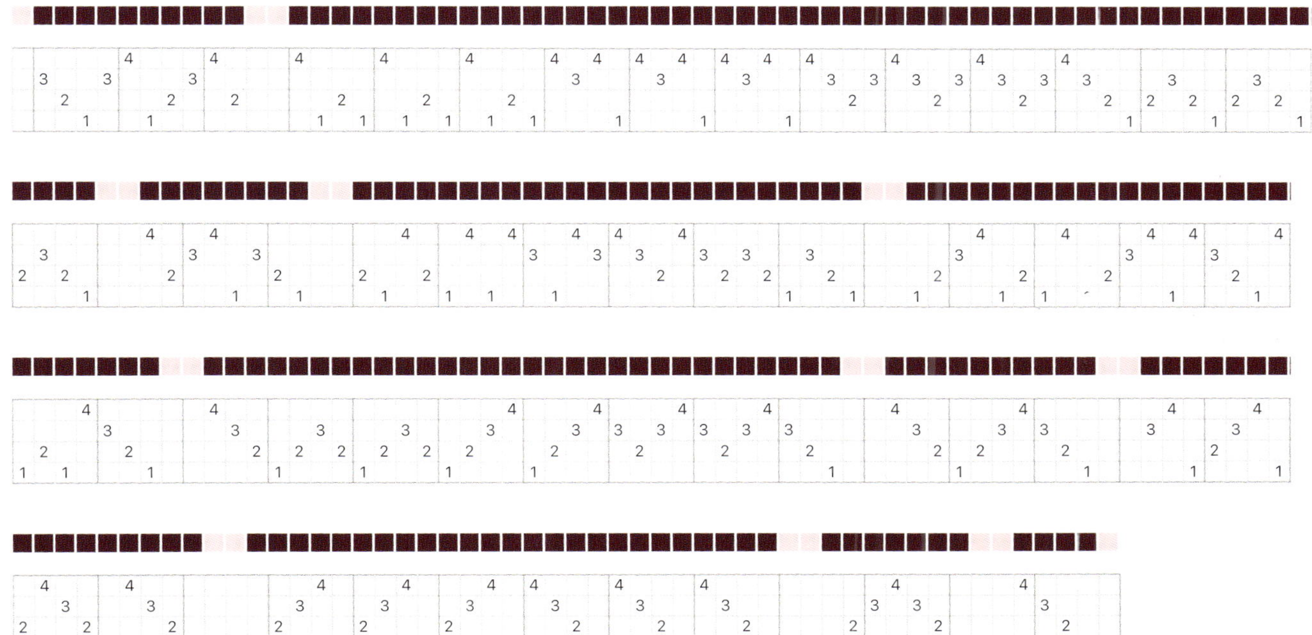

Figure 81 *Threading of the gamp*

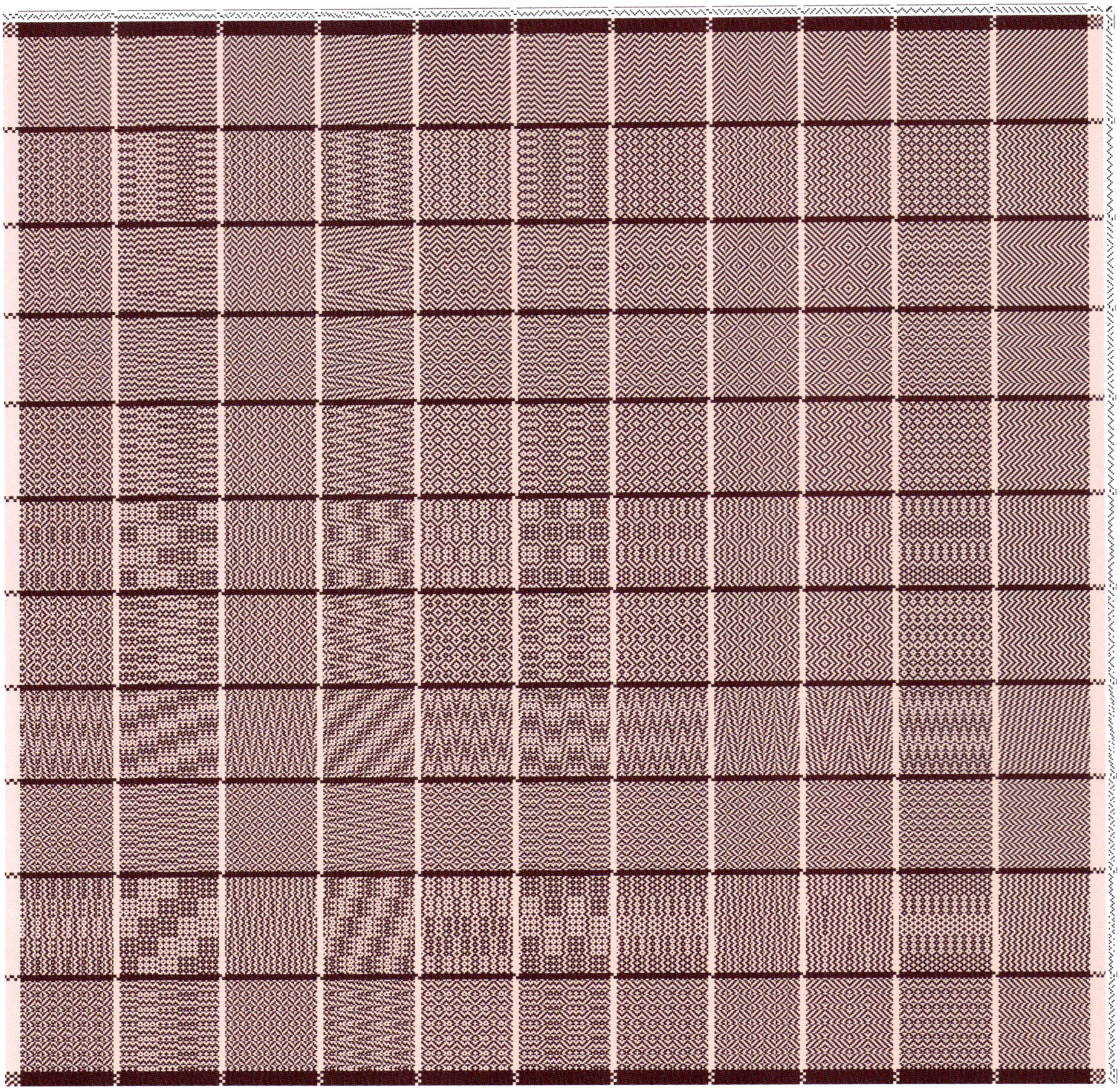

The entire gamp

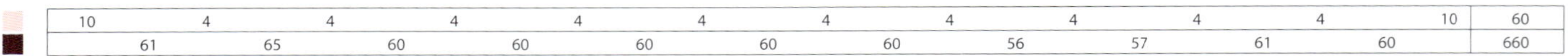

10		4		4		4		4		4		4		4		4		4		4		10	60
	61		65		60		60		60		60		60		56		57		61		60		660

Figure 82 *Warp color order for winding warp for entire gamp*

An Interlude Suggested by William G. Bateman

The work of William G. Bateman is incredibly substantial and remarkable. He left a legacy of manuscripts that his daughter had published, and while most of the patterns presented often require at least 8 shafts, there are a few gems in 4 shafts. To oversimplify, one could say that the originality of his work lies in the fact that he separates the threading into two parts: one ensures that the woven fabric is durable while the other highlights the floats. He was inspired by the Summer and Winter structure.

Each draft is a testament to a method and to research that are very analytical. Although it may seem complex at first, if we work on summarizing and simplifying it into blocks, it can be made more easily. We always find blocks in warp and weft, in which groups of threads woven with the same thread as the one used in warp provide a kind of plain weave, and other groups make the floats.

Sincerely, the assurance of obtaining a well-thought-out fabric, where the composition of the floats gives a delicate result and where the would-be plain weave provides sturdiness, is worth the effort of analyzing and deciphering.

Figure 83 *Twill weave inspired by an example from William G. Bateman on 4 shafts. Fonty 100% merino lace, 4,465 yd/lb (9,000 m/kg)*

Figure 84 *Variations of tie-ups with an M & W threading on 8 shafts*

The Orchestra Is Growing: Twill on an 8-Shaft Loom!

It is very satisfying to spread out the twill from 4 shafts to 8 shafts. The 1-2-3-4 can easily be imagined as 1-2-3-4-5-6-7-8. This logic can certainly apply to reverse twill or broken twill. The M & W will be stretched out in the same way. No worries with all these possibilities. And playing with the tie-up is even more amazing—it's infinite!

With much more surprising results, I like to work the **8 shafts as two times 4 shafts**, by blocks and combinations of blocks. This way, the weaving area threaded on the first 4 shafts will show one pattern, while the area right next to it will show a completely different pattern.

Let's take a simple example to start, with straight threading in each block. The treadling copies the threading, tromp as writ. The **tie-up draft** is divided into four quadrants, each tied up in 1/3 or 3/1 twill. This allows shafts 1-2-3-4 to work together, and shafts 5-6-7-8 to do the same, but each group is independent and different. So, two areas are different from each other in warp and weft depending on the choices made in each quadrant of the tie-up draft. When one is a warp-faced weave with the slant in one direction, the other is weft-faced with the slant in the other direction. These contrasts enhance each other.

The edges of each block must be impeccably sharp and deserve some attention when moving from one quadrant to the other. Each float stops at its block without spilling over into its neighbor!

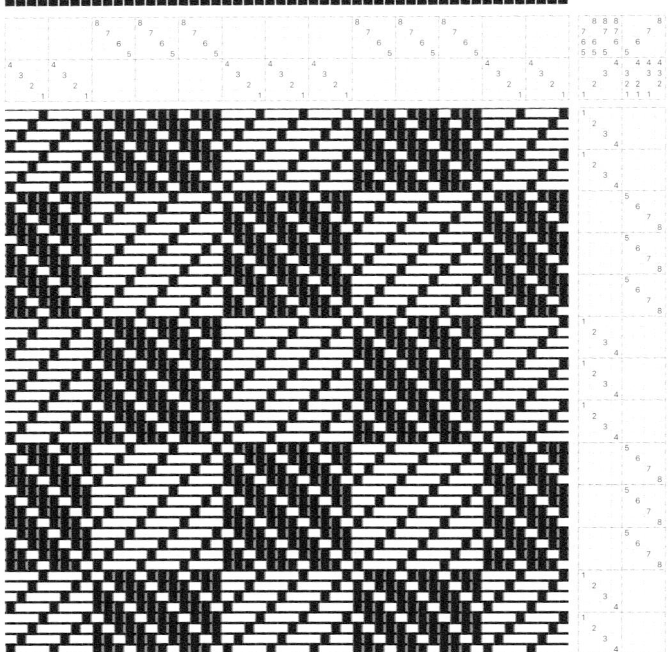

Figure 85 ***Two blocks of 4 shafts put together to make 8 shafts***

To work more comfortably, the draft profile is the ideal tool. The group of shafts 1-2-3-4 becomes block A and the group of shafts 5-6-7-8 becomes block B. The complete draft shown in this way becomes very legible and it is easy to move the blocks to modify the design (Figure 86).

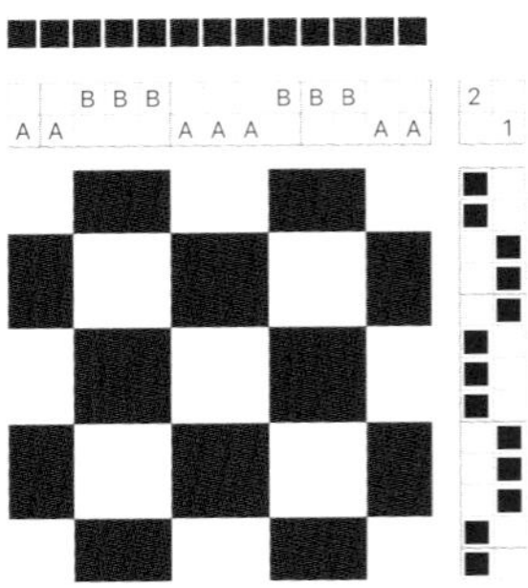

Figure 86 ***Profile draft with 2 blocks assembled***

Working with a profile draft means drawing in two rows and two columns. Here are some examples where the size of the blocks is different, and where the repetition is organized (see Figure 87).

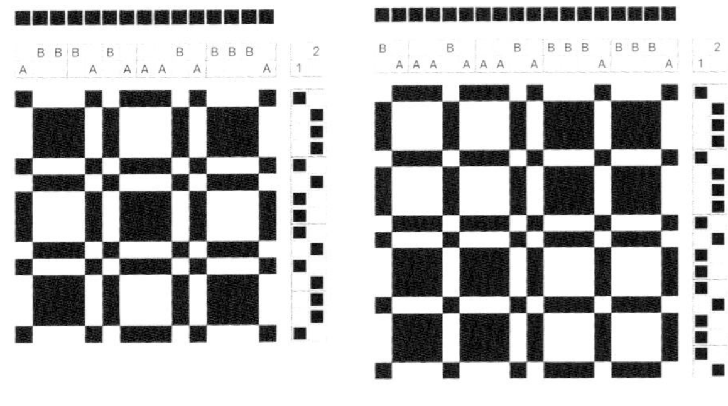

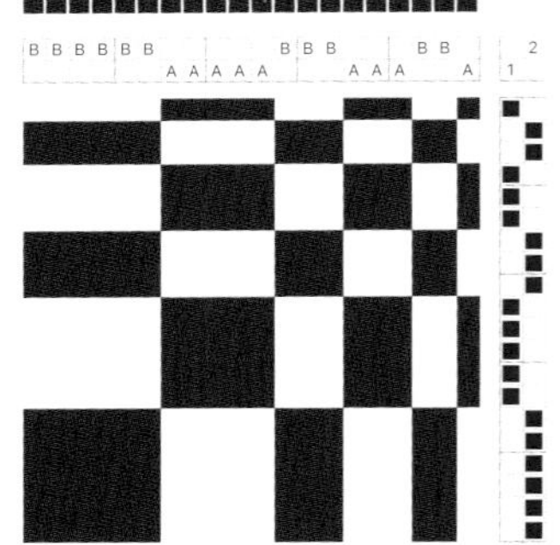

Figure 87 ***A few variations of twill profile drafts: 2 blocks of 4 shafts***

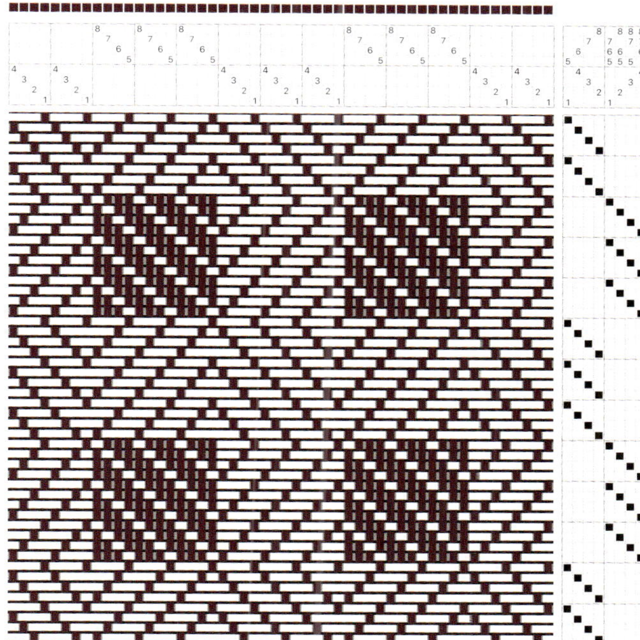

Another way to work is to not vary the size of the blocks, neither in threading nor in treadling, but to have fun just with the tie-up. Everything is done by arranging the quadrants of the tie-up draft. It's amazing how this simple change radically transforms the look of the fabric.

My favorite effect is achieved by working with the contrasts in each of the quadrants by:

- putting the 1/3 twill and the 3/1 twill next to each other;
- reversing the direction of the slope;
- watching the edges of each quadrant so that there is a real break between each block.

Figure 88 *Twill, 8 shafts. Soie de Marie, 50% wool, 50% Madagascar silk*

I would like to present the remarkable work of Alice Schlein. In addition to varying the blocks and the tie-ups, she introduces the use of multiple colors in warp and in weft to magnify the complexity of the pattern. Unobtrusively, in a first example, the color matches the block. Then the color is shifted to the adjacent block, in the middle of it. Finally, she dares to move the position of the color just a bit, both in warp and weft. It is this "just a bit" that gives real character to this composition. The block and color are paired on a ratio of one third to two thirds.

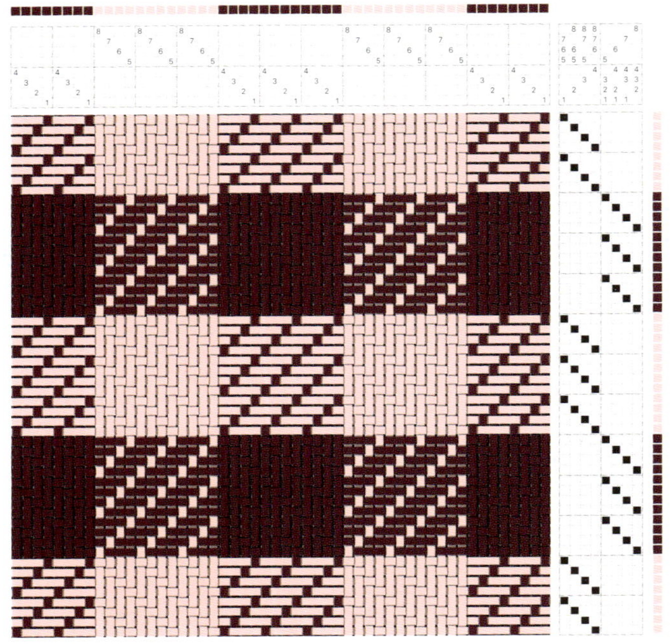

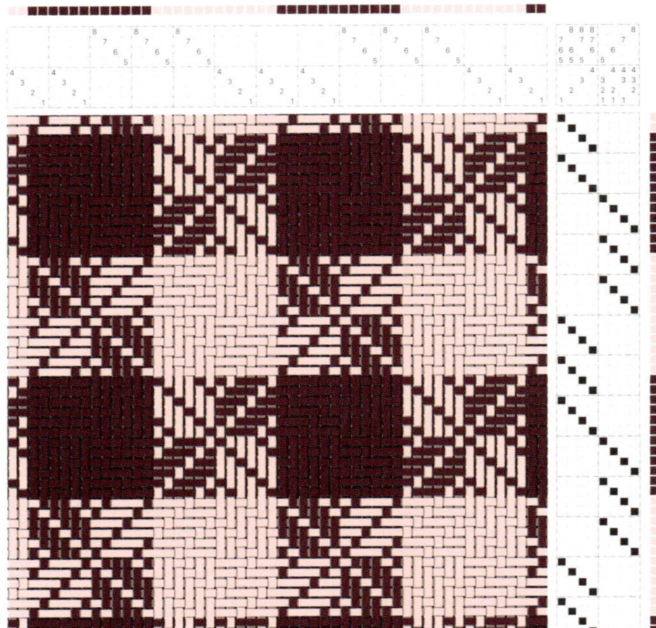

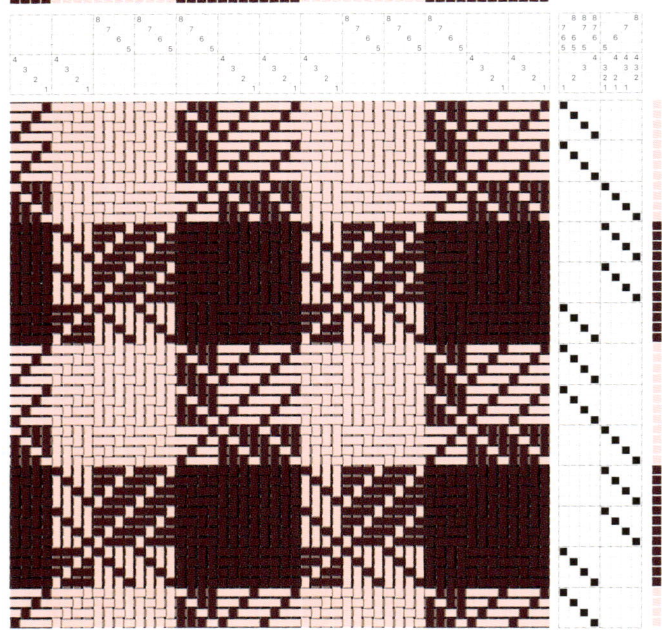

Figure 89 ***Fun with threading and treadling blocks and yarn colors. Hand towel inspired by the work of Alice Schlein, 8 shafts. Venne 22/2 Cottolin.***

Undulating Twill: New Vocalizations

With the presence of floats and the shifting of the binding point, twill brings a nice fluidity to the fabric. We can encourage this characteristic by threading or treadling more gradually. We could thread several ends in a row on the same shaft or, conversely, skip a shaft. This will immediately break the usual uniformity of the diagonal, and will tilt or straighten the 45 degree angle we are taught to aim for.

It is generally not a good idea to bring too much inventiveness to one project, and it would be advisable to choose a simple tie-up with this varied threading. Once again, this structure is possible on 4 shafts but much more fun on 8 shafts.

By threading several adjacent threads on the same shaft, we remove binding or interlacing points. This removes some of the fabric's stability, making it very flexible. Fewer binding points means floats, which can rather quickly become very long. So don't overdo it, and limit it to a few threads side by side. By decreasing the number of intersections, the space needed for the weft to pass through is also decreased. The density of this type of weave should then be increased to give it durability.

The yarn used also has a great impact. Viscose will excessively accentuate the fluidity of this structure, while wool floats will be locked in place by washing. You can enjoy the visual aspect of the wavy lines without suffering too much from the disadvantages.

It can be tricky to find the right balance for this fabric.

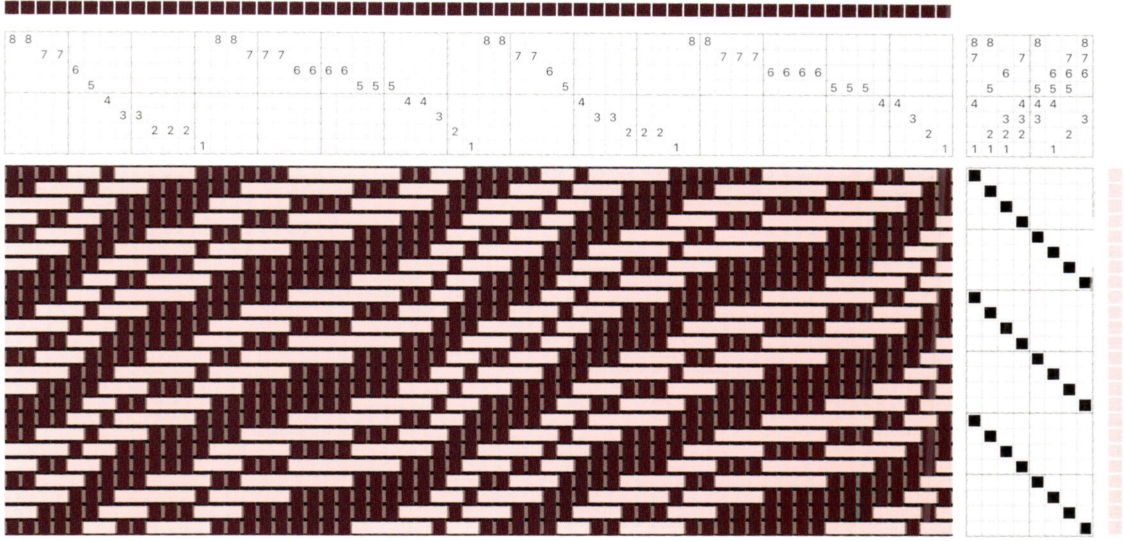

Figure 90 **Undulating (wavy) twill**

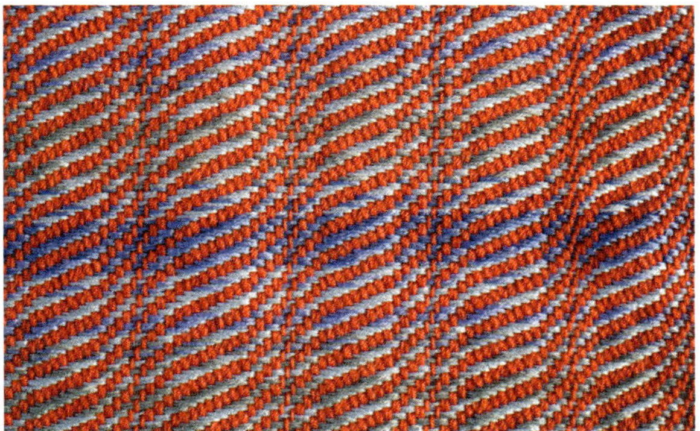

Figure 91 **Undulating twill. Various yarns.**

Plaited Twills: The Weaver's Braid

As its name suggests, the organization of the warp and weft threads shows a kind of braiding, which resembles some contemporary Japanese fabric prints.

In the style of William G. Bateman, the threading is divided into two groups. On the first two shafts, every other thread is placed in a consistent order as for a plain weave, while the other threads are laid as for a reverse or broken twill.

Multiple variations are possible and it is simply amazing to see how a single thread added to the threading completely transforms the pattern. The example in Figure 92 shows this with three threadings where the changes are very minimal. Not to be missed as you explore the possibilities!

Figure 92 ***Three threadings for plaited (braided) twills***

Figure 93 ***Plaited twills, 8 shafts. Japanese silk, 8,433 yd/lb (17,000 m/kg)***

Figure 94 ***Miniature kimono in braided twill***

Twill in Weft-Faced Rep: A Key Change!

Let's go back to the conventional threadings from the beginning of the chapter, with straight, point, M & W, and fishbone threadings. Another world to explore within them is **weft-faced weaves**. We have already discussed this possibility with plain weave. We choose a warp density that is so low that the weft threads will set down on top of each other until they completely cover the warp. With 4 shafts, the possibilities are no longer limited to only 2 columns, but to 4. With 5 or 6 shafts, the definition of our designs shows more details. With more than 6, the floats in the back often become bothersome and we don't really play with this technique anymore.

This weft-faced weave is very instinctive. Start carefully at the beginning by following a pattern, then invent! The following is a very brief introduction to this technique, which is already covered in many books, especially the one by Nancy Arthur Hoskins, *Weft-Faced Pattern Weaves*.

Figure 95 ***Weft-faced rep in rotation, 2/2 twill, 4 shafts. Fonty BB Merinos, 1,985 yd/lb (4,000 m/kg)***

Threading, Tie-Up, Treadling: Some Points of Reference

With plain weave weft-faced rep, remember that the warp ends were alternately threaded in shaft 1 and shaft 2. We alternated two treadlings, one to cover the ends threaded in shaft 1, the other for those threaded in shaft 2. We used two shuttles, and only two colors per pick.

With 4 or more shafts, the threading can be done in straight or repeat twill or in rosepath. The warp ends are covered one by one, shaft by shaft. The first weft only covers the thread from shaft 1. The second covers those from shaft 2 and so on. A treadling sequence is complete when all warp ends from the four shafts are covered. The treadling sequence is always the same. Only the color of the weft changes and reveals the pattern. The number of colors used together on the same row becomes more important and it is then necessary not to mix the shuttles. This sequence will be repeated until the desired pattern is obtained.

Traditionally, **the weft rep tie-up** is for a sinking shed and the symbol for this is a cross in the tie-up draft. Of course, it is possible to weave with a rising shed loom. To do this, all shafts except the one indicated are raised, i.e., those that are threaded with the ends that are not to be covered by the weft.

Two Tie-Ups Are Used

When only **one shaft** is lowered (or one is not raised!), this is 3/1 or 4/1 or 5/1 twill, depending on the number of shafts used. A line in the drawing then corresponds to as many weft passes as there are shafts to cover all the warp ends.

In the following example, one pattern row corresponds to 4 weft passes; the ends from shaft **1 are covered**, then those from shaft 2, then those from shaft 3, then those from shaft 4. This order is respected until the end of the weaving! It is only the order of the colors that changes according to the desired pattern:

- first line of the pattern: weft 1 - orange, weft 2 – blue, weft 3 – blue, weft 4 – blue. Sequence to be repeated as many times as needed until pattern is completed. Five times in the example in Figure 96;
- second line: weft 1 – orange, weft 2 – orange, weft 3 – blue, weft 4 – blue. With the same number of repeats;
- third line: weft 1 – blue, weft 2 – orange, weft 3 – orange, weft 4 – blue;
- and so on!

Figure 96 ***Weft-faced rep in rotation, 3/1 twill, 4 shafts. Fonty BB Mérinos, 1,985 yd/lb (4,000 m/kg)***

Two adjacent shafts are lowered (or not raised) with the regular 2/2 twill. As for the preceding weave, the order of the picks does not change. Only the order of the colors changes. Depending on the examples, 4-1 treadling is or is not used. One row of pattern is then composed of three or four wefts.

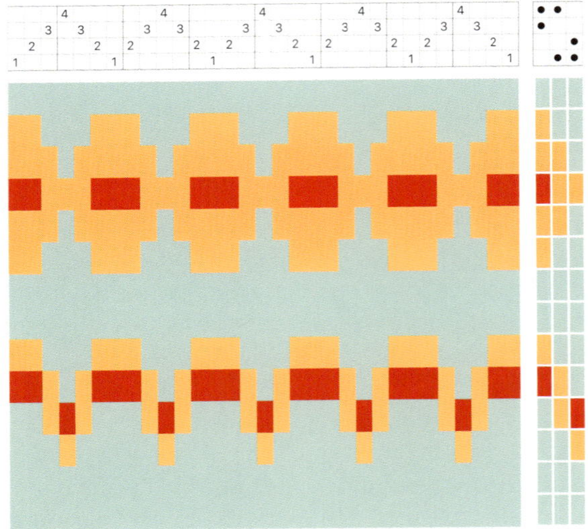

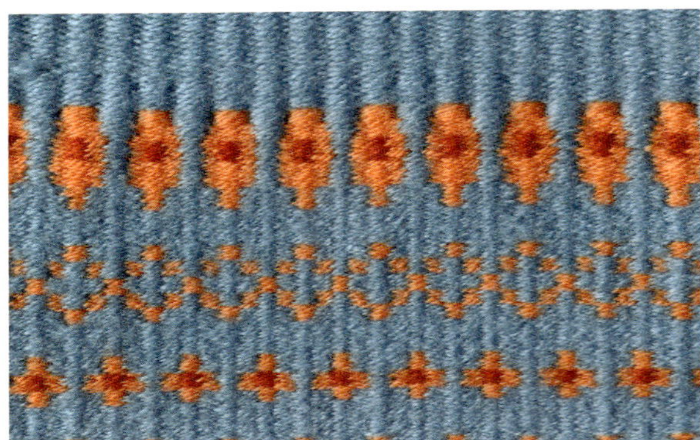

Figure 97 ***Weft-faced rep in rotation, 2/2 twill, 4 shafts. Fonty BB Mérinos, 1,985 yd/lb (4,000 m/kg)***

Two Types of Treadling Are Used

The most natural is **treadling in rotation**, like the examples in Figure 96. We follow the order of the treadles 1, 2, 3, and 4, each tied up to two or three shafts. With each new shed, the shuttle is passed with the color of your choice, then this rotation consistently starts again, with only the weft colors changing. With this treadling, 3/1 twill is more suitable, and in this case, the image is created as if you were drawing with a pencil. When we use 2/2 twill, the weave is softer, but less precise.

Treadling on opposites is only done with a 2/2 tie-up. It is sometimes called flamepoint, a term more traditionally used with the overshot or on opposites threading. On four shafts, a pattern line consists of two passes. The first weft covers the threads of two adjacent shafts with one color, immediately followed by a different color weft with the opposite shed. Again, it is easier to explain with a profile draft:

- Block A: the threads of shafts 1 + 2 are covered with the orange wool, then immediately after, the threads of shafts 3 + 4 are covered with the blue. This row is repeated as many times as needed to complete the pattern chosen;
- Block B: the threads of shafts 2 + 3 are covered with the orange wool, followed by the blue on the threads of shafts 4 + 1;
- Block C: the weft with the orange wool covers the threads of shafts 3 + 4, then the blue weft covers the threads of shafts 1 + 2;
- Block D: the weft with the orange wool covers the threads of shafts 4 + 1, then the blue weft covers the threads of shafts 2 + 3;
- each sequence is repeated as many times as needed according to the pattern.

This sample is made on the same reverse twill threading of the previous example, but this time with treadling on opposites.

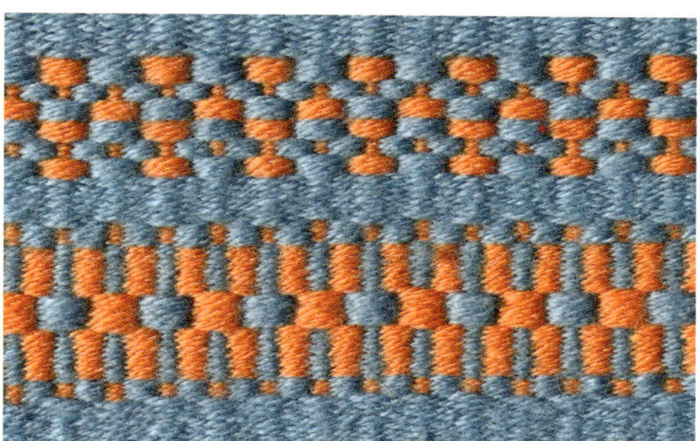

Figure 98 *Weft-faced rep on opposites, 2/2 twill, 4 shafts. Fonty BB Mérinos, 1,985 yd/lb*

To Your Instruments: First Picks in G Major

The purpose of these very simple examples is to introduce you to weft reps by showing you a few ways to decipher some works and launch you on your way in these very gratifying and delightful weaves. I have relied heavily on the remarkable publications of Clotilde Barret and Nancy Arthur Hoskins.

Get started with reverse twill threading 1-2-3-4-3-2, etc. Get some shuttles with colored yarns, and place your colored wefts on the warp threads not raised. Try the 3/1 tie-up first as it is very intuitive. You will cover the threads of shaft 1 that have remained lowered, then those of shaft 2, shaft 3, and shaft 4. With each pass, you will choose to keep the same color or not. And depending on your choice of pattern or yarn, you will need to repeat this sequence of picks for as long as needed to see your design appear.

Figure 99 *Weft-faced rep in rotation, 3/1 twill, 4 shafts*

One day you will try the same threading but on 5 or 6 shafts. The more shafts you have, the sharper the outline, but the more substantial the floats are on the back.

Figure 100 *Weft-faced rep in rotation, 5/1 twill, 6 shafts. Fonty BB Mérinos, 1,985 yd/lb (4,000 m/kg)*

Then you will try the 2/2 twill tie-up, with the same colors and the same order. And why not try out treadling on opposites? This weave in red and black is made on this threading. Repetitions of the treadling reveal this wavy rep.

Figure 101 ***Weft-faced rep on opposites, 4 shafts, 2/2 twill. Fonty BB Mérinos, 1,985 yd/lb (4,000 m/kg)***

Figure 102 ***Krokbragd weft-faced rep in rotation, 3 shafts, 2/1 twill. Fonty Zéphir wool, 3,720 yd/lb (7,500 m/kg)***

Krokbragd is a popular weave in the northern European countries. It is woven on 3 shafts, with **reverse twill threading, 2/1 tie-up, and 1-2-3 rotation treadling**. With two or three colors, you will see small geometric patterns emerge. In Scandinavia, when you work on more than 3 shafts with rosepath threading, this is traditionally called ***boundweave***. When the patterns are geometric with a straight twill threading on 4 shafts, it is called ***Indian saddle blanket***, referring to the blankets used by the Navajos.

When the Question of Density Comes Up Again and Again

The great difficulty of this weaving is choosing the right correlation between the weft yarn and the warp density. So you will have to make a sample to find the exact balance between these two choices. Is the density too low? The weave will be soft. Is it too high? The warp will not be completely covered. The less the weft is twisted, the more it can be pressed down on the previous weft, the more it can spread out and the more the warp will be covered.

If you have 6 shafts, quickly test the 1-2-3-4-5-6-5-4-3-2 threading. Realize that you will need 6 shafts to make a pattern row. Equip yourself with a large number of shuttles wrapped with colored yarn. Practice with existing patterns and then, inevitably, have fun creating your own designs. Test the difference between 5/1 and 4/2 tie-ups, not forgetting to adjust the density.

Remember that to cover a single row, you need to have as many passes of weft as you have shafts threaded. And to cover 1 inch, you have to repeat this sequence several times. It is not unusual to have a weft density of 60 ppi (24 per cm). This weaving will take a long time to complete, and it consumes a lot of yarn. But it is so much fun to make! And the result is always visually appealing.

Finishing the Ends: The Final Arrangements

The warp is subjected to high tension and a lot of friction from the reed. A highly twisted cabled cotton is ideal for a rug. It is not necessary to use a thick yarn, but rather a strong yarn.

A **floating selvedge** is recommended, and it can even be doubled to resist wear and tear from the reed. For this reason, the use of a **temple** is really desirable.

The warp is not subject to much shrinkage because it does not go around the weft. Because of this, the weft will tend to slide. Finishing the ends should prevent the fabric from fraying. Paris stitch alone may not be enough. I often weave about 2 inches (4 to 5 cm) of plain weave with a very thin weft, which I finish with the Paris stitch. This border is folded under the weave as a hem. Sometimes, I sew a border that I turn over. That said, making knots with the warp ends, or a kind of macramé, is still the easiest and most secure. We just want everything to be solid!

Weft reps are great for a rug. Nevertheless, it deserves to be tried out with a fine yarn, usually mercerized cotton or wool. Of course, it will take a long time, but the result is sublime.

Satin

And so, on a clear summer's day,
The great sun, complicit in my joy,
Shall make, amid the satin and silk,
Your dear beauty more beautiful still.

Verlaine, *La Bonne Chanson*, 1870

Figure 103 *Satin, 10 shafts. Mercerized cotton*

Satin is the third and last basic structure.

Its uniqueness lies in the fact that it is never **offset** by 1 like in twill. Unlike the latter, where we want to see the perfectly diagonal ribs, here the **binding points** are scattered as much as possible so that the floats are free, so they can move and get closer to each other more easily, until those interlacings are hidden. The result is a plain, smooth, shiny fabric.

Satin is not a structure commonly used by weavers because its **density** is necessarily high. It therefore uses up a lot of yarn and time. It also requires **at least 5 shafts**. I am going to present some properties that will help you get to know it, recognize it, and weave it a little for those who dare!

More visible, the threads show themselves as they are, and it is an opportunity to use beautiful materials. This is why satin is often associated with silk, a thread whose shine is magnified by this structure. But all yarns are welcome!

Warp- or weft-faced satin? We have two different terms for this: satin for warp-faced and sateen for weft-faced. Of course, we can instinctively see the difference. But we are faced with a dilemma. Warp satin is the most lustrous, and therefore the most sought after. On the other hand, it is also the most physically demanding on the loom, as it requires the most shafts to be raised.

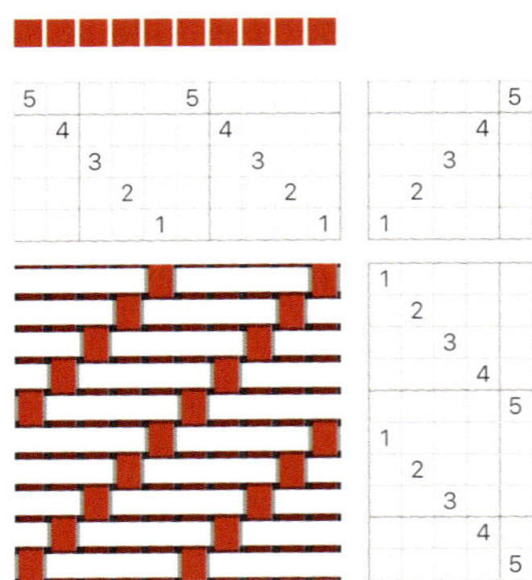

Figure 104 ***Straight twill on 5 shafts***

Creating a Satin Without Cacophony

Consecutive combinations of sounds are called melody; simultaneous combinations are called harmony, in general, and chords specifically.

François-Joseph Fétis, *Traité d'Harmonie*, 1849

Once again, those who are not interested in mathematics can skip this section, and let the others have fun! For that is what it is all about: looking for mathematical arrangements.

First off, for our study, we will take a five-shaft satin. Let's remember that the general rule is that the offset cannot be 1, or "n," or "n-1,"—"n" being the weave unit. In the case of the satin we will be looking at here, n = 5; we weave on 5 shafts, so the offsets of 1, 5, and 4 are impossible. We are left with offsets of 2 and 3.

Let's go step by step and work on a satin with offset of 2.

First Movement: Composing a Satin from a Straight Twill

Five shafts, straight threading, tromp as writ, 1/4 twill. That's everything! The rib of the diagonal is clearly visible. It is perfectly diagonal. With each weft, a warp end is followed by a 4-thread weft float.

Let's transform this order and spread out the binding points. For the first pick, raise shaft 1; the weft covers the four other threads that have stayed in place.

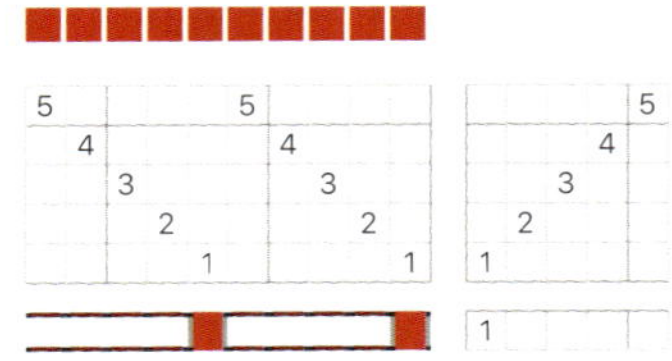

Figure 105 ***Straight twill on 5 shafts, satin tie-up, first pick***

For the second pick, we don't want to raise the adjacent shaft 2, or 5, also adjacent—don't forget. Having chosen an offset of 2, we raise shaft 3.

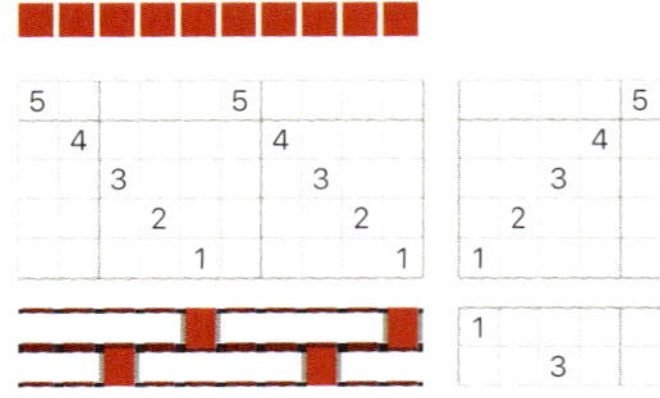

Figure 106 ***Straight twill on 5 shafts, satin tie-up, second pick***

The same logic applies to the third pick. We offset by 2, raising shaft 5.

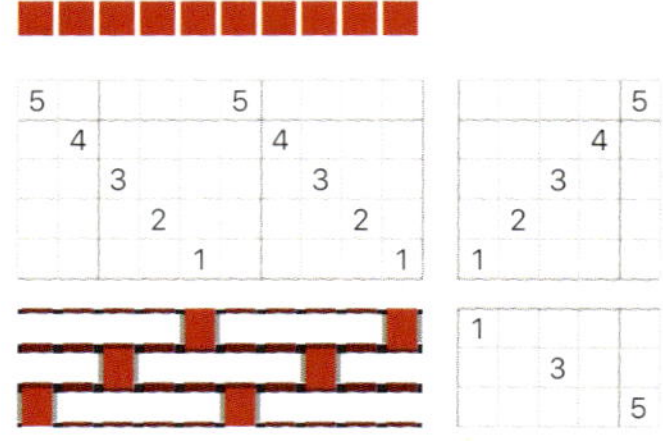

Figure 107 ***Straight twill on 5 shafts, satin tie-up, third pick***

Let's continue with the last shafts and raise shaft 2 then 4. The 5 weft picks have been placed and the weave unit is finished. We can start again at the beginning by raising shaft 1.

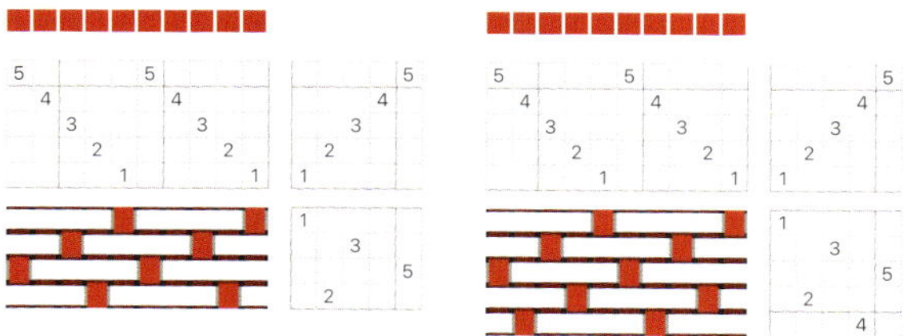

Figure 108 ***Straight twill on 5 shafts, satin tie-up, fourth and fifth picks***

Second Movement: Sateen Tie-Up!

The change is obviously smaller and some will not see it. However, I like to follow the tromp as writ or "treadle as drawn in" approach. And my inner reasoning is calmer when the tie-up clearly and precisely shows what is happening. This is also how it is very frequently written.

So here is the new version of the previous draft. Consider the advantage of this presentation. The offset of 2 is very visible. The sequence is 1-3-5-2-4.

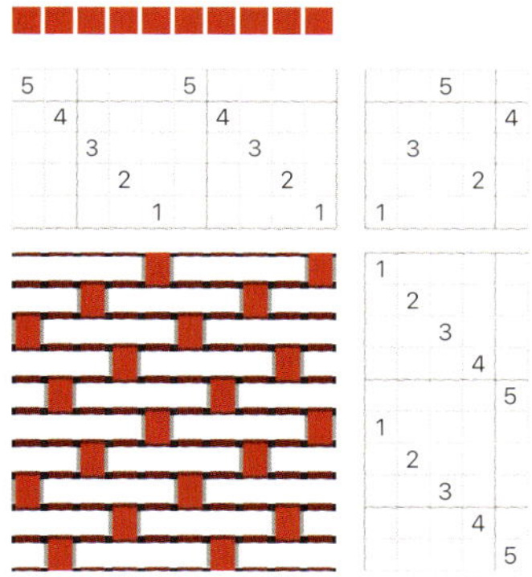

Figure 109 ***Sateen with offset of 2***

It is now easy to show the 3 satin. The offset of 3 in 3 will give the following sequence: 1-4-2-5-3. This changes little, except for the direction of the diagonal; we can play with it.

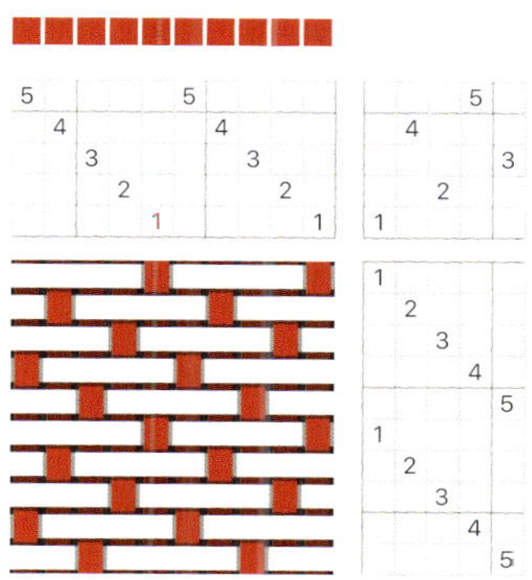

Figure 110 ***Sateen with offset of 3***

Third Movement *Allegretto moderato*: Adding Shafts

The larger the number of shafts, the more dispersed and distant the binding points are from each other. As a result, the floats are longer and have more room to cover the interlacing points.

With 6 shafts, you cannot make satin. The 1, "n," and "n-1" rule stated above helps us to check this mathematically.

With 7 shafts, we cannot choose offsets of 1, 6, and 7. Four types of satin remain, those with offsets of 2, 3, 4, or 5. They go in pairs, within which only the slope of the diagonal changes.

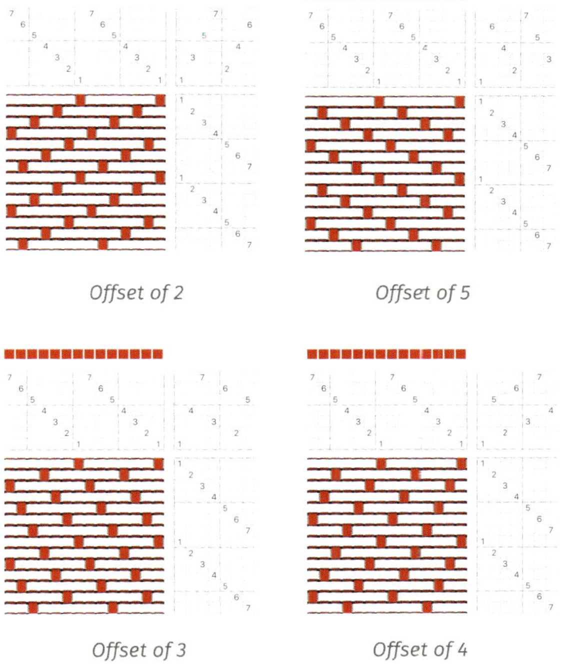

Figure 111 ***Various offsets in 7-shaft sateen***

For an 8-shaft satin, there cannot be offsets of 1, 2, 4, 6, 7, or 8. I know some who will want to verify that!

Last Movement: Warp-Faced Satin

Regardless of the offset, by transforming the 1/4 tie-up into a 4/1 on 5 shafts, we get a warp-faced satin. For a 7-shaft satin, we will choose 6/1 to get the warp effect.

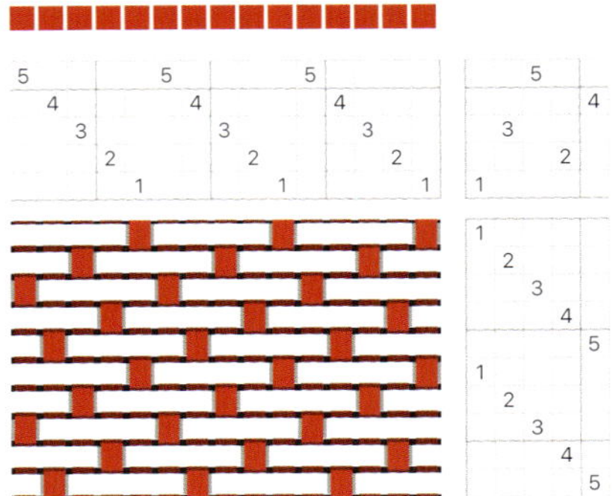

Weft-faced satin (sateen)

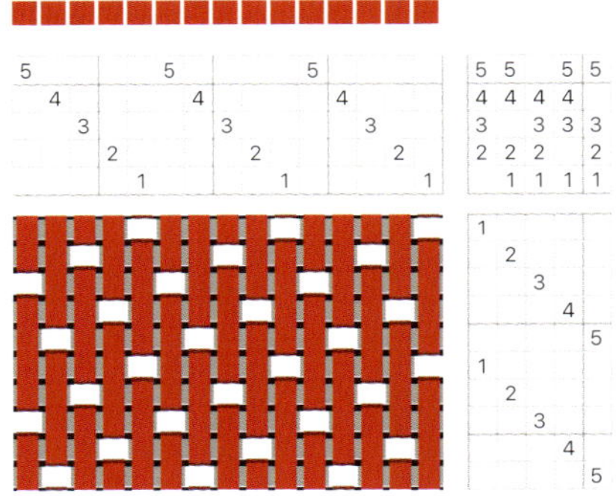

Warp-faced satin

Figure 112 *Tie-ups for weft-faced satin (sateen) and warp-faced satin*

How do you choose one or the other?

- The first criterion is undoubtedly your loom. Is lifting six shafts heavier and more difficult than lifting one shaft?
- If you want to highlight your warp, you will naturally choose the warp-faced satin.
- The reverse side of warp satin is sateen, even though in reality it is difficult to find the perfect balance of density to make it look just right.
- With the same yarn in warp and weft, warp satin shines more than sateen, probably due to the fact that the yarn is more taut on the loom.

Summary of the Characteristics of Satin

- At least five shafts are needed. Thanks to mathematics, it is easy to verify that not all satins are possible to make.
- The binding points are unobtrusive; they go around a single yarn and they are scattered in such a way as to allow the adjacent floats to cover them.
- For a 5-shaft with a 1/4 tie-up, the sateen is on the front side of the fabric, warp-faced on the reverse side. To obtain a satin with a warp effect, the tie-up is in 4/1.
- The number of interlacings in a weave unit is low, so much so that the density in warp and weft is high, and therefore the fabric is heavier and uses up more materials.
- Fewer interlacings and freer floats make the fabric more voluptuous and brighter, but fragile and more difficult to cut for clothing.
- The more shafts you have, the larger the offset, the further away the binding points are from each other and the more the floats can hide them by moving as close together as possible.

Weaving a Satin: Precious and Prized

Even though it's very likely that you won't often weave satin, for the reasons mentioned above, I suggest you try it anyway, playing with its distinctiveness—the very visible floats, a strong contrast between the warp floats and weft floats, very different front and back sides, almost pure colors, barely altered by the thread that crosses.

A Pair of Contrasts by Column or by Row

Plain weave shows as much warp as weft; 2/2 does as well, but by showing off the yarn using floats. Warp-faced satin shows almost exclusively the warp threads on the top of the fabric and weft floats underneath. While continuing to be very careful because of the different densities depending on the structure, it is very enjoyable to thread areas of plain weave alternating with areas of satin or weave in weft strips with a different tie-up. For other reasons, Hermès squares are made this way. In fact, the pure satin squares were too slippery and women lost them. Inserting small strips of plain weave limits this inconvenience.

Here is a very simple way to make this project. The first 5 shafts are reserved for the satin; shafts 6 and 7 are reserved for the plain weave.

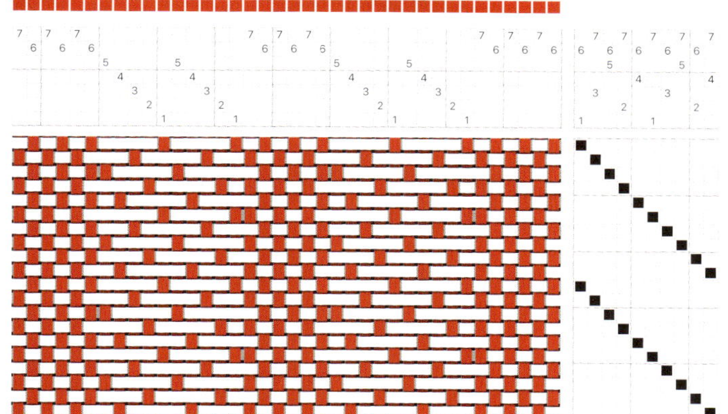

Figure 113 ***Satin alternating with plain weave on 7 shafts***

Figure 114 ***Satin alternating with plain weave on 7 shafts***

There is one small thing nonetheless. The weave unit of plain weave is 2, while the satin weave ratio is 5. In this example, you have to think about 10 weft shots to complete the whole weave unit of the two adjacent structures.

For the lucky owners of a 10-shaft loom, and to simplify the treadling of the preceding draft, it is easier to make an 8 satin and the plain weave on shafts 9 and 10. And to use 8 treadles. This way, the break between the strips of plain weave and satin is sharper.

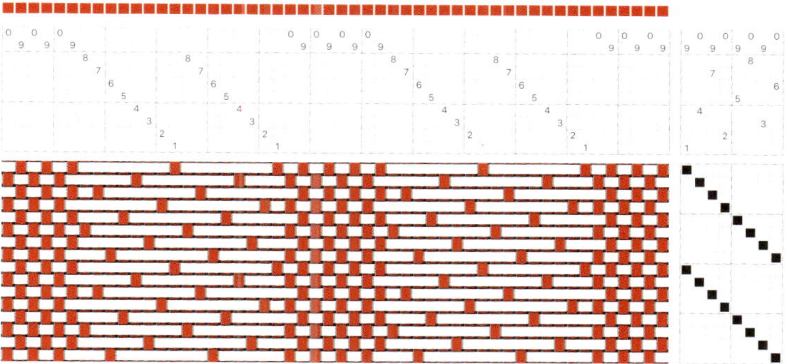

Figure 115 ***Satin alternating with plain weave on 10 shafts***

Later we will see how to manage densities as well as take-up, which are different for plain weave and for satin when you alternate between them for the threading.

To conclude this part of the duet between plain weave and satin, let's alternate them in warp and weft, and weave a Hermès-style scarf.

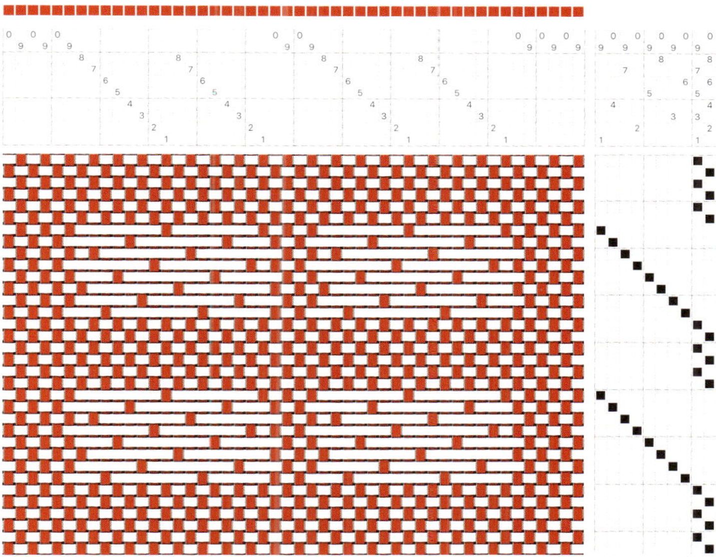

Figure 116 ***Satin alternating with plain weave in warp and weft on 10 shafts***

The main idea, which is not the simplest, is to find the right density to obtain a balanced satin and a balanced plain weave! Everything will be explained in a bit.

It is also necessary to pay particular attention to the place the two blocks meet so that no float goes over the edge into the adjacent block, so there is a real break between the two. It's through the tie-up draft that we can keep an eye on things.

Patterned Satins Almost Within Reach

Often on velvet and silky damask
We see the most hasty of the happy guests
Sit down early at the banquet.

Victor Hugo, *Odes*, 1828

Go to the Textile Museum in Lyon, look at the upholstery and soft furnishings fabrics from castles, stroll in an exhibition organized by Tours Cité de la Soie, and admire how a pattern is created simply from the opposition between warp-faced satin and weft-faced satin or sateen. In our own way, without wishing to attempt the gold weft brocades made in the Syrian city of Damascus between the 17th and 19th centuries, without imagining creating what the jacquard machine now can weave, it is possible for us to juxtapose blocks of warp-faced satin with weft-faced satin (sateen) and come close to damask.

It takes 5 shafts to make a satin, so we need 10 if we want to alternate warp and weft satins. I am well aware that there are not many of us who own a loom of this kind, so I will not elaborate too much on this.

To attempt this weave, use the section found under twills called "The Orchestra Is Growing: Twill on an 8-Shaft Loom" (p. 159). The idea is exactly the same: to thread a series of A blocks in 1-2-3-4-5, followed by a series of B blocks in 6-7-8-9-10. Treadle as drawn in. The tie-up draft is again divided into quadrants in which we tie up either weft- or warp-faced. Some examples follow..

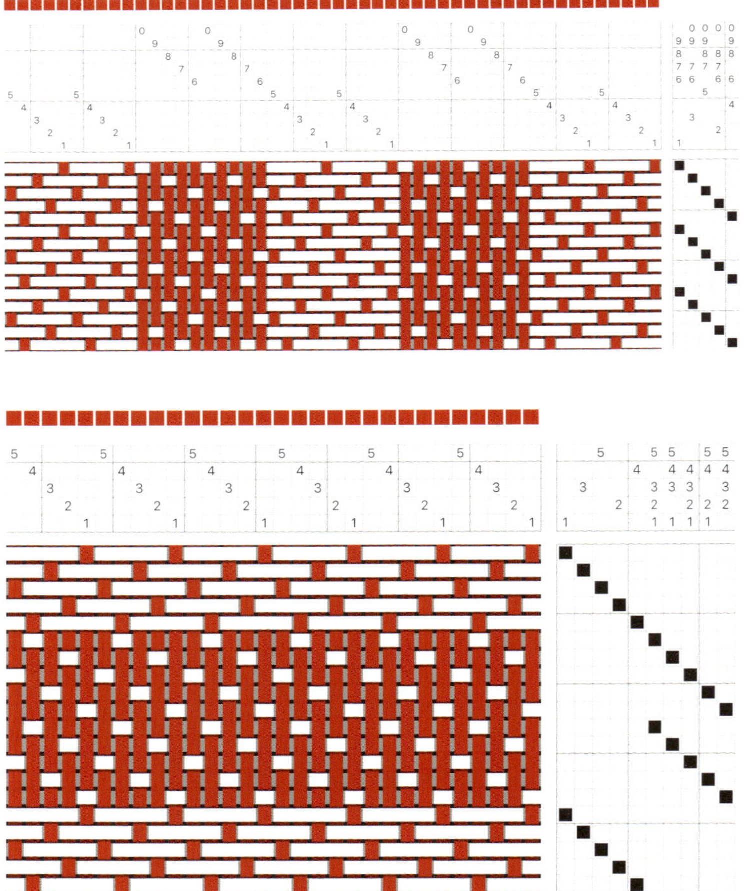

Figure 117 ***Warp- and weft-faced satin in rows and warp- and weft-faced satin in columns***

By condensing these two previous drafts, we can imagine playing in the big leagues. Without a jacquard loom, it's impossible to make true damask. Nevertheless, weaving this fabric makes you dream! Like twill, the quality of the patterns will be seen where they join. Everything is done in the tie-up draft. No warp float should spill over into its neighboring weft strip.

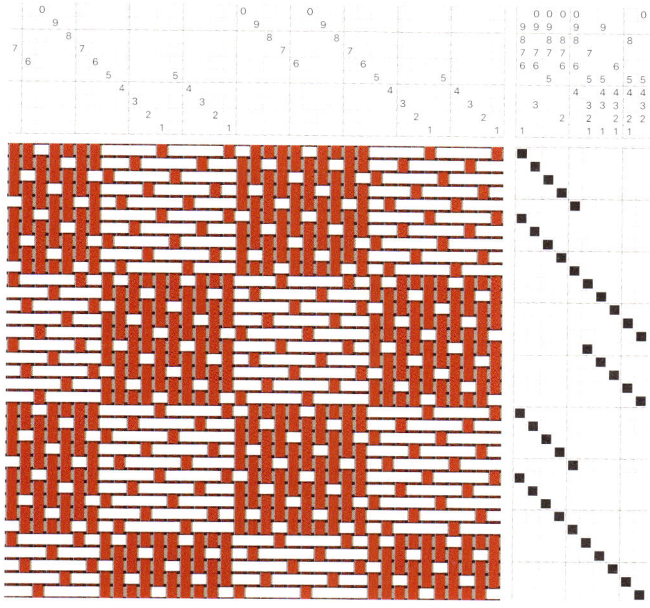

Figure 118 ***Damask, 10 shafts. MERO 266 Royal Linen Nm, 100% pure fine linen, 1,989 yd/lb***

When the Satin Draft Becomes a Base for Improvisation: Satinés

This type of structure was widely used, for some number of years, in the manufacture of worsted wool fabrics. The remarkable success of the corkscrews had no equal except that of *casimir* fabrics.

R. Beaumont, *Fabrication des lainages*, 1893

It is something that my analytical mind very much appreciates, redirecting the function of a draft and getting inspired about something else. Here are a few examples on 8 shafts.

Let's take the tie-up of an 8 satin with an offset of 3 and add some new binding points in the tie-up draft. For example, a new interlacing above and another one next to it on the right around each of the existing 8 binding points. They are symbolized here by a gray square.

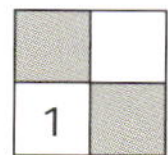

Figure 119 ***Addition of two binding points***

Figure 120 ***The new tie-up grid***

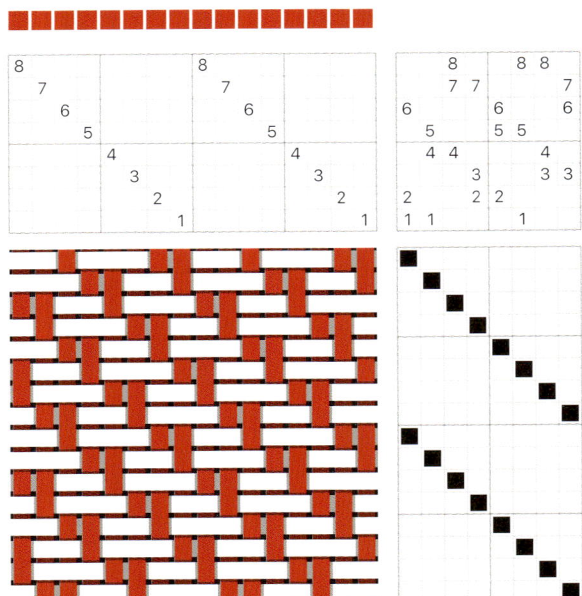

Figure 121 ***The weaving***

You can alter this tie-up by adding three binding points to the satin draft. An example of this is shown in Figures 121 and 124.

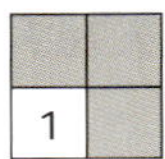

Figure 122 ***Addition of three binding points***

					8		
		7					
							6
				5			
	4						
						3	
			2				
1							

Figure 123 ***The new tie-up grid***

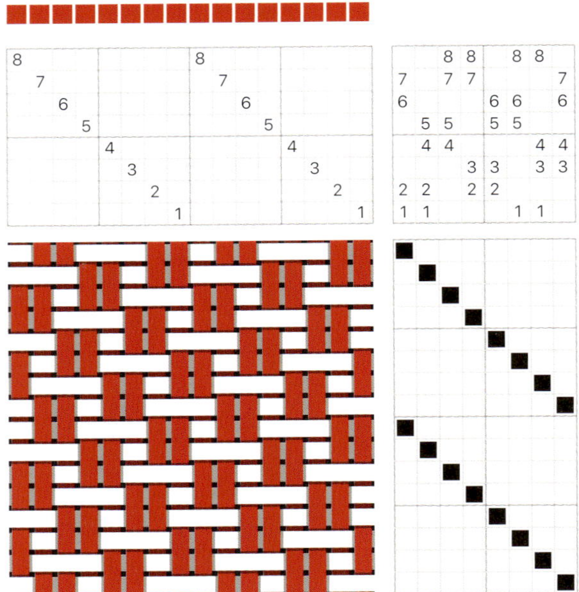

Figure 124 ***The weaving***

You will definitely get a balanced, sturdy, and yet original weave. This is really something to try with a beautiful worsted wool. Depending on the book, this can be called a derivative, transposed, satiné, or huckaback twill, etc. Sometimes, depending on the number of shafts, the offset and transformations, some tie-ups have their own name, including crepe, diagonal panama, corkscrew, whipcord, venetian, etc.

Figure 125 ***Huckaback twill, 8 shafts, Bart & Francis Linny Scott, 3,472 yd/lb (7,000 m/kg)***

With these new structures, we are walking a fine line between twill and satin. Similarly, with a 4- or 6-shaft loom, when it is impossible to make a real satin, we can make what we call a false satin or irregular satin. In a true satin, the offset is the same for the entire tie-up. In false satin, the offsets are irregular: 2, 3, or 4, as needed.

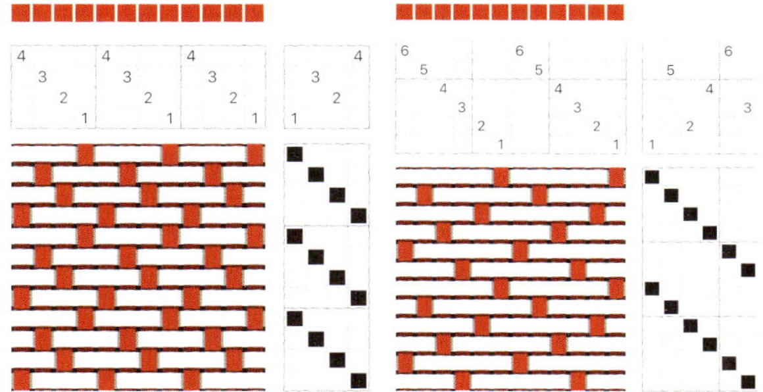

Figure 126 *False satin on 4 and 6 shafts*

Mastering a Satin

Density: The Perpetual Defining Moment of a Fabric!

Satin is a balanced weave and even if the diagonal line from the interlacings is less visible, we must be careful to create a fabric where the warp count and weft count are the same.

The principle does not change. The fewer the binding points, the closer the threads can move toward each other, and the higher the density.

I encourage you to use Ashenhurst's formula, wrapping a ruler with the yarn you've chosen. Be sure to keep the wraps close together and use the following formula:

$$\text{Density} = \frac{\text{No. of wraps of yarn around the Ruler} \times \text{No. of Warp ends in a weave unit}}{\text{No. of Warp ends} + \text{No. of Weft threads in this same weave unit}}$$

$$D = \frac{R \times Wa}{Wa + We}$$

With a 5-shaft satin, the number of warp ends in a weave unit is 5; the number of wefts is always 2. To get the density, you multiply the number of times the yarn wraps around 1 inch of the ruler by the number of warp ends, which varies depending on the number of shafts used: $D = R \times \frac{5}{5 + 2} = 0.72$.

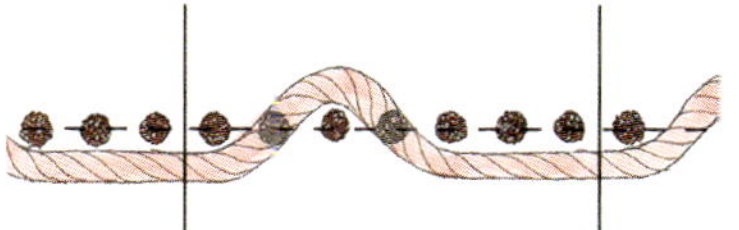

Figure 127 *Number of interlacings in a 5-shaft satin*

With an 8-shaft satin, the number of warp ends is 8, and weft is always 2. The percentage to be applied to the number of threads wrapped over 1 inch is: $D = R \times \frac{8}{8 + 2} = 0.80$.

Finally, for satins on 10 shafts in damask, we have two blocks of 5 satin. The density will thus be the number of threads × 0.72.

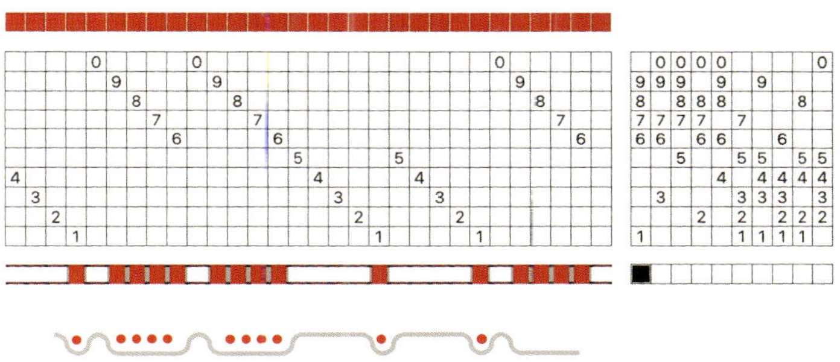

Figure 128 *Illustration of damask interlacing*

A bit more perilous is putting **plain weave and satin next to each other**. Neither the warp nor the weft density is the same for these two structures. We then decide to which of these two weaves we assign a square construction, the satin for example. Then, for adjacent areas in plain weave, we make a quick average between this weft density adapted to the satin and the ideal plain weave density, the one that will become the warp density for the plain weave.

It is also a good idea to put plain weave or cannelé on the selvedge to bring each weft to the ends by intertwining them. And to apply this change of density. The refrain is still the same: a sample is necessary!!! The sleying will be more dense for the satin. If it is decided to alternate weft, it will be necessary to have the control for a less firm beat to obtain a balanced plain weave.

Also take advantage of this sample to introduce colors and enjoy a warp effect or weft effect to highlight this new element. This is an uncommon structure where the thread color appears almost pure.

Different Types of Take-Up: The Risks of Slipping Up

Binding points are relatively rare in satin, which forces us to use a high density. The shrinkage, or take-up, is so small that it can be neglected when calculating the length of the warp.

Everything is fine until you place some plain weave in the middle of areas of warp satin. The more systematic intersecting of the warp with the weft requires a longer warp length. As you weave, there comes a time when the warp for the satin will float, will be less taut. However, unless you are weaving a very long project, it is not necessary to wind these two different warps separately on two warp beams. A little manipulation should do the trick. Lift the layer that is slack, slide in a solid slat under this layer, have it go around the back beam, and attach a weight to it that will hang off the back. This slat will act like a second warp beam.

The smallest event unfolds like fate, and fate itself unfolds like a wonderful, wide fabric in which every thread, guided by an infinitely tender hand, is held and supported by a hundred others.

Rainer Maria Rilke, *Letters to a Young Poet*, 1903

7

A Proliferation of Structures: The Orchestra Diversifies

It is absolutely necessary for the virtuoso to step aside before the composer, as the orchestra does in symphonies.

Hector Berlioz, *Studies on Beethoven, Gluck and Weber*, 1844

After these long instructions to understand what a weaving is, how a structure is built, how to think about the interlacing, how to find the right density, we will now cherry-pick from among these combinations to weave the usual structures or to invent as we please.

Threading has been straight until this point, and now it will be organized in a completely different order. You will even have to accept that plain weave is not only done by alternating odd and even shafts, as was the case until now.

What follows is an introduction to some of the most popular structures. I would have liked to describe them in as much detail as the previous ones, but that's a future book project. In order to not weigh down the aim of this book, only the fundamental characteristics will be briefly discussed—what gives them their particular identity—followed by some examples in the form of patterns.

A Concert of Compound Structures

Summer and Winter, overshot, and monk's belt are all weave patterns with floats built on a plain weave background—thus the name "compound structures." Two shafts, and therefore two shuttles, alternate to build the fabric to form:

- the plain weave with the same yarns as the warp;
- the pattern with a yarn that is a different thickness, color, or type.

The plain weave provides the ground cloth. It is sometimes called "tabby" or "binding pick." The patterns, made with floats, are placed as for a supplementary weft.

Depending on how the threading, treadling, and tie-up are organized, the patterns unfold differently and the floats are longer or shorter. Each structure was named based on these characteristics. However, these are primarily plain weave embellished with floats, and we will first try to determine the density of this plain weave.

Summer and Winter: The Two Seasons of a Weaver

If you spend all summer singing, you'll dance supperless to bed all winter.

Aesop, *Fables*

Figure 1 Summer and Winter weave. Design by Ineke Elsinga. Vlak-in-Vlak-in-Vlak

American colonists named this structure Summer and Winter because it traditionally has a light warp and a darker weft pattern thread, which gives the weave a distinctly lighter and darker side. You can almost imagine there are two blankets, simply turning it over to match the season. Traditionally woven in linen with dark wool floats, Summer and Winter can be worked with any yarn, as long as it suits the purpose: a cotton and linen table runner, a blanket in wool or alpaca, a silk scarf.

This is a structure that I particularly like because it is simple to design, the fabric is durable thanks to the tabby, the float length is secure, the treadlings are varied, and it is easy to change the design of the draft.

The drawdown in a profile draft simplifies both the design of the pattern and the weaving process: a straightforward outline to follow. There are as many blocks as shafts, minus two. The first two shafts are reserved for the foundation of this weave in tabby. With four shafts, we have two possible threading blocks.

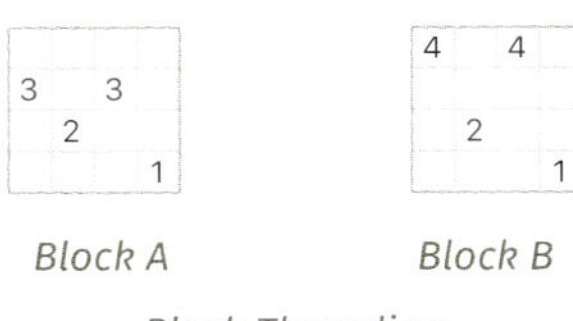

Block Threading

You can repeat these blocks as many times as you want; the floats will never exceed three threads. Below is an example of threading in a profile draft, and then the same expanded on the shafts.

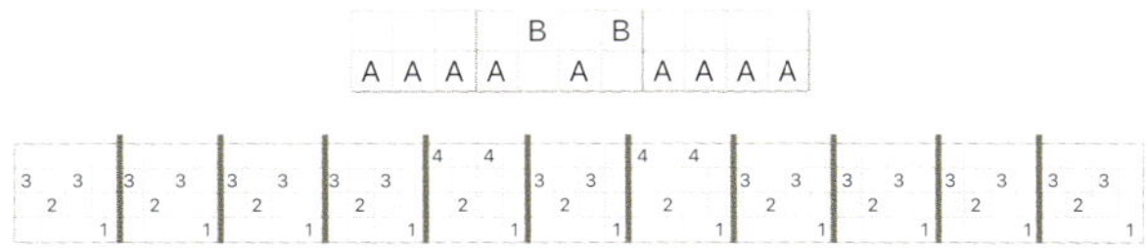

Figure 2 Threading in profile draft and then in expanded version

It is common to choose a light-colored thread for the warp so the colored pattern will really pop out.

Treadling

Two shuttles are needed, one for the tabby and the other for the float thread that will reveal the pattern. Traditionally, the tabby is made with the same yarn as the warp—same type, same color, same count—and the floats with a thicker, more voluptuous thread. Once you have experimented with this structure, you can change these norms to your liking.

As we know, plain weave is the regular alternating of odd-numbered threads (1st, 3rd, 5th, etc. warp end) and even-numbered threads (2nd, 4th, 6th, etc. warp end). In this structure, the odd ones are on shafts 1 and 2 and the even ones on all other shafts.

Four treadling groups are used: alternating, "X," "O," and in a column (also called dukagång). The drafts shown here show the two tabby picks, seen in the first two columns of each draft. Later we will opt to not show the tabby picks.

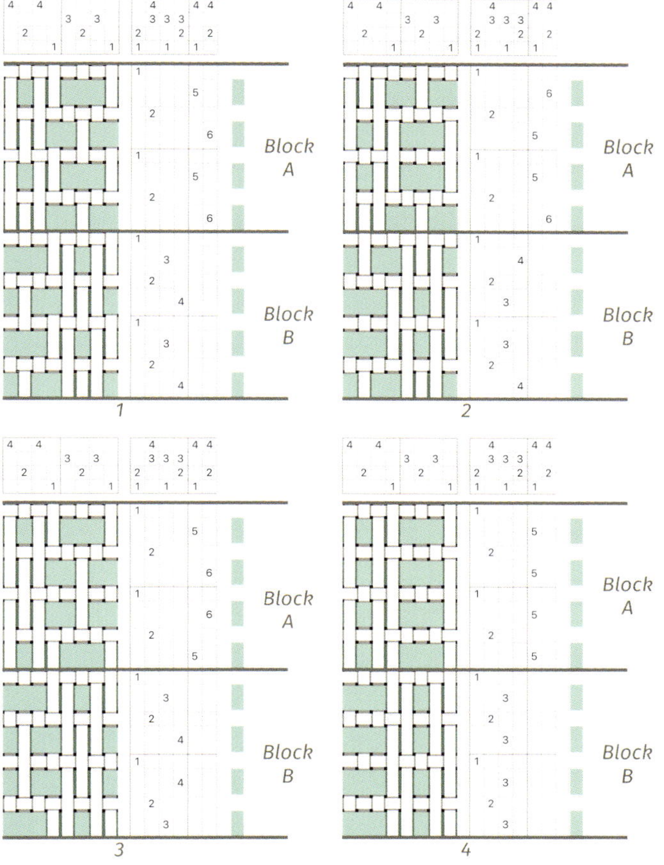

Figure 3 *The four treadlings for Summer and Winter: alternating (1), "X" (2), "O" (3), column (or dukagång, 4)*

Again, the profile draft is the ideal tool and again, the famous tromp as writ ensures a sharp, refined design.

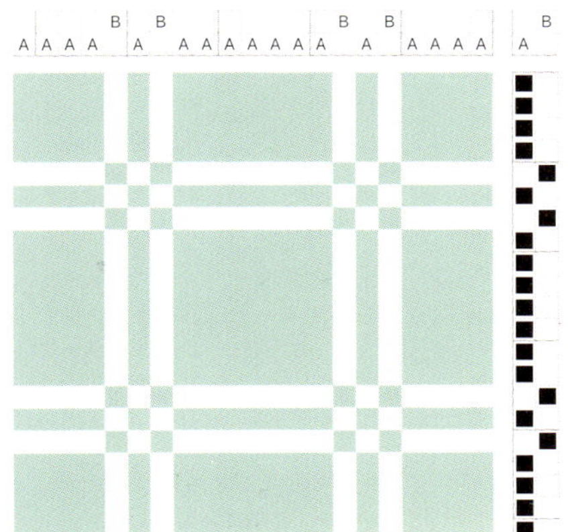

Figure 4 *An example of a symmetrical profile draft*

Each treadling block shown in the profile draft is a series of 8 picks: one tabby pick alternating with one pattern pick, the whole thing repeated four times. Let's simplify and agree that the first tabby pick raises the odd ends that are on shafts 1+2. Let's call it Odd tabby = O. The second tabby pick raises the even ends on shafts 3+4 and will be the Even tabby = E. These two picks will be woven with the same yarn as used for the warp.

Each tabby pick is consistently followed by a pattern pick. For each of these **pattern picks**, we alternate shaft 1 and then 2, each being accompanied by shafts 3 and/or 4. Because of this order where 1 and 2 alternate, the floats will never cross more than 3 threads! This way, we can repeat identical blocks in threading without risk of getting a float that's too long. Then we will change the order of shafts 1 and 2 in treadling and the appearance of the pattern will be transformed. With **alternating treadling**, shafts 1-2-1-2 follow each other along with pattern shafts 3 and/or 4. With **"X" treadling**, the order is 2-1-1-2. With **"O" treadling**, the order is 1-2-2-1, and with dukagång, only shaft 1 is raised. Nevertheless, in these four pattern picks, the more or less regular alternating of 1 and 2 ensures sensible floats.

With four shafts, we then have two blocks. The example below is based on **alternating treadling**, the preferred treadling when you're first starting to familiarize yourself with this structure, and shows the eight picks of each block:

- alternating treadling of block A: **O**dd tabby pick, pattern pick (shafts **1**+4), **E**ven tabby pick, pattern pick (shafts **2**+4). These four picks are repeated once so that block A is then complete. This sequence is then duplicated as many times as indicated in the profile draft;
- alternating treadling of block B: **O**dd tabby pick, pattern pick (shafts **1**+3), **E**ven tabby pick, pattern pick (shafts **2**+3). These four picks are repeated once to make block B complete, and then duplicated as many times as indicated in the profile draft.

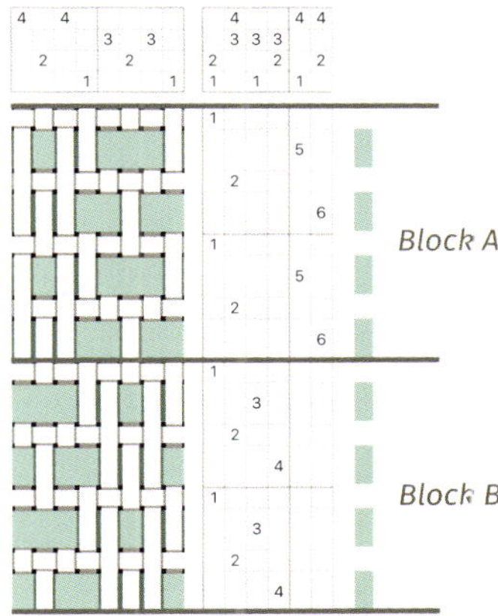

We can be systematic about throwing the shuttles. When the shuttle is to the left of the weaving, the shed of the odd tabby is opened, and conversely, when the shuttle is on the right side, we prepare the even tabby. We can also get used to always having the pattern shuttle "follow" the tabby shuttle. These are little mnemonic devices that are always welcome when weaving and that will quickly become a kind of reflex.

Here is the suggested sequence of movements of the two shuttles:

- **O**dd tabby shuttle (1+2) with tabby yarn: ⟶
- shuttle with pattern yarn (1+_): ⟶
- **E**ven tabby shuttle (3+4) with tabby yarn: ⟵
- shuttle with pattern yarn (2+_): ⟵

Be careful: very often treadling blocks are shown simplified, without the tabby. You may be reminded of this by the phrase "use tabby" or "binding pick." In any case, don't forget it!

Tie-Up

Summer and Winter is so powerful that with only four shafts and two blocks, we can choose to cover A blocks, B blocks, or both blocks with floats, remembering that what is not seen on the front is seen on the back.

So here are the ten possible tie-up combinations with four shafts.

1	2	3	4	5	6	7	8	9	10
	4			4	4			4	4
	3					3	3	3	3
2			2		2		2		2
1		1		1		1		1	

Figure 5 *The ten tie-ups for a Summer and Winter*

On this tie-up draft, the two columns on the left are reserved for the tabby. Pattern floats will appear on blocks A and B using the tie-up of columns 3 and 4. They will appear only in the threaded areas in block A with the tie-up of columns 5 and 6. They will be seen only in the areas threaded in block B with the tie-up of columns 7 and 8. They will only be visible on the back with the tie-up of columns 9 and 10.

With Summer and Winter, the order of the columns in the draft corresponds exactly to the order of the treadles on the loom: column 1, treadle 1, column 2, treadle 2, and so on. So the left foot will swing back and forth over the two treadles reserved for the tabby and the right foot will walk over the next four pairs of treadles, the two feet working together perfectly, alternating from one to the other.

Unfortunately, it's very rare to have 10 treadles on a 4-shaft loom. Often, with 6 treadles, the design may be limited by placing floats either in Block A (columns 5 and 6), or in Block B (columns 7 and 8). If you want to add the other two patterns (floats on the whole row on the front or back), the skeleton tie-up, shown on p. 258, will help you out.

Changes with 8 Shafts

As with other structures, having 8 shafts opens up a huge field of possibilities; you just have to expand each explanation given for a 4-shaft. We will now have 6 threading blocks; each one keeps its foundation of 1, n, 2, n. The "n" was 3 or 4 in our previous explanations on 4 shafts; it will become 5, 6, 7, or 8. The 1-3-2-3, 1-4-2-4 refrain will be expanded to 1-5-2-5, 1-6-2-6, 1-7-2-7, etc.

Concerning the tie-up, we keep in mind that the shafts not raised will receive the float; that is where the patterns will appear. If 8 pattern tie-ups are different with 4 shafts, imagine how many are possible with 8 shafts! And what an incredible freedom this brings to pattern design!

For treadling, we can always choose between alternating, "X," "O," or *dukagång* treadling, remembering that it is only the position of the 1 or the 2 in the sequence of 8 picks that changes the appearance of the pattern: 1-2-1-2 for alternating treadling, 1-2-2-1 for "O" treadling, 2-1-2-1 for "X" treadling, and 1-1-1-1 for *dukagång*.

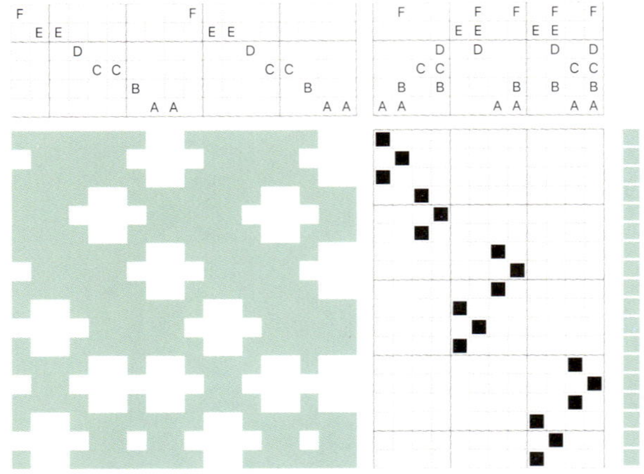

Figure 6 *A profile draft on 6 blocks and its expansion to 8 shafts with alternating treadling in the following figure*

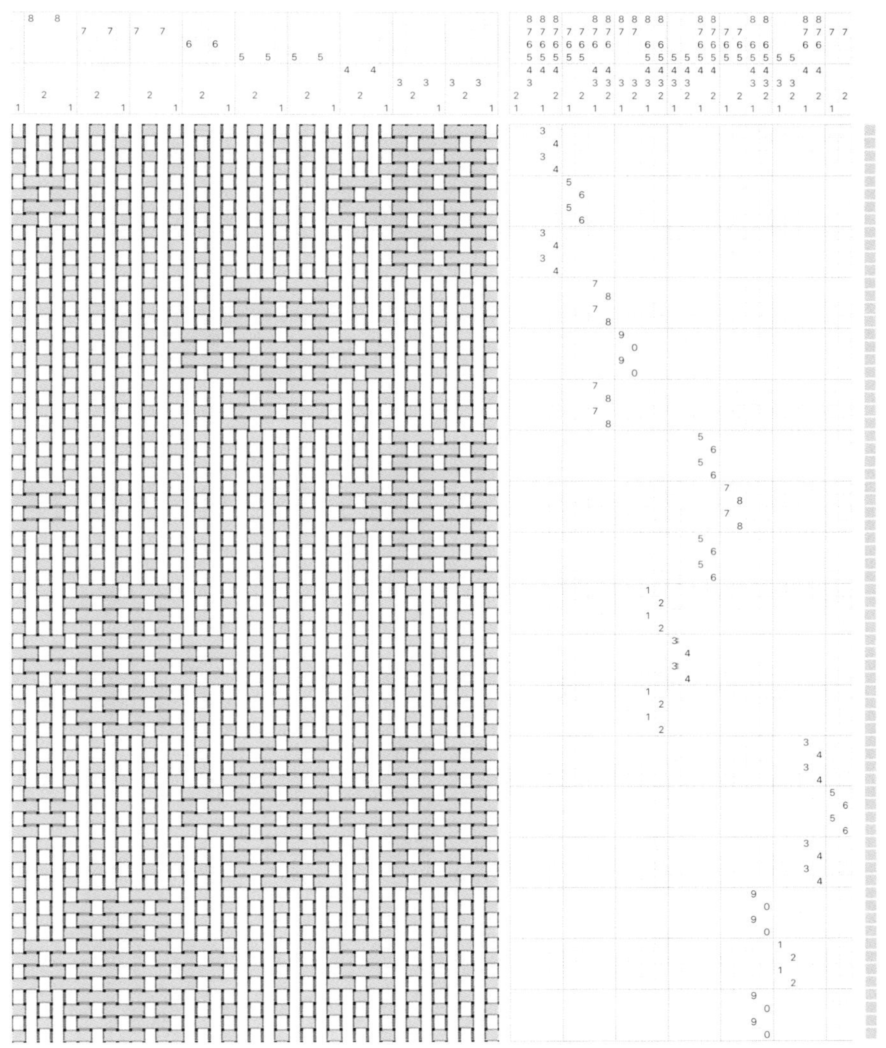

A Sample Woven on 4 Shafts

I propose this 4-shaft Summer and Winter as a sample weave, with which we will be able to practice transforming a profile draft into a regular weaving draft, try out a few different tie-ups, and check out the differences between the four treadlings.

PROJECT RECORD SHEET—A SUMMER AND WINTER WEAVE

Plain weave warp and weft: Venne 22/2 cottolin, pink

Pattern weft: Fonty Cotton Club 3, purple

Sett: 18 epi (7 per cm)

Width in reed: 11¾ in. (30 cm)

Total number of ends: 210

Project length: 51 in. (130 cm)

Warp length: 87 in. (220 cm)

% of shrinkage when taken off loom: 3%

% of shrinkage after washing: 3%

Fringe: ¾ in. (2 cm)

Loss due to front tie-on and at back of loom: 24 in. (60 cm)

Quantity of cottolin: 3.5 oz. (100 g)

Quantity of Cotton Club 3, purple: 1.75 oz. (50 g)

This is woven on 4 shafts; the profile draft shows 2 blocks.

Figure 7 **Profile draft on 4 shafts**

Of course, we could write up an expanded threading, but I am adamant that you should try to thread by referring to this simple version, which forces you to step back, and will undoubtedly keep you from making threading errors! To help, here is the transcription of the first six blocks only.

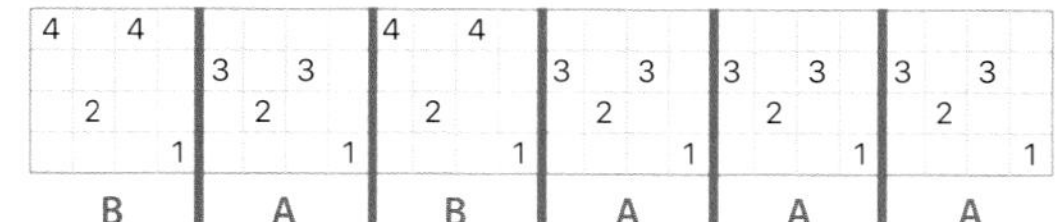

Figure 8 **Start of expanded threading**

Here are the four different tie-ups. As you weave, you will recognize the strip where the floats cover the two blocks, the one where the floats are seen on the back only, the strip where only the A blocks are covered, and then the one where the B blocks are covered.

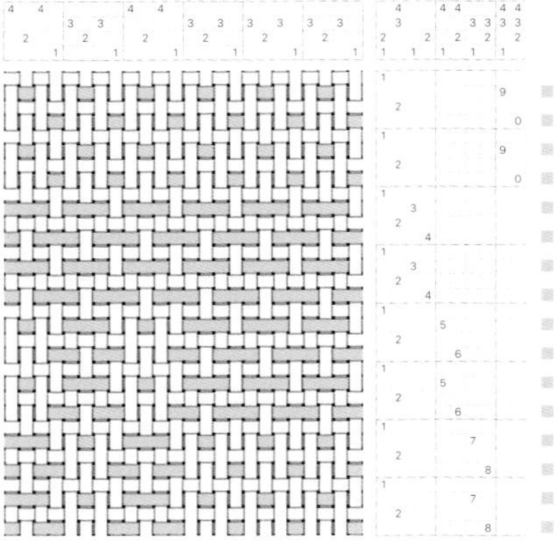

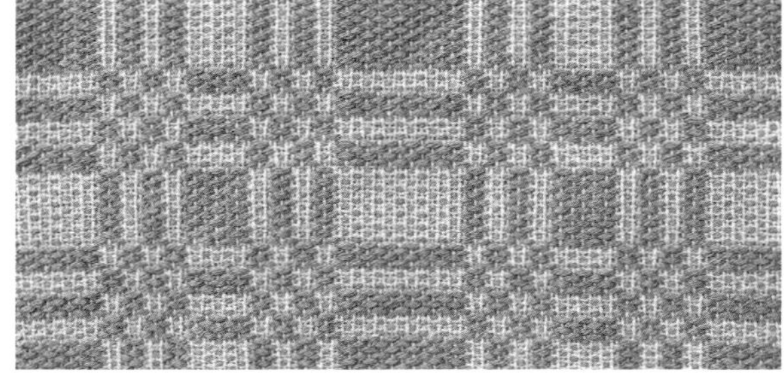

Figure 9 **Weave with alternating treadling and the 4 possible tie-ups**

To complete this example, here are the drafts of the three other treadlings.

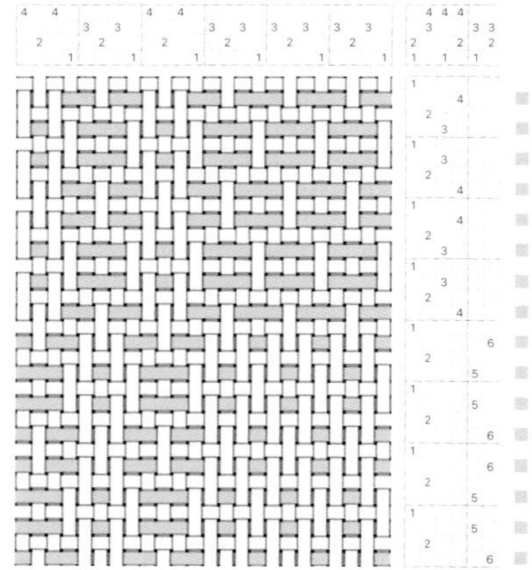

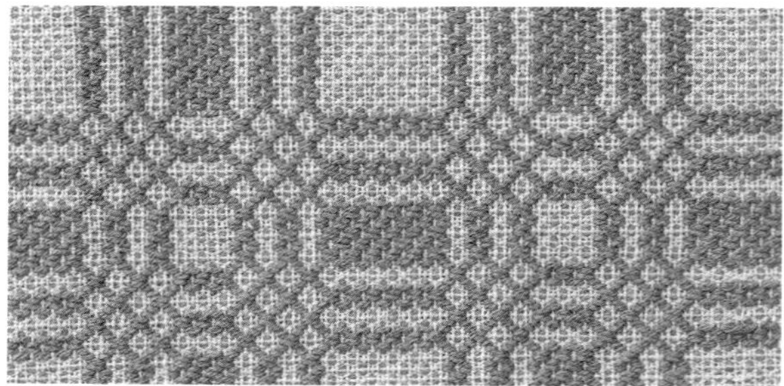

Figure 10 **"X" treadling**

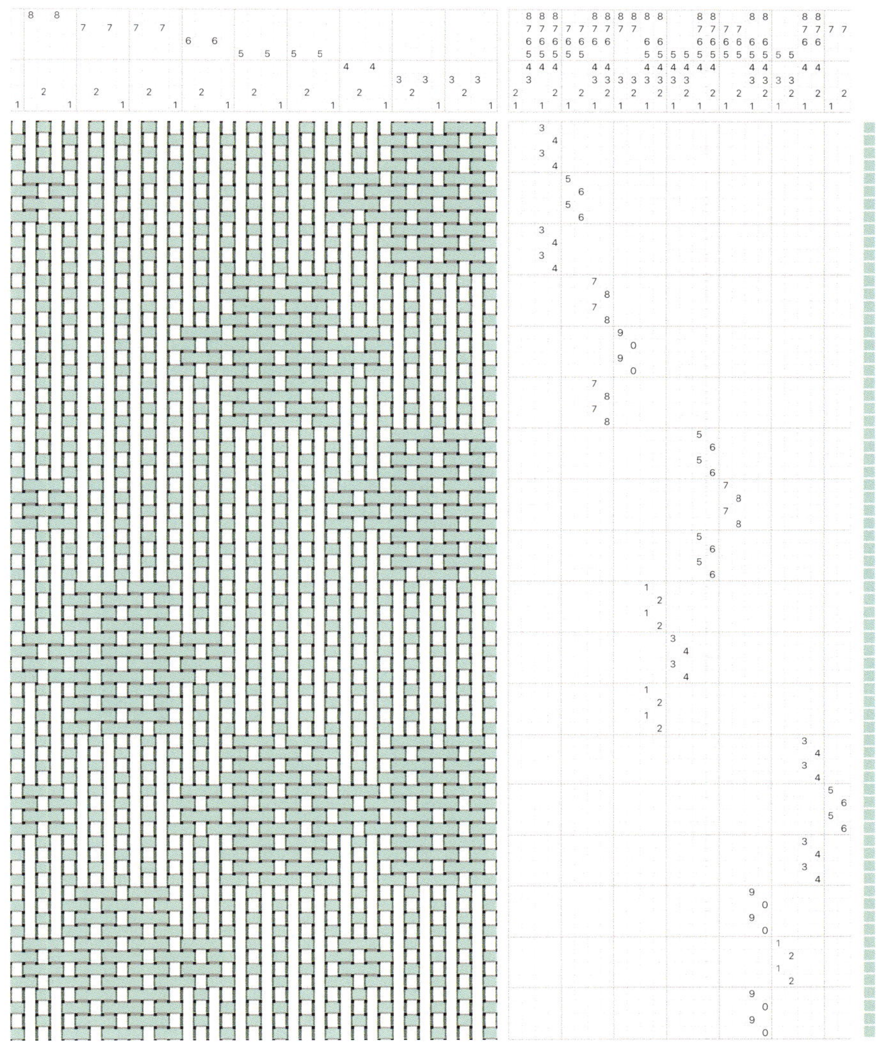

A Sample Woven on 4 Shafts

I propose this 4-shaft Summer and Winter as a sample weave, with which we will be able to practice transforming a profile draft into a regular weaving draft, try out a few different tie-ups, and check out the differences between the four treadlings.

PROJECT RECORD SHEET—A SUMMER AND WINTER WEAVE

Plain weave warp and weft: Venne 22/2 cottolin, pink

Pattern weft: Fonty Cotton Club 3, purple

Sett: 18 epi (7 per cm)

Width in reed: 11¾ in. (30 cm)

Total number of ends: 210

Project length: 51 in. (130 cm)

Warp length: 87 in. (220 cm)

% of shrinkage when taken off loom: 3%

% of shrinkage after washing: 3%

Fringe: ¾ in. (2 cm)

Loss due to front tie-on and at back of loom: 24 in. (60 cm)

Quantity of cottolin: 3.5 oz. (100 g)

Quantity of Cotton Club 3, purple: 1.75 oz. (50 g)

This is woven on 4 shafts; the profile draft shows 2 blocks.

Figure 7 ***Profile draft on 4 shafts***

Of course, we could write up an expanded threading, but I am adamant that you should try to thread by referring to this simple version, which forces you to step back, and will undoubtedly keep you from making threading errors! To help, here is the transcription of the first six blocks only.

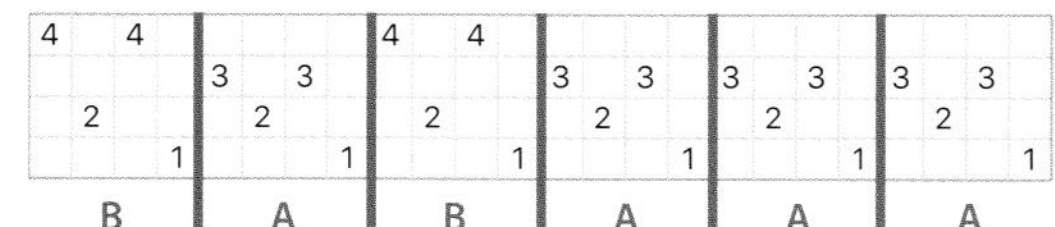

Figure 8 ***Start of expanded threading***

Here are the four different tie-ups. As you weave, you will recognize the strip where the floats cover the two blocks, the one where the floats are seen on the back only, the strip where only the A blocks are covered, and then the one where the B blocks are covered.

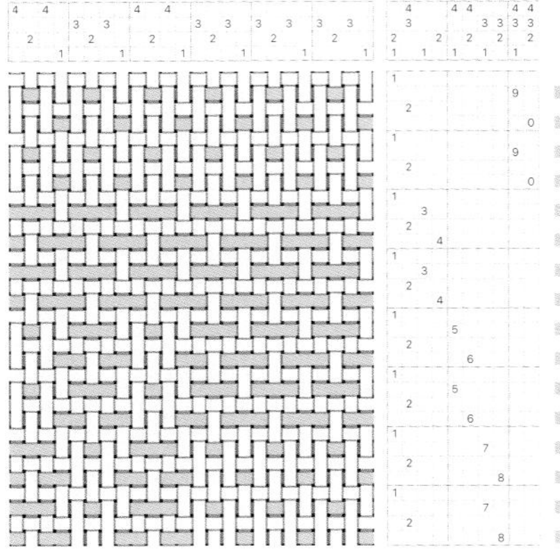

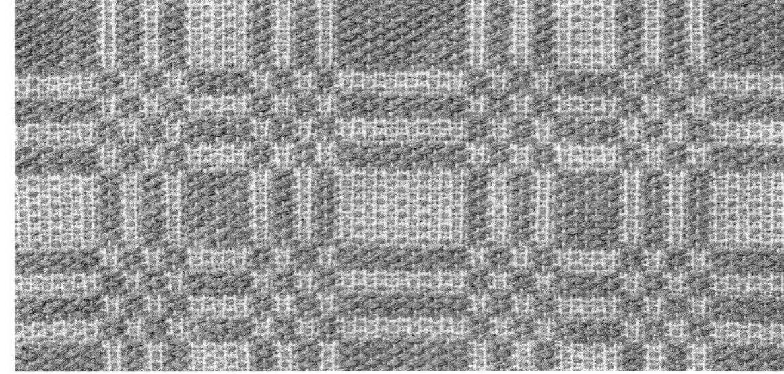

Figure 9 ***Weave with alternating treadling and the 4 possible tie-ups***

To complete this example, here are the drafts of the three other treadlings.

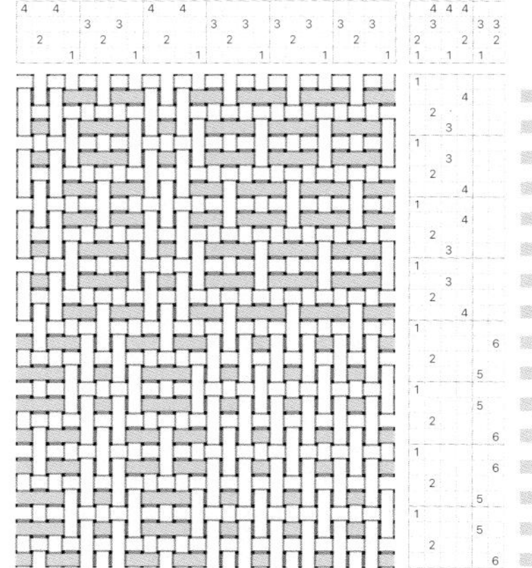

Figure 10 ***"X" treadling***

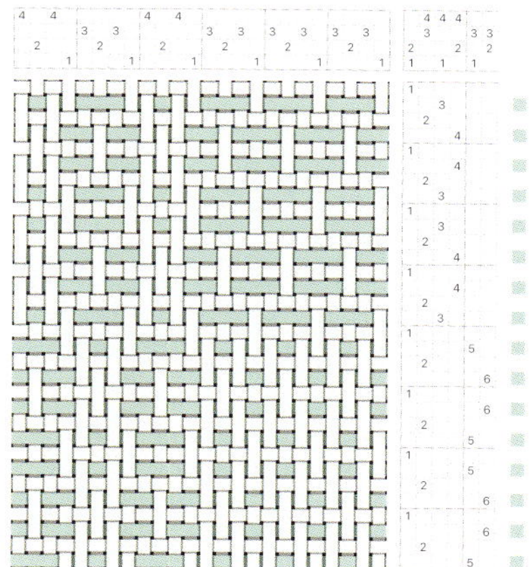

Figure 11 *"O" treadling*

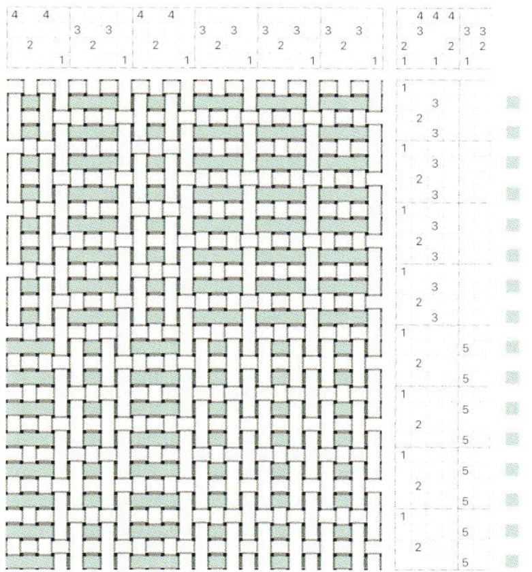

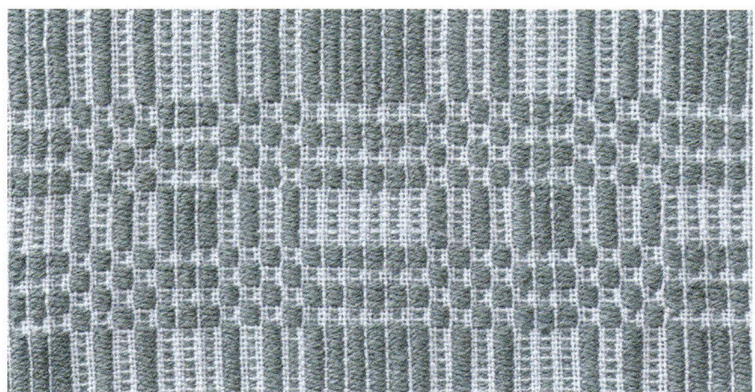

Figure 12 Dukagång *treadling*

Taqueté: Summer and Winter Without the Tabby

Figure 13 *Taqueté, 4 shafts, Venne 22/2 Cottolin*

Taqueté is not really a compound structure. However, I like to couple it with Summer and Winter because the threading is the same, which explains its place in this chapter. It is probably more comparable to a weft-faced rep woven on opposites (see page 166), since the warp ends are entirely covered by the two pattern picks in contrasting colors. The front and back are the exact opposite of each other. The alternating placement of the floats resembles a plain weave.

Compared to the traditional Summer and Winter that we just looked at:

- the threading is identical—we keep the two A and B blocks on 4 shafts;
- we don't weave tabby picks;
- two pattern picks of different colors follow each other, covering the width of the fabric. When block A is covered by the first color; block B is immediately covered by the second color. The order of the two colors is always the same;
- just as with Summer and Winter, shafts 1 and 2 are for the foundation, and no float will cross more than 3 ends;
- the weft spreads completely over the warp, which we want to hide. Nonetheless, to ensure that it will not be seen, choose warp in the same color as one used for the pattern.

Four treadling blocks are shown in the draft: the one where the orange yarn covers the A blocks, the one where it covers the B blocks, the one where it covers both, and the one where it is only visible on the back.

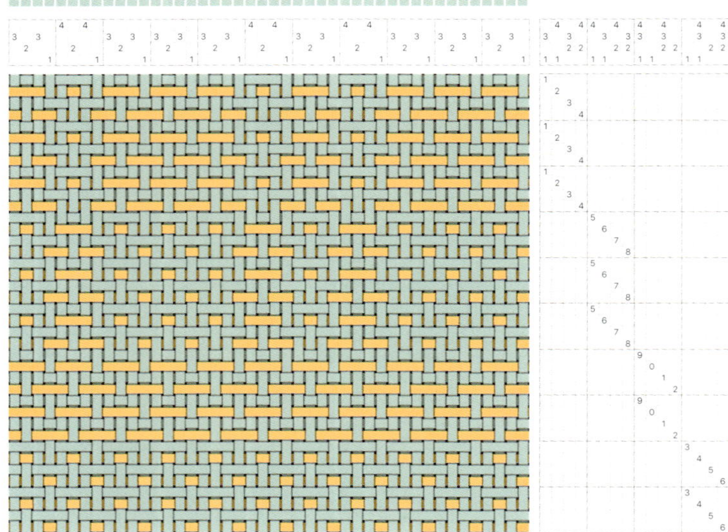

Figure 14 *Taqueté draft*

The entire sequence of a Taqueté block is done with four picks, a sequence that may be repeated as many times as desired depending on the pattern. Even though the sequence of picks is not the same as in Summer and Winter, it does have some similarities. Let's take the example where we would like to cover block A in orange and B in celadon:

- shuttle pass with celadon yarn: 1 + 3 ⟶
- shuttle pass with orange yarn: 1 + 4 ⟶
- shuttle return with celadon yarn: 2 + 3 ⟵
- shuttle return with orange yarn: 2 + 4 ⟵

Two rhythms are happening at once:

- the one with the **foundation yarn** (shafts 1 and 2): on the first two passes, shaft 1 remains lifted for both colors to pass through, then shaft 2 is raised for the shuttles to return;
- the one with the **pattern yarn** (shafts 3 and 4): in our example, with the celadon color, shaft 3 is raised and with the orange, shaft 4 is raised.

Depending on the pattern selected, if shaft 3 is raised for the first color to pass through, then shaft 4 is lifted for the second color. If all the pattern shafts are lifted for the first color, then neither 3 or 4 is raised for the second color. When changing colors, we always use the opposite pattern shafts.

The density is quite different from that of Summer and Winter, and the sleying will need to be changed if you want to weave a Taqueté immediately after a Summer and Winter. Depending on the pattern yarn being used, you should probably decrease the density to spread the warp ends further apart to allow the pattern wefts to move closer together in order to completely cover the warp.

Beating should be fairly firm. This technique is obviously appropriate when making rugs, but when using lightweight yarns, it is ideal for many other projects.

As with Summer and Winter, pattern definition becomes more precise with a larger number of shafts. With an 8-shaft loom, you have 6 blocks, which allows for an increased choice of shapes.

Figure 15 *Taqueté, 8 shafts. Tides, Holstgarn wool and silk, 2,828 yd/lb (5,700 m/kg)*

The Taqueté threading block is composed of 4 ends. Its cousin, samitum, from the Byzantine Greek word *examitos*, which means 6 threads, is threaded over 6 ends and floats are placed with the offset used for twill.

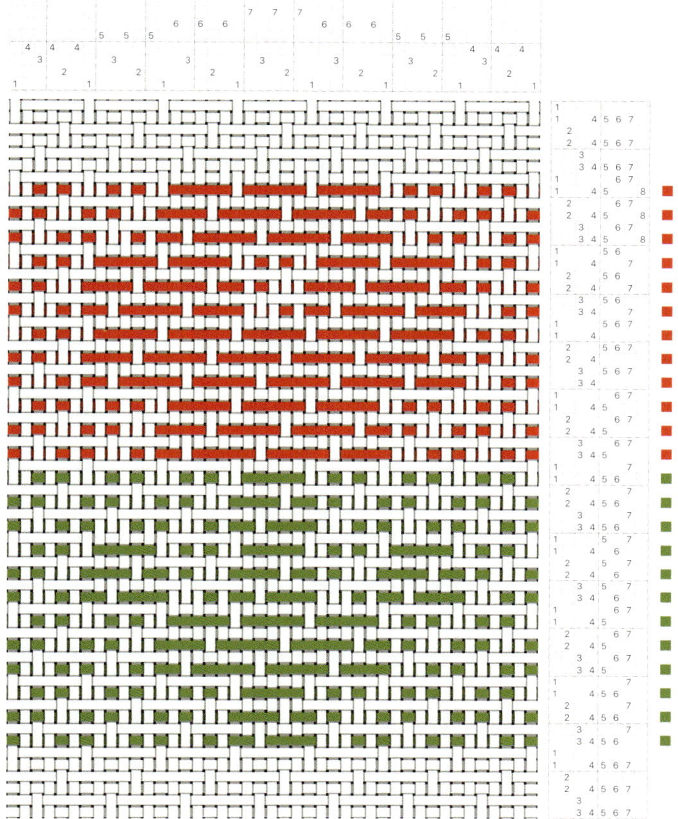

Figure 16 *A simple example of samitum on 8 shafts*

Overshot and Monk's Belt: Playing in Major or Minor Key

It would really be odd to consider a symphony minor solely because it is written in major.

Olivier Bellamy, *Requiem pour un chat*, 2018

Overshot, *reps lancé*, *frappé colonial*, and *daldräll* are some of the names given to many woven blankets, depending on the area of the world in which they were created. Traditionally, the plain weave was in an ecru cotton or linen and the patterns in a dark wool. Overshot is so popular that many weavers make it without knowing.

Figure 17 *Overshot, 4 shafts, Venne 22/2 Cottolin and novelty yarn for the pattern*

It certainly has many advantages. With only 4 shafts, you can design 4 blocks, and through float placement and repetition you can create curves, almost circles, which is quite unusual in weaving. There is a sizable variety of patterns. In her book *A Handweaver's Pattern Book*, Marguerite Davison presents a great number of them. It is easy to refresh their sometimes old-fashioned appearance, or to change them using the usual profile draft by trying new threads, new shapes. Here, the pattern thread floats freely and is highlighted. Let's play with it!

Like Summer and Winter, overshot is a three-thread structure: the warp; the tabby weft or binding pick (often the same as the warp thread), which together constitute the plain weave base; and the pattern thread, softer and usually thicker. The design is made by the pattern thread, which is woven in such a way that it makes floats. The length of the floats is determined by the size of the block.

Building a Pattern with Blocks and a Profile Draft

Overshot is a derivative of straight or point twill on two shafts; two adjacent yarns are threaded on two neighboring shafts, but instead of having straight threading like a twill, overshot makes short back-and-forth trips on two adjacent shafts, which will become blocks. Each block is composed of at least two ends.

Block A : shafts 1 and 2, or 2 and 1

Block B : shafts 2 and 3, or 3 and 2

Block C : shafts 3 and 4, or 4 and 3

Block D : shafts 4 and 1, or 1 and 4

Figure 18 ***Threading of overshot pine bloom, thread-by-thread***

The profile draft of an overshot resembles twill threading. Let's take the example of a fairly common pattern called pine bloom. These drafts show a threading in three different shapes that you can find in the literature: fully drawn out thread-by-thread draft, the same threading with circles that groups the threads by block, and the corresponding profile draft, written in blocks.

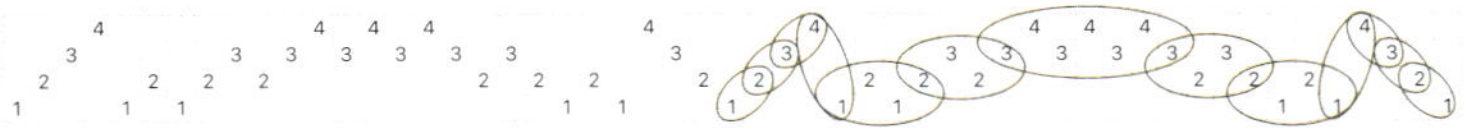

Figure 19 ***Threading of pine bloom with threads grouped together in blocks***

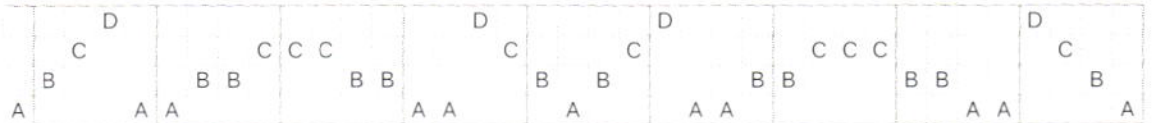

Figure 20 ***Threading of pine bloom in profile draft***

Writing with circles highlights the fact that the threads on the edges of the blocks are shared by two blocks. This is the characteristic of overshot, that the warp end shared by two adjacent blocks is covered by the two consecutive floats. The first warp end of each block is also the last of the preceding block. It is this layering that can give a rounded shape to the design, and also is what gives it the name "overshot."

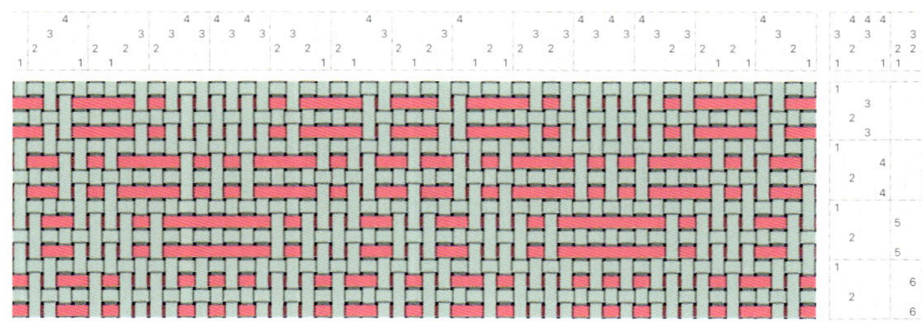

Each initial block will be repeated as many times as desired, limited by **the length of the float**, as it covers the entire length of the block. In our example, the length of block C is almost risky, as it is composed of 7 threads. This is both the disadvantage of this structure, with floats that take away from the stability of the whole, and the advantage for the freedom they bring to the design! The longest acceptable length of a float depends on the thread count and the use of your weaving project. For example, watch out for a ring that can snag! However, it is because this yarn is left free and flowing that its quality shines. This is an opportunity to use a distinctive yarn. This structure is not wise like its neighbor Summer and Winter, which has a securing point every 3 ends. The word "float" takes on its true meaning here.

On each band, the fabric exposes three different zones: an area entirely covered by the weft floats, an area of solid plain weave, where the pattern thread appears only on the reverse side, and an area where the pattern thread is woven in a "halftone" plain weave, as visible on the front as on the back of the fabric.

Most weaves are symmetrical, with the pattern developed around the center and repeats on each side thereafter. But any other arrangement of the threading blocks is of course possible, either repetitive or entirely at your discretion.

Threading

Threading following the profile draft may seem uncomfortable. However, by following a few rules, this simplified draft makes reading easier and threading more sure.

Each block is threaded so that the warp ends are systematically on an odd shaft and then on an even shaft. This is the golden rule! This way, true plain weave is always possible. The order of the blocks doesn't really matter, even though A, B, C, and D are often in sequence.

A block consists of at least 2 threads and the maximum depends on the thread count. If the density of the fabric is 25 threads per inch (10 per cm), a block made of 10 threads produces a float of only ⅜ inch (1 cm). With a thicker thread, and therefore a lower density, this float could quickly exceed ¾ inch (2 cm) in length—a danger of snagging and risk of the float drooping!

If the patterns are symmetrical, they must be centered or evenly distributed around the center of the weave, even calculating the width of the weave to suit this pattern. With each change of direction or each time the pattern is reversed, a thread must be added to the center block so that the following blocks start in the exact opposite direction. The symmetry must be perfect. In our example, the center block 3-4-3-4-3-4-3 consists of 7 threads. If the block that precedes it is 3-2-3-2, the block that follows it is 2-3-2-3. In the beginning, this inversion is a bit confusing when threading.

Treadling

Overshot is a compound structure, which means that we systematically alternate one pick of plain weave with the same yarn used for the warp and one pattern pick with a more vivid yarn. Two shuttles work together.

Because these plain weave picks are systematic, and because they don't make the sketch easier to read, I won't draw them in. But they are there! Sometimes they are called tabby or binding picks, but I usually think of them as plain weave picks. If this is a balanced plain weave, if the warp density is the same as the weft density, which is expected, then we can obtain a balanced pattern where each treadling block will be the same size as the threading block. We still look for the famous diagonal that shows it is balanced.

Just as I don't draw the plain weave in the drafts, I don't think about the plain weave anymore and it is just included as part of my systematic, consistent movements. When the shuttle passes from left to right, I do the odd tabby, and the even tabby when it starts from the right.

A thicker float yarn, less twisted than the one for plain weave, is appreciated. We look for a yarn that will have a visual impact due to its texture, color, or different yarn count than the plain weave. This doesn't often influence the density selected for the plain weave. Nevertheless, this should be verified by the sample.

The traditional tromp as writ once again ensures the best appearance of the pattern. The profile draft is the ideal tool to visualize it.

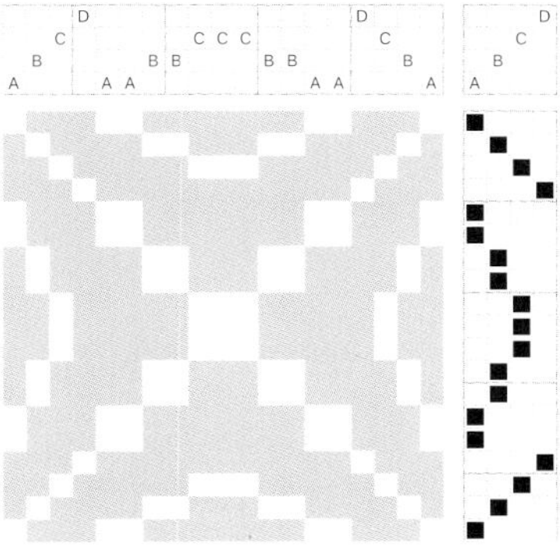

Figure 21 *A balanced profile draft*

To convert the profile draft into a treadling draft, we weave as many picks of floats as we have warp ends in this same block, minus one. This way, the pattern will be balanced. If there are 4 threads in threading block A, the corresponding treadling block will have 3 picks of tabby and its associated 3 picks of floats.

Of course, there is nothing to prevent you from doing as you wish and avoiding the mirror effect! It's the size of the blocks and their placement that design the pattern, and it's how circles and curves become possible.

For flexible and smooth working movements, the left foot remains on the two left treadles used for the plain weave, and the right foot is for making the pattern with the four other treadles. The left foot will move systematically, while the right will be able to rest on the same treadle for several picks in a row.

The treadling draft can be presented in different formats. Some authors indicate the number of repetitions of the pick in the treadling columns instead of the treadle number. As for other structures, I indicate the number of the treadle, and I like to see this number repeated as many times as necessary. In this way, you can directly visualize the shape of the pattern.

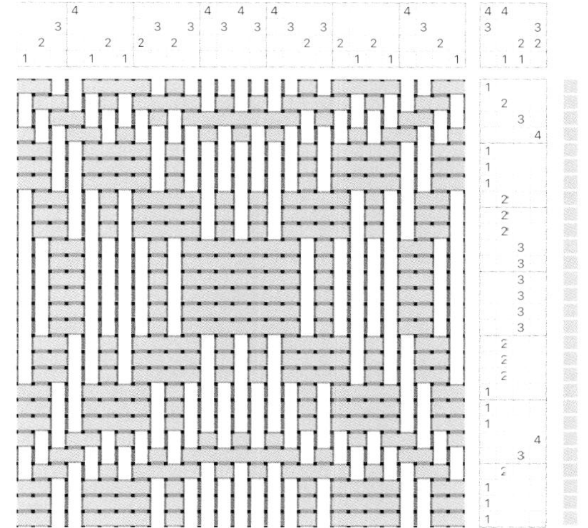

Figure 22 *Treadling for an overshot*

Tie-Up

We will always lift two shafts together: the tabby with the pairs 1-3 and 2-4, alternating with twill tie-ups: 1-2, 2-3, 3-4, and 4-1. The same shed from a pattern can be repeated since the tabby pick inserted prevents any warp float—the tabby is playing its role as ground cloth!

As always, it is necessary to check that pattern instructions are for a rising or sinking shed loom. A draft can easily be retranscribed from rising to sinking by changing the marked squares to empty squares and vice versa.

The richness of overshot, already quite substantial with the floats whose length is chosen when threading and whose number of repeats is chosen during treadling, is increased with the tie-up. Let's look at that with the profile draft, and continue with the usual code: A = 1-2, B = 2-3, C = 3-4, and D = 4-1.

Figure 23 *Tie-up for an overshot in profile draft and its expanded draft*

The appearance of the pattern can be changed incredibly by simply changing the order of the blocks in the tie-up draft, to give it a curved or an angular appearance. Let's limit ourselves to only two traditional tie-ups, the "rose" and the "star," and note how much bigger the curve is with the rose tie-up, while the angles have more impact with the star tie-up.

Figure 24 ***Rose and star tie-ups***

The pattern determines how much the rose or star motif stands out. Honestly, what a luxury. With the same threading and treadling, this one change in the tie-up transforms your pattern. Would you try a DCAB or ABDC tie-up to get a star motif on some blocks and a rose motif on the others?

Density

The pattern yarn does not really matter for the density when weaving an overshot structure. Unless it is very thick or your weave needs to be flexible, the desired density is the one that you would choose for the simple plain weave ground cloth. In any case, you will need an equal density in warp and weft to obtain a balanced and well-proportioned pattern. Only a sample with the complete pattern that should appear square will be able to confirm your initial choice. Using a triangle ruler when you begin the weaving will help with adjusting your beat to get a 45-degree diagonal.

Adding a floating selvedge is recommended. This way, the yarn used for the floats will systematically go around the selvedge. Remember, overshot is a twill derivative, where the floating selvedge has the same function, to make the pattern yarn go all the way to the ends. However, if you wish to stop the pattern before the edge, you can put in a strip of plain weave on each side by threading warp ends on shafts 5 and 6.

An Example on 4 Shafts

The example on page 191 is the overshot pine bloom that was described above. In the draft, the darker shaded green warp yarn and pink weft yarn frame the part of the pattern that will be repeated as many times as needed to obtain the desired width.

Monk's Belt, the Minor Key of This Structure

Like overshot, monk's belt is a compound weave composed of a plain weave in which the warp and weft yarns are the same, and a supplementary weft that creates the pattern. In the same way, the pattern yarn used is generally thicker or more visible. It is different from its cousin due to a simplification. It uses only two of the four blocks: blocks A and C. This way, there are no longer any halftone parts. The pattern floats completely cover the blocks on the front and back.

Block A: shafts 1 and 2, or 2 and 1

Block C: shafts 3 and 4, or 4 and 3

The profile draft is composed of 2 rows and 2 columns. It is a really perfect tool as it is the exact reproduction of the pattern. The design is therefore very simple, and ideal practice for creating designs.

PROJECT RECORD SHEET—AN EXAMPLE IN OVERSHOT

Plain weave warp and weft: Fonty Merlin 3,720 yd/lb (7,500 m/kg)

Pattern weft: MERO 266 Royal Linen, 100% pure fine linen, 1,989 yd/lb

Sett: 18 epi (7 per cm)

Width in reed: 15¾ in. (40 cm)

Total number of ends: 287

Project length: 75 in. (190 cm)

Warp length: 118 in. (300 cm)

% of shrinkage when taken off loom: 3%

% of shrinkage after washing: 3%

Fringe: ¾ in. (2 cm)

Loss due to front tie-on and at back of loom: 24 in. (60 cm)

Quantity of Merlin: 6.35 oz. (180 g)

Quantity of Royal Linen: 2.8 oz. (80 g)

Figure 25 *Overshot pine bloom, 4 shafts. Merlin, 3,720 yd/lb (7,500 m/kg) and MERO 266 Royal Linen, 100% pure fine linen, 1,989 yd/lb*

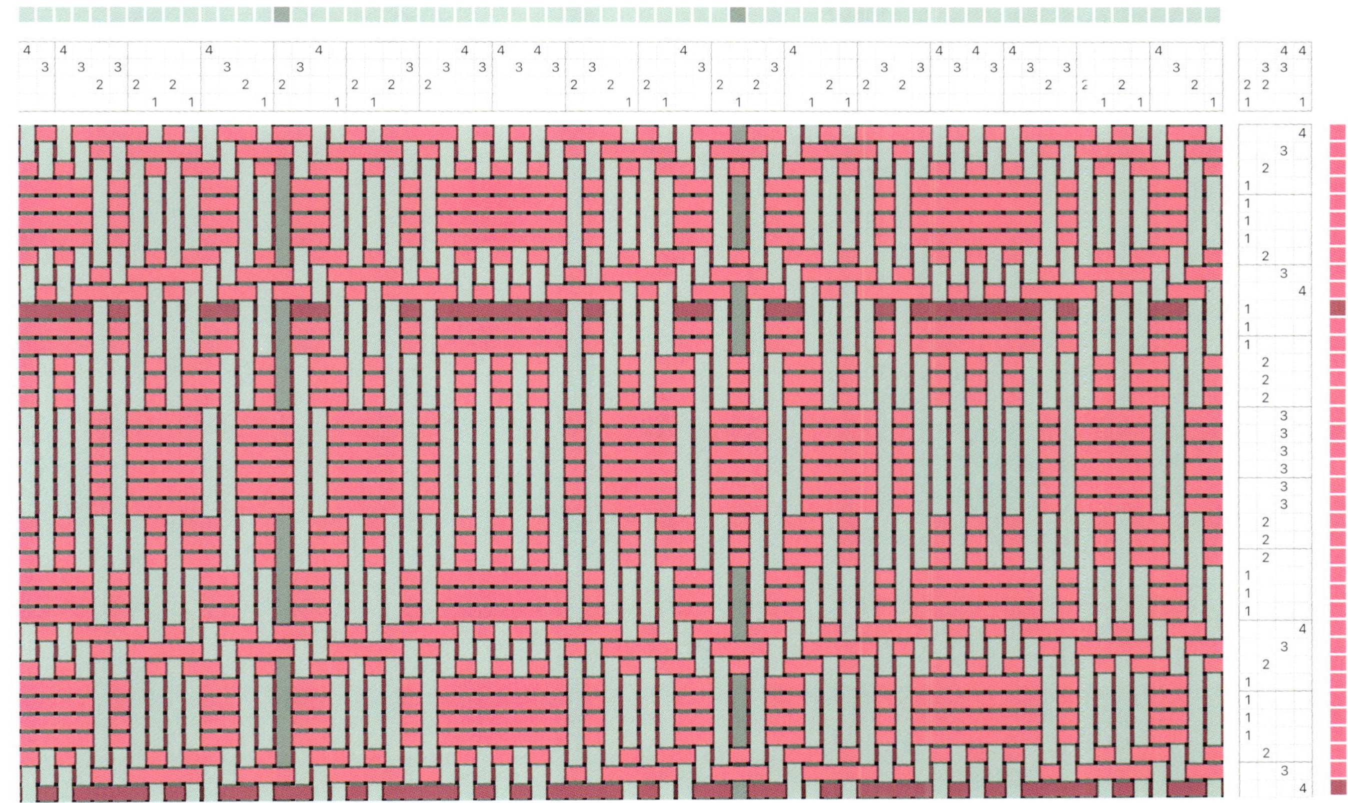

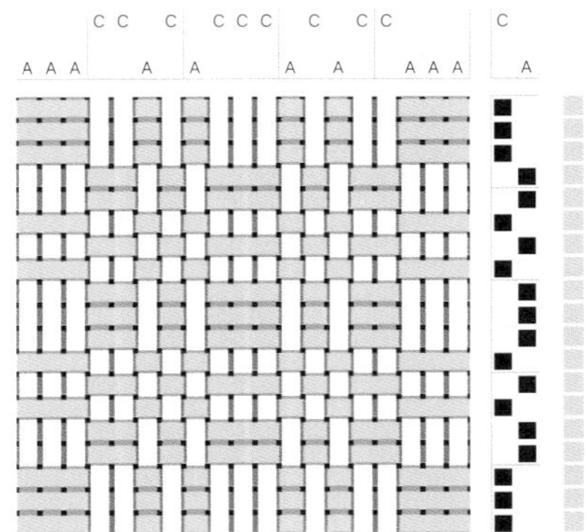

Figure 26 *Profile draft for weaving monk's belt*

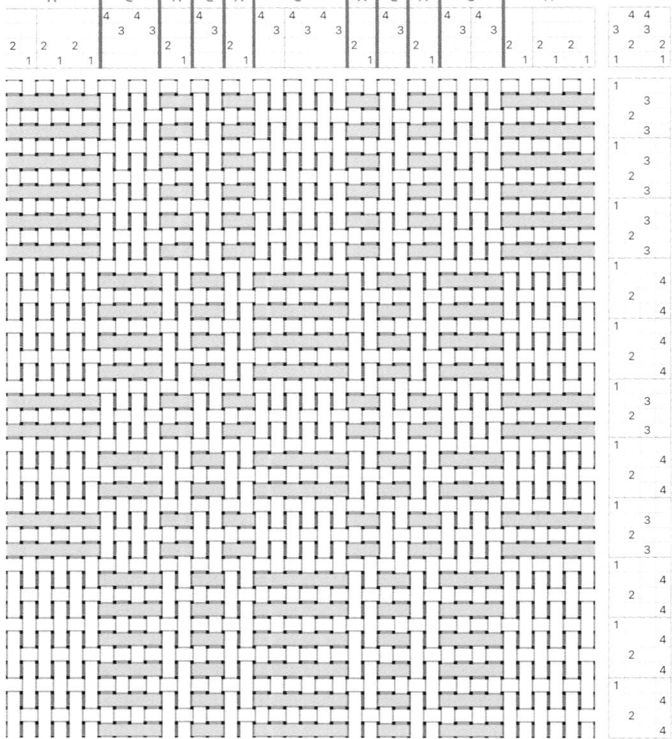

Figure 27 *Expansion of this profile draft*

As with all these compound plain weave structures, it is much easier to not draw the plain weave on the drafts so that the patterns can be seen clearly; the following drafts are therefore shown without the tabby. Two shuttles are needed, one for the plain weave and the other for the pattern. And keep the movement of the pattern shuttle systematic, from left to right for the odd tabby and from right to left for the even tabby. This way I only have to remember the number of float picks. And in this case, following the profile draft is sufficient.

To cover Block A, we lift shafts 3+4, and shafts 1+2 to cover Block C. The floats run the total width of the block. Depending on the yarn count and the density in the reed, you will adjust their maximum acceptable length. The small float is over two warp ends. The number of threads per block is not necessarily even. However, it is absolutely necessary to keep alternating the ends threaded in an even shaft then an odd shaft so that the plain weave will always be perfect.

As for all compound structures, I keep the two left treadles for weaving the tabby and two others for the pattern that the right foot makes. Thus, the left foot's rhythm is consistently treadle 1/treadle 2, while the right foot must remain for several picks in a row on the same treadle, following what is indicated on the profile draft.

Monk's belt, made with very thin yarn, makes an impressive visual impact for household linens. Probably of Swedish origin, this *munkabälte mönster* is commonly woven for tablecloths and curtains, with traditional motifs such a star or cross.

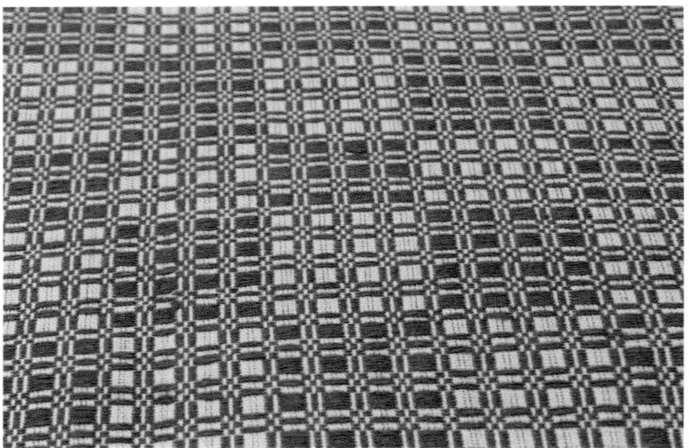

Figure 28 *Monk's belt, 4 shafts, Venne 34/2 cotton*

Changing Density, Weaving on Opposites, Flamepoint, and Boundweave

On opposites and flamepoint weaves are to overshot what taqueté is to Summer and Winter. The threading is the same, there are no tabby picks, there are several pattern picks in a row, and the density is lower, leaving room for the weft picks to get as close to each other as possible. All the following examples are made with this overshot pattern, the draft of which is included below. It will serve as a guide.

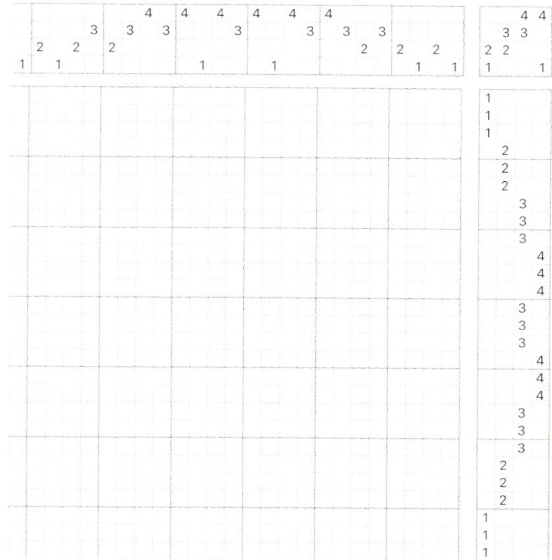

Figure 29 *Overshot draft to be used as a guide for the following three weaves*

The first weft rep in overshot threading is **weaving on opposites**: one pick of one color is immediately followed by one pick of another color in the exact opposite shed. Two shuttles and two different colored yarns are required. **The order of the two colors is always the same!** Only the treadling order changes.

Let's agree on a new block code for this project. A block is made up of two picks. In this example, the first is in orange, the second in green. Let's call:

- **block 1**: pairs shafts 1-2 in orange and shafts 3-4 in green;
- **block 2**: pairs shafts 2-3 in orange and shafts 4-1 in green;
- **block 3**: pairs shafts 3-4 in orange and shafts 1-2 in green;
- **block 4**: pairs shafts 4-1 in orange and shafts 2-3 in green.

No matter what they are called, you can change the number or code if that seems more clear to you, but keep the idea of four pairs.

Just as in overshot, patterns are pleasing when they are symmetrical and square. The classic tromp as writ again fits well here and working with the profile draft is of course perfect. Otherwise, the idea is to follow the treadling draft of the initial overshot pattern, but changing the code. The number 1, in the column, no longer indicates treadle 1 as usual, but block 1 (pairs 1-2 in orange and 3-4 in green), the number 2 indicates block 2, etc.

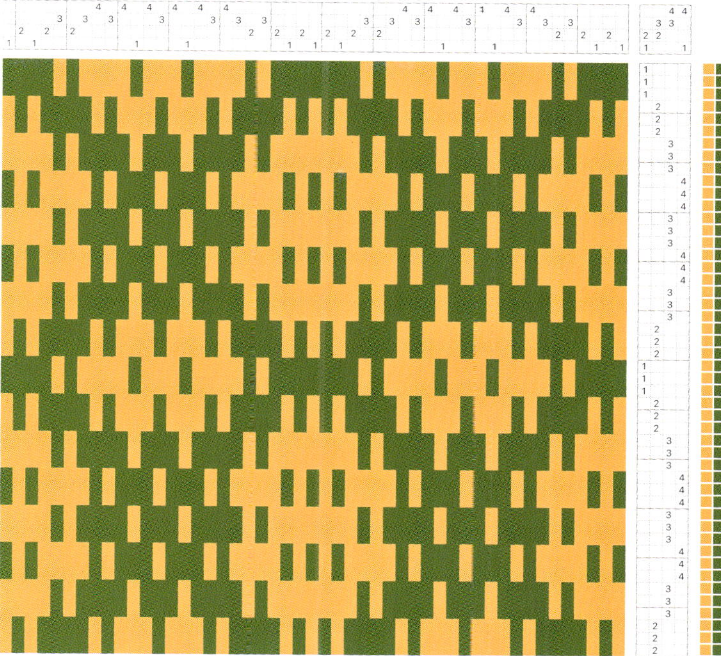

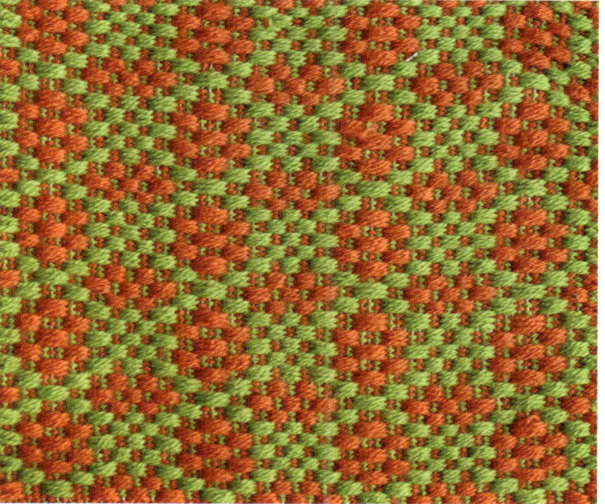

Figure 30 *Draft for a weave on opposites*

The second overshot weft rep is flamepoint weaving. To make it you will need four shuttles with four different colors. This time, it is **the order of the treadles that is always the same**; only the order of the colors changes!

The order of the treadles will always be **1** (shafts 1-2), **2** (shafts 2-3), **3** (shafts 3-4) and **4** (shafts 4-1) i.e., a 2/2 twill. We keep the same overshot pattern for reading.

Let's transform the coding into blocks that will now refer to the order of the colors:

- **block 1**: red (1+2), orange (2+3), yellow (3+4), and green (4+1);

- **block 2**: green (1+2), red (2+3), orange (3+4), and yellow (4+1);
- **block 3**: yellow, green, red, and orange;
- **block 4**: orange, yellow, green, and red.

As for weaving on opposites, the simplest is to follow the treadling in Figure 31 or the profile draft, again using this new code. Each time you read 1 in the overshot treadling column, you will weave the four picks of block 1. Weave block 2 when you read 2, and so forth. A sort of quartet of picks is being played here.

The following draft represents only the first 6 groups of 4 picks on the 27 quartets of picks in the example's complete overshot draft.

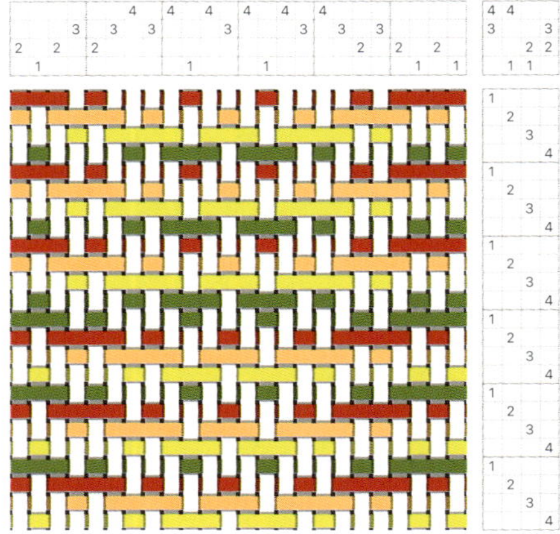

Figure 31 ***The first six blocks of a flamepoint weave***

For weft rep weaves, it is traditional to indicate the four colors on the same line, and once you understand the code, this draft is really more visual and therefore easier to follow when weaving. This is the one found in the literature.

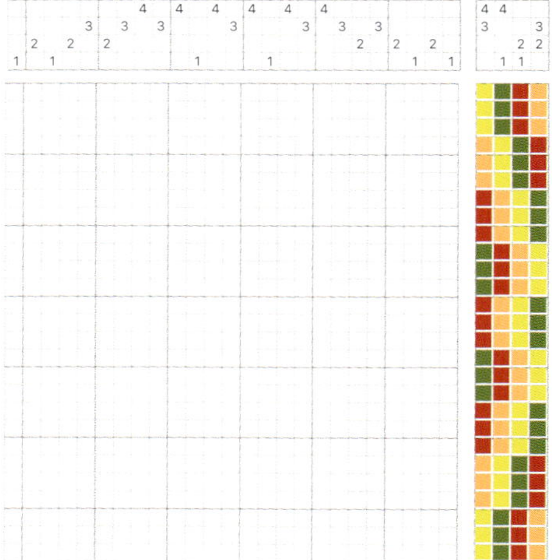

Figure 32 ***The 27 quartets of the flamepoint diagram***

Some people weave this pattern adding a tabby. The effect is not the same, and in this case the density will need to be adjusted again. But the same rule still applies: the density is good when the pattern is square or when the diagonal is 45 degrees!

When weaving overshot, we transformed the tie-up square to obtain a rose or star motif. We can also test these tie-up variations. See how varied and exciting the possibilities are for creating patterns.

A third possibility for weft-faced rep with overshot threading is similar to this flamepoint example with a treadling rhythm that does not change. This time, it is the number and the order of colors that are totally unrestricted and make it possible to make a large number of patterns on the same threading. Called boundweave, or sometimes "square within a square" when using tromp as writ, we can draw up a design on a simple piece of graph paper. I again recommend using a profile draft or the draft guide from previous weaves.

This type of weaving is much easier to think about with a sinking shed loom. In this example, Block A indicates that it is the threads from shafts 1 and 2 that are covered by the weft. With a rising shed loom, it is then shafts 3 and 4 that are activated. Sometimes we can get lost in these gymnastics; these sketches are instinctive and following the drawing on paper is often enough, by asking yourself which warp block you want to see covered by which color. When the drawing is not really started, it is a bit difficult to find reference points, but that will come quickly.

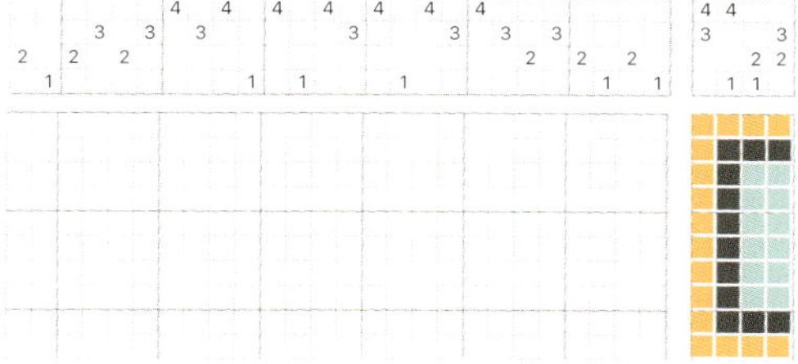

Figure 33 ***Draft and profile draft for a boundweave***

For these three weft-faced weaves, a sample will really be necessary to find the appropriate density to create a balanced weave. This density will depend on the suppleness of the weft yarn, its ability to pack into the previous weft rows, and what the use of the fabric will be. Finding the right density is tricky because it needs to be low enough to allow the weft picks to get close to each other, but it also must be high enough to result in a solid, durable fabric. Finding a good compromise can take a lot of research! Using a temple helps to protect the selvedge threads and to maintain the initial width of the weave.

Overshot and its derivatives, woven so often by generations of weavers, still inspire many. These few lines above are far from presenting the richness of its heritage. While it is relatively easy to invent your own pattern, the publications are so numerous that a lifetime would not be enough to take advantage of all the possible examples. So be adventurous and weave a long warp of samples and marvel at these multiple variations. A beautiful project, for sure!

Just as with many other structures, having 8 shafts increases the possibilities, just as with overshot, a 4-shaft loom offers an abundant polyphony.

Figure 34 ***Boundweave rug, 4 shafts, 8/2 wool with little twist***

Interlude with Lace Structures

To be sure, weaving is an intertwining of threads. When weaving, we separate warp ends so that the weft can repeatedly cross these layers of threads. And when the threads do not have to cross, then they float. I like to say that threads are good companions and like to stay close together. Free from the constraint of interlacing, the floats move closer together. The big family of lace weaves plays on this property of floats, letting them move close together and thus creating openwork. These areas of openwork combined with areas of plain weave produce a lace effect.

These structures have different names, depending on how the floats or groups of floats are laid out among the areas of plain weave. It is difficult to know exactly what to call them, between what some people are accustomed to and the translations of others. And a new difficulty added on top of that is that structures are threaded differently depending on the country or author, amplifying the confusion.

So, let's get into the dance with laces, huck lace, Bronson lace, Atwater-Bronson lace, huckaback or huck-a-buck, spot Bronson, Swedish lace, and barley corn weave. Once again, the naming system doesn't help us much. These structures are very similar and sometimes can only be distinguished by very small differences.

Openwork structures are often associated with household linens woven in linen or cotton. Plain weave provides durability and floats produce delicate patterns. However, using soft yarn with little twist, this weave becomes light and airy, and is well-suited for wraps and throws.

Only huck lace and Bronson lace will be presented here with the intention of explaining the general principle of these lace structures. Some of you will undoubtedly try to analyze the other lace structures; there are certainly plenty of books and patterns on the Internet!

Huck Lace

Huck lace is a plain weave in which small openwork areas with warp and/or weft floats are inserted. Again we will talk about blocks and units. With a 4-shaft loom, we have two blocks, A and B. The first two shafts are used to build the ground cloth, while shafts 3 and 4 produce the floats. With 8 shafts, we have 6 different blocks and as always, this larger number gives greater creative freedom.

Figure 35 ***Huck lace, 8 shafts. 16/1 linen***

Threading

I am going to use an example on 8 shafts to explain the principle of constructing this weave. **Two types of blocks** follow one another, those where the floats are placed on the odd shafts, 3 or 5 or 7, alternating with the threads on shaft 2, and those where the floats are placed on the even shafts, 4 or 6 or 8, alternating with the threads on shaft 1. We will therefore follow the sequence 2-3-2-3-2, then 1-4-1-4-1, 2-5-2-5-2, etc.

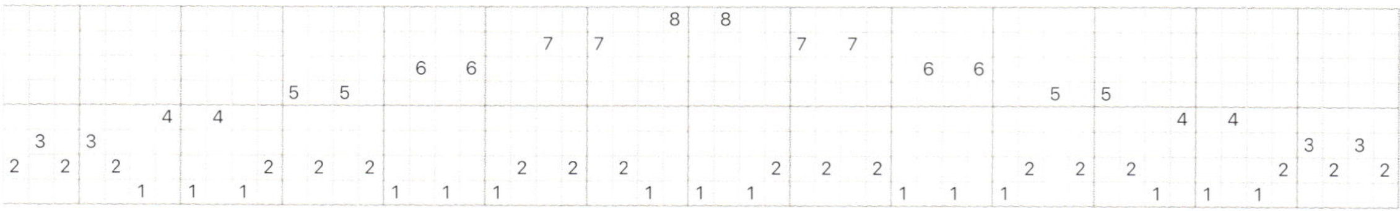

Figure 36 ***Principle of threading a huck lace on 8 shafts***

Huck is defined by the number of threads in a **base unit**. The above example is a huck with a unit of 5: 2-3-2-3-2, 1-4-1-4-1, etc. In this group of 5, the three ends threaded on shafts 1 or 2 are the ones that continuously provide the plain weave. The other two threads form the floats. Changing the size of the base unit means adding or removing a pair of threads: one plain weave thread and one float thread. The latter floats across the entire width of this block; the size of the unit is adapted according to the acceptable length of the float and the thread count. Each unit is composed of an odd number of threads so that it is always possible to do plain weave and that between two blocks, the threads of shafts 1 and 2 are always adjacent!

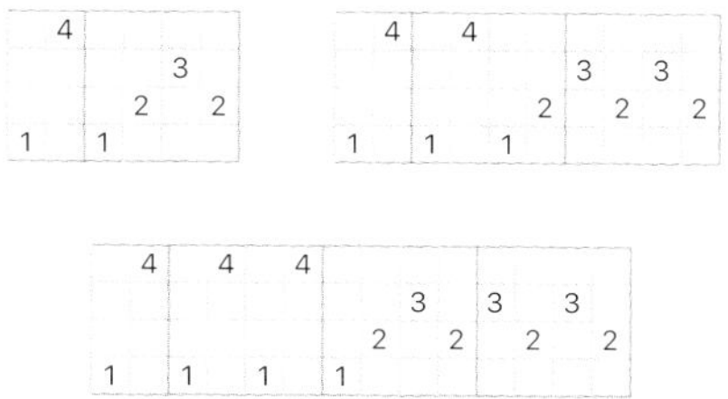

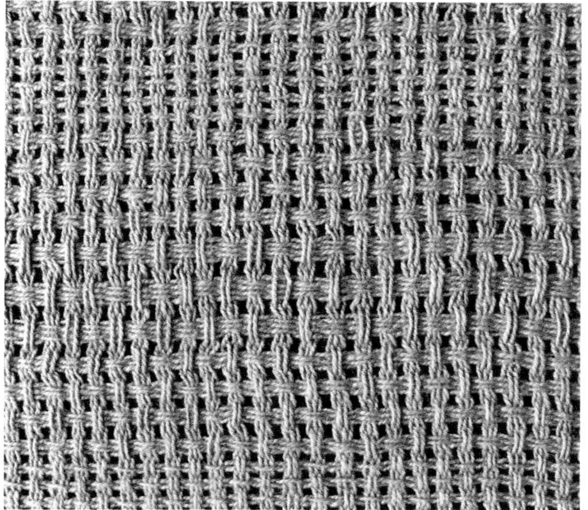

Figure 37 *Huck with 3-, 5-, or 7-thread units*

In a 3-unit huck, a single float passes over three threads. In a 5-unit, there are two floats that pass over five threads. In a 7-unit, three floats pass over seven threads.

In the same threading, even and odd blocks must always follow each other, no matter the order of the blocks. With a 4-shaft loom, it is only possible to alternate Block A/ Block B, and this limits the pattern. Varying the size of the blocks in the threading helps break up this monotony and gives the pattern some movement. With 8 shafts, there is much more freedom in the placement of openwork and a pattern can take shape.

Sleying and Density

Huck is first and foremost a plain weave. The density is therefore similar to that of a plain weave in most projects. You divide the number of threads wrapped around a ruler by two. This is the density that is used for household linens in cotton or linen.

However, it may be that, wishing to take advantage of the suppleness of the floats, we choose a density that is a little lower. This is particularly good for wraps in wool, mohair, or alpaca. It is also a structure that can be used when you're short on yarn as it doesn't use as much as other structures.

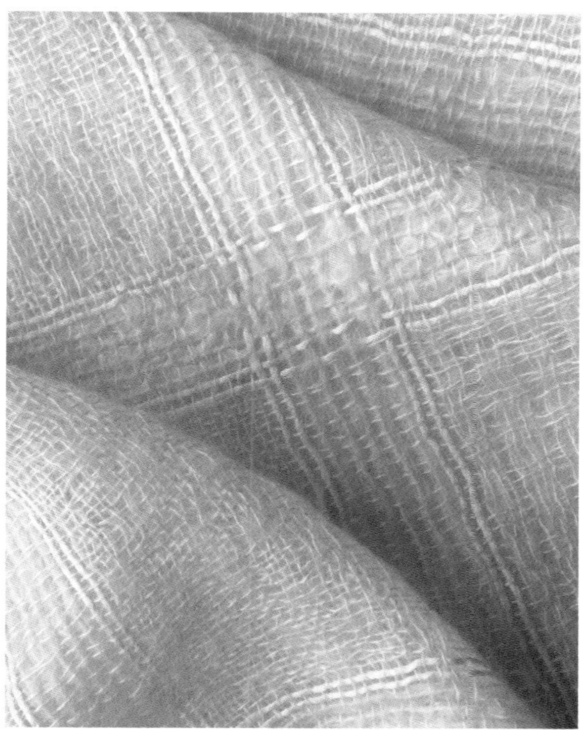

Figure 38 *Huck lace, 4 shafts. Soie de Marie Tana and Anny Blatt Vogue*

As with plain weave, the density of warp and weft must be balanced. This way, each area of plain weave or of floats will be square.

Tie-Up and Treadling

Again, let's talk blocks. In each one, we alternate weft–plain weave / weft–plain weave / weft–plain weave. Each block begins and ends with plain weave. There is an odd number of picks in a block. In Block A, the even plain weave (shafts 2-4) alternates with the pattern pick that raises the thread from shaft 1. In Block B, the odd plain weave (shafts 1-3) alternates with the pattern pick that raises the thread from shaft 2. So, shafts 1 and 2 are systematically raised alternately for the entire weave.

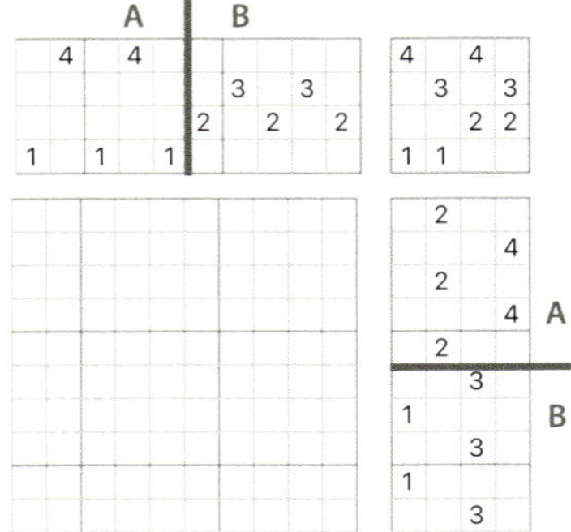

Figure 39 ***Huck lace basic draft***

By tying up the treadles in the order shown in this example, the right and left feet work in cadence with a rhythm that is easy on the body and not stressful to remember. The left foot stays on treadle 2 three times in a row while the right foot stays twice in a row on treadle 4, the two alternating for these five picks. Then the right foot moves to treadle 3 and alternates with the left foot that makes floats with treadle 1.

In each block, you can choose to weave plain weave, warp floats, weft floats, or both warp and weft floats at the same time. Everything is decided in this tie-up square by combining or not combining shafts 3 and/or 4 with the other 2 foundation shafts.

This is the magical thing about this structure, that there is a solid foundation thanks to the plain weave and there is a wide variety of patterns, whether or not you add shafts 3 and/or 4. With only 4 shafts, we can already have fun with numerous possibilities. With 8 shafts, the choice of combinations explodes.

In these drafts, I have assigned a color to the floats to make them more visible. When warp and weft floats are combined in the same block, you get the true huck lace.

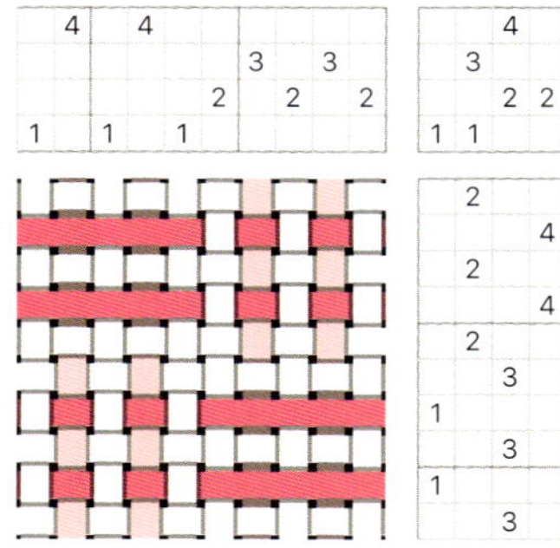

Figure 40 ***Weft floats in huck***

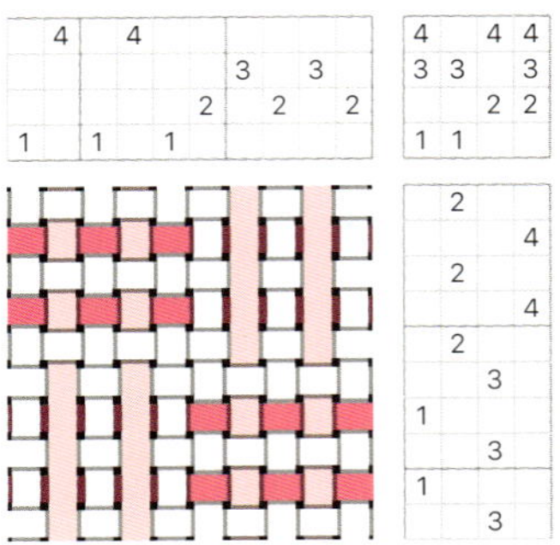

Figure 41 ***Warp floats in huck***

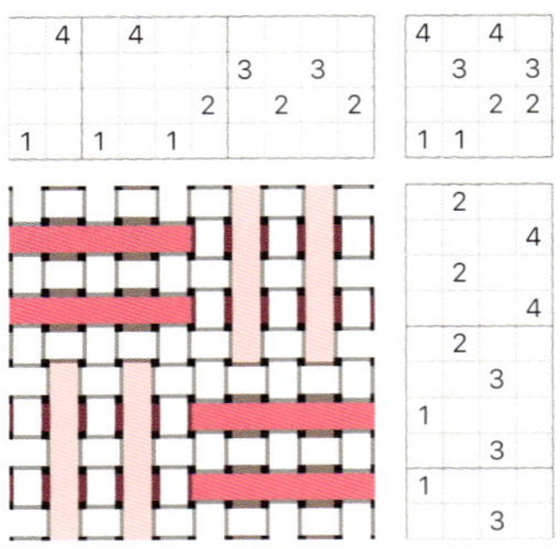

Figure 42 ***Warp and weft floats: huck lace***

When weaving, the lack of visibility of these single-color floats is a disadvantage. With the warp under tension, it is indeed difficult to distinguish between the pattern and the plain weave, which really requires attention when weaving. It helps considerably to do some things automatically, like always starting from the left to weave Block A and from the right for Block B. On the other hand, as soon as this weaving is off the loom and soaked in water, the floats move closer together and finally, the openwork is revealed! It is often a very emotional moment.

It is always possible to weave strips of plain weave in weft by treadling 1-3 and 2-4. It is also possible to plan for areas of plain weave at the selvedges or between the pattern areas by threading the warp on shafts 1 and 2 only, and making sure to always alternate even and odd shafts for two adjacent threads when starting to thread blocks.

As with threading, the treadling blocks can be made up of three, five, or seven picks.

Many other combinations can be imagined: weft floats on Block A and warp floats on Block B, no floats on block A and floats on Block B. Madelyn van der Hoogt shows many projects in the book *Huck Lace* from "The Best of Weaver's" collection.

While with four shafts one is forced to put Blocks A and B next to each other, with more shafts you have more freedom in where to place the pattern areas and it becomes really exciting to construct your pattern.

PROJECT RECORD SHEET—AN EXAMPLE IN HUCK

Plain weave warp and weft: Fonty Merlin linen, 3,720 yd/lb (7,500 m/kg)

Sett: 22 epi (9 per cm)

Width in reed: 11 in. (28 cm)

Total number of ends: 252

Project length: 59 in. (150 cm)

Warp length: 83 in. (210 cm)

% of shrinkage when taken off loom: 3%

% of shrinkage after washing: 0.5%

Fringe: ¾ in. (2 cm)

Loss due to front tie-on and at back of loom: 24 in. (60 cm)

Quantity of Merlin: 2.8 oz. (80 g) of color 0560; 1.6 oz. (45 g) of color 056

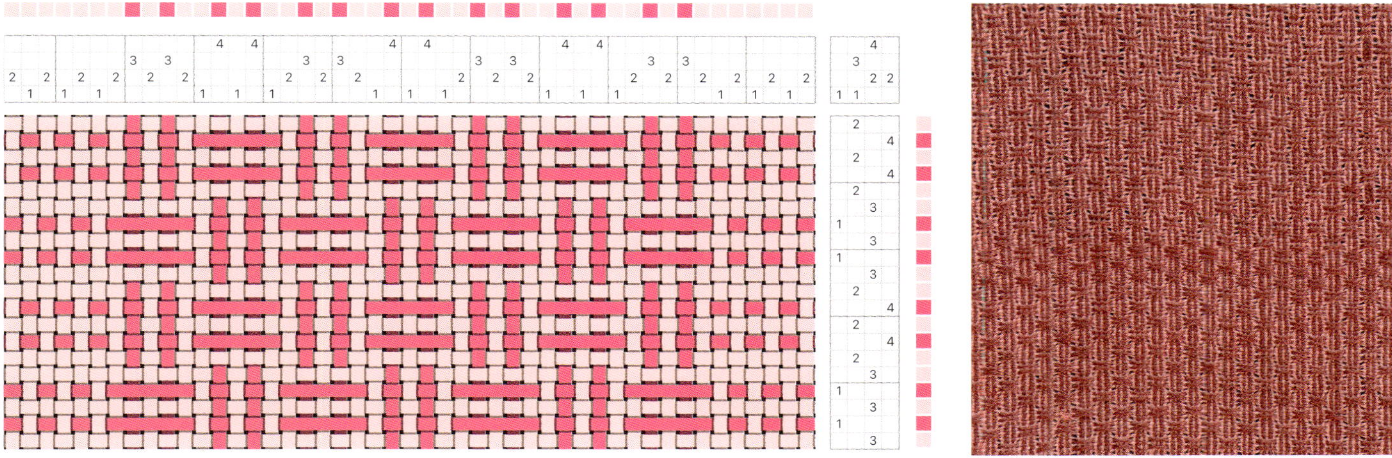

Figure 43 *Threading and treadling of huck in linen. Tie-up in weft floats.*

Weft floats

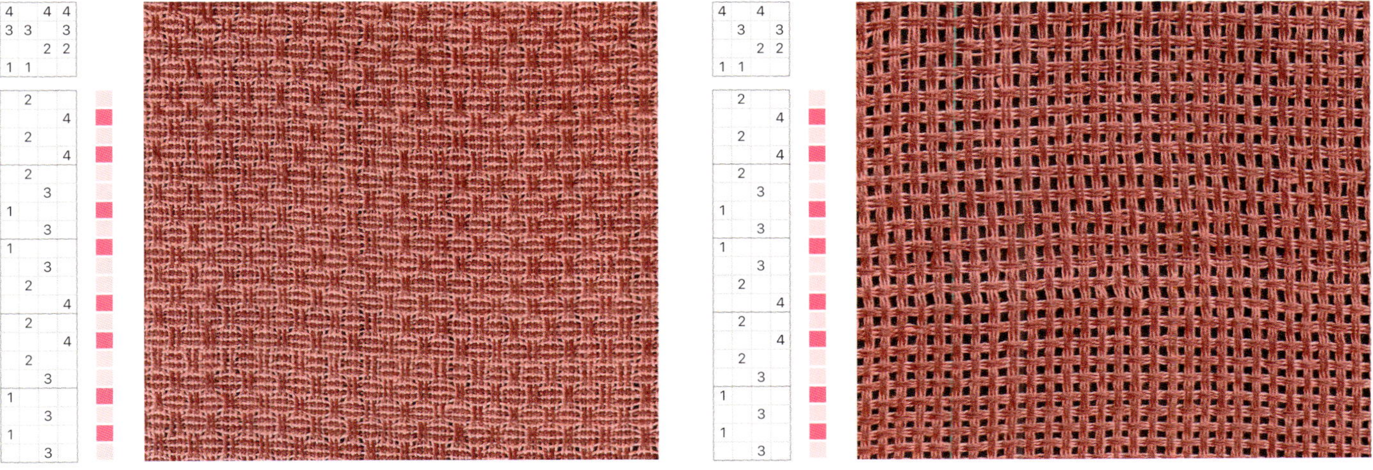

Warp floats

Huck lace floats

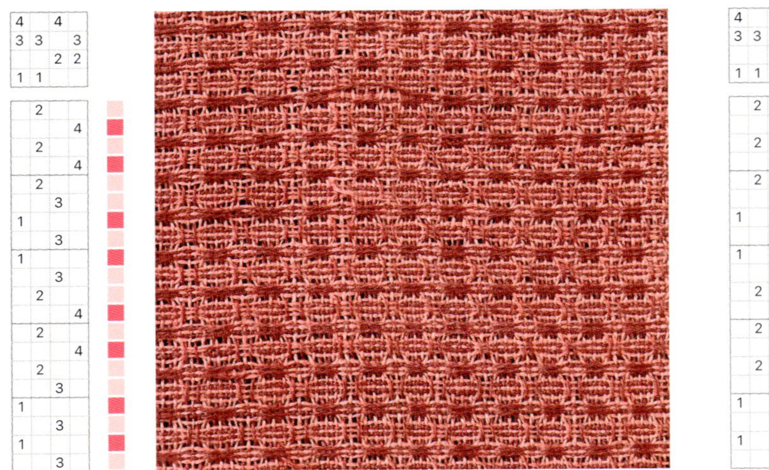

Line of warp floats on Block B and line with warp and weft floats in A and B

Another layout

Figure 44 ***Huck, 4 shafts, Fonty Merlin, 3,720 yd/lb (7,500 m/kg)***

Bronson Lace

In the huck structure, floats pass over the entire block of 3, 5, or more threads, depending on the unit chosen. With 4 shafts, it is imperative to systematically alternate Block A with Block B. Conversely, threading ends on shaft 2 for the Bronson lace structure (sometimes called Atwater-Bronson lace) allows several identical blocks to be placed in a row.

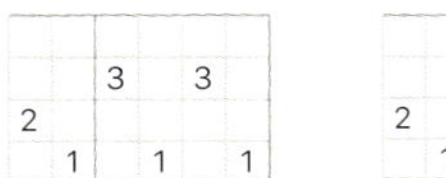

Figure 45 ***Threading of Blocks A and B in Bronson Lace***

As with the huck, the float ends are threaded in both shafts 3 and 4. With 4 shafts, only two blocks are possible. Unlike huck, each block is stabilized by an end threaded on shaft 2, a precaution to make sure the weft float interlaces at the end of each block. Thus the float does not cover the whole block but stops at this single thread. This way, it is possible to place several identical blocks side by side and to design elaborate patterns. Blocks A and B will no longer alternate systematically. The profile draft becomes the ideal tool for designing a project that will be a replica of the weaving.

Let me make a small analogy with the Summer and Winter structure. Just like the latter, Bronson lace is a very reassuring structure because a float will ever exceed the size of the block. These two structures only have two blocks with a 4-shaft loom. Despite that, it is possible to thread several identical blocks in a row. In addition, four different areas can be woven: no float, floats on Block A, floats on Block B, or floats on the two blocks. Then, just like in huck, lengthening or decreasing the size of the block, and therefore the length of the float, is an additional option. Be careful: as with huck, if you add an area of plain weave in threading between the blocks and/or at the selvedges, be sure to alternate threading in shaft 1 then two at the joins. A true plain weave is always possible in weft. Also pay attention to the fact that half the heddles will be on shaft 1. Counting the heddles before starting to thread will be more than necessary.

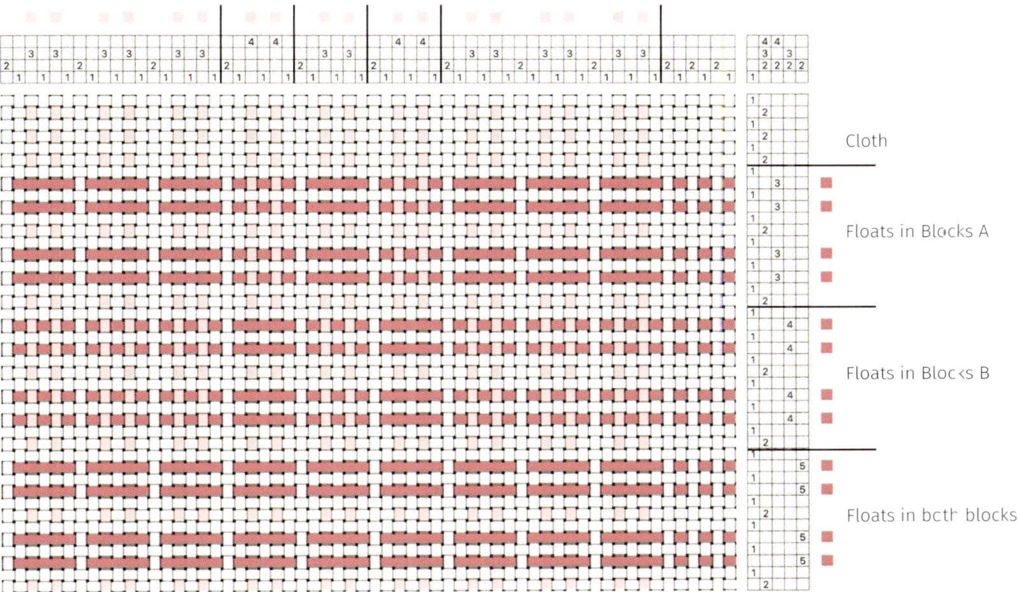

Figure 46 ***Profile draft to design a pattern in Bronson lace, expanded to its weaving draft, in part***

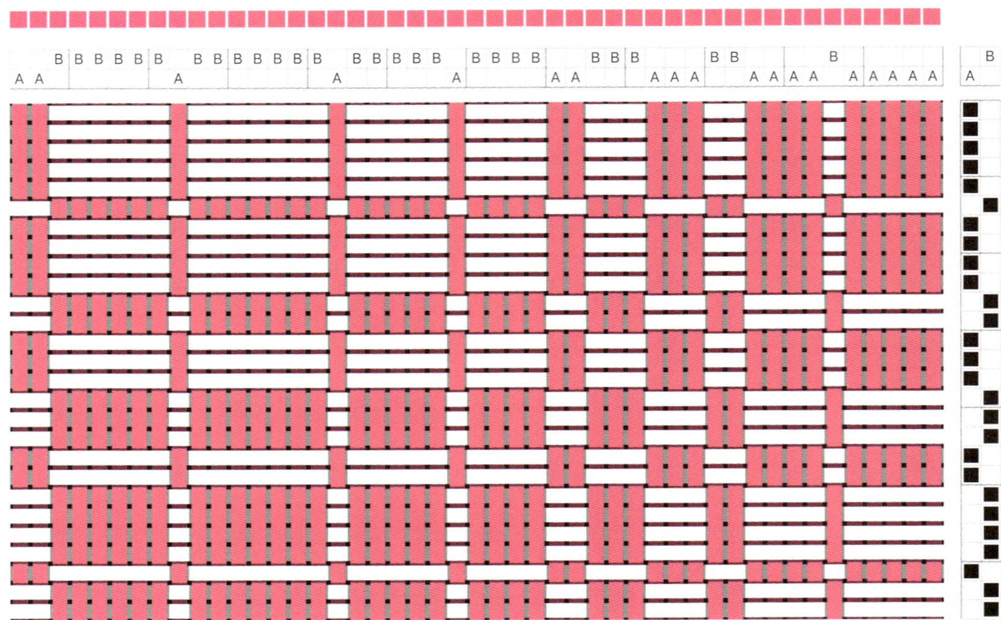

Figure 47 *Part of the profile draft for the Bronson lace weave*

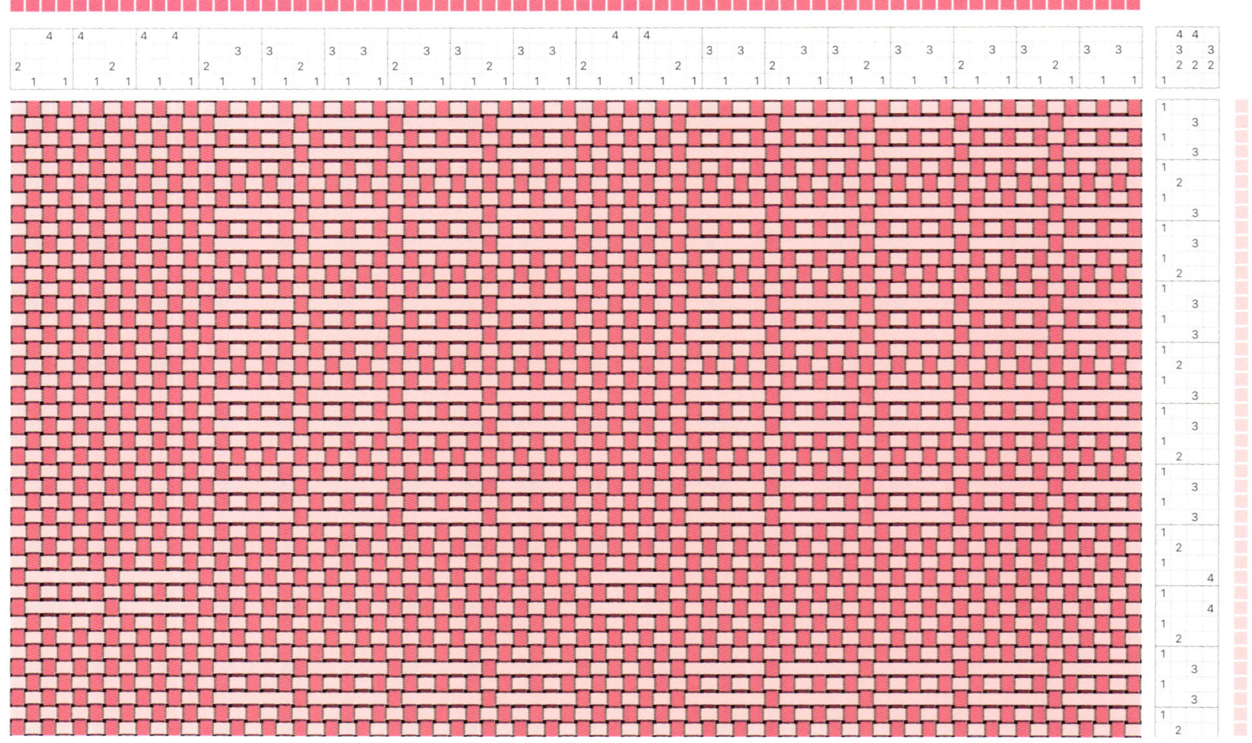

Figure 48 *Draft from part of the profile draft, expanded*

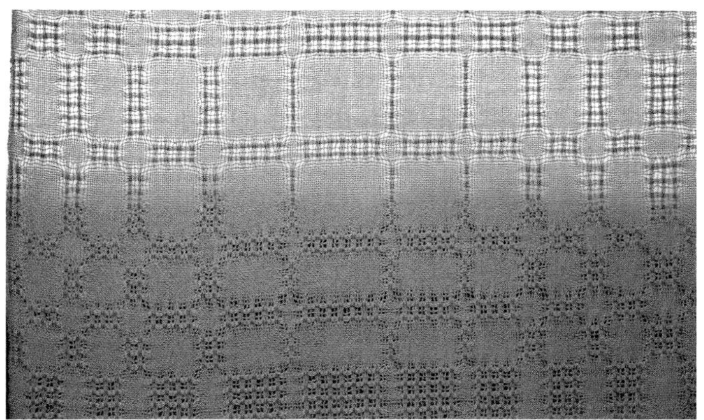

Figure 49 ***Bronson lace curtain, 4 shafts, 34/2 Tencel***

To conclude this section, I want to emphasize that a 4-shaft loom offers an abundance of patterns, a single shuttle will suffice, a large number of fibers can be used, and the weaving rhythm is so regular that it can be quickly etched in our minds and in our weaving motions. Color can be added in many ways, including by area to make stripes, by block, on the plain weave only with shafts 1 or 2, or only on warp or weft floats. Depending on the yarn, the density can be slightly lower than that of a plain weave, so it is economical in its use of yarn. Honestly, don't overlook these structures—they are terrific.

Other Laces

We might automatically think that sleying with a low density, no matter what the structure, would be enough to make openwork weaves. This is often impossible, as the choice of density is such a deciding factor in the quality of a fabric. However, it can be done, with some restrictions, by choosing a yarn or a threading that allows the warp and weft yarns to stay put without risk of sliding around with use and over time. It's difficult to see that happening with a slippery viscose yarn! On the other hand, wool will be blocked by washing and a slight felting; mohair will do this all by itself. Some low-twist linens cling together easily and would be nicely suited. These yarns are ideal for this alternative to weaving a lace. There is not enough interlacing in a satin to allow for openwork by decreasing density. Plain weave is the ideal structure as well as twill with its very specific sleying.

The following project was made with a reverse twill threading 1-2-3-4-3-2 (-1). The density chosen was that of plain weave, but the **sleying is unique**, following a very precise order. Take a reed that would be suitable for sleying one thread per dent or choose a yarn that would work with a reed that you have. Then sley the yarn threaded in shaft 1, with only one thread per dent. Leave the two dents on either side empty, put the ends from shafts 2 and 3 in the same dent, and leave the thread from shaft 4 in a dent by itself:

Empty dent	Thread from shaft 1	Empty dent	Threads from shafts 2 and 3 in the same dent	Thread from shaft 4	2 and 3 in the same dent

Thread repeat in reed dents

The pattern is made in six picks with the following treadling: 1-3/4/1-3/4/1-3/2-4.

Figure 50 ***Reverse twill, 4 shafts. 16/1 linen***

Another way to create openwork in weaving is inspired by the **pulled thread** embroidery technique. Areas of the fabric are left without weaving in weft, leaving the warp threads open. The edges of woven parts will then be secured by a Paris stitch or blanket stitch. Supplementary threads can be used to add embellishments and some kinds of knots or loops.

Bead Leno

A very simple way to create openwork is to replace some picks with a yarn you insert with a needle or by hand, with which you create twists between warp ends. Securing this way by twisting prevents adjacent wefts from moving too close and produces an airy weave. Several techniques are inspired by this method, such as Spanish lace, the bouquets of Marguerite G. Brooks, Danish medallions, or leno.

We can "mechanize" the weaving of leno by using beads when installing the warp, which will force its threads to twist systematically. This is getting close to the very curious gauze where an unusual interlacing was created by very sophisticated looms, with certain warp ends going around other warp ends, which then no longer remain parallel. These beads are inserted between the heddles and reed and only have a mechanical action; they are not woven and are removed from the loom with the warp end threads when the weave is taken off the loom. They must be small enough to not interfere with the weaving, have a hole that is big enough for two warp threads to easily pass through, and be solid enough to withstand a lot of friction.

The warp is wound onto the beam as usual, threading is straight (1-2-3-4). Each group of four threads will be **sleyed in the same reed dent**; this is absolutely essential. But before that, the threads from shafts 1 and 4 must be threaded together in a bead. These two threads must first be passed **under the threads of shafts 2 and 3**, otherwise the twist will not happen. This is a rather tricky operation, I admit, one where you'd like to have three hands. The density in the reed depends on the yarn, but it is very likely that you will have to leave one or two dents between the sleying of each group of four threads.

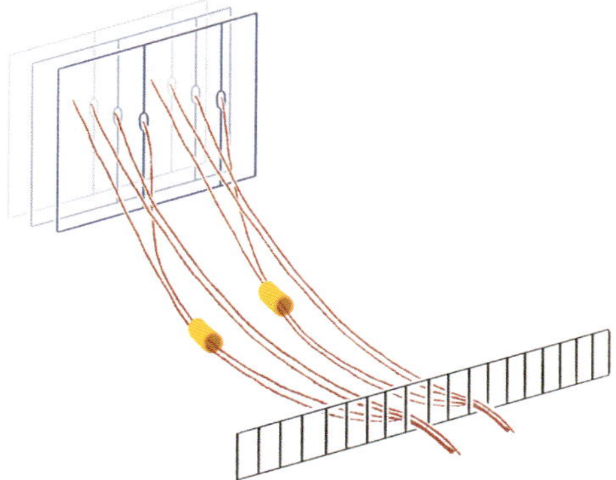

Figure 51 *Inserting beads between heddles and reed*

Several treadlings and tie-ups are possible. But the principle remains the same. By lifting shaft 1, the bead pulls the thread from shaft 4, crossing under the pair of warp ends from shafts 2-3 to the right. By then lifting shaft 4, it is the thread from shaft 1 that crosses under to the left, pulled along by the thread from shaft 4. Threads 2 and 3 remain straight with the other threads always crossing under them.

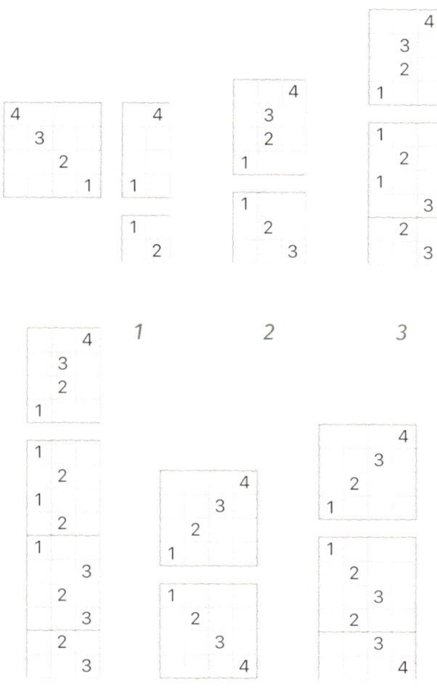

Figure 52 *Threading, tie-ups, and treadlings of a bead leno weave*

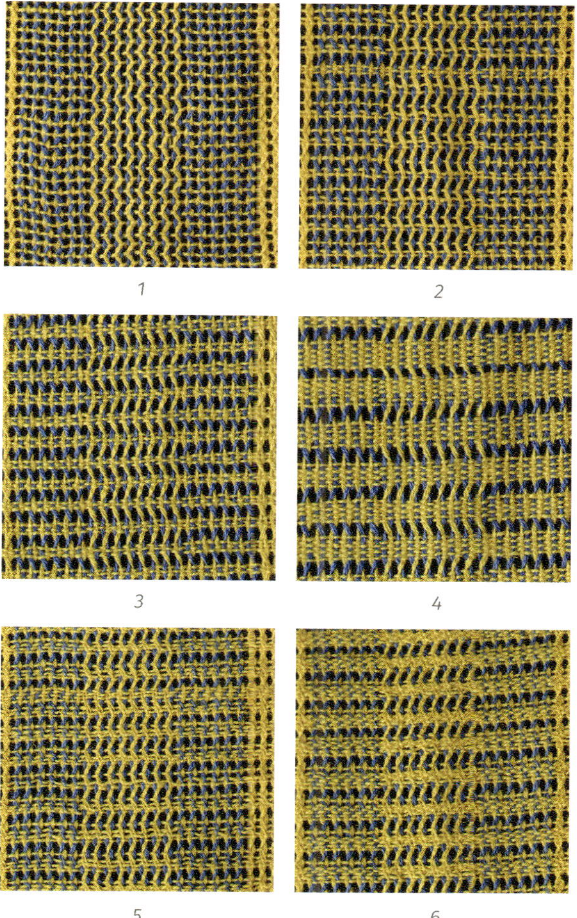

Figure 53 *A few variations of bead leno*

True plain weave is not possible as the warp threads always work in pairs. It is not foolish to double the weft to balance the weave; in this case, putting in floating selvedges is essential.

Figure 54 *Treadling and tie-up of the "plain weave" in leno*

The shed is always very narrow, a bit more open if the warp is not too tight. The use of a flat shuttle is recommended. The yarn used must be strong and cabled so as to withstand the considerable friction and risk of wear and tear. It is necessary, however, to often separate warp ends by hand, which may seem long and tedious. But the number of weft per inch is so low that the weaving process goes incredibly fast. It is a magical weave as the fabric becomes so light and airy when removed from the loom.

Fugues with Deflected Structures

Like the lace structures just presented, deflected structures have areas of plain weave that adjoin areas of floats. Here, the purpose of this proximity is no longer to create openwork areas, but to create volume or movement in the fabric. We are entering the third dimension.

Again, we have questions of terminology. Honeycomb is called waffle weave in Europe, and what is called waffle weave in the U.S. is honeycomb in Europe. So you might want to be aware of the origin of any publication you are reading on these weaves. To limit confusion, I suggest that you also rely on the threading and treadling drafts that are very identifiable. Textile vocabulary does not always help us. So we will agree here that waffle weave creates squares that are a bit puffed up and bulky, while the honeycomb pattern shows floats forming waves with long floats on the reverse side. Another dimensional structure, deflected doubleweave, plays with floats that twist around areas of plain weave.

As with lace structures, the threads are under tension on the loom and it is difficult to anticipate the result. Only after the weave is cut from the loom and especially after it is washed is the effect really seen.

Waffle Weave

This structure is undoubtedly the one that most easily gives us volume. It is recognized by its small hollowed squares and is often associated with household linens. Waffle weave towels are appreciated for their good absorption.

Each small square is bordered with floats in warp and weft and its two diagonals are made in plain weave. As we know, plain weave has the most interlacings possible and its density is low. Conversely, floats require a higher density to be held in place. The waffle weave plays on these opposites. By juxtaposing plain weave and fairly long floats, and by using a density similar to that of a twill, the floats are constantly trying to move closer together and away from the plain weave. This is how volume is created.

During weaving, warp ends are not subjected to this contraction due to the tension on the loom. As for the weft, it must be helped to resist this inevitable draw-in, and placing a temple on the weave is recommended to protect the selvedge threads from wear and tear due to friction from the reed. This also helps maintain the initial density of the warp so the wefts can be beaten without difficulty. The higher the density, the more puffy the fabric will look. However, if this draw-in is not anticipated, it is likely that the width of your fabric, once off the loom and after washing, will be much smaller than your original design. Making samples is essential!

Although we are looking for a high density, the main objective is to weave in such a way as to obtain balanced squares. This is often the most difficult thing to achieve on small looms: a high density to obtain bulk and a balanced density to obtain the square. This difficulty will be increased by using more than five shafts. When the number of shafts increases, the square cell is deeper, the force of beating quickly becomes painful and getting a square difficult with a light beater.

All yarns are suitable for this structure and will be chosen depending on the use of the fabric. In unmercerized cotton or linen, the woven fabric will be suitable for household linens and will be absorbent. In wool and alpaca, we obtain a soft and warm fabric as this volume gives it insulating properties. The softer the yarn, the greater the swelling. For a beautiful symmetry, we use the same yarn in warp and weft.

Threading and Treadling

Threading is that of a simple reverse twill. It can be done on 4 shafts. In this case, the squares are not very deep, but the longest float of 5 threads is reasonable. In warp, the threading block is over 6 threads, while in treadling, the pattern is in 8 weft rows so that it is symmetrical. Treadling is similar to reverse twill threading and is done with 5 treadles.

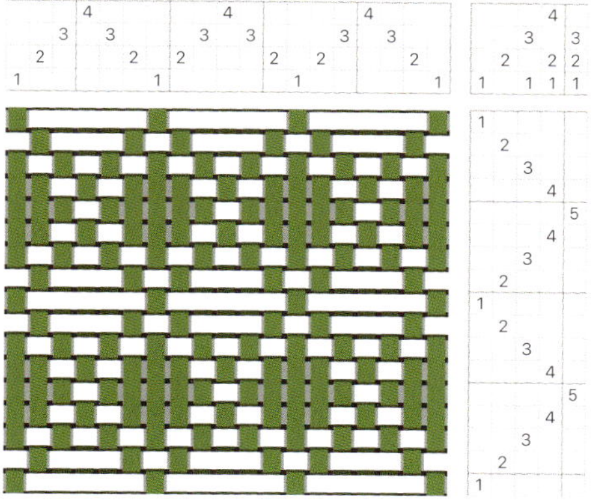

Figure 55 ***Draft for waffle weave on 4 shafts***

As the number of shafts increases, the length of the floats increases, more treadles are required, shrinkage becomes more substantial, but the depth of the cells increases. The number of treadles required to obtain symmetry in warp and weft is the number of shafts plus 1. The length of the floats is twice the number of shafts minus 3. The deeper the cell, the more elastic the fabric and the greater the need for a temple.

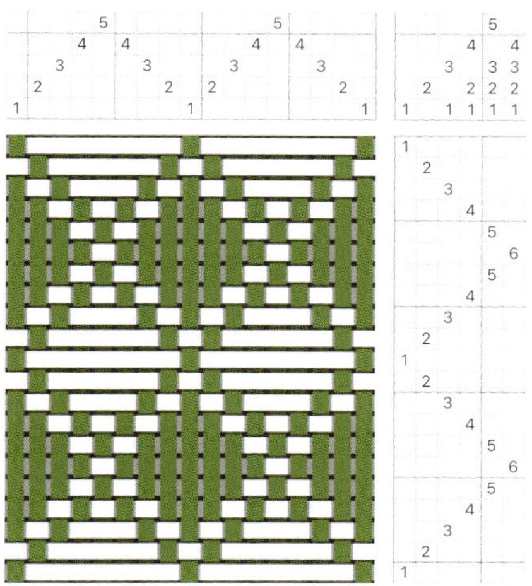

Figure 56 ***Draft for waffle weave on 5 shafts***

Tie-Up

The tie-up is very logical. On five shafts, each end threaded on shaft 1 remains raised until it floats over seven weft threads. It defines the left and right edges of the square. When treadle 1 is pressed, each weft passed covers seven warp ends not lifted. It defines the top and bottom of the square. Between these two ends, the floats are smaller and smaller, always bordered by plain weave.

The plain weave is made on the diagonal; it structures the cell. Around these points of plain weave, the interlacing of the warp and weft is systematic!

- Pick **1**: Shaft **1** is raised.
- Pick **2**: Shaft **2** is raised, but not its direct neighbor below, shaft 1.
- Pick **3**: Shaft **3** is raised, but not its direct neighbor below, shaft 2. Then the one below, shaft 1, is raised.
- Pick **4**: Shaft **4** is raised, but not its direct neighbor below, shaft 3. Then all of those below, shafts 1 and 2, are raised.
- Pick **5**: Shaft **5** is raised but not its direct neighbor below, shaft 4. Then all of those below, shafts 1, 2, and 3, are raised.
- Pick **6**: We imagine a shaft "**6**" raised but not its direct neighbor below, shaft 5. Then all of those below, shafts 1, 2, 3, and 4, are raised.

« 6 »

				5	
			4		4
		3		3	3
	2		2	2	2
1		1	1	1	1

When weaving with a treadle loom, the tie-up is done so that the left foot alternates with the right foot with each pick.

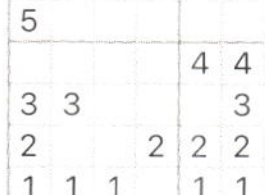

5					
				4	4
3	3				3
2			2	2	2
1	1	1		1	1

Figure 57 ***Tie-up of treadles so left and right feet alternate***

Density

The higher the density, the deeper the cells. However, a waffle weave is successful when the cell is square. It is thus a question of finding the highest possible density to meet these two objectives. With few shafts, using the same yarn, it is almost the same as twill density. The higher the number of shafts, the higher the density of the cell. Several samples will likely be needed to determine the proper density.

Weavers will often want to begin and end their project with a few strips in plain weave. Although it is always possible to weave them by alternating even and odd shafts, the densities of plain weave and waffle weave are not the same. Unless you want to have a wavy strip of plain weave, you will need to choose a finer weft yarn to get a clean border. For hand towels, a cotton sewing thread works well. You will be able to create an unobtrusive hem by weaving the first inch or two with this fine thread.

Playing with Color

This structure is so geometric that it calls for the introduction of color in a thoughtful way. Of course, there is nothing to stop you from arranging colored stripes of different widths as in any other fabric, being sure to make changes on shaft 1 or 5, so that it's on the crest of the square.

Nevertheless, knowing that the shaft 1 thread floats more than the adjacent threads and becomes so much more visible, encourages us to differentiate it and highlight it. To do this, it can be given the same color all the time. For the same reason, the thread on shaft 5 will also be very visible, but on the reverse, and it would be good for it to have its own color as well. By choosing a dark color inside the square cell, you can accentuate its depth. You can also pair each cell with a different color. This way, the lines are clean and regular. A final choice is having a solid color on a large part of the fabric and bringing in touches of color on the first part of the blocks: 1-2-3-4.

Figure 58 ***Assortment of hand towels in colorful waffle weave***

So you'll have to wait until the fabric is off the loom, washed and dried, to enter this third dimension. Then hope that you have anticipated the shrinkage enough not to discover with disappointment that the dimensions of the fabric are much smaller than expected.

PROJECT RECORD SHEET—POTHOLDERS IN WAFFLE WEAVE ON 6 SHAFTS

Warp and weft: Venne 22/2 Cottolin

Sett: 30 epi (12 per cm)

Width in reed: 10 in. (25 cm)

Total number of ends: 293

Dimensions of each potholder: 7 × 7 in. (18 × 18 cm)

Warp length: 73 in. (184 cm)

% of shrinkage when taken off loom: 16%

% of shrinkage after washing: 10%

Hem: 1¼ in. (3 cm) on each end

Loss due to front tie-on and at back of loom: 24 in. (60 cm)

Quantity of Cottolin: colors 2009 and 4006: 2.3 oz. (65 g) of each

Follow the draft in Figure 56.

Honeycomb Weave

With honeycomb, or *hälkrus* in Sweden, the deviation of the weft thread does not generate the depth seen in the waffle weave, but brings it out of the normal straight line and draws zigzags or waves from one selvedge to the other.

Figure 59 ***Honeycomb, 8 shafts. FIR Group Linen and Nepal nettle yarn or lacing.***

The idea is to create plain weave with the same yarn in warp and weft and to add a softer or thicker supplementary weft at regular intervals that will go around the blocks of plain weave. The placement of the blocks makes this added thread twist around them and outline the cells.

Normally, with 4 shafts, there are 2 different blocks. When Block A is woven in plain weave, the threads from Block B float. The warp is raised on Block B and the weft passes under. Then Block B is woven is plain weave while the weft passes under the threads from Block A, which float. These two blocks are alternated and, before each change, plain weave is woven on all blocks with the different yarn. This supplementary yarn is pushed back by the block of plain weave—it is diverted and that is how the actual wave or undulation is formed in honeycomb weave. It is worth trying out any special or novelty yarn here. Anything is possible depending on the use of the fabric. This is the time to be bold and daring.

However, this fabric is not reversible. Weft that has not been woven in floats on the reverse side. Unless you play with these long floats by embroidering the fabric, a lining is often used to hide them as they are long and unattractive.

Threading, Treadling, and Tie-Up

With 4 shafts, **threading** is done in 2 blocks: Block A, which groups together the threads of shafts 1 and 2, and Block B, which groups together the threads of shafts 3 and 4. It is essential that even shaft and odd shaft alternate since weaving a real plain weave must always be possible; this is closely watched where the two blocks are joined.

There is no obligation to tromp as writ, but as is often the case, it provides uniformity. There are also two blocks in **treadling**: Block A, which makes the plain weave is woven with the yarn threaded on 1 and 2 and Block B, where the plain weave is woven with the ends from the other two shafts. While plain weave is woven on one block, the warp ends remain raised on the other block.

Between each change in block, the supplementary thread is woven in plain weave on the two blocks at the same time, by one back-and-forth. It is shown in color on the draft.

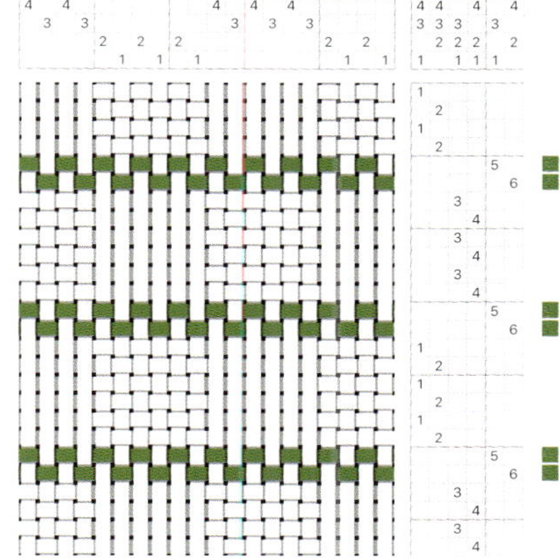

Figure 60 ***Draft of a honeycomb weave in two blocks on 4 shafts***

In the same way that, on the loom, the tension of the threads prevents us from seeing the movement of this added thread, it is difficult on the diagram as well to imagine that this green thread is going to wave around the two blocks. To understand what is going on, remember that threads are good companions and that as soon as they can, they move closer.

Where warp ends have remained raised, and when the fabric is taken off the loom and not under tension, the wefts that have been diverted will be able to move toward each other, while the blocks of plain weave will push them back to their original place.

When Block A is woven in plain weave, the diverted threads are drawn into the Block B area. Then we weave Block B in plain weave, and the opposite happens. This repeated alternation causes the fancy yarn to waver between the blocks and to give it this look of a wave. When weaving, we are careful not to stretch this weft yarn too much. Thus, freed from the tension of the loom, it will have the suppleness to go around the blocks of plain weave and sail freely.

This thread that sails the waves has little influence on density. The density of the plain weave will be chosen to make the weave balanced, meaning as many threads in warp as in weft per inch.

Possible Changes

As long as the conditions discussed above are followed, it is easy to change this structure and create your own personal pattern. In threading, the size of the blocks doesn't really matter; it is a minimum of two threads. On the other hand, in treadling, you cannot stay on the same block for too long; otherwise the wave would become too deep and the deflected threads could no longer get close enough to each other. Depending on the yarn used, it is necessary to test this. Four or six picks are often a good compromise between a flat sea and a rough sea.

As more shafts are used, the number of blocks and thus the number of different cells increases. Two shafts are needed to make a block. With 8 shafts, 4 blocks are possible. The blocks need not follow the order A-B-C-D; you just have to be sure to alternate even and odd shafts! The length of the floats on the reverse side of the fabric can be impressive since the weft can pass under three adjacent blocks.

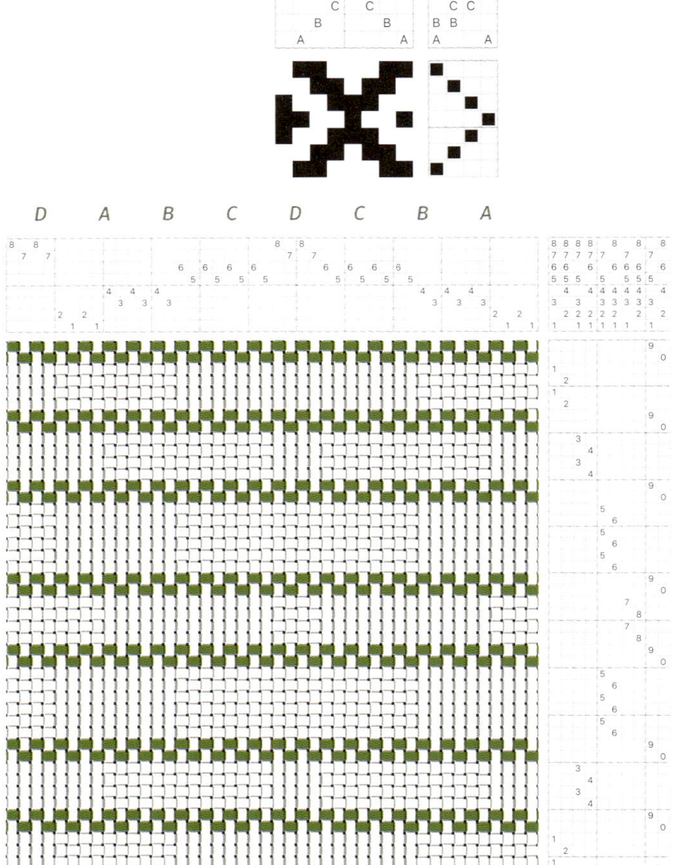

Figure 61 ***Honeycomb, 8 shafts. Fonty Zephir 17/2 wool***

To draw up a new threading, we can base the construction of a honeycomb profile draft on a twill threading (straight, reverse, rosepath, etc.), by matching each block of the honeycomb A, B, C, and D to the number of the shafts from the twill 1, 2, 3, and 4. Then we replace each block by one or more pairs of shafts. The treadling can follow this same logic. With 4 blocks, the tie-up diversifies quite a bit. The preceding example shows that the shafts of two adjacent blocks remain raised for the entire treadling sequence of a block. Feel free to test this example by raising a single block or two or three neighboring blocks. The long floats on the back are a concern but do not affect the weave visible on the front.

The same yarn is often used in warp and in weft to make the plain weave ground cloth, but this is not a rule. The opposite can be done by weaving the diverted wefts with the same yarns as that in warp and weaving the inside of the cells with a fine thread—why not in color?

Except for the floats on the reverse side of the fabric that prevent it from being reversible, this structure is quite strong and uncomplicated.

Deflected Doubleweave

This structure always appeals to me. Is it the way the threads from one weave float over the groups of threads from the other in both warp and weft? Is it the way the threads deflect from their vertical and horizontal positions when removed from the loom? I can't find any disadvantages to this structure, except perhaps for the selvedges, which require special care. Like honeycomb, the thread deviations are very attractive because they are a rare departure from the usual straight warps and wefts.

All yarns are suitable here. This is the time to use yarns together that are very different types, colors, or thicknesses. The floats go around the areas of plain weave and while we usually try to minimize their fullness, in deflected doubleweave they are inherent to the structure and we study them as much as the parts in plain weave. It is because there are areas of plain weave that adjoin areas of floats that this distortion effect is possible, both in warp and weft. Two different yarns are usually chosen, each on its own block and constantly alternating. However, each area of plain weave will be woven with the same yarn in warp and weft to obtain a uniform fabric.

Building a Pattern with the Profile Draft

Deflected doubleweave is a structure that is worked in blocks. Each block is built with two shafts. Block A: shafts 1 and 2, Block B: shafts 3 and 4, Block C: shafts 5 and 6, etc. The float is the total length of the block. Each block is made up of at least 2 threads. Depending on the use of the fabric and the yarn count, the length of the block will be adjusted (1-2-1-2-1-2, etc.). Blocks A and C are made of the same yarn, blocks B and D of the other yarn, both in warp and weft.

Even if you can weave the deflected doubleweave on 4 shafts, the effect is more apparent when you use 6 shafts, and it becomes really magical with 8 shafts. On the following drafts, each block is differentiated by color, but don't forget that for once you can also contrast the blocks by yarn size and type.

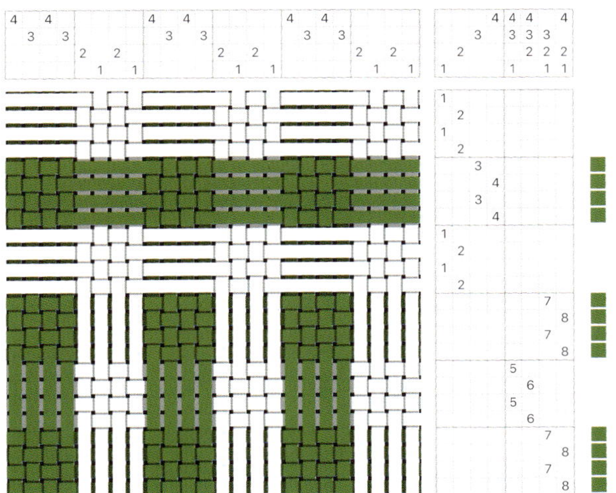

Figure 62 **Example of a deflected doubleweave on 4 shafts**

When using blocks, it is easier to work with a profile draft. With 2 blocks, it is inevitable that A and B will alternate. Only the size of the blocks can vary. With 3 blocks, we can break this methodical sequence. With 4 blocks we start to have a lot of freedom! One fun way to draw a profile draft is to arrange the blocks like twill, for this profile to be straight, reverse, or broken.

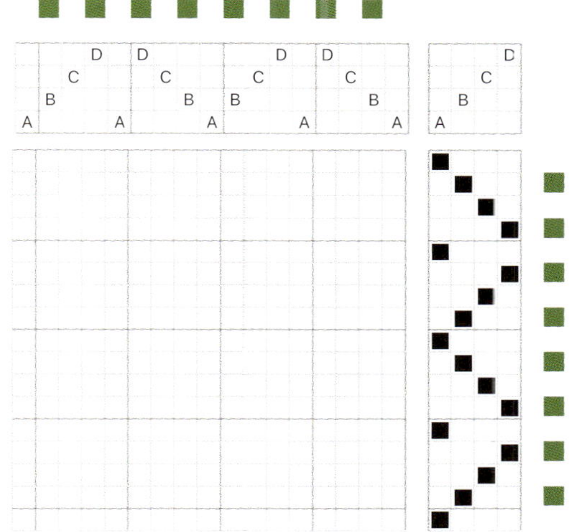

Figure 63 **Profile draft with placement of blocks in reverse twill**

Expanding the profile draft into threading and then treadling must at least follow one rule, that it must systematically alternate odd and even threads: even shaft/odd shaft for threading then even plain weave/odd plain weave for weaving, to obtain a perfect plain weave. For now, let's not dwell on the size of the blocks, but let's make sure that each one is composed of an even number of threads.

Blocks A and C will be threaded with the same yarn, then blocks B and D with their own yarn. This alternation will be followed identically in weft. This is essential so that the areas of plain weave will be uniform.

Tromp as writ ensures a balanced pattern. This is a comfortable way to discover the deflected. Later, the treadling can evolve in a spontaneous and risk-free way.

Threading, Treadling, and Tie-Up

To keep it simple, I'm going to draw inspiration from the profile draft shown above and expand it. Deliberately, to show that it is really possible, the blocks are not the same size.

Figure 64 ***Draft of a deflected doubleweave***

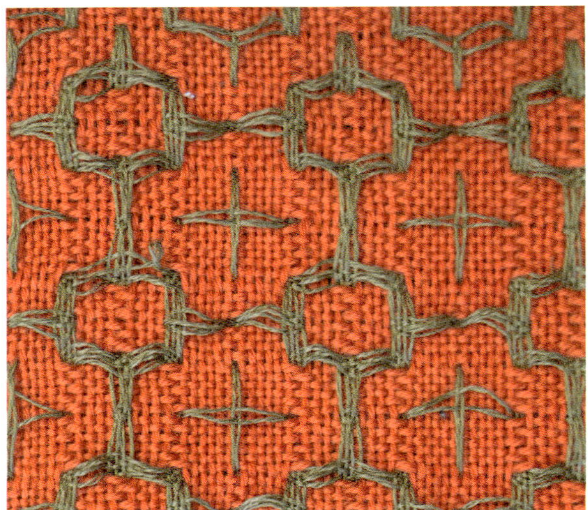

When the yarn is under tension on the loom, you can't see the movement of the floats that jog around the plain weave areas, just like on this draft. But when the fabric comes off the loom, the floats try to move closer to each other, and sometimes even more after washing. As for the threads in the plain weave blocks, not being forced to stay in their place thanks to these liberating floats, they try to move closer to the threads from the other blocks of plain weave, however far away they may be, by slipping under the floats. It is the addition of these two deviations that give the pattern its curve, sometimes even forming circles around the plain weave squares.

Figure 65 ***Circles that can be made with deflected doubleweave***

The treadling follows the same reasoning as the threading. Each block has its own color, different from that of the neighboring block. When weaving **the treadling of Block A**, shafts 1-2 and 5-6 of Blocks A and C will be operated alternately to produce the plain weave. In Block B, the warp floats will pass over and in Block D below for this entire sequence. Then, when weaving the **treadling of Block B**, we change shuttles to again obtain the solid color plain weave on Blocks B and D by alternating shafts 3-4 and 7-8, while the warp ends of Block C float above and those from Block A below during the entire sequence. Then, we go back to the first shuttle to weave **treadling block C**, weaving plain weave on blocks A and C, the warp floats passing above or below, the opposite of treadling Block A. For **treadling Block D**, the plain weave is woven on Blocks B and D and the warp floats on Blocks A and C, the opposite of treadling Block B.

The tie-up draft shows this movement by blocks fairly well. Let's look at the first two treadles that weave treadling Block A: treadles 1 and 2 operate shafts 1-2 and 5-6 alternately so that the solid plain weave is made on Blocks A and C. The threads of shafts 3 and 4 remain raised, so there are warp floats above and weft floats below the fabric. The threads from shafts 7 and 8 remain lowered, thus receiving weft floats above, while below they form warp floats.

When weaving the next treadling Block B, the second thread is used and the solid color plain weave is made with the threads from the shafts of Blocks B and D. The threads from Block A float below and those from Block C remain raised. And so on for the other two treadling blocks. This little tie-up square is very self-explanatory. Again, I encourage you to really understand it. It will help you gain some perspective and you will weave with fluidity.

Balanced Density

Despite its name, deflected doubleweave is not truly a doubleweave in the sense that two fabrics are not woven simultaneously. The woven blocks are surrounded by blocks of floats, which are not part of density calculations.

On the other hand, all the blocks of plain weave must be woven with their specific density and must stick to the famous balanced density in warp and weft! Therefore, there are two density calculations to be made: one for the plain weave of the first yarn and then the one for the other yarn.

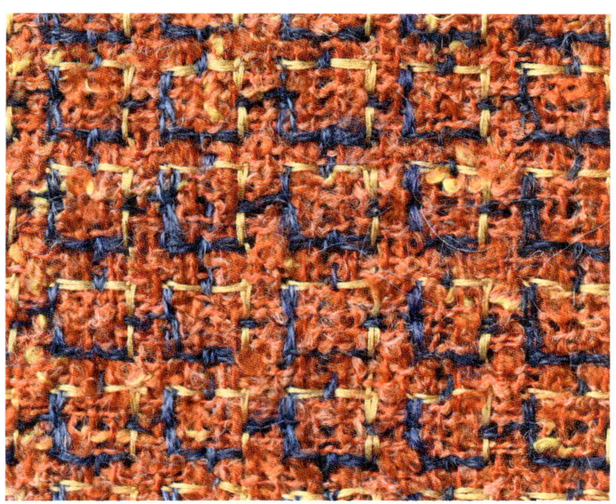

Figure 66 ***A different density appropriate for each yarn***

If the yarns chosen are very similar, they will of course be averaged over the width of the weave and that will give the approximate density of a simple plain weave. However, when the two yarns are very different, it is better to assign the appropriate density to each block in order to get perfect little squares in plain weave. You must take this into account when calculating your project, apply it when you sley the reed, and keep an eye out for it when you're weaving. However, it is best to start by weaving two yarns that are similar in size and choose to create contrast with color by applying the density of the plain weave across the entire width of the fabric.

Selvedges

Selvedges are very tricky to get right and require a lot of attention. With the yarn from Blocks A and C, there's no problem, since the plain weave is woven right up to the edge. However, when the thread from Blocks B and D is woven, it should not be taken to the edge of the weaving. It is not allowed to cross the border with Block B. The selvedge is made naturally and stops itself at the end of Block B.

But just before changing blocks and shuttles, sometimes the shuttle will be brought out above the weaving, sometimes below, so that this weft thread accompanies the warp thread, which is similar to it, throughout all the weaving of the following block, without it overflowing into Block A. Thus, the selvedge of Block A is not disturbed by this thread from Block B and it stays consistent. The edge of Block B is shifted toward the inside of the fabric.

Figure 67 *Selvedge of the deflected doubleweave*

There is no need to put in a floating selvedge, unless you want to sew your fabric; this edge will then be hidden in the seam. In this case, you can get rid of the back-and-forth of the shuttle from the front side to the back side of the fabric. This will save you time.

Changing Treadling or Tie-Up: Inventions at Your Fingertips

To start, tromp as writ is the guarantee to a balanced weave. But nothing prevents you from changing the tempo. Let's go back to the analogy at the beginning. The profile draft shows a sequence of blocks that look like a twill sequence. This is the time to try a "straight" or "reverse" or "broken" treadling, being careful not to make the floats dangerously long by always alternating the shuttles each time treadling blocks are changed to get pure color plain weaves. With more experience, you will juggle the blocks more freely and take some risks.

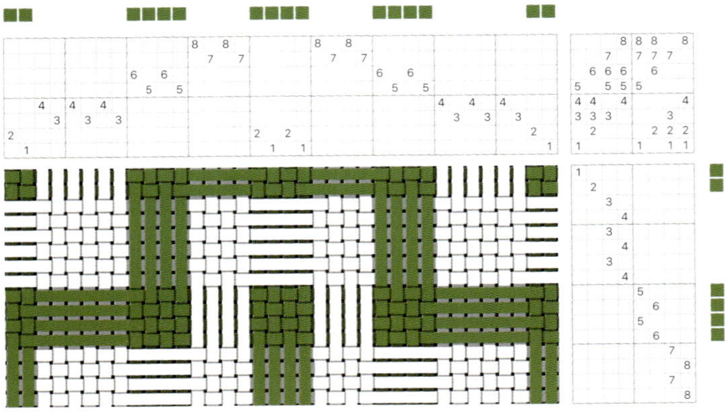

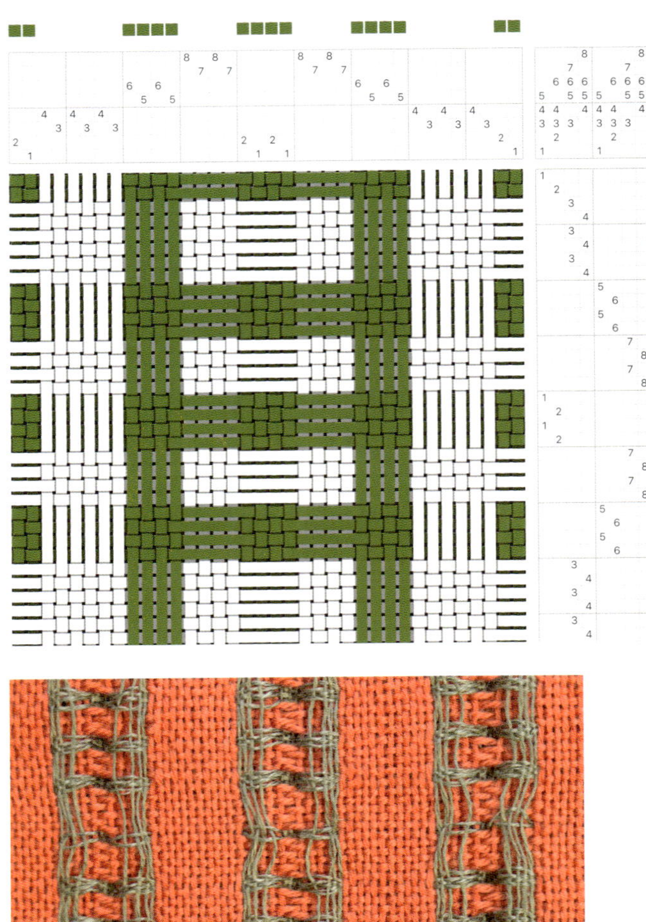

Figure 68 ***Some suggestions for treadlings***

Another way to transform your weave is to modify the tie-up draft. Although we often want to keep plain weave unadorned, we can choose to slide floats in more freely above or below the weaving. Here are a few examples.

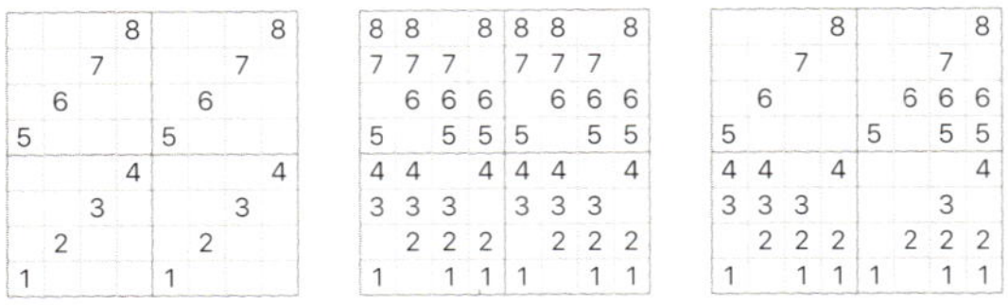

Figure 69 ***Some suggestions for tie-ups***

PROJECT RECORD SHEET—A SCARF IN DEFLECTED DOUBLEWEAVE

Warp and weft Blocks A and C: Alpacone alpaca, 6,944 yd/lb (14,000 m/kg)

Warp and weft Blocks B and D: Soies de Marie silk, 5,953 yd/lb (12,000 m/kg)

Sett: 20 epi (8 per cm)

Width in reed: 13 in. (33 cm)

Total number of ends: 265

Length of the scarf: 2 yds. (180 cm)

Warp length: 3 yds. (270 cm)

% of shrinkage when taken off loom: 5%

% of shrinkage after washing: 4%

Fringe: 2.5 in. (6 cm) on each end

Loss due to front tie-on and at back of loom: 24 in. (60 cm)

Quantity of alpaca: 2.1 oz. (60 g)

Quantity of silk: 1.1 oz. (30 g)

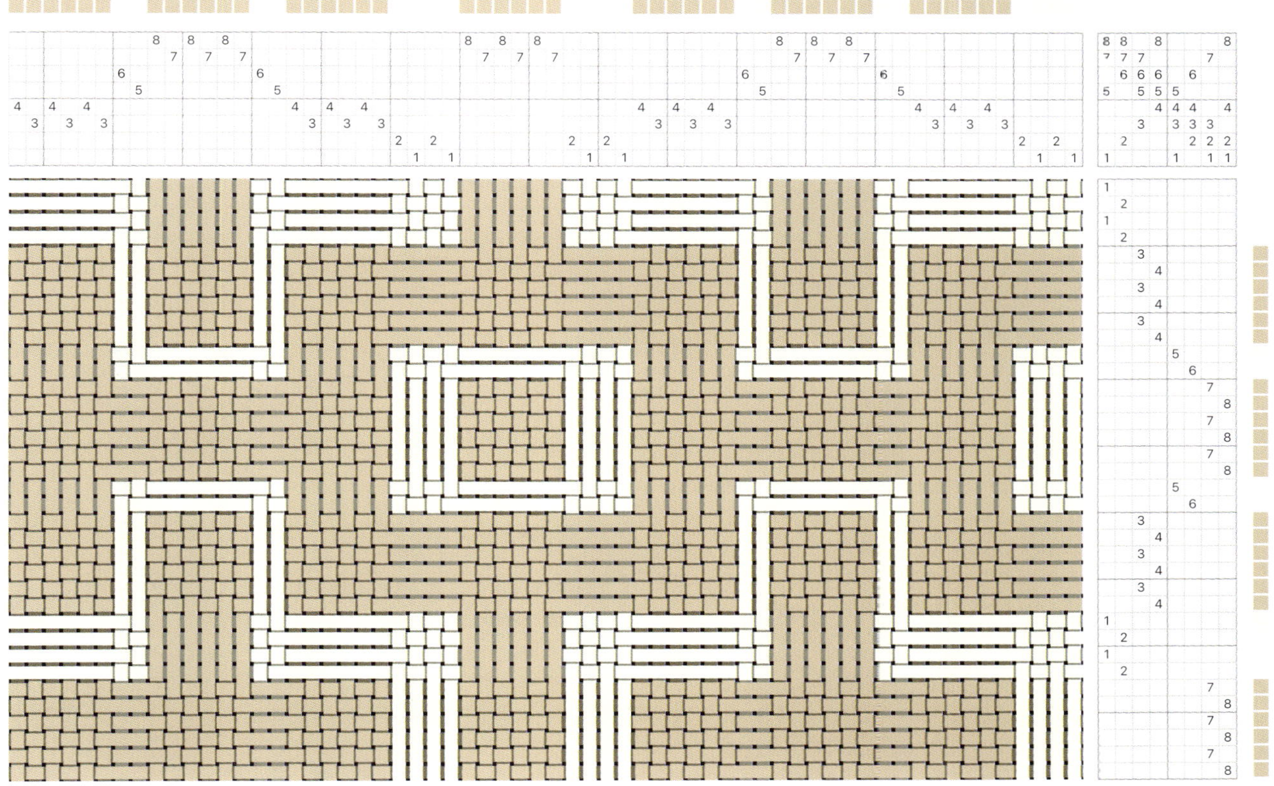

*Figure 70 - **Scarf in deflected doubleweave, 8 shafts. Alpaca and silk, 6,944 yd/lb (14,000 m/kg)***

Deflected doubleweave, depending on the yarn used, can produce any type of fabric: a soft shawl, an absorbent towel, a colorful pillow a durable rug, a scarf with bold colors. Its design is simole and it is easy to change. Don't be afraid to improvise.

Doubleweave: A Waltz in Two Beats

There are two sorts of time: the time that waits and the time that hopes.

Jacques Brel, *L'Ostendaise*, 1968

Doubleweave is a powerful structure because it has many qualities that allow it to adapt to very different projects. Do you want to weave something twice as wide as your loom allows? Do you want to weave a seamless tube? Would you like to slide some padding between two fabrics to give it volume? Or do you want to alternate weft or warp bands of different colors while keeping the colors pure? Double weaving grants all these wishes.

It consists of weaving two fabrics at the same time, one on top of the other, which are called layers, and which can be joined together either by interweaving the two layers, or by joining them on one or both selvedges to double the width or to weave in a tube.

Theory on 4 Shafts: A Little Sight Reading

At first, it seems quite mysterious and even difficult. The enigma will probably be solved more easily by weaving the two layers with two very different colors; it will then be impossible to weave the wrong layer without realizing it!

It seems to me that by understanding the principle that I explain here for four shafts, it becomes easier to extrapolate and navigate on more shafts, to also control which plain weave, which block, or which part of the warp to highlight. Let's agree on the basic concepts.

First Movement

If you have a loom with two shafts, you can weave plain weave. So you can think of a loom with four shafts as two 2-shaft looms on top of each other so you can weave two plain weaves one on top of the other at exactly the same time. With six shafts, you can have fun weaving three plain weaves one on top of the other or two layers of twill. With eight, ten, or more shafts, you need to be a bit of an expert, but you can split your work into blocks and it is pure fun.

First, we will study the mechanism with only four shafts and two identical yarns but each a different color, one light for the first plain weave, the other dark for the second one.

Threading

According to some authors, you will find there are two ways to thread the heddles:

- The first plain weave is threaded on shafts 1 and 2 and the other on shafts 3 and 4. This is the notation used by Jennifer Moore and others;

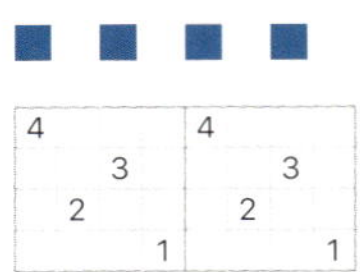

Figure 71 ***First way to thread heddles***

- The first plain weave is threaded on the odd shafts and the second on the even shafts. Many of us prefer this notation because it makes the tie-up more logical and easier to remember: the threads of the first layer are on shafts 1 and 3, and the threads for the second layer are on shafts 2 and 4.

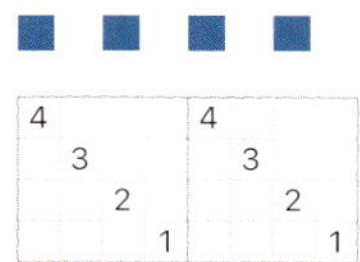

Figure 72 ***Second way to thread heddles***

Every author has their own routines, and it's up to you to try them out and choose the one that is most natural for you. Nevertheless, whatever the method, the colors must systematically alternate. The light yarn is threaded first, then the dark, and this rhythm is repeated until the end.

For those who are skilled in winding the warp, both threads can be wound at the same time, making sure that they do not cross between the bobbins and the warping board. Ideally, the bobbins will be installed on a creel or in separate boxes so that each stays in its place. Throughout the warping process, keep a finger between the two threads to prevent them from becoming entangled. You can separate the two strands with a cross. With thicker yarns, I leave the two yarns together in the same cross, knowing that during threading I will keep up the light/dark rhythm unremittingly!

Some people prefer to wind and place the two warps separately. Installing the warp on the loom then requires two sets of cross sticks and tie-on rods. It's a bit of a work-out, but there's no risk of the threads getting tangled up.

Density

It's an obvious fact, but we need to think about it carefully and I assure you that sometimes you can get muddled up doing the calculations—doubleweave means double density! If the plain weave with the yarn chosen requires a density of 20 epi, then 40 epi will need to be prepared in order to allocate 20 epi to each of the two plain weave fabrics.

The reed will be sleyed following these densities. It is highly likely that you will have to thread several ends through the same dent. Because the number of ends per inch is high, there is a lot of friction. Choosing a low-density reed and putting several threads together reduces the risk of wear.

Treadling and Tie-Up

To make it clearer to understand, we are weaving the two plain weaves in pure color. The first one, whose light-colored threads were threaded on the odd shafts, will be woven with the same light thread in weft, and the second one, threaded on the even shafts, will be woven with this same dark thread in weft.

Let's find a weaving rhythm that is easy to understand and remember. The first warp end and the first pick are light. The second warp end and the second pick are dark. The third warp end and third pick are again light, and the fourth warp end and fourth pick dark.

Let's also make the order of the shuttles easier. To start, the two shuttles are set up on the same side, on the left for example. Both plain weaves are woven simultaneously! We weave the first pick of light plain weave, followed by the first pick of the dark plain weave, then the return of the light plain weave followed by the return of the dark plain weave. A treadling sequence consists of 4 wefts, being absolutely certain to keep the same rhythm of color as the warp: light/dark!

In the following explanation, I indicate the basic rhythm, the framework that is applied systematically, specifying for each pick which minimum shaft is raised. When we have determined which layer is woven above or below, then we will have to lift other additional shafts. All this will be explained as we go.

- weft 1 creates the "out" pick for the light plain weave: the light shuttle goes from left to right and "at least" shaft 1 is raised;
- weft 2 creates the "out" pick for the dark plain weave: the dark shuttle goes from left to right and "at least" shaft 2 is raised;
- weft 3 creates the "return" pick for the light plain weave: the light shuttle goes from right to left and "at least" shaft 3 is raised;
- weft 4 creates the "return" pick for the dark plain weave: the dark shuttle goes from right to left and "at least" shaft 4 is raised.

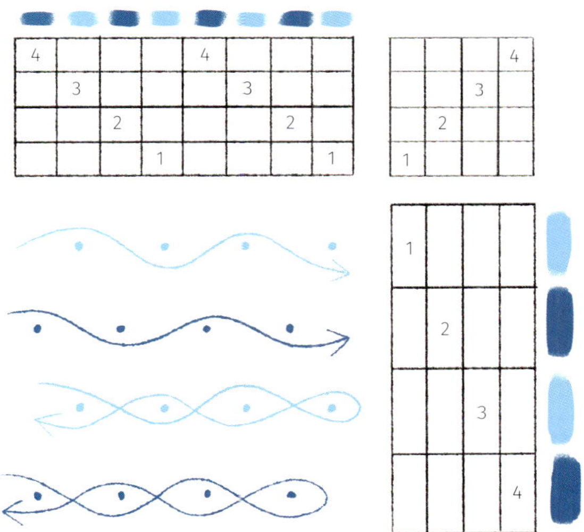

Figure 73 ***Sketch of weft passes***

If we look at the shed, here is what see for each weft pass. I venture to insist that this diagram will be completed whether it's the light or dark plain weave that is woven above.

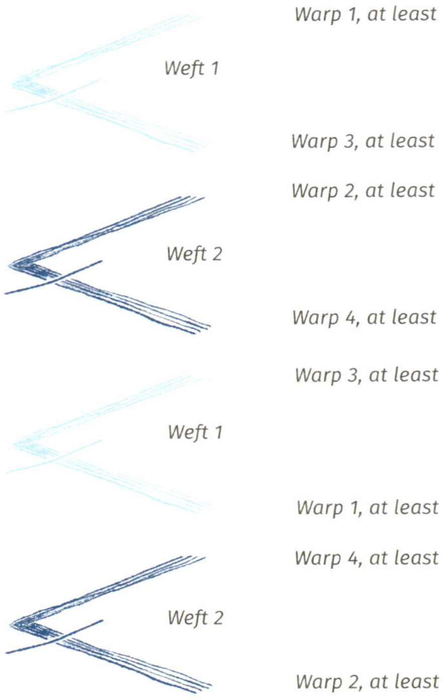

Figure 74 *Basic diagram: the four weft picks in their respective sheds*

Two different weaves are possible. Either the light fabric is visible above, or it is the opposite.

First choice: **light fabric on top**. The weaving method and the order of the weft picks shown above are used, **but the odd shafts are added** each time a dark weft is woven. The light plain weave is raised so that the dark plain weave can be woven independently underneath. I use the framework just shown, to which I add the odd shafts for the picks of dark weft. Here's how it looks:

1. weft **1, "out" pick for light plain weave**: light weft and shaft 1 only;
2. weft **2, "out" pick for dark plain weave**: dark weft and **shaft 2 + the two odd shafts (1-3)** in which the light warp is threaded;
3. weft **3, "return" pick for light plain weave**: light weft and shaft 3 only;
4. weft **4, "return" pick for dark plain weave**: dark weft and **shaft 4 + the two odd shafts (1-3)** with the light warp.

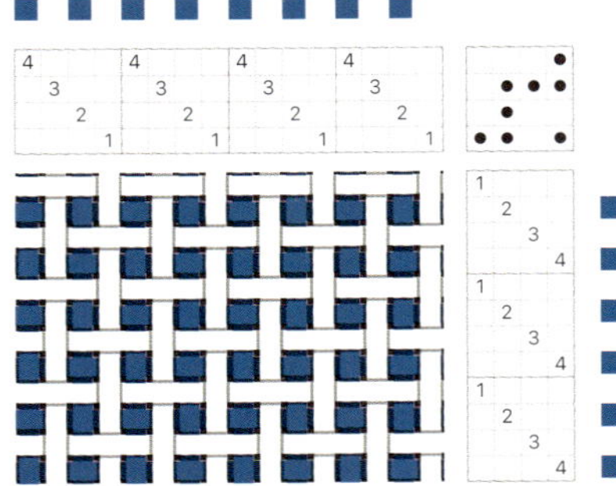

Figure 75 *The light plain weave is visible above.*

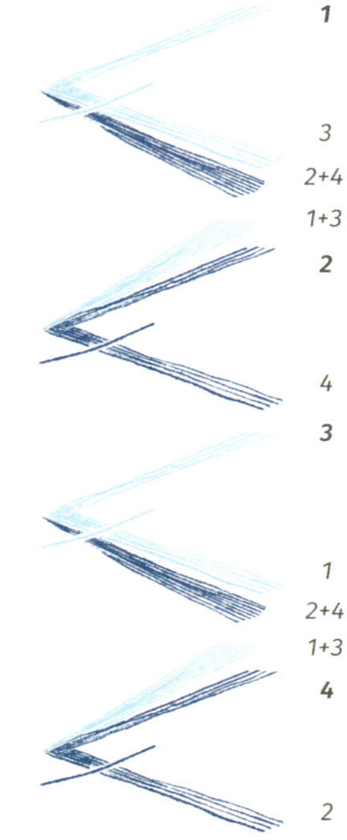

Figure 76 *Diagram of the shed: the light warp is always visible above.*

Second choice: **dark fabric on top**. Same method, same order of shafts, but even shafts are added each time the light plain weave is woven and they are raised alone when the dark plain weave is woven:

1. weft **1, "out" pick for light plain weave**: light weft and **shaft 1 + the two even shafts (2-4)** in which the dark warp is threaded;
2. weft **2, "out" pick for dark plain weave**: dark weft and **shaft 2 only**;
3. weft **3, "return" pick for light plain weave**: light weft and **shaft 3 + the two even shafts (2-4)** with the dark warp;
4. weft **4, "return" pick for dark plain weave**: dark weft and **shaft 4 only**.

Again, watching the shed helps to better understand what is taking place.

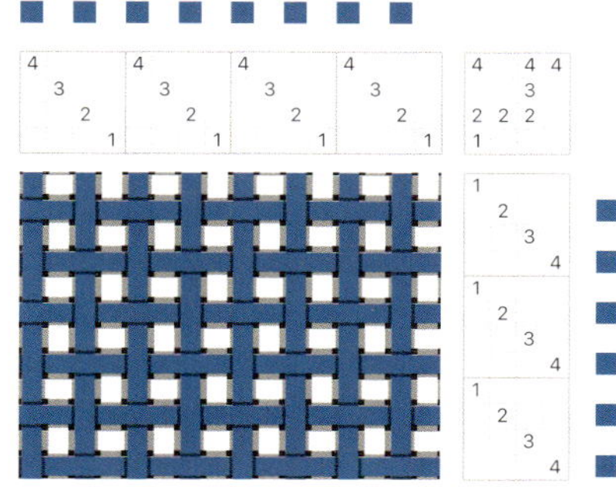

Figure 77 *The dark plain weave is visible above.*

Whichever plain weave you want to see above, you always and systematically have shaft 1 for pick 1, shaft 2 for pick 2, shaft 3 for pick 3, and shaft 4 for pick 4. Depending on whether you want the light or dark plain weave to show above, you add the pair of light or dark shafts. The regularity of this rhythm helps to understand the mechanism and to extrapolate it when you have more shafts.

The place the shuttles are also helps you to find your way around. Are the two shuttles on the left? Then you are ready to weave pick 1. Are the two shuttles on the right? Then you are ready to weave pick 3. If one shuttle is on one side and one on the other, you know by the color whether you should weave pick 2 or 4.

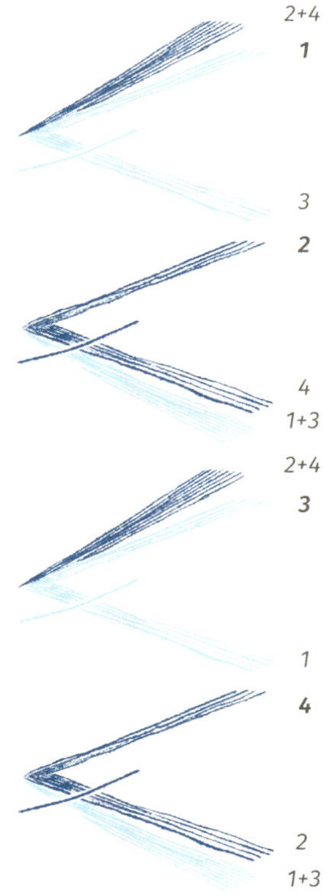

Figure 78 *Diagram of the shed: the dark warp is always visible above.*

PROJECT RECORD SHEET—A SAMPLE IN DOUBLEWEAVE

Warp and weft: Holstgarn Tides wool and silk, 2,828 yd/lb (5,700 m/kg)

Sett for each layer: 12 epi (5 per cm)

Width in reed: 8 in. (20 cm)

Total number of ends: 100 light and 100 dark

Item length: 37.5 in. (95 cm)

Warp length: 63 in. (160 cm)

% of shrinkage when taken off loom: 3%

% of shrinkage after washing: 2%

Fringe: 1.5 in. (4 cm) on each end

Loss due to front tie-on and at back of loom: 24 in. (60 cm)

Quantity of Tides: 44 g 0.8 oz. (22 g) each of cream and lapis

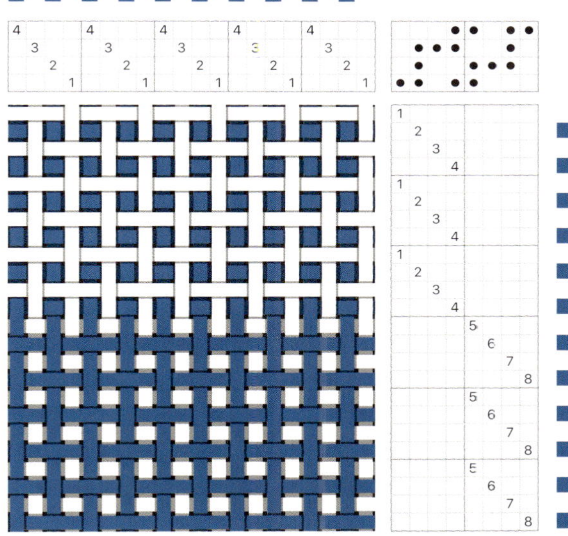

Figure 79 *Sample of doubleweave, 4 shafts. Holstgarn Tides wool and silk, 2,828 yd/lb (5,700 m/kg)*

Double-Width or Tubular Fabric

Double-Width Fabric

Often interest in double weaving comes from a loom not being wide enough. By weaving the two layers of cloth one on top of the other but connecting them only along one selvedge, we double the width of the fabric, which opens up like at book when taken off the loom. One of the edges becomes the middle of the fabric. Thus, even on a small loom, you can weave throws or blankets. The double weaving technique explained above can be followed with a few nuances:

- First of all, it is woven with a single shuttle so that the two layers are connected; there is therefore only one color of weft. Because of this, it is usual to have only one color in warp, except when weaving a plaid pattern, so that when the fabric is unfolded it is identical from one edge to the other.
- Then, we are careful to bind together the side of the fabric where the selvedge looks best. It is indeed common to be more comfortable with one of the two selvedges. The one that is bound and that will be in the middle of the unfolded fabric must be perfect.
- Finally, there must be an odd number of warp ends threaded. If it is connected on the right, the threading is started on shaft 2 and then we stay with the usual rhythm of 1, 2, 3, 4. If it is connected on the left, the last end will be threaded on shaft 3. So you should check very carefully where the two fabrics are joined after having woven a few picks so that there is a real plain weave. At this point, keep a close eye on each selvedge thread of both layers, being sure that one goes over and the other under. If you see a mistake, it is probably necessary to remove the extra warp thread to make it perfect.
- To finish, the treadling order shown so far changes a little so that both layers are not woven simultaneously, but the "out" of the upper layer, the "out-and-back" of the lower layer, and then the "back" of the upper layer. We start weaving on the opposite side of the side bound together.

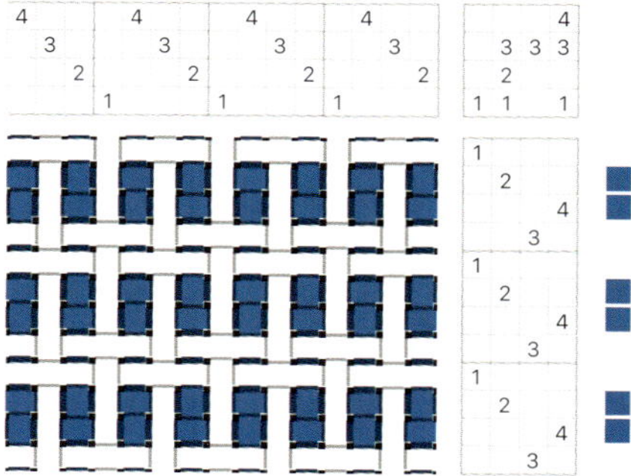

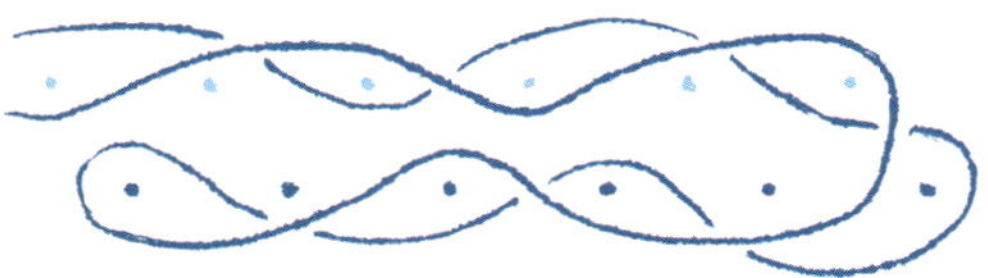

Figure 80 ***Double-width weaving***

The weaving must be very consistent, the density chosen very carefully, and the shuttles unwound without jerking. Otherwise, the fabric is likely to shrink and the center join will be permanently affected. Another way to take care of the "center selvedge" is to put in a fishing line through the reed that is slightly more taut and used as a floating selvedge for support. This line will naturally be removed at the end of the weaving process.

Tubular Fabric

A few years ago, it was common to find pillows or bags, sometimes even tunics, without seams. These items had been woven in tubes. This technique has been around since antiquity and was used to weave garments such as the Holy Shroud of Christ. In fact, it is the same technique as double-width weaving, except that this time the selvedges are closed on each side. A single shuttle is used and the upper fabric is woven followed by the bottom layer, turning in a spiral and alternating the even and odd warps of the two layers.

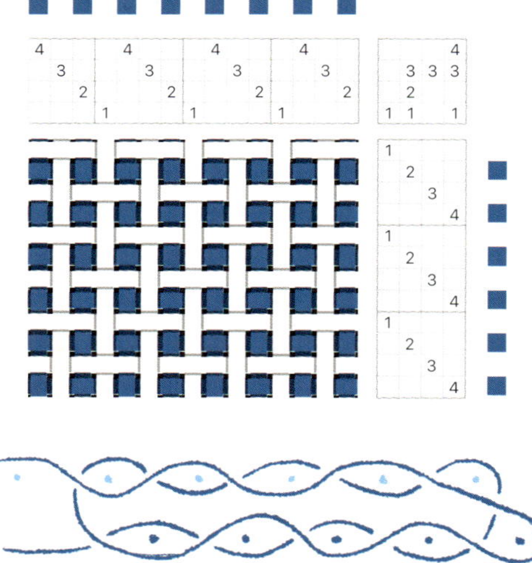

Figure 81 ***Tubular weaving***

Pay close attention to the two selvedges throughout the weaving process so that they are perfect. As for double-width weaving, you can put two floating selvedges in that are taut and slippery. Make sure that the yarns alternate at the selvedge so that you get a real plain weave.

Even if this weave seems a bit old-fashioned, I can imagine wearing an intriguing scarf or wrap ending with this tube that would serve as a sleeve or pocket. A project to try one day!

Structured Doubleweave

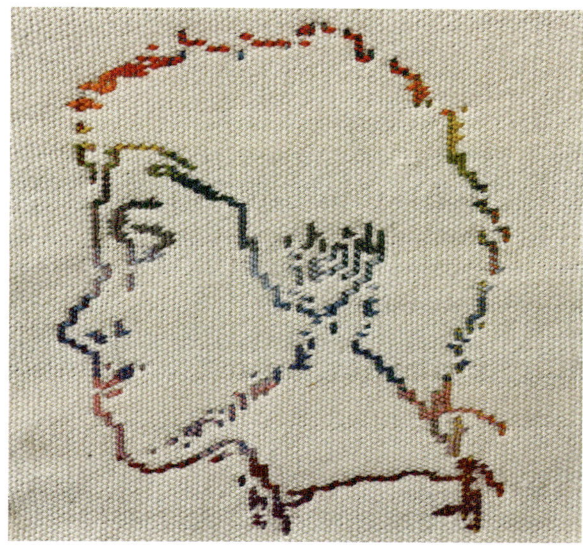

This weaving technique appeared in China over a thousand years ago and then spread in western Europe, but was developed in particular in Scandinavia. With this technique you can weave patterns using pickup sticks for interchanging threads. The idea is to thread two warps of very contrasting colors and, drawing inspiration from a sketch on heavy graph paper, to reproduce this drawing by making the warp ends on the back appear on the front and vice versa. Each of these warps, interchanged or left in its original place, is woven in plain weave with its own color; two shuttles are therefore used. When pairs of threads are interchanged, the right and wrong sides are completely identical but in opposite colors, like the positive/negative of a photo. The design reproduced is more precise when interchanging the threads one by one, but obviously this is more time consuming.

In both cases, with the help of pick-up sticks and manipulations at the front of the loom and between the reed and the heddles, you select warp ends from below that you want to see on the top. Then the **top plain weave is woven** between the threads selected from the bottom warp, weaving the "out" weft with the same color as the top warp. It's as if there were three layers:

- the warp ends from the bottom that we brought up to be seen on the top, which are not woven by this first weft by simply put on hold;
- the other ends from this same warp that we want to remain underneath so that they appear on the reverse side and which are not woven either;
- between these two layers of selected warp, the top plain weave is woven across the entire width with the weft yarn in the same color as the corresponding warp.

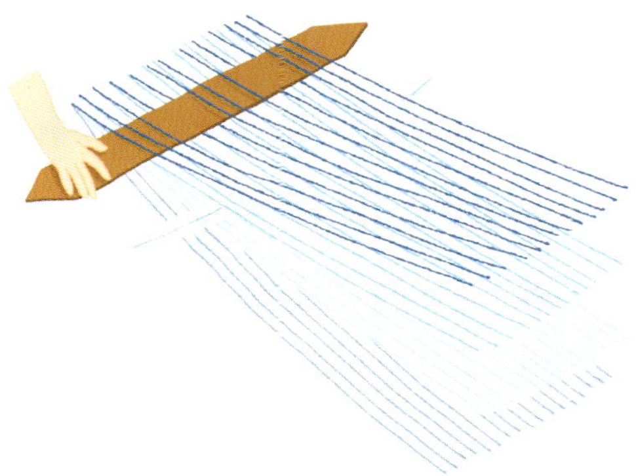

The same procedure is used to weave **the top plain weave**. Any interchanges are made to the top layer, separating what we want to see on the top and what remains below, and between these groups we weave the "out" of the bottom plain weave. Each pick is woven with the opposite color as the sorted ends. We start this sequence again to weave the shuttle's "return" trip for each of these two plain weaves with their respective warp, between the warp ends of the opposite plain weave sorted and put on hold.

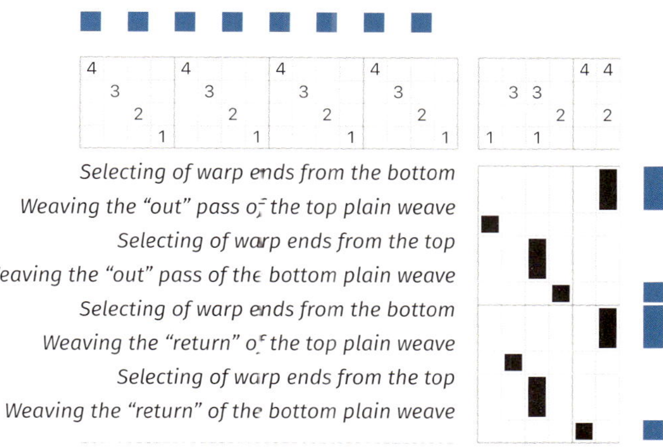

The pattern is made by intermittently making the bottom plain weave appear on the top and vice versa. These exchanges of parts of the warps reduce the opening of the shed. With a little practice, the manipulations are done without too much trouble, but the work does take a long time. Nevertheless, it is interesting to continue to practice this little-known technique to preserve this ancestral know-how. Moreover, it is always a pleasure to make a weaving almost as good as a jacquard weaving. An old Swedish book, *Fins Weven* by Ingrid Arlenborg and Ulla Feltzing published by Zomer & Keuning in 1973, shows step by step how to design, interchange, and weave thread by thread in the ancestral Finnish way.

With 8 or More Shafts, the Second Movement

Wherever I turn my head I behold
the vast octave of Creation!

Paul Claudel, *Cinq grandes odes*, 1910

Let's go back to the basics: a plain weave is made with 2 shafts. With 8 shafts, you can weave four plain weaves on top of each other that cross whenever you want. You can also make a double-width throw in twill; in this case you have to pay attention to where these two layers are joined.

What attracts me most with 8 shafts or a multiple of 4 is especially that I can arrange my warp in blocks and work on the weaving by splitting it into several areas. This means that we can imagine reversing the layers, not only with the weft, as is possible with doubleweave on 4 shafts, but also the warp, and thus weave checkerboards or columns and not just rows.

Profile Draft and Threading Blocks

The technique studied earlier on 4 shafts will now be extended to 8 shafts in the form of 2 blocks. Block A is threaded on shafts 1, 2, 3, and 4 and Block B on shafts 5, 6, 7, and 8. With 12 shafts, we have block C on shafts 9, 10, 11, and 12, and so on. To simplify and to help us acquire reflexes, we will keep the same points of reference, meaning the light threads are on the odd shafts and the dark threads are on the even shafts. The blocks are distributed and repeated with no risk and no rules; they can be small or large, repeated often or simply on the edges! While easier to understand on 8 shafts, the logic with 12 or 16 shafts is exactly the same.

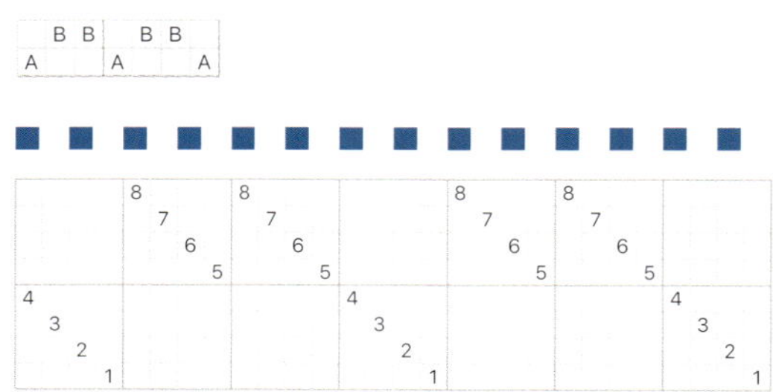

Figure 82 ***Profile draft on two blocks and related threading on 8 shafts***

Tie-Up

Remember that with 4 shafts, you can choose to have either the light or the dark plain weave appear on top. We had these two possible tie-ups.

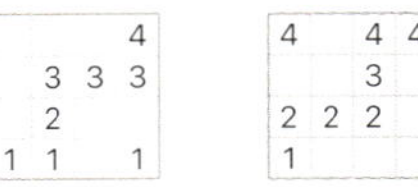

Figure 83 ***Tie-up on 4 shafts: light plain weave or dark plain weave visible on top***

To transpose these notations to Block B and to the other blocks, you could simply replace the number 1 with 5 or 9, number 2 with 6 or 10, number 3 with 7 or 11, and number 4 with 8 or 12. I suggest you use a type of code by substituting colored squares for the numbers in the tie-up draft. This way, we keep the characteristic shape of the two configurations without the risk of confusing the numbers. This more general and abstract notation can be adapted to any type of project regardless of the number of shafts that are multiples of 4.

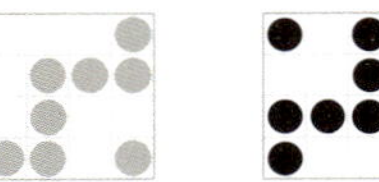

Figure 84 ***Simplified notation of the tie-up: light plain weave L or dark plain weave D visible on top***

As you become more comfortable with this notation, I would encourage you to replace this diagram with the letter L when you want the light plain weave on top and D for the dark plain weave on top. Keep this basic rhythm in mind:

1. **weft 1** is used for the **"out" pick for the light plain weave**: the light shuttle goes from left to right and at least **shafts 1 and 5** are raised;
2. **weft 2** is used for the **"out" pick for the dark plain weave**: the dark shuttle goes from left to right and at least **shafts 2 and 6** are raised;
3. **weft 3** is used for the **"return" pick for the light plain weave**: the light shuttle goes from right to left and at least **shafts 3 and 7** are raised;
4. **weft 4** is used for the **"return" pick for the dark plain weave**: the dark shuttle goes from right to left and at least **shafts 4 and 8** are raised.

To this basic sequence, you will add the odd or even shafts, in the blocks you choose, depending on whether you want to show the light or dark plain weave on top.

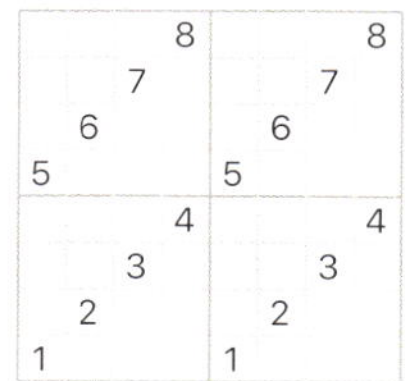

Figure 85 ***Basic minimum structure for the tie-up***

Playing with Checkerboards: Treadling and Tie-Up

To acquire certain reflexes, here are a few simple exercises when starting out. If you have a table loom, it may take a little time before your movements become fluid. But definitely, once you get the hang of it and no longer need to look at your paper, you will be proud of yourself! If you have a floor loom, I recommend tying up the left treadles for each light pick and the right ones for each dark pick. This way, your feet will easily find a rhythm.

First sequence: Blocks A and B are identical. If you want to see the light cloth on top across the entire width, draw the tie-up square intended for the light plain weave for each of the two blocks, in simplified writing or with numbers. Do the same for the dark plain weave. We can make it easier by using the code L for light and D for dark in the tie-up grid of the profile draft.

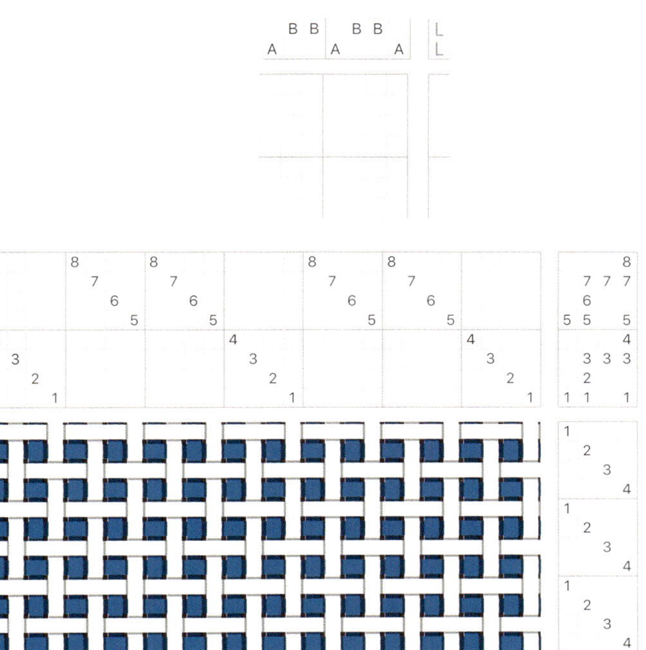

Figure 86 ***The light plain weave is on top in the two blocks***

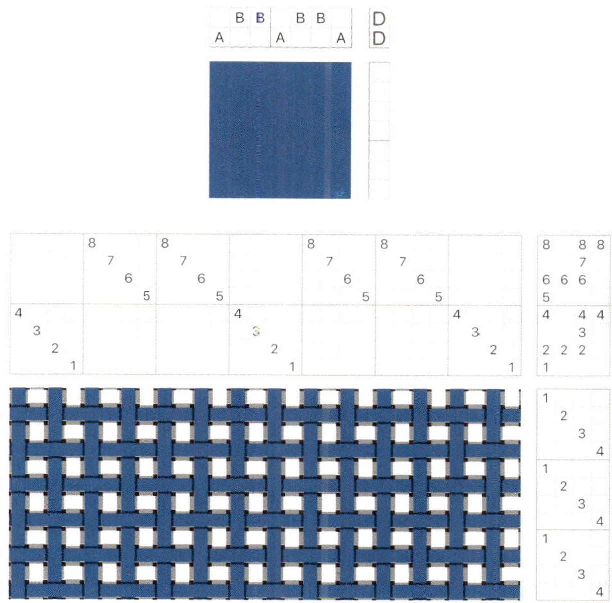

Figure 87 ***The dark plain weave is on top in the two blocks***

Second sequence: The two blocks are woven differently and the colors appear in a column along the length of the weave. In this case, the shafts do the work of mechanically sorting and separating the two layers. With this draft, we can see how the wefts can be woven with the correct warp. The profile draft clearly indicates the dark or light areas.

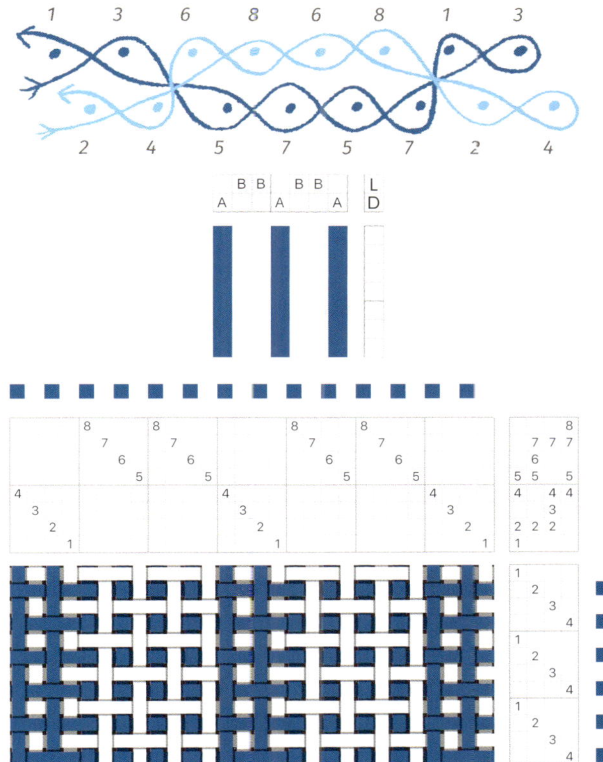

Figure 88 ***The plain weave is dark in Block A and light in Block B***

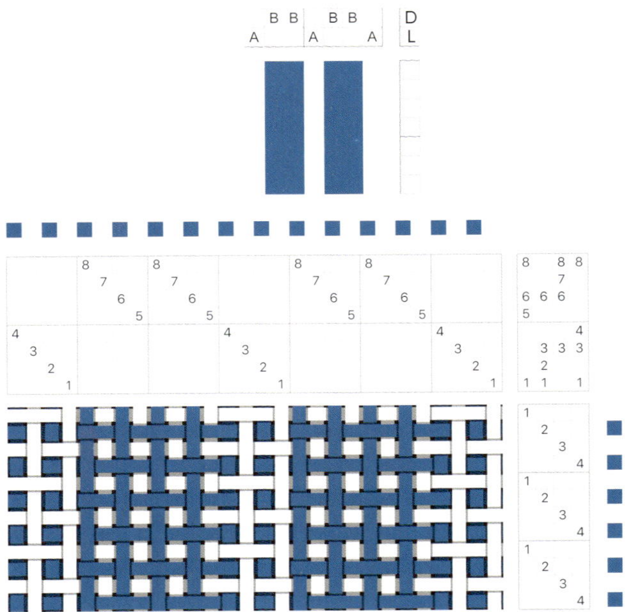

Figure 89 ***The plain weave is light in Block A and dark in Block B***

Third sequence: improvisation. By following a drawn profile draft and applying our code of L or D with the simplified tie-up grid, we quickly find the reflexes to reproduce the sketch. Here are a few examples that are often used with 8 treadles.

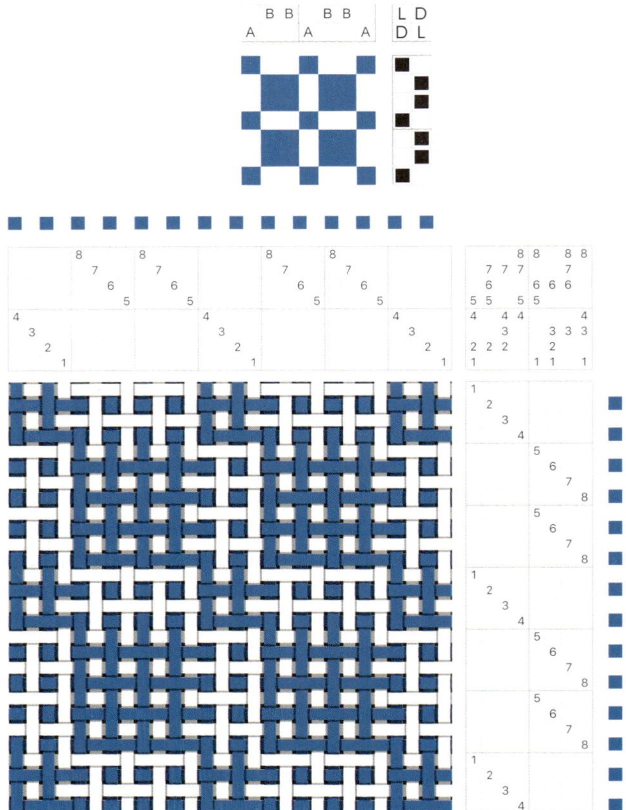

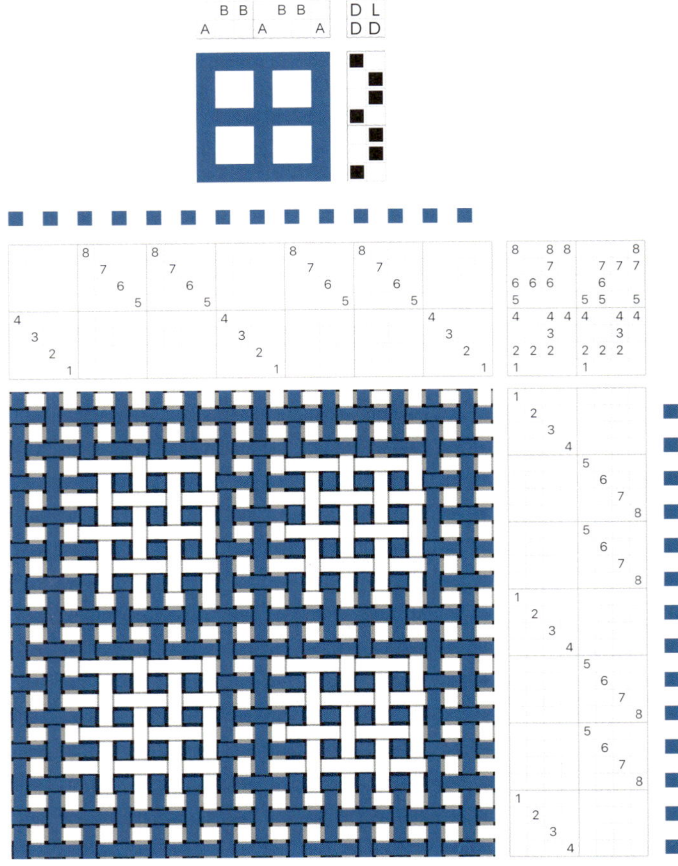

Certainly these manipulations and tie-ups will require a little practice before the movement flows naturally, but as soon as the logic is understood, it quickly becomes very simple to transform these drawings and to invent your own, just as it will be fairly spontaneous to transform these attempts using more shafts if you are the lucky owner of a loom with 12, 16, or 24 shafts! Work on remembering the simplified writing with the codes L and D because once you have a lot of shafts, it's fantastic.

Doubleweave Allegretto

As its name indicates, doubleweave fabric can be separated. Once the technique is well understood, it quickly becomes tempting to push this distinctive characteristic.

As the two layers are completely separate from each other, you can slip some batting in to add volume. In the previous example, before closing the small pockets formed with the B Blocks, we can stuff in some fiberfill and transform this weaving into a pillow or very soft rug.

We can also imagine the bottom layer to be quite simple and plain, and work with color effects such as log cabin and shadow-weave on the other layer. Depending on what choices are made for the tie-up, this structure will appear like a checkerboard on the top, a very pretty effect!

You can also choose to weave one of the layers with wool and the other with a much finer thread, so that this thread appears to be delicately placed on the firmer fabric. In this case, we can no longer follow the alternating binary rhythm of light yarn/dark yarn, and the density will be calculated for each yarn. This example shows the rhythm 1 light thread/2 dark threads.

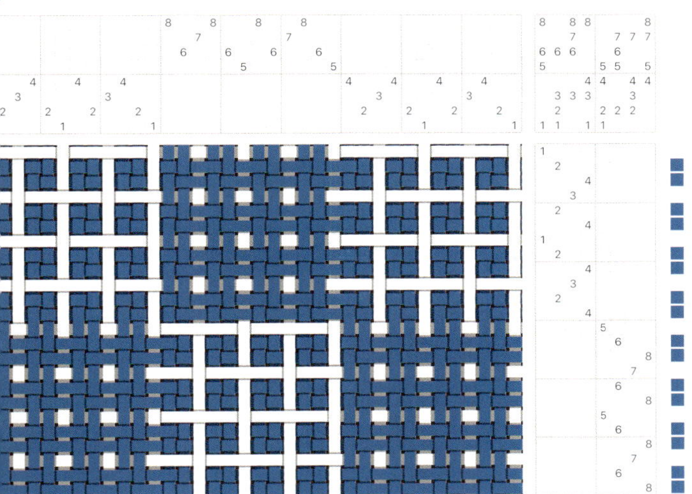

Figure 90 ***Doubleweave with two very different yarns: adjusting threading and sleying***

One of the layers can also be woven in twill and the other in plain weave. Again, the density will be different for each fabric.

Some designers, like Kay Sekimachi, have had so much fun by separating the layers and then connecting them back together that they have created three-dimensional sculptural pieces. Others let small parts of the plain weave show here and there and construct an origami-like fabric.

Eva Stossel and Marian Stubenitsky have explored an overabundance of double weaving by working with multiple shafts, breaking the rigidity of four-shaft blocks, and threading with four or eight colors. Their work is wonderful. The breaks between each layer are so minute, the merger of colors so fine, that their weavings are similar to moiré or ikat.

About-face: A double-sided overshot

For just a moment, let's leave the world of 8-shaft blocks and come back to 4. Threading the light yarn in overshot on 4 shafts and then threading the dark yarn between each light end, following the same threading but offset, produces a really stunning result. The simplest way, as is often the case, is to work on a profile draft following a classic 4-block overshot pattern.

The pattern will no longer appear with the floats like in overshot, but in plain weave, light on the back and dark on the front. The density is that of a balanced plain weave for each of the two layers. Any overshot draft will work and you follow it by threading the light ends while inserting a dark thread between each of them on its opposite even or odd shaft. When a light one is threaded on shaft 1, the dark one immediately goes on shaft 3; when the light one is on 2, the dark is on 4, etc.

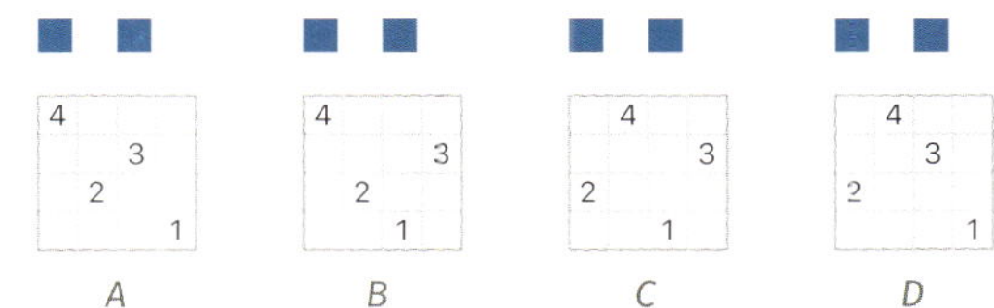

Figure 91 ***The four overshot threading blocks in echo***

The treadling is also broken down into four blocks, just like the tie-up. At first glance, the latter seems a bit complex, but on analyzing it, we notice that in each block, a single shaft is raised to weave the first color, then three shafts are raised to weave the second color, this same shaft and the two that "surround" it. For example, when you raise shaft 2 with the first color, you then raise shafts 1-2-3 for the second color. Each of these treadling blocks is repeated to follow the initial overshot pattern.

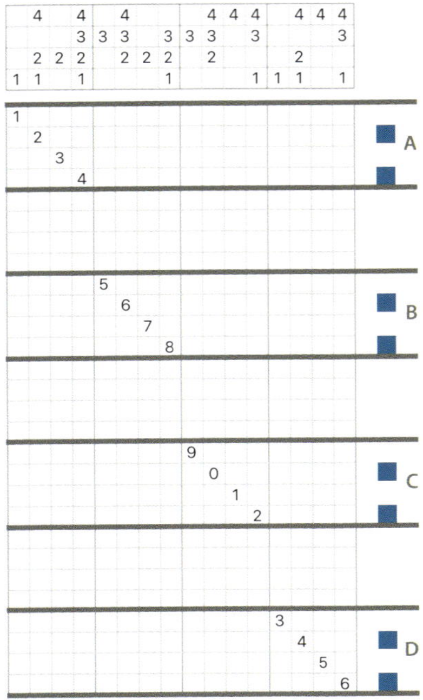

Figure 92 ***Treadling and tie-up of an overshot pattern***

You can try this doubleweave technique with any overshot pattern by converting its threading, tie-up, and treadling draft into a profile draft. The same pattern is formed in one color or the front side and in the other color on the reverse side. In this draft, only the blocks of the overshot profile draft are expanded.

The "vast octave of creation," wrote Paul Claudel. Doubleweave is without a doubt a powerful structure. It offers a great freedom and stimulates our creativity in many directions. Of course, it requires a lot of thought and conceptualization. If your mind is stimulated by this kind of exercise, no doubt one idea will lead to another, and nothing will seem impossible . . . except when you are lacking a certain number of shafts.

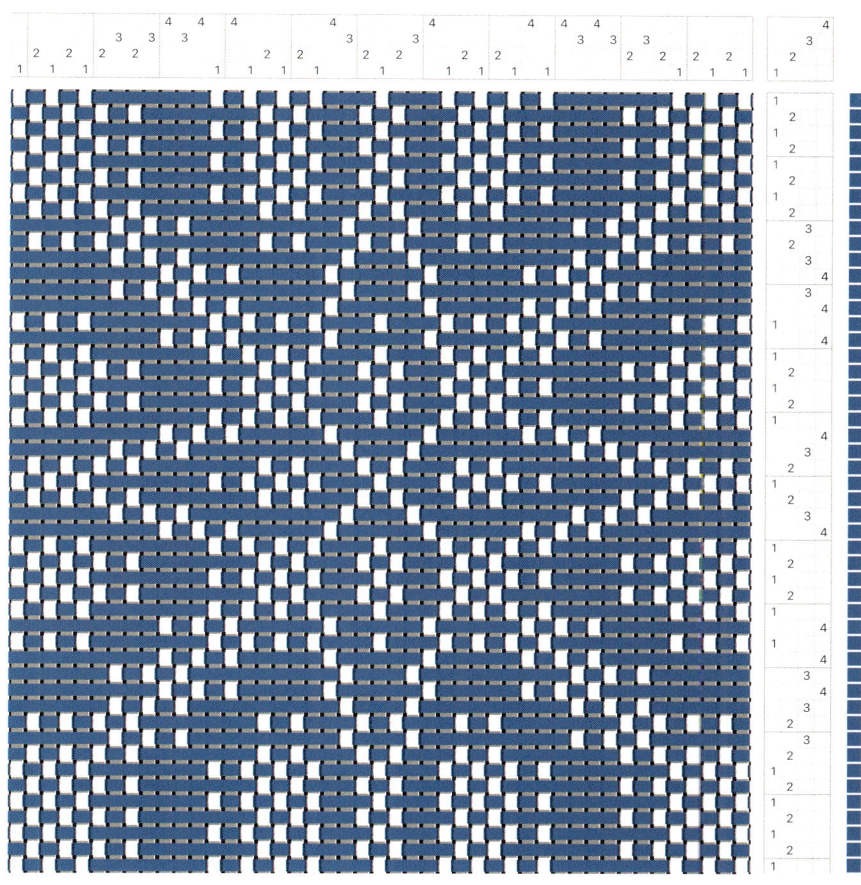

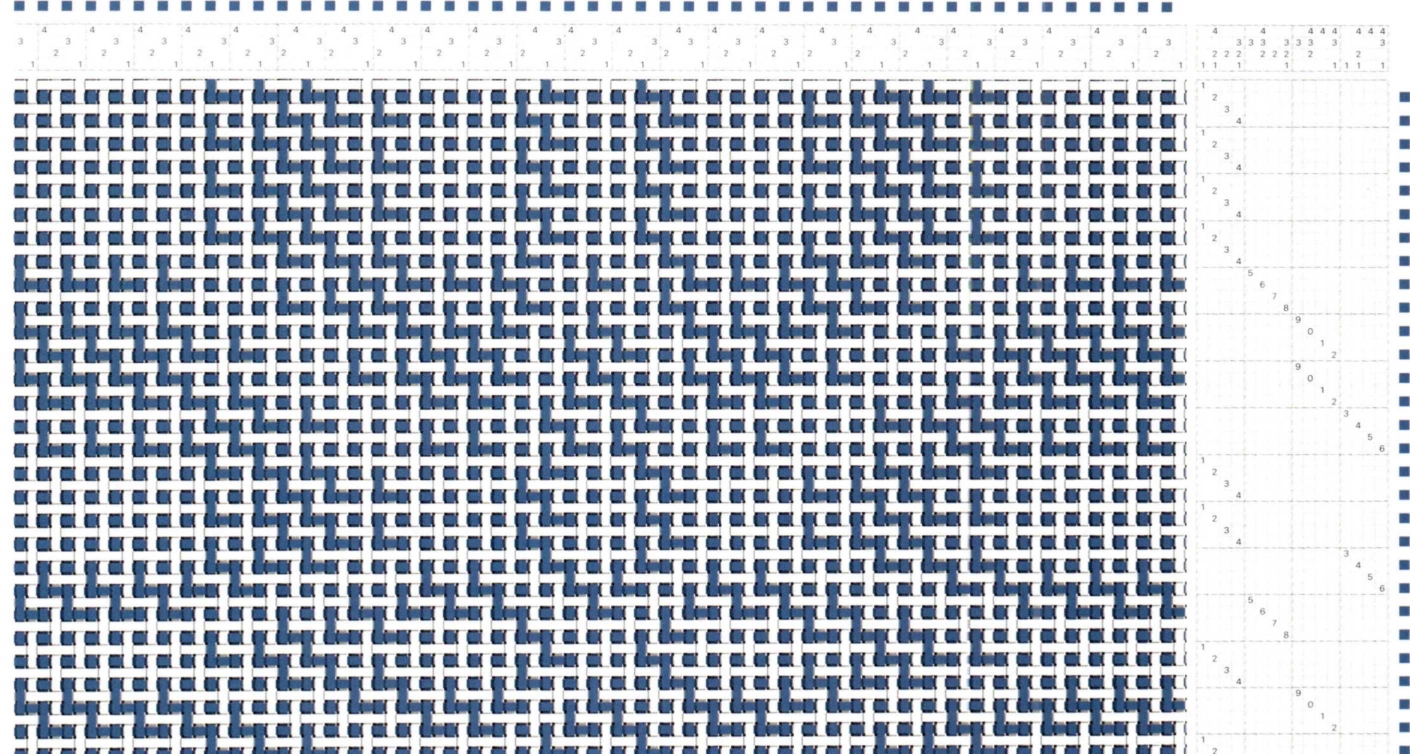

Figure 93 ***The usual overshot draft and its expansion in double weave***

Theo Moorman: One More for the Road

The technique to which my name has been given is so simple that I hesitate to claim it as a discovery. It has, however, dominated my work for the last twenty years . . . But I know only too well how easy it is to discover for oneself something in common use.

Theo Moorman, *Weaving as an Art Form*, 1975

Theo Moorman was an English weaver born in 1907. Regretting that she had not received any art education in her youth and feeling frustrated at not knowing how to draw, she felt very comfortable in weaving classes, where the teaching was practical. However, she soon felt limited. At the time, weaving was for making clothing and soft furnishings. During this difficult period in England around World War II, she had a variety of odd jobs, some of which allowed her to meet artists. Asking them for help to overcome her timidity toward designing, and recreating their drawings, she developed a technique that is now named after her.

This method allowed her to create monumental pieces of textile art from freehand drawing, in a way that is relatively simple and quick. It comes a bit close to tapestry in the sense that one recreates a drawing using yarn inlays. Unlike tapestry, a plain weave woven from selvedge to selvedge acts as support for the motifs and facilitates the work. The fabric is constructed with two different warps that separate at the place where the motif is placed on the ground cloth and held there by the other warp.

A Bit of Technique

To create this structure, there are two warps, one on top of the other. There is the **base warp** used in the plain weave ground cloth and the **tie-down warp**. The latter uses a yarn two times thinner than the one used in the ground cloth. The sole purpose of this almost invisible warp is to secure the inlay yarns that will be placed on the ground cloth. It must be strong enough to withstand the unequal tensions, fine enough to be invisible, and elastic enough to equally hold the different inlay threads. A 20/2 cotton is perfect.

You will change and develop all this as you go along, imagining it with other weaving structures or other yarn. Let's begin with a plain weave on four shafts. The base warp yarn is threaded on the first two shafts. After each 1-2 pair, the fine yarn is threaded on shafts 3 or 4 alternately.

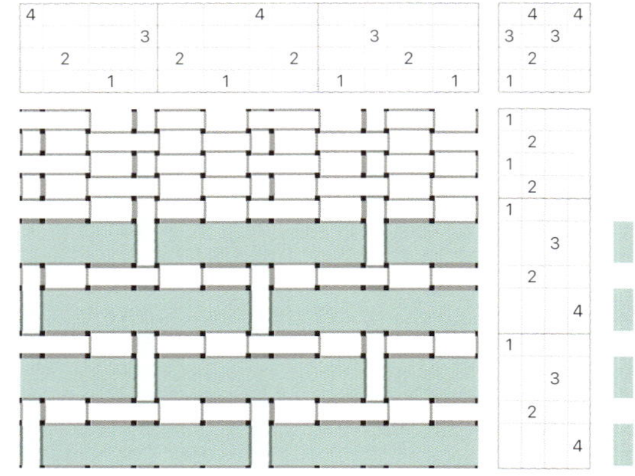

Figure 94 ***Basic draft of Moorman weaving***

When weaving the ground cloth, the same yarn is used for the weft as for the base warp, and its density is calculated for this yarn. The treadling is 1-3/2-4. The ends threaded on shafts 1 and 2 form the plain weave; the fine yarn threaded on shafts 3 and 4 are pulled into this plain weave and simply duplicate the thicker yarn of the base warp. But they are so thin that they are not visible, nor do they influence the density.

It is helpful to use something to hold the **inlay thread**. It can be wound on tapestry bobbins or small boat shuttles, fishing net needles, or little bobbins used in stranded knitting. The yarn is woven between the ground cloth and the tie-on warp, not from selvedge to selvedge but only on the pattern area. If you are not yet an expert, choose yarns that are low-twist, soft, thicker than those of the ground cloth, though the type of yarn doesn't matter. Later on, it will be fun to use bouclé yarn or, on the contrary, a very thin yarn that will create a slight interplay of shadows. This inlay yarn is only woven with shafts 3 and 4.

Figure 95 *Moorman technique, 4 shafts. Inlay in Bart & Francis silk 150 den, and plainweave in Linières St Martin 24/2 linen*

The square design is the ideal shape to start with. Straight edges are easier to achieve than curves. It is also advisable to spread out the inlay areas as much as possible. If all the designs are in the same area, it is likely that the unused tie-down warp will slacken on the fabric while the rest will become tighter, still busy holding the inlay. For this reason, and for large weaves, it is reasonable to use two warp beams at the back.

Density is only calculated with the ground cloth yarn, without taking the fine tie-down warp into consideration. You wrap your yarn around a ruler and divide this number by two, as per Ashenhurst's formula. Then you check the density by making a sample, first with the plain weave only, then with an inlay. If the density of the weft is the same as that of the warp. Through this sample you can check that the yarn used for the inlay is not too thick and does not disrupt the balance of the plain weave.

Choose a reed that will allow you to put the two threads of the ground warp and the tie-down warp in the same dent. When that's not possible, sley the ground warp threads with the appropriate density for a balanced plain weave, bringing together the fine yarn with the adjacent ground warp yarn in the order in which it appears. The fine yarn will never be by itself in a reed dent.

Inlays

There are several ways to place inlaid designs. They can be scattered over the weaving, which is probably the easiest method and the one to start with. Later, it is tempting to layer a few designs on top of each other. If you chose a single weft color, the place where the two designs overlap will be darker. If the wefts are different colors, you will see a new color appear where there is an overlap. You can also cover the entire width of the weaving and place the inlay areas next to each other, like a tapestry. The area where the motifs join up requires some attention to ensure that all warp threads are properly covered. This can be done using tapestry methods.

When you use several shuttles, you have to work methodically. I usually start my weaving with all shuttles on the left. I weave the plain weave ground cloth pick (shafts 1+3),

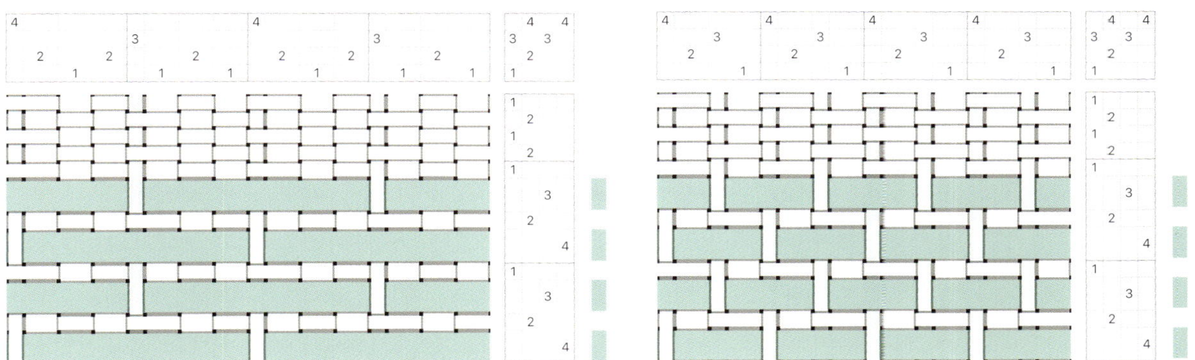

Figure 96 *Variations for threading the tie-down warp to vary the length of the float*

then often all the inlay shuttles follow with only shaft 3 still raised. They will also go from the left to the right, starting with the one that is the furthest to the right. For the return, all the shuttles, the one for the ground cloth (shafts 2+4), then those for the inlays, with shaft 4 remaining raised, go from right to left, but as for the previous pick, I first weave my little shuttles that are the farthest to the left. This way, we protect ourselves from creating somewhat of a mish-mash and ensure nice joins between each motif.

Each time the weaving of these inlays starts and stops, we do as we normally would when starting a weft: we split this yarn for a short length, then go back and forth over an inch or two of width with this split yarn (see p. 115).

Taking It Just a Bit Further

While we started looking at this technique with a plain weave threaded in shafts 1 and 2 and the tie-down warp in shafts 3 and 4, once you have the possibility of using more shafts, it is tempting to replace the plain weave ground cloth with a **twill** and to keep the inlays in plain weave. Depending on what the use of the fabric will be, this suggestion will elevate any plain fabric, being sure to use inlay threads that will react identically if this fabric is to be washed.

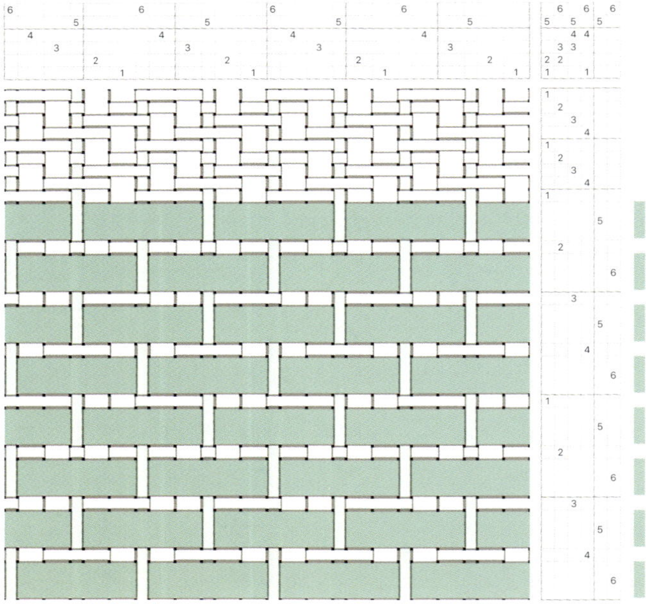

Figure 97 ***Inlays in plain weave on twill base***

Jacques Plasse and Bilou Le Caisne transformed many cartoons, particularly those by painter Alfred Manessier, into tapestries. They used an 8-shaft loom. The plain weave ground cloth was entirely covered with adjacent inlays that were woven in twill. They alternated one pick of plain weave and one of brocade. I can't imagine the number of shuttles needed for the inlays, since their weaving-tapestry could be almost 8 feet (2.4 m) wide!

Figure 98 ***The Plasse Le Caisne workshop and a tapestry cartoon by Manessier***

In the basic example shown at the beginning of this section, the inlay thread floats over two warp ends. Depending on the thread count of the plain weave ground cloth and on the density, the **length of the float** varies. If you want to have more apparent floats or if the inlay yarn is very thick and bulky, it may be desirable to lengthen this float and decrease the number of interlacing points to allow the yarn to open up naturally. In this case, the alternation will no longer be 2 ground warp ends/1 tie-down warp, but 3 ground warp ends/1 tie-down warp, or more if necessary. Conversely, if the inlay thread is very thin and you want to reproduce a pattern with great precision, you can then systematically alternate 1 ground thread with 1 tie-down thread.

Another small adjustment can be made if the **inlay weft is so thick** that it cannot be beaten properly and the ground cloth is distorted, or if the plain weave cannot be beaten as it should be. We can then throw several picks of plain weave before inserting the pattern thread. This technique was very helpful when I wove a photo that I had cut into ⅜-inch (1-cm) strips. I had to be careful to leave shaft 3 or shaft 4 raised during all background weft picks up until I inserted the photo strips.

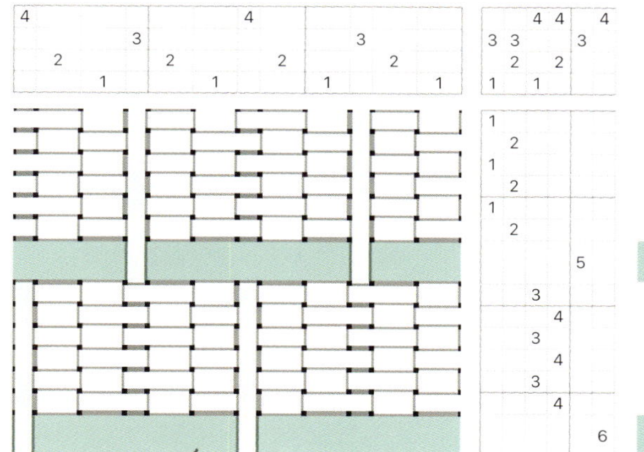

Figure 99 ***Inserting very thick wefts***

One last tip in case the tie-down thread can be seen in the plain weave ground cloth. Insert the same yarn used for the tie-down warp as **supplementary ground weft**. The order of insertion will be the same as the threading order. If the ratio between ground warp ends and tie-down warp is 2 to 1, then this same sequence will be used for the weft.

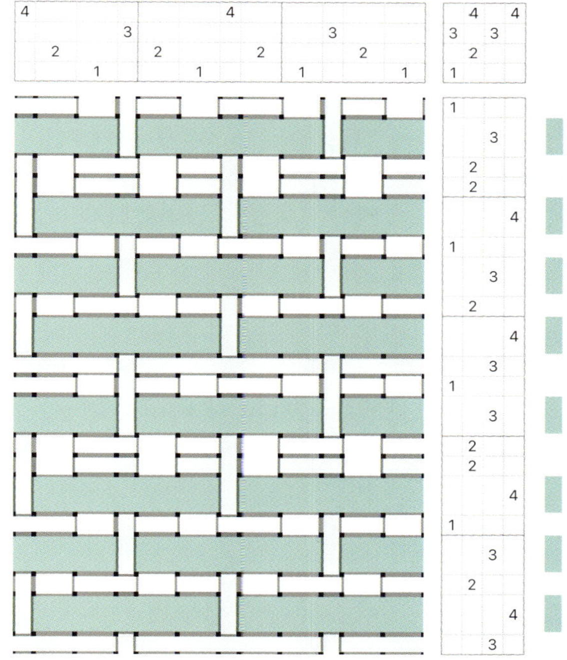

Figure 100 ***Inserting a second ground weft***

PART THREE

TAKING A GIANT LEAP

One may leap to heaven from the very slums.

Seneca

Nothing makes me happier that the smile of a course participant inventing their own personal weaving! This is surely the reason the large blackboard has an honored place in my classroom. Structures, when understood, can then be arranged and given a twist.

This part of the book makes me think of the leaps of principal dancers in prestigious ballets—all of the training, the rehearsals, the long hours spent at the barre, to then be able to leap into the air with a great feeling of freedom.

In the beginning, of course, we reproduce patterns shown in magazines or found on the Internet. Then, we are simply inspired by these examples and change up the yarn, the color order, or the density. The day comes when we really want to create, a day when, like the dancer in Swan Lake, we dare to take the leap. The day of the first ballet on stage.

In the following pages, I will present some elements that can help you to detach yourself little by little from patterns. Sometimes, you may feel that you have not done something satisfying, that you didn't choose the right yarn or the right structure. But still, a nice pride settles in, knowing that you made it and invented it. A unique piece!

Some tools, some methods are good partners in what now looks like a solo!

8

Looking at the Bigger Picture, Sketching Your Design

The profile draft is a fundamental tool. You may have already looked at a weaving draft and not recognized or understood anything. That's because it was probably not a weaving draft, but a profile draft. Using this tool, we can work on a sketch for a future weaving project, taking a step back and working on it not thread by thread, but block by block. It is not yet a question of structure, or of threading, but simply a first sketch of your pattern.

So, we are now going to talk about blocks and the profile draft, and enter the world of a diagram made up of little squares.

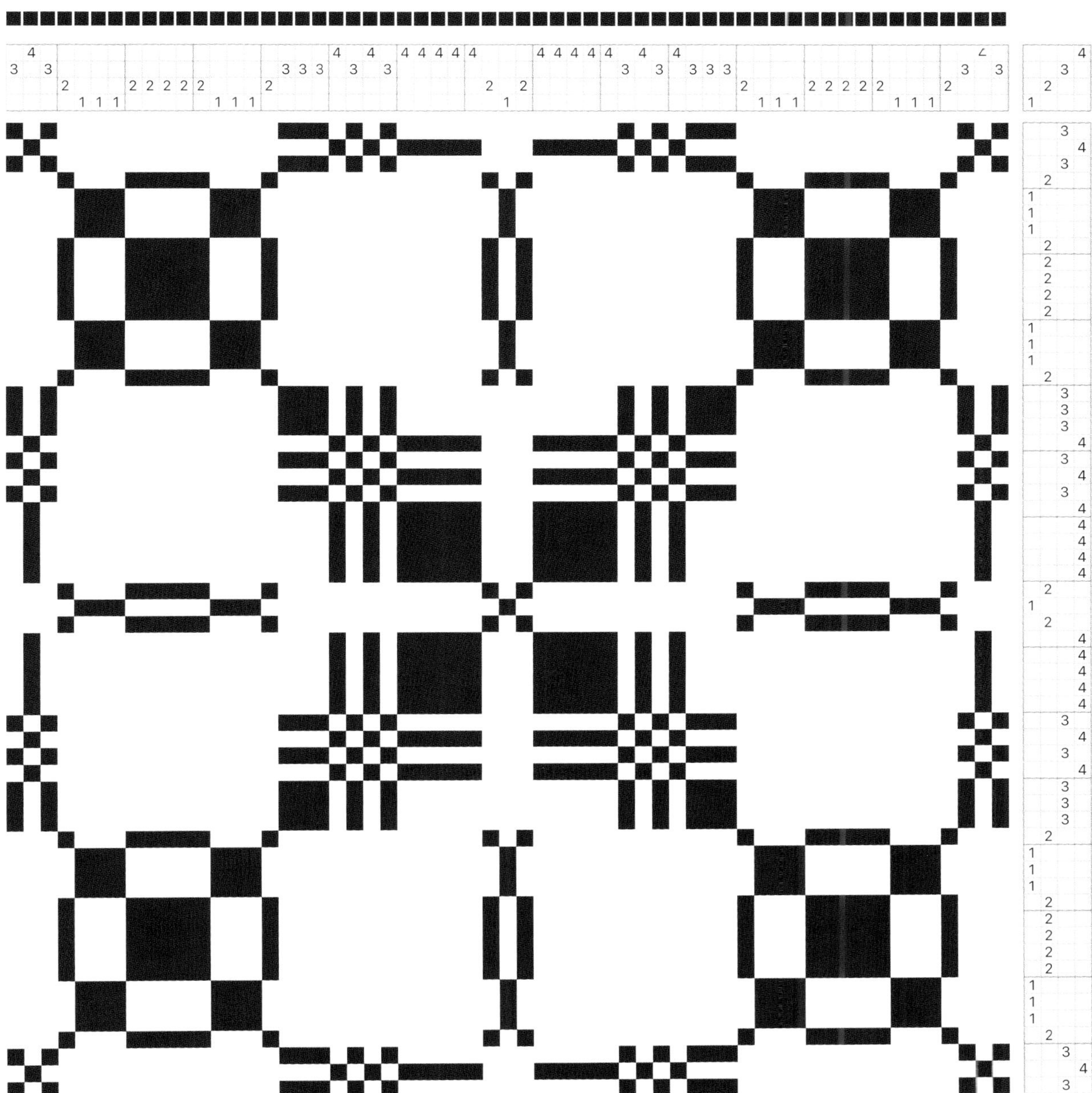

Figure 1 **Example of a profile draft**

Drawing a Profile Draft

Although there are a multitude of profile draft templates online or in specialized books, which are useful to use as a starting point, it's a lot of fun to take out your graph paper, pencil, and eraser and create one from scratch. There is no need for color at first.

A Few Definitions

A **block** is the basic unit of the preliminary draft. It is drawn in the shape of a small square. It is the schematic representation of a group of threads that always work in the same way, in warp, in weft, and in tie-up. Each different block means that the threads that make it up form a new pattern. They are usually called A, B, C, or D.

The **profile draft** is the diagram in which we place the blocks. It looks like the classic weaving draft, but there, where each spot usually represents a thread, in a profile draft, **each square represents a group of threads**. Looking at the profile draft of a weave is like stepping back and seeing the design as a whole.

Using a profile draft allows you to organize your weaving project. This is particularly useful with some structures called unit weaves. It's a very comfortable and efficient way to choose a color pattern or to organize color effect weaves such as a rep or a log cabin. This is how I presented the design of the tea towels in Chapter 4, "Staging Without Stage Fright," on p. 70.

Using a profile draft to create requires a good knowledge of weaving structures and deserves a bit of effort to conceptualize. I suggest that you create a profile draft, illustrate it with some structures, then transform it into several weaving drafts.

First Duet: Profile Draft and Blocks

The profile draft uses the same configuration as the usual weaving drafts. The rows on top are for the threading, the columns to the right are for treadling, the square at the top right is for the tie-up, and the large area at the bottom lower left shows the pattern design. An alphabetical notation is generally used. Each letter or square represents a block, a group of threads, and never a single thread or a single pick! This similarity between a weaving draft and the profile draft is sometimes confusing. Don't let yourself get thrown by it.

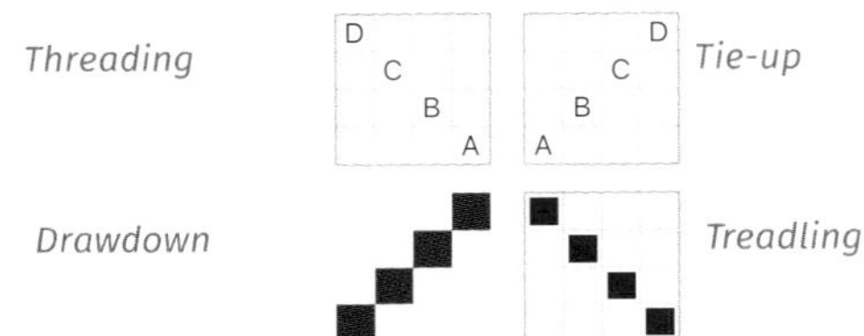

Figure 2 ***Presentation of a profile draft***

The number of rows of threading depends on the structure and the number of shafts. Here are two profile drafts for 4-shaft looms that we will use as examples for the following explanations.

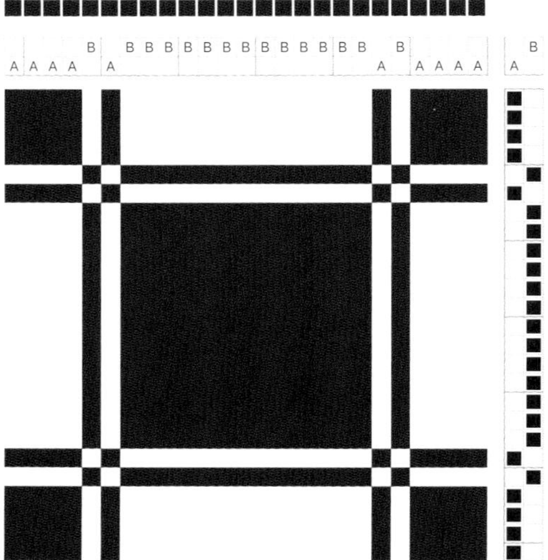

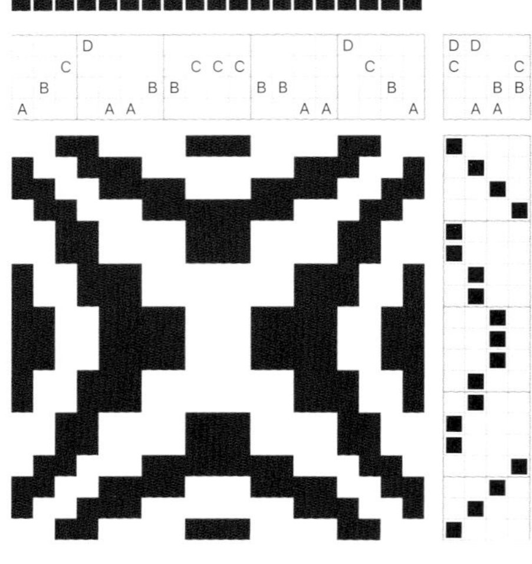

Figure 3 ***Profile draft with 2 and 4 blocks***

Some of us describe a structure by the threading order, its identity card in a way. This is what we are going to clarify by now studying some structures so that we can replace the letters or squares of the profile draft with a threading or treadling draft. To do this, let's dissect some basic unit structures. The following examples are mainly for looms with four shafts.

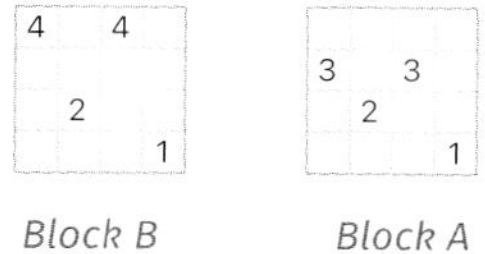

Block B *Block A*

Figure 4 ***The two threading blocks for Summer and Winter***

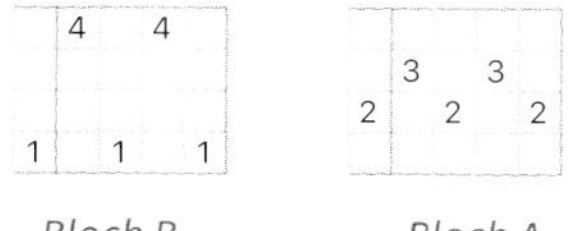

Block B *Block A*

Figure 5 ***The two threading blocks for huck lace***

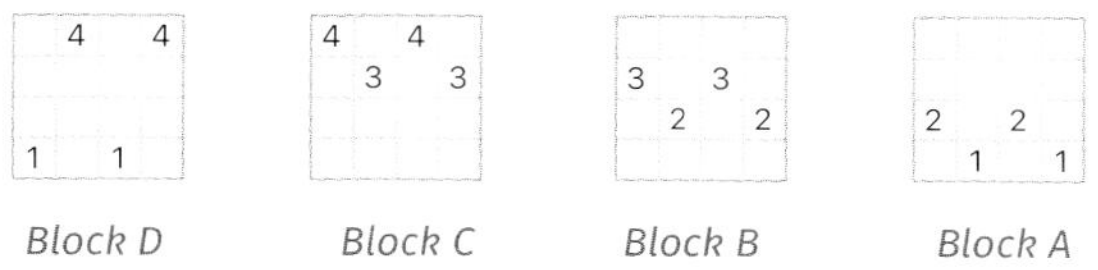

Block D *Block C* *Block B* *Block A*

Figure 6 ***The four threading blocks for overshot***

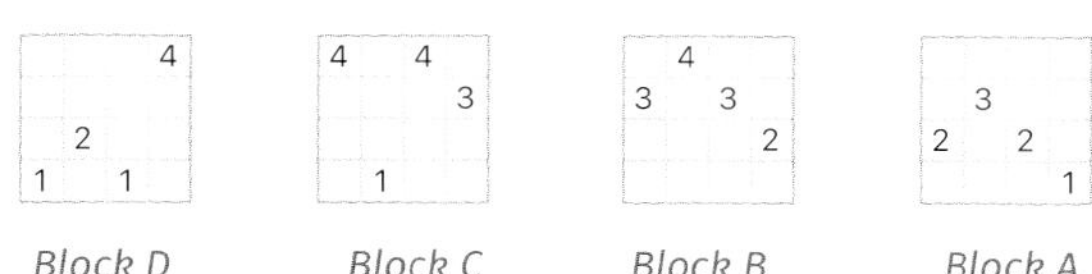

Block D *Block C* *Block B* *Block A*

Figure 7 ***The four threading blocks for crackle***

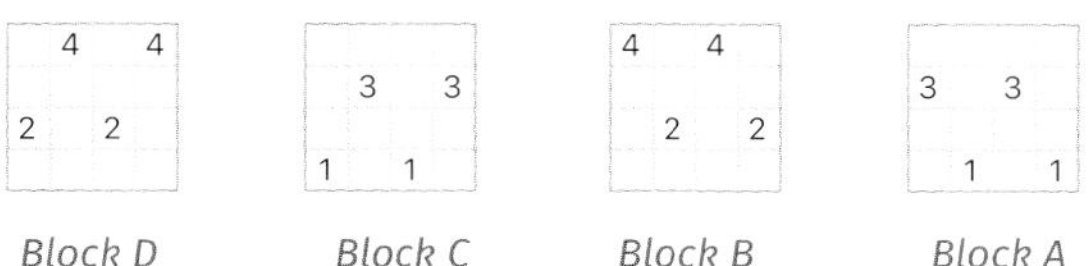

Block D *Block C* *Block B* *Block A*

Figure 8 ***The four threading blocks for rep***

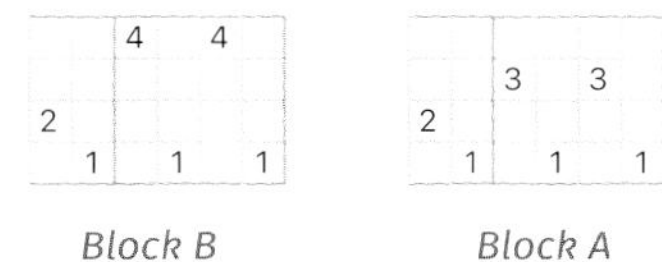

Block B *Block A*

Figure 9 ***The two threading blocks for Bronson***

The more shafts the loom has, the greater the number of blocks. Nevertheless, the coding generally makes it easy to find your way around. Let's take the example of Summer and Winter. All blocks will have this structure: 1-n-2-n. For Block A, we replace n by 3, for Block B, by 4, for C, by 5, then for D, by 6. This is the usual way of writing the threading: Block A = 1-3-2-3, Block B = 1-4-2-4, C = 1-5-2-5, D = 1-6-2-6.

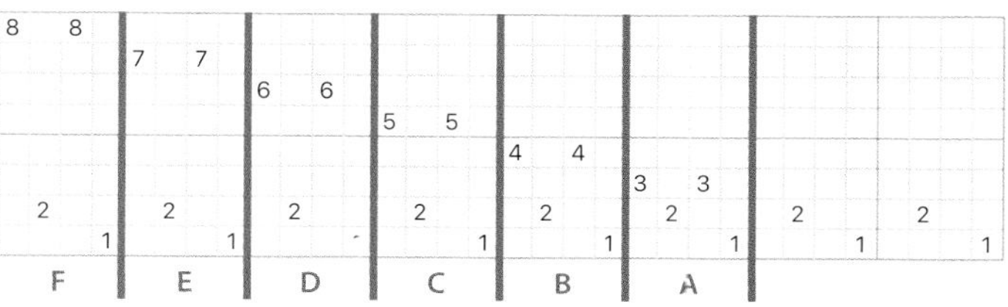

Figure 10 ***Threading of a Summer and Winter on eight shafts***

I suggest you learn to identify how each block, each basic unit, is constructed and to memorize them. Then I recommend that you only follow the profile draft for the threading and treadling. I assure you that stepping back and looking at the big picture in this way of course requires a little effort in conceptualization in the beginning, but it allows you to avoid drowning in a very detailed threading draft. Peace of mind and safety assured!

The Choreography Falls into Place

Once the profile draft has been drawn and once the weave structure has been chosen, you will have to replace the A in the profile draft with the corresponding block, and the same for the B and so on. Let's look at an example with the two-block profile draft, shown in Figure 11, using the Bronson structure.

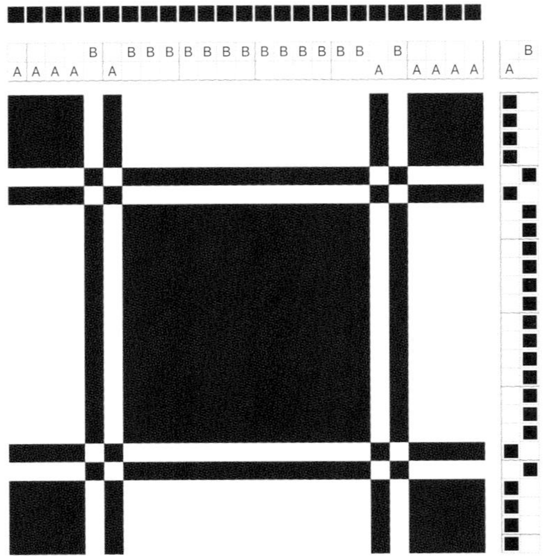

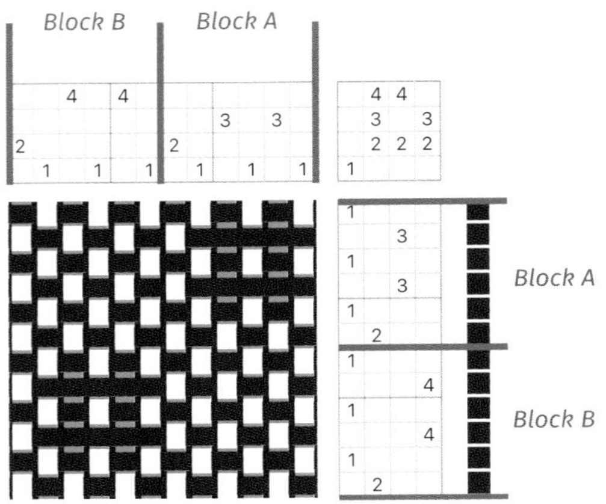

Figure 11 ***Threading and treadling of two blocks of Bronson***

The black areas of the profile draft are those where the pattern is visible. Thus, with this structure, the black squares represent the openwork part of the weave made by the floats, and the white squares symbolize the parts in plain weave.

Sometimes we have to adapt the block of the structure to follow certain constraints. This is the case for overshot, where even thread/odd thread alternate systematically in the weaving. When the pattern of the draft profile is symmetrical, the central block around which the pattern is reflected must be transformed. If the initial block is made of 4 threads, then the one around which the symmetry is made is 5 threads. I suggest you refer to the section on overshot (see p. 187).

For some structures, the length of the float is the length of the block. It is therefore not possible to place the same block several times in a row; otherwise the float will be too long. This is the case for overshot and also huck lace. We therefore know that a serious understanding of the structures is needed to adapt the profile draft to the chosen structure. Weaving software is a great help to check on a future project, as it automatically indicates the length of the longest floats. A drawing on a sheet of graph paper can of course be sufficient.

On the other hand, for other structures, it is essential to place several of the same blocks side by side or the pattern will not appear. This is the case for rep weave or color effects.

One last comment concerns structures like crackle. Between certain blocks, we slip in what is called an incidental thread in order to always alternate a warp thread of an odd shaft with a warp thread of an even shaft.

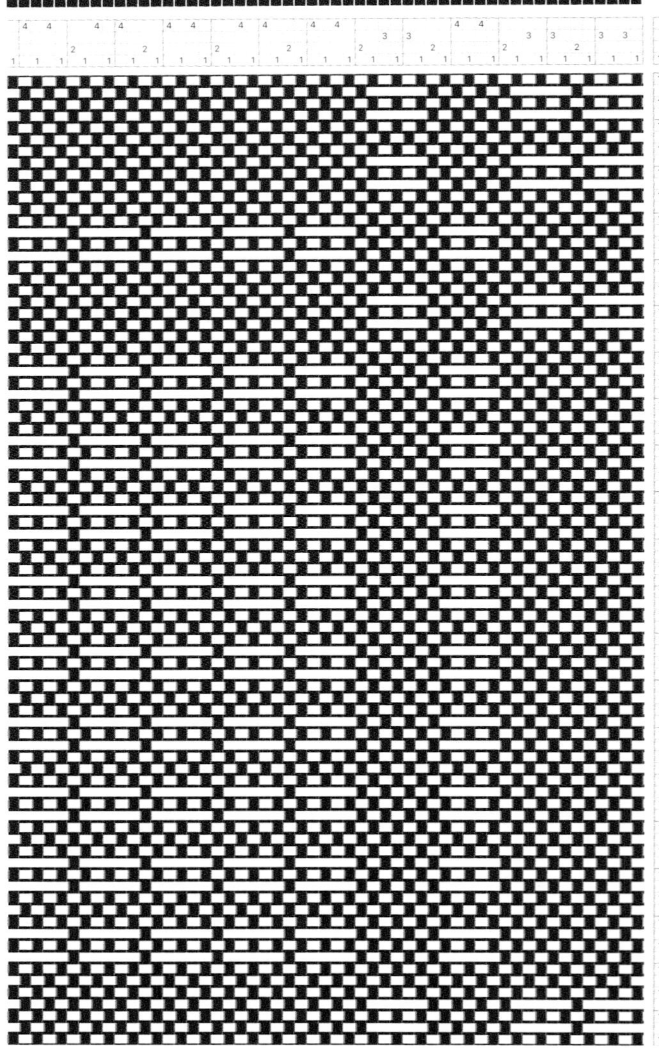

Figure 12 ***Expanded profile draft in Bronson***

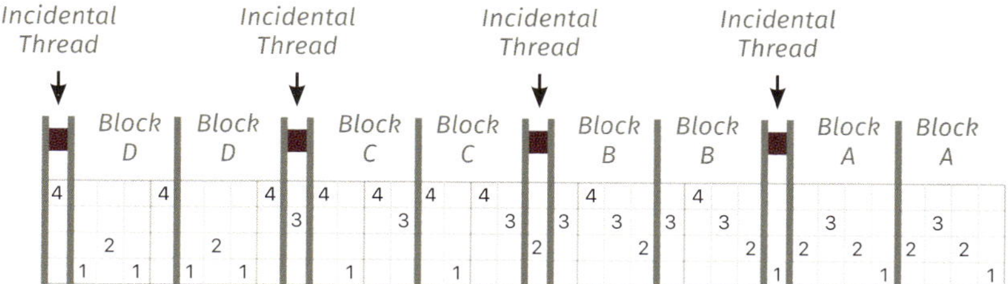

Figure 13 ***Insertion of incidental threads between each different block of a crackle***

But these comments should not frighten you, as a profile draft is very convenient to use. I imagine that you will try it, cautiously at first, by drawing sensible profile drafts. Then with the lightness of a trained dancer, you'll dare to make daring arabesques. A little tip, however: any very simple threading such as a twill can easily be turned into a pattern for a profile draft. Let's keep the example on two blocks already used above, and see what a twill on eight shafts looks like. Really, I urge you to try it—it's so magical!

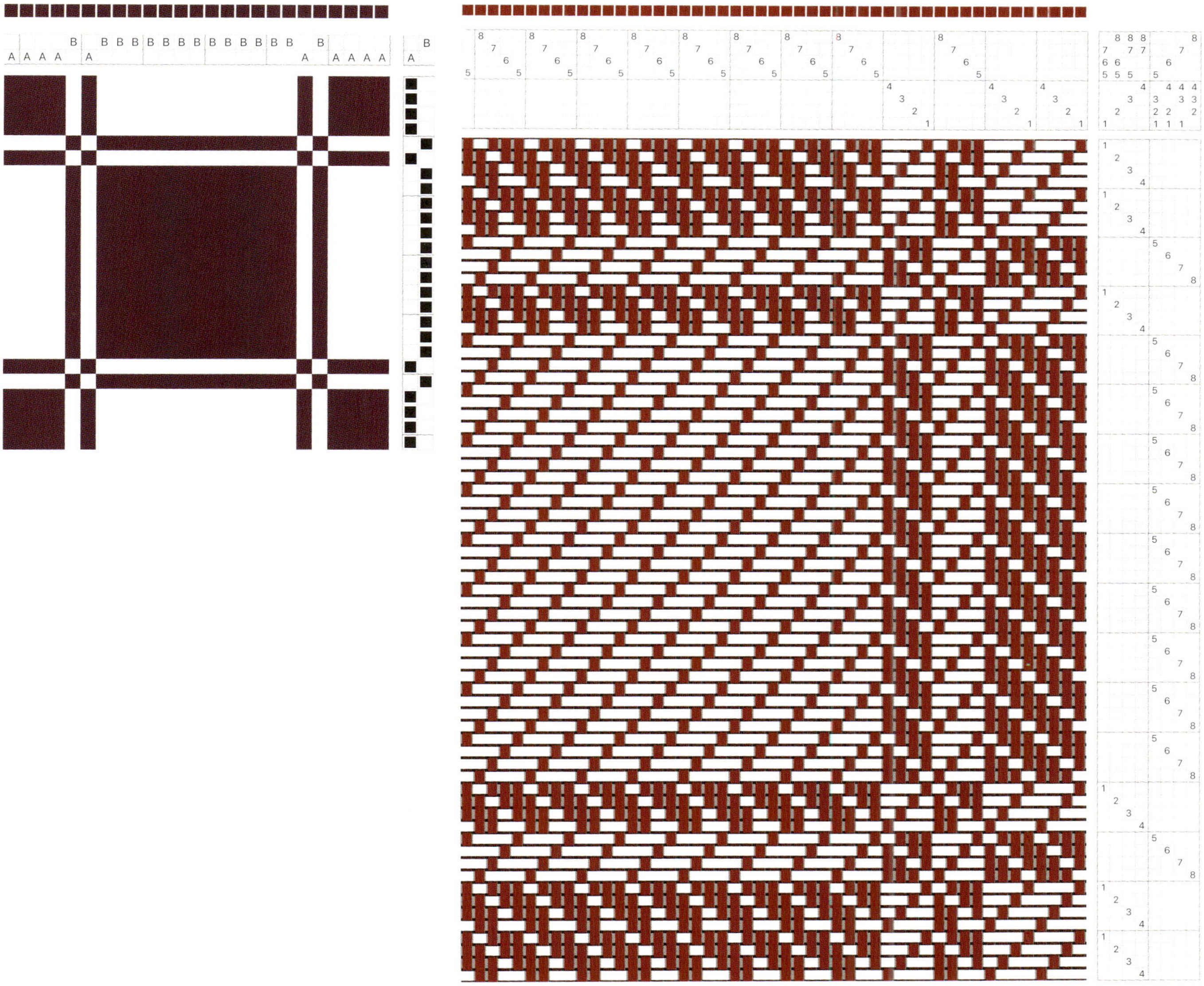

Figure 14 ***Straight twill profile draft on eight shafts***

Analyzing Fabrics

What would be this rare reality which connects in my hand the sensory and the intelligible? A piece of fabric with a surprisingly compelling presence, whose structure deserves to immediately be observed and analyzed with a linen tester.

Patrice Hugues, *Le Langage du tissu*, 1982

We are surrounded by fabrics, and we become real detectives as soon as we master the weaving structures. Sometimes even standing in line can turn into a pleasure if by chance the garment worn by the person right in front of us inspires us or poses a challenge for us! How many times have I taken out my camera and my sketchbook to remember a fabric in order to recreate it one day?

At first, it is the textures or colors that catch our eye. Then comes the moment when you will be tempted to recreate the structure. This is an exercise that entertains me a lot. My analytical mind immediately gets excited!

In the following few lines, I would like to give you a taste for this as well as a little method to initiate you to this practice. Analyzing a fabric is not very difficult, except that it requires a lot of strict precision. It is laborious but undoubtedly is a way to become an autonomous weaver!

A Few Warm-up Exercises

As with any practice, you have to start slowly with exercises that seem monotonous, but are very instructive. I invite you take a simple weave that you have made yourself and whose structure you are familiar with.

What are we looking for? We want to know the threading, as well as the number of shafts needed, then the treadling, and finally the tie-up. All of this can be deduced from analyzing the fabric. Where are the binding points, what floats are there and over how many threads, in warp and weft?

Of course, we are not going to analyze the whole fabric, because it is likely that a small part of it will be enough. So here's the first step: mark the base unit on the fabric. To do this, you will take two pins and slide them into the fabric, horizontally and vertically, as if defining the corner of a rectangle. Then, probably with the help of a magnifying glass, or at least with a very good light, you will draw the warp and weft floats on a piece of graph paper. I admit that it is not always easy.

Now let's work step by step.

1. Let's transfer the design from your fabric to the usual weaving draft. To do this, read each warp, column by column, and note it as you go on your graph paper. Here, in Figure 15, is what we get.

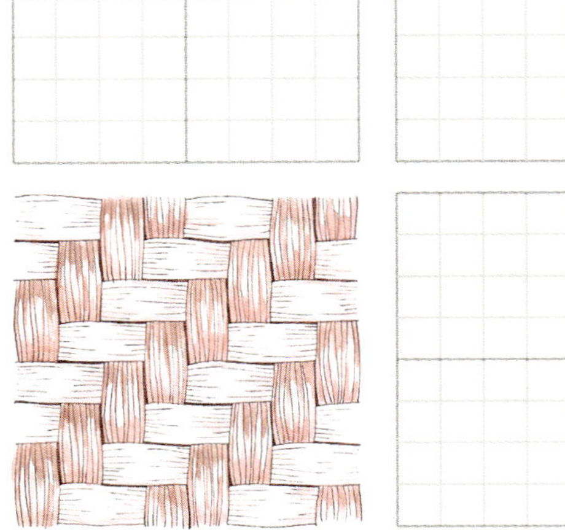

Figure 15 ***Method for analyzing a fabric***

2. Let's notate each column from right to left, assigning a number to each one. Above the first column, let's note the number 1. Is the second column different from the first? Yes! So, let's write the number 2 above. Same question for all the columns. When we look at the fifth column, we realize that it is the same as the first column, so we assign it the number 1.

3. Let's do the same for the rows and notate the picks in the same way. Here, in Figure 16, is what we get.

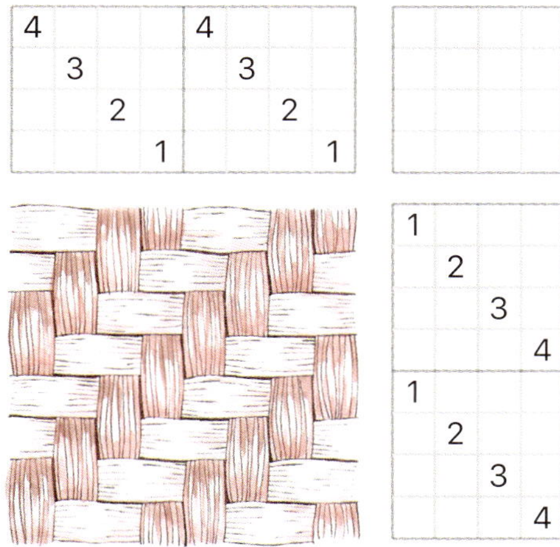

Figure 16 ***Notating the warp and then the weft***

It is obvious that this twill is a simple weave to notate and that the threading order is written naturally in straight twill. With a more complex weave, your threading or treadling numbers may become very messy as you decipher. You will need to take a breath and reverse the numbers between two columns in order to get the straightest threading and treadling possible. This is probably what is most unnerving. Even though the stakes are low, as in the end it doesn't matter if your threading or treadling is very conventional. It makes little difference! The main idea is to put together a threading that is practically easy when you are putting ends through heddles, and if possible to find the threading that matches a known structure.

4. Now let's transfer this information to the tie-up square. This is the part of the work that I find most fun. Let's continue very methodically.

– First treadle: which warp ends are raised? The ones in shafts 1 and 2.

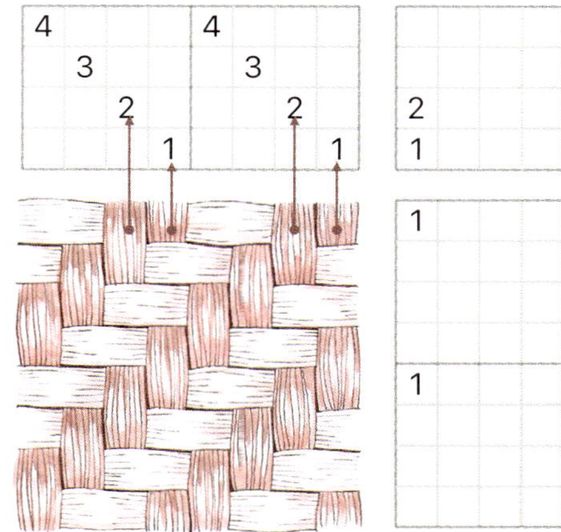

– Second treadle: same question! The answer is 2 and 3.

– Third treadle: shafts 3 and 4.

– Fourth treadle: shafts 4 and 1.

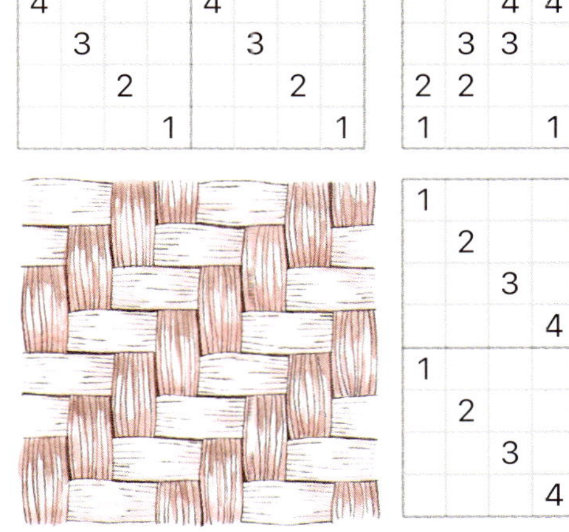

Figure 17 ***Notating the tie-up***

A New Set Design

Let's try an exercise together with actual fabric: a wool pillow cover. I happened to see this gray and ecru upholstery fabric on a couch one day. I liked it a lot and took a picture of it while waiting for the right moment to try to recreate it.

I'm going to use this weaving that I made myself in purple and yellow wool to put into practice the process described above. I hope to give you a few more hints so that you will challenge yourself to try it as well.

Figure 18 ***Pins and magnifying glass: tools for analyzing fabric***

The first step is to delineate the pattern. The colors are very helpful here. I choose the purple strips to mark and slide two needles into the fabric. With a very good light, it appears that the pattern is made over 12 warp and 12 weft threads. Then, on graph paper, I transfer the threads that seem to be floats and those that seem interlaced in plain weave. I choose colored pencils that I can easily erase. The eraser is an indispensable tool! This fabric is complex to decipher as the threads go underneath and then reappear. Nothing is obvious at first and we have to wait for the next step to validate our assumptions.

When the fabric seems to be drawn, I start notating the threading. First column: shaft 1, second column: shaft 2, etc. You have to pay particular attention to the columns that are repeated. The pattern is over 12 threads and it is tempting to spread out the threading on 12 shafts. Always ask yourself this question, "Is this column new or have I already found these same interlacing patterns, regardless of the colors?

I repeat this process for the weft. I lean on the fact that often the weaving is tromp as writ, meaning "treadle as drawn in."

Once this work is done, and not yet being certain that I have interpreted everything correctly, I fill in the tie-up square. Everything is long, tricky, and I sometimes feel like the alchemist making the philosopher's stone! A first draft appears.

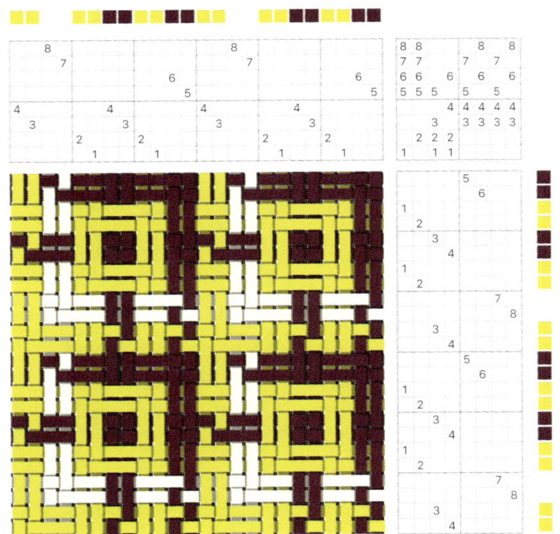

Figure 19 ***Deciphering the fabric***

At this stage, a knowledge of weave structures is of great benefit and helps reorganize the notation. This weave is not a very conventional deflected doubleweave but the sliding of the threads from the front toward the back and the presence of areas of plain weave is a clue. It allowed me to reorganize the whole thing in order to find points of reference for the deflected. Finally, I transformed the previous sketch to end up with this draft (Figure 20). The whole threading, tie-up, and treadling seemed logical to me and easy to remember. This proved to be true, as I turned this draft into a weaving.

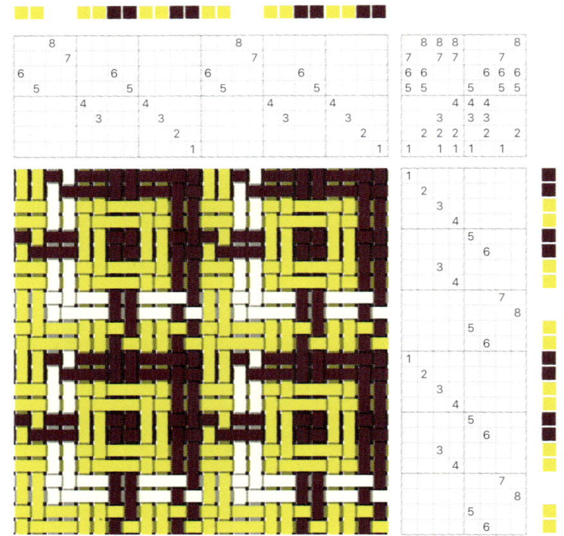

Figure 20 ***Transformed and simplified notation***

To conclude this section on fabric analysis, I can't deny the effort it takes on somewhat complex fabrics, but above all, I can't hide the immense pleasure of doing it. It's long and confusing, but stimulating!

Weaving Software: Switching Roles

In Chapter 3, "The Reading and Writing of Weaving: Stage Left then Stage Right," I touched a little on this question of weaving software (see p. 66). Throughout this book, many weaving drafts illustrate the explanations. They have been made with the help of software.

There are several software programs on the market, which can be downloaded depending on your computer equipment. Often created by weavers, they have been built according to their needs. None is ideal or perfect! Some features are in different stages of improvement or have seen upgrades, such as the choice of colors, the work on structures, or the yarn size. Weavers must find the one that suits them best.

What they all have in common is that they allow you to visualize the graphic representation of your weaving project. Like on your graph paper, you have rows to break down the threading, columns to show the treadling order, and the tie-up square. You can often first try out the free demo version, which has a good number of functions, except that it cannot be saved or printed, so a screenshot will have to do. This will allow you to try out several programs and then one day, perhaps, to buy a license. I first tested pixeLoom before buying it. All the examples in this book are made using this program.

First of all, in the properties tab, you select whether it is a rising or sinking shed loom and indicate the number of shafts used. Some programs allow you to select whether it is a balanced weave, a rep weave, or doubleweave.

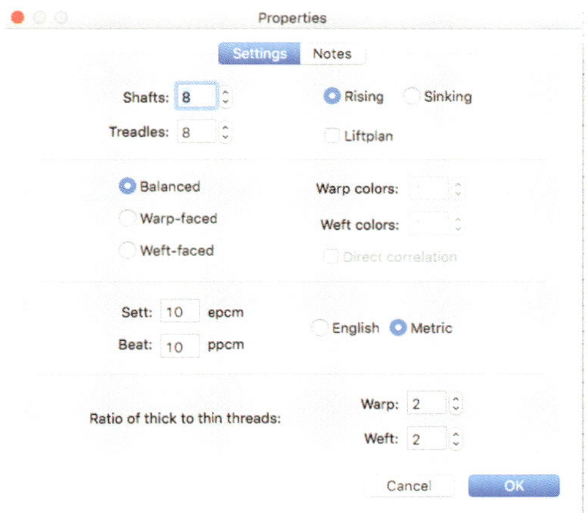

Figure 21 ***File properties***

Then you click to fill in the threading draft, as if with a pencil. You can choose to use numbers, letters, or symbols. There are often tools to duplicate a part of the threading or to change it; all these settings are discovered as you use them. The same operations are possible for treadling and for tie-up. And immediately, the magic happens and the depiction of the weaving appears.

Then, it is possible to refine the image by adding colors and adjusting the yarn size. The technical calculations are obtained by entering the density, the thread count, and the dimensions of the project to be made.

Why use such a tool? Unlike a pencil on paper, you will instantly see the pattern of your weaving as you work on the project, and I must admit that it is quite exhilarating. For example, changing threading on the screen with your mouse allows you to refine the pattern right away. The work is done quickly!

With complex structures, it's a great tool to analyze the length of floats and thus protect yourself from a design error.

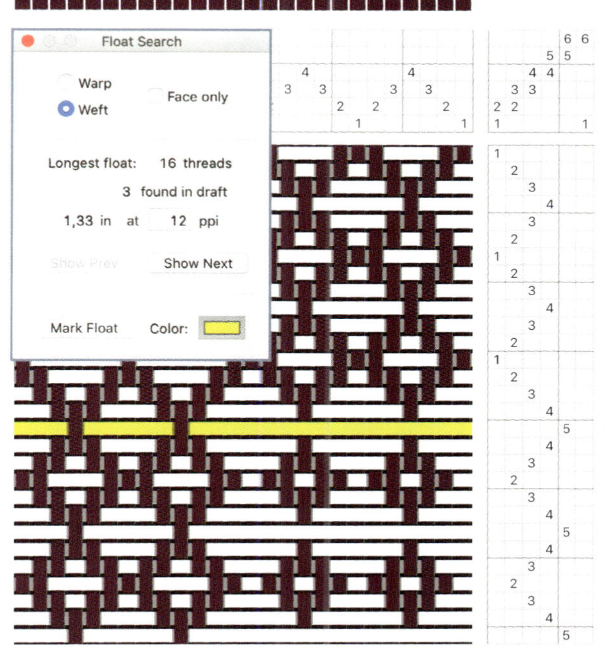

Figure 22 ***Tool to search for floats and calculate their length***

It is also a great help for all calculations. Simply enter the type of yarn used, the density chosen, and the width and length of the project! Immediately, the machine calculates the required amount of yarn and the number of heddles per shaft.

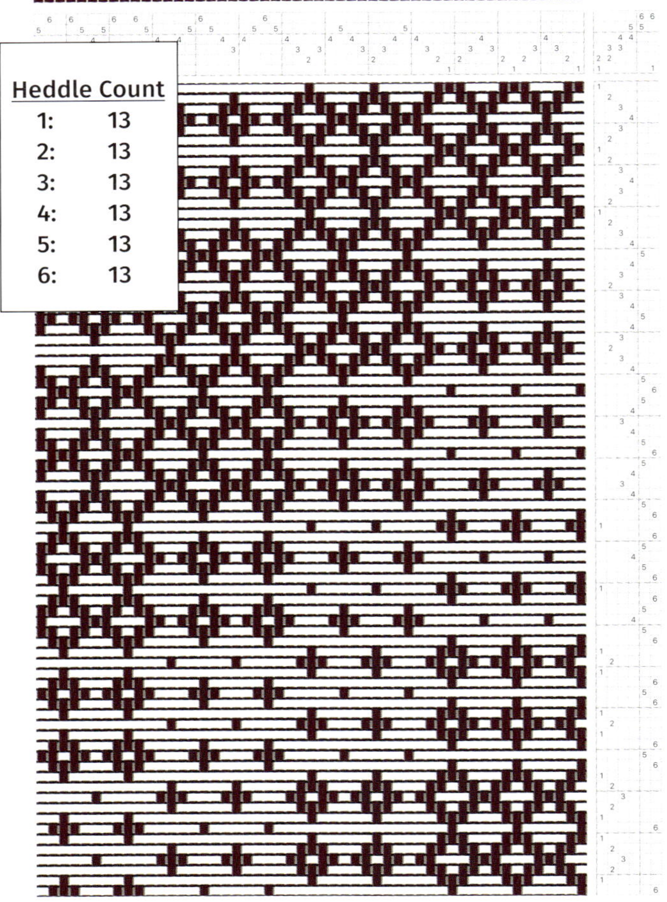

Figure 23 ***Automatic calculation of the number of heddles per shaft***

This is quite useful when you are low on yarn in a certain color. Any change immediately impacts the results, and you can instantly check if you have enough yarn or if you need to change the size of the column to reduce the amount of the color.

But Then, Why Not Use It?

It's impossible for me to deny the efficiency of this software, the time savings, and the flexibility in doing searches! I use them daily. But I am probably affected by the fact that I grew up without a computer. This computer tool does not completely replace my pencils or my graph paper.

By drawing the threading on a paper, by penciling in the floats, these slower actions help us understand what is going on and already help lead to memorizing. I assure you that having ticked 1-2-3-4-3-2-1 twice in the threading draft, and then 2-3-4-5-4-3-2 twice, etc., your memory has retained what your hands will do a little later when threading. Likewise, having drawn the weave with your colored pencils, you will know what should appear very naturally in your weaving and you will have a much better eye for seeing the effect or the error. It's definitely a time saver!

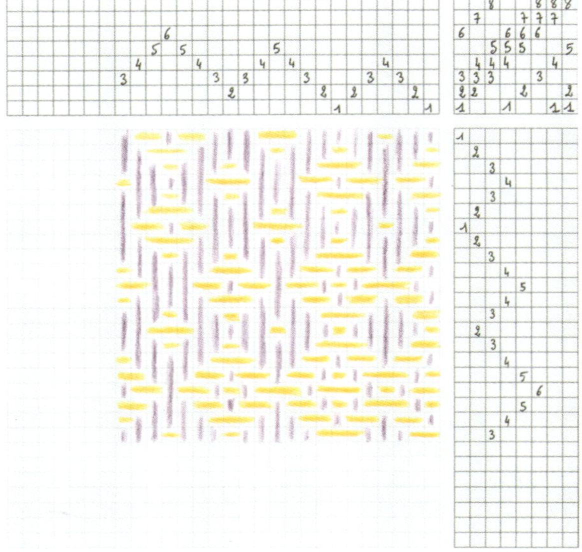

Figure 24 ***Drawing by hand prepares for the work of understanding and weaving.***

Finally, these software programs do not show the yarn exactly as it is, not its size or color. It is often deceiving to choose your yarn after testing it out on screen. To do this, nothing is better than pencil or watercolor.

For me, the conclusion is obvious: use these two tools together. A pencil goes with creativity, the software reaffirms the calculations and accuracy of the choice of structure.

Look Around You to Find Inspiration

My inspiration has always been based on everyday realities. I have always been faithful to my time, to my era.

Interview of Yves Saint Laurent, *La Croix*, January 2007

Mastering technique to be completely free to create: we made it! It is the purpose of this book to have scattered many pointers and suggestions, numerous examples, and to have led you through the vast world of technique to finally arrive at the stage of creation.

We are entering a dance that becomes so personal that these following lines will not be enough to really describe it. Nevertheless, they are based on my work and I share them for whatever benefit they may bring.

Figure 25 ***Inspiration: from a mosaic to a fabric***

Choose Your Ballet Master

Your first weaving projects were likely inspired by patterns. There are plenty to be found in **books**. A bibliography at the end of this book lists some of the books in my library. There are also **magazines** to which you can subscribe, in paper or digital format. Each time you get these patterns, it's like a call to recreate them.

It is impossible to describe all the suggestions for weaving projects that are found on the Internet, on **blogs, forums, podcasts, websites**, etc. It is both a fun trip to see weaving throughout the world and a great frustration as we will never have the time to work on all the patterns offered. Not being an expert in wandering this web, I will not present many resources here. But I would like to thank the many people who share, who show their work, their research, their results! I know that there are also groups on Facebook.

My favorite sites are handweaving.net and arizona.edu, where an impressive number of documents are scanned or written directly in digital, classified, and put online. An inexhaustible source, it is worth going there to look for explanations or patterns before starting a new project. I also like to browse the websites of weaving schools or sites that publish magazines, then with one click, I subscribe to some newsletters. Still, I find this very time-consuming and prefer to surf the "web" of fabric waiting for me on my loom.

Meetings among weavers are also an excellent opportunity to look at one's work in a new way, letting yourself be questioned by the work of others. Once a year we organize a get-together with a few weavers that we call "Shared Weavings." A new theme is suggested each year: a word, a photo, a structure, a material, etc. Each participant makes a weaving on this theme then gifts it to another through a drawing. Each person leaves with a different weaving than the one she brought. It is joyful and very fruitful!

In the same vein, **workshops** have always been real "sparks" for me, because in addition to being a place of dense learning, the exchanges between course participants, during which each one shows one another what they have made, are very formative. I have stirring memories of "Show and Tell" times during my workshops with Erica de Ruiter. The exchange groups made possible by the Internet are just as valuable.

I would like to finish this list by thanking the students who attend my workshops in Chinon. I must admit that assisting with their projects, answering questions when I present a structure, but especially seeing the weavings they make from two sessions, are all inspiring!

Dance Like No One Is Watching

Let's put away the books and magazines, leave the universe of weavings that already exists, open up our eyes and ears, and change perspectives. Let us be led by what surrounds us.

This is about inspiration and not reproduction. While a painter draws a cartoon for a tapestry weaver to reproduce, for the rest of us weavers, an image is only a source of inspiration. The color? Shape? Composition? It's all about letting our creative spirit turn away from what it knows to dare to transform our habits.

In Scotland's Hebrides Islands, the landscape is a strong source of inspiration for making the famous tweed. The story goes that the nobles wore this garment to go hunting or fishing, and that it was meant to serve as camouflage. Green grassy hills, emerald lagoons, brown sandy beaches, white clouds, blond or black peat bogs, gray rocks covered with red or yellow lichen, a palette of colors with soft tones that plant dyes know how to reproduce. You could say that tweed weaves the landscape.

Figure 26 ***Countryside and Harris Tweed from the Hebrides***

Any source of inspiration will do, as long as it pushes us, takes us away from our habits and out of our comfort zone where we are simply content to copy rather than create. It's a lot of fun and reinvigorating to allow your instincts to guide.

In the example of the tweed, the structure is a herringbone woven in twill. The threading stays the same; it is the color palette that transforms the fabric. Knowing the structures is definitely handy when choosing the one that will best bring out what inspires you. Twill emphasizes lines, Summer and Winter highlights squares or geometric shapes, circles or stars are specialties of overshot, and with echo weave, you can draw waves.

Knowledge of and experience with many structures are undeniable assets for this work of pure creativity. The lines of the sea, the sky, and the wall in the scene found in the photo below were quite simple to draw with colors. The lichen deserved flat areas of color without too much geometry, with nuances. Crackle is a structure that shows a little blur in the pattern. It took a few tries to arrive at these weavings, which, mounted as a screen, evoke this seaside image.

Figure 27 ***Low wall with lichen transformed into a screen***

Many other sources of inspiration surround us, and discovering them to hijack them quickly becomes a game: a poster in town, a musical score, a cobblestone street, a painting in a museum, the countryside during a hike, a child's drawing, etc. So open a notebook or a folder in your computer and collect. Collect everything that jumps out at you. Classify by color, by structure, by yarn type, and come back to it often to let your mind wander.

Build Up Your Knowledge of Choreography

Thinking of yourself as a star dancer capable of improvisation can be scary. Sometime we think it is not within our grasp. When describing plain weave (see p. 129), I offered many tips to help find color rhythms, through geometry, the golden ratio, mathematical sequences, or letters of the alphabet, a whole range of creative support. Similarly, these arrangements can inspire the distribution of blocks in a profile draft.

In this example of a curtain, Bronson lace was woven on four shafts. With this structure, we are limited to two blocks. I used the Fibonacci sequence to draw the profile draft.

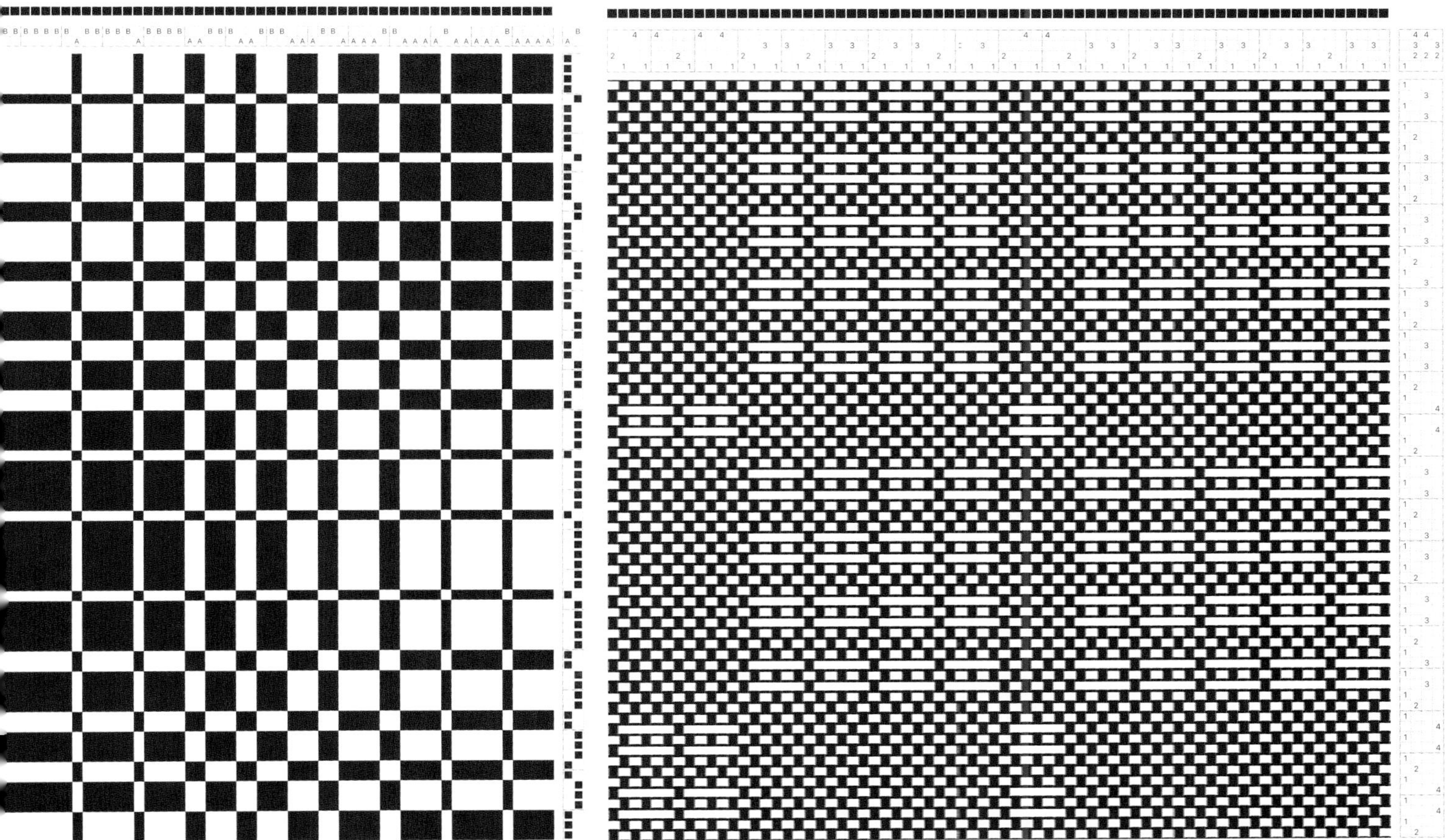

Figure 28 ***Profile draft on the Fibonacci sequence and its expanded draft***

Figure 29 ***Curtain in Bronson lace, four shafts. 34/2 Tencel***

At the beginning of this experiment with improvisation, we can quite easily transform a pattern found in a magazine. It's almost a required exercise in my classes: change the colors of the pattern, change the suggested structure, lengthen a block, add a detail, etc. Try it with no worries: take a pattern you like, analyze a bit what attracted you to it, and exaggerate it.

Changing up the use of the item in the pattern is often the first step. You see a cotton table runner in a log cabin? You don't need a table runner, but your curiosity is pushing you to try out this pattern. Why not try weaving this in alpaca and make a throw blanket. During my classes, I have a lot of fun using the same pattern in different ways. Sometimes there is a kind of wave within the workshop that makes me think of a fashion trend and I have the joy of witnessing a parade of waffle weaves in cotton, in wool, in alpaca, each obviously with a very different use.

The profile draft is a true help when creating. It allows us to dissect and analyze the steps. First, draw the sketch by determining the number of blocks allowed by the structure and possibly by your loom. Then replace the blocks by the basic unit of the structure you want to use.

Placing the order of the structure on the order of the colors, or the reverse, is a sure way to obtain a balanced result. This way, we don't take big risks by opening up Block A in warp with a single color and then Block B with another color. Stretching an overshot or crackle design to fit the width of the colored stripe is a very nice effect. Or reserving a color for the pattern thread adds a delicacy to the weave. In the above Bronson lace example, all the threads on shafts 1 and 2 could be in ecru, while the threads on shafts 3 and 4 would be in burgundy. This color placement is particularly interesting on a waffle weave, where we can choose to always put the same color on shaft 1 in order to accentuate the cells.

In the same vein, we can bring nuances to a structure not by changing color but by changing the type of yarn. In the Bronson structure in Figure 12 on page 238, the yarns reserved for the pattern, arranged in shafts 3 and 4, could be silk on an alpaca plain weave for a single-color wrap. A sumptuous effect is guaranteed. The deflected doubleweave is a structure that allows a great deal of freedom in the choice of colors as well as materials: daring games are possible.

Figure 30 ***Scarf in deflected doubleweave: alpaca, mohair, and gold thread***

The purpose of these previous paragraphs has been to suggest a few avenues to explore. There are so many others!

To conclude, I would like to express a few reservations: don't overdo it! Playing with color, practicing with structure, daring to use different yarns are all pretexts for creation. But know anyway how to be understated and moderate. It's a bit like a dance performance. It's neither the technical performance nor the abundance of jumps and arabesques that arouse our emotion.

I will finish with our usual companion, while hoping not to bore you: the sample! While it is essential as a confirmation of our choices of colors, structure, and density, it is also the perfect tool for exploring and inventing. I have repeatedly found that new ideas come to me when working on a sample. Usually, the width of the sample does not exceed 8 to 10 in. (20 to 25 cm). Re-weaving is therefore not too onerous. That's why I recommend installing a fairly long sample warp, in order to keep the beginning of the warp for technical adjustments and then get to the game of creating. I have already brought up the concept of serendipity: taking advantage of a discovery, going along with a crazy idea, making the most of a mistake.

There is no security on this earth; there is only opportunity.

General Douglas MacArthur, Chief of Staff of the U.S. Army during the 1930s

9

Details That Change Everything: Mastery Becomes Possible

Sometimes you don't have all the equipment you need. Perhaps you don't have enough shafts to make a pattern that has inspired you, or the loom only has ten treadles when you need twelve. Sometimes you find yourself at an impasse. These last few pages will show you not to lose hope—think hard, make several sketches of your project, even talk to other weavers before getting to what you want. I'm really excited about solving these conundrums!

Changing the Threading

Your loom has four shafts, but the pattern you want to weave needs eight. There is no way to transcribe a threading designed for an 8-shaft loom into a threading for a 4-shaft loom. You can't copy a design made with eight colors if you only have four pencils! Nevertheless, it is possible to rework the threading, treadling, and tie-up to approximate the shapes of the pattern.

A twill intended for an 8-shaft loom can be written out quite well for a 4-shaft loom. With this example of an M & W, we show that the conversion is possible, while realizing that it is not an exact reproduction!

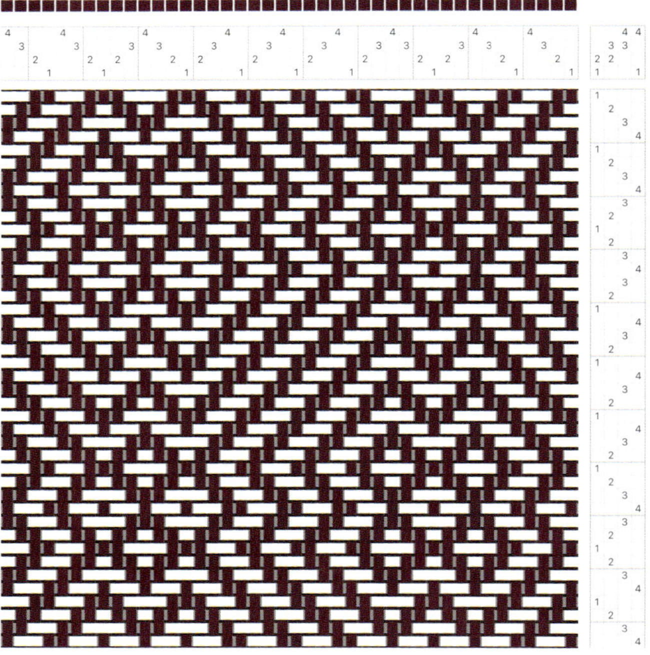

Figure 1 ***Conversion of an 8-shaft draft into a 4-shaft draft***

For more complex patterns, using a profile draft is valuable. In the following example, the pattern is initially made on eight blocks. There are two methods to reduce the number of blocks and, consequently, the number of shafts: digitizing and telescoping.

These two examples show that a decrease in the number of shafts transforms the result and eliminates some detail. However, the general shape is not altered. Having four pencils only prevents us from coloring with all the different shades of color.

Figure 2 ***Digitizing and telescoping: two methods of converting an eight-block profile draft into a four-block profile draft***

Memorizing a Complex Treadling by Creating Codes

Detaching yourself from having to read the treadling diagram by memorizing it instead contributes so much to the fluidity of your movements and the consistency of the weaving that I cannot help but encourage you to make this effort. I know how much this puts some people off because they find following the treadling draft with a pencil or a needle reassuring. I actually quite admire all the ways people have found to keep track of where they are! Yet, despite this ingenuity, I persevere and encourage my students to memorize. A dose of method, a dash of confidence, and a bit of practice!

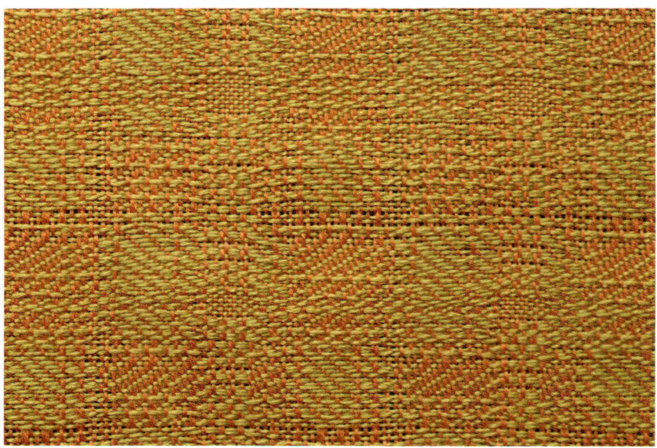

The use of a floor loom, where you tie-up several shafts to each treadle, simplifies this task a bit since there is only one action: pressing on a single treadle that will raise several shafts simultaneously instead of operating several levers. In any case, you need to find some mnemonic devices to remember the sequence. Here are some tips.

Make a code for the tie-up. The idea is to simplify to facilitate memorization. For example, when plain weave is on shafts 1-3, then 2-4, I find it easier to memorize Odd then Even. This is even more true when there are 8 shafts. Odd is easier to memorize than 1-3-5-7!

To make a code for 2/2 twill, as soon as I can, in my mind I replace 1-2 with **1**, 2-3 with **2**, 3-4 with 3, and 4-1 with **4**.

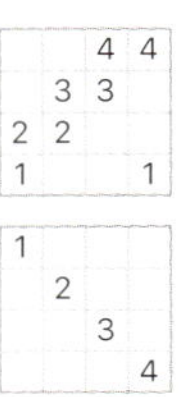

Figure 3 ***Simplification for reading the tie-up of a 2/2 twill***

With eight shafts, it's even more important to make myself find a way to replace several numbers with one. In the chapter dealing with twill (see p. 151), I indicated how to recognize and simplify the different twills. In this example, the point is to remember two things:

- the **structure of the twill**. This a 2/2/1/3 compound twill, which means that the first two threads are raised, the next two are lowered, the next one is raised, then the last three are lowered. When this rhythm 2 under/2 over/1 under/3 over is used, remember the order rather than the numbers of the shafts used; so remember 2/2/1/3 and "forget" shafts numbers 1-2-5;
- the **number of the treadle** used. If it is treadle **1**, then the rhythm of this 2/2/1/3 twill settles on 1. The first two shafts raised are 1-2, the next two remain lowered, 5 is raised and 6-7-8 remain lowered. When it's time for treadle **6**, then you can deduce that you lift shafts **6**-7, leave 8-1, raise shaft 2, and leave 3-4-5.

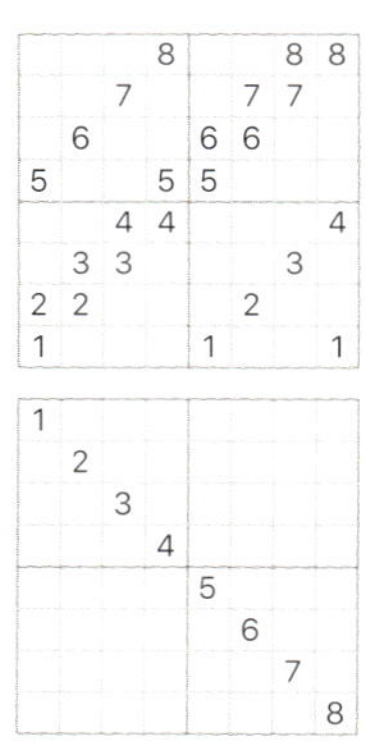

Figure 4 ***Simplification for reading the tie-up of a 2/2/1/3 twill***

Memorize the treadling. The above example is really easy to remember: 1, 2, 3, 4, etc. Obviously, it is often not that simple. Nevertheless, it is rare that you can't find some trick or rhythm or notation.

Let's look at another example with huck lace, where the plain weave doesn't play the role of a grid and see how we can simplify the treadling.

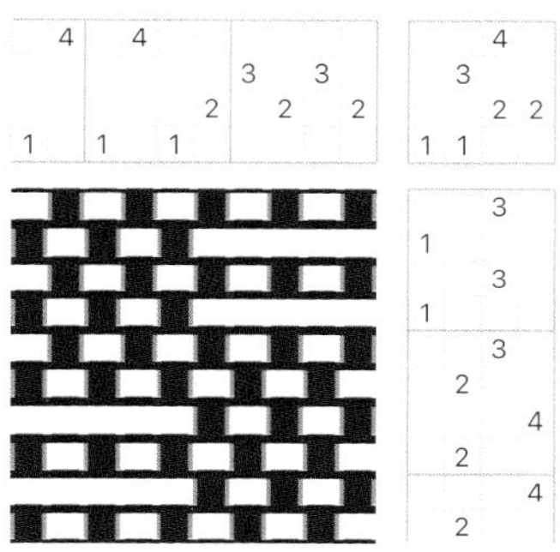

Figure 5 ***Example of giving a code to huck lace***

From top to bottom, we read the treadle numbers:

- Block A: Even plain weave (shafts 2-4), 1 (shaft 1), Even plain weave, 1, Even plain weave;
- Block B: Odd plain weave (shafts 1-3), 4 (shaft 2), Odd plain weave, 4, Odd plain weave.

Finally, these 10 lines of treadling can be simplified into two blocks: A for the first 5 picks, and B for the last 5. We can simplify the memorization by forcing ourselves to weave the group of 5 picks without interruption!

If by chance your weaving is based on a sketch drawn by a profile draft, you have a key to reading. Try to remember how each of the blocks is organized, then check the progress of your weaving using only the letters A and B. Otherwise, take the time to find a group, an order, a point of reference.

Sometimes, these groupings are not obvious, so we are reluctant to look for some pattern that will make memorization easier. And yet! The fluidity of reading a draft affects one's movements and they can become very smooth and effortless. I see this too often not to emphasize its importance. Stopping at each pick to mark the progress of our work with a sheet of paper and a pencil prevents us from acquiring this regular rhythm which makes a beautiful weaving.

Invent a reminder that will be a real help. It must be effective! A simple glance should be enough to find your way. Move the draft next to your loom and place it at eye level. A piece of paper stuck to the frame is often enough. Use different colors depending on the block, put a green or red arrow depending on the order, etc. Find very visible things!

Also look for what is always repeated and don't write it down anymore! For example, in compound structures that use tabby, such as Summer and Winter or overshot, agree that the shuttle goes from left to right for the odd tabby and from right to left for the even tabby. Thus, depending on where the shuttle is, you know which tabby to do.

I like to simplify and I can spend a lot of time looking for solutions. I especially like to weave and I enjoy the pleasure of smooth, natural movements.

Installing Supplementary Warp and Rotating the Weaving Draft

Maybe you were once bothered by the use of two shuttles at the same time for a compound weave, maybe you would have liked to have stripes in the warp direction instead of in the weft direction and thus avoid the handling of shuttles at each weft color change. Maybe you don't have enough treadles or shafts. When I discovered the subtlety of this pattern rotation, I quickly realized that it would be very useful.

Rotating the weaving draft simply means that you take your usual draft and rotate it 90 degrees. So, warp ends shown vertically in the original draft end up in the rows and become weft threads. The weft threads shown horizontally are turned vertical to become warp ends.

Here are the steps for a Summer and Winter weave. To make it easier to read, I have changed the numerical notation into symbols.

1. Make the initial weaving draft without forgetting the tabby.

Figure 6 ***Draft for a Summer and Winter weave on four shafts***

2. Turn this draft 90 degrees clockwise.

Figure 7 ***90-degree rotation of the drawing***

3. Rearrange to return to the traditional layout. Move the tie-up lines to the top of the draft, putting them back in the usual order and replace the symbols with the numbers of the corresponding shafts and treadles. This will give you the new draft.

Figure 8 The same draft after all the changes

You can get a little lost at first; you have to work methodically. I find that the easiest way is to have a draft on paper and to actually rotate it.

Doing this rotation for compound structures of plain weave and patterns requires two important comments:

- Structures such as Summer and Winter or overshot are in fact weaves with a supplementary weft. Calculating the density is based on the yarn used in the plain weave. By turning the draft, we are now in a weave configuration with a supplementary warp. We must therefore **double the density** of the warp compared to the initial calculation;
- The colored yarns are pattern yarns. They are interlaced much less than the adjacent threads used for the plain weave. It is possible that during a long weave, this yarn will become a little slack. You can then **tighten up this supplementary warp**. Lift all the shafts in which the pattern yarn is threaded, in this case shafts 3-4-5-6, slide a fairly strong slat under these threads at the back of the loom, move this slat behind the back beam and weight it down reasonably with weights. As the weaving progresses, this rod will move down and will restore the necessary tension on these stretched threads. Lucky owners of a double warp beam will know how to use it for this purpose.

Reorganizing the pattern so that the pattern threads initially installed in weft are now in warp has the great advantage of no longer having to handle two shuttles. This saves time, makes the weaving easier, without worrying about mixing up the shuttles, and especially, the selvedges are clean and impeccable.

Tying Up a Countermarch Loom

I would like to come back to this type of loom because the tie-up can be intimidating. The countermarch loom is a great tool as it offers a clean shed and equal tension on both layers of warp threads. All the shafts work at the same time. Some rise while others sink, an ideal and balanced movement. However, this loom intimidates. How many people get discouraged because they don't understand the mechanism, and do not know what to connect or how.

First, let's try to solve the difficulties of terminology. Depending on the country, the manufacturer, and the use, we do not name all the parts of this type of loom the same way.

As for me, here are the terms I have adopted:

- **shafts**: the part of the loom that holds the heddles and that rises or falls depending on the weave structure;
- **jacks**: the wooden bars at the top of the loom that hinge around an axis. They allow the shaft to rise. Each shaft is connected to two jacks. They are installed in the upper part of the loom called the castle. On some looms, this pair of jacks is replaced by a single one or a system of pulleys;
- **lower lamm**: the wooden bar that is connected to the treadles and the jacks. To help, we can remember that Lower Lamms Lift the shaft.
- **upper lamm**: the wooden bar that is connected to the treadle and to the shafts directly. It lowers, or sinks, the shaft.

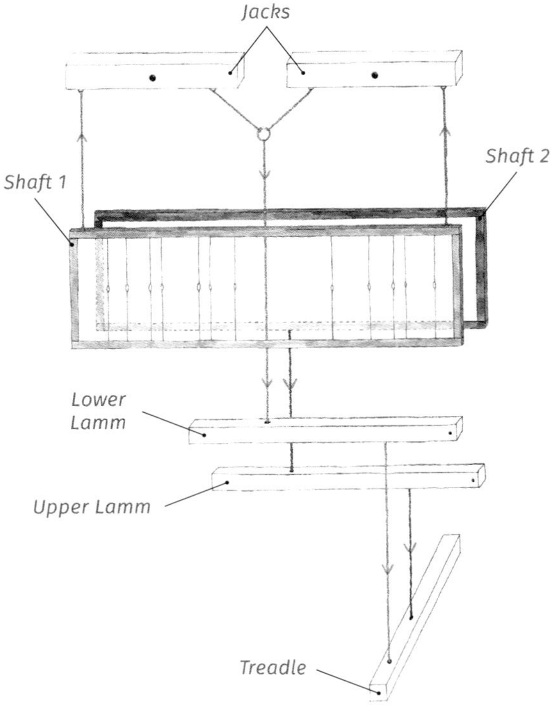

Figure 9 ***Tie-up of a countermarch loom***

There are as many shafts as there are lower and upper lamms and pairs of jacks. These three tools are positioned vertically to each other. The jacks are just above the shaft, above the lower lamm and above the upper lamm. On some looms, the lower and upper lamms are next to each other instead. On the Louet looms from the Netherlands or some Leclerc looms from Canada, the jacks are replaced with a nylon pulley and cable system, with two sets of cables per shaft, one connected to the lower lamm to lift the shaft, the other to the upper lamm to lower it.

The shafts and their related mechanisms are arranged from the front to the back of the loom. Shaft 1 and its pair of jacks, its lower and upper lamm are in the front.

The treadles are aligned along the width of the loom. Treadle 1 is on the left. Each treadle is hooked up either to the lower lamm or to the upper lamm of the shafts being operated, with a connection that is perfectly vertical.

The lower and upper lamms are relays that allow the treadles to activate the shafts so that they remain horizontal. These relays pull the shafts down from the middle thanks to the upper lamm or pull them up thanks to the center jack rod, even though the treadles are not in line with this center. Without these relays, the shafts would be pulled askew.

Several tie-ups are **unchangeable**:

- each shaft is connected to the corresponding jacks;
- each pair of jacks is connected to its lower lamm;
- each shaft is connected to its upper lamm.

The shaft is therefore systematically connected to its upper lamm, **and** to its lower lamm via the jacks. On some looms, these connections are metal, which sets the heights of the whole system. No more questions asked, everything is preset. When this is not the case, using Texsolv cords makes the work easier compared to the old hemp ties.

Each loom, and therefore how to set up each one, is different. The first adjustments are explained in the assembly instructions. Without this guide, adjustments are generally made so that the shafts, the lower lamms, and the upper lamms are horizontal. The height of the shafts can be adjusted after having threaded a few warp ends. The thread must pass through the center of the eye in the heddle and through the middle of the reed. I make these adjustments without blocking the jacks, which would tilt and throw everything out of order as soon as I would release them.

Only the tie-ups of the treadles to the lower and upper lamms change depending on the weave structure: plain weave, twill, Summer and Winter, etc. It is precisely here that we use the tie-up square from the weaving drafts! And it is to tie-up these treadles that the weaver will have to find a comfortable position. Being on the floor, enclosed in the loom, is inconvenient and can unfortunately be discouraging!

It is important to remember that each necessary treadle is connected to all the shafts, via the lower lamm for shafts that rise, via the upper lamm for those that sink. As in this example, imagine weaving a twill that alternates with a plain weave on four shafts. You need six treadles.

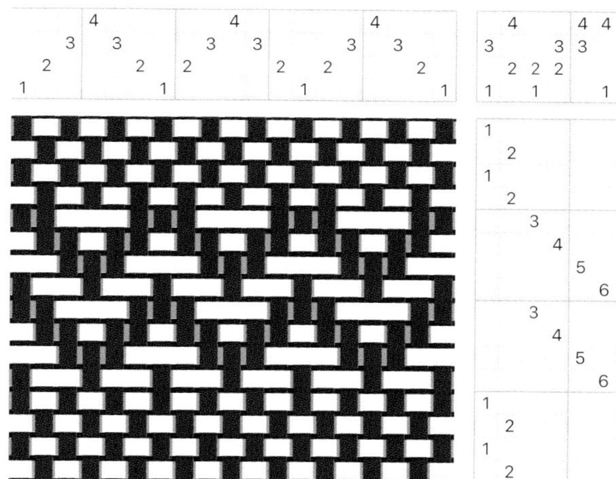

This draft is very useful for reading the treadling, but much less so for the footwork. Also, the placement of the treadles must be readjusted so that the body is comfortable and the feet find a comfortable rhythm:

- treadle 1 is connected to lower lamms 1 and 3 and to upper lamms 2 and 4;
- treadle 2 is connected to lower lamms 3-4 and to upper lamms 1-2;
- treadle 3 is connected to lower lamms 1 and 2 and to upper lamms 3 and 4;
- treadle 4 is connected to lower lamms 2 and 3 and to upper lamms 1 and 4;
- treadle 5 is connected to lower lamms 4 and 1 and to upper lamms 2 and 3;
- treadle 6 is connected to lower lamms 2 and 4 and to upper lamms 1 and 3 as indicated in the tie-up square.

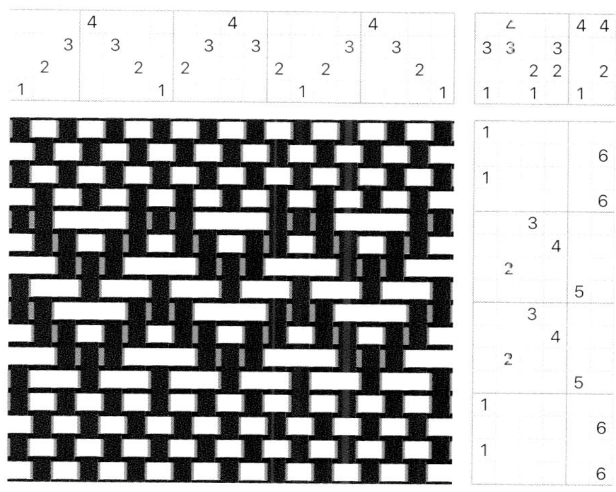

Figure 10 ***Regular tie-up of a twill–plain weave pair***

This tie-up order for the treadles may be surprising but I chose it because it allows me to weave plain weave with the two outside treadles, 1 and 6, and to weave twill with the four middle treadles, systematically alternating left foot/right foot. Weaving with a regular step!

Here again, we find certain writing conventions. An "O" to symbolize the shaft that rises and an "X" for the one that falls. To avoid confusion, I prefer to indicate only the shafts that rise by designating them by their number. It is up to the weaver to tie up any shafts that sink that are not noted.

The verdict of how the treadles are tied up comes back quickly! By pressing on a treadle, you give the order to each of the shafts to either rise (treadles connected to the lower lamm), or to fall (treadles connected to the upper lamm). If by mistake you have attached both the upper and lower lamm of the same shaft to a treadle, nothing will happen, because a shaft that receives the command to both rise and fall will block the treadle. Nothing serious except that you have to contort yourself again to move a tie.

Since with this loom, one layer of yarn rises and the other falls, the height of the reed is adjusted so that, at rest, the entire warp passes through the middle of the reed.

I really prefer the countermarch loom for two reasons: the tension is balanced between the two layers of yarn, the one that rises and the one that falls, and the pressure on the treadles requires less effort. The body works more smoothly and the threads are less stressed. And I thank the manufacturers who have put the user's comfort first with a quick and easy tie-up system!

The Skeleton

Here is a nice trick to know when you have a lot of shafts. The day will come when you don't have enough treadles. Using a skeleton tie-up allows you to isolate certain treadles by grouping together those that are used systematically in each block.

To explain this method simply, tying up a Summer and Winter project on eight shafts is ideal.

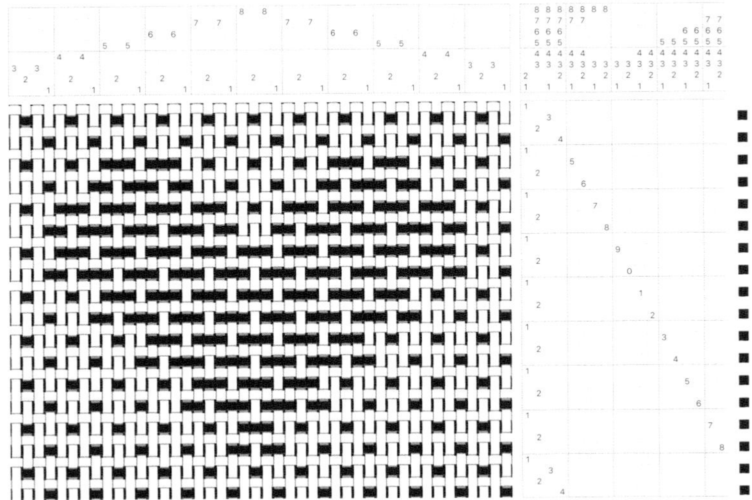

Figure 11 ***Complete draft of a Summer and Winter weave***

The main idea of a skeleton tie-up is to look for repeats and separate them from the overall tying. In this example, we distinguish that the treadling is composed of blocks of four picks. Each block is systematically constructed as follows:

- first pick: shafts 1-2;
- third pick: shafts 3-4-5-6-7-8, which is all the other shafts;
- these two picks make the plain weave or what some call the tabby;
- second pick: shaft 1, to which other shafts are added to make the pattern;
- fourth pick: shaft 2, to which we add the same other shafts for the pattern. Depending on the pattern, the "other shafts" are chosen from 3-4-5-6-7-8.

To create the foundations of this structure, we therefore reserve **four treadles**. Later we will see which ones to choose.

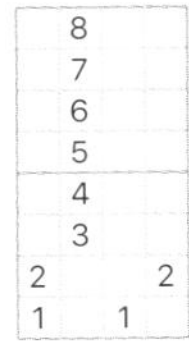

Figure 12 ***Foundation of the tie-up for the Summer and Winter structure***

To analyze the rest of the tie-up, it is very helpful to go through the profile draft because it summarizes the whole thing. This is how we discover that this pattern is made up of eight configurations.

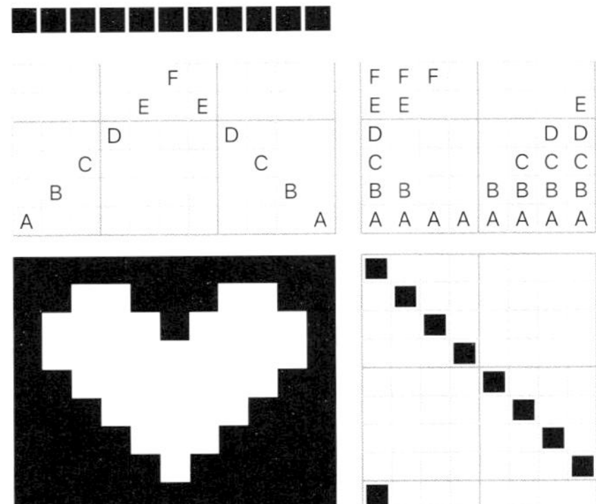

Figure 13 ***Profile draft of this project in Summer and Winter***

Up until now, I've always encouraged you to tie up shafts that move together on a single treadle so that you can use one foot per pick. For these structures that use a lot of shafts, from now on we will use two feet simultaneously for each pattern pick: the left foot for the four left treadles that work the foundation plain weave and the right foot for all the other treadles that make the pattern.

You will probably be hesitant at first; you'll have to learn to work with both feet. For this example, the treadles are

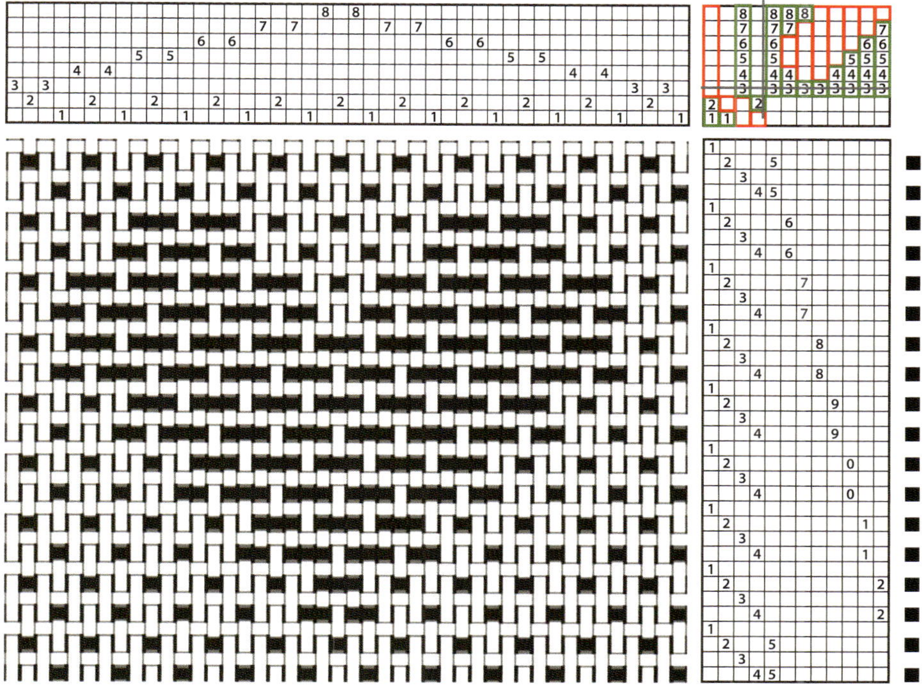

Figure 14 ***Project in Summer and Winter with a skeleton tie-up***

numbered 1 through 12 from the left. The left foot keeps the following constant cadence: treadle 1, then 2, then 3, then 4 and moves from left to right. When it is on treadle 2 or 4, the right foot comes into action at the same time and presses on one of the treadles from 1 to 12, following the pattern. Here is the sequence of the four picks from the first block:

- **First tabby pick**. Left foot only: treadle 1 (shafts 1-2);
- **First pattern pick**. Left foot: treadle 2 (shaft 1) and right foot: treadle 5 (shafts 3-4-5-6-7-8);
- **Second tabby pick**. Left foot only: treadle 3 (shafts 3-4-5-6-7-8);
- **Second pattern pick**. Left foot: treadle 4 (shaft 2) **and** right foot: treadle 5 (shafts 3-4-5-6-7-8).

This group of treadlings is repeated twice to balance the pattern in this Summer and Winter example.

Reducing the number of treadles in skeleton tie-up requires some thought. Some people like to get help from applications found on the Internet. Tim's Rudimentary Treadle Reducer is often appreciated. Personally, I find that doing this research with paper and pencil better comes alongside the work of understanding and reinforces the relevance of the choice of treadle order.

Reducing this tie-up on a countermarch loom requires "splitting" the loom into two parts. When we weave the pattern picks, we imagine being on a loom with two shafts for the left foot and on another loom with six shafts for the right foot. To treadle 2, we tie up shaft 1 to rise and shaft 2 to fall. To treadle 4, shaft 2 is tied up to rise, while shaft 1 is tied up to fall. We do not tie-up the other shafts to these two treadles. Only the first two shafts are operated, which is really unusual on a countermarch loom, when usually **all** the shafts are attached to each treadle used!

Only treadles 1 and 3 are attached to all the shafts as usual on a riser loom: **at treadle 1**, shafts 1 and 2 are attached to the rise, while the other 6 shafts are attached to the fall. And **at treadle 3**, shafts 1 and 2 are attached to the fall, while the other 6 frames are attached to the rise.

Treadles 5, 6, 7, 8, 9, 10, 11, and 12 are all tied up to the last six shafts only. The first two shafts are not used at all by these eight pattern treadles. In this example, treadle 5 lifts these six shafts and does not lower any of them. Treadle 6 lifts shafts 3, 4, 7, and 8 and lowers shafts 5 and 6.

This method is ideal in many cases, but it is likely that one day you will run out of treadles again. Choosing to do this weaving on a table loom is the easiest solution. Or, if you are used to complex treadlings, the dobby loom might be a gift to yourself.

The Network and the Initials Method

Different weaving methods observe the initial without fully using it or defining it.

Brandon and Guiguet, *La méthode des initiales—Un aspect mathematique du tissage à lames*, 1938

I am quite happy to end this book by mentioning the work of two Frenchmen being talked about in North America: Olivier Masson and François Roussel who, inspired by Brandon and Guiguet's research, have created the French software Poincarré. Even if it is absolutely impossible to describe this method in detail in a few lines, I would like to present what is called the network, network weaving, or weaving with the initial.

The Principle

The representation of **network** weaving is a different way of drawing threading or treadling than what we usually do. It is a method that relies on complex mathematical reasoning, which you can read about in Brandon and Guiguet's book, *La méthode des initiales—Un aspect mathematique du tissage à lames* (The Initials Method—A Mathematical Aspect of Shaft Weaving). Networking allows us to break free from the usual rectilinear geometry of weaving to enter the work of curves. It also makes it possible to transform patterns that use a lot of shafts into weave that can be made on a simple eight-shaft loom. To do this, we use a block of four squares, called an **initial**, which is placed on both a graphic line and on a grid called a **network**.

Drawing a network threading makes use of three things:

- The **initial** is like a brick that will be used to build the network. Here are three examples of four-thread initials:

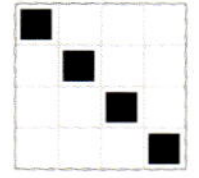
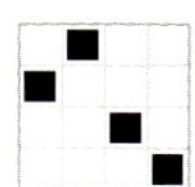
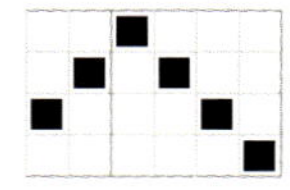

Figure 15 ***Three examples of initials***

- The network is built with an initial duplicated and juxtaposed to itself. The following example uses the initial 1 as a brick. The result is the representation of a straight twill on eight shafts. The gray squares form the network.

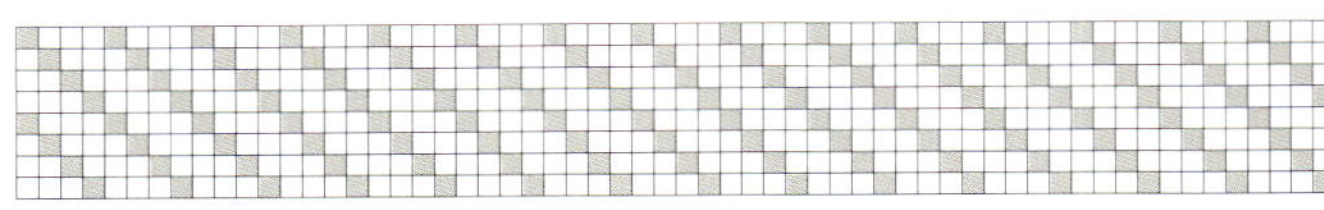

Figure 16 ***Network on eight shafts***

- A line is drawn freehand, a curving line that will go from one end of the network to the other.

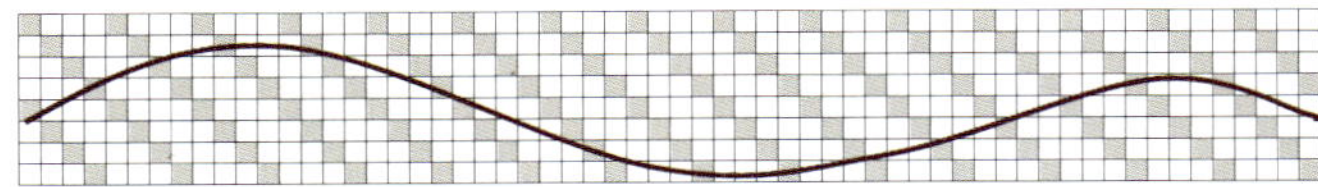

Figure 17 ***The design line is drawn on the network***

Building the Complete Draft Step by Step

On this network, we will now determine the **threading**. Each time the line passes over a gray square of the network, we color it red. Then, each gray square of the network that is above this pattern line in a column without a red square is colored green.

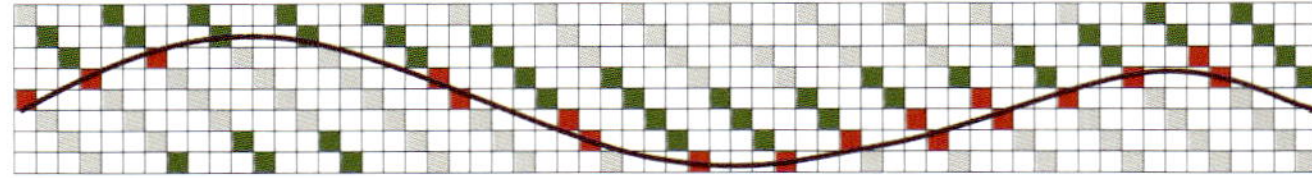

Then we clean up this grid by replacing the colored squares with the number of their line to obtain the threading as usual.

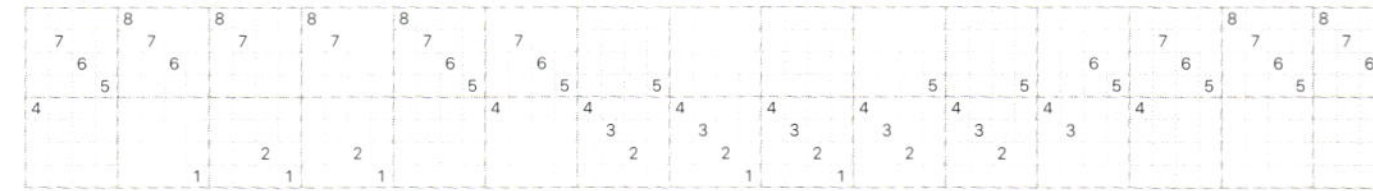

Figure 18 ***Translation into threading***

As is often the case, it is very simple to adopt the tromp as writ, or treadle as drawn in, method. It is a method that ensures harmony in the design. The treadling may be an exact copy of the threading.

The construction of network weaving is based on two notions: the appearance of the pattern, which we have just constructed, and the making of the fabric by the choice of structure and the type of interlacing. Twill is very suitable when you have eight shafts. Here I show a compound twill: 3/3/1/1 and a combined twill, playing on the weft effect of the 1/3 twill and the warp effect of the 3/1 twill.

	8				8	8	8
7				7	7	7	
			6	6	6		6
		5	5	5		5	
	4	4	4		4		
3	3	3		3			
2	2		2				2
1		1				1	1

	8	8	8				8
7		7	7			7	
6	6		6		6		
5	5	5		5			
			4		4	4	4
		3		3		3	3
	2			2	2		2
1				1	1	1	

Figure 19 ***Two possible tie-ups: compound twill and combined twill***

The two resulting images show how different the patterns are depending on the tie-up chosen. No doubt you will try to change this little magic square.

The amazing thing about this method is that you can weave curves and still have the security of a sufficiently interlaced weave that is therefore sturdy. No float exceeds three threads!

This method explained succinctly can be improved in many ways:

- by changing the network grid to be based on another initial;
- by defining the threading points between two curves and not only above a single line as in the example;
- by adding bands of color either in warp or weft;
- by superimposing two different networks and by alternating the threading of two colors in order to create a moiré effect. Marian Stubenitsky is a specialist in this technique and has published two books on the subject (see Bibliography, p. 275).

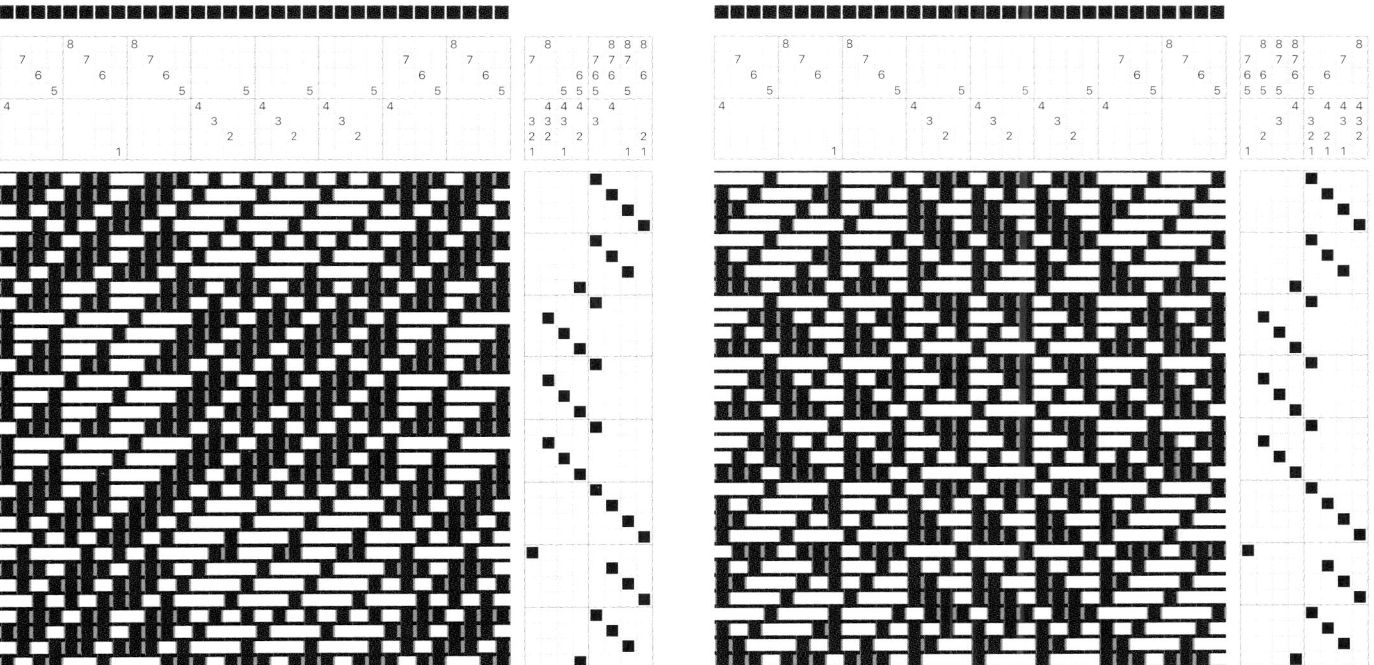

Figure 20 ***Network weaves on eight shafts: compound twill and combined twill tie-ups***

Even if this method can be used with a four-shaft loom, even if the design possibilities explode with eight shafts, once you are lucky enough to have a loom with twelve or more shafts, you really start to have fun! The treadles of a conventional loom alone will quickly become insufficient. A table (lever) loom, or even better a dobby loom, is perfect to enjoy this technique. With them, you can finally draw curves that are more inspired by what nature offers, to escape the usual lines and angles of classic weaving.

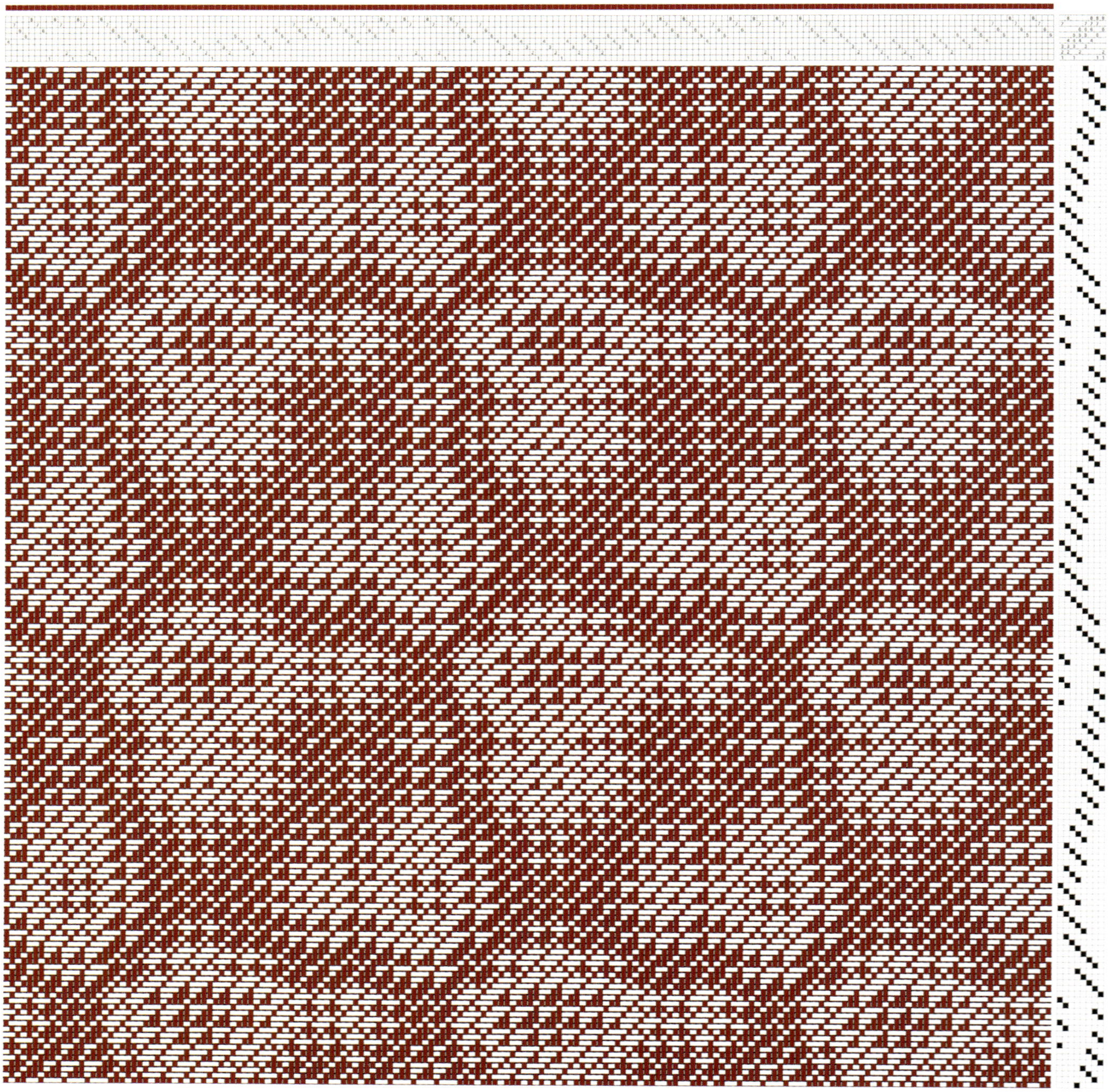

Figure 21 **Network weave in silk on eight shafts**

CONCLUSION

The best way to fill time is to waste it.

Marguerite Duras, *La Vie matérielle (Practicalities)*, 1987

How long does it take to make a weaving? This is probably the question I have been asked the most often by people who do not weave. I have often liked to answer, "A whole lifetime!" because stating a specific number of hours reveals very little about the reality of the exercise. What about the pleasure of searching for and designing a project, of thinking about its structure, of choosing the yarn to make it? What can we say about the experience that had to be acquired over time so that setting up the loom and working on it becomes natural and fluid? What can we say about the happiness of seeing the fabric being made before our eyes and with our hands with each weft passage? What about the satisfaction of a job well done when we unroll the finished fabric from the loom? What about the satisfaction of using or looking at your own textile creation every day?

Taking up a hobby or creative pastime is essential; weaving is something else entirely. You need only to see how many founding texts are written around weaving all over the world. You need only to remember Athena, Arachne, Penelope, Philomena, and many other characters from Greco-Roman mythology, as well as the stories and legends of so many other countries. You need only to observe how much the vocabulary of weaving permeates our everyday life: to weave a story, to spin a yarn, to pick up the threads of a conversation, to feel something with every fiber of your being. I have always been very sensitive to the relationship between text and textile, between *mots* and *motifs* [words and patterns]. This back-and-forth between language and fabric suggests that this activity goes beyond mere manual work.

How long did it take me to write this book? Here again, I would say: a lifetime. For many years, I have been composing this work, my thoughts unfolding with perseverance like yarn unwinding from a skein. I have been constantly seeking how to share what I have been able to discover and understand about weaving with as much method, precision, and as many examples as possible. I have often found that explaining orally with a blackboard and chalk is much easier than writing. In spite of the difficulties, I hope that this manual will accompany you in your exploration of weaving, so that you in turn can enjoy it as much as I do.

My dearest wish is that this collection becomes yours. So, write in it, add to it, turn down the page corners, and may it become a good companion in this wonderful adventure that is the art of weaving.

APPENDICES

Glossary

Balanced weave: A weave where the density of the weft is the same as the density of the warp.

Beam: Wooden crosspiece of the loom over which, at the back, the warp passes after leaving the warp beam and over which, at the front, the woven cloth passes before winding onto the cloth beam.

Beaming the warp: Winding the warp under tension onto the warp beam or roller.

Beat: Action performed after each weft pick by pulling the reed toward you in order to press the weft in place.

Beater: Frame that holds the reed, either hanging from the top of the loom frame or pivoting from the bottom.

Binding, intersection: Interlacing of the warp and the weft by passage of the weft between the warp threads.

Block: Basic unit of a pattern, consisting of a group of threads that have an identity either in threading, treadling, or tie-up. It is used to simplify the weaving draft and to make a profile draft.

Broadcloth: Plain woven fabric historically made of wool, but also made of cotton or hemp.

Brocade: Silk fabric enhanced with brocaded designs on a taffeta, gros de Tours, or satin background. Common and commercial name with no technical meaning.

Brocatelle: Fabric made with raised satin patterns on a flat twill background.

Cannelé: Weave structure that is a derivative of plain weave, where several picks pass through the same shed, the warp floats giving it a ribbed appearance. Gros de Tours is a cannelé.

Carded: After being sorted and washed, wool is carded. This operation, done with carders, wooden paddles covered in pin cloth, or with rollers in industry, consists of untangling the fibers and removing impurities. Once the fibers are in ribbon form, they are ready to be spun. Carded wools are rustic, matte, airy, and warm. They have a tendency to pill.

Compound weaves: Compound weaves are those made up of a tabby pick alternating with a pattern pick. Summer and Winter and overshot are compound weaves.

Counterbalance: A mechanism with pulleys installed above the shafts of the loom that allows certain shafts to be raised and the others to be lowered.

Countermarch: System of wooden lamms installed between the shafts and the treadles of a loom that allows certain shafts to be raised and all others to be lowered. These looms have even sheds.

Creel: Frame with movable pegs on which bobbins can be placed to wind the warp.

Crepe: Highly twisted thread giving the fabric a textured effect. By extension, crepe is also a fabric with an irregular elastic effect. The crepe effect is obtained by a crepe weave structure, by crepe yarns, or by alternating S- and Z-twisted yarns.

Cross: Separation of warp threads into two layers (even and odd threads) obtained by crossing the threads between two pegs when winding the warp. This cross is kept on the loom using lease sticks or cross sticks. Each thread is thus kept in its place.

Damask: Twill or satin fabric with alternating warp and weft effects. Originally, this fabric came from Damascus, Syria.

Degumming, scouring: Action of removing the sericin from the silk by dipping it in an alkaline solution. Degummed silk is soft and off-white.

Denier: Unit of measurement for silk corresponding to the weight in grams of 9,000 meters of thread.

Dents: The narrow parallel spaces between the metal or stainless steel dividers in the reed through which the warp ends are passed.

Dobby: A mechanism attached to a loom that controls the movement of the shafts, either mechanically or electronically. The mechanical dobby is a bar with holes in which pegs are inserted that select the shafts that you want to activate. It is an indispensable device when the loom has too many shafts for the number of treadles available.

Draft or grid: graphic representation of the threading, treadling, and tie-up.

Eye of a heddle: Metal or polyester ring on a heddle through which a warp end is threaded so it can be guided by the heddle.

Flat shuttle: Elongated, flat tool made of wood, metal, or bone around which the weft yarn is wound for weaving.

Float: Warp or weft thread that spans and floats above or below several threads without interlacing between them. The corresponding shafts remain raised or lowered for several wefts.

Flying shuttle: Elongated, hollow wooden tool into which a bobbin of weft thread is inserted.

Gauze: Light, open-weave fabric, in which the warp is made up of straight threads and threads that undulate. The weft blocks in the undulating warp. This name comes from the city of Gaza.

Heddle: A wire or polyester cord with an eye in the center through which a warp end is threaded. These heddles are suspended on shafts and together they guide the warp end.

Heddle hook: Flat hook used to help thread warp ends through the eyes of the heddles and through the reed.

Inkle loom: Table loom for weaving belts and bands.

Inlay (brocading): Weaving method used to form raised patterns from supplementary weft.

Interlacing, intersection, binding: Passage of the weft threads between the warp threads.

Jacquard: Loom developed by Joseph Marie Jacquard of Lyon in 1801 with a punch card programming mechanism that directly triggers warp threads to be lifted individually.

Lampas: Figured fabric in several colors whose design is formed by patterns in twill or taffeta on a taffeta or satin background or any other structures. Two warps are necessary: one for the ground cloth and the other for the interlacing of pattern threads. The second one is not very visible and we only see the weft.

Layer: Set of warp threads that divides into upper and lower layers depending on the movement of the shafts.

Lease sticks or cross sticks: Flat wooden slats used to keep warp ends in warping order, separating the even and odd threads.

Louisine: A weave structure that is a derivative of taffeta. The weft forms floats covering two or more threads.

Mercerization: Finishing treatment for yarn, mainly cotton, with caustic soda to give it shine, strength, and flexibility.

Metric number (Nm): A unit of measurement of a length of yarn for one gram of this yarn. The number following the fraction bar indicates the number of strands making up this yarn. Nm 40/2 means that the yarn consists of 2 strands and measures 20 m/g (40 ÷ 2). Unit used for wool.

Offset: Regular shift of the interlacing or binding points from one pick to the next.

Overshot or *dalldräl:* Weave structure made with two wefts, one for the plain weave and the other to make patterns with floats.

Pick: Weft yarn inserted in the shed from one selvedge to the other. Note that in tapestry the pick corresponds to two passages of weft yarn, so that the warp ends are completely covered by this back-and-forth trip since it is a plain weave. By extension, in weaving, the term "pick" often replaces the word "weft."

Plain weave: One of the three basic weave structures, in which each weft pick interlaces over and under each warp end, alternating each row. It is called taffeta when woven from silk.

Profile draft: Graphic representation or sketch of the weaving pattern, not thread-by-thread but block-by-block. It is a work tool from which the regular threading, tie-up, and treadling draft can then be developed according to the structure chosen.

Raddle: A sort of open comb with pegs or metal pins every ½ inch or so. This tool is used to spread out the warp evenly on the warp beam at the intended density. It is indispensable for winding the warp onto the warp beam (roller).

Reed: Metal or stainless steel part with dents or slots that are more or less narrow used to impose the desired density of the warp. It is also used to beat each weft pick.

Rep weave: Fabric with a structure that is a derivative of plain weave. Warp rep typically has a very dense warp, which creates ribs in the direction of the weft. Take-up is very important since the warp goes around weft that is sometimes fairly thick. Weft rep, conversely, has a warp density that is so low that the weft is packed down tightly and completely covers the warp, as it does in tapestries.

Roller or beam: The warp is wound on the warp roller or beam at the back of the loom and the fabric is wound on the cloth roller or beam at the front of the loom.

Satin: Formerly called Atlas, this is one of the three basic weave structures. The binding points are so far apart that the floats hide them, making the surface smooth and shiny. Warp effect satin is the brightest.

Section: Group of warp ends, the number of which often matches the density of the warp for one inch.

Selvedge: Edge of the fabric, often reinforced by a higher density in the reed. Sometimes it is reinforced by a floating selvedge, which is not threaded through a heddle. It is not raised or lowered, and the weft always wraps around it with each passage.

Shaft or harness: Part of the loom supporting the heddles, rising or sinking depending on the type of loom.

Shed: Space opened by the shafts between the two layers of warp threads through which the shuttle passes.

Shrinkage: There are two types of shrinkage. Shrinkage from being taken off the loom is the difference between the width of the fabric in the reed and the width of the fabric after it is released from the tension of the loom. Shrinkage from post-weaving finishing processes is the difference between the width of the fabric and the width of the fabric after washing, ironing, or any other treatment. They are expressed as a percentage.

Silk noil: Silk thread drawn from cocoon waste.

Silk throwing: Operation that consists of twisting several silk threads together.

Sleying the reed: Passage of warp ends through the dents of the reed.

Structure or Weave Pattern: The way in which the warp and weft yarns are interwoven. Plain weave, twill, and satin are the three basic weave structures.

Tabby pick: intermediate pick, usually in plain weave, used to reinforce the fabric and to split up floats that are too long.

Taffeta: Plain-woven fabric made from silk.

Take-up: Loss of length of warp threads during weaving due to the interlacing of warp and weft. It is calculated by unweaving a warp thread and measuring the difference in length between the extracted thread and this same thread in the fabric. It is expressed as a percentage.

Temple: Tool placed over the width of the weaving between the breast beam and the reed to keep the fabric at its initial width and to prevent draw-in and protect the selvedge threads from wear due to friction from the reed.

Thread count of a fabric: This is defined by the number of warp and weft threads per square inch of fabric and by the thread count in metric number (Nm). In artisanal weaving, the term "thread count" is often used instead of warp count.

Threading: Passage of the warp ends through the eyes of the heddles following the order on a weaving draft, often with the help of a threading hook.

Tie-up: Connecting treadles to shafts by a system of cords, jacks, or lamms, following the tie-up draft. On the draft, the tie-up shows which shaft will be tied up to be lifted by the treadle or the lever.

Treadling: Sequence of manipulating the treadles or levers. The treadling draft is on the right side of the weaving draft, in columns.

Twill: One of the three basic weave structures, it is characterized by diagonal lines, created by the pattern shifting over one end for each pick.

Upper lamm: Horizontal wooden slat placed between the shafts and treadles of the loom that allows the shafts of a rising shed loom to be raised.

Waffle weave: Weave structure that creates a textured fabric that looks like a waffle.

Warp: The lengthwise threads of the fabric, stretched on the loom between the two beams or rollers, passed through the heddles and through the dents of the reed.

Warp count or density or sett: Number of warp ends per inch (epi).

Warp sticks: Thin wooden slats used when beaming the warp to help keep the warp ends in place when winding onto the warp beam.

Warping board or warping mill: Instrument for winding the warp for indirect warping. Wooden frame (board) for short warps, warping mill for others.

Weave pattern or structure: The way in which the warp and weft yarns are interwoven. Plain weave, twill, and satin are the three basic weave structures.

Weave unit: The smallest group of warp ends and picks needed to make up the weave pattern. This is the basic unit that will be repeated in threading and treadling.

Weft: The threads that cross the fabric widthwise.

Winding the warp: Preparation of the warp threads using a warping board, for indirect warping, or a creel, for direct warping, so that all warp threads are prepared, having the same length and tension.

Worsted: Worsted wool is the result of a combing process. The fleece has first been sorted, washed, and carded. The long and fine fibers are then passed through combs to remove impurities and short fibers. They are put into ribbons. The resulting yarn is very soft, bright, and durable.

Yarn count: This indicates the size of the yarn. Depending on the type of yarn, it is expressed in length per unit of weight or weight per unit of length. The metric number (Nm) is used for wool, denier for silk, NeL for linen, NeC for cotton. Tex is the legal yarn count unit, but is struggling to replace other measurement systems.

Yarn swift: An instrument used to unwind skeins or hanks of yarn.

Project Record Sheet

Fabric project			
My source of inspiration			
Final measurements of the fabric			
Warp yarn used		Yarn count	
Weft yarn used		Yarn count	
Structure			
Warp sett / in.			**epi**
Reed: dents / in.		Number of threads per dent	
Weft density / in.			**ppi**

Calculation of the Warp

Warp width	**Desired width of finished fabric**			**in.**
	+ added amount due to finishing processes	%	+	in.
	= width of raw fabric off the loom		=	in.
	+ added amount due to draw-in	%	+	in.
	= Width of warp in the reed		**=**	**in.**

Warp length	**Desired length of finished fabric**			**in.**
	+ added amount due to finishing processes	%	+	in.
	= length of fabric off the loom		=	in.
	+ added amount due to shrinkage	%	+	in.
	= Length of woven warp per item		**=**	**in.**
	+ fringe		+	in.
	= warp length needed per item		=	in.
	× number of items	%	=	in.
	+ losses due to tying on at the front and back of the loom		+	8 + 16 = 24 in.
	= length of warp needed		**=**	**ft.**

Number of warp ends	**Width of fabric in the reed in inches × density**	=		**in. ×**	**ends/in. = ends**
Quantity in yards	Number of warp ends × length of warp	=	ends ×	yd. =	yd.
Quantity in oz. (lb.)	Quantity in yards ÷ warp yarn count	=	yd. ÷	yd./lb. =	lb.
Cost of the warp	Quantity in lb. × price per lb.	=	lb. ×	$/lb. =	$

Calculation of the Weft

Number of weft threads	= length of woven warp in inches × density × number of items	= picks
Quantity of threads in yds.	Number of picks × width in reed	= picks × yd. = yd.
Quantity in oz. (lb.)	Quantity in yards ÷ weft yarn count	= yd. ÷ yd. /lb. = kg
Cost of the weft	Quantity in lb. × price per lb.	= lb. × $/lb. = $

Warp Color Order Chart

Color 1															=
Color 2															=
Color 3															=
															=
															=
															=

Heddle Counting Table

Shafts	Heddles per Group			× number of repeats of each pattern			+ rest not in pattern	= total heddles per shaft
	Pattern 1	Pattern 2	Pattern 3	Pattern 1	Pattern 2	Pattern 3		
8								
7								
6								
5								
4								
3								
2								
1								
Total								heddles

Threading, Tie-Up, and Treadling Draft

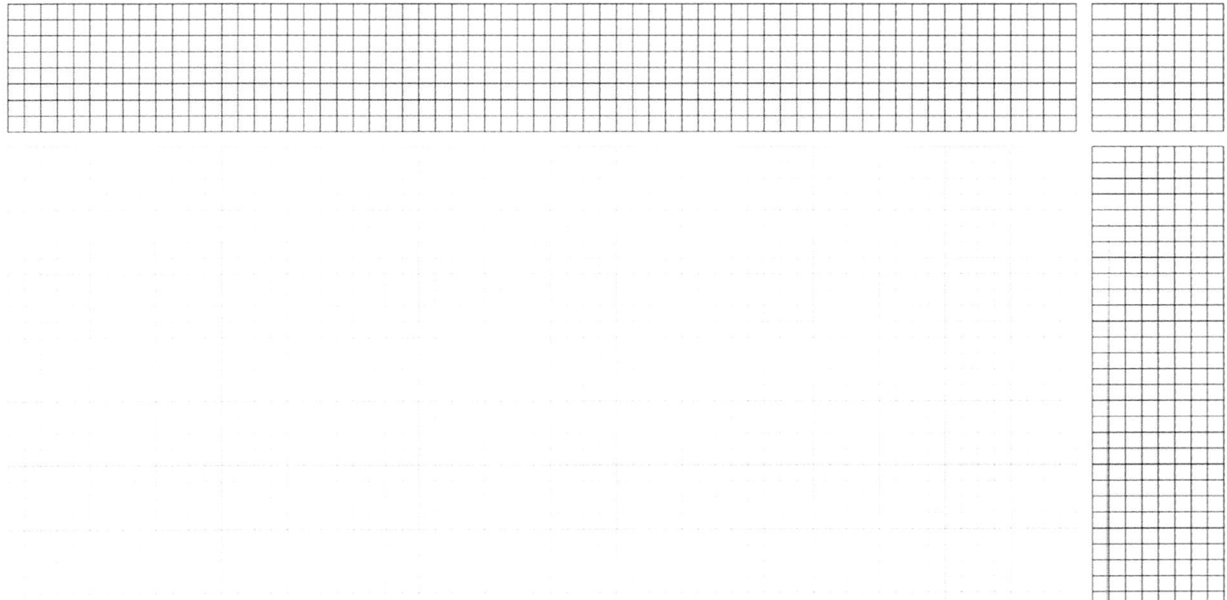

Equivalent Imperial and Metric Measurements

1 meter (m) = 1.09 yards

1 yard (yd) = 0.914 meters

1 meter (m) = 3.28 feet or 1.09 yards or 39 inches

1 foot (ft) = 30.5 centimeters

1 centimeter = 0.394 inches

1 inch (in.) = 2.54 centimeters

1 gram (g) = 0.035 ounces

1 ounce (oz.) = 28.35 grams

1 kilogram (kg) = 2.205 pounds

1 pound (lb) = 0.454 kilograms

Equivalent Imperial and Metric Measurements for the Reed

Dents/10 cm	Dents/1 inch
60	15
50	12.5
40	10
30	7.5
20	5

Dents/1 inch	Dents/10 cm
16	64
12	48
10	40
8	32
6	24

Equivalent Imperial and Metric Yarn Counts

Wool	
Yd/lb	m/kg
Nm 36/2 8,940	18,000
Nm 26/2 5,960	13,000
Nm 8/2 1,985	4,000

Cotton and cotton/linen	
Yd/lb	m/kg
Ne 20/2 8,400	17,000
Ne 16/2 6,720	13,500
Ne 8/2 3,360	6,500
NeL 22/2 2,740	6,400

Composition of Yarns and Burn Test

Natural Fibers

Animal

Wool: Fiber from the fleece of sheep.

Hair: Goat (cashmere, mohair), alpaca, llama, vicuna, camel, rabbit (angora), horse, yak, beaver, and otter among others.

Silk: Bombyx mori, spider, mollusks, feathers.

Animal fibers burn poorly, sizzle, and smell like burnt horn. They leave a charred residue with a black crumbly ball.

Plant

Stems – barks: Bamboo, hemp, jute, flax, nettle, ramie.

Pods and fruits: Cotton, kapok, coconut.

Leaves: Aloe, pineapple, banana, palm, sisal, raffia.

Vegetable fibers burn quickly with a bright flame and give off an odor of burned paper. After combustion, the cut is clean, with no residue stuck to the fiber and white or gray ashes remain.

Mineral

Metals: Gold, silver, copper, stainless steel.

Asbestos.

Artificial Fibers

Cellulose fibers

Viscose was originally derived from tree pulp cellulose modified with soda. Today, it is often produced artificially and is used in the composition of many synthetic fibers. Depending on the chemical treatment used, the name of the fiber changes.

Rayon: First term designating "artificial silk" of a cellulosic nature. This viscose thread is continuous.

Lyocell: Fiber produced from wood pulp (bamboo, hardwood, eucalyptus, etc.); tencel is the most widely used.

Acetate: Made from a mixture of wood pulp and cotton.

Fibranne: Regenerated cellulose obtained from cut viscose.

Vegetable: Algae.

Rayon burns quickly, without melting, produces a yellow flame, leaves a black ball, and gives off a slight odor. Acetate burns weakly, continues to burn after the flame is removed, leaves a black ball like wool but hard, and gives off an odor of vinegar.

Cellulose ester fibers

Cellulose fiber is treated with a acetic ester and produces a silk-like yarn. Acetate fabrics are not very strong and tear easily, but are wrinkle-free.

Noncellulose fibers

Sap: Rubber (rubber tree sap).

Animal: Fibers derived from milk or feathers

Synthetic Fibers

Synthetic fibers are obtained by synthesis of chemical compounds, mainly from hydrocarbons, and more recently from starch.

Organic polymers

Polyamides: Antron, caprolan, Cordura, nylon, perlon. Spinning of polymers resulting from the reaction of an acid on a product derived from petroleum, which allows molecules to be chemically linked together.

Polyesters: Dacron, tergal, terylene. Generally molded polymers, these fibers are more resistant to abrasion and wrinkling than polyamides.

Acrylics : Courtelle, crylor, dolon, dralon, orlon. Designates fibers obtained by polymerization of acrylic nitrile, which is widely used by the Japanese.

The chemists of this very young textile industry experimented with many molecules and chemical processes. Other fibers followed: polypropylene, modacrylic, chlorofibers, elastane, fluorofiber, aramids, etc.

Polyamides do not ignite much, give off an odor of celery, and leave a hard ball. Polyesters burn slowly as they melt, give off an aromatic odor, and leave a hard ball. Acrylics burn as they melt, emitting black smoke, and smell bad. They leave a black, rubbery ash.

Inorganic polymers

Glass, carbon, ceramic and various metals.

Grid for Warp-Faced Rep Weave

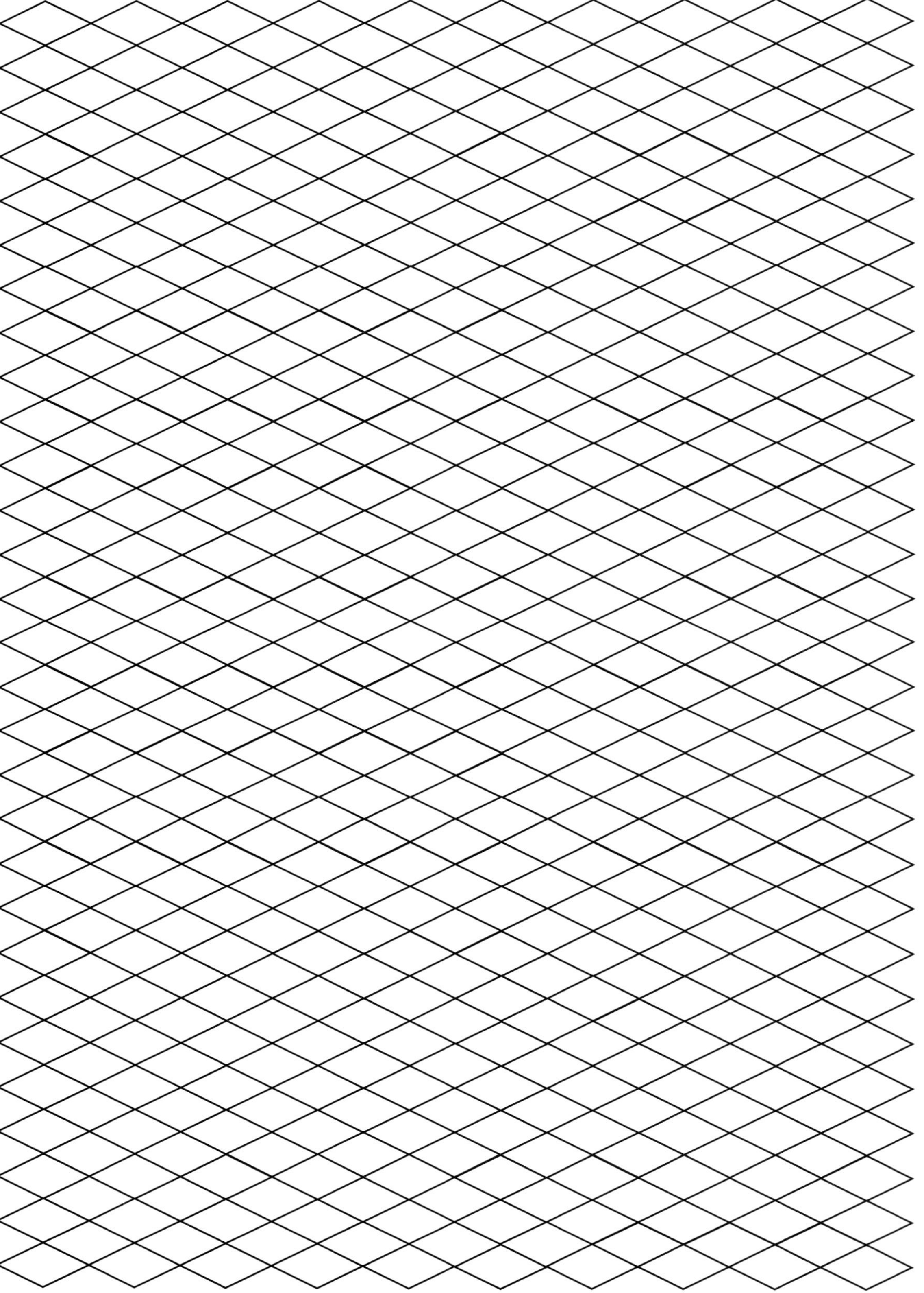

Bibliography

Alderman Sharon, *Mastering Weave Structures—Transforming Ideas into Great Cloth*, Interweave, 2004

Anquetil Jacques, *Mémoires d'un tisserand*, Nil Éditions, 1997

Anquetil Jacques, *Le tissage*, Dessain et Tolra/Chêne, 1977

Atwater Mary Meigs, *Byways in Hand-Weaving*, Macmillan, 1954

Atwater Mary Meigs, *Design and the Handweavers*, Shuttle Craft Books, 1961

Atwater Mary Meigs, *The Shuttle-Craft Book of American Hand Weaving Being an Account of the Rise, Development, Eclipse, & Modern Revival of a National Popular Art Together with Information of Interest & Value to Collectors, Technical Notes for the Use of Weavers*, MacMillan, 1951

Barrett Clotilde, "Boundweave," *Weavers Journal*, 1982

Barrett Clotilde and Smith Eunice, "Double Two-tie Unit Weaves," Weaver's Journal Publications, 1983

Bateman William, *Extended Manifold Twill Weaves*, Virginia I. Harvey, 1981

Baum Maggy, Boyeldieu Chantal, *Dictionnaire encyclopédique des textiles*, Éditions Eyrolles, 2018

Black, Mary E., *The Key to Weaving—A Textbook of Hand Weaving for the Beginning Weaver*, Macmillan, 1945

Boekholt Albert, *Premiers tissages*, Éditions du Centurion, 1976

Bort Françoise et Dupont Valérie (sous la direction de), *Texte, texture, textile*, Éditions universitaires de Dijon, 2013

Brandon-Guiguet, *Méthode des initiales—Un aspect mathématique du tissage à lames*, Joannès Desvignes & Cie, 1938

Chandler Deborah, *Learning to Weave*, Interweave, 2009

Collectif, *Couleurs et motifs dans l'art textile*, éditions Pyramyd, 2018

Collectif, *Les secrets du tissage*, Les Cercles des Fermières du Québec, 2009

Collingwood Peter, *The Techniques of Rug Weaving*, Faber and Faber, 1968

Complex Weavers, *Greatest Hits*, Judie Eatought & Wanda J. Shelp, 2000

Cyrus-Zetterström Ulla, *Manuel de tissage à la main*, LTs förlag, 1977

Davison Marguerite Porter, *A Handweaver's Pattern Book*, Marguerite Davison, 1950

Debétaz-Grünig Erika, *Apprenons à tisser*, Dessain et Tolra, 1977

Dixon Anne, Tissage—*600 diagrammes*, Éditions Eyrolles, 2020

Dixon Anne, *The Weaver's Inkle Pattern Directory*, Interweave, 2012

Duchemin Mad, *Le tissage à la main sur 2, 3 ou 4 lames*, Dessain et Tolra, 1975

Durand Jean-Pierre, *Auto-apprentissage du tissage*, Éditions de la Lanterne, 1979

Emery Irene, *The Primary Structures of Fabrics: An Illustrated Classification*, Thames & Hudson, 2009

Eriksson Mariana, Gustavsson Gunnel, Lovallius Kerstin, *Warp and Weft: Lessons in Drafting for Handweaving*, Trafalgar Square Books, 2011

Essen Deb, *Easy Weaving with Supplemental Warps—Overshot, Velvet, Shibori, and More*, Interweave, 2016

Fauque Claude, *Les mots du textile*, Belin, 2013

Graver Pattie, *Next Steps in Weaving*, Interweave, 2015

Greenlaw Debby, *Krokbragd: How to Design & Weave*, Independently published, 2019

Hardouin-Fugier Élisabeth, Berthod Bernard, Chavent-Fusaro Martine, *Les Étoffes—Dictionnaire historique,* Les Éditions de l'amateur, 1994

Hoskins Nancy Arthur, *Weft-faced Pattern Weaves: Tabby to Taquete,* Schiffer Publishing, 2011

Hugues Patrice, Debray Régis, *Dictionnaire culturel du tissu,* Babylone/Fayard, 2005

Hugues Patrice, *Le langage du tissu,* Patrice Hugues, 1982

Hugues Patrice, *Tissu et travail de Civilisation,* Éditions Médianes, 1996

Ignell Tina, *Favorite Rag Rug,* Trafalgar Square Books, 2007

Ignell Tina, *Favorite Scandinavian Projects to Weave: 45 Stylish Designs for the Modern Home,* Trafalgar Square Books, 2018

Irwin Bobbie, *Weaving Iridescence: Color Play for the Handweaver,* Stackpole Books, 2017

Keasbey Doramay, *Designing with Blocks for Handweaving,* Keasbey Publication, 1993

Keasbey Doramay, *Sheer Delight: Handwoven Transparencies,* Stellar Pub House, 1990

Knisely Tom, *Handwoven Baby Blankets,* Stackpole Books, 2015

Knisely Tom, *Handwoven Table Linens,* Stackpole Books, 2017

Labrife Charles, *Manuel de tissage,* Baillère & Fils, 1923

Laughlin Mary Elisabeth, *More Than Four: A Book for Multiple Harness Weavers,* Rubin and Russ Handweavers, 1976

Legrand Catherine, *Textiles et vêtements du monde—Carnet de voyage d'une styliste,* Éditions de la Martinière, 2010

Lundell Laila & Windesjö Elisabeth, *The Big Book of Weaving,* Collins & Brown, 2005

Marshall Kelly, *Custom Woven Interiors Bringing Color and Design Home with Rep Weave,* Custom Woven Interiors, 2012

McEneely Naomi, *Compendium of Finishing Techniques*, Interweave, 2003

Menz Deb, *Color Works—The Crafter's Guide to Color,* Interweave, 2004

Moore Jennifer, *Double Weave,* Interweave, 2010

Moorman Theo, *Weaving as an Art Form— A Personal Statement,* Schiffer, 1975

O'Connor Paul R., *Weft-Faced Designs,* Coe Produced, 2012

Oelsner G. H., *A Handbook of Weaves, 1875 Illustrations,* Macmillan, 1915

Osterkamp Peggy, *Weaving & Drafting Your Own Cloth,* Lease Sticks Press, 2005

Parcineau Martine, *Fibres, fils, tissus—De l'artisanat à l'industrie, Mémento à l'usage des designers textile,* Éditions Eyrolles, 2015

Patrick Jane, *A Handwoven Treasury,* Interweave Press, 1989

Philips Janet, *Designing Woven Fabrics,* Natural Time Out Publications, Somerset, 2009

Proux Bibiane April, *Reps—Technique de création de tissage traditionnel et moderne*, Éditions La Treille, 1979

Regensteiner Else, *L'art du tissage,* Dessain et Tolra, 1979

Robert Leclerc, *Warp and Weave,* Ottawa, 1971

Roque Geaorges, *Art et science de la couleur,* Gallimard, 2009

de Ruiter Erica, *Weven op 3 schachten,* Erica de Ruiter, 2017

Ryall Pierre, *Le tissage à la main,* Ryall, 1975

Selby Margo, *Contempory Weaving Patterns,* A&C Black, 2011

Smit Jo, *Internationale Weefdictionaire—623 begrippen verklaard en vertaald,* Rostrum Haarlem, 1981

Snyder Mary E., *Crackle Weave,* Robin & Russ Handweavers, 1961

Spady Robin, Tracy Nancy A., Fiddler Marjorie, *Weaving Innovations from the Bateman Collection,* Schiffer, 2015

Strickler Carol, *A Weaver's Book of 8-Shaft Patterns: From the Friends of Handwoven,* Interweave, 1991

Stubenitsky Marian, *Stubenitsky Code,* Weefschool De Hoeve, 2018

Stubenitsky Marian, *Weaving with Echo and Iris,* Rap God, 2014

Sutton Ann, *Ideas in Weaving,* Interweave, 1989

Sutton Ann, *The Structure of Weaving,* Bastsford, 1082

Tallarovic Joanne, *Rep Weave and Beyond,* Interweave Press, 2004

Tassinari Bernard, *La soie à Lyon—De la Grande Fabrique aux textiles du xxie siècle,* Éditions Lyonnaises d'Art et d'Histoire, 2012

Tours, cité de la Soie, *La soie en Touraine,* Éditions La Simarre, 1992

Van der Hoogt Madelyn, *The Best of Weaver's—Fabrics That Go Bump*, XRX Books, 2002

Van der Hoogt Madelyn, *The Best of Weaver's—Huck Lace*, XRX Books, 2000

Van der Hoogt Madelyn, *The Best of Weaver's—The Magic of Double Weave*, XRX Books, 2007

Van der Hoogt Madelyn, *The Best of Weaver's—Overshot Is Hot*, XRX Books, 2008

Van der Hoogt Madelyn, *The Best of Weaver's—Summer & Winter*, XRX Books, 2010

Van der Hoogt Madelyn, *The Best of Weaver's—Thick'n Thin,* XRX Books, 2001

Van der Hoogt Madelyn, *The Best of Weaver's—Twill Thrills,* XRX Books, 2004

Van der Hoogt Madelyn, *The Complete Book of Drafting for Handweavers,* Shuttle Craft Books, 1993

Weidmann Daniel, *Guide pratique des Textiles,* Dunod, 2015

Weidmann Daniel, *Technologies des textiles—De la fibre à l'article,* Dunod, 2009

Wilson Jean, *Joinings, Edges, and Trims,* Van Nostrand Reinhold Company, 1983

Wilson Susan, *Weave Classic Crackle & More,* Schiffer, 2011

Windeknecht Margaret B., *Creative Overshot,* HTH Publishers, 1978

Index

Y

Photo, Illustration, and Weaving Credits

Photo Credits

© Jacques Péré : pages 18, 33, 34, 39, 40, 44, 94, 120, 125, 128, 129, 130, 131, 132, 133, 134, 135, 136, 137, 138, 139, 141, 142, 143, 146, 147, 148, 149, 150, 151, 153, 154, 157, 159, 161, 162, 163, 164, 165, 166, 167, 168, 169, 173, 175, 176, 180, 182, 184, 185, 186, 187, 190, 191, 192, 193, 194, 195, 196, 197, 199, 200, 203, 204, 205, 206, 208, 209, 210 (bottom left) 212, 213, 214, 215, 216, 219, 221, 225, 226, 228, 229, 232, 242, 245, 246 (upper right), 248, 252, 254, 262

© Antoinette Roze : page 126

© Petra Marciniak : page 168 (bottom right)

© Antoine Albrespy : page 246 (bottom left)

© Agnès His : page 210 (on the right)

© Michel-Georges Bernard : page 230 (on the right), https://fr.wikipedia.org/wiki/Atelier_Plasse_Le_Caisne

© Shutterstock/EQRoy : page 246 (upper left)

© DR : page 38

Illustration Credits

© Angèle Coquerie : pages 21, 22, 23, 24, 25, 26, 32, 35, 35, 41, 42, 43, 45, 46, 71, 81 (bottom left), 124, 128, 129, 141, 142, 147, 177, 240, 241, 256

© Alix Boiron-Albrespy : pages 36, 46, 48, 49, 50, 51, 53, 58, 69, 73, 74, 75, 76, 77, 78, 79, 80, 81 (top), 82, 83, 84, 85, 86, 88, 90, 91, 92, 94, 95, 101, 102, 103, 104, 105, 106, 107, 109, 110, 111, 113, 114, 115, 116, 117, 137, 148, 205. 217, 218, 219, 220, 221, 223

© Agnès His : page 37

© Guillemette Hueber : page 122 (portion of sheet music)

Weaving Credits

The weaving drafts were all made by the author using pixeLoom software.

The weavings photographed in this book are by Betty Briand and also by:

© Christine Bouvet : pages 42, 134 (left), 149 (top), 167 (right), 173

© Gilles De Laage : pages 110, 197 (on right)

© Pierrette Barré : pages 131, 138, 139, 149 (bottom), 156 (top), 176, 187, 190 (left), 191, 215

© Véronique Chollet : pages 133 (bottom right), 136 (right)

© Évelyne Péré : pages 135 (top), 150, 196, 206, 246

© Juliette Nozières : page 137

© Valérie Coquerie : pages 141 (bottom right), 148, 165

© Elyane Quervet-Sommer : pages 163, 169

© Petra Marciniak : page 168 (bottom right)

© Irina Kartlelishvili : page 185 (top right)

© Annette Bossard : page 186

© Stéphanie Bry : pages 197 (left), 208 (top)